A H

THE INQUISITION
OF
THE MIDDLE AGES

BY
HENRY CHARLES LEA
IN THREE VOLUMES
VOL. II

THE INQUISITION.
BOOK II.
THE INQUISITION IN THE SEVERAL LANDS OF CHRISTENDOM.
CHAPTER I.

LANGUEDOC.

THE men who laid the foundations of the Inquisition in Languedoc had before them an apparently hopeless task. The whole organization and procedure of the institution were to be developed as experience might dictate and without precedents for guidance. Their uncertain and undefined powers were to be exercised under peculiar difficulties. Heresy was everywhere and all-pervading. An unknown but certainly large portion of the population was addicted to Catharism or Waldensianism, while even the orthodox could not, for the most part, be relied upon for sympathy or aid. Practical toleration had existed for so many generations, and so many families had heretic members, that the population at large was yet to be educated in the holy horror of doctrinal aberrations. National feeling, moreover, and the memory of common wrongs suffered during twenty years of bitter contest with invading soldiers of the Cross, during which Catholic and Catharan had stood side by side in defence of the fatherland, had created the strongest bonds of sympathy between the different sects. In the cities the magistrates were, if not heretics, inclined to toleration and jealous of their municipal rights and liberties. Throughout the country many powerful nobles were avowedly or secretly heretics, and Raymond of Toulouse himself was regarded as little better than a[2] heretic. The Inquisition was the symbol of a hated foreign domination which could look for no cordial support from any of these classes. It was welcomed, indeed, by such Frenchmen as had succeeded in planting themselves in the land, but they were scattered, and were themselves the objects of detestation to their neighbors. The popular feeling is voiced by the Troubadours, who delight in expressing contempt for the French and hostility to the friars and their methods. As Guillem de Montanagout says: "Now have the clerks become inquisitors and condemn men at their pleasure. I have naught against the inquests if they would but condemn errors with soft words, lead the wanderers back to the faith without wrath, and allow the penitent to find mercy." The bolder Pierre Cardinal describes the Dominicans as disputing after dinner over the quality of their wines: "They have created a court of judgment, and whoever attacks them they declare to be a Waldensian; they seek to penetrate into the secrets of all men, so as to render themselves dreaded."[1]

The lands which Raymond had succeeded in retaining were, moreover, drained by the enormous sums exacted of him in the pacification. To enable him to meet these demands he was authorized to levy taxes on the subjects of the Church, in spite of their immunities, and this and the other expedients requisite for the discharge of his engagements could not fail to excite widespread discontent with the settlement and hostility to all that represented it. That it was hard to extort these payments from a population exhausted by twenty years of war is manifest when, in 1231, two years after the treaty, the Abbey of Citeaux had not as yet received any part of the two thousand marks which were its share of the plunder, and it was forced to agree to a settlement under which Raymond promised to pay in annual instalments of two hundred marks, giving as security his revenues from the manor of Marmande.[2]

The Inquisition, it is true, was at first warmly greeted by the Church, but the Church had grown so discredited during the[3] events of the past half-century that its influence was less than in any other spot in Christendom. Even in Aragon the Council of Tarragona, in 1238, felt itself compelled to decree excommunication against those who composed or applauded lampoons against the clergy. The abuse of the interdict had grown to such proportions that Innocent IV., in 1243, and again in 1245, was obliged to forbid its employment throughout southern France, in all places suspected of heresy, because it afforded to heretics so manifold an occasion of asserting that it was used for private interests, and not for the salvation of souls. During the troubles which followed after the crusade of Louis VIII. the bishops had taken advantage of the confusion to seize many lands to which they had no claim, and this involved them in endless quarrels with the royal fisc in the territories which fell to the king, while in those which remained to Raymond, the pious St. Louis was forced to interfere to obtain for him a restoration of what they obstinately refused to surrender. The Church itself was so deeply tainted with heresy that the faithful were scandalized at seeing the practical immunity enjoyed by heretical clerks, owing to the difficulty of assembling a sufficient number of bishops to officiate at their degradation, and Gregory IX. felt it necessary, in 1233, to decree that in such cases a single bishop, with some of his abbots, should have power to deprive them of holy orders and deliver them to the secular arm to be burned—a provision which he subsequently embodied in the canon law. Innocent IV., moreover, in 1245, felt called upon to order his legate in Languedoc to see that no one suspected of heresy was elected or consecrated as bishop. On the other hand, priests who were zealous in aiding the Inquisition sometimes found that the enmities thus excited rendered it impossible for them to reside in their parishes, as occurred in the case of Guillem Pierre, a priest of Narbonne, in 1246, who on this account was allowed to employ a vicar and to hold a plurality of benefices. About the same time Innocent IV. felt obliged to express his surprise that the prelates disobeyed his repeated commands to assist the Inquisition; he has trustworthy information that they neglect to do so, and he threatens them roundly with his displeasure unless they manifest greater zeal. Bernard Gui, indeed, speaks of the bishops who favored Count Raymond as among the craftiest and most dangerous enemies of the inquisitors. The natural antagonism[4] between the Mendicants and the secular clergy was, moreover, increased by the pretension of the inquisitors to supervise the priesthood and see that they performed their neglected duty in all that pertained to the extension of the faith. That under such circumstances the Dominicans employed in the pious work should suffer constant molestation scarce needs the explanation given by the pope that it was through the influence of the Arch Enemy.[3]

Another serious impediment to the operations of the Inquisition lay in the absence of places of detention for those accused and of prisons for those condemned. We have already seen how the bishops shirked their duty in providing jails for the multitudes of prisoners until St. Louis was obliged to step in and construct them, and during this prolonged interval the sentences of the inquisitors show, in the number of contumacious absentees after a preliminary hearing, how impossible it often was to retain hold of heretics who had been arrested.[4]

To undertake, in such an environment, the apparently hopeless task of suppressing heresy required men of exceptional character, and they were not wanting. Repulsive as their acts must seem to us, we cannot refuse to them the tribute due to their fearless fanaticism. No labor was too arduous for their unflagging zeal, no danger too great for their unshrinking courage. Regarding themselves as elected to perform God's work, they set about it with a sublime self-confidence which lifted them above the weakness of humanity. As the mouthpiece of God, the mendicant friar, who lived on charity, spoke to prince and people with all the awful authority of the Church, and exacted obedience or punished contumacy unhesitatingly and absolutely. Such men as{5} Pierre Cella, Guillem Arnaud, Arnaud Catala, Ferrer the Catalan, Pons de Saint-Gilles, Pons de l'Esparre, and Bernard de Caux, bearded prince and prelate, were as ready to endure as merciless to inflict, were veritable Maccabees in the internecine strife with heresy, and yet were kind and pitiful to the miserable and overflowing with tears in their prayers and discourses. They were the culminating development of the influences which produced the Church Militant of the Middle Ages, and in their hands the Inquisition was the most effective instrument whereby it maintained its supremacy. A secondary result was the complete subjugation of the South to the King of Paris, and its unification with the rest of France.

If the faithful had imagined that the Treaty of 1229 had ended the contest with heresy they were quickly undeceived. The blood-money for the capture of heretics, promised by Count Raymond, was indeed paid when earned, for the Inquisition undertook to see that this was done, but the earning of it was dangerous. Nobles and burghers alike protected and defended the proscribed class, and those who hunted them were slain without mercy when occasion offered. The heretics continued as numerous as ever, and we have already seen the fruitless efforts put forth by the Cardinal Legate Romano and the Council of Toulouse. Even the university which Raymond bound himself to establish in Toulouse for the propagation of the faith, though it subsequently performed its work, was at first a failure. Learned theologians were brought from Paris to fill its chairs, but their scholastic subtleties were laughed at by the mocking Southrons as absurd novelties, and the heretics were bold enough to contend with them in debate. After a few years Raymond neglected to continue the stipends, and for a time the university was suspended.[5]{6}

The most encouraging feature of the situation, one, indeed, full of promise, was the steady progress of the Dominican Order. It had outgrown the modest Church of St. Romano, bestowed upon it by Bishop Foulques; and in 1230 the piety of a prominent burgher of Toulouse, Pons de Capdenier, provided for it more commodious quarters in an extensive garden, situated partly in the city and partly in the suburbs. The inmates of the convent, some forty in number, were always ready to furnish champions of the Cross, whose ardent zeal shrank from neither toil nor peril; and when, in 1232, the fanatic Bishop Foulques died and was succeeded by the yet more fiery fanatic, the Dominican Provincial Raymond du Fauga, the Order was fully prepared to enter upon the exterminating war with heresy which was to last for a hundred years.[6]

The eager zeal of the friars did not wait to be armed with the organized authorization of inquisitorial powers. Their leading duty was to combat heresy, and their assaults on it were unintermitting. In 1231 a friar, in a sermon, declared that Toulouse was full of heretics, who held their assemblies there and disseminated their errors without hindrance. Already the magistrates seem to have looked askance on these pious efforts, for this assertion was made the occasion of a decided attempt at repression. The consuls of the city met and summoned before them, in the capitole, or town-hall, the prior, Pierre d'Alais. There they roundly scolded and threatened him, declaring that it was false to assert the existence of heresy in the town, and forbidding such utterances for the future. Trivial as was the occurrence, it has interest as the commencement of the ill-will between the authorities of Toulouse and the Inquisition, and as illustrating the sense of municipal pride and independence still cherished in the cities of the South. It required but a few years" struggle to trammel the civic liberties which had held their own against feudalism, but which could not stand against the subtler despotism of the Church.[7]

Even thus early Dominican ardor refused to be thus restrained. Master Roland of Cremona, noted as the first Dominican licentiate of the University of Paris, who had been brought to Toulouse to teach theology in the infant University, was scandalized when he{7} heard of the insolent language of the consuls, and exclaimed that it was only a fresh incentive to preach against heresy more bitterly than ever. He set the example in this, and was eagerly followed by many of the brethren. He soon, too, had an opportunity of proving the falsity of the consuls" disclaimer. It transpired that Jean Pierre Donat, a canon of the ancient Church of Saint Sernin, who had recently died and been buried in the cloister, had been secretly hereticated on his death-bed. Without authority, and apparently without legal investigation, Master Roland assembled some friars and clerks, exhumed the body from the cloister, dragged it through the streets, and publicly burned it. Soon afterwards he heard of

2

the death of a prominent Waldensian minister named Galvan. After stirring up popular passion in a sermon, he marched at the head of a motley mob to the house where the heretic had died and levelled it to the ground; then proceeding to the Cemetery of Villeneuve, where the body was interred, he dug it up and dragged it through the city, accompanied by an immense procession, to the public place of execution beyond the walls, where it was solemnly burned.[8]

All this was volunteer persecution. The episcopal court was as yet the only tribunal having power to act in such matters, and it, as we have seen, could only authorize the secular arm to do its duty in the final execution. Yet the episcopal court seems to have been in no way invoked in these proceedings, and no protest is recorded as having been uttered against such irregular enforcements of the law by the mob. There was, in fact, no organization for the steady repression of heresy. Bishop Raymond appears to have satisfied himself with an occasional raid against heretics outside of the city, and to have allowed those within it virtual immunity under the protection of the consuls, though he had, in virtue of his office, all the powers requisite for the purpose, and the machinery for their effective use could have readily been developed. No permanent results were to be expected from fitful bursts of zeal, and the suppression of heresy might well seem to be as far off as ever.

Urgent as was evidently the need of some organized body devoted exclusively to persecution, the appointment of the first{8} inquisitors, in 1233, seems not to have been regarded as possessing any special significance. It was merely an experiment, from which no great results were anticipated. Frère Guillem Pelisson, who shared in the labors and perils of the nascent Inquisition, and who enthusiastically chronicled them, evidently does not consider it as an innovation worthy of particular attention. It was so natural an evolution from the interaction of the forces and materials of the period, and its future importance was so little suspected, that he passes over its founding as an incident of less moment than the succession to the Priory of Toulouse. "Frère Pons de Saint Gilles," he says, "was made Prior of Toulouse, who bore himself manfully and effectively for the faith against the heretics, together with Frère Pierre Cella of Toulouse and Frère Guillem Arnaud of Montpellier, whom the lord pope made inquisitors against the heretics in the dioceses of Toulouse and Cahors. Also, the Legate Archbishop of Vienne made Frère Arnaud Catala, who was then of the Convent of Toulouse, inquisitor against the heretics." Thus colorless is the only contemporary account of the establishment of the Holy Office.[9]

How little the functions of these new officials were at first understood is manifested by an occurrence, which is also highly suggestive of the tension of public feeling. In a quarrel between two citizens, one of them, Bernard Peitevin, called the other, Bernard de Solier, a heretic. This was a dangerous reputation to have, and the offended man summoned his antagonist before the consuls. The heretical party, we are told, had obtained the upper hand in Toulouse, and the magistrates were all either sympathizers with or believers in heresy. Bernard Peitevin was condemned to exile for a term of years, to pay a fine both to the complainant and to the city, and to swear publicly in the town-hall that he had lied, and that de Solier was a good Catholic. The sentence was a trifle vindictive, and Peitevin sought counsel of the Dominicans, who recommended him to appeal to the bishop. Episcopal jurisdiction in such a matter was perhaps doubtful, but Raymond du Fauga entertained the appeal. A few years later, if any cognizance had been taken of the case it would have been by the Inquisition, but{9} now the inquisitors, Pierre Cella and Guillem Arnaud, appeared as advocates of the appellant in the bishop's court, and so clearly proved de Solier's heresy that the miserable wretch fled to Lombardy.[10]

Similar indefiniteness of procedure is visible in the next attempt. The inquisitors, Pierre and Guillem, began to make an inquest through the city, and cited numerous suspects, all of whom found defenders among the chief citizens. The hearings took place before them, but seem as yet to have been in public. One of the accused, named Jean Teisseire, asserted himself to be a good Catholic because he had no scruples in maintaining marital relations with his wife, in eating flesh, and in lying and swearing, and he warned the crowd that they were liable to the same charge, and that it would be wiser for them to make common cause than to abandon him. When he was condemned, and the viguier, the official representative of the count, was about to conduct him to the stake, so threatening a clamor arose that the prisoner was hurried to the bishop's prison, still proclaiming his orthodoxy. Intense excitement pervaded the city, and menaces were freely uttered to destroy the Dominican convent and to stone all the friars, who were accused of persecuting the innocent. While in prison Teisseire pretended to fall mortally sick, and asked for the sacraments; but when the bailli of Lavaur brought to Toulouse some perfected heretics and delivered them to the bishop, Teisseire allowed himself to be hereticated by them in prison, and grew so ardent in the faith under their exhortations that when they were taken out for examination he accompanied them, declaring that he would share their fate. The bishop assembled the magistrates and many citizens, in whose presence he examined the prisoners. They were all condemned, including Teisseire, who obstinately refused to recant, and no further opposition was offered when they were all duly burned.[11]

Here we see the inquisitorial jurisdiction completely subordinate to that of the bishop, but when the inquisitors soon afterwards left Toulouse to hold inquests elsewhere they acted with full independence. At Cahors we hear nothing of the Bishop of Querci taking part in the proceedings under which they condemned{10} a number of the dead, exhuming and burning their bodies, and inspiring such fear that a prominent believer, Raymond de Broleas, fled to Rome. At Moissac they condemned Jean du Gard, who fled to Montségur, and they cited a certain Folquet, who, in terror, entered the convent of Belleperche as a Cistercian monk, and, finding that this was of no avail, finally fled to Lombardy. Meanwhile Frère Arnaud Catala and our

3

chronicler, Guillem Pelisson, descended upon Albi, where they penanced a dozen citizens by ordering them to Palestine, and in conjunction with another inquisitor, Guillem de Lombers, burned two heretics, Pierre de Puechperdut and Pierre Bomassipio.[12]

The absence of the inquisitors from Toulouse made no difference in the good work, for their duties were assumed by their prior, Pons de Saint-Gilles. Under what authority he acted is not stated, but we find him, in conjunction with another friar, trying and condemning a certain Arnaud Sancier, who was burned, in spite of his protests to the last that he was a good Catholic, causing great agitation in the city, but no tumultuous uprising.[13]

The terror which Pelisson boasts that these proceedings spread through the land was probably owing not only to the evidence they afforded of an organized system of persecution, but also to their introduction of a much more effective method of prosecution than had heretofore been known. The "heretic," so called, was the perfected teacher who disdained to deny his faith, and his burning was accepted by all as a matter of course, as also was that of the "credens," or believer, who defiantly contumacious and persisted in admitting and adhering to his creed. Hitherto, however, the believer who professed orthodoxy seems generally to have escaped, in the imperfection of the judicial means of proving his guilt. The friars, trained in the subtleties of disputation and learned in both civil and canon law, were specially fitted for the detection of this particularly dangerous secret misbelief, and their persistence in worrying their victims to the death was well calculated to spread alarm, not only among the guilty, but among the innocent.

How reasonable were the fears inspired by the speedy informality of the justice accorded to the heretic is well illustrated by{11} a case occurring in 1234. When the canonization of St. Dominic was announced in Toulouse it was celebrated in a solemn mass performed by Bishop Raymond in the Dominican convent. St. Dominic, however, desired to mark the occasion with some more edifying manifestation of his peculiar functions, and caused word to be brought to the bishop, as the latter was leaving the church for the refectory to partake of a meal, that a woman had just been hereticated in a house hard by, in the Rue de l'Olmet sec. The bishop, with the prior and some others, hurried thither. It was the house of Peitavin Borsier, the general messenger of the heretics of Toulouse, whose mother-in-law lay dying of fever. So sudden was the entrance of the intruders that the woman's friends could only tell her "the bishop is coming," and she, who expected a visit from the heretic bishop, was easily led on by Raymond to make a full declaration of her heresy and to pledge herself to be steadfast in it. Then, revealing himself, he ordered her to recant, and, on her refusal, he summoned the viguier, condemned her as a heretic, and had the satisfaction of seeing the dying creature carried off on her bed and burned at the place of execution. Borsier and his colleague, Bernard Aldric of Drémil, were captured, and betrayed many of their friends; and then Raymond and the friars returned to their neglected dinner, giving thanks to God and to St. Dominic for so signal a manifestation in favor of the faith.[14]

The ferocious exultation with which these extra-judicial horrors were perpetrated is well reflected in a poem of the period by Isarn, the Dominican Prior of Villemier. He represents himself as disputing with Sicard de Figueras, a Catharan bishop, and each of his theological arguments is clinched with a threat—

"E" s'aquest no vols creyre vec te 'l foc aizinat
Que art tos companhos,
Aras vuelh que m"respondas en un mot o en dos,
Si cauziras et foc o remanras ab nos."

"If you will not believe this, look at that raging fire which is consuming your comrades. Now I wish you to reply to me in one word or two, for you will burn in the fire or join us." Or again,{12} "If you do not confess at once, the flames are already lighted; your name is proclaimed throughout the city with the blast of trumpets, and the people are gathering to see you burn." In this terrible poem, Isarn only turned into verse what he felt in his own heart, and what he saw passing under his eyes almost daily.[15]

As the holy work assumed shape and its prospects of results grew more encouraging, the zeal of the hunters of men increased, while the fear and hatred of the hunted became more threatening. On both sides passion was fanned into flame. Already, in 1233, two Dominicans, sent to Cordes to seek out heretics, had been slain by the terrified citizens. At Albi the people, excited by the burning of the two heretics already referred to, rose, June 14, 1234, when Arnaud Catala ordered the episcopal bailli to dig up the bones of a heretic woman named Beissera whom he had condemned. The bailli sent back word that he dared not do it. Arnaud left the episcopal synod in which he was sitting, coolly went to the cemetery, himself gave the first strokes of the mattock, and then, ordering the officials to proceed with the work, returned to the synod. The officials quickly rushed after him, saying that they had been ejected from the burial-ground by the mob. Arnaud returned and found it occupied by a crowd of howling sons of Belial, who quickly closed in on him, striking him in the face and pummelling him on all sides, with shouts of "Kill him! he has no right to live!" Some endeavored to drag him into the shops hard by to slay him; others wished to throw him into the river Tarn, but he was rescued and taken back to the synod, followed by a mass of men fiercely shouting for his death. The whole city, indeed, seemed to be of one mind, and many of the principal burghers were leaders of the tumult. It is satisfactory to learn that, although Arnaud mercifully withdrew the excommunication which he launched at the rebellious city, his successor, Frère Ferrer, wrought the judgment of God upon the guilty, imprisoning many of them and burning others.[16]{13}

4

In Narbonne disturbances arose even more serious, although special inquisitors had not yet been sent there. In March, 1234, the Dominican prior, François Ferrer, undertook a volunteer inquisition and threw in prison a citizen named Raymond d'Argens. Fifteen years previous the artisans of the suburb had organized a confederation for mutual support called the Amistance, and this body arose as one man and forcibly rescued the prisoner. The archbishop, Pierre Amiel, and the viscount, Aimery of Narbonne, undertook to rearrest him, but found his house guarded by the Amistance, which rushed upon their followers with shouts of "Kill! kill!" and drove them away after a brief skirmish, in which the prior was badly handled. The archbishop had recourse to excommunication and interdict, but to little purpose, for the Amistance seized his domains and drove him from the city. Both sides sought allies. Gregory IX. appealed to King Jayme of Aragon, while a complaint from the consuls of Narbonne to those of Nîmes looks as though they were endeavoring to effect a confederation of the cities against the Inquisition, of whose arbitrary and illegal methods of procedure they give abundant details. A kind of truce was patched up in October, but the troubles recommenced when the prior, in obedience to an order from his provincial, undertook a fresh inquisition, and made a number of arrests. In December a suspension was obtained by the citizens appealing to the pope, the king, and the legate, but in 1235 the people rose against the Dominicans, drove them from the city, sacked their convent, and destroyed all the records of the proceedings against heresy. Archbishop Pierre had cunningly separated the city from the suburb, about equal in population, by confining the inquisition to the latter, and this bore fruit in his securing the armed support of the former. The suburb placed itself under the protection of Count Raymond, who, nothing loath to aggravate the trouble, came there and gave to the people as leaders Olivier de Termes and Guiraud de Niort, two notorious defenders of heretics. A bloody civil war broke out between the two sections, which lasted until April, 1237, when a truce for a year was agreed upon. In the following August the Count of Toulouse and the Seneschal of Carcassonne were called in as arbitrators, and in March, 1238, a peace was concluded. That the Church triumphed is shown by the conditions which imposed upon some of the participators{14} in the troubles a year's service in Palestine or against the Moors of Spain.[17]

In Toulouse, the centre both of heresy and persecution, in spite of mutterings and menaces, open opposition to the Inquisition was postponed longer than elsewhere. Although Count Raymond is constantly represented by the Church party as the chief opponent of the Holy Office, it was probably his influence that succeeded in staving off so long the inevitable rupture. Hard experience from childhood could scarce have rendered him a fervent Catholic, yet that experience had shown him that the favor and protection of the Church were indispensable if he would retain the remnant of territory and power that had been left to him. He could not as yet be at heart a persecutor of heresy, yet he could not afford to antagonize the Church. It was important for him to retain the love and good-will of his subjects and to prevent the desolation of his cities and lordships, but it was yet more important for him to escape the stigma of favoring heresy, and to avoid calling down upon his head a renewal of the storm in which he had been so nearly wrecked. Few princes have had a more difficult part to play, with dangers besetting him on every side, and if he earned the reputation of a trimmer without religious convictions, that reputation and his retention of his position till his death are perhaps the best proof of the fundamental wisdom which guided his necessarily tortuous course. Pierre Cardinal, the Troubadour, describes him as defending himself from the assaults of the worst of men, as fearing neither the Frenchman nor the ecclesiastic, and as humble only with the good.[18]

He was always at odds with his prelates. Intricate questions with regard to the temporalities were a constant source of quarrel, and he lived under a perpetual reduplication of excommunications,{15} for he had been so long under the ban of the Church that no bishop hesitated for a moment in anathematizing him. Then, one of the conditions of the treaty of 1229 had been that within two years he should proceed to Palestine and wage war there with the infidel for five years. The two years had passed away without his performing the vow; the state of the country at no time seemed to render so prolonged an absence safe, and for years a leading object of his policy was to obtain a postponement of his crusade or immunity for the non-observance of his vow. Moreover, from the date of the peace of Paris until the end of his life he earnestly and vainly endeavored to obtain from Rome permission for the sepulture of his father's body. These complications crippled him in multitudinous ways and exposed him to immense disadvantage in his fencing with the hierarchy.

As early as 1230 he was taxed by the legate with inobservance of the conditions of the peace, and was forced to promise amendment of his ways. In 1232 we see Gregory IX. imperiously ordering him to be energetic in the duty of persecution, and, possibly in obedience to this, during the same year, we find him personally accompanying Bishop Raymond of Toulouse in a nocturnal expedition among the mountains, which was rewarded with the capture of nineteen perfected heretics, male and female, including one of their most important leaders, Pagan, Seigneur de Bécède, whose castle we saw captured in 1227. All these expiated their errors at the stake. Yet not long afterwards the Bishop of Tournay, as papal legate, assembled the prelates of Languedoc and formally cited Raymond before King Louis to answer for his slackness in carrying out the provisions of the treaty. The result of this was the drawing up of severe enactments against heretics, which he was obliged to promulgate in February, 1234. In spite of this, and of a letter from Gregory to the bishops ordering them no longer to excommunicate him so freely as before, he was visited within a twelvemonth with two fresh excommunications, for purely temporal causes. Then came fresh urgency from the pope for the extirpation of heresy, with which Raymond doubtless made a show of compliance, as his heart was bent on obtaining from Rome a restoration of the Marquisate of Provence. In this he was strongly backed by King Louis, whose brother Alfonse was to be Raymond's heir, and towards the close of the year he sought an{16}interview with Gregory and succeeded in effecting it. His reconciliation with the papacy appeared to be complete. His military reputation stood high, and Gregory made use of his visit to confide to him the leadership of the papal troops in a campaign against the rebellious citizens of Rome, who had expelled the head of the Church from their city. Though he did not succeed in restoring the pope, they parted on the best of terms, and he returned to Toulouse as a favored son of the Church, ready on all points to obey her behests.[19]

There he found matters rapidly approaching a crisis which tested to the utmost his skill in temporizing. Passions on both sides were rising to an uncontrollable point. At Easter, 1235, the promise of grace for voluntary confession brought forward such crowds of penitent heretics that the Dominicans were insufficient to take their testimony, and were obliged to call in the aid of the Franciscans and of all the parish priests of the city. Encouraged by this, the prior, Pons de Saint-Gilles, commenced to seize those who had not come forward spontaneously. Among these was a certain Arnaud Dominique, who, to save his life, promised to betray eleven heretics residing in a house at Cassers. This he fulfilled, though four of them escaped through the aid of the neighboring peasants, and he was set at liberty. The long-suffering of the heretics, however, was at last exhausted, and shortly afterwards he was murdered in his bed at Aigrefeuille by the friends of those whom he had thus sacrificed. Still more significant of the dangerous tension of popular feeling was a mob which, under the guidance of two leading citizens, forcibly rescued Pierre-Guillem Delort from the hands of the viguier and of the Abbot of Saint-Sernin, who had arrested him and were conveying him to prison. The situation was becoming unbearable, and soon the ceremony of dragging through the streets and burning the bodies of some dead heretics aroused an agitation so general and so menacing that Count Raymond was sent for in hopes that his interposition{17} might avert the most deplorable consequences. Thus far, although perhaps somewhat lacking in alacrity of persecution, no serious charges could be laid against him. His officials, his baillis and viguiers, had responded to all appeals of the inquisitors and had lent the aid of the secular arm in seizing heretics, in burning them, and in confiscating their property. Yet when he came to Toulouse and begged the inquisitors to suspend for a time the vigor of their operations he was not listened to. Then he turned to the papal legate, Jean, Archbishop of Vienne, complaining specially of Pierre Cella, whom he considered to be inspired with personal enmity to himself, and whom he regarded as the chief author of the troubles. His request that Cella's operations should be confined to Querci was granted. That inquisitor was sent to Cahors, where, with the assistance of Pons Delmont and Guillem Pelisson he vigorously traversed the land and forced multitudes to confess their guilt.[20]

This expedient was of no avail. Persecution continued as aggressive as ever, and popular indignation steadily rose. The inevitable crisis soon came which should determine whether the Inquisition should sink into insignificance, as had been the case with so many previous efforts, or whether it should triumph over all opposition and become the dominating power in the land.

Guillem Arnaud was in no way abashed by the banishment of his colleague. Returning from a brief absence at Carcassonne, of which more anon, he summoned for trial as believers twelve of the leading citizens of Toulouse, one of them a consul. They refused to appear, and threatened him with violence unless he should desist. On his persisting, word was sent him, with the assent of Count Raymond, that he must either leave the city or abandon his functions as inquisitor. He took council with his Dominican brethren, when it was unanimously agreed that he should proceed manfully in his duty. The consuls then ejected him by force from the city; he was accompanied to the bridge over the Garonne by all the friars, and as he departed the consuls recorded a protest to the effect that if he would desist from the inquisition he could remain; otherwise, in the name of the count and in their own, they ordered him to leave the city. He went to Carcassonne, whence{18} he ordered the Prior of Saint-Étienne and the parish priests to repeat the citations to the parties already summoned. This order was bravely obeyed in spite of threats, when the consuls sent for the prior and priests, and after keeping them in the town-hall part of a night, expelled them from the town, and publicly proclaimed that any one daring to repeat the citations should be put to death, and that any one obeying the summons of an inquisitor should answer for it in body and goods. Another proclamation followed, in which the name of Count Raymond was used, prohibiting that any one should give or sell anything to the bishop, the Dominicans, or the canons of Saint-Étienne. This forced the bishop to leave the city, as we are told that no one dared even to bake a loaf of bread for him, and the populace, moreover, invaded his house, beat his clerks, and stole his horses. The Dominicans fared better, for they had friends hardy enough to supply them with necessaries, and when the consuls posted guards around their house, still bread and cheese and other food was thrown over their walls in spite of the arrest of some of those engaged in it. Their principal suffering was from lack of water, which had to be brought from the Garonne, and as this source of supply was cut off, they were unable to boil their vegetables. For three weeks they thus exultingly endured their martyrdom in a holy cause. Matters became more serious when the indomitable Guillem Arnaud sent from Carcassonne a letter to the prior saying, that as no one dared to cite the contumacious citizens, he was forced to order two of the friars to summon them to appear before him personally in Carcassonne to answer for their faith, and that two others must accompany them as witnesses. Tolling the convent bell, the prior assembled the brethren, and said to them with a joyful countenance: "Brethren, rejoice, for I must send four of you through martyrdom to the throne of the Most High. Such are the

6

commands of our brother, Guillem the inquisitor, and whoever obeys them will be slain on the spot, as threatened by the consuls. Let those who are ready to die for Christ ask pardon." With a common impulse the whole body cast themselves on the ground, which was the Dominican form of asking pardon, and the prior selected four, Raymond de Foix, Jean de Saint-Michel, Gui de Navarre, and Guillem Pelisson. These intrepidly performed their duty, even penetrating when necessary into the bed-chambers of the accused. Only in one{19} house were they ill-treated, and even there, when the sons of the person cited drew knives upon them, the bystanders interfered.

There was evidently nothing to be done with men who thus courted martyrdom. To gratify them would be suicidal, and the consuls decided to expel them. On being informed of this the prior distributed among trusty friends the books and sacred vessels and vestments of the convent. The next day (Nov. 5 or 6, 1235) the friars, after mass, sat down to their simple meal, during which the consuls came with a great crowd and threatened to break in the door. The friars marched in procession to their church, where they took their seats, and when the consuls entered and commanded them to depart they refused. Then each was seized and violently led forth, two of them who threw themselves on the ground near the door being picked up by the hands and feet and carried out. Thus they were accompanied through the town, but not otherwise maltreated, and they turned the affair into a procession, marching two by two and singing Te Deum and Salve Regina. At first they went to a farm belonging to the church of Saint-Étienne, but the consuls posted guards to see that nothing was furnished to them, and the next day the prior distributed them among the convents of the province. That the whole affair enlisted for them the sympathies of the faithful was shown by two persons of consideration joining them and entering the Order while it was going on.[21]

It is significant of the position which Guillem Arnaud's steadfastness had already won for his office that to him was conceded the vindication of this series of outrages on the immunity of the Church. Bishop Raymond had joined him in Carcassonne without anathematizing the authors of his exile, but now the anathema promptly went forth, November 10, 1235, uttered by the inquisitor with the names of the Bishops of Toulouse and Carcassonne appended as assenting witnesses. It was confined to the consuls, but Count Raymond was not allowed to escape the responsibility. The excommunication was sent to the Franciscans of Toulouse for publication, and when they obeyed they too were expelled, in no gentle{20} fashion, and the rebellious city was virtually left without ecclesiastics. Further excommunications followed, now including the count, and Prior Pons de Saint-Gilles hastened to Italy to pour the story of his woes into the sympathizing ears of the pope and the sacred college. Gregory assailed the count as the chief offender. A minatory brief of April 28, 1236, addressed to him, is couched in the severest language. He is held responsible for the audacious acts of the consuls; he is significantly reminded of the unperformed vow of the crusade; not only has he failed to extirpate heresy according to his pledges, but he is a manifest fautor and protector of heretics; his favorites and officers are suspect of heresy; he protects those who have been condemned; his lands are a place of refuge for those flying from persecution elsewhere, so that heresy is daily spreading and conversions from Catholicism are frequent, while zealous churchmen seeking to restrain them are slain and abused with impunity. All this he is peremptorily ordered to correct and to sail with his knights to the Holy Land in the "general passage" of the following March. It scarcely needed the reminder, which the pope did not spare him, of the labors which the Church and its Crusaders had undergone to purge his lands of heresy. He had too keen a recollection of the abyss from which he had escaped to risk another plunge. He had gone as far as he dared in the effort to protect his subjects, and it were manifest folly to draw upon his head and theirs another inroad of the marauders whom the pope with a word could let loose upon him to earn salvation with the sword.[22]

The epistle to Raymond was accompanied with one to the legate, instructing him to compel the count to make amends and perform the crusade. To Frederic II. he wrote forbidding him to call on Raymond for feudal services, as the count was under excommunication and virtually a heretic, to which the emperor replied, reasonably enough, that, so long as Raymond enjoyed possession of fiefs held under the empire, excommunication should not{21} confer on him the advantage of release from their burdens. King Louis was also appealed to and was urged to hasten the marriage between his brother Alfonse and Raymond's daughter Jeanne. With the spectre of all Europe in arms looming up before him Raymond could do nothing but yield. When, therefore, the legate summoned him to meet the inquisitors at Carcassonne he meekly went there and conferred with them and the bishops. The conference ended with his promise to return the bishop and friars and clergy to Toulouse, and this promise he kept. The friars were duly reinstated September 4, after ten months of exile. That Guillem Arnaud returned with them is a matter of course.[23]

Pierre Cella was still restricted to his diocese of Querci, and as Guillem required a colleague, a concession was made to popular feeling by the legate in appointing a Franciscan, it being imagined that the comparative mildness of that Order might serve to modify the hatred felt towards the Dominicans. The post was conferred on the provincial minister, Jean de Notoyra, but his other duties were too engrossing, and he substituted Frère Étienne de Saint-Thibery, who had the reputation of being a modest and courteous man. If hopes were entertained that thus the severity of the Inquisition would be tempered, they were disappointed. The two men worked cordially together, with a single purpose and perfect unanimity.[24]

Guillem Arnaud's activity was untiring. During his exile in Carcassonne he occupied himself with the trial of the Seigneur de Niort, whom he sentenced in February or March, 1236.[25] In the early months of 1237 we

7

hear of him in Querci, co-operating with Pierre Cella in harrying the heretics of Montauban. During his absence there occurred a crowning mercy in Toulouse, which threw the heretics into a spasm of terror and contributed greatly to their destruction. Raymond Gros, who had been a perfected heretic for more than twenty years, one of the most loved and trusted leaders of the sect, was suddenly converted. Tradition relates that a quarter of a century before he had been seized and consigned{22} to the stake, when the prophetic spirit of St. Dominic, foreseeing that he would return to the Church and perform shining service in the cause of God, rescued him from the flames. On April 2, without heralding, he presented himself at the Dominican convent, humbly begged to be received into the Church, and promised to do whatever should be required of him. With the eagerness of an impassioned convert he proceeded to reveal all that lifelong intercourse with the Cathari had brought to his knowledge. So full were his recollections that several days were required to write down all the names and facts that crowded to his lips. The lists were long and embraced prominent nobles and citizens, confirming suspicion in many cases, and revealing heresy in other quarters where it was wholly unlooked for.

Guillem Arnaud hurried back from Montauban to take full advantage of this act of Providence. The heretics were stunned. None of them dared to deny the truth of the accusations made by Raymond Gros. Many fled, some of whose names reappear in the massacre of Avignonet and the final catastrophe of Montségur. Many recanted and furnished further revelations. Long lists were made out of those who had been hereticated on their death-beds, and multitudes of corpses were exhumed and burned, with the resultant harvest of confiscations. It is difficult to exaggerate the severity of the blow thus received by heresy. Toulouse was its headquarters. Here were the nobles and knights, the consuls and rich burghers who had thus far defied scrutiny and had protected their less fortunate comrades. Now scattered and persecuted, forced to recant, or burned, the power of the secret organization was broken irrevocably. We can well appreciate the pious exultation of the chronicler as he winds up his account of the consternation and destruction thus visited upon the heretical community—"Their names are not written in the Book of Life, but their bodies here were burned and their souls are tortured in hell!" A single sentence of February 19, 1238, in which more than twenty penitents were consigned *en masse* to perpetual imprisonment, shows the extent of the harvest and the haste of the harvesters.[26]{23}

The Inquisition thus had overcome the popular horror which its proceedings had excited; it had braved the shock and triumphed over the opposition of the secular authorities, and had planted itself firmly in the soil. After the harvest had been gathered in Toulouse it was evident to the indefatigable activity of the inquisitors that they could best perform their functions by riding circuit and holding assizes in all the towns subject to their jurisdiction, and this was represented as a concession to avert the complaints of those who deemed it a hardship to be summoned to distant places. Their incessant labors began to tell. Heretics were leaving the lands of Raymond at last and seeking a refuge elsewhere. Possibly some of them found it in the domains which had fallen to the crown, for in this year we find Gregory scolding the royal officials for their slackness of zeal in executing sentences against powerful heretics. Elsewhere, however, there was no rest for them. In Provence this year Pons de l'Esparre made himself conspicuous for the energy and effectiveness with which he confounded the enemies of the faith; while Montpellier, alarmed at the influx of heretics and their success in propagating their errors, appealed to Gregory to favor them with some assistance that should effectively resist the rising tide, and Gregory at once ordered his legate Jean de Vienne to go thither and take the necessary measures.[27]

The progress of the Inquisition, however, was not destined to be uninterrupted. Count Raymond, apparently reckless of the numerous excommunications under which he lay, so far from sailing for Palestine in March, had seized Marseilles, which was in rebellion against its suzerain, the Count of Provence. This aroused anew the indignation of Gregory, not only because of its interference with the war against the Saracens in Spain and the Holy Land, but because of the immunity which heretics would enjoy{24} during the quarrel of the Christian princes. He peremptorily ordered Raymond to desist from his enterprise on Marseilles, and to perform his Crusader's vow. An appeal was made to King Louis and Queen Blanche, whose intervention procured for Raymond not only a postponement of the crusade for another year, but an order to the legate empowering him to grant the count's request to take the Inquisition entirely out of the hands of the Dominicans, if, on investigation, he should find justification for Raymond's assertion that they were actuated by hatred towards himself. Fresh troubles had arisen at Toulouse. July 24, 1237, the inquisitors had again excommunicated the viguier and consuls, because they had not arrested and burned Alaman de Roaix and some other heretics, condemned *in absentia*, and Raymond was resolved, if possible, to relieve himself and his subjects from the cruel oppression to which they were exposed.[28]

In this his efforts were crowned with most unlooked-for success. May 13, 1238, he obtained a suspension for three months of all inquisitorial proceedings, during which time his envoys sent to Gregory were to be heard. They seem to have used most persuasive arguments, for Gregory wrote to the Bishop of Toulouse to continue the suspension until the new legate, the Cardinal-bishop of Palestrina, should examine into the complaints against the Dominicans and consider the advisability of granting Raymond's request that the business of persecution should be confined, as formerly, to the bishops. Raymond's crusade was also reduced to three years, to be performed voluntarily, provided he would give to King Louis sufficient security that he would sail the following year: by performing this, and making amends for the wrongs inflicted on the Church, he was to earn absolution from his numerous excommunications.[29]

The temporary suspension was unexpectedly prolonged, for, {25} owing to hostilities with Frederic II., the cardinal-legate's departure was postponed for a year. When at least he came, in 1239, he brought special orders to the inquisitors to obey his commands. What investigation he made and what were his conclusions we have no means of knowing, but this at least is certain, that until late in 1241 the Inquisition was effectually muzzled. No traces remain of its activity during these years, and Catholic and Catharan alike could draw a freer breath, relieved of apprehension from its ever-present supervision and the seemingly superhuman energy of the friars.[30]

We can readily conjecture the reasons which impelled its reinstatement. Doubtless the bishops were as negligent as of old, and looked after their temporalities to the exclusion of their duties in preserving the purity of the faith. Doubtless, too, the heretics, encouraged by virtual toleration, grew bolder, and cherished hopes of a return to the good old times, when, secure under their native princes, they could safely defy distant Paris and yet more distant Rome. The condition of the country was, in fact, by no means reassuring, especially in the regions which had become domains of the crown. The land was full of knights and barons who were more or less openly heretics, and who knew not when the blow might fall on them; of seigneurs who had been proscribed for heresy; of enforced converts who secretly longed to avow their hidden faith, and to regain their confiscated lands; of penitents burning to throw off the crosses imposed on them, and to avenge the humiliations which they had endured. Refugees, *faidits*, and heretic teachers were wandering through the mountains, dwelling in caverns and in the recesses of the forests. Scarce a family but had some kinsman to avenge, who had fallen in the field or had perished at the stake. The lack of prisons and the parsimony of the prelates had prevented a general resort to imprisonment, and the burnings had not been numerous enough to notably reduce the numbers of those who were of necessity bitterly opposed to the existing order. Suddenly, in 1240, an insurrection appeared, headed by Trencavel, son of that Viscount of Béziers whom we have seen entrapped by Simon de Montfort and dying opportunely in {26} his hands, not without suspicion of poison. He brought with him from Catalonia troops of proscribed knights and gentlemen, and was greeted enthusiastically by the vassals and subjects of his house. Count Raymond, his cousin, held aloof; but his ambiguous conduct showed plainly that he was prepared to act on either side as success or defeat might render advisable. At first the rising seemed to prosper. Trencavel laid siege to his ancestral town of Carcassonne, and the spirit of his followers was shown when, on the surrender of the suburb, they slaughtered in cold blood thirty ecclesiastics who had received solemn assurance of free egress to Narbonne.[31]

It required but a small force of royal troops under Jean de Beaumont to crush the insurrection as quickly as it had arisen, and to inflict a vengeance which virtually annihilated the *petite noblesse* of the region; but, nevertheless, the lesson which it taught was not to be neglected. The civil order, as now established in the south of France, evidently rested in the religious order, and the maintenance of this required hands more vigorous and watchful than those of the self-seeking prelates. A great assembly of the Cathari held in 1241, on the bank of the Larneta, under the presidency of Aymeri de Collet, heretic Bishop of Albi, showed how bold they had become, and how confidently they looked to the future. Church and State both could see now, if not before, that the Inquisition was a necessary factor in securing to both the advantages gained in the crusades.[32]

Gregory IX., the founder of the Inquisition, died August 22, 1241. It is probable that, before his death, he had put an end to the suspension of the Inquisition and slipped the hounds from the leash, for his immediate successor, Celestin IV., enjoyed a pontificate of but nineteen days—from September 20 to October 8—and then followed an interregnum until the election of Innocent IV., June 28, 1243, so that for nearly two years the papal throne {27} was practically vacant. Raymond's policy, for the moment, had leaned towards gratifying the papacy, for he desired from Gregory not only the removal of his four excommunications and forbearance in the matter of the crusade, but also a dispensation to enable him to carry out a contract of marriage into which he entered with Sanche, daughter and heiress of the Count of Provence, not foreseeing that Queen Blanche would juggle him in this, and, by securing the brilliant match for her son Charles, found the House of Anjou-Provence, and win for the royal family another large portion of the South. Full of these projects, which promised so well for the rehabilitation of his power, he signed, April 18, 1241, with Jayme I. of Aragon, a treaty of alliance for the defence of the Holy See and the Catholic faith, and against the heretics. Under such influences he was not likely to oppose the renewal of active persecution. Besides, he had been compromised in Trencavel's insurrection; he had been summoned to answer for his conduct before King Louis, when, on March 14, he had been forced to take an oath to banish from his lands the *faidits* and enemies of the king, and to capture without delay the castle of Montségur, the last refuge of heresy.[33]

The case of the Seigneurs de Niort, powerful nobles of Fenouillèdes, who had taken part in Trencavel's insurrection, is interesting from the light which it throws upon the connection between the religion and the politics of the time, the difficulties which the Inquisition experienced in dealing with stubborn heresy and patriotism, and the damage inflicted on the heretic cause by the abortive revolt. The three brothers—Guillem Guiraud, Bernard Otho, and Guiraud Bernard—with their mother, Esclarmonde, had long been a quarry which both the inquisitors and the royal seneschal of Carcassonne had been eager to capture. Guillem had earned the reputation of a valiant knight in the wars of the crusades, and the brothers had managed to hold their castles and their power through all the vicissitudes of the time. In the general inquisition made by Cardinal Romano in 1229 they were described as among the chief leaders of the heretics, and the Council of Toulouse, at the same time,

9

denounced two of them as enemies of the faith, and declared them excommunicate if they did not submit within{28} fifteen days. In 1233 we hear of their having, not long before, laid waste with fire and sword the territories of Pierre Amiel, Archbishop of Narbonne, and they had assailed and wounded him while on his way to the Holy See, an exploit which led Gregory IX. to order the archbishop, in conjunction with the Bishop of Toulouse, to proceed against them energetically, while at the same time he invoked the secular arm by a pressing command to Count Raymond. It was probably under this authority that Bishop Raymond du Fauga and the Provost of Toulouse held an inquest on them, in which was taken the testimony of Pierre Amiel and of one hundred and seven other witnesses. The evidence was conflicting. The archbishop swore at great length as to the misdeeds of his enemies. They were all heretics. At one time they kept in their Castle of Dourne no less than thirty perfected heretics, and they had procured the assassination of André Chaulet, Seneschal of Carcassonne, because he had endeavored to obtain evidence against them. Other witnesses were equally emphatic. Bernard Otho on one occasion had silenced a priest in his own church, and had replaced him in the pulpit with a heretic, who had preached to the congregation. On the other hand, there were not wanting witnesses who boldly defended them. The preceptor of the Hospital at Puységur swore to the orthodoxy of Bernard Otho, and declared that what he had done for the faith and for peace had caused the death of a thousand heretics. A priest swore to having seen him assist in capturing heretics, and an archdeacon declared that he would not have remained in the land but for the army which Bernard raised after the death of the late king, adding that he believed the prosecution arose rather from hate than from charity. Nothing came of this attempt, and in 1234 we meet with Bernard Otho as a witness to a transaction between the royal Seneschal of Carcassonne and the Monastery of Alet; but when the Inquisition was established it was promptly brought to bear on the nobles who persisted in maintaining their feudal independence in spite of the fact that their immediate suzerain was now the king. In 1235 Guillem Arnaud, the inquisitor, while in Carcassonne, with the Archdeacon of Carcassonne as assistant, cited the three brothers and their mother to answer before him. Bernard Otho and Guillem obeyed the summons, but would confess nothing. Then the seneschal seized them; under compulsion{29} Guillem made confession ample to warrant the inquisitor in sentencing him to perpetual prison (March 2, 1236), while Bernard, remaining obdurate, was condemned as a contumacious heretic (February 13, 1236), and the seneschal made preparations to burn him. Guiraud and his mother, Esclarmonde, were further condemned, March 2, for contumacious absence. Guiraud, however, who had wisely kept at large, began to fortify his castles and make warlike demonstrations so formidable that the Frenchmen scattered through the land took alarm. The Maréchal de la Foi, Levis of Mirepoix, stood firm, but the rest so worked upon the seneschal that the brothers were released, and the inquisitors had only the barren satisfaction of condemning the whole family on paper—a disappointment alleviated, it is true, by gathering for the stake a rich harvest of less formidable heretics, both clerks and laymen. Equally vain was an effort made two years later by the inquisitors to compel Count Raymond to carry out their sentence by confiscating the lands of the contumacious nobles, but the failure of Trencavel's revolt forced them to sue for peace. Bernard Otho was again brought before the Inquisition, and Guillem de Niort made submission for himself and brothers, surrendering their castles to the king on condition that he would procure their reconciliation with the Church, and that of their mother, nephews, and allies, and, failing to accomplish this by the next Pentecost, that he would restore their castles and grant them a month of truce to put themselves in defence. King Louis ratified the treaty in January, 1241, but refused, when the time came, to restore the castles, only agreeing to pay over the revenues on consideration that the brothers should reside outside of Fenouillèdes. Guillem died in 1256, when Louis kept both castles and revenues, under pretext that the treaty had been a personal one with Guillem. The new order of things by this time had become so firmly established that no further resistance was to be dreaded. The extinction of this powerful family is a typical example of the manner in which the independence of the local seigneurie was gradually broken down by means of the Inquisition, and the authority of crown and Church was extended over the land.[34]{30}

Under the reaction consequent upon Trencavel's failure, and emboldened by the ruin of the local protectors of the people, the inquisitors returned to their work with sharpened zeal and redoubled energy. Chance has preserved for us a record of sentences pronounced by Pierre Cella, during a circuit of a few months in Querci, from Advent, 1241, to Ascension, 1242, which affords us a singularly instructive insight into one phase of inquisitorial operations. We have seen that, when an inquisitor visited a town, he proclaimed a "time of grace," during which those who voluntarily came forward and confessed were spared the harsher punishments of prison, confiscation, or the stake, and that the Inquisition found this expedient exceedingly fruitful, not only in the number of penitents which it brought in, but in the testimony which was gathered concerning the more contumacious. The record in question consists of cases of this kind, and its crowded calendar justifies the esteem in which the method was held.[35]

Summarized, the record shows—

In Gourdon	19	sentences pronounced in Advent, 1241.
In Montcucq	4	" " " Lent, 1242.
In		

In Sauveterre	.	
In Belcayre	.	
In Montauban	54	sentences pronounced in week before Ascension (May 21-28, 1242).
In Moissac	9	" " " week of Ascension (May 28-June 5, 1242).
In Montpezat	2	" " " Lent, 1242.
In Montaut	3	" " " " "
In Castelnau	1	" " " " "
Total	24	

{31}

Of these penitents four hundred and twenty-seven were ordered to make the distant pilgrimage to Compostella, in the northwestern corner of Spain—some four hundred or five hundred miles of mountainous roads. One hundred and eight were sent to Canterbury, this pilgrimage, in all but three or four cases, being superimposed on that to Compostella. Only two penitents were required to visit Rome, but seventy-nine were ordered to serve in the crusades for terms varying from one to eight years.

The first thing that impresses one in considering this record is the extraordinary speed with which the work was done. The whole was despatched in six months, and there is no evidence that the labor was continuous—in fact, it could not have been so, for the inquisitor had to move from place to place, to grant the necessary delays, and must have been frequently interrupted to gather in the results of testimony which implicated recusants. With what reckless lack of consideration the penances were imposed is shown by the two hundred and nineteen penitents of Gourdon, whose confessions were taken down and whose sentences were pronounced within the four weeks of Advent; and even this is outstripped by the two hundred and fifty-two of Montauban, despatched in the week before Ascension, at the rate of forty-two for each working-day. In several cases two culprits are included in the same sentence.

Even more significant than this, however, are the enormous numbers—two hundred and nineteen for a small town like Gourdon and eighty-four for Montcucq. The number of these who were really heretics, both Catharan and Waldensian, is large, and shows how thoroughly the population was interpenetrated with heresy. Even more, however, were good Catholics whose cases prove how amicably the various sects associated together, and how impossible it was for the most orthodox to avoid the association with heretics which rendered him liable to punishment. This friendly intercourse is peculiarly notable in the case of a priest who confessed to having gone to some heretics in a vineyard, where he read in their books and ate pears with them. He was rudely reminded of his indiscretion by being suspended from his functions, sent to Compostella and thence to Rome, with letters from the inquisitors which doubtless were not for his benefit, for apparently they felt unable to decide what ought to be done for{32} an offence so enormous. Even the smallest derelictions of this sort were rigorously penanced. A citizen of Sauveterre had seen three heretics entering the house of a sick man, and heard that they had hereticated him, but knew nothing of his own knowledge, yet he was subjected to the disgrace of a penitential pilgrimage to Puy. Another, of Belcayre, had carried a message between two heretics, and was sent to Puy, St. Gilles, and Compostella. A physician of Montauban had bound up the arm of a heretic and was subjected to the same three pilgrimages, and the same penance was inflicted on a woman who had simply eaten at a table with heretics. The same was prescribed in several cases of boatmen who had ignorantly transported heretics, without recognizing them until the voyage was under way or finished. A woman who had eaten and drunk with another woman who she heard was a heretic was sentenced to the pilgrimages of Puy and St. Gilles, and the same penance was ordered for a man who had once seen heretics, and for a woman who had consulted a Waldensian about her sick son. The Waldenses had great reputation as skilful leeches, and two men who had called them in for their wives and children were penanced with the pilgrimages of Puy, St. Gilles, and Compostella. A man who had seen heretics two or three times, and had already purchased reconciliation by a gift to a monastery, was sent on a long series of pilgrimages, embracing both Compostella and Canterbury, besides wearing the yellow cross for a year. Another was sent to Compostella because he had once been thrown into company with heretics in a boat, although he had left them on hearing their heresies; and yet another because, when a boy, he had spent part of a day and night with heretics. One who had seen heretics when he was twelve years old was sent to Puy; while a woman who had seen them in her father's house was obliged to go to Puy and St. Gilles. A man who had seen two heretics leaving a place which he had rented was sent to Compostella, and another who had allowed his Waldensian mother to visit him and had given her an ell of cloth was forced to expiate it with pilgrimages to Puy, St. Gilles, and Compostella.[36] The list might be prolonged

11

almost indefinitely, but these cases will suffice to {33} show the character of the offence and the nature of the grace proffered for voluntary confession. There is no pretence that any of these particular culprits themselves were not wholly orthodox, but the people were to be taught that the toleration which had existed for generations was at an end; that the neighborly intercourse which had established itself between Catholic and Catharan and Waldensian was in itself a sin; that the heretic was to be tracked and captured like a wild beast, or at least to be shunned like a leper.

When such was the measure meted out to spontaneous penitents within the time of grace, with harsher measures in reserve for those subsequently detected, we can easily imagine the feelings inspired by the Inquisition in the whole population, without distinction of creed, and the terror common to all when the rumor spread that the inquisitors were coming. Scarce any one but was conscious of some act—perhaps of neighborly charity—that rendered him a criminal to the awful fanaticism of Pierre Cella or Guillem Arnaud. The heretics themselves would look to be imprisoned for life, with confiscation, or to be burned, or sent to Constantinople to support the tottering Latin Empire; while the Catholics were likely to fare little better on the distant pilgrimages to which they were sentenced, even though they were spared the sterner punishments or the humiliation of the saffron cross. Such a visit would bring, even to the faithful, the desolation of a pestilence. The inquisitors would pass calmly on, leaving a neighborhood well-nigh depopulated—fathers and mothers despatched to distant shrines for months or years, leaving dependent families to starve, or harvests ungathered to be the prey of the first-comer, all the relations of a life, hard enough at the best, disturbed and broken up. Even such a record as that of Pierre Cella's sentences rendered within the time of grace shows but a portion of the work. A year or two later we find the Council of Narbonne beseeching the inquisitors to delay rendering sentences of incarceration, because the numbers of those flocking in for reconciliation after the expiration of the term of grace were so great that it would be impossible to raise funds for their maintenance, or to find stones enough, even in that mountainous land, to build prisons to contain them.[37] {34} That a whole vicinage, when it had timely notice, should bind itself in a league to defeat the purpose of the inquisitors, as at Castelnaudary, must have been a frequent experience; that, sooner or later, despair should bring about a catastrophe like that of Avignonet was inevitable.

Montségur for years had been the Mount Tabor of the Cathari—the place of refuge in which, as its name implies, they could feel secure when safety could be hoped for nowhere else. It had been destroyed, but early in the century Raymond de Péreille had rebuilt it, and for forty years he held it as an asylum for heretics, whom he defended to the utmost of his ability. In 1232 the Catharan bishops Tento of Agen and Guillabert de Castres of Toulouse, with a number of ministers, foreseeing, in the daily increasing pressure of persecution, the necessity of some stronghold which should serve as an asylum, arranged with Raymond that he should receive and shelter all fugitives of the sect and guard the common treasure to be deposited there. His castle, situated in the territories of the marshals of Mirepoix, had never opened its gates to the Frenchmen. Its almost inaccessible peak had been sedulously strengthened with all that military experience could suggest or earnest devotion could execute. Ever since the persecutions of the Inquisition commenced we hear of those who fled to Montségur when they found the inquisitor's hand descending upon them. Dispossessed knights, *faidits* of all kinds, brought their swords to its defence; Catharan bishops and ministers sought it when hard pressed, or made it a resting-place in their arduous and dangerous mission-work. Raymond de Péreille himself sought its shelter when, compromised by the revelations of Raymond Gros, he fled from Toulouse, in 1237, with his wife Corba; the devotion of his race to heresy being further proved by the fate of his daughter Esclarmonde, who perished for her faith at the stake, and by the Catharan episcopate of his brother Arnaud Roger. Such a stronghold in the hands of desperate men, fired with the fiercest fanaticism, was a menace to the stability of the new order in the State; to the Church it was an accursed spot whence heresy might at any moment burst forth to overspread the land again. Its destruction had long been the desire of all good Catholics, and Raymond's pledge to King Louis, March 14, 1241, to capture it had {35} been one of the conditions on which his suspicious relations with Trencavel had been condoned. In fact, he made some show of besieging it during the same year, but success would have been most damaging to the plans which he was nursing, and his efforts can scarce have been more than a cover for military preparations destined to a far different object. The French army, after the suppression of the rising, also laid siege to Montségur, but were unable to effect its reduction.[38]

On Ascension night, 1242, while Pierre Cella was tranquilly winding up his work at Montauban, the world was startled with the news that a holocaust of the terrible inquisitors had been made at Avignonet, a little town about twelve leagues from Toulouse. The stern Guillem Arnaud and the courteous Étienne de Saint-Thibery were making, like their colleague Pierre Cella, a circuit through the district subjected to their mercy. Some of their sentences which have been preserved show that in November, 1241, they were laboring at Lavaur and at Saint-Paul de Caujoux, and in the spring of 1242 they came to Avignonet.[39] Raymond d'Alfaro was its bailli for the count, who was his uncle through his mother, Guillemetta, a natural daughter of Raymond VI. When he heard that the inquisitors and their assistants were coming he lost no time in preparing for their destruction. A swift messenger was despatched to the heretics of Montségur, and in answer to his summons Pierre Roger of Mirepoix, with a number of knights and their retainers, started at once. They halted in the forest of Gaiac, near Avignonet, where food was brought them, and they were joined by about thirty armed men of the vicinage, who waited with them till after nightfall. Had this plot failed, d'Alfaro had arranged another for an ambuscade on the road to Castelnaudary, and the fact that so extensive a conspiracy could be organized on the spot, without finding a traitor to betray it, shows how general was the hate that had been earned by the cruel work of the Inquisition. Not less significant is the fact that on their return to Montségur the murderers were hospitably entertained at the Château de Saint-Félix by a priest who was cognizant of their bloody deed.

The victims came unsuspectingly to the trap. There were {36} eleven in all. The two inquisitors, with two Dominican friars, and one Franciscan, the Benedictine Prior of Avignonet, Raymond de Costiran, Archdeacon of Lezat, a former troubadour, of whose verses only a single obscene song remains, a clerk of the archdeacon, a notary, and two apparitors—in all a court fully furnished for the despatch of business. They were hospitably received and housed in the castle of the count, where on the morrow they were to open their dread tribunal for the trembling inhabitants. When darkness came a selected band of twelve, armed with axes, left the forest and stole cautiously to a postern of the castle, where they were met by Golairan, a comrade of d'Alfaro, who assured himself that all was right, and returned to see what the inquisitors were doing. Coming back, he reported that they were drinking; but a second visit, after an interval, brought the welcome news that they were going to bed. As though apprehensive of danger, they had remained together in the great hall, and had barricaded the door. The gate was opened, the men of Montségur were admitted and were joined by d'Alfaro, armed with a mace, and twenty-five men of Avignonet, and the fact that an esquire in the service of the inquisitors was with him indicates that there was treachery at work. The hall-door was quickly broken down, the wild band of assassins rushed in, and, after despatching their victims, there was a fierce chorus of gratified vengeance, each man boasting of his share in the bloody deed—d'Alfaro especially, who shouted "*Va be, esta be,*" and claimed that his mace had done its full duty in the murderous work. Its crushing of Guillem Arnaud's skull had deprived Pierre Roger de Mirepoix, the second in command at Montségur, of the drinking-cup which he had demanded as his reward for the assistance furnished. The plunder of the victims was eagerly shared between the assassins—their horses, books, garments—even to their scapulars. When the news reached Rome, the College of Cardinals made haste to express their belief that the victims had become blessed martyrs of Jesus Christ, and one of the first acts of Innocent IV., after his installation in June, 1243, was to repeat this declaration; but they never were canonized, in spite of frequent requests to the Holy See, and of the numerous miracles which attested their sanctity in the popular cult, until, in 1866, Pius IX. gave them tardy recognition.[40]{37}

Like the murder of the legate Pierre de Castelnau, in 1208, the massacre of Avignonet was a fatal error. Its violation of the traditional sanctity of the ecclesiastic sent a thrill of horror even among those who had small sympathy with the cruelty of the Inquisition, while the deliberateness of its planning and its unsparing ferocity gave color to the belief that heresy was only to be extirpated by force. Sympathy, indeed, for a time might well change sides, for the massacre was practically unavenged. Frère Ferrer, the Inquisitor of Carcassonne, made due inquest into the affair, and after the capture of Montségur, in 1244, some of the participants confessed all the details, but the real culprits escaped. Count Raymond, it is true, when he had leisure from pressing business, hanged a few of the underlings, but we find Raymond d'Alfaro, in 1247, promoted to be Viguier of Toulouse, and representing his master in the proceedings with regard to the burial of the old count, and, finally, he was one of the nine witnesses to Raymond's last will. Another ringleader, Guillem du Mas-Saintes-Puelles, is recorded as taking the oath of allegiance to Count Alfonse, in 1249, after the death of Raymond. Guillem's participation in the murders has special interest, as showing the antagonism created by the violence of the Inquisition, for in 1233, as Bailli of Lavaur, he had dutifully seized a number of heretics and carried them to Toulouse, where they were promptly burned.[41]

The massacre of Avignonet came at a time peculiarly unfortunate for Count Raymond, who was nursing comprehensive and far-reaching plans, then ripe for execution, for the rehabilitation of his house and the independence of his land. He could not escape the responsibility for the catastrophe which public opinion {38} everywhere attached to him. Although he had recently, on March 14, solemnly sworn to persecute heresy with his whole strength when, apparently sick unto death, he had sought absolution at the hands of the episcopal official of Agen, yet he was known to be hostile to the Dominicans as inquisitors, and had bitterly opposed the restoration of their functions. On May 1, just four weeks before the event, he had made a solemn declaration in the presence of numerous prelates and nobles to the effect that he had appealed to Rome against the commission of Dominican inquisitors by the provincial in his territories, and that he intended to prosecute that appeal. He protested that he earnestly desired the eradication of heresy, and urged the bishops to exercise energetically their ordinary power to that end, promising his full support to them and the execution of the law both as to confiscation and the death-penalty. He would even accept the friars as inquisitors provided they acted independently of their Orders, and not under the authority of their provincials. One of his baillis even threatened, in the church of Moissac, seizure of person and property for all who should submit to the penalties imposed by the inquisitors, as they were not authorized by the count to administer justice. Such being his position, it was inevitable that he should be regarded as an accomplice in the murders, and that the cause which he represented should suffer greatly in the revulsion of public feeling which it occasioned.[42]

Raymond had been busy in effecting a widespread alliance which should wring from the House of Capet its conquests of the last quarter of a century. He had been joined by the Kings of England, Castile, and Aragon, and the Count de la Marche, and everything bid fair for his reconquest of his old domains. The massacre of

Avignonet was a most untoward precursor of the revolt which burst forth immediately afterwards. It shook the fidelity of some of his vassals, who withdrew their support; and, to counteract its impression, he felt obliged to convert his sham siege of Montségur into an active one, thus employing troops which he could ill spare. Yet the rising, for a while, promised success, and Raymond even reassumed his old title of Duke of{39} Narbonne. King Louis, however, was equal to the occasion, and allowed the allies no time to concentrate their forces. His victories over the English and Gascons at Taillebourg and Saintes, July 19 and 23, deprived Raymond of all hope of assistance from that quarter. Pestilence forced the withdrawal of the main army of Louis, but a force under the veteran Imbert de Beaujeu operated actively against Raymond, who, without help from his allies and deserted by many of his vassals, was obliged to lay down his arms, December 22. When suing for peace he pledged himself to extirpate heresy and to punish the assassins of Avignonet with an effusiveness which shows the importance attached to these conditions. The sagacity and moderation of King Louis granted him easy terms, but one of the stipulations of settlement was that every male inhabitant over the age of fifteen should take an oath to assist the Church against heresy, and the king against Raymond, in case of another revolt. Thus the purity of the faith and the supremacy of the foreign domination were once again recognized as inseparably allied.[43]

The triumph of both had been secured. This ended the last serious effort of the South to recover its independence. Henceforth, under the treaty of Paris, it was to pass irrevocably into the hands of the stranger, and the Inquisition was to have unrestricted opportunity to enforce conformity in religion. It was in vain that Raymond again, at the Council of Béziers, April 20, 1243, summoned the bishops of his dominions—those of Toulouse, Agen, Cahors, Albi, and Rodez—urging them personally or through proper deputies, whether Cistercians, Dominicans, or Franciscans, to make diligent inquisition after heresy, and pledged the assistance of the secular arm for its extirpation. It was equally in vain that, immediately on the accession of Innocent IV., in June, a deputation of Dominicans, frightened by the warning of Avignonet, earnestly alleged many reasons why the dangerous burden should be lifted from their shoulders. The pope peremptorily refused, and ordered them to continue their holy labors, even at the risk of martyrdom.[44]{40}

Despite this single exhibition of hesitation and weakness, the Order was not lacking in men whose eager fanaticism rendered them fully prepared to accept the perilous post. The peril, indeed, was apparent rather than real—it had passed away in the revulsion which followed the useless bloodshed of Avignonet and the failure of Raymond's rebellion. There was a rising tide in favor of orthodoxy. A confraternity organized in October, 1243, by Durand, Bishop of Albi, is probably only the expression of what was going on in many places. Organized under the protection of St. Cecilia, the members of the association pledged themselves not only to mutual protection, but to aid the bishop to execute justice on heretics, Vaudois and their fautors, and to defend inquisitors as they would their own bodies. Any member suspected of heresy was to be incontinently ejected, and a reward of a silver mark was offered for every heretic captured and delivered to the association. The new pope had, moreover, spoken in no uncertain tone. His refusal to relieve the Dominicans was accompanied with a peremptory command to all the prelates of the region to extend favor, assistance, and protection to the inquisitors in their toils and tribulations. Any slackness in this was freely threatened with the papal vengeance, while favor was significantly promised as the reward of zeal. The Dominicans were urged to fresh exertion to overcome the threatened recrudescence of heresy. A new legate, Zoen, Bishop-elect of Avignon, was also despatched to Languedoc, with instructions to act vigorously. His predecessor had been complained of by the inquisitors for having, in spite of their remonstrances, released many of their prisoners and remitted penances indiscriminately. All such acts of misplaced mercy were pronounced void, and Zoen was ordered to reimpose all such penalties without appeal.[45]

Still more menacing to the heretic cause was the reconciliation at last effected between Raymond and the papacy. In September, 1243, the count visited Italy, where he had an interview with Frederic II. in Apulia, and with Innocent in Rome. For ten years{41} he had been under excommunication, and had carried on an unavailing struggle. He could no longer cherish illusions, and was doubtless ready to give whatever assurances might be required of him. On the other hand, the new pope was free from the predispositions which the long strife had engendered in Gregory IX. There seems to have been little difficulty in reaching an understanding, to which the good offices of Louis IX. powerfully contributed. December 2, Raymond was released from his various excommunications; January 1, 1244, the absolution was announced to King Louis and the prelates of the kingdom, who were ordered to publish it in all the churches, and January 7 the Legate Zoen was instructed to treat him with fatherly affection and not permit him to be molested. In all this absolution had only been given *ad cautelam*, or provisionally, for a special excommunication had been decreed against him as a fautor of heretics, after the massacre of Avignonet, by the inquisitors Ferrer and Guillem Raymond. Against this he had made a special appeal to the Holy See in April, 1243, and a special bull of May 16, 1244, was required for its abrogation. No conditions seem to have been imposed respecting the long-deferred crusade, and thenceforth Raymond lived in perfect harmony with the Holy See. Indeed, he was the recipient of many favors. A bull of March 18, 1244, granted him the privilege that for five years he should not be forced by apostolic letters to answer in judgment outside of his own dominions; another of April 27, 1245, took him, his family, and lands under the special protection of St. Peter and the papacy; and yet another of May 12, 1245, provided that no delegate of the Apostolic See should have power to utter excommunication or any other sentence against him without a special mandate. Besides this, one of April 21, 1245, imposed some limitations on the power of inquisitors, limitations which they seem never to have observed. Raymond was fairly won over. He had evidently resolved to accommodate himself to the necessities of the time, and the heretic had nothing further to hope or the inquisitor to fear from him. The preparation for increased and systematic vigor of operations is seen in the elaborate provisions, so often referred to above, of the Council of Narbonne, held at this period.[46] {42}

Yet so long as heresy retained the stronghold of Montségur as a refuge and rallying-point its secret and powerful organization could not be broken. The capture of that den of outlaws was a necessity of the first order, and as soon as the confusion of the rebellion of 1242 had subsided it was undertaken as a crusade, not by Raymond, but by the Archbishop of Narbonne, the Bishop of Albi, the Seneschal of Carcassonne, and some nobles, either led by zeal or by the hope of salvation. The heretics, on their side, were not idle. Some baillis of Count Raymond sent them Bertrand de la Bacalairia, a skilful maker of military engines, to aid them in the defence, who made no scruple in affirming that he came with the assent of the count, and from every side money, provisions, arms, and munitions of war were poured into the stronghold. In the spring of 1243 the siege began, prosecuted with indefatigable ardor by the besiegers, and resisted with desperate resolution by the besieged. As in the old combats at Toulouse, the women assisted their warriors, and the venerable Catharan bishop, Bertrand Martin, animated their devoted courage with promises of eternal bliss. It is significant of the public temper that sympathizers in the besiegers" camp permitted tolerably free communication between the besieged and their friends, and gave them warning of the plans of attack. Even the treasure which had been stored up in Montségur was conveyed away safely through the investing lines, about Christmas, 1243, to Pons Arnaud de Châteauverdun in the Savartès. Secret relations were maintained with Count Raymond, and the besieged were buoyed up with promises that if they would hold out until Easter, 1244, he would march to their relief with forces supplied by the Emperor Frederic II. It was all in vain. The siege dragged on its weary length for nearly a year, till, on the night of March 1, 1244, guided by some shepherds who betrayed their fellow-countrymen, by almost inaccessible paths among the cliffs, the crusaders surprised and carried one of the outworks. The castle was no longer tenable. A brief parley ensued, and the garrison agreed to surrender at dawn, delivering up to the archbishop all the perfected heretics among them, {43} on condition that the lives of the rest should be spared. Although a few were let down from the walls with ropes and thus escaped, the capitulation was carried out, and the archbishop's shrift was short. At the foot of the mountain-peak an enclosure of stakes was formed, piled high with wood, and set on fire. The Perfect were asked to renounce their faith, and on their refusal were cast into the flames. Thus perished two hundred and five men and women. The conquerors might well write exultingly to the pope, "We have crushed the head of the dragon!"[47]

Although the lives of the rest of the captives were guaranteed, they were utilized to the utmost. For months the inquisitors Ferrer and P. Durant devoted themselves to the examinations to secure evidence against heretics far and near, dead and alive. From the aged Raymond de Péreille to a child ten years of age, they were forced, under repeated interrogatories, to recall every case of adoration and heretication that they could remember, and page after page was covered with interminable lists of names of those present at sermons and *consolamenta* through a period extending back to thirty or forty years before, and embracing the whole land as far as Catalonia. Even those who had brought victual to Montségur and sold it were carefully looked after and set down. It can readily be conceived what an accession was made to the terrible records of the Inquisition, and how valuable was the insight obtained into the ramifications of heresy throughout the land during more than a generation—what digging up of bones would follow with confiscation of estates, and with what unerring certainty the inquisitors would be able to seize their victims and confound their denials. We can only guess at the means by which this information was extracted from the prisoners. Torture had not yet been introduced; life had been promised, and perpetual imprisonment was inevitable for such pronounced heretics; and when we see Raymond de Péreille himself, who had endured unflinchingly the vicissitudes of the crusades, and had bravely held out to the last, ransacking his memory to betray all whom he had ever seen adore a minister, we can imagine the horrors of the two {44} months" preliminary captivity which had so broken his spirit as to bring him to this depth of degradation. Even a perfected heretic, Arnaud de Bretos, captured while flying to Lombardy, was induced to reveal the names of all who had given him shelter and attended his ministrations during his missionary wanderings.[48]

Henceforth the Cathari could hope only in God. All chance of resistance was over. One by one their supports had broken, and there was only left the passive resistance of martyrdom. The Inquisition could track and seize its victims at leisure, and king and count could follow with decrees of confiscation which were gradually to transfer the lands of the South to orthodox and loyal subjects. The strongest testimony that can be given to the living earnestness of the Catharan faith is to be found in the prolongation of this struggle yet through three hopeless generations. It is no wonder, however, if the immediate effect of these crowding events was to fill the heretics with despair. In the poem of Isarn de Villemur, written about this period, the heretic, Sicard de Figueras is represented as saying that their best and most trusted friends are turning against them and betraying them. How many believers at this juncture abandoned their religion, even at the cost of lifelong imprisonment, we have no means of accurately estimating, but the number must have been enormous, to judge from the request, already alluded to, of the Council of Narbonne about this time to the inquisitors to postpone their sentences in view of the impossibility of building prisons sufficient to contain the crowds who hurried in to

15

accuse themselves and seek reconciliation, after the expiration of the time of grace, which Innocent IV., in December, 1243, had ordered to be designated afresh.[49]

Yet, in a population so thoroughly leavened with heresy, these thousands of voluntary penitents still left an ample field of activity for the zeal of the inquisitors. Each one who confessed was bound to give the names of all whom he had seen engaged in heretical acts, and of all who had been hereticated on the death-bed. Innumerable clews were thus obtained to bring to trial those who failed to accuse themselves, and to exhume and burn the bones of those who were beyond the ability to recant. For the next few{45} years the life of the inquisitors was a busy one. The stunned populations no longer offered resistance, and grew used to the despair of the penitents sentenced to perpetual prison, the dragging of decomposed corpses through the streets, and the horror of the Tophets where the victims passed through temporal to eternal flame. Still there is a slight indication that the service was not wholly without danger from the goadings of vengeance or the courage of despair, when the Council of Béziers, in 1246, ordering travelling inquests, makes exception in the cases when it may not be safe for the inquisitors to personally visit the places where the inquisition should be held; and Innocent IV., in 1247, authorizes the inquisitors to cite the accused to come to them, in view of the perils arising from the ambushes of heretics.[50]

The fearless and indefatigable men who now performed the functions of inquisitor in Languedoc can rarely have taken advantage of this concession to weakness. Bernard de Caux, who so well earned the title of the hammer of heretics, was at this time the leading spirit of the Inquisition of Toulouse, after a term of service in Montpellier and Agen, and he had for colleague a kindred spirit in Jean de Saint-Pierre. Together they made a thorough inquest over the whole province, passing the population through a sieve with a completeness which must have left few guilty consciences unexamined. There is extant a fragmentary record of this inquest, covering the years 1245 and 1246, during which no less than six hundred places were investigated, embracing about one half of Languedoc. The magnitude of the work thus undertaken, and the incredible energy with which it was pushed, is seen in the enormous number of interrogatories recorded in petty towns. Thus at Avignonet there are two hundred and thirty; at Fanjoux, one hundred; at Mas-Saintes-Puelles, four hundred and twenty. M. Molinier, to whom we are indebted for an account of this interesting document, has not made an accurate count of the whole number of cases, but estimates that the total cannot fall far short of eight thousand to ten thousand. When we consider what all this involved in the duty of examination and comparison we may well feel wonder at the superhuman energy of these founders of the Inquisition; but we may also assume, as{46} with the sentences of Pierre Cella, that the fate of the victims who were sifted out of this mass of testimony must have been passed upon with no proper or conscientious scrutiny. At least, however, they must have escaped the long and torturing delays customary in the later and more leisurely stages of the Inquisition. With such a record before us it is not easy to understand the complaint of the bishops of Languedoc, in 1245, that the Inquisition was too merciful, that heresy was increasing, and that the inquisitors ought to be urged to greater exertions. It was possibly in consequence of the lack of harmony thus revealed between the episcopate and the Inquisition that Innocent, in April of the same year, ordered the Inquisitors of Languedoc to proceed as usual in cases of manifest heresy, and in those involving slight punishment, while he directed them to suspend proceedings in matters requiring imprisonment, crosses, long pilgrimages, and confiscation until definite rules should be laid down in the Council of Lyons, which he was about to open. These questions, however, were settled in that of Béziers, which met in 1246, and issued a new code of procedure.[51]

In all this Count Raymond, now thoroughly fitted in the Catholic groove, was an earnest participant. As his stormy life drew to its close, harmony with the Church was too great an element of comfort and prosperity for him to hesitate in purchasing it with the blood of a few of his subjects, whom, indeed, he could scarce have saved had he so willed. He gave conspicuous evidence of his hatred of heresy. In 1247 he ordered his officials to compel the attendance of the inhabitants at the sermons of the friars in all towns and villages through which they passed, and in 1249, at Berlaiges, near Agen, he coldly ordered the burning of eighty believers who had confessed their errors in his presence—a piece of cruelty far transcending that habitual with the inquisitors. About the same time King Jayme of Aragon effected a change in the Inquisition in the territories of Narbonne. Possibly this may have had some connection with the murder by the citizens of two{47} officials of the Inquisition and the destruction of its records, giving endless trouble in the effort to reconstruct the lists of sentences and the invaluable accumulation of evidence against suspects. Be this as it may, Innocent IV., at the request of the king, forbade the archbishop and inquisitors from further proceedings against heresy, and then empowered the Dominican Provincial of Spain and Raymond of Pennaforte to appoint new ones for the French possessions of Aragon.[52]

When St. Louis undertook his disastrous crusade to Damietta he was unwilling to leave behind him so dangerous a vassal as Raymond. The vow of service to Palestine had long since been remitted by Innocent IV., but the count was open to persuasion, and the bribes offered show at once the importance attached to his presence with the host and to his absence from home. The king promised him twenty thousand to thirty thousand livres for his expenses and the restitution of the duchy of Narbonne on his return. The pope agreed to pay him two thousand marks on his arrival beyond seas, and that he should have during his absence all the proceeds of the redemption of vows and all legacies bequeathed to the crusade. The prohibition of imposing penitential crusades on converted heretics was also suspended for his benefit, while the other long pilgrimages

16

customarily employed as penances were not to be enjoined while he was in service. Stimulated by these dazzling rewards, he assumed the cross in earnest, and his ardor for the purity of the faith grew stronger. Even the tireless activity of Bernard de Caux was insufficient to satisfy him. While that incomparable persecutor was devoting all his energies to working up the results of his tremendous inquests, Raymond, early in 1248, complained to Innocent that the Inquisition was neglecting its duty; that heretics, both living and dead, remained uncondemned; that others from abroad were coming into his own and neighboring territories and spreading their pestilence, so that the land which had been well-nigh purified was again filled with heresy.[53]

Death spared Raymond the misfortunes of the ill-starred Egyptian crusade. When his preparations were almost complete he{48} was seized with mortal illness and died, September 27, 1249, with his latest breath ordering his heirs to restore the sums which he had received for the expedition, and to send fifty knights to serve in Palestine for a year. That his death was generally regretted by his subjects we can readily believe. Not only was it the extinction of the great house which had bravely held its own from Carlovingian times, but the people felt that the last barrier between them and the hated Frenchmen was removed. The heiress Jeanne had been educated at the royal court, and was French in all but birth. Moreover, she seems to have been a nonentity whose influence is imperceptible, and the sceptre of the South passed into the hands of Alphonse of Poitiers, an avaricious and politic prince, whose zeal for orthodoxy was greatly stimulated by the profitable confiscations resulting from persecution. Raymond had required repeated urging to induce him to employ this dreaded penalty with the needful severity. No such watchfulness was necessary in the case of Alphonse. When the rich heritage fell in, he and his wife were with his brother, King Louis, in Egypt, but the vigilant regent, Queen Blanche, promptly took possession in their name, and on their return, in 1251, they personally received the homage of their subjects. By a legal subtlety Alphonse evaded the payment of the pious legacies of Raymond's will, and compounded for it by leaving, on his departure for the North, a large sum to provide for the expenses of the Inquisition, and to furnish wood for the execution of its sentences. Not long afterwards we find him urging his bishops to render more efficient support to the labors of the inquisitors; in his chancery there was a regular formula of a commission for inquisitors, to be sent to Rome for the papal signature; and throughout his twenty years of reign he pursued the same policy without deviation. The urgency with which, in December, 1268, he wrote to Pons de Poyet and Étienne de Gâtine, stimulating them to redoubled activity in clearing his dominions of heretics, was wholly superfluous, but it is characteristic of the line of action which he carried out consistently to the end.[54]

The fate of Languedoc was now irrevocably sealed. Hitherto{49} there had been hopes that perhaps Raymond's inconstancy might lead him to retrace the steps of the last few years. Moreover, his subjects had shared in the desire, manifested in his repeated marriage projects, that he should have an heir to inherit the lands not pledged in succession to his daughter. He was but in his fifty-first year, and the expectation was not unreasonable that his line might be perpetuated and the southern nationality be preserved. All this was now seen to be a delusion, and the most sanguine Catharan could look forward to nothing but a life of concealment ending in prison or fire. Yet the heretic Church stubbornly held its own, though with greatly diminished numbers. Many of its members fled to Lombardy, where, even after the death of Frederic II., the civic troubles and the policy of local despots, such as Ezzelin da Romano, afforded some shelter from the Inquisition. Yet many remained and pursued their wandering missions among the faithful, perpetually tracked by inquisitorial spies, but rarely betrayed. These humble and forgotten men, hopelessly braving hardship, toil, and peril in what they deemed the cause of God, were true martyrs, and their steadfast heroism shows how little relation the truth of a religion bears to the self-devotion of its followers. Rainerio Saccone, the converted Catharan, who had the best means of ascertaining the facts, computes, about this time, that there were in Lombardy one hundred and fifty "perfected" refugees from France, while the churches of Toulouse, Carcassonne, and Albi, including that of Agen, then nearly destroyed, numbered two hundred more. These figures would indicate that a very considerable congregation of believers still existed in spite of the systematic and ruthless proscription of the past twenty years. Their earnestness was kept alive, not only by the occasional and dearly-prized visits of the travelling ministers, but by the frequent intercourse which was maintained with Lombardy. Until the disappearance of the sect on this side of the Alps, there is, in the confessions of penitents, perpetual allusion to these pilgrimages back and forth, which kept up the relations between the refugees and those left at home. Thus, in 1254, Guillem Fournier, in an interrogatory before the Inquisition of Toulouse, relates that he started for Italy with five companions, including two women. His first resting-place was at Coni, where he met many heretics; then at Pavia, where he was hereticated by Raymond{50} Mercier, former deacon of Toulouse. At Cremona he lived for a year with Vivien, the much-loved Bishop of Toulouse, with whom he found a number of noble refugees. At Pisa he stayed for eight months; at Piacenza he again met Vivien, and he finally returned to Languedoc with messages from the refugees to their friends at home. In 1300, at Albi, Étienne Mascot confesses that he had been sent to Lombardy by Master Raymond Calverie to bring back Raymond André, or some other perfected heretic. At Genoa he met Bertrand Fabri, who had been sent on the same errand by Guillem Golfier. They proceeded together and met other old acquaintances, now refugees, who conducted them to a spot where, in a wood, were several houses of refuge for heretics. The lord of the place gave them a Lombard, Guglielmo Pagani, who returned with them. In 1309 Guillem Falquet confessed at Toulouse to having been four times to Como, and even to Sicily, organizing the Church. He was caught while visiting a sick believer, and condemned to imprisonment in chains, but managed to escape in 1313. At the same time was sentenced Raymond de Verdun, who had likewise been four times to Lombardy.[55]

The proscribed heretics, thus nursing their faith in secret, gave the inquisitors ample occupation. As their ranks were thinned by persecution and flight, and as their skill in concealment increased with experience, there could no longer be the immense harvests of penitents reaped by Pierre Gella and Bernard de Caux, but there were enough to reward the energies of the friars and to tax{51} the adroitness of their spies. The organization of the Inquisition, moreover, was gradually perfected. In 1254 the Council of Albi carefully revised the regulations concerning it. Fixed tribunals were established, and the limitations of the inquisitorial districts were strictly defined. For Provence and the territories east of the Rhone, Marseilles was the headquarters, eventually confided to the Franciscans. The rest of the infected regions were left to the Dominicans, with tribunals at Toulouse, Carcassonne, and Narbonne; and, from such fragmentary documents as have reached us, at this time the Inquisition at Carcassonne rivalled that of Toulouse in energy and effectiveness. For a while safety was sought by heretics in northern France, but the increasing vigor of the Inquisition established there drove the unfortunate refugees back, and in 1255 a bull of Alexander IV. authorized the Provincial of Paris and his inquisitors to pursue the fugitives in the territories of the Count of Toulouse. At the same time the special functions of the inquisitors were jealously guarded against all encroachments. We have seen how, in its early days, it was subjected to the control of papal legates, but now that it was firmly established and thoroughly organized it was held independent; and when the legate Zoen, Bishop of Avignon, in 1257, endeavored, in virtue of his legatine authority, which fourteen years before had been so absolute, to perform inquisitorial work, he was rudely reminded by Alexander IV. that he could do so if he pleased in his own diocese, but that outside of it he must not interfere with the Inquisition. To this period is also to be ascribed the complete subjection of all secular officials to the behests of the inquisitors. The piety of St. Louis and the greed of Alphonse of Poitiers and Charles of Anjou rivalled each other in placing all the powers of the State at the disposal of the Holy Office, and in providing for its expenses. It was virtually supreme in the land, and, as we have seen, it was a law unto itself.[56]

The last shadow of open resistance was dissipated in the year 1255. After the fall of Montségur the proscribed and disinherited{52} knights, the *faidits*, and the heretics had sought to establish among the mountains some stronghold where they could feel safe for a moment. Driven from one retreat after another, they finally took possession of the castle of Quéribus, in the Pyrenees of Fenouillèdes. In the early spring of 1255 this last refuge was besieged by Pierre d'Auteuil, the royal Seneschal of Carcassonne. The defence was stubborn. May 5 the seneschal appealed to the bishops sitting in council at Béziers to give him assistance, as they had done so energetically at Montségur. The reply of the prelates was commendably cautious. They were not bound, they said, to render military service to the king, and when they had joined his armies it had been by command of a legate or of their primate, the Archbishop of Narbonne. Nevertheless, as common report described Quéribus as a receptacle of heretics, thieves, and robbers, and its reduction was a good work for the faith and for peace, they would each one, without derogating from his rights, furnish such assistance as seemed to him fitting. It may be assumed from this that the seneschal had to do the work unaided; in fact, he complained to the king that the prelates rather impeded than assisted him, but by August the place was in his hands, and nothing remained for the outlaws but the forest and the caverns. In that savage region the dense undergrowth afforded many a hiding-place, and an attempt was made to cut away the briers and thorns which served as shelter for ruined noble and hunted Catharan. The work was undertaken by a certain Bernard, who thence acquired the name of Espinasser or thorn-cutter. Popular hatred has preserved his remembrance, and expresses its sentiment in a myth which gibbets him in the moon.[57]

With the land at its feet, the Inquisition, in the plenitude of its power, had no hesitation in attacking the loftiest nobles, for all men were on a level in the eyes of the Most High, and the Holy Office was the avenger of God. The most powerful vassal of the houses of Toulouse and Aragon was the Count of Foix, whose extensive territories on both sides of the Pyrenees rendered him almost independent in his mountain fastnesses. Count Roger Bernard II., known as the Great, had been one of the bravest and{53} most obstinate defenders of the land, and, after the pacification of 1229, Raymond had been obliged to threaten him with war to force him to submit. His memory was proudly treasured in the land as *"Rogier Bernat lo pros et sens dengun reproche."* His family was deeply tinctured with heresy. His wife and one of his sisters were Waldenses, another sister was a Catharan, and the monk of Vaux-Cernay describes him as an enemy of God and a cruel persecutor of the Church. Yet, when he yielded in 1229, although he does not seem to have energetically fulfilled his oath to persecute heresy in his domains, for in 1233 we hear of his holding a personal conference at Aix with the heretic bishop Bertrand Martin, he was in other respects a loyal subject and faithful son of the Church. In 1237 he counselled his son, then Vizconde de Castelbo in Aragon, to allow the Inquisition in his lands, which had resulted in the condemnation of many heretics, although Ponce, Bishop of Urgel, his personal enemy, had refused to relieve him of excommunication as a fautor of heresy until 1240, when he submitted to the conditions imposed, abjured heresy, and was reconciled. At his death, in 1241, he left liberal bequests to the Church, and especially to his ancestral Cistercian Abbey of Bolbonne, in which he died in monkish habit, after duly receiving the sacraments. His son, Roger IV., gave the *coup de grâce* to the rising of 1242, by placing himself under the immediate sovereignty of the crown, and defeating Raymond after the victories of St. Louis had driven back the English and Gascons. He had some troubles with the Inquisition, but a bull of Innocent IV., in 1248, eulogizes his devotion to the Holy See, and rewards him with the power to release from the saffron crosses six penitents of his choice; and in 1261 he issued an edict commanding the enforcement of the rule that no office within his domains should be held by any one condemned to wear crosses, any one suspected of heresy, or the son of any one similarly defamed.[58]

All this would seem to give ample guarantee of the orthodoxy and loyalty of the House of Foix, but the Inquisition could not{54} condone its ancient patriotism and tolerance. Besides, if Roger Bernard the Great could be convicted of heresy, the confiscation of the broad inheritance would effect a great political object and afford ample spoils for all concerned. Twenty-two years after his death, therefore, in 1263, proceedings were commenced against his memory. A faithful servitor of the old count still survived, Raymond Bernard de Flascan, bailli of Mazères, who had attended his lord day and night during his last sickness. If he could be brought to swear that he had seen heretication performed on the death-bed, the desirable object would be attained. Frère Pons, the Inquisitor of Carcassonne, came to Mazères, found the old man an unsatisfactory witness, and threw him into a dungeon. Suffering under a severe strangury, he was starved and tormented with all the cruel ingenuity of the Inquisition, and interrogated at intervals, without his resolution giving way. This was continued for thirty-two days, when Pons resolved to carry him back to Carcassonne, where possibly the appliances for bringing refractory witnesses to terms were more efficacious. Before the journey, which he expected to be his last, the faithful bailli was given a day's respite at the Abbey of Bolbonne, which he utilized by executing a notarial instrument, November 26, 1263, attested by two abbots and a number of monks, in which he recited the trials already endured, solemnly declared that he had never seen the old count do anything contrary to the faith of Rome, but that he had died as a good Catholic, and that if, under the severe torture to which he expected to be subjected, human weakness should lead him to assert anything else, he would be a liar and a traitor, and no credence should be given to his words. It would be difficult to conceive of a more damning revelation of inquisitorial methods; yet fifty years later, when those methods had been perfected, all concerned in the preparation of the instrument, whether as notary or witnesses, would have been prosecuted as impeders of the Inquisition, to be severely punished as fautors of heresy.[59]

What became of the poor wretch does not appear. Doubtless he perished in the terrible Mura of Carcassonne under the combination of disease, torture, and starvation. His judicial murder, however, was gratuitous, for the old count's memory remained uncondemned.{55} Yet Roger Bernard III., despite the papal favor and the proofs he had given of adhesion to the new order of things, was a perpetual target for inquisitorial malice. When lying in mortal illness at Mazères, in December, 1264, he received from Étienne de Gâtine, then Inquisitor of Narbonne, an imperious order, with threats of prosecution in case of failure, to capture and deliver up his bailli of Foix, Pierre André, who was suspect of heresy and had fled on being cited to appear. The count dared only in reply to express surprise that no notice had been given him that his bailli was wanted, adding that he had issued orders for his arrest, and would have personally joined in the pursuit had not sickness rendered him incapable. At the same time he requested "Apostoli," and appealed to the pope, to whom he retailed his grievances. The inquisitors, he said, had never ceased persecuting him; at the head of armed forces they were in the habit of devastating his lands under pretext of searching for heretics, and they would bring in their train and under their protection his special enemies, until his territories were nearly ruined and his jurisdiction set at naught. He, therefore, placed himself and his dominions under the protection of the Holy See. He probably escaped further personal troubles, for he died two months later, in February, 1265, like his father, in the Cistercian habit, and in the Abbey of Bolbonne; but in 1292 his memory was assailed before Bertrand de Clermont, Inquisitor of Carcassonne. The effort was fruitless, for in 1297 Bertrand gave to his son, Roger Bernard IV., a declaration that the accusation had been disproved, and that neither he nor his father should suffer in person or property in consequence of it.[60]

When such were the persecutions to which the greatest were exposed it is easy to understand the tyranny exercised over the whole land by the irresponsible power of the inquisitors. No one was so loftily placed as to be beyond their reach, no one so humble as to escape their spies. When once they had cause of enmity with a man there was no further peace for him. The only appeal from them was to the pope, and not only was Rome distant, but the avenue to it lay, as we have seen, in their own hands. Human wickedness and folly have erected, in the world's history, more violent{56} despotisms, but never one more cruel, more benumbing, or more all-pervading.

For the next twenty years there is little worthy of special note in the operations of the Inquisition of Languedoc. It pursued its work continuously with occasional outbursts of energy. Étienne de Gâtine, and Pons de Poyet, who presided over its tribunals for many years, were no sluggards, and the period from 1373 to 1375 rewarded their industry with an abundant harvest. Though heretics naturally grew scarcer with the unintermitting pursuit of so many years, there was still the exhaustless catalogue of the dead, whose exhumation furnished an impressive spectacle for the mob, while their confiscations were welcome to the pious princes, and contributed largely to the change of ownership of land which was a political consummation so desirable. Yet heresy with incredible stubbornness maintained itself, though its concealment grew ever more difficult, and Italy grew less safe as a refuge and less prolific as a source of inspiration.[61]

19

In 1271 Alphonse and Jeanne, who had accompanied St. Louis in his unlucky crusade to Tunis, died without issue, during the homeward journey. The line of Raymond was thus extinct, and the land passed irrevocably to the crown. Philippe le Hardi took possession even of the territories which Jeanne had endeavored, as was her right, to alienate by will, and though he surrendered the Agenois to Henry III., he succeeded in retaining Querci. No opposition was made to the change of masters. When, October 8, 1271, Guillaume de Cobardon, royal Seneschal of Carcassonne, issued his orders regulating the new *régime*, one of the first things thought of was the confiscations. All castles and villages which had been forfeited for heresy were taken into the king's hand, without prejudice to the right of those to whom they might belong, thus throwing the burden of proof upon all claimants, and cutting out assigns under alienations. In 1272 Philippe paid a visit to his new territories; it was designed to be peaceful, but some violences committed by Roger Bernard IV. of Foix caused him to come at the head of an army, with which he easily overcame the resistance of the count, occupied his lands, and threw him into a dungeon. Released in 1273, the count in 1276 rendered such assistance in the{57} invasion of Navarre that Philippe took him into favor and restored his castles, on his renouncing all allegiance to Aragon. Thus the last show of independence in the South was broken down, and the monarchy was securely planted on its ruins.{62}

This consolidation of the south of France under the kings of Paris was not without compensating advantages. The monarch was rapidly acquiring a centralized power, which was very different from the overlordship of a feudal suzerain. The study of the Roman law was beginning to bear fruit in the State as well as in the Church, and the imperial theories of absolutism as inherent in kingship were gradually altering all the old relations. The king's court was expanding into the Parlement, and was training a school of subtle and resolute civil lawyers who lost no opportunity of extending the royal jurisdiction, and of legislating for the whole land in the guise of rendering judgments. In the appeals which came ever more thickly crowding into the Parlement from every quarter, the mailed baron found himself hopelessly entangled in the legal intricacies which were robbing him of his seignorial rights almost without his knowledge; and the Ordonnances, or general laws, which emanated from the throne, were constantly encroaching on old privileges, weakening local jurisdictions, and giving to the whole country a body of jurisprudence in which the crown combined both the legislative and the executive functions. If it thus was enabled to oppress, it was likewise stronger to defend, while the immense extension of the royal domains since the beginning of the century gave it the physical ability to enforce its growing prerogatives.

It was impossible that this metamorphosis in the national institutions could be effected without greatly modifying the relations between Church and State. Thus even the saintliness of Louis IX. did not prevent him from defending himself and his subjects from ecclesiastical domination in a spirit very different from that which any French monarch had ventured to exhibit since the days of Charlemagne. The change became still more manifest under his grandson, Philippe le Bel. Though but seventeen years of age when he succeeded to the throne in 1286, his rare ability and vigorous{58} temper soon led him to assert the royal power in incisive fashion. He recognized, within the boundaries of his kingdom, no superior, secular or spiritual. Had he entertained any scruples of conscience, his legal counsellors could easily remove them. To such men as Pierre Flotte and Guillaume de Nogaret the true position of the Church was that of subjection to the State, as it had been under the successors of Constantine, and in their eyes Boniface VIII. was to their master scarce more than Pope Vigilius had been to Justinian. Few among the revenges of time are more satisfying than the catastrophe of Anagni, in 1303, when Nogaret and Sciarra Colonna laid hands on the vicegerent of God, and Boniface passionately replied to Nogaret's reproaches, "I can patiently endure to be condemned and deposed by a Patarin"—for Nogaret was born at St. Felix de Caraman, and his ancestors were said to have been burned as Cathari. If this be true he must have been more than human if he did not feel special gratification when, at command of his master, he appeared before Clement V. with a formal accusation of heresy against Boniface, and demanded that the dead pope's bones be dug up and burned. The citizens of Toulouse recognized him as an avenger of their wrongs when they placed his bust in the gallery of their illustrious men in the Hôtel-de-ville.{63}

It was to the royal power, thus rising to supremacy, that the people instinctively turned for relief from the inquisitorial tyranny which was becoming insupportable. The authority lodged in the hands of the inquisitor was so arbitrary and irresponsible that even with the purest intentions it could not but be unpopular, while to the unworthy it afforded unlimited opportunity for oppression and the gratification of the basest passions. Dangerous as was any manifestation of discontent, the people of Albi and Carcassonne, reduced to despair by the cruelty of the inquisitors, Jean Galande and Jean Vigoureux, mustered courage, and in 1280 presented their complaints to Philippe le Hardi. It was difficult to{59} sustain their charges with specific proofs, and after a brief investigation their reiterated requests for relief were dismissed as frivolous. In the agitation against the Inquisition thus commenced, it must be borne in mind that heretics had little to do. By this time they were completely cowed and were quite satisfied if they could enjoy their faith in secret. The opposition arose from good Catholics, the magistrates of cities and substantial burghers, who saw the prosperity of the land withering under the deadly grasp of the Holy Office, and who felt that no man was safe whose wealth might arouse cupidity or whose independence might provoke revenge. The introduction of the use of torture impressed the popular imagination with special horror, and it was widely believed that confessions were habitually extorted by insufferable torment from rich men whose faith was unblemished. The cruel provisions which brought confiscation on the descendants of heretics, moreover, were peculiarly hard to endure, for ruin impended over every one against whom the inquisitor might see fit to produce from his records evidence of ancestral heresy. It was against these records that the next attempt was directed. Foiled in their appeal to the throne, the consuls of Carcassonne and some of its prominent ecclesiastics, in 1283 or 1284, formed a conspiracy to destroy the books of the Inquisition containing the confessions and depositions. How far this was organized it would be difficult now to say. The statements of the witnesses conflict so hopelessly on material points, even as to dates, that there is little dependence to be placed on them. They were evidently extracted under torture, and if they are credible the consuls of the city and the archdeacon, Sanche Morlana, the episcopal Ordinary, Guillem Brunet, other episcopal officials and many of the secular clergy were not only implicated in the plot, but were heretics in full affiliation with the Cathari. Whether true or false they show that there was the sharpest antagonism between the Inquisition and the local Church. The whole has an air of unreality which renders one doubtful about accepting any portion, but there must have been some foundation for the story. According to the evidence Bernard Garric, who had been a perfected heretic and a *filius major*, but had been converted and was now a familiar of the Inquisition, was selected as the instrument. He was approached, and after some bargaining he agreed to deliver the{60} books for two hundred livres Tournois, for the payment of which the consuls went security. How the attempt failed and how it was discovered does not appear, but probably Bernard at the first overtures confided the plot to his superiors and led on the conspirators to their ruin.[64]

The whole community was now at the mercy of the Inquisition, and it was not disposed to be lenient in its triumph. While the trials were yet going on, the citizens made a fresh appeal to Pierre Chalus, the royal chancellor, who was passing through Toulouse on a mission from the court of Paris to that of Aragon. This was easily disposed of, for on September 13, 1285, the inquisitors triumphantly brought before him Bernard Garric to repeat the confession made a week previous. He had thoroughly learned his lesson, and the only conclusion which the royal representative could reach was that Carcassonne was a hopeless nest of heretics, deserving the severest measures of repression. As a last resort recourse was had to Honorius IV., but the only result was a brief from him to the inquisitors expressing his grief that the people of Carcassonne should be impeding the Inquisition with all their strength, and ordering the punishment of the recalcitrants irrespective of their station, order, or condition, an expression which shows that the opposition had not arisen from heretics.[65]

In reply to these complaints the inquisitors could urge with some truth that heresy, though hidden, was still busy. Although heretic seigneurs and nobles had been by this time well-nigh destroyed and their lands had passed to others, there was still infection among the bourgeoisie of the cities and the peasantry. It is one of the noteworthy features of Catharism, moreover, that at{61} no time during its existence were lacking earnest and devoted ministers, who took their lives in their hands and wandered around in secret among the faithful, administering spiritual comfort and instruction, making converts where they could, exhorting the young and hereticating the old. In toil and hardship and peril they pursued their work, gliding by night from one place of concealment to another, and their self-devotion was rivalled by that of their disciples. Few more touching narratives can be conceived than those which could be constructed from the artless confessions extorted from the peasant-folk who fell into the hands of the inquisitors—the humble alms which they gave, pieces of bread, fish, scraps of cloth, or small coins, the hiding-places which they constructed in their cabins, the guidance given by night through places of danger, and, more than all, the steadfast fidelity which refused to betray their pastors when the inquisitor suddenly appeared and offered the alternative of free pardon or the dungeon and confiscation. The self-devotion of the minister was well matched with the quiet heroism of the believer. To this fidelity and the complete network of secret organization which extended over the land may be attributed the marvellously long exemption which many of these ministers enjoyed in their proselyting missions. Two of the most prominent of them at this period, Raymond Delboc and Raymond Godayl, or Didier, had already, in 1276, been condemned by the Inquisition of Carcassonne as perfected heretics and fugitives, but they kept at their work until the explosion of 1300, incessantly active, with the inquisitors always in pursuit but unable to overtake them. Guillem Pagès is another whose name constantly recurs in the confessions of heretications during an almost equally long period. The inquisitors might well urge that their utmost efforts were needed, but their methods were such that even the best intentions would not have saved the innocent from suffering with the guilty.[66]

The secretly guilty were quite sufficiently influential, and the innocent sufficiently apprehensive, to keep up the agitation which had been commenced, and at last it began to bear fruit. A new inquisitor of Carcassonne, Nicholas d'Abbeville, was quite as cruel{62} and arbitrary as his predecessors, and when the people prepared an appeal to the king he promptly threw into jail the notary who drew up the paper. In their desperation they disregarded this warning; a deputation was sent to the court, and this time they were listened to. May 13, 1291, Philippe addressed a letter to his Seneschal of Carcassonne reciting the injuries inflicted by the Inquisition on the innocent through the newly-invented system of torture, by means of which the living and the dead were fraudulently convicted and the whole land scandalized and rendered desolate. The royal officials were therefore ordered no longer to obey the commands of the inquisitors in making arrests, unless the accused be a confessed heretic or persons worthy of faith vouch for his being publicly defamed for heresy. A month later he reiterated these orders even more precisely, and announced his intention of sending deputies to Languedoc armed with full authority to make permanent provision in the matter. It is impossible to exaggerate the importance of these manifestoes as marking a new era in the relations between the temporal and spiritual authorities. For far less than this all the chivalry and scum of Europe had been promised salvation if they would drive Raymond of Toulouse from his inheritance.[67]

It was probably to break in some degree the force of this unheard-of interference with inquisitorial supremacy that in September, 1292, Guillem de Saint-Seine, Inquisitor of Carcassonne, ordered all the parish priests in his district for three weeks on{63} Sundays and feast-days to denounce as excommunicate all who should impede the business of the Inquisition and all notaries who should wickedly draw up revocations of confessions for heretics. This could not effect much, nor was anything accomplished by a Parlement held April 14, 1293, at Montpellier, by the royal chamberlain, Alphonse de Ronceyrac, of all the royal officials and inquisitors of Toulouse and Carcassonne to reform the abuses of all jurisdictions.[68]

Shortly after this, in September, 1293, Philippe went a step further and threw his ægis over the unfortunate Jew. Although Jews as a class were not liable to persecution by the Inquisition, still, if after being once converted they reverted to Judaism, or if they proselyted among Christians to obtain converts, or if they were themselves converts from Christianity, they were heretics in the eyes of the Church, and fell under inquisitorial jurisdiction, and were liable to be abandoned to the secular arm. All these classes were a source of endless trouble to the Church, especially the "neophytes" or converted Jews, for feigned conversions were frequent, either for worldly advantage or to escape the incessant persecution visited upon the unlucky children of Israel.[69] The bull *Turbato corde*, ordering the inquisitors to be active and vigilant in prosecuting all who were guilty of these offences, issued in 1268 by Clement IV., was reissued by successive popes with a pertinacity showing the importance attached to it, and when we see Frère Bertrand de la Roche, in 1274, officially described as inquisitor in Provence against heretics and wicked Christians who{64} embrace Judaism, and Frère Guillaume d'Auxerre, in 1285, qualified as "Inquisitor of Heretics and Apostate Jews in France," it is evident that these cases formed a large portion of inquisitorial business. As the Jews were peculiarly defenceless, this jurisdiction gave wide opportunity for abuse and extortion which was doubtless turned fully to account. Philippe owed them protection, for in 1291 he had deprived them of their own judges and ordered them to plead in the royal courts, and now he proceeded to protect them in the most emphatic manner. To Simon Brisetête, Seneschal of Carcassonne, he sent a copy of the bull *Turbato corde*, with instructions that while this was to be implicitly obeyed, no Jew was to be arrested for any cause not specified therein, and, if there was any doubt, the matter was to be referred to the royal council. He further enclosed an Ordonnance directing that no Jew in France was to be arrested on the requisition of any person or friar of any Order, no matter what his office might be, without notifying the seneschal or bailli, who was to decide whether the case was sufficiently clear to be acted upon without reference to the royal council. Simon Brisetête thereupon ordered all officials to defend the Jews, not to allow any exactions to be imposed on them whereby their ability to pay their taxes might be impaired, and not to arrest them at the mandate of any one without informing him of the cause. It would not have been easy to limit more skilfully the inquisitorial power to oppress a despised class.[70]

Philippe had thus intervened in the most decided manner, and the oppressed populations of Languedoc might reasonably hope for permanent relief, but his subsequent policy belied their hopes. It vacillated in a manner which is only partially explicable by the{65} shifting political exigencies of the times so far as we can penetrate them. In this same year, 1293, the Seneschal of Carcassonne is found instructing Aimeric, the Viscount of Narbonne, to execute royal letters ordering aid to be rendered to the inquisitors there. This may have been a mere local matter, and Philippe, for a while at least, adhered to his position. Towards the end of 1295 there was issued an Ordonnance of the royal court, applicable to the whole kingdom, forbidding the arrest of any one on the demand of a friar of any Order, no matter what his position might be, unless the seneschal or bailli of the jurisdiction was satisfied that the arrest should be made, and the person asking it showed a commission from the pope. This was sent to all the royal officials with strict injunctions to obey it, although, if the accused were likely to fly, he might be detained, but not surrendered until the decision of the court could be had. Moreover, if any persons were then in durance contrary to the provisions of the Ordonnance, they were to be set at liberty. Even this did not effect its object sufficiently, and a few months later, in 1296, Philippe complained to his Seneschal of Carcassonne of the numbers who were arrested by the royal officers, and confined in the royal prisons on insufficient grounds, causing scandal and the heavy infliction of infamy on the innocent. To prevent this arrests were forbidden except in cases of such violent presumption of heresy that they could not be postponed, and the officials were instructed, when called upon by the inquisitors, to make such excuses as they could. These orders were obeyed, for when, about this time, Foulques de Saint-Georges, Vice-inquisitor of Carcassonne, ordered the arrest of sundry suspects by Adam de Marolles, the deputy seneschal, the latter referred the matter to his principal, Henri de Elisia, who, after consultation with Robert d'Artois, lieutenant of the king in Languedoc and Gascony, refused the demand.[71]

No previous sovereign had ventured thus to trammel the Inquisition. These regulations, in fact, rendered it virtually powerless, for it had no organization of its own; even its prisons were the king's and might be withdrawn at any time, and it depended{66}wholly upon the secular arm for physical force. In some places, as at Albi, it might rely upon episcopal assistance, but elsewhere it could do nothing of itself. Philippe had, moreover, been careful not to excite the ill-will of his bishops, for his Ordonnances and instructions alluded simply to the friars, thus excluding the Inquisition from royal aid without specifically naming it. His quarrel with Boniface

22

VIII. was now beginning. Between January, 1296, and February, 1297, appeared the celebrated bulls *Clericis laicos*, *Ineffabilis amoris*, *Excitat nos*, and *Exiit a te*, whose arrogant encroachments on the secular power aroused him to resistance, and this doubtless gave a sharper zest to his desire to diminish in his dominions the authority of so purely papal an institution as the Inquisition. So shrewd a prince could readily see its effectiveness as an instrument of papal aggression, for the Church could make what definition it pleased of heresy; and Boniface did not hesitate to give him fair warning, when, in October, 1297, he ordered the Inquisitor of Carcassonne to proceed against certain officials of Béziers who had rendered themselves in the papal eyes suspect of heresy because they remained under excommunication, incurred for imposing taxes on the clergy, boasting that food had not lost its savor to them nor sleep its sweetness, and who, moreover, dared with polluted lips to revile the Holy See itself. Under such an extension of jurisdiction Philippe himself might not be safe, and it is no wonder that tentative efforts made in 1296 and 1297 to find some method of reconciling the recent royal Ordonnances with the time-honored absolutism of the Inquisition proved failures.[72]

Meanwhile, the exigencies of Italian politics caused Boniface suddenly to retrace his steps. His quarrel with the Cardinals Giacomo and Pietro Colonna rendered it advisable to propitiate Philippe. In May, 1297, he assented to a tithe conceded to the king by his bishops, and in the bull *Noveritis* (July, 1297) he exempted France from the operation of the *Clericis laicos*, while in *Licet per speciales* (July, 1298) he withdrew his arrogant pretension imperatively to prolong the armistice between France and {67} England. A truce was thus patched up with Philippe, who hastened to manifest his good-will to the Holy See by abandoning his subjects again to the inquisitors. In the Liber Sextus of the Decretals, published by Boniface March 3, 1298, the pope included, with customary imperiousness, a canon commanding the absolute obedience of all secular officials to the orders of inquisitors under penalty of excommunication, which if endured for a year carried with it condemnation for heresy. This was his answer to the French monarch's insubordinate legislation, and Philippe at the moment was not inclined to contest the matter. In September he meekly enclosed the canon to his officials with instructions to obey it in every point, arresting and imprisoning all whom inquisitors or bishops might designate, and punishing all whom they might condemn. A letter of Frère Arnaud Jean, Inquisitor of Pamiers, dated March 2, of the same year, assuring the Jews that they need dread no novel measures of severity, would seem to indicate that the royal protection had been previously withdrawn from them. The good understanding between king and pope lasted until 1300, when the quarrel broke out afresh with greater acrimony than ever. In December of that year the provisions of *Clericis laicos* were renewed by the bull *Nuper ex rationalibus*, followed by the short one, of which the authenticity is disputed, *Scire te volumus*, asserting Philippe's subjection in temporal affairs and calling forth his celebrated rejoinder, *Sciat tua maxima fatuitas*. The strife continued with increasing violence till the seizure of Boniface at Anagni, September 8, 1303, and his death in the following month.[73]

Under this varying policy the fate of the people of Languedoc was hard. Nicholas d'Abbeville, the Inquisitor of Carcassonne, was a man of inflexible severity, arrogantly bent on pushing his prerogatives to the utmost. He had an assistant worthy of him in Foulques de Saint-Georges, the Prior of the Convent of Albi, which was under his jurisdiction. He had virtually another assistant in the bishop, Bernard de Castanet, who delighted to act as inquisitor, impelled alike by fanaticism and by greed, for, as we have {68} seen, the bishops of Albi, by a special transaction with St. Louis, enjoyed a half of the confiscations. Prior to his elevation in 1276 Bernard had been auditor of the papal camera, which shows him to have been an accomplished legist, and he was also a patron of art and literature, but he was ever in trouble with his people. Already, in 1277, he had succeeded in so exasperating them that his palace was swept by a howling mob, and he barely escaped with his life. In 1282 he commenced the erection of the cathedral of St. Cecilia, a gigantic building, half church, half fortress, which swallowed enormous sums, and stimulated his hatred of heresy by supplying a pious use for the estates of heretics.[74]

To such men the protection granted to his subjects by Philippe was most distasteful, and not without reason. Heretics naturally took advantage of the restrictions imposed on the Inquisition and redoubled their activity. It might seem, indeed, to them that the day of supremacy of the Church was past, and that the rising independence of the secular power might usher in an era of comparative toleration, in which their persecuted religion would at length find its oft-deferred opportunity of converting mankind—a dream in which they indulged to the last. More demonstrative, if not more earnest, was the feeling which the royal policy aroused in Carcassonne. The Ordonnances had not only crippled the Inquisition, but had shown the disfavor with which it was regarded by the king, and in 1295 some of the leading citizens, who had been compromised in the trials of 1285, found no difficulty in arousing the people to open resistance. For a while they controlled the city, and inflicted no little injury on the Dominicans, and on all who ventured to support them. Nicholas d'Abbeville was driven from the pulpit when preaching, pelted with stones and pursued with drawn swords, and the judges of the royal court on one occasion were glad to escape with their lives, while the friars were beaten and insulted when they appeared in public and were practically segregated as excommunicates. Bernard Gui, an {69} eye-witness, naturally attributes this to the influence of heresy, but it is impossible for us now to conjecture how much may have been due to religious antagonism, and how much to the natural reaction among the orthodox against the intolerable oppression of the inquisitorial methods.[75]

For some years the Inquisition of Carcassonne was suspended. As soon as secular support was withdrawn public opinion was too strong, and it succumbed. This lasted until the truce between king and pope again placed the royal power at the disposal of the inquisitors. In their despair the citizens then sent envoys to Boniface VIII., with Aimeric Castel at their head, supported by a number of Franciscans. Boniface listened to their complaints and proposed to depute the Bishop of Vicenza as commissioner to examine and report, but the papal referendary, afterwards Cardinal of S. Sabina, required a bribe of ten thousand florins as a preliminary. It was promised him, but Aimeric, having secured the good offices of Pierre Flotte and the Duke of Burgundy, thought he could obtain his purpose for less, and refused to pay it. When Boniface heard of the refusal he angrily exclaimed, "We know in whom they trust, but by God all the kings in Christendom shall not save the people of Carcassonne from being burned, and specially the father of that Aimeric Castel!" The negotiation fell through, and Nicholas d'Abbeville had his triumph. A large portion of the citizens were wearied with the disturbances, and were impatient under the excommunication which rested on the community. The prosperity of the town was declining, and there were not wanting those who predicted its ruin. The hopelessness of further resistance was apparent, and matters being thus ripe for a settlement, a solemn assembly was held, April 27, 1299, when the civic magistrates met the inquisitor in the presence of the Bishops of Albi and Béziers, Bertrand de Clermont, Inquisitor of Toulouse, the royal officials, sundry abbots and other notables. Nicholas dictated his own terms for the absolution asked at his hands, nor were they seemingly harsh. Those who were manifest heretics, or specially defamed, or convicted by legal proof must take their chance. The rest were to be penanced as the bishops and the Abbot{70} of Fontfroide might advise, excluding confiscation and personal or humiliating penalties. All this was reasonable enough from an ecclesiastical point of view, but so deep-seated was the distrust, or so strong the heretical influence, that the people asked twenty-four hours for consideration, and on reassembling the next day refused the terms. Six months passed, their helplessness and isolation each day becoming more apparent, until, October 8, they reassembled, and the consuls asked for absolution in the name of the community. Nicholas was not severe. The penance imposed on the town was the building of a chapel in honor of St. Louis, which was accomplished in the year 1300 at the cost of ninety livres Tournois. The consuls, in the name of the community, secretly abjured heresy. Twelve of the most guilty citizens were reserved for special penances, viz., four of the old consuls, four councillors, two advocates, and two notaries. Of these the fate was doubtless deplorable. Chance has preserved to us the sentence passed on one of the authors of the troubles, Guillem Garric, by which we find that he rotted in the horrible dungeon of Carcassonne for twenty-two years before he was brought forward for judgment in 1321, when in consideration of his long confinement he was given the choice between the crusade and exile, and the crushed old man fell on his knees and gave thanks to Jesus Christ and to the inquisitors for the mercy vouchsafed him. Some years later intense excitement was created when Frère Bernard Délicieux obtained sight of the agreement, and discovered that the consuls had been represented in it as confessing that the whole community had given aid to manifest heretics, that they had abjured in the name of all, and thus that all citizens were incapacitated for office and were exposed to the penalties of relapse in case of further trouble. This excited the people to such a point that the inquisitor, Geoffroi d'Ablis, was obliged to issue a solemn declaration, August 10, 1303, disclaiming any intention of thus taking advantage of the settlement; and notwithstanding this, when King Philippe came to Carcassonne in 1305 the agreement was pronounced fraudulent, the seneschal Gui Caprier was dismissed for having affixed his seal to it, and confessed that he had been bribed to do so by Nicholas d'Abbeville with a thousand livres Tournois.[76]{71}

Encouraged by the crippling and suspension of the Inquisition, the Catharan propaganda had been at work with renewed vigor. In 1299 the Council of Béziers sounded the alarm by announcing that perfected heretics had made their appearance in the land, and ordering close search made after them. At Albi, Bishop Bernard was, as usual, at variance with his flock, who were pleading against him in the royal court to preserve their jurisdiction. The occasion was opportune. He called to his assistance the inquisitors Nicholas d'Abbeville and Bertrand de Clermont, and towards the close of the year 1299 the town was startled by the arrest of twenty-five of the wealthiest and most respected citizens, whose regular attendance at mass and observance of all religious duties had rendered them above suspicion. The trials were pushed with unusual celerity, and, from the manner in which those who at first denied were speedily brought to confession and to revealing the names of their associates, there was doubtless good ground for the popular belief that torture was ruthlessly and unsparingly used; in fact, allusions to it in the final sentence of Guillem Calverie, one of the victims, leave no doubt on the subject. Abjuration saved them from the stake, but the sentence of perpetual imprisonment in chains was a doubtful mercy for those who were sentenced, while a number were kept interminably in jail awaiting judgment.[77]

The whole country was ripe for revolt. The revival of Philippe's quarrel with Boniface soon gave assurance that help might be expected from the throne; but if this should fail there would be scant hesitation on the part of desperate men in looking for some other sovereign who would lend an ear to their complaints. The arrest and trial for treason of the Bishop of Pamiers, in 1301, shows us what was then the undercurrent of popular feeling in Languedoc, where the Frenchman was still a hated stranger, the king a foreign despot, and the people discontented and ready to shift their allegiance to either England or Aragon whenever they could see their advantage in it. The fragile tenure with which{72} the land was still held by the Kings of Paris must be kept in view if we would understand Philippe's shifting policy.[78]

24

The prosecutions of Albi caused general terror, for the victims were universally thought to be good Catholics, selected for spoliation on account of their wealth. The conviction was widespread that such inquisitors as Jean de Faugoux, Guillem de Mulceone, Jean de Saint-Seine, Jean Galande, Nicholas d'Abbeville, and Foulques de Saint-Georges had long had no scruple in obtaining, by threats and torture, such testimony as they might desire against any one whom they might wish to ruin, and that their records were falsified, and filled with fictitious entries for that purpose. Some years before, Frère Jean Martin, a Dominican, had invoked the interposition of Pierre de Montbrun, Archbishop of Narbonne (died 1286), to put a stop to this iniquity. Some investigation was made, and the truth of the charges was established. The dead were found to be the special prey of these vultures, who had prepared their frauds in advance. Even the fierce orthodoxy of the Maréchaux de la Foi could not save Gui de Levis of Mirepoix from this posthumous attack; and, when Gautier de Montbrun, Bishop of Carcassonne, died, they produced from their records proof that he had adored heretics and had been hereticated on his death-bed. In this latter case, fortunately, the archbishop happened to know that one of the witnesses, Jourdain Ferrolh, had been absent at the time when, by his alleged testimony, he had seen the act of adoration. Frère Jean Martin urged the archbishop to destroy all the records and cause the Dominicans to be deprived of their functions, and the prelate made some attempt at Rome to effect this, contenting himself meanwhile with issuing some regulations and sequestrating some of the books. It was probably during this flurry that the Inquisitors of Carcassonne and Toulouse, Nicholas d'Abbeville and Pierre de Mulceone, hearing that they were likely to be convicted of fraud, retired with their records to the safe retreat of Prouille and busied themselves in making a transcript, with the compromising entries omitted, which they ingeniously bound in the covers stripped from the old volumes.[79]{73}

About this time occurred a case which confirms the popular belief in inquisitorial iniquity, and which had results of vastly greater importance than its promoters anticipated. When the disappointed Boniface VIII. swore that he would cause the burning of Aimeric Castel's father, he uttered no idle threat. Nicholas d'Abbeville, a fitting instrument, was at hand, and to him he privately gave the necessary verbal instructions. Castel Fabri, the father, had been a citizen of Carcassonne distinguished for piety and benevolence no less than for wealth. A friend of the Franciscan Order, after duly receiving the sacraments, he had died, in 1278, in the hands of its friars, six of whom kept watch in the sick-room until his death, and he had been buried in the Franciscan cemetery. We have seen in the case of the Count of Foix how easily all these precautions could be brushed aside, and Nicholas found no difficulty in discovering or making the evidence he required.[80] Suddenly, in 1300, the people of Carcassonne were startled by a notice, read in all the parish churches, summoning those wishing to defend the memory of Castel Fabri to appear before the Inquisition on a day named, as the deceased was proved to have been hereticated on his death-bed. The moment was well chosen, as Aimeric Castel, the son, was absent. The Franciscans, for whom the accused had doubtless provided liberally in his will, felt themselves called upon to assume his defence. Hastily consulting, they determined to send their lector, Bernard de Liegossi, or Délicieux, to the General Chapter then assembling at Marseilles, for instructions, as, in the chronic antagonism between the Mendicants, the matter seemed to be regarded as an assault on the Order. The wife of Aimeric Castel provided for the expenses of the journey, and Bernard returned with instructions from the provincial to defend the memory of the deceased, while Eléazar de{74} Clermont, the syndic of the convent, was deputed by the Guardian of Narbonne to co-operate with him. Meanwhile Nicholas had proceeded to condemnation, and when, July 4, 1300, Bernard and Eléazar presented themselves to offer the testimony of the friars who had watched the dying man, Nicholas received them standing, refused to listen to them, and on their urging their evidence left the room in the most contemptuous manner. In the afternoon they returned to ask for a certificate of their offer and its refusal, but found the door of the Inquisition closed, and could not effect an entrance.

The next step was to take an appeal to the Holy See and ask for "Apostoli," but this was no easy matter. So general was the terror inspired by Nicholas that the doctor of decretals, Jean de Penne, to whom they applied to draw the paper, refused unless his name should be kept inviolably secret, and nineteen years afterwards Bernard when on trial refused to reveal it until compelled to do so. To obtain a notary to authenticate the appeal was still harder. All those in Carcassonne absolutely refused, and it was found necessary to bring one from a distance, so that it was not until July 16 that the document was ready for service. How seriously, indeed, all parties regarded what should have been a very simple business is shown by the winding-up of the appeal, which places, until the case is decided, not only the body of Castel Fabri, but the appellants and the whole Franciscan convent, under the protection of the Holy See. When they went to serve the instrument on Nicholas the doors, as before, were found closed and entrance could not be effected. It was therefore read in the street and left tacked on the door, to be taken down and treasured and brought forward in evidence against Bernard in 1319. We have no further records of the case, but that the appeal was ineffectual is visible in the fact that in 1322-3 the accounts of Arnaud Assalit show that the royal treasury was still receiving an income from the confiscated estates of Castel Fabri; while in 1329 the still unsatisfied vengeance of the Inquisition ordered the bones of his wife Rixende to be exhumed.[81]{75}

The case of Castel Fabri might have passed unnoticed, like thousands of others, had it not chanced to bring into collision with the Inquisition the lector of the convent of Carcassonne. Bernard Délicieux was no ordinary man, in fact a contemporary assures us that in the whole Franciscan Order there were few who were his equals. Entering the Order about 1284, his position of lector or teacher shows the esteem felt for his learning, for the Mendicants were ever careful in selecting those to whom they confided such functions; and, moreover, we find him in relations with the leading minds of the age, such as Raymond Lully and Arnaldo de Vilanova. His eloquence made him much in request as preacher; his persuasiveness enabled him to control those with whom he came in contact, while his enthusiastic ardor prompted him to make any sacrifices necessary to a cause which had once enlisted his sympathies. He was no latitudinarian or time-server, for when the split came in his own Order he embraced, to his ruin, the side of the Spiritual Franciscans, with the same disregard of self as he had manifested in his dealings with the Inquisition. He was no admirer of toleration, for he devoutly wished the extermination of heresy, but experience and observation had convinced him that in Dominican hands the Inquisition was merely an instrument of oppression and extortion, and he imagined that by transferring it to the Franciscans its usefulness would be preserved while its evils would be removed. Boniface VIII., as we have seen, about this time replaced the Franciscan inquisitors of Padua and Vicenza with Dominicans for the purpose of repressing similar evils, and in the jealousy and antagonism between the two orders the converse operation might seem worth attempting in Languedoc. In the hope of alleviating the sufferings of the people, Bernard devoted himself to the cause for years, incurring obloquy, persecution, and ingratitude. Those whom he sought to serve allowed him to sell his books in their service, and to cripple himself with debt, while the enmities which he excited hounded him relentlessly to the death. Yet in the struggle he had the sympathies of his own Order which everywhere throughout Languedoc manifested itself{76} the enemy of the Dominican Inquisition. Already, in 1291, Franciscans in Carcassonne had endeavored to intervene in cases of heresy, and had been sharply reproved by Philippe le Bel at the instance of the Inquisitor Guillaume de Saint-Seine. In 1298 they had supported the appeal of the men of Carcassonne to Boniface VIII., and throughout the whole of Bernard's agitation the Franciscan convents are seen to be rallying-points of the opposition. It is there that Bernard preaches his fiery sermons; it is there that meetings are held to plan resistance. During the troubles in Carcassonne Foulques de Saint-Georges went with twenty-five men to the Franciscan convent to cite the opponents of the Inquisition. The friars would not admit them, but tolled the bell and an angry crowd assembled, while those inside the convent assailed them with stones and quarrels, and they were glad to escape with their lives.[82]

Vainly the inquisitors complained to the Franciscan prelates of Bernard as an impeder of the Holy Office. The form of a trial would be gone through, and the offender would be furnished with letters attesting his innocence. The Dominicans asserted that Franciscan zeal was solely caused by jealousy; the Franciscans retorted that their friends were the special objects of inquisitorial persecution. King Philippe's confessor was a Dominican, Queen Joanna's a Franciscan, and the two courtly friars took part, for and against the Inquisition, with a zeal which rendered them important factors in the struggle. The undying hostility between the two Orders always led them to opposite sides in every question of dogma or practice, and this was one which afforded the amplest scope to bitterness.[83]

The *coup-de-main* executed on the so-called heretics of Albi, in December, 1299, and the early months of 1300, had excited consternation too general for the matter to be passed over. King Philippe's quarrel with Boniface was breaking out afresh, and he might not be averse to making his subjects feel that they had a{77} protector in the throne. With the advice of his council an investigation was ordered, and confided to the Bishops of Béziers and Maguelonne, but the inquisitors arrogantly and persistently refused to allow the secrets of their office to be invaded. This was not calculated to remove popular disquiet, and in 1301 Philippe sent to Languedoc two officials armed with supreme powers, under the name of Reformers. As the royal authority extended and established itself, special deputies for the investigation and correction of abuses were frequently despatched to the provinces. In the present case those who came to Languedoc perhaps had for their chief business the arrest of the Bishop of Pamiers, accused of treasonable practices, but the colorable pretext for their mission was the correction of inquisitorial abuses. One of them, Jean de Pequigny, Vidame of Amiens, was a man of high character for probity and sagacity; the other was Richard Nepveu, Archdeacon of Lisieux, of whom we hear little in the following years, except that he quietly slipped into the vacant episcopate of Béziers. He must have done his duty to some extent, however, for Bernard Gui tells us that he died in 1309 of leprosy, as a judgment of God for his hostility to the Inquisition.[84]

The Reformers established themselves at Toulouse, where Foulques de Saint-Georges had been inquisitor since Michaelmas, 1300, and speedily gathered much damaging testimony against him, for he was accused not only of unduly torturing persons for purposes of extortion, but of gratifying his lusts by arresting women whose virtue he failed otherwise to overcome. Thither flocked representatives of Albi, with the wives and children of the prisoners, beseeching and imploring the representatives of the{78} king for justice, and promising revelations if they would issue letters of safety to those who would give information—for the terror inspired by the Inquisition was such that no one dared to testify concerning it unless he was assured of protection against its vengeance. The Bishop of Albi came also to justify himself, and on his return to his episcopal seat he was welcomed with a manifestation of the feeling entertained for him by his flock, whom the coming of the Reformers encouraged in the expression or their sentiments. When his approach was announced a crowd of men and women rushed forth from the gates to meet him with shouts of "Death, death, death to the traitor!" It may perhaps be doubted whether, as reported, he bore the threats and insults with patience akin to that of Christ, ordering his followers to keep their weapons down; certain it is that he was roughly handled, and had difficulty in safely reaching his palace. A conspiracy was formed to burn the palace, in order, during the confusion, to liberate the prisoners, but the hearts of the conspirators failed them and the project was abandoned. Even more menacing was the action of a number of the chief citizens, who bound themselves by a notarial instrument to prosecute him and Nicholas d'Abbeville in the king's court. As a consequence, the bishop's temporalities were sequestrated, and eventually the enormous fine of twenty thousand livres stripped him of a portion of his ill-gotten gains for the benefit of the king, who was bitterly reproached by Bernard Délicieux for thus preferring money to justice. Bernard de Castanet retained his uneasy seat until 1308, when, seeing under Clement V. no prospect of better times, he procured a transfer to the quieter see of Puy. One of the earliest signs of the revulsion under John XXII. was his advancement, in December, 1316, to the Cardinalate of Porto, which he held for only eight months, his death occurring in August, 1317.[85]

The Reformers, meanwhile, had sent for Bernard Délicieux, who was then quietly performing his duties as lector in the convent of Narbonne. He must already have made himself conspicuous[79] in the affair of Castel Fabri, and was evidently regarded as a desirable ally in the impending struggle. According to his own story he advised Pequigny to let the Inquisition alone, as experience had shown that effort was useless; but on being called again to Toulouse on some business connected with the Priory of la Daurade, and having to visit Paris in connection with the will of Louis, Bishop of Toulouse, it was arranged, at Pequigny's suggestion, that he should accompany a deputation which the citizens of Albi were sending to the king to invoke his active intervention. The court was at Senlis, whither they repaired, and there came also Pequigny to justify himself, and Frère Foulques with several Dominicans, eager to establish the innocence of the Inquisition.[86]

The battle was fought out before the king. Bernard urged the suspension of the inquisitors during an investigation, or that the Dominicans should be permanently declared ineligible while awaiting final action by the Holy See. Supported by Frère Guillaume, the king's Dominican confessor, Foulques preferred charges against Pequigny, but could furnish no proofs. Pequigny retorted with accusations against Foulques, and a commission, consisting of the Archbishop of Narbonne and the Constable of France, was appointed to hear both sides. After due deliberation, it reported in favor of Pequigny, and the king took the unheard-of step of removing the inquisitor. He at first requested this of the Dominican Provincial of Paris, who possessed the power to do so, but that official called together a chapter, which contented itself with appointing an adjunct, and ordering Foulques to retain office till the middle of the following Lent, in order to complete the trials which he had already commenced. This gave Philippe great offence, which he expressed in the most outspoken terms in letters to his chaplain and to the Bishop of Toulouse, whom he bitterly reproached for advising acceptance of the terms. He did not content himself with words, for simultaneously, December 8, 1301, he wrote to the bishop, the Inquisitor of Toulouse, and the seneschals of Toulouse and Albi, stating that the imploring cries of his subjects, including prelates and ecclesiastics, counts, barons, and other distinguished men, convinced him that Foulques was guilty of the charges preferred against him, including crimes[80] abhorrent to the human mind. He afflicted the people with numerous exactions and oppressions; he was accustomed to commence proceedings with torture inconceivable and incredible, and thus compel confession from those whom he suspected, and when this failed he suborned witnesses to testify falsely. His detestable excesses had created such general terror that a rising of the people was to be apprehended unless some speedy remedy was had. Some further unavailing opposition was made to Foulques's removal, but not much was gained by the appointment of his successor, Guillaume de Morières, who had previously succeeded him in the Priory of Albi. Foulques was gratified with the important Priory of Avignon, and when he subsequently died in poverty at Lyons he was regarded by his Order almost in the light of a martyr.[87]

Philippe had not contented himself with getting rid of Foulques, but had endeavored to introduce reforms which are interesting not only as a manifestation of the royal supremacy which he assumed, but also as the model of all subsequent endeavors to curb the abuses of the Inquisition. It was natural that this should take the shape of reviving the episcopal power which had become so completely suppressed. Firstly, the prison which the crown had built on its own land in Toulouse for the use of the Inquisition was to be placed under the charge of some one selected by both bishop and inquisitor, and in case of their disagreement by the royal seneschal. The inquisitor was deprived of the power of arbitrary arrest. He was obliged to consult the bishop, and when they could not agree the question was to be decided by a majority vote in an assemblage consisting of certain officials of the cathedral and of the Franciscan and Dominican convents. Arrests were only to be made by the seneschal, after these preliminaries had been observed, except in case of foreign heretics who might escape. The question of bail was to be settled in the same way as that of arrest. In no case was either bishop or inquisitor entitled to obedience when acting individually, for, as the king declared,[81] "We cannot endure that the life and death of our subjects shall be abandoned to the discretion of a single individual, who, even if not actuated by cupidity, may be insufficiently informed." Inadequate as these reforms eventually proved, they had an excellent temporary effect. For a time the Inquisition was paralyzed, and arrests which had been taking place every week were suddenly brought to an end, for during 1302 these provisions were embodied in a general Ordonnance, and the legislation of 1293 protecting the Jews was repeated. At the same time Philippe was careful to manifest due solicitude for the suppression of heresy, for he published anew the severe edict of St. Louis; and on the appointment of Guillaume de Morières to the Inquisition of Toulouse he wrote to the seneschal instructing him to place the royal prisons at the inquisitor's disposal, to pay him the customary stipend, and to aid him in every way until further orders.[88]

While the new regulations may have promised relief elsewhere, they gave little comfort at Albi, the inquisitorial proceedings of whose bishop had given rise to the whole disturbance. Its citizens were still languishing in the prison of the Inquisition of Carcassonne, and a numerous deputation of both sexes was sent to the king, accompanied by two Franciscans, Jean Hector and Bertrand de Villedelle. Again Bernard Délicieux was present, having this time been opportunely chosen to represent the Order on a summons from Philippe for consultation on the subject of his quarrel with Pope Boniface. They all followed the king to Pierrefonds and then to Compiègne. He gave them fair words, promised a speedy visit to Languedoc, when he would settle matters, and consoled them with a donation of one thousand livres, which he could well afford to do, for the confiscated estates of the prisoners were in his hands, and were never released.[89]

All this, of course, gave little satisfaction; nor were the people placated by the removal of Nicholas d'Abbeville, for he was succeeded in the Inquisition of Carcassonne by Geoffroi d'Ablis,{82} who was as energetic and unsparing as his predecessor, and who brought royal letters, dated January 1, 1303, ordering all officials to render him the customary obedience. Popular excitement grew more and more threatening, and as Albi had no local inquisitors of its own, being within the jurisdiction of the tribunal of Carcassonne, the discontent vented itself on the Dominicans, who were regarded as the representatives of the hated tribunal. On the first Sunday in Advent, December 2, 1302, when the friars went as usual to preach in the churches they were violently ejected and assailed with cries of "Death to the traitors!" and deemed themselves at length fortunate in being able to regain their convent. This state of things continued for several years, during which they scarce dared to show themselves in the streets, and were never secure from insult. All alms and burial-fees were withdrawn, and the people refused even to attend mass in their church. The names of Dominic and Peter Martyr were erased from the crucifix at the principal gate of the town, and were replaced with those of Pequigny and Nepveu, and of two citizens who were leaders in the disturbances—Arnaud Garsia and Pierre Probi of Castres.[90]

The prisoners of Albi were still as far as ever from liberation, and Bernard Délicieux urged Pequigny to come to Carcassonne and consider their case on the spot. In the summer of 1303 he did so, and was met by a large number of the people of Albi, men and women, praying him to liberate them. While he was investigating the subject he came upon the instrument of pacification between Nicholas d'Abbeville and the consuls of Carcassonne in 1299. This was communicated to the people by Frère Bernard in a fiery sermon, and a knowledge of its conditions aroused them almost to frenzy. Riots ensued in which the houses of some of the old consuls and of those who were regarded as friends of the Inquisition were destroyed; the Dominican church was assailed, its windows broken, the statues in its porch overthrown, and the friars maltreated. To violate the prisons of the Inquisition was so serious a matter that Pequigny seems to have wished the backing of an enraged populace before he would venture on the step: and{83} when he resolved upon it he anticipated resistance so confidently that with his privity Bernard assembled fourscore men, with skilled mechanics, in the Franciscan convent, ready to break open the jails in case of necessity. Their services were not needed. Geoffroi d'Ablis yielded, and in August, 1303, Pequigny removed the prisoners of Albi. He did not discharge them, however, but merely transferred them to the royal prisons, and refused to carry them to the king as Bernard advised. Possibly their treatment for a while may have been gentler, but they derived no permanent advantage from the movement. The grasp of the Inquisition was unrelaxing. It obtained possession of them again, and we shall see that it held them to the last.[91]

Meanwhile advantage was taken of the access obtained to them to procure from them statements of the tortures which they had endured, and lists were made of the names of those whom they had been forced to accuse as heretics. These were circulated throughout the land and excited general alarm, the Franciscans being especially active in giving them publicity. On the other hand, the inquisitor Geoffroi d'Ablis was equal to the emergency. He cited Pequigny to appear and stand trial for impeding the Inquisition, and on his refusal excommunicated him, September 29; and as soon as word could be carried to Paris he was published as excommunicate by the Dominicans there. This audacious act brought all parties to a sense of the nature of the conflict which had sprung up between Church and State. The consuls and people of Albi addressed to the queen an earnest petition beseeching her to prevail upon the king not to abandon them by withdrawing the Reformers, who had already done so much good and on whom depended their last hope. A fruitless effort also was made to prevent the publication of the excommunication. At Castres, October 13, Jean Ricoles, stipendiary priest of the Church of St. Mary, published it from the pulpit, as he was bound to do, and was promptly arrested by the deputy of the royal viguier of Albi and carried to the Franciscan convent, where he was threatened{84} and maltreated, and the friars used every effort to persuade him to withdraw it. This in itself was a grave violation of clerical immunity, and it was soon recognized that such proceedings were worse than useless. Pequigny's authority was paralyzed until the excommunication should be removed, and this could only be done by the man who had uttered it, or by the pope himself.[92]

The prospect of relief was darkened by the election, October 21, of Benedict XI., himself a Dominican and necessarily pre-disposed in favor of the Inquisition. Special exertions evidently were required unless all that had been gained was to be lost, and, at the best, litigation in the Roman court was a costly business. Pequigny had appealed to the pope, and, October 29, he wrote from Paris to the cities of Languedoc asking for their aid in the persecution which he had brought upon himself in their cause. Bernard Délicieux promptly busied himself to obtain the required assistance. By his exertions the three cities of Carcassonne, Albi, and Cordes entered into an alliance and pledged themselves to furnish the sum of three thousand livres, one half by Carcassonne and the rest by the other two, and to continue in the same proportions as long as the affair should last. After Pequigny's death they renewed their obligation to his oldest son Renaud; but as the matter was much protracted, they grew tired, and Bernard, who had raised some of the money on his own responsibility, was left with heavy obligations, of which he vainly sought restitution at the hands of the ungrateful cities.[93]

The quarrel was thus for a time transferred to Rome. Pequigny went to Italy with envoys from the king and from Carcassonne and Albi to plead his cause, and was opposed by Guillaume de Morières, the Inquisitor of Toulouse, sent thither to manage the case against him. Benedict was not slow in showing on|85| which side his sympathies lay. At Perugia, while the pope was conducting the solemnities of Pentecost, May 17, 1304, Pequigny ventured to enter the church. Benedict saw him, and, pointing to him, said to his marshal, P. de Brayda, "Turn out that Patarin!" an order which the marshal zealously obeyed. The significance of the incident was not small, and after the death of both Benedict and Pequigny, Geoffroi d'Ablis caused a notarial instrument recounting it to be drawn up and duly authenticated as one of the documents of the process. The climate of Italy was very unhealthy for Transmontanes. Morières died at Perugia, and Pequigny followed him at Abruzzo, September 29, 1304, the anniversary of his excommunication. Having remained for a year under the ban for impeding the Inquisition, he was legally a heretic, and his burial in consecrated ground is only to be explained by the death of Benedict a short time before. Geoffroi d'Ablis demanded that his bones be exhumed and burned, while Pequigny's sons carried on the appeal for the rehabilitation of his memory. The matter dragged on till Clement V. referred it to a commission of three cardinals. These gave a patient hearing to both sides, who argued the matter exhaustively, and submitted all the necessary documents and papers. At last, July 23, 1308, they rendered their decision to the effect that the sentence of excommunication had been unjust and iniquitous, and that its revocation should be published in all places where it had been announced. Geoffroi fruitlessly endeavored to appeal from this, which was the most complete justification possible of all that had been said and done against the Inquisition, emphasized by Clement's cutting refusal to listen to his statements—"It is false: the land never wished to rebel, but was in evil case in consequence of the doings of the Inquisition," while a cardinal told him that for fifty years the people had been goaded to resistance by the excesses of his predecessors, and that when a corrective was applied they only added evil to evil.[94]

Benedict XI. had given other proofs of partisanship. It is true that in answer to the complaints of the oppressed people he|86| appointed a commission of cardinals to investigate the matter, but there is no trace of their labors, which were probably cut short by his death, July 7, 1304. No commissioners of his selection would have been likely to report adversely to the Inquisition, for he manifested his prejudgment by ordering the Minister of Aquitaine, under pain of forfeiture of office and future disability, to arrest Frère Bernard without warning and send him under sufficient guard to the papal court, as a fautor of heretics and presumably a heretic. The leading citizens of Albi, including G. de Pesenches the viguier and Gaillard Étienne the royal judge, who had sought to aid Pequigny, were also involved in the papal condemnation. The Minister of Aquitaine intrusted to Frère Jean Rigaud the execution of the arrest, which he duly performed, June, 1304, in the convent of Carcassonne, adding an excommunication when Bernard, encouraged by the active sympathy of the people, delayed in obeying the papal summons. He never went, and it is a curious illustration of Franciscan tendencies to see that the minister absolved him from the excommunication, and that the provincial chapter of his Order at Albi decided that he had done all that was requisite, though perhaps Benedict's death in July had relieved them from fears as to the immediate consequences of their contumacy.[95]

Meanwhile Philippe le Bel had at last fulfilled his promise to visit in person his southern provinces and rectify on the spot the wrongs of which his subjects had so long complained. He was expecting a favorable termination to his negotiation with Benedict for the removal of the excommunications launched by Boniface VIII. against himself and his subjects and chief agents, a result which he obtained May 13, 1304, with exception of the censure inflicted on Guillaume de Nogaret and Sciarra Colonna. When, therefore, he reached Toulouse on Christmas Day, 1303, he was not disposed to excite unnecessarily Benedict's prejudices. From Albi and Carcassonne multitudes flocked to him with cries for redress and protection, and Pequigny spoke eloquently in their behalf. The inquisitors were represented by Guillem Pierre, the|87| Dominican provincial, while Bernard Délicieux was foremost in the debate. It was on this occasion that he made his celebrated assertion that St. Peter and St. Paul would be convicted of heresy if tried with inquisitorial methods, and when the scandalized Bishop of Auxerre tartly reproved him, he stoutly maintained the truth of what he had said. Friar Nicholas, the king's Dominican confessor, was suspected of exercising undue influence in favor of the Inquisition, and Bernard endeavored to discredit him by accusing him of betraying to the Flemings all the secrets of the royal council. Geoffroi d'Ablis, the Inquisitor of Carcassonne, moreover, was ingratiating himself with Philippe at the moment by skilful negotiations to bring about a reconciliation with Rome.[96]

Philippe patiently heard both sides, and recorded his conclusions in an edict of January 13, 1304, which was in the nature of a compromise. It recited that the king had come to Languedoc for the purpose of pacifying the country excited by the action of the Inquisition, and had had prolonged consultation on the subject with all who were entitled to express an opinion. The result thus reached was that the prisoners of the Inquisition should be visited by royal deputies in company with inquisitors; the prisons were to be safe, but not punitive. In the case of prisoners not yet sentenced the trials were to be carried to conclusion under the conjoined supervision of the bishops and inquisitors, and this co-operation was to be observed in the future, except at Albi, where the bishop, being suspected, was to be replaced by Arnaud Novelli, the Cistercian Abbot of Fontfroide. The royal officials were strictly ordered to aid in every way the inquisitors and episcopal ordinaries when called upon, and to protect from injury and violence the Dominicans, their churches and houses.[97]

At Albi the change had the wished-for effect. No more heretics were found and no further prosecutions were required. Yet the refusal of the king to entertain any project of reform other than his previous one of curbing the Inquisition with an illusory{88} episcopal supervision was a grievous disappointment. Men naturally argued that if the Dominicans had done right they ought not to be insulted by the proposed episcopal co-operation; and if they had done wrong they ought to be replaced. If any change was called for, the projected one was insufficient. So many hopes had been built upon the royal presence in the land, that the result caused universal dismay, which was not relieved by Philippe's subsequent action. When he visited Carcassonne he was urged to see the unfortunate captives whose persecution had been the prominent cause of the troubles, but he refused, and sent his brother Louis to look at them. Worse than all, the citizens had designed to propitiate him and demonstrate their loyalty by offering him some elaborate silver vessels. These were yet in the hands of the gold-smiths of Montpellier when the royal party came to Carcassonne, so they were sent after him to Béziers, where the presentation was made, a portion to him and the rest to the queen. She accepted the offering, but he not only rejected it, but, when he learned what the queen had done, forced her to return the present. This threw the consuls of Carcassonne into despair. Offerings of this kind from municipalities to the sovereign were so customary and their gracious acceptance so much a matter of course, that refusal in this instance seemed to argue some most unfavorable intentions on the part of the king, which was not unlikely, seeing that Elias Patrice, the leading citizen of Carcassonne, had plainly told him when there that if he did not render them speedy justice against the Inquisition they would be forced to seek another lord, and when Philippe ordered him from his presence the citizens obeyed Patrice's command to remove the decorations from the streets. Imagining that he had been won over by the Dominicans and that his protection would be withdrawn, the prospect of being abandoned to the mercy of the Inquisition seemed so terrible that they wildly declared that if they could not find another lord to protect them they would burn the town and with the inhabitants seek some place of refuge. In consultation with Frère Bernard it was hastily determined to offer their allegiance to Ferrand, son of the King of Majorca.

The younger branch of the House of Aragon, which drew its title from the Balearic Isles, held the remnants of the old French possessions of the Catalans, including Montpellier and Perpignan.{89} It had old claims to much of the land, and its rule might well be hailed by the people as much more welcome than the foreign domination to which they had been unwillingly subjected. Had the whole region agreed to transfer its allegiance, its reduction might have cost Philippe a doubtful struggle, embarrassed as he was with the chronic disaffection of the Flemings. When, however, the project was broached to the men of Albi, they refused peremptorily to embark in it, and there can be no stronger proof of the desperation of the Carcassais than their resolution to persist in it single-handed. Ferrand and his father were at Montpellier entertaining the French court, which they accompanied to Nîmes. He eagerly listened to the overtures, and asked Frère Bernard to come to him at Perpignan. Bernard went thither with a letter of credence from the consuls, which he prudently destroyed on the road. The King of Majorca, when he heard of the offer, chastened his son's ambition by boxing his ears and pulling him around by the hair, and he ingratiated himself with his powerful neighbor by communicating the plot to Philippe.[98]

Although there could have been no real danger from so crazy a project, the relation of the southern provinces to the crown were too strained for the king not to exact a vengeance which should prove a warning. A court was assembled at Carcassonne which sat through the summer of 1305 and made free use of torture in its investigations. Albi, which had taken no part in the plot, escaped an investigation by a bribe of one thousand livres to the seneschal, Jean d'Alnet, but the damage inflicted on the Franciscan convent shows that the Dominicans were keen to make reprisals for what they had suffered. The town of Limoux had been concerned in the affair; it was fined and disfranchised, and{90} forty of its citizens were hanged. As for Carcassonne, all of its eight consuls, with Elias Patrice at their head, and seven other citizens were hanged in their official robes, the city was deprived of self-government and subjected to the enormous fine of sixty thousand livres, a sentence from which it vainly appealed to the Parlement. As Bernard Gui observes with savage exultation, those who had croaked like ravens against the Dominicans were exposed to the ravens. Aimeric Castel, who had sought in this way to obtain redress for the wrong done to his father's memory and estate, escaped by flight, but was captured and long lay a prisoner, finally making his peace with a heavy ransom, and a harvest of fines was gathered into the royal exchequer from all who could be accused of privity. As for Frère Bernard, he received early intelligence from Frère Durand, the queen's confessor, of the discovery of the plot, when he boldly headed a delegation of citizens of Albi who went to Paris to protest their innocence. There Durand informed them that Albi was not implicated, when they returned, leaving Bernard. At the request of the king, Clement V. had him arrested and carried to Lyons, whence he was taken by the papal court to Bordeaux; and when it went to Poitiers he was confined in the convent of St. Junian of Limoges. In May, 1307, at the instance of Clement, Philippe issued letters of amnesty to all concerned, and remitted to Carcassonne the portion of its fine not yet paid, and in Lent, 1308, Bernard was allowed to come to Poitiers. On the king's arrival there he boldly complained to him of his arrest and of the punishment which had involved the innocent with the guilty. As he still had no license to leave the papal court, he accompanied it to Avignon, and was at length discharged with the royal assent—the heavy bribes paid to three cardinals by his friends of Albi having perhaps something to do with his immunity. He returned to Toulouse, and we hear of no further activity on his part. His narrow escape probably sobered his restless enthusiasm, and as the reform of the Inquisition seemed to have been taken resolutely in hand by Clement V. he might well persuade himself that there was no further call for self-sacrifice.[99]{91}

The death of Benedict XI., in July, 1304, had given fresh hopes to the sufferers from the Inquisition. There was an interregnum of nearly a year before the election of his successor, Clement V., June 5, 1305. During this period a petition to the College of Cardinals was presented by seventeen of the religious bodies of the Albigeois, including the canons of the cathedral of Albi, those of the church of St. Salvi, the convent of Gaillac, etc., imploring in the most pressing terms the Sacred College to intervene and avert the fearful dangers threatening the community. The land, they declare, is Catholic, the people are faithful, cherishing the religion of Rome in their hearts, and professing it with their lips. Yet so fierce are the dissensions between them and the inquisitors, that they are aroused to wrath and are eager to put to the sword those whom they have learned to regard as enemies. Doubtless the inquisitors had taken advantage of the revulsion consequent upon the fruitless treason of Carcassonne and of the altered attitude of the king. Philippe thenceforth interfered no further, save to urge his representatives to renewed vigilance in enforcing the laws against heretics and the disabilities inflicted upon their descendants. It was not only the treason of Carcassonne which indisposed him to interfere; from 1307 onward he needed the indispensable aid of the Inquisition to carry out his designs against the Templars, and he could afford neither to antagonize it nor to limit its powers.[100]

The Sacred College, monopolized by electioneering intrigues, paid no heed to the imploring prayer of the Albigensian clergy, but when the year's turmoil was ended by the triumph of the French party in the election of Clement V. the hopes raised by the death of his predecessor might reasonably seem destined to fruition. Bertrand de Goth, Cardinal-Archbishop of Bordeaux, was a Gascon by birth, and, though an English subject, was doubtless more familiar than the Italians with the miseries and needs of Languedoc. His transfer of the papacy to French soil was also {92} of good augury. Hardly had the news of his election reached Albi, when Frère Bernard was busy in organizing a mission to represent to him in the name of the city the necessity of relief, and when he visited Toulouse the wives of the prisoners, still languishing in confinement, were taken thither to make their woes emphatically known. Hardly had he been consecrated at Lyons when these complaints poured in and were substantiated by two Dominicans, Bertrand Blanc and François Aimeric, who were as emphatic as the representatives of Albi in their denunciations of inquisitorial methods and abuses. Geoffroi d'Ablis hurried thither from Carcassonne to defend himself in such haste that he left no one to take his place, and was obliged to send from Lyons, September 29, 1305, a commission to Jean de Faugoux and Gerald de Blumac to act in his stead. In this paper his fiery fanaticism breathes forth in his denunciations of the horrid beasts, the cruel beasts, who are ravaging the vineyard of the Lord, and who are to be tracked to their dens and extirpated with unsparing rigor.[101]

His efforts to justify the Inquisition were unavailing, more especially, perhaps, because the people of Albi bribed Cardinal Raymond de Goth, the pope's nephew, with two thousand livres Tournois, the Cardinal of Santa Croce with as much, and the Cardinal Pier Colonna with five hundred. March 13, 1306, Clement commissioned two cardinals, Pierre of San Vitale (afterwards of Palestrina) and Berenger of SS. Nereo and Achille (afterwards of Frascati), who were about to pass through Languedoc on a mission, to investigate and make such temporary changes as they should find necessary. The people of Carcassonne, Albi, and Cordes had offered to prove that good Catholics were forced to confess heresy through the stress of torture and the horrors of the prisons, and further that the records of the Inquisition were altered and falsified. Until the investigation was completed, the inquisitors were not to consign to strict prison or to inflict torture on {93} any one except in conjunction with the diocesan, and in the place of the Bishop of Albi the Abbot of Fontfroide was subrogated.

On April 16, 1306, the cardinals held a public session at Carcassonne in presence of all the notables of the place. The consuls of Carcassonne and the delegates of Albi preferred their complaints and were supported by the two Dominicans, Blanc and Aimeric, who had appeared before the pope. On the other hand, Geoffroi d'Ablis and the deputy of the Bishop of Albi defended themselves and complained of the popular riots and the ill-treatment to which they had been exposed. After hearing both sides the cardinals adjourned further proceedings until January 25, at Bordeaux, where Carcassonne, Albi, and Cordes were each to send four procurators to conduct the matter. As this office was a most dangerous one, the cardinals gave security to them against the Inquisition during the performance of their duty. This was no idle precaution, and Aimeric Castel, one of the representatives of Carcassonne, found himself in such danger that in September, 1308, he was obliged to procure from Clement a special bull forbidding the inquisitors to assail him until the termination of the affair. Even greater danger impended over any witnesses called upon to prove the falsification of records, as they were bound to silence under oaths which exposed them to the stake as relapsed heretics in case they revealed their evidence, and the cardinals were asked to absolve them from these oaths.[102]

If there were any further formal proceedings in this matter, which thus assumed the shape of a litigation between the people and the Inquisition, they have not reached us. Yet the cardinals, before continuing their journey, took some steps which showed that they were convinced of the truth of the accusations. They visited the prison of Carcassonne, and caused the prisoners, forty in number, of whom three were women, to be brought before them. Some of these were sick, others worn with age, and all tearfully complaining of the horrors of their lot, the insufficiency of food and bedding, and the cruelty of their keepers. The cardinals were moved to dismiss all the jailers and attendants except the chief,{94} and to put the prison under the control of the Bishop of Carcassonne. It is significant that the oath imposed on the new officials bound them never to speak to a prisoner except in the presence of an associate, and not to steal any of the food destined for those under their charge. One of the cardinals visited the prison of the Bishop of Albi, where he found the jailers well spoken of, but was shocked with the condition of the prisoners. Many of them were in chains and all in narrow, dark cells, where some of them had been confined for five years or more without being yet condemned. He ordered all chains removed, that light should be introduced in the cells, and that new and less inhuman ones should be built within a month. As regards general amelioration in inquisitorial proceedings, the only regulation which they issued was a confirmation of Philippe's expedient, requiring the co-operation of the diocesan with the inquisitor, and this was withdrawn by Clement, August 12, 1308, in an apologetic bull declaring that the cardinals had exceeded his intentions.[103]

The existence of the evils complained of was thus admitted, but the Church shrank from applying a remedy, and, after the struggle of years, relief was as illusory as ever. Even with regard to the crying and inexcusable abuse of the detention of prisoners in these fearful dungeons for long years without conviction or sentence, Clement found himself powerless to effect reform in the most flagrant cases. The inquisitors had in their archives a bull of Innocent IV. authorizing them to defer indefinitely passing sentence when they deemed that delay was in the interest of the faith, and of this they took full advantage. Of the captives seized by the Bishop of Albi in 1299, many were still unsentenced when the Cardinal of San Vitale examined his prisons. This visit passed away without result. Five years afterwards, in 1310, Clement wrote to the Bishop of Albi and Geoffroi d'Ablis that the citizens{95} of Albi, whom he names, had repeatedly appealed to him, after more than eight years of imprisonment, to have their trials completed either to condemnation or absolution. He therefore orders the trials proceeded with at once and the results submitted for confirmation to the Cardinals of Palestrina and Frascati, his former commissioners. Bertrand de Bordes, Bishop of Albi, and Geoffroi d'Ablis contemptuously disregarded this command, because some of the prisoners named in it had died before its date, whence they argued that the papal letter had been surreptitiously obtained. When this contumacy reached the ears of Clement, some year or two later, he wrote to Geraud, then Bishop of Albi, and Geoffroi, peremptorily reiterating his commands and ordering them to try both living and dead. In spite of this, Geoffroi maintained his sullen contumacy. We have no means of knowing the fate of most of these unfortunates, who probably rotted to death in their dungeons without their trials being concluded; but of some of them we have traces, as related in a former chapter. After Clement and his cardinals had passed away, and no further interference was to be dreaded, in 1319 two surviving ones, Guillem Salavert and Isarn Colli, were brought out for further examination, when the former confirmed his confession and the latter retracted it as extorted under torture. Six months later, Guillem Calverie of Cordes, who had been imprisoned in 1301, was abandoned to the secular arm for retracting his confession (probably before Clement's cardinals), and Guillem Salavert was allowed to escape with wearing crosses, in consideration of his nineteen years" imprisonment without conviction. Even as late as 1328 attested copies made by order of the royal judge of Carcassonne, of inventories of personal property of Raymond Calverie and Jean Baudier, two of the prisoners of 1299-1300, show that their cases were still the subject of litigation. Even more remarkable as a manifestation of contumacy is the case of Guillem Garric, held in prison for complicity in the attempt to destroy the records at Carcassonne in 1284. Royal letters of 1312 recite that his merits and piety had caused Clement V. to grant him full pardon, wherefore the king restores to him and his descendants his confiscated castle of Monteirat. Yet the Inquisition did not relax its grip, but waited until 1321, when he was brought forth from prison, and in consideration of his contrition Bernard Gui{96} mercifully sentenced the old man to perpetual banishment from France within thirty days.[104]

Another endeavor was made by Clement to repress the abuses of the Inquisition by transferring from its jurisdiction to that of the bishops the Jews of the provinces of Toulouse and Narbonne on account of the undue molestation to which they were continually subjected. This transfer even included cases then pending, but after Clement's death a bull was produced in which he annulled the previous one and restored the jurisdiction of the Inquisition.[105]

The outcome of all this struggle and investigation is to be found in the measures of reform adopted in 1312 by the Council of Vienne at Clement's instance. The five books of canon law known as the "Clementines," which were enacted by the council, were retained for revision by Clement, who was on the point of publishing them when he died, April 20, 1314. They were held in suspense during the long interregnum which followed, and were not authoritatively given to the world until October 25, 1317, by John XXII. The canons relating to the Inquisition have been alluded to above, and it will be remembered that they only restricted the power of the inquisitor by requiring episcopal concurrence in the use of torture, or of harsh confinement equivalent to torture, and in the custody of prisoners. There was a *brutum fulmen* of excommunication denounced against those who should abuse their power for purposes of hate, affection, or extortion, and the importance of the whole lies far less in the remedies it proposes than in its emphatic testimony of the existence of cruelty and{97} corruption in every detail of inquisitorial practice. Bernard Gui vainly raised his voice in an earnest and elaborate protest against the publication of the new rules, and after their promulgation he did not hesitate openly to tell his brethren that they required to be modified or rather wholly suspended by the Holy See, but his expostulations were totally uncalled for. The closest examination of inquisitorial methods before and after the publication of the Clementines fails to reveal any influence exercised by them for good or for evil. No trace of any practical effort for their enforcement is to be found, and inquisitors went on, as was their wont, in the arbitrary fashion for which their office gave them such unlimited opportunity.[106]

One case may indeed be cited to show a special relaxation of the procedure against heretics. Philippe's hatred of Boniface VIII. was undying, and could not be quenched even by the miserable end of his enemy. Yet the one thing which he failed to wring from his tool in the papal chair was the condemnation of the memory of Boniface as a heretic. After repeated efforts he compelled Clement to take testimony on the subject, and a cloud of witnesses were produced who swore with minute detail to the unbelief of the late pope in the immortality of the soul, and in all the doctrines of the incarnation and the atonement, and to his worship of demons, to his cynical and unnatural lasciviousness, and to the common fame which existed in the community as to his evil beliefs and habits. The witnesses were reputable churchmen for the most part, and their evidence was precise. A tithe of such testimony would have sufficed to burn the bones and disinherit the heirs of a score of ordinary culprits, but for once the recognized rules of procedure were set aside. Philippe was forced{98} to desist from the pursuit, though Clement in his final bull of April 27, 1311, declared that the king and his witnesses had been actuated solely by zeal for the Church, and the affair fell through. The pretensions put forth by Boniface in his offensive decretals were formally withdrawn, and Guillaume de Nogaret obtained his long-withheld absolution.[107]

Clement died at Carpentras April 20, 1314, carrying with him the shame and guilt of the ruin of the Templars, and was followed in about seven months (November 29) by his tempter and accomplice, Philippe le Bel. The cardinals on whom devolved the choice of a successor to St. Peter were torn with dissensions. The Italians demanded that the election should be held in the Eternal City. The French, or Gascons, as they were called, insisted on the observance of the rule that the selection should be made on the spot where the last pontiff had expired, knowing that in Italy they would be exposed to the same insults and annoyances as were inflicted in France on their Italian brethren. Shut up in the episcopal palace of Carpentras, the conclave awaited in vain the inspiration of the Holy Ghost, even though those outside tried the gentle expedient of cutting off the food of the members and pillaging their houses. The situation grew so insupportable that, as a last desperate resort, on July 23, 1314, the Gascon faction, under the lead of Clement's nephews, set fire to the palace and threatened the Italians with death, so that the latter were glad to escape with their lives by breaking a passage through the rear wall. Two years passed away without the election of a visible head of the Church, and the faithful might well fear that they had seen the last of the popes. The French court, however, had found itself so well abetted by a French pope that its policy required the chair of St. Peter to be filled, and in 1316 Louis Hutin sent his brother, Philippe le Long, then Count of Poitiers, to Lyons with orders to get the cardinals together. To accomplish this Philippe was obliged to swear that he would neither do them violence nor imprison them, and they, having thus secured their independence, were no more disposed to accord than before. For six months the business thus lagged without prospect of result, when Philippe received the news of the sudden death of his brother, and that the{99}widowed queen claimed to be pregnant. The prospect of a vacant throne, or at least of a regency, awaiting him in Paris rendered further dallying in Lyons insupportable, nor could he well depart without bringing his errand to a successful issue. Hastily counselling with his lawyers, it was discovered that his oath was unlawful and therefore not to be observed. Consequently he invited the reverend fathers to a colloquy in the Dominican convent, and when they were thus safely hived he sternly told them that they should not depart till they had chosen a pope. His guards blocked every entrance, and he hastened off to Paris, leaving them to deliberate in captivity. Thus entrapped they made a merit of necessity, though forty days were still required before they proclaimed Jacques d'Ozo, Cardinal of Porto, as the Vicar of Christ—the Italians having been won over by his oath that he would never mount a horse or mule except to go to Rome. This oath he kept during his whole pontificate of eighteen years, for he slipped down the Rhone to Avignon by boat, ascended on foot to the palace, and never left it except to visit the cathedral which adjoined it. Such a process of selection was not likely to result in the evolution of a saint, and John XXII. was its natural exponent. His distinguished learning and vigorous abilities had elevated him from the humblest origin, while his boundless ambition and imperious temper provoked endless quarrels from which his daring spirit never shrank.[108]

With his election the troubles of the Inquisition of Languedoc were over. Though he published the Clementines, he soon let it be seen that the inquisitors had nothing to fear from him, and they made haste to pay off the accumulated scores of vengeance. The first victim was Bernard Délicieux. During the pontificate of Clement and the interregnum he had lived in peace, and might well imagine that his enthusiasm for the people of Languedoc had been forgotten. His earnest nature had led him to join the section of his order known as the Spirituals, and he had been prominent{100} in the movements by which, during the vacancy of the Holy See, they had gained possession of the convents of Béziers and Narbonne. One of the first cares of John XXII. was to heal this schism in the Order, and he promptly summoned before him the friars of Béziers and Narbonne. Bernard had not hesitated in signing an appeal to the pope, and he now boldly came before him at the head of his brethren. When he undertook to argue their cause he was accused of having impeded the Inquisition and was promptly arrested. Besides the charge of impeding the Inquisition, others of encompassing by magic arts the death of Benedict XI., and of treason in the affair of Carcassonne, were brought against him. A papal commission was formed to investigate these matters, and for more than two years he was held in close prison while the examination went slowly on. At length it was ready for trial, and September 3, 1319, a court was convened at Castelnaudari consisting of the Archbishop of Toulouse and the Bishops of Pamiers and St. Papoul, when the archbishop excused himself and left the matter in the hands of his associates, who transferred the court to Carcassonne, September 12. The importance attached to the trial is shown by the fact that at it the Inquisition was represented by the inquisitor Jean de Beaune, and the king by his Seneschal of Carcassonne and Toulouse and his "Reformers," Raoul, Bishop of Laon, and Jean, Count of Forez.[109]

The official report of the trial has been preserved in all its immense prolixity, and there are few documents of that age more instructive as to what was then regarded as justice. Some of Bernard's old accomplices, such as Arnaud Garsia, Guillem Fransa, Pierre Probi, and others, who had already been seized by the Inquisition, were brought forward to be tried with him and were used as witnesses to save their own lives by swearing his away. The old man, worn with two years of imprisonment and constant examination, was subjected for two months to the sharpest cross-questioning on occurrences dating from twelve to eighteen years previous, the subjects of the multiform charges being ingeniously intermingled in the most confusing manner. Under pretext of{101} seeking the salvation of his soul he was solemnly and repeatedly admonished that he was legally a heretic for remaining for more than a year under the *ipso facto* excommunication incurred by impeding the Inquisition, and that nothing could save him from the stake but absolute submission and full confession. Twice he was tortured, the first time, October 3, on the charge of treason, and the second, November 20, on that of necromancy; and though the torture was ordered to be "moderate," the notaries who assisted at it are careful to report that the shrieks of the victim attested its sufficiency. In neither case was anything extracted from him, but the efficacy of the combined pressure thus brought to bear on a man weakened by age and suffering is shown by the manner in which he was brought day by day to contradict and criminate himself, until at last he threw himself on the mercy of the court, and humbly begged for absolution.[110]

In the sentence, rendered December 8, he was acquitted of attempting the life of Benedict XI., while on the other charges his guilt was aggravated by no less than seventy perjuries committed under examination. After abjuration, he was duly absolved and condemned to degradation from holy orders and imprisonment for life, in chains and on bread and water, in the inquisitorial prison of Carcassonne. Considering the amnesty proclaimed in 1307 by Philippe le Bel, and the discharge of Frère Bernard in 1308, it seems strange that now the representatives of Philippe le Long at once protested against the sentence as too mild, and appealed to the pope. The judges themselves did not think so, for in delivering the prisoner to Jean de Beaune they humanely ordered that in view of his age and debility, and especially the weakness of his hands (doubtless crippled in the torture-chamber), the penance of chains and bread and water should be omitted. Jean de Beaune may be pardoned if he felt a fierce exultation when the ancient enemy of his office was thus placed in his hands to expiate the offence which had so harassed his predecessors; and that exultation was perhaps increased when, February 26, 1320, the relentless{102} pope, possibly to gratify the king, countermanded the pitying order of the bishops, and required the sentence to be executed in all its terrible rigor. Under these hardships the frail body which had been animated by so dauntless a spirit soon gave way, and in a few months merciful death released the only man who had dared to carry on a systematic warfare with the Inquisition.[111]

The progress of reaction had been rapid. In 1315 Louis Hutin had issued an edict in which were embodied most of the provisions of the laws of Frederic II. This piece of legislation, perfectly superfluous in view of the eighty years" career of the Inquisition in his dominions, is only of interest as showing the influence already obtained by the Dominicans during the papal interregnum. With the election of John XXII., notwithstanding his publication of the Clementines, all fear of interference disappeared, and the populations were surrendered again to the unchecked authority of the inquisitors. There was a significant notice to this effect in the withdrawal by the new pope, March 30, 1318, of the security given by Clement's cardinals to Aimeric Castel and the other citizens of Carcassonne, Albi, and Cordes, who were deputed to carry on the case of those cities against the inquisitors, and the latter were directed to prosecute them diligently. The Inquisition recognized that its hour of triumph had come, and took in hand the survivors of those who had been conspicuous in the disturbances of fifteen years before. The unconvicted prisoners of 1299 and 1300, whom it had held in defiance of the reiterated orders of Clement—at least those who had not rotted to death in its dungeons—were brought forth and disposed of. A still more emphatic assertion of its renewed mastery was the subjection and "reconciliation" of the rebellious towns. Of what took place at Carcassonne we have no record, but it probably was the same as the ceremonies performed at Albi. There, March 11, 1319, the consuls and councillors and a great crowd of citizens were assembled in the cathedral cemetery, before Bishop Bernard and the inquisitor Jean de Beaune. There, with uplifted hands, they all professed repentance in the most humiliating terms, and swore to accept whatever penance{103} might be imposed upon them, and thereafter to obey implicitly the bishop and inquisitor. Then those present, together with the dead who had shown signs of penitence, were relieved from excommunication, the rest of the population being required to apply for absolution within a month. The announcement of the penances followed. The town was to make good all expenses and losses accruing to the episcopate and Inquisition by reason of the troubles; it was to build and complete within two years a chapel to the cathedral, and a portal to the Dominican church; to give fifty livres to the Carmelites to be expended on their church, and, finally, to construct marble tombs for Nicholas d'Abbeville, and Foulques de Saint-Georges at Lyons and Carcassonne, where those inquisitors had died in poverty and exile by reason of the rebellion of the inhabitants. Ten pilgrimages, moreover, were designated for the survivors of those who in 1301 had bound themselves to prosecute Bishop Bertrand and Nicholas d'Abbeville in the royal court, as well as for those who had served as consuls and councillors from 1302 to 1304. Jean de Beaune seems to have considered it a special grace when, in December, 1320, he postponed the performance of their pilgrimages during the year from Easter, 1321, to 1322. The town of Cordes, June 29, 1321, was "reconciled" with a similar humiliating ceremony and pledges of future obedience. Thus the Inquisition celebrated its triumph in the long struggle. It had won the victory, and its opponents could only save themselves by unconditional surrender.[112]

Whether the citizens of Albi whose arrest in 1299 gave rise to so many troubles were really heretics or not cannot now be determined. Their confessions were precise and detailed, but, as their defenders alleged, the Inquisition had ample means of extorting what it pleased from its victims, and the long delay in convicting them would seem to argue that the tribunal had good reason for not wishing its sentences to see the light while there was chance of their being subjected to scrutiny under Clement V. The inquisitors urged in justification a single case, that of Lambert de{104} Foyssenx, who complained to Clement's cardinals that he had been unjustly accused, but who subsequently asserted his heresy defiantly, refused to recant, and was burned in 1309. This is the only instance of the kind, for the wretched survivors who were led to abjure and recant in 1319 were broken by prison and torture, and their evidence is worthless.[113]

Yet Bernard Gui was undoubtedly correct when he asserted that the troubles and limitations imposed on the Inquisition under Philippe le Bel led to the recrudescence of a heresy which had been nearly extinguished. In the debate before the king at Toulouse, in 1304, Guillem Pierre, the Dominican provincial, asserted that there were then in Languedoc no heretics except some forty or fifty in Albi, Carcassonne, and Cordes, and for a few leagues around them. This was doubtless an exaggeration, but with improved prospects of immunity perfected missionaries were invited from Lombardy and Sicily, and the number of believers rapidly increased. Bernard Gui boasts that from 1301 to 1315 there were more than a thousand detected by the Inquisition, who confessed and were publicly punished.[114]

The registers of Geoffroi d'Ablis at Carcassonne in 1308-9 show great activity rewarded by abundant results, and one of the witnesses in the trial of Bernard Délicieux tells us that, when the Inquisition was able to resume its labors there, many heretics and believers were promptly discovered.[115] About the same period commence the sentences of the Inquisition of Toulouse published by Limborch. In 1306 Bernard Gui had been appointed inquisitor at Toulouse. His numerous works attest his wide range of learning and incessant mental activity, while his practical skill in affairs was animated with a profound conviction of the wickedness of heresy and of the duty of his Order to enforce, at every cost, submission to Rome. Two missions as papal legate, one to Italy and the other to France, and two bishoprics, those of Tuy and Lodève, attest the value set on his services by John XXII. With his appointment at Toulouse he promptly commenced the long campaign{105} which resulted in the virtual extirpation of Catharism in Languedoc. Yet, though stern and unsparing when the occasion seemed to demand it, his record bears no trace of useless cruelty or abusive extortion.[116]

Catharism by this time had been forced back to the humbler class among whom it had found its first disciples. The nobles and gentlemen who had so long upheld it had perished or been impoverished by the remorseless confiscations of three quarters of a century. The rich burghers of the cities—merchants and professional men—had learned the temptations held out by their wealth and the impossibility of avoiding detection. The fascinations of martyrdom have their limits, and the martyrs among them had been gradually but surely weeded out. Yet the old beliefs were still rooted among the simple folk of country hamlets and especially in the wild valleys among the foothills of the eastern Pyrenees. The active intercourse with Lombardy, and even with Sicily, was still kept up, and there were not wanting earnest ministers who braved every danger to administer to believers the consolations of their religion and to spread the faith in the fastnesses which were its last refuge. Chief among these was Pierre Autier, formerly a notary of Ax (Pamiers). His early life had not been pure, for we hear of his *druda*, or mistress, and his natural children, but with advancing years he embraced all the asceticism of the sect, to which he devoted his life. Driven to Lombardy in 1295, he returned in 1298 to remain on his native soil to the end, and to endure a war to the knife from the Inquisition. His property was confiscated and his family dispersed and ruined. The region to which he belonged lay at the foot of the Pyrenees, rugged, with few roads and many caves and hiding-places, whence escape across the frontier to Aragon was comparatively facile; it was full of his kindred who were devoted to him, and here for eleven years he maintained himself, lurking in disguise and wandering from place to place with the emissaries of the Holy Office ever on his track. He had been ordained to the ministry at Como, and speedily acquired authority in the sect of which he became one of the most zealous, indefatigable, and intrepid missionaries. Already, in 1300, he was{106} so conspicuous that every effort was made for his apprehension. A certain Guillem Jean offered the Dominicans of

Pamiers to betray him, but the treachery became known among the faithful, two of whom, Pierre d'Aère and Philippe de Larnat enticed Guillem to the bridge at Alliat by night, seized him, gagged him, carried him off to the mountains, and, after extorting a confession, cast him over a precipice. Worthy lieutenants of Pierre Autier were his brother Guillem and his son Jacques, Amiel de Perles, Pierre Sanche, and Sanche Mercadier, whose names occur everywhere throughout the confessions as active missionaries. Jacques Autier on one occasion had the boldness to preach at midnight to a gathering of heretic women in the Church of Sainte-Croix in Toulouse, the spot being selected as one in which they could best hold their meeting undisturbed.[117]

The work of Geoffroi d'Ablis in Carcassonne seems to be principally directed to determining the protectors and refuges of Pierre Autier. At Toulouse Bernard Gui was energetically employed in the same direction. The heretic was driven from place to place, but the wonderful fidelity of his disciples seemed to render all efforts vain, and finally Bernard was driven to the expedient of issuing, August 10, 1309, a special proclamation as an incitement for his capture.

"Friar Bernard Gui, Dominican, Inquisitor of Toulouse, to all worshippers of Christ, the reward and crown of eternal life. Gird yourselves, Sons of God; arise with me, Soldiers of Christ, against the enemies of his Cross, those corrupters of the truth and purity of Catholic faith, Pierre Autier, the heresiarch, and his coheretics and accomplices, Pierre Sanche and Sanche Mercadier. Hiding in concealment and walking in darkness, I order them by the virtue of God, to be tracked and seized wherever they may be found, promising eternal reward from God, and also a fitting temporal payment to those who will capture and produce them. Watch, therefore, O pastors, lest the wolves snatch away the sheep of your flock! Act manfully, faithful zealots, lest the adversaries of the faith fly and escape!"

This stirring exhortation was probably superfluous, for the prey was captured before it could have been published throughout the land. The arrest of nearly all his family and friends, in 1308-9, had driven Pierre Autier from his accustomed haunts.{107} About St. John's Day (June 24), 1309, he found refuge with Perrin Maurel of Belpech, near Castelnaudari, where he lay for five weeks or more. Thither came his daughter Guillelma, who remained with him a short time, and the two departed together. The next day he was captured. Perrin Maurel was likewise seized, and with customary fidelity stoutly denied everything until Pierre Autier, in prison, advised him in December to confess.[118]

This triumph was followed in October by the capture of Amiel de Perles, who forthwith placed himself in *endura*, refusing to eat or drink, and, as he was fast sinking, to prevent the stake from being robbed of its prey, a special *auto de fé* was hurriedly arranged for his burning, October 23. While yet his strength lasted, however, Bernard Gui enjoyed the ghastly amusement of making the two heresiarchs in his presence perform the act of heretical "adoration."[119]

Pierre Autier was not burned until the great *auto de fé* of April, 1310, when Geoffroi d'Ablis came from Carcassonne to share in the triumph. The heresiarch had not sought to conceal his faith, but had boldly declared his obnoxious tenets and had pronounced the Church of Rome the synagogue of Satan. That he was subjected to the extremity of torture, however, there can be no reasonable doubt—not to extract a confession, for this was superfluous, but to force him to betray his disciples and those who had given him refuge. His intimate acquaintance with all the heretics of the land was a source of information too important for Bernard Gui to shrink from any means of acquiring it; and the copious details thus obtained are alluded to in too many subsequent sentences for us to hesitate as to the methods by which the heresiarch was brought to place his friends and associates at the mercy of his tormentors.[120]

This may be said to close the bloody drama of Catharism in Languedoc. Armed with the revelations thus obtained, Bernard Gui and Geoffroi d'Ablis required but a few years more to convert or burn the remnant of Pierre Autier's disciples who could be caught, and to drive into exile those who eluded their spies. No new and self-devoted missionaries arose to take his place, and{108} after 1315 the Patarin almost disappears from the records of the Inquisition in France. Some few scattering cases subsequently occur, but their offences are of old date and almost invariably revert to the missionary work of Pierre Autier and his associates. One of the latest of these is recorded in an undated sentence, probably of 1327 or 1328, in which Jean Duprat, Inquisitor of Carcassonne, condemns Guillelma Tornière. She had abjured and had been long confined in prison, where she was detected in making converts and praising Guillem Autier and Guillem Balibaste as good and saintly men. Under interrogation she refused to take an oath, and was accordingly burned. In 1328, Henri de Chamay of Carcassonne condemned to prison Guillem Amiel for Catharism, and in 1329 he sentenced two Cathari, Bartolomé Pays and Raymond Garric of Albi, whose offences had been committed respectively thirty-five and forty years before. In the same year he ordered four houses and a farm to be demolished because their owners had been hereticated in them, but these acts had doubtless been performed long previous. Confiscations still continued for ancestral offences, but Catharism as an existing belief may be said at this period to be virtually extinct in Languedoc, where it had a hundred and fifty years before had a reasonable prospect of becoming the dominant religion.[121]

In the same year, 1329, occurred a case which is not without interest as showing how an earnest but unstable brain pondering over the crime and misery of the world, wove some of the cruder elements of Catharism and Averrhoism into a fantastic theory.{109} Limoux Noir, of Saint-Paul in the diocese of Alet, had already been tried by his bishop in 1326, but had been able to evade the unskilled officials of the episcopal tribunal. The Inquisition had surer methods and speedily brought him to confession. He had formed a philosophy of the Universe which superseded all religion. God had created the archangels, these the angels, and the latter the sun and moon. These heavenly bodies, as being unstable and corruptible, were females. Out of their urine the world was formed, and was necessarily corrupt, with all that sprang from it. Moses, Mahomet, and Christ were all sent by the sun and were teachers of equal authority. In the under world Christ and Mahomet are now disputing and seeking to gain followers. Baptism was of no more use than the circumcision of Israel or the blessing of Islam, for those who renounced evil in baptism grew up to be robbers and strumpets. The Eucharist was naught, for God would not let himself be handled by adulterers such as the priests. Matrimony was to be shunned, for from it sprang robbers and strumpets. Thus he explained away and rejected all the doctrines and practices of the Church. To see whether the Saviour's fast of forty days was possible, he had fasted in a cabin ten days and nights, at the end of which this system of philosophy had been revealed to him by God. Again, in 1327, he had placed himself in *endura*, with the resolve to carry it to the end, but had been persuaded by his brother to take the Eucharist, to save his bones from being burned after his death. He was sixty years old, and his crazy doctrines had brought him a few disciples, but the sect was crushed at the outset. He declared to the inquisitor that he would rather be flayed alive than believe in transubstantiation, and he proved his resolute character by resisting all attempts to induce him to recant, so that there was no alternative but to abandon him to the secular arm, which was duly done and his belief perished with him.[122]

Thus the Inquisition triumphed, as force will generally do when it is sufficiently strong, skilfully applied, and systematically continued without interruption to the end. In the twelfth century the south of France had been the most civilized land of Europe.{110}There commerce, industry, art, science, had been far in advance of the age. The cities had won virtual self-government, were proud of their wealth and strength, jealous of their liberties, and self-sacrificing in their patriotism. The nobles, for the most part, were cultivated men, poets themselves or patrons of poetry, who had learned that their prosperity depended on the prosperity of their subjects, and that municipal liberties were a safeguard, rather than a menace, to the wise ruler. The crusaders came, and their unfinished work was taken up and executed to the bitter end by the Inquisition. It left a ruined and impoverished country, with shattered industry and failing commerce. The native nobles were broken by confiscation and replaced by strangers, who occupied the soil, introducing the harsh customs of Northern feudalism, or the despotic principles of the Roman law, in the extensive domains acquired by the crown. A people of rare natural gifts had been tortured, decimated, humiliated, despoiled, for a century and more. The precocious civilization which had promised to lead Europe in the path of culture was gone, and to Italy was transferred the honor of the Renaissance. In return for this was unity of faith and a Church which had been hardened and vitiated and secularized in the strife. Such was the work and such the outcome of the Inquisition in the field which afforded it the widest scope for its activity, and the fullest opportunity for developing its powers.

Yet in the very triumph of the Inquisition was the assurance of its decline. Supported by the State, it had earned and repaid the royal favor by the endless stream of confiscations which it poured into the royal coffers. Perhaps nothing contributed more to the consolidation of the royal supremacy than the change of ownership which threw into new hands so large a portion of the lands of the South. In the territories of the great vassals the right to the confiscations for heresy became recognized as an important portion of the *droits seigneurioux*. In the domains of the crown they were granted to favorites or sold at moderate prices to those who thus became interested in the new order of things. The royal officials grasped everything on which they could lay their hands, whether on the excuse of treason or of heresy, with little regard to any rights; and although the integrity of Louis IX. caused an inquest to be held in 1262 which restored a vast amount{111} of property illegally held, this was but a small fraction of the whole. To assist his Parlement in settling the innumerable cases which arose, he ordered, in 1260, the charters and letters of greatest importance to be sent to Paris. Those of each of the six senechaussées filled a coffer, and the six coffers were deposited in the treasury of the Sainte-Chapelle. In this process of absorption the case of the extensive Viscounty of Fenouillèdes may be taken as an illustration of the zeal with which the Inquisition co-operated in securing the political results desired by the crown. Fenouillèdes had been seized during the crusades and given to Nuñez Sancho of Roussillon, from whom it passed, through the King of Aragon, into the hands of St. Louis. In 1264 Beatrix, widow of Hugues, son of the former Viscount Pierre, applied to the Parlement for her rights and dower and those of her children. Immediately the inquisitor, Pons de Poyet, commenced a prosecution against the memory of Pierre, who had died more than twenty years previously in the bosom of the Church, and had been buried with the Templars of Mas Deu, after assuming the religious habit and receiving the last sacraments. He was condemned for having held relations with heretics, his bones were dug up and burned, and the Parlement rejected the claim of the daughter-in-law and grandchildren. Pierre, the eldest of these, in 1300, made a claim for the ancestral estates, and Boniface VIII. espoused his quarrel with the object of giving trouble to Philippe le Bel; but, though the affair was pursued for some years, the inquisitorial sentence held good. It was not only the actual heretics and their descendants who were dispossessed. The land had been so deeply tinctured with heresy that there were few indeed whose ancestors could not be shown, by the records of the Inquisition, to have incurred the fatal taint of associating with them.[123]{112}

The rich bourgeoisie of the cities were ruined in the same way. Some inventories have been preserved of the goods and chattels sequestrated when the arrests were made at Albi in 1299 and 1300, which show how thoroughly everything was swept into the maelstrom. That of Raymond Calverie, a notary, gives us every detail of the plenishing of a well-to-do burgher's house—every pillow, sheet, and coverlet is enumerated, every article of kitchen gear, the salted provisions and grain, even his wife's little trinkets. His farm or bastide was subjected to the same minuteness of seizure. Then we have a similar insight into the stock and goods of Jean Baudier, a rich merchant. Every fragment of stuff is duly measured—cloths of Ghent, Ypres, Amiens, Cambray, St. Omer, Rouen, Montcornet, etc., with their valuation—pieces of miniver, and other articles of trade. His town house and farm were inventoried with the same conscientious care. It is easy to see how prosperous cities were reduced to poverty, how industry languished, and how the independence of the municipalities was broken into subjection in the awful uncertainty which hung over the head of every man.[124]

In this respect the Inquisition was building better than it knew. In thus aiding to establish the royal power over the newly-acquired provinces, it was contributing to erect an authority which was destined in the end to reduce it to comparative insignificance. With the disappearance of Catharism, Languedoc became as much a part of the monarchy as l'Isle de France, and the career of its Inquisition merges into that of the rest of the kingdom. It need not, therefore, be pursued separately further.{113}

CHAPTER II.

FRANCE.

ALTHOUGH Catharism never obtained in the North sufficient foothold to render it threatening to the Church, yet the crusades and the efforts which followed the pacification of 1229 must have driven many heretics to seek refuge in places where they might escape suspicion. In organizing persecution in the South, therefore, it was necessary to provide some supervision more watchful than episcopal negligence was likely to supply, over the regions whither heretics might fly when pursued at home, or the efforts made in Languedoc would only be scattering the infection. Vigilant guardians of the faith were consequently requisite in lands where heretics were few and hidden, as well as in those where they were numerous and enjoyed protection from noble and city. Under the pious king, St. Louis, who declared that the only argument a layman could use with a heretic was to thrust a sword into him up to the hilt, they were sure of ample support from the secular power.[125]

Accordingly when, in 1233, the experiment was tried of appointing Pierre Cella and Guillem Arnaud as inquisitors in Toulouse, a similar tentative effort was made in the northern part of the kingdom. Here also it was the Dominican Order which was called upon to furnish the necessary zealots. I have already alluded to the failure of the attempt to induce the Friars of Franche-Comté to undertake the work. In western Burgundy, however, the Church was more fortunate in finding a proper instrument. Like Rainerio Saccone, Frère Robert, known as le Bugre, had been a Patarin. The peculiar fitness thence derived for detecting the hidden heretic was rendered still more effective by the special gift which he is said to have claimed, of being able to recognize{114} them by their speech and carriage. In addition, he was fitted for the work by the ardent fanaticism of the convert, by his learning, his fiery eloquence, and his mercilessness. When, early in 1233, instructions to persecute heresy were sent to the Prior of Besançon, Robert was nominated to represent him and act as his substitute; and, eager to manifest his zeal, he lost no time in making a descent upon La Charité. It will be remembered that this place was notorious as a centre of heresy in the twelfth century, and that repeated efforts had been made to purify it. These had proved fruitless against the stubbornness of the misbelievers, and Frère Robert found Stephen, the Cluniac prior, vainly endeavoring to win or force them over. The new inquisitor seems to have been armed with no special powers, but his energy speedily made a profound impression, and heretics came forward and confessed their errors in crowds, husbands and wives, parents and children, accusing themselves and each other without reserve. He reported to Gregory IX. that the reality was far worse than had been rumored; that the whole town was a stinking nest of heretical wickedness, where the Catholic faith was almost wholly set aside and the people in their secret conventicles had thrown off its yoke. Under a specious appearance of piety they deceived the wisest, and their earnest missionary efforts, extending over the whole of France, were seducing souls from Flanders to Britanny. Uncertain as to his authority, he applied to Gregory for instructions and was told to act energetically in conjunction with the bishops, and, under the statutes recently issued by the Holy See, to extirpate heresy thoroughly from the whole region, invoking the aid of the secular arm, and coercing it if necessary with the censures of the Church.[126]

We have no means of knowing what measures Robert adopted, but there can be no doubt that under this stimulus, and clothed with this authority, he was active and unsparing. His crazy fanaticism probably exaggerated greatly the extent of the evil and confounded the innocent with the guilty. It was not long before the Archbishop of Sens, in whose province La Charité lay, expostulated with Gregory upon this interference with his jurisdiction, and in this he was joined by other prelates, alarmed at the authority{115}given to the Dominican Provincial of Paris to appoint inquisitors for all portions of the kingdom. They assured the pope that there was no heresy in their provinces and no necessity for these extraordinary measures. Gregory thereupon revoked all commissions early in February, 1234, and urged the prelates to be vigilant, recommending them to make use of Dominicans in all cases where action appeared desirable, as the friars were specially skilled in the refutation of heresy. Had Robert been an ordinary man this might have postponed for some time the extension of the

38

Inquisition in France, but he was too ardent to be repressed. In June, 1234, we find St. Louis paying for the maintenance of heretics in prison at St. Pierre-le-Moutier, near Nevers, which would seem as though Frère Robert had succeeded in getting to work again on his old field of operations. Meanwhile he had not been idle elsewhere. King Louis furnished him with an armed guard to protect him from the enmities which he aroused, and, secure in the royal favor, he traversed the country carrying terror everywhere. At Péronne he burned five victims; at Elincourt, four, besides a pregnant woman who was spared for a time at the intercession of the queen. His methods were speedy, for before Lent was out we find him at Cambrai, where, with the assistance of the Archbishop of Reims and three bishops, he burned about twenty and condemned others to crosses and prison. Thence he hastened to Douai, where, in May, he had the satisfaction of burning ten more, and condemning numerous others to crosses and prison in the presence of the Count of Flanders, the Archbishop of Reims, sundry bishops and an immense multitude who crowded to the spectacle. Thence he hurried to Lille, where more executions followed. All this was sufficient to convince Gregory that he had been misinformed as to the absence of heresy. Undisturbed by the severe experience which he had just undergone with a similar apostle of persecution, Conrad of Marburg, we find him, in August, 1235, excitedly announcing to the Dominican provincial that God had revealed to him that the whole of France was boiling with the venom of heretical reptiles, and that the business of the Inquisition must be resumed with loosened rein. Frère Robert was to be commissioned again, with fitting colleagues to scour the whole kingdom, aided by the prelates, so that innocence should not suffer nor guilt escape. The Archbishop of Sens was strictly ordered to lend efficient{116} help to Robert, whom God had gifted with especial grace in these matters, and Robert himself was honored with a special papal commission empowering him to act throughout the whole of France. The pope, moreover, spurred him on with exhortations to spare no labor in the work, and not to shrink from martyrdom if necessary for the salvation of souls.[127]

This was pouring oil upon the flames. Robert's untempered fanaticism had required no stimulus, and now it raged beyond all bounds. The kingdom, by Gregory's thoughtless zeal, was delivered up to one who was little better than a madman. Supported by the piety of St. Louis, the prelates were obliged to aid him and carry out his behests, and for several years he traversed the provinces of Flanders, Champagne, Burgundy, and France with none to curb or oppose him. The crazy ardor of such a man was not likely to be discriminating or to require much proof of guilt. Those whom he designated as heretics had the alternative of abjuration with perpetual imprisonment or of the stake—varied occasionally with burial alive. In one term of two or three months he is said to have thus despatched about fifty unfortunates of either sex, and the whole number of his victims during his unchecked career of several years must have been large. The terror spread by his arbitrary and pitiless proceedings rendered him formidable to high and low alike, until at length the evident confounding of the innocent with the guilty raised a clamor to which even Gregory IX. was forced to listen. An investigation was held in 1238 which exposed his misdeeds, though not before he had time, in 1239, to burn a number of heretics at Montmorillon in Vienne, and twenty-seven, or, according to other accounts, one hundred and eighty-three, at Mont-Wimer—the original seat of Catharism in the eleventh century—where, at this holocaust pleasing to God, there were present the King of Navarre with a crowd of prelates and nobles and a multitude wildly estimated at seven hundred thousand souls. Robert's commission was withdrawn, and he expiated his insane cruelties in perpetual prison. The case ought to have proved, like{117} that of Conrad of Marburg, a wholesome warning. Unfortunately the spirit which he had aroused survived him, and for three or four years after his fall active persecution raged from the Rhine to the Loire, under the belief that the land was full of heretics.[128]

The unlucky termination of Robert's career did not affect his colleagues, and thenceforth the Inquisition was permanently established throughout France in Dominican hands. The prelates at first were stimulated to some show of rivalry in the performance of their neglected duties. Thus the provincial council of Tours, in 1239, endeavored to revive the forgotten system of synodal witnesses. Every bishop was instructed to appoint in each parish three clerks—or, if such could not be had, three laymen worthy of trust—who were to be sworn to reveal to the officials all ecclesiastical offences, especially those concerning the faith. Such devices, however, were too cumbrous and obsolete to be of any avail against a crime so sedulously and so easily concealed as heresy, even if the prelates had been zealous and earnest persecutors. The Dominicans remained undisputed masters of the field, always on the alert, travelling from place to place, scrutinizing and questioning, searching the truth and dragging it from unwilling hearts. Yet scarce a trace of their strenuous labors has been left to us. Heretics throughout the North were comparatively few and scattered; the chroniclers of the period take no note of their discovery and punishment, nor even of the establishment of the Inquisition itself. That a few friars should be deputed to the duty of hunting heretics was too unimpressive a fact to be worthy of record. We know, however, that the pious King Louis welcomed them in his old hereditary dominions, as he did in the newly-acquired territories of Languedoc, and stimulated their zeal by defraying their expenses. In the accounts of the royal baillis for 1248 we find entries{118} of sums disbursed for them in Paris, Orleans, Issoudun, Senlis, Amiens, Tours, Yèvre-le-Chatel, Beaumont, St. Quentin, Laon, and Macon, showing that his liberality furnished them with means to do their work, not only in the domains of the crown, but in those of the great vassals; and these items further illustrate their activity in every corner of the land. That their sharp pursuit rendered heresy unsafe is seen in the permission already alluded to, in 1255, to pursue their quarry across the border into the territories of Alphonse of Toulouse, thus disregarding the limitations of inquisitorial districts.[129]

This shows us that already the Inquisition was becoming organized in a systematic manner. In Provence, where Pons de l'Esparre, the Dominican prior, had at first carried on a kind of volunteer chase after heretics, we see an inquisitor officially acting in 1245. This district, comprising the whole southeastern portion of modern France, with Savoy, was confided to the Franciscans. In 1266, when they were engaged in Marseilles in mortal strife with the Dominicans, the business of persecution would seem to have been neglected, for we find Clement IV. ordering the Benedictines of St. Victor to make provision for extirpating the numerous heretics of the valley of Rousset, where they had a dependency. The Inquisition of Provence was extended in 1288 over Avignon and the Comtat Venaissin, whose governor was ordered to defray from the confiscations the moderate expenses of the inquisitors, Bertrand de Cigotier and Guillem de Saint-Marcel. In 1292 Dauphiné was likewise included, thus completing the organization in the territories east of the Rhone. The attention of the inquisitors was specially called to the superstition which led many Christians to frequent the Jewish synagogues with lighted candles, offering oblations and watching through the vigils of the Sabbath, when afflicted with sickness or other tribulations, anxious for friends at sea or for approaching childbirth. All such observances, even in Jews, were idolatry and heresy, and those who practised them were to be duly prosecuted.[130]{119}

With this exception the whole of France was confided to the Dominicans. In 1253 a bull of Innocent IV. renders the Provincial of Paris supreme over the rest of the kingdom, including the territories of Alphonse of Toulouse. Numerous bulls follow during the next few years which speak of the growth of heresy requiring increased efforts for its suppression and of the solicitude of King Louis that the Inquisition should be effective. Elaborate instructions are sent for its management, and various changes are made and unmade in a manner to show that a watchful eye was kept on the institution in France, and that there was a constant effort to render it as efficient as possible. By a papal brief of 1255 we see that at that time the Inquisition of Languedoc was independent of the Paris provincial; in 1257 it is again under his authority; in 1261 it is once more removed, and in 1264 it is restored to him—a provision which became final, rendering him in some sort a grand-inquisitor for the whole of France. In 1255 the Franciscan provincial was adjoined to the Dominican, thus dividing the functions between the two Orders; but this arrangement, as might be expected, does not seem to have worked well, and in 1256 we find the power again concentrated in the hands of the Dominicans. The number of inquisitors to be appointed was always strictly limited by the popes, and it varied with the apparent exigencies of the times and also with the extent of territory. In 1256 only two are specified; in 1258 this is pronounced insufficient for so extensive a region, and the provincial is empowered to appoint four more. In 1261, when Languedoc was withdrawn, the number is reduced to two; in 1266 it is increased to four, exclusive of Languedoc and Provence, to whom in 1267 associates were adjoined, and in 1273 the number was made six, including Languedoc, but excluding Provence. This seems to have been the final organization, but it does not appear that the Northern kingdom was divided into districts, strictly delimitated as those of the South.[131]

The Inquisition at Besançon appears to have been at first independent{120} of that of Paris. After the failure to establish it in 1233 it seems to have remained in abeyance until 1247, when Innocent IV. ordered the Prior of Besançon to send friars throughout Burgundy and Lorraine for the extirpation of heresy. The next year John Count of Burgundy urged greater activity, but his zeal does not seem to have been supplemented with liberality, and in 1255 the Dominicans asked to be relieved of the thankless task, which proved unsuccessful for lack of funds, and Alexander IV. acceded to their request. There are some evidences of an Inquisition being in operation there about 1283, and in 1290 Nicholas IV. ordered the Provincial of Paris to select three inquisitors to serve in the dioceses of Besançon, Geneva, Lausanne, Sion, Metz, Toul, and Verdun, thus placing Lorraine and the French Cantons of Switzerland, as well as Franche Comté, under the Inquisition of France, an arrangement which seems to have lasted for more than a century.[132]

Little remains to us of the organization thus perfected over the wide territory stretching from the Bay of Biscay to the Rhine. The laborers were vigorous, and labored according to the light which was in them, but the men and their acts are buried beneath the dust of the forgotten past. That they did their duty is visible in the fact that heresy makes so little figure in France, and that the slow but remorseless extermination of Catharism in Languedoc was not accompanied by its perpetuation in the North. We hear constantly of refugees from Toulouse and Carcassonne flying for safety to Lombardy and even to Sicily, but never to Touraine or Champagne, nor do we ever meet with cases in which the earnest missionaries of Catharism sought converts beyond the Cevennes. This may fairly be ascribed to the vigilance of the inquisitors, who were ever on the watch. Chance has preserved for us as models in a book of formulas some documents issued by Frère Simon Duval, in 1277 and 1278, which afford us a momentary glimpse at his proceedings and enable us to estimate the activity requisite for the functions of his office. He styles himself inquisitor "*in regno Franciæ*," which indicates that his commission extended throughout the kingdom north of Languedoc, and{121} he speaks of himself as acting in virtue of the apostolical authority and royal power, showing that Philippe le Hardi had dutifully commissioned him to summon the whole forces of the State to his assistance when requisite. November 23, 1277, he gives public notice that two canons of Liège, Suger de Verbanque and Berner de Niville, had fled on being suspected of heresy, and he cites them to appear for trial at St. Quentin in Vermandois on the 23d of the ensuing January. This trial was apparently postponed, for on January 21, 1278, we find him summoning the people and clergy of Caen to attend his sermon on the 23d. Here he at least found an apostate Jewess who fled, and we have his proclamation calling upon every one to aid Copin, sergeant of the Bailli of Caen, who had been

40

despatched in her pursuit. Frère Duval was apparently making an extended inquest, for July 5 he summons the people and clergy of Orleans to attend his sermon on the 7th. A fortnight later he is back in Normandy and has discovered a nest of heretics near Evreux, for on July 21 we have his citation of thirteen persons from a little village hard by to appear before him. These fragmentary and accidental remains show that his life was a busy one and that his labors were not unfruitful. A letter of the young Philippe le Bel, in February, 1285, to his officials in Champagne and Brie, ordering them to lend all aid to the inquisitor Frère Guillaume d'Auxerre, indicates that those provinces were about to undergo a searching examination.[133]

The inquisitors of France complained that their work was impeded by the universal right of asylum which gave protection to criminals who succeeded in entering a church. No officer of the law dared to follow and make an arrest within the sacred walls, for a violation of this privilege entailed excommunication, removable only after exemplary punishment. Heretics were not slow in availing themselves of the immunity thus mercifully afforded by the Church which they had wronged, and in the jealousy which existed between the secular clergy and the inquisitors there was apparently no effort made to restrict the abuse. Martin IV. was accordingly appealed to, and in 1281 he issued a bull addressed to all the prelates of France, declaring that such perversion of the{122} right of asylum was no longer to be permitted; that in such cases the inquisitors were to have full opportunity to vindicate the faith, and that so far from being impeded in the performance of their duty, they were to be aided in every way. The special mention in this bull of apostate Jews along with other heretics indicates that this unfortunate class formed a notable portion of the objects of inquisitorial zeal. Several of them, in fact, were burned or otherwise penanced in Paris between 1307 and 1310.[134]

There was one class of offenders who would have afforded the Inquisition an ample field for its activity, had it been disposed to take cognizance of them. By the canons, any one who had endured excommunication for a year without submission and seeking absolution was pronounced suspect of heresy, and we have seen Boniface VIII., in 1297, directing the inquisitors of Carcassonne to prosecute the authorities of Béziers for this cause. The land was full of such excommunicates, for the shocking abuse of the anathema by priest and prelate for personal interests had indurated the people, and in a countless number of cases absolution was only to be procured by the sacrifice of rights which even faithful sons of the Church were not prepared to make. This growing disregard of the censure was aggravating to the last degree, but the inquisitors do not seem to have been disposed to come forward in aid of the secular clergy, nor did the latter call upon them for assistance. In 1301 the Council of Reims directed that proceedings should be commenced, when it next should meet, against all who had been under excommunication for two years, as being suspect of heresy; and in 1303 it called upon all such to come forward and purge themselves of the suspicion, but the court in which this was to be done was that of the bishops and not of the Inquisition. Mutual jealousy was seemingly too strong to admit of such co-operation.[135]

In 1308 we hear of a certain Étienne de Verberie of Soissons, accused before the inquisitor of blasphemous expressions concerning the body of Christ. He alleged drunkenness in excuse, and was mercifully treated. Shortly afterwards occurred the first{123} formal *auto de fé* of which we have cognizance at Paris, on May 31, 1310. A renegade Jew was burned, but the principal victim was Marguerite de Hainault, or la Porete. She is described as a "*béguine clergesse*," the first apostle in France of the German sect of Brethren of the Free Spirit, whom we shall consider more fully hereafter. Her chief error was the doctrine that the soul, absorbed in Divine love, could yield without sin or remorse to all the demands of the flesh, and she regarded with insufficient veneration the sacrifice of the altar. She had written a book to propagate these doctrines which had, before the year 1305, been condemned as heretical and burned by Gui II., Bishop of Cambrai. He had mercifully spared her, while forbidding her under pain of the stake from circulating it in future or disseminating its doctrines. In spite of this she had again been brought before Gui's successor, Philippe de Marigny, and the Inquisitor of Lorraine, for spreading it among the simple folk called Begghards, and she had again escaped. Unwearied in her missionary work, she had even ventured to present the forbidden volume to Jean, Bishop of Chalons, without suffering the penalty due to her obstinacy. In 1308 she extended her propaganda to Paris and fell into the hands of Frère Guillaume de Paris, the inquisitor, before whom she persistently refused to take the preliminary oath requisite to her examination. He was probably too preoccupied with the affair of the Templars to give her prompt justice, and for eighteen months she lay in the inquisitorial dungeons under the consequent excommunication. This would alone have sufficed for her conviction as an impenitent heretic, but her previous career rendered her a relapsed heretic. Instead of calling an assembly of experts, as was customary in Languedoc, the inquisitor laid a written statement of the case before the canonists of the University, who unanimously decided, May 30, that if the facts as stated were true, she was a relapsed heretic, to be relaxed to the secular arm. Accordingly, on May 31, she was handed over, with the customary adjuration for mercy, to the prévôt of Paris, who duly burned her the next day, when her noble manifestation of devotion moved the people to tears of compassion. Another actor in the tragedy was a disciple of Marguerite, a clerk of the diocese of Beauvais named Guion de Cressonessart. He had endeavored to save Marguerite from the clutches of the Inquisition, and on being seized had, like her,{124} refused to take the oath during eighteen months" imprisonment. His brain seems to have turned during his detention, for at length he astonished the inquisitor by proclaiming himself the Angel of Philadelphia and an envoy of God, who alone could save mankind. The inquisitor in vain pointed out that this was a function reserved solely for the pope, and as Guion would not withdraw his claims he was convicted as a heretic. For some reason, however, not specified in the sentence, he was only condemned to degradation from orders and to perpetual imprisonment.[136]

The next case of which we hear is that of the Sieur de Partenay, in 1323, to which allusion has already been made. Its importance to us lies in its revealing the enormous and almost irresponsible authority wielded by the Inquisition at this period. The most powerful noble of Poitou, when designated as a heretic by Frère Maurice, the Inquisitor of Paris, is at once thrown into the prison of the Temple by the king, and all his estates are sequestrated to await the result. Fortunately for Partenay he had a large circle of influential friends and kindred, among them the Bishop of Noyon, who labored strenuously in his behalf. He was able to appeal to the pope, alleging personal hatred on the part of Frère Maurice; he was sent under guard to Avignon, where his friends succeeded in inducing John XXII. to assign certain bishops as assessors to try the case with the inquisitor, and after infinite delays he was at length set free—probably not without the use of means which greatly diminished his wealth. When such a man could be so handled at the mere word of an angry friar, meaner victims stood little chance.[137] This case in the North and the close of Bernard Gui's career in Toulouse, about the same time, mark the apogee of the Inquisition in France. Thenceforth we have to follow its decline.

Yet for some years longer there was a show of activity at Carcassonne, where Henri de Chamay was a worthy representative of the older inquisitors. January 16, 1329, in conjunction with Pierre Bruni he celebrated an *auto de fé* at Pamiers, where thirty-five persons were permitted to lay aside crosses, and twelve were released{125} from prison with crosses, six were pardoned, seven were condemned to perpetual imprisonment, together with four false witnesses, eight had arbitrary penances assigned them, four dead persons were sentenced, and a friar and a priest were degraded. As the see of Pamiers, to which this *auto* was confined, was a small one, the number of sentences uttered indicates active work. December 12, of the same year, Henri de Chamay held another at Narbonne, where the fate of some forty delinquents was decided. Then, January 7, 1329, he held another at Pamiers; May 19, one at Béziers; September 8, one at Carcassonne, where six unfortunates were burned and twenty-one condemned to perpetual prison. Shortly afterwards he burned three at Albi, and towards the end of the year he held another *auto* at a place not named, where eight persons were sentenced to prison, three to prison in chains, and two were burned. Some collisions seem to have occurred about this time with the royal officials, for, in 1334, the inquisitors complained to Philippe de Valois that their functions were impeded, and Philippe issued orders to the seneschals of Nîmes, Toulouse, and Carcassonne that the Inquisition must be maintained in the full enjoyment of its ancient privileges.[138]

Activity continued for some little time longer, but the records have perished which would supply the details. We happen to have the accounts of the Sénéchaussée of Toulouse, for 1337, which show that Pierre Bruni, the inquisitor, was by no means idle. The receiver of confiscations enumerates the estates of thirty heretics from which collections are in hand; there was an *auto de fé* celebrated and paid for; the number of prisoners in the inquisitorial jail is stated at eighty-two, but as their maintenance during eleven months amounted to the sum of three hundred and sixty-five livres fourteen sols, the average number at three deniers per diem must have been ninety. The terrible vicissitudes of the English war doubtless soon afterwards slackened the energy of the inquisitors, but we know that there were *autos de fé* celebrated at Carcassonne in 1346, 1357, and 1383, and one at Toulouse in 1374. The office of inquisitor continued to be filled, but its functions diminished greatly in importance, as we may guess from the fact that it is related of{126} Pierre de Mercalme, who was Provincial of Toulouse from 1350 to 1363, that during more than two years of this period he also served as inquisitor.[139]

In the North we hear little of the Inquisition during this period. The English wars, in fact, must have seriously interfered with its activity, but we have an evidence that it was not neglecting its duty in a complaint made by the Provincial of Paris to Clement VI., in 1351, that the practice of excepting the territories of Charles of Anjou from the commissions issued to inquisitors deprived the provinces of Touraine and Maine of the blessings of the institution and allowed heresy to flourish there, whereupon the pope promptly extended the authority of Frère Guillaume Chevalier and of all future inquisitors to those regions.[140]

With the return of peace under Charles le Sage the Inquisition had freer scope. The Begghards, or Brethren of the Free Spirit, undeterred by the martyrdom of Marguerite la Porete, had continued to exist in secret. In September, 1365, Urban V. notified the prelates and inquisitors throughout France that they were actively at work propagating their doctrines, and he sent detailed information as to their tenets and the places where they were to be found to the Bishop of Paris, with orders to communicate it to his fellow-prelates and the Inquisition. If any immediate response to this was made, the result has not reached us, but in 1372 we find Frère Jacques de More, "*inquisiteur des Bougres*," busy in eradicating them. They called themselves the Company of Poverty, and were popularly known by the name of Turelupins; as in Germany, they were distinguished by their peculiar vestments, and they propagated their doctrines largely by their devotional writings in the vernacular. Charles V. rewarded the labors of the inquisitor with a donation of fifty francs, and received the thanks of Gregory XI. for his zeal. The outcome of the affair was the burning of the books and garments of the heretics in the swine-market beyond the Porte Saint-Honoré, together with the female leader of the sect, Jeanne Daubenton. Her male colleague escaped by death in prison, but his body was preserved in quicklime for fifteen{127} days, in order that he might accompany his partner in guilt in the flames. That such a spectacle was sufficiently infrequent to render it a matter of importance is shown by its being recorded in the doggerel of a contemporary chronicler—

"L'an MDCCCLXXII. je vous dis tout pour voir
Furent les Turelupins condannez pour ardoir,
Pour ce qu'ils desvoient le people à decepvoir
Par feaultes heresies, l'Eveque en soult levoir."

The sect was a stubborn one, however, especially in Germany, as we shall see hereafter, and in the early part of the next century Chancellor Gerson still considers it of sufficient importance to combat its errors repeatedly. Its mystic libertinism was dangerously seducing, and he was especially alarmed by the incredible subtlety with which it was presented in a book written by a woman known as Mary of Valenciennes. In May, 1421, twenty-five of these sectaries were condemned at Douai by the Bishop of Arras. Twenty of them recanted and were penanced with crosses and banishment or imprisonment, but five were stubborn and sealed their faith with martyrdom in the flames.[141]

In 1381 Frère Jacques de More had a more illustrious victim in Hugues Aubriot. A Burgundian by birth, Aubriot's energy and ability had won for him the confidence of the wise King Charles, who had made him Prévôt of Paris. This office he filled with unprecedented vigor. To him the city owed the first system of sewerage that had been attempted, as well as the Bastille, which he built as a bulwark against the English, and he imposed some limitation on the flourishing industry of the *filles de vie*. His good government gained him the respect and affection of the people, but he made a mortal enemy of the University by disregarding{128} the immunities on the preservation of which, in the previous century, it had staked its existence. In savage mockery of its wrath, when building the Petit-Châtelet, he named two foul dungeons after two of the principal quarters of the University, le Clos Bruneau and la Rue du Foing, saying that they were intended for the students. Under the strong rule of Charles V. the University had to digest its wrongs as best it could, but after his death, in 1380, it eagerly watched its opportunity. This was not long in coming, nor, in the rivalry between the Dukes of Berri and Burgundy, was it difficult to enlist the former against Aubriot as a Burgundian. The rule of the princes, at once feeble and despotic, invited disorder, and when the people, November 25, 1380, rose against the Jews, pillaged their houses, and forcibly baptized their children, Aubriot incurred the implacable enmity of the Church by forcing a restoration of the infants to their parents. The combination against him thus became too strong for the court to resist. It yielded, and on January 21, 1381, he was cited to appear before the bishop and inquisitor. He disdained to obey the summons, and his excommunication for contumacy was published in all the churches of Paris. This compelled obedience, and when he came before the inquisitor, on February 1, he was at once thrown into the episcopal prison while his trial proceeded. The charges were most frivolous, except the affair of the Jewish children and his having released from the Châtelet a prisoner accused of heresy, placed there by the inquisitor. It was alleged that on one occasion one of his sergeants had excused himself for delay by saying that he had waited at church to see God (the elevation of the Host), when Aubriot angrily rejoined, "Sirrah, know ye not that I have more power to harm you than God to help;" and again that when some one had told him that they would see God in a mass celebrated by Silvestre de la Cervelle, Bishop of Coutances, he replied that God would not permit himself to be handled by such a man as the bishop. His enemies were so exasperated that on the strength of this flimsy gossip he was actually condemned to be burned without the privilege allowed to all heretics of saving himself by abjuration; but the princes intervened and succeeded in obtaining this for him. He had no reason to complain of undue delay. On May 17 a solemn *auto de fé* was held. On a scaffold erected in front of Nôtre Dame, Aubriot humbly confessed{129} and recanted the heresies of which he had been convicted, and received the sentence of perpetual imprisonment, which of course carried with it the confiscation of his wealth, while the rejoicing scholars of the University lampooned him in halting verses. He was thence conveyed to a dungeon in the episcopal prison, where he lay until 1382, when the insurrection of the Maillotins occurred. The first thought of the people was of their old prévôt. They broke open the prison, drew him forth and placed him at their head. He accepted the post, but the same night he quietly withdrew and escaped to his native Burgundy, where his adventurous life ended in peaceful obscurity. The story is instructive as showing how efficient an instrument was the Inquisition for the gratification of malice. In fact, its functions as a factor in political strife were of sufficient importance to require more detailed consideration hereafter.[142]

After this we hear little more of the Inquisition of Paris, although it continued to exist. When, in 1388, the eloquence of Thomas of Apulia drew wondering crowds to listen with veneration to his teaching that the law of the Gospel was simply love, with the deduction that the sacraments, the invocation of saints, and all the inventions of the current theology were useless; when he wrote a book inveighing against the sins of prelate and pope, and asserting, with the Everlasting Gospel, that the reign of the Holy Ghost had supplanted that of the Father and the Son, and when he boldly announced himself as the envoy of the Holy Ghost sent to reform the world, the Inquisition was not called upon to silence even this revolutionary heretic. It was the Prévôt of Paris who ordered him to desist from preaching and, when he refused, it was the bishop and University who tried him, ordered his book to be burned on the Place de Grève, and would have him burned had not the medical alienists of the day testified to his insanity and procured for him a commutation of his punishment to perpetual imprisonment.[143]

Various causes had long been contributing to deprive the Inquisition{130} in France of the importance which it had once enjoyed. It no longer as of old poured into the royal fisc a stream of confiscations and co-operated efficiently in consolidating the monarchy. It had done its work too well, and not only had it become superfluous as an instrument for the throne, but the throne which it had aided to establish had become supreme and had reduced it to subjection. Even in the plenitude of inquisitorial power the tendency to regard the royal court as possessing a jurisdiction higher than that of the Holy Office is shown in the case of Amiel de Lautrec, Abbot of S. Sernin. In 1322 the Viguier of Toulouse accused him to the Inquisition for having preached the doctrine that the soul is mortal in essence and only immortal through grace. The Inquisition examined the matter and decided that this was not heresy. The royal *procureur-général*, dissatisfied with this, appealed from the decision, not to the pope but to the Parlement or royal court. No question more purely spiritual can well be conceived, and yet the Parlement gravely entertained the appeal and asserted its jurisdiction by confirming the decree of the Inquisition.[144]

This was ominous of the future, although the indefatigable Henri de Chamay, apparently alarmed at the efforts successfully made by Philippe de Valois to control and limit spiritual jurisdictions, procured from that monarch, in November, 1329, a *Mandement* confirming the privileges of the Inquisition, placing all temporal nobles and officials afresh at its disposal, and annulling all letters emanating from the royal court, whether past or future, which should in any way impede inquisitors from performing their functions in accordance with their commissions from the Holy See. The evolution of the monarchy was proceeding too rapidly to be checked. Henri de Chamay himself, in 1328, had officially qualified himself as inquisitor, deputed, not by the pope, as had always been the formula proudly employed, but by the king, and a judicial decision to this effect followed soon after. It was Philippe's settled policy to enforce and extend the jurisdiction of the crown, and in pursuance of this he sent Guillaume de Villars to Toulouse to reform the encroachments of the ecclesiastical tribunals over the royal courts. In 1330 de Villars, in the performance of his duty, caused the registers of the ecclesiastical{131} courts to be submitted to him, after which he demanded those of the Inquisition. When we remember how jealously these were guarded, how arrogantly Nicholas d'Abbeville had refused a sight of them to the bishops sent by Philippe le Bel, and how long Jean de Pequigny hesitated before he interfered with Geoffroi d'Ablis, we can measure the extent of the silent revolution which had occurred during the interval in the relations between Church and State, by the fact that de Villars, on being refused, coolly proceeded to break open the door of the chamber in which the registers were kept. The inquisitor appealed, and again it was not to the pope, but to the Parlement, and that body, in condemning de Villars to pay the costs and damages, did so on the ground that the Inquisition was a royal and not an ecclesiastical court. This was a Pyrrhic victory; the State had absorbed the Inquisition. It was the same when, in 1334, Philippe listened to the complaints of the inquisitors that his seneschals disturbed them in their jurisdiction, and gave orders that they should enjoy all their ancient privileges, for these are treated as derived wholly from the royal power. Henceforth the Inquisition could exist only on sufferance, subject to the supervision of the Parlement, while the Captivity of Avignon, followed by the Great Schism, constantly gave to the temporal powers increased authority in spiritual matters.[145]

How completely the Inquisition was becoming an affair of state is indicated by two incidents. In 1340, when the lieutenant of the king in Languedoc, Louis of Poitou, Count of Die and Valentinois, was making his entry into the good city of Toulouse, he found the gate closed. Dismounting and kneeling bareheaded on a cushion, he took an oath on the Gospels, in the hands of the inquisitor, to preserve the privileges of the Inquisition, and then another oath to the consuls to maintain the liberties of the city. Thus both institutions were on the same footing and required the same illusory guarantee, the very suggestion of which would have been laughed to scorn by Bernard Gui. Again, in 1368, when the royal revenues were depleted by the English wars and the ravages of the Free Companies, and were insufficient to pay the wages of the Inquisitor of Carcassonne, Pierre Scatisse, the royal{132} treasurer, ordered a levy by the consuls of twenty-six livres tournois to complete the payment. Confiscations had long since ceased to meet the expenditures, but the inquisitor was a royal official and must be paid by the city if not by the state.[146]

How thorough was the subjection of all ecclesiastical institutions, and how fallen the Inquisition from its high estate, is manifested by an occurrence in 1364, at a moment when the royal authority was at the lowest ebb. King John had died a prisoner in London, April 8, and the young Charles V. was not crowned until May 19, while his kingdom was reduced almost to anarchy by foreign aggression and internal dissensions. Yet, April 16, Marshal Arnaud d'Audeneham, Lieutenant du Roi in Languedoc, convoked at Nîmes an assembly of the Three Estates presided over by the Archbishop of Narbonne. One of the questions discussed was a quarrel between the Archbishop of Toulouse and the inquisitor whom he had prohibited from exercising his functions, saying that the Inquisition had been established at the request of the province of Languedoc, and that now it had become an injury. All the prelates, except Aymeri, Bishop of Viviers, sided with the archbishop, while the representatives of Toulouse asked to be admitted as parties to the suit on the side of the inquisitor. No one seems to have doubted that the marshal, as royal deputy, had full jurisdiction over the matter, and his decision was against the archbishop.[147]

Even in Carcassonne, where the Dominicans had lorded it so imperiously, all fear of them had disappeared so utterly that in 1354 a sturdy blacksmith named Hugues erected a shop close to the church of the Friars, and carried on his noisy avocation so vigorously as to interrupt their services and interfere with their studies. Remonstrances and threats were of no avail, and they were obliged to appeal, not to the bishop or the inquisitor, but to the king, who graciously sent a peremptory order to his seneschal to remove the smithy or to prevent Hugues from working in it.[148]

Towards the end of the century some cases occurring in Reims illustrate how completely the Inquisition was falling into abeyance{133} throughout the kingdom, and how the jurisdiction of the royal court of the Parlement was accepted as supreme in spiritual matters. In 1385 there arose a dispute between the magistrates of the city and the archbishop as to jurisdiction over blasphemy, which was claimed by both. This was settled by an agreement recognizing it as belonging to the archbishop, but twenty years later the quarrel broke out afresh over the case of Drouet Largèle, who was guilty of blasphemy savoring of heresy as to the Passion and the Virgin. The matter was appealed to the Parlement, which decided in favor of the archbishop, and no allusion throughout the whole affair occurs as to any claim that the Inquisition might have to interpose, showing that at this time it was practically disregarded. Yet we chance to know that Reims was the seat of an Inquisition, for in 1419 Pierre Florée was inquisitor there, and preached, October 13, the funeral sermon at the obsequies of Jean sans Peur of Burgundy, giving great offence by urging Philippe le Bon not to avenge the murder of his father. We see also the scruples of the Inquisition on the subject of blasphemy in 1423 at Toulouse, where it had become the custom to submit to the inquisitor the names of all successful candidates in municipal elections in order to ascertain whether they were in any way suspect of heresy. Among the capitouls elected in 1423 was a certain François Albert, who was objected to by the acting inquisitor, Frère Bartolomé Guiscard, on account of habitual use of the expletives *Tête-Dieu* and *Ventre-Dieu*, whereupon the citizens substituted Pierre de Sarlat. Albert appealed to the Parlement, which approved of the action of the inquisitor.[149]

Still more emphatic as to the supreme authority of the Parlement was the case of Marie du Canech of Cambrai, to which I have already had occasion to refer. For maintaining that when under oath she was not bound to tell the truth to the prejudice of her honor, she was prosecuted for heresy by the Bishop of Cambrai and Frère Nicholas de Péronne, styling himself deputy of the inquisitor-general or Provincial of Paris. Being severely mulcted, she appealed to the Archbishop of Reims, as the metropolitan,{134} and he issued inhibitory letters. Then the bishop and inquisitor appealed from the archbishop to the Parlement. The matter was elaborately argued on both sides, the archbishop alleging that there was at that time no inquisitor in France, and drawing a number of subtle distinctions. The Parlement had no hesitation in accepting jurisdiction over this purely spiritual question. It paid no attention to the cautious arguments of the archbishop, but decided broadly that the bishop and inquisitor had no grounds for disobeying the citation of the archbishop evoking the case to his own court, and it condemned them in costs. Thus the ancient supremacy of the episcopal jurisdiction was reasserted over that of the Inquisition.[150]

The Great Schism, followed by the councils of Constance and Basle, did much to shake the papal power on which that of the Inquisition was founded. The position of Charles VII. towards Rome was consistently insubordinate, and the Pragmatic Sanction which he published in 1438 secured the independence of the Gallican Church, and strengthened the jurisdiction of the Parlement. When Louis XI. abrogated it, in 1461, the remonstrances of his Parlement form a singularly free-spoken indictment of papal vices, and that body continued to treat the instrument as practically in force, while Louis himself, by successive measures of 1463, 1470, 1472, 1474, 1475, and 1479, gradually re-established its principles. Had not the Concordat of Francis I., in 1516, swept it away, when he conspired with Leo X. to divide the spoils of the Church, it would eventually have rendered France independent of Rome. Francis knew so well the opposition which it would excite that he hesitated for a year to submit the measure to his Parlement for registration, and the Parlement deferred the registration for another year, till at last the negotiator of the concordat, Cardinal Duprat, brought to bear sufficient pressure to accomplish the object. During the discussion the University had the boldness to protest publicly against it, and to lodge with the Parlement an appeal to the next general council.[151]{135}

During this period of antagonism to Rome the University of Paris had contributed no little to the abasement of the Inquisition by supplanting it as an investigator of doctrine and judge of heresy. Its ancient renown, fully maintained by an uninterrupted succession of ardent and learned teachers, gave it great authority. It was a national institution of which clergy and laity alike might well be proud, and at one time it appeared as though it might rival the Parlement in growing into one of the recognized powers of the State. In the fearful anarchy which accompanied the insanity of Charles VI. it boldly assumed a right to speak on public affairs, and its interference was welcomed. In 1411 the king, who chanced at the time to be in the hands of the Burgundians, appealed to it to excommunicate the Armagnacs, and the University zealously did so. In 1412 it presented a remonstrance to the king on the subject of the financial disorders of the time and demanded a reform. Supported by the Parisians, at its dictate the financiers{136} and thieves of the government, with the exception of the chancellor, were dismissed in 1413, greatly to the discontent of the courtiers, who ridiculed the theologians as bookworms; and in the same year it co-operated with the Parlement in securing momentary peace between the angry factions of the land. The thanks which the heir-apparent, the Duke of Guienne, accompanied by the Dukes of Berri, Burgundy, Bavaria, and Bar, solemnly rendered to the assembled Faculty, virtually recognized it as a part of the State. But when, in 1415, it sent a deputation to remonstrate against the oppression of the people through excessive taxation, the Duke of Guienne, who was angry at the part taken by it, without consulting the court, in degrading John XXIII. at the Council of Constance, curtly told the spokesmen that they were interfering in matters beyond their competence; and when the official orator attempted to reply, the duke had him arrested on the spot and kept in prison for several days.[152]

Though its temporary ambition to rival the Parlement in state affairs was fortunately not gratified, in theology such a body as this was supreme. It would naturally be called upon, either as a whole or by delegates, to furnish the experts whose counsel was to guide bishop and inquisitor in the decision of cases; and as the old heresies died out and new ones were evolved, every deviation from orthodoxy came to be submitted to it as a matter of course, when its decision was received as final. These were for the most part scholastic subtleties to which I shall recur hereafter, as well as to the great controversies over the Immaculate Conception of the Virgin, and over Nominalism and Realism, in which it took a distinguished part. Sometimes, however, the questions were more practical. When some insolent wretch, in 1432, impudently told Frère Pierre de Voie, the deputy-inquisitor of Evreux, that his citations were simply abuses, the offended functionary, in place of promptly clapping the recalcitrant into prison, plaintively referred the case to the University, and had the satisfaction of receiving a solemn decision that the words were audacious, presumptuous, scandalous, and tending to rebellion (it did not say heretical), and that the utterer was liable to punishment. Bernard{137}Gui or Nicholas d'Abbeville would have asked for no such warrant.[153]

To what an extent the University in time replaced the Inquisition in its neglected and forgotten functions is shown in 1498, in the case of the Observantine Franciscan, Jean Vitrier. In the restlessness and insubordination which heralded the Reformation, this obscure friar anticipated Luther even more than did John of Wesel, although in the strictness of his asceticism he taught that a wife might better break her marriage-vow than her fasts. In his preaching at Tournay he counselled the people to drag the concubines and their priests from their houses with shame and derision; he affirmed that it was a mortal sin to listen to the masses of concubinary priests. Pardons and indulgences were the offspring of hell: the faithful ought not to purchase them, for they were not intended for the maintenance of brothels. Even the intercession of the saints was not to be sought. These were old heresies for which any inquisitor would promptly offer the utterer the alternative of abjuration or the stake; but the prelates and magistrates of Tournay referred the matter to the University, which laboriously extracted from Vitrier's sermons sixteen propositions for condemnation.[154]

Even more significant of the growing authority of the University and the waning power of the Papacy was a decision rendered in 1502. Alexander VI. had levied a tithe on the clergy of France, with the customary excuse of prosecuting the war against the Turks. The clergy, whose consent had not been asked, refused to pay. The pope rejoined by excommunicating them, and they applied to the University to know whether such a papal excommunication was valid, whether it was to be feared, and whether they should consequently abstain from the performance of divine service. On all these points the University replied in the negative, unanimously and without hesitation. Had circumstances permitted the same independence in Germany, a little more progress in this direction would have rendered Luther superfluous.[155]

It is not to be supposed, however, that the Inquisition, though fallen from its former dignity, had ceased to exist or to perform{138} its functions after a fashion. It was to the interest of the popes to maintain it, and the position of inquisitor, though humble in comparison with that which his predecessors enjoyed, was yet a source of influence, and possibly of profit, which led to its being eagerly sought. In 1414 we find two contestants for the post at Toulouse, and in 1424 an unseemly quarrel between two rivals at Carcassonne. The diocese of Geneva was also the subject of contention embittered by the traditional rivalry between the two Mendicant Orders. It will be remembered that in 1290 this, with other French cantons, was included by Nicholas IV. in the inquisitorial province of Besançon, which was Dominican. Geneva belonged, however, ecclesiastically to the metropolis of Vienne, which was under the Franciscan Inquisition of Provence, and Gregory XI. so treated it in 1375. When Pons Feugeyron was commissioned, in 1409, Geneva was not mentioned in the enumeration of the dioceses under him; but when his commission was renewed by Martin V., in 1418, it was included, and he began to exercise his powers there. There at once arose the threat of a most scandalous quarrel between the combative Orders; the Dominicans appealed to Martin, and in 1419 he restored Geneva to them. Yet in 1434, when Eugenius IV. again confirmed Pons Feugeyron's commission, the name of Geneva once more slipped in. The Dominicans must again have successfully reclaimed it, for in 1472, when there was a sudden resumption of inquisitorial activity under Sixtus IV., in confirming Frère Jean Vaylette as Inquisitor of Provence, with the same powers as Pons Feugeyron, Geneva was omitted in the list of his jurisdictions, while the Dominicans, Victor Rufi and Claude Rufi, were appointed respectively at Geneva and Lausanne; and in 1491 another Dominican, François Granet, was commissioned at Geneva.[156]

Yet the position thus eagerly sought had no legitimate means of support. In the terrible disorders of the times the royal stipends had been withdrawn. Alexander V., in 1409, instructed his legate, the Cardinal of S. Susanna, that some method must be devised of meeting the expenses of the inquisitor, his associate, his notary, and his servant. He suggests either levying three hundred{139} gold florins on the Jews of Avignon; or that each bishop shall defray the cost as the inquisitor moves from one diocese to another; or that each bishop shall contribute ten florins annually out of the legacies for pious uses. Which device was adopted does not appear, but they all seem to have proved fruitless, for in 1418 Martin V. wrote to the Archbishop of Narbonne that he must find some means of supplying the necessary expenses of the Inquisition. Under such circumstances the attraction of the office may, perhaps, be discerned from a petition, in this same year 1418, from the citizens of

Avignon in favor of the Jews. The protection afforded by the Avignonese popes to this proscribed class had rendered the city a Jewish centre, and they were found of much utility; but they were constantly molested by the inquisitors, who instituted frivolous prosecutions against them, doubtless not without profit. Martin listened kindly to the appeal, and it proves the degradation of the Inquisition that he gave the Jews a right to appoint an assessor who should sit with the inquisitor in all cases in which they were concerned.[157]

Still the Inquisition was not wholly without evidence of activity in its purposed sphere of duty. We shall see hereafter that Pierre d'Ailly, Bishop of Cambrai, when, in 1411, he prosecuted the Men of Intelligence, duly called in the inquisitor of the province, who was Dominican Prior of St. Quentin in Vermandois, to join in the sentence. In 1430 we hear of a number of heretics who had been burned at Lille by the deputy-inquisitor and the Bishop of Tournay; and in 1431 Philippe le Bon ordered his officials to execute all sentences pronounced by Brother Heinrich Kaleyser, who had been appointed Inquisitor of Cambrai and Lille by the Dominican Provincial of Germany—a manifest invasion of the rights of his colleague of Paris, doubtless due to the political complications of the times. This order of Philippe le Bon, however, shows that the example of supervision set by the Parlement was not lost on the feudatories, for the officials are only instructed to make arrests when there has been a proper preliminary inquest, with observance of all the forms of law. I shall have occasion hereafter to speak of the part played by the Inquisition in the tragedy of Joan of Arc, and need here only allude to the appointment,{140} in 1431, by Eugenius IV., of Frère Jean Graveran to be Inquisitor of Rouen, where he was already exercising the functions of the office, and where he was succeeded in 1433 by Frère Sébastien l'Abbé, who had been papal penitentiary and chaplain—another evidence of the partition of France during the disastrous English war. People were growing more careless about excommunication than ever. About 1415, a number of ecclesiastics of Limoges were prosecuted by the inquisitor, Jean du Puy, as suspect of heresy for this cause; they appealed to the Council of Constance, and in 1418 the matter was referred back to the archbishop. Still the indifference to excommunication grew, and in 1435 Eugenius IV. instructed the Inquisitor of Carcassonne to prosecute all who remained under the censure of the Church for several years without seeking absolution.[158]

With the pacification of France and the final expulsion of the English, Nicholas V. seems to have thought the occasion opportune for reviving and establishing the Inquisition on a firmer and broader basis. A bull of August 1, 1451, to Hugues le Noir, Inquisitor of France, defines his jurisdiction as extending not only over the Kingdom of France, but also over the Duchy of Aquitaine and all Gascony and Languedoc. Thus, with the exception of the eastern provinces, the whole was consolidated into one district, with its principal seat probably in Toulouse. The jurisdiction of the inquisitor was likewise extended over all offences that had hitherto been considered doubtful—blasphemy, sacrilege, divination, even when not savoring of heresy, and unnatural crimes. He was further released from the necessity of episcopal co-operation, and was empowered to carry on all proceedings and render judgment without calling the bishops into consultation. Two centuries earlier these enormous powers would have rendered Hugues almost omnipotent, but now it was too late. The Inquisition had sunk beyond resuscitation. In 1458 the Franciscan Minister of Burgundy represented to Pius II. the deplorable condition of the institution in the extensive territories confided to his Order, comprising the great archiepiscopates of Lyons, Vienne, Arles, Aix, Embrun, and Tarantaise, and covering both sides of{141} the Rhone and a considerable portion of Savoy. In the thirteenth century Clement IV. had placed this region under the control of the Burgundian Minister, but with the lapse of time his supervision had become nominal. Ambitious friars had obtained directly from the popes commissions to act as inquisitors in special districts, and therefore acknowledged no authority but their own. Others had assumed the office without appointment from any one. There was no power to correct their excesses; scandals were numerous, the people were oppressed, and the Order exposed to opprobrium. Pius hastened to put an end to these abuses by renewing the obsolete authority of the minister, with full power of removal, even of those who enjoyed papal commissions.[159]

The Inquisition was thus reorganized, but its time had passed. To so low an ebb had it fallen that in this same year, 1458, Frère Bérard Tremoux, Inquisitor of Lyons, who had aroused general hostility by the rigor with which he exercised his office, was thrown in prison through the efforts of the citizens, and it required the active interposition of Pius II. and his legate, Cardinal Alano, to effect his release. The venality and corruption of the papal curia, moreover, was so ineradicable that no reform was possible in anything subject to its control. But three years after Pius had placed the whole district under the Minister of Burgundy we find him renewing the old abuses by a special appointment of Brother Bartholomäus of Eger as Inquisitor of Grenoble. That such commissions were sold, or conferred as a matter of favor, there can be no reasonable doubt, and the appointees were turned loose upon their districts to wring what miserable gains they could from the fears of the people. Only this can explain a form of appointment which became common as "inquisitor in the Kingdom of France," "without prejudice to other inquisitors authorized by us or by others"—a sort of letter-of-marque to cruise at large and make what the appointees could from the faithful. Similarly significant is the appointment of Frère Pierre Cordrat, confessor of Jean, Duke of Bourbon, in 1478, to be Inquisitor of Bourges, thus wholly disregarding the consolidation of the kingdom by Nicholas V. It is hardly necessary to extend the list further. Inquisitors were appointed by the popes in constant succession,{142} either for the kingdom of France or for special districts, as though the institution were at the height of its power and activity. That something was to be gained by all this there can be no question, but there is little risk in assuming that the gainer was not religion.[160]

Several cases occurring about this period are interesting as illustrations of the spread of the spirit of inquiry and independence, and of the subordinate position to which the Inquisition had sunk. In 1459, at Lille, there was burned a heretic known as Alphonse of Portugal, who led an austere life as an anchorite and frequented the churches assiduously, but who declared that since Gregory the Great there had been no true pope, and consequently no valid administration of the sacraments. In the account which has reached us of his trial and execution there is no allusion to the intervention of the Holy Office. Still more significant is the case, in 1484, of Jean Laillier, a priest in Paris, a theological licentiate, and an applicant for the doctorate in theology. In his sermons he had been singularly free-spoken. He denied the validity of the rule of celibacy; he quoted Wickliff as a great doctor; he rejected the supremacy of Rome and the binding force of tradition and decretal; John XXII., he said, had had no power to condemn Jean de Poilly; so far from St. Francis occupying the vacant throne of Lucifer in heaven, he was rather with Lucifer in hell; since the time of Silvester the Holy See had been the church of avarice and of imperial power, where canonization could be obtained for money. So weak had become the traditional hold of the Church on the consciences of men that this revolutionary preaching seems to have aroused no opposition, even on the part of the Inquisition; but Laillier, not content with simple toleration, applied to the University for the doctorate, and was refused admission to the preliminary disputations unless he should purge himself, undergo penance, and obtain the assent of the Holy See.{143}Laillier thereupon boldly applied to the Parlement, now by tacit assent clothed with supreme jurisdiction in ecclesiastical matters, asking it to compel the University to admit him. The Parlement entertained no doubts as to its own competence, but decided the case in a manner not looked for by the hardy priest. It ordered Louis, Bishop of Paris, in conjunction with the inquisitor and four doctors selected by the University, to prosecute Laillier to due punishment. The bishop and inquisitor agreed to proceed separately and communicate their processes to each other; but Laillier must have had powerful backers, for Bishop Louis, without conferring with his colleague or the experts, allowed Laillier to make a partial recantation and a public abjuration couched in the most free and easy terms, absolved him, June 23, 1486, pronounced him free from suspicion of heresy, restored him to his functions, and declared him capable of promotion to all grades and honors. Frère Jean Cossart, the inquisitor, who had been diligently collecting evidence of many scandalous doctrines of Laillier's and vainly communicating them to the bishop, was forced to swallow this affront in silence, but the University felt its honor engaged and was not inclined to submit. November 6, 1486, it issued a formal protest against the action of the bishop, appealed to the pope, and demanded "Apostoli." Innocent VIII. promptly came to the rescue. He annulled the decision of the bishop and ordered the inquisitor, in conjunction with the Archbishop of Sens and the Bishop of Meaux, to throw Laillier into prison, while they should investigate the unrecanted heresies and send the papers to Rome for decision. Very suggestive of the strong influences supporting Laillier is the pope's expression of fear lest the pressure brought to bear on the University should have forced it to admit him to the doctorate; if so, such action is pronounced void, and all engaged in the attempt are ordered to desist under pain of incurring suspicion of heresy. It is not a little singular that the Bishop of Meaux, who was thus selected to sit in judgment on Laillier, was at this very time under censure by the University for reviving the Donatist heresy of the insufficiency of the sacraments in polluted hands—the Eucharist of a fornicating priest was of no more account, he said, than the barking of a dog. Many an unfortunate Waldensian had been burned for less than this, but the inquisitor had not dared to hold him to account. Nor do we hear{144} of his intervention in the case of Jean Langlois, priest of St. Crispin, who, when celebrating mass, June 3, 1491, horrified his flock by casting on the floor and trampling the consecrated wine and host. On his arrest he gave as his reason that the body and blood of Christ were not in the elements, and as he stubbornly refused to recant, he expiated his error at the stake. Similar was the fate of Aymon Picard, who, at the feast of St. Louis in the Sainte-Chapelle, August 25, 1503, snatched the host from the celebrant and cast it in pieces on the floor, and obstinately declined to abjure. All this was significant of the time coming when the Inquisition would be more necessary than ever.[161]

The present degradation which it shared with the rest of the Church in the constantly growing supremacy of the State is manifested by a commission issued in 1485, by Frère Antoine de Clède, appointing a vicar to act for him in Rodez and Vabres. In this document he styles himself Inquisitor of France, Aquitaine, Gascony, and Languedoc, deputed by the Holy See and the Parlement. The two bodies are thus equal sources of authority, and the appointment by the pope would have been insufficient without the confirmation by the royal court. How contemptible, indeed, the Inquisition had become, even in the eyes of ecclesiastics, is brought instructively before us in a petty quarrel between the Inquisitor Raymond Gozin and his Dominican brethren. When he succeeded Frère Gaillard de la Roche, somewhere about 1516, he found that the house of the Inquisition at Toulouse had been stripped of its furniture and utensils by the friars of the Dominican convent. He made a reclamation, and some of the articles were restored; but the friars subsequently demanded them back, and on his refusal procured from the General Master instructions to the vicar, under which the latter proceeded to extremities with him, wholly disregarding his appeal to the pope, though he finally, in 1520, succeeded in obtaining the intervention of Leo X. Imagination could scarcely furnish a more convincing proof of decadence than this exhibition of the successor of Bernard de Caux and Bernard Gui vainly endeavoring to defend his kitchen gear from the rapacious hands of his brethren.[162]{145}

It is quite probable that this dispute was envenomed by the inevitable jealousy between the main body of the Order and its puritan section known as the Reformed Congregation. Of this latter Raymond Gozin was vicar-general, and his anxiety to regain his furnishings was probably due to the fact that he was altering the house of the Inquisition so as to accommodate within it a Reformed convent. The vast buildings which it had required in the plenitude of its power had become a world too wide for its shrunken needs. The original home of the Dominican Order, before the removal in 1230 through the liberality of Pons de Capdenier, it contained a church with three altars, a refectory, cells (or prison), chambers, guest-rooms, cloisters, and two gardens. In approving of the proposed alterations, Leo X. stipulated that some kind of retiring-room with convenient offices must still be reserved for the use of the Inquisition. This epitomizes the history of the institution. Yet it had by no means wholly lost its power of evil, for in 1521 Johann Bomm, Dominican Prior of Poligny, and inquisitor at Besançon had the satisfaction of despatching two lycanthropists, or wer-wolves.[163]

The career of the Waldenses forms so interesting and well-defined an episode in the history of persecution that I have hitherto omitted all reference to that sect, in order to present a brief, continuous outline of its relations with the Inquisition, which found in it, after the disappearance of the Cathari, the only really important field of labor in France.

Although by no means as numerous or as powerful in Languedoc as the Cathari, the Waldenses formed an important heretical element. They were, however, mostly confined to the humbler classes, and we hear of few nobles belonging to the sect. In the sentences of Pierre Cella, rendered in Querci in 1241 and 1242, we have abundant testimony as to their numbers and activity. Thus, references occur to them—

{146}

At		cases out of
Gourdon in	5	219
At		" "
Montcucq in	4 "	84
At		case " "
Sauveterre in	5	
At		cases out
Belcayre in	of	7
At		" "
Montauban in	75 "	252
At		case " "
Moissac in	94	
At		" "
Montpezat in	o "	22
At		" "
Montaut in	o "	23
At		" "
Castelnau in	"	11

and although many of these are mere allusions to having seen them or had dealings with them, the comparative frequency of the reference indicates the places where their heresy was most flourishing. Thus, Montauban was evidently its headquarters in the district, and at Gourdon and Montcucq there were vigorous colonies.

They had a regular organization—schools for the young where their doctrines were doubtless implanted in the children of orthodox parents; cemeteries where their dead were buried; missionaries who traversed the land diligently to spread the faith, and who customarily refused all alms, save hospitality. A certain Pierre des Vaux is frequently referred to as one of the most active and most beloved of these, regarded, according to one of his disciples, as an angel of light. Public preaching in the streets was constant, and numerous allusions are made to disputations held between the Waldensian ministers and the Catharan perfects. Still, the utmost good feeling existed between the two persecuted sects. Men were found who confessed to believing in the Waldenses and to performing acts of adoration to the Cathari—in the common enmity to Rome any faith which was not orthodox was regarded as good. The reputation of the Waldenses as skilful leeches was a powerful aid in their missionary labors. They were constantly consulted in cases of disease or injury, and almost without exception they refused payment for their ministrations, save food. One woman confessed to giving forty sols to a Catharan for medical services, while to Waldenses she gave only wine and bread. We learn also that they heard confessions and imposed penance; that they celebrated a sacramental supper in which bread and fish were blessed and partaken of, and that bread which they consecrated with the sign of the cross was regarded as holy by their disciples. Notwithstanding the strength and organization of the sect, the Waldenses were evidently looked upon by Pierre Cella with a less {147} unfavorable eye than the Cathari, and the penances imposed on them were habitually lighter.[164]

From Lyons the Waldensian belief had spread to the North and East, as well as to the South and West. It is a curious fact that while the Cathari never succeeded in establishing themselves to any extent beyond the Romance territories, the Waldenses were already, in 1192, so numerous in Lorraine that Eudes, Bishop of Toul, in ordering them to be captured and brought to him in chains for judgment, not only promises remission of sins as a reward, but feels obliged to add that if, for rendering this service, the faithful are driven away from their homes, he will find them in food and clothing. In Franche Comté, John, Count of Burgundy, bears emphatic testimony to their numbers in 1248, when he solicited of Innocent IV. the introduction of the Inquisition in his dominions, and its discontinuance in 1257 doubtless left them to multiply in peace. In 1251 we find the Archbishop of Narbonne condemning some female Waldenses to perpetual imprisonment. It was, however, in the mountains of Auvergne and the Alpine and sub-Alpine regions stretching between Geneva and the Mediterranean that they found the surest refuge. While Pierre Cella was penancing those of Querci, the Archbishop of Embrun was busy with their brethren of Freyssinières, Argentière, and Val-Pute, which so long continued to be their strongholds. In 1251, when Alphonse and Jeanne, on their accession, guaranteed at Beaucaire the liberties of Avignon and the Comtat Venaissin, the Bishop-legate Zoen earnestly urged them to destroy the Waldenses there. There were ample laws on the municipal statute-books of Avignon and Arles for the extermination of "heretics and Waldenses," but the local magistracy was slack in their enforcement and was obliged to swear to extirpate the sectaries. The Waldenses were mostly simple mountain folk, with{148} possessions that offered no temptation for confiscation, and persecuting energy was more profitable and more usefully directed against the richer Cathari. We hear, indeed, that from 1271 to 1274 the zeal of Guillaume de Cobardon, Seneschal of Carcassonne, urged the inquisitors to active work against the Waldenses, resulting in numerous convictions, but among the far more populous communities near the Rhone the Inquisition was not introduced into the Comtat Venaissin until 1288, nor into Dauphiné until 1292, and in both cases we are told that it was caused by the alarming spread of heresy. In 1288 the same increase is alluded to in the provinces of Arles, Aix, and Embrun, when Nicholas IV. sent to the nobles and magistrates there the laws of Frederic II., with orders for their enforcement, and to the inquisitors a code of instructions for procedure.[165]

About the same period there is a curious case of a priest named Jean Philibert, who was sent from Burgundy into Gascony to track a fugitive Waldensian. He followed his quarry as far as Ausch, where he found a numerous community of the sectaries, holding regular assemblies and preaching and performing their rites, although they attended the parish churches to avert suspicion. Their evangelical piety so won upon him that, after going home, he returned to Ausch and formally joined them. He wandered back to Burgundy, where he fell under suspicion, and in 1298 he was brought before Gui de Reims, the Inquisitor of Besançon, when he refused to take an oath and was consigned to prison. Here he abjured, and on being liberated returned to the Waldenses of Gascony, was again arrested, and brought before Bernard Gui in 1311, who finally burned him in 1319 as a relapsed. In 1302 we hear of two Waldensian ministers haunting the region near Castres, in the Albigeois, wandering around by night and zealously propagating their doctrines. Still, in spite of these evidences of activity, little effort at repression is visible at{149} this period. The Inquisition was crippled for a while by its contest with Philippe le Bel and Clement V., and when it resumed unrestricted operations, Pierre Autier and his Catharan disciples absorbed its energies. Although the sentences of Bernard Gui at Toulouse commence in 1308, it is not until the *auto de fé* of 1316 that any Waldenses appear among its victims, when one was condemned to perpetual imprisonment and one was burned as an unrepentant heretic. The *auto* of 1319 appears to have been a jail-delivery, for poor wretches appear in it whose confessions date back to 1309, 1311, 1312, and 1315. On this occasion eighteen Waldenses were condemned to pilgrimages with or without crosses, twenty-six to perpetual prison, and three were burned. In the *auto* of 1321 a man and his wife who obstinately refused to abjure were burned. In that of 1322 eight were sentenced to pilgrimages, of whom five had crosses, two to prison, six dead bodies were exhumed and burned, and there is an allusion to the brother of one of the prisoners who had been burned at Avignon. This comprises the whole work of Bernard Gui from 1308 to 1323, and does not indicate any very active persecution. It is perhaps noteworthy that all of those punished in 1319 were from Ausch, while the popular name of "Burgundians," by which the Waldenses were known, indicates that the headquarters of the sect were still in Franche Comté. In fact, an allusion to a certain Jean de Lorraine as a successful missionary indicates that region as busy in proselyting efforts, and there are not wanting facts to prove that the Inquisition of Besançon was active during this period. In the *auto* of 1322 many of the sufferers were refugees from Burgundy, and we learn that they had a provincial named Girard, showing that the Waldensian Church of that region had a regular organization and hierarchy.[166]

In his "*Practica*" Bernard Gui gives a clear and detailed statement of the Waldensian belief as it existed at this time, the chief points of which may be worth enumerating as affording us a definite view of the development of the faith in its original seat after a century and a half of persecution. There was no longer any self-deceit as to connection with the Roman Church. Persecution{150} had done its work, and the Waldenses were permanently severed. Theirs was the true Church, and that of the pope was but a house of lies, whose excommunication was not to be regarded, and whose decrees were not to be obeyed. They had a complete organization, consisting of bishops, priests, and deacons, and they held in some large city one or two general chapters every year, in which orders were conferred and measures for mission work were perfected. The

Waldensian orders, however, did not confer exclusive supernatural power. Although they still believed in transubstantiation, the making of the body and blood of Christ depended on the purity of the ministrant; a sinner was impotent to effect it, while it could be done by any righteous man or woman. It was the same with absolution: they held the power of the keys direct from Christ, and heard confessions and imposed penance. Their antisacerdotalism was strongly expressed in the simplification of their faith. There was no purgatory, and consequently masses for the dead or the invocation of the suffrages of the saints were of no avail; the saints, in fact, neither heard nor helped man, and the miracles performed in their name in the churches were fictitious. The fasts and feasts prescribed in the calendar were not to be observed, and the indulgences so lavishly sold were useless. As of old, oaths and homicide were forbidden. Yet enough of the traditional ascetic tendencies were preserved to lead to the existence of a monastic fraternity whose members divested themselves of all individual property, and promised chastity, with obedience to a superior. Bernard Gui refers, with a brevity which shows how little importance he attached to them, to stories about sexual abominations performed in nocturnal assemblies, and he indicates the growth of popular superstition by a brief allusion to a dog which appears in these gatherings and sprinkles the sectaries with his tail.[167]

The non-resistance doctrines of the Waldenses rendered them, as a rule, a comparatively easy prey, but human nature sometimes asserted itself, and a sharp persecution carried on at this period by Frère Jacques Bernard, Inquisitor of Provence, provoked a bloody reprisal. In 1321 he sent two deputies—Frères Catalan Fabri and Pierre Paschal—to the diocese of Valence to make inquisition{151} there. Former raids had left the people in an angry mood. Multitudes had been subjected to the humiliation of crosses, and these and their friends vowed revenge on the appearance of the new persecutors. A plot was rapidly formed to assassinate the inquisitors at a village where they were to pass the night. For some reason, however, they changed their plans, and passed on to the Priory of Montoison. The conspirators followed them, broke down the doors, and slew them. Strangely enough, the Prior of Montoison was accused of complicity in the murder, and was arrested when the murderers were seized. The bodies of the martyrs were solemnly buried in the Franciscan convent at Valence, where they soon began to manifest their sanctity in miracles, and they would have been canonized by John XXII. had not the quarrel which soon afterwards sprang up between him and the Franciscans rendered it impolitic for him to increase the number of Franciscan saints.[168]

A few Waldenses appear in the prosecutions of Henri de Chamay of Carcassonne in 1328 and 1329, and, from the occasional notices which have reached us in the succeeding years, we may conclude that persecution, more or less fitful, never wholly ceased; while, in spite of this, the heresy kept constantly growing. After the disappearance of Catharism, indeed, it was the only refuge for ordinary humanity when dissatisfied with Rome. The Begghards were mystics whose speculations were attractive only to a certain order of minds. The Spirituals and Fraticelli were Franciscan ascetics. The Waldenses sought only to restore Christianity to its simplicity; their doctrines could be understood by the poor and illiterate, groaning under the burdens of sacerdotalism, and they found constantly wider acceptance among the people, in spite of all the efforts put forth by the waning power of the Inquisition. Benedict XII., in 1335, summoned Humbert II., Dauphin of Viennois, and Adhémar of Poitou to assist the inquisitors. Humbert obeyed, and from 1336 to 1346 there were expeditions sent against them which drove them from their homes and captured some of them. Of these a portion abjured and the rest were burned; their possessions were confiscated and the bones of the dead exhumed. The secular and ecclesiastical officials of Embrun joined in these{152} efforts, but they had no permanent result. In Languedoc Frère Jean Dumoulin, Inquisitor of Toulouse, in 1344 attacked them vigorously, but only succeeded in scattering them throughout Béarn, Foix, and Aragon. In 1348 Clement VI. again urged Humbert, who responded with strict orders to his officers to aid the ecclesiastical authorities with what force might be necessary, and this time we hear of twelve Waldenses brought to Embrun, and burned on the square in front of the cathedral. When Dauphiné became a possession of the crown the royal officials were equally ready to assist. Letters of October 20, 1351, from the governor, order the authorities of Briançon to give the inquisitor armed support in his operations against the heretics of the Briançonnais, but this seems to have been ineffective; and the next year Clement VI. appealed to the Dauphin Charles, and to Louis and Joanna of Naples, to aid Frère Pierre Dumont, the Inquisitor of Provence, and summoned prelates and magistrates to co-operate in the good work. The only recorded result of this was the penancing of seven Waldenses by Dumont in 1353. More successful were the Christian labors of Guillaume de Bordes, Archbishop of Embrun from 1352 to 1363, surnamed the Apostle of the Waldenses, who tried the unusual expedient of kindness and persuasion. He personally visited the mountain valleys, and had the satisfaction of winning over a number of the heretics. With his death his methods were abandoned, and Urban V., from 1363 to 1365, was earnest in calling upon the civil power and in stimulating the zeal of the Provençal inquisitors, Frères Hugues Cardilion and Jean Richard. The celebrated inquisitor François Borel now appears upon the scene. Armed expeditions were sent into the mountains which had considerable success. Many of the heretics were obstinate and were burned, while others saved their lives by abjuration. Their pitiful little properties were confiscated; one had a cow, another two cows and clothes of white cloth. In the purse of another, more wealthy, were found two florins—a booty which scarce proved profitable, for the wood to burn him and a comrade cost sixty-two sols and six deniers. One woman named Juven who was burned possessed a vineyard. The vintage was gathered and the must stored in her cabin, when the wrathful neighbors fired it at night and destroyed the product.[169]{153}

All this was of no avail. When Gregory XI. ascended the pontifical throne, in 1370, his attention was early directed to the deplorable condition of the Church in Provence, Dauphiné, and the Lyonnais. The whole region was full of Waldenses, and many nobles were now beginning to embrace the heresy. The prelates were powerless or negligent, and the Inquisition ineffective. He set to work vigorously, appointing inquisitors and stimulating their zeal, but the whole system by this time was so discredited that his labors were ineffectual. The royal officials, so far from aiding the inquisitors, had no scruple in impeding them. Unsafe places were assigned to them in which to conduct their operations; they were forced to permit secular judges to act as assessors with them; their proceedings were submitted for revision to the secular courts, and even their prisoners were set at liberty without consulting them. The secular officials refused to take oaths to purge the land of heresy, and openly protected heretics, especially nobles, when prosecutions were commenced against them.[170]

Gregory duly complained of this to Charles le Sage in 1373, but to little purpose at first. The evil continued unabated, and in 1375 he returned to the charge still more vigorously. No stone was left unturned. Not only was the king requested to send a special deputy to the infected district, but the pope wrote directly to the royal lieutenant, Charles de Banville, reproaching him for his protection of heretics, and threatening him if he did not mend his ways. Certain nobles who had become conspicuous as favorers of heresy were significantly reminded of the fate of Raymond of Toulouse; the prelates were scolded and stimulated; Amedeo of Savoy was summoned to assist, and the Tarantaise was added to the district of Provence that nothing might interfere with the projected campaign. As the spread of heresy was attributable to the lack of preachers, and to the neglect of prelates and clergy in instructing their flocks, the inquisitor was empowered to call in the services of Dominicans, Franciscans, Carmelites, and Augustinians, to spread over the land and teach the people the truths of religion.{154} These multiplied efforts at length began to tell. Charles issued orders to enforce the laws against heresy, and when Gregory sent a special Apostolic Internuncio, Antonio, Bishop of Massa, to direct operations, persecution began in earnest. Frère François Borel, the Inquisitor of Provence, had long been struggling against the indifference of the prelates and the hostility of the secular power. Now that he was sure of efficient seconding be was like a hound slipped from the leash. His forays against the miserable populations of Freyssinières, l'Argentière, and Val-Pute (or Val-Louise) have conferred on him a sinister reputation, unredeemed by the efficient aid which he contributed to regaining the liberties of his native town of Gap.[171]

The immediate success which rewarded these efforts was so overwhelming as to bring new cause for solicitude. The Bishop of Massa's mission commenced early in May, 1375, and already, by June 17, Gregory is concerned about the housing and support of the crowds of wretches who had been captured. In spite of numerous burnings of those who proved obstinate, the prisons of the land were insufficient for the detention of the captives, and Gregory at once ordered new and strong ones to be built in Embrun, Avignon, and Vienne. To solve the financial complications which immediately arose, the bishops, whose negligence was accountable for the growth of heresy, were summoned within three months to furnish four thousand gold florins to build the prisons, and eight hundred florins per annum for five years for the support of the prisoners. This they were allowed to take from the legacies for pious uses, and the restitutions of wrongly-acquired funds, with a threat, if they should demur, that they should be deprived of these sources of income and be excommunicated besides. The bishops, however, were no more amenable to such arguments than those of Languedoc had been in 1245, and, after the three months had passed, Gregory answers, October 5, the anxious inquiry of the Bishop of Massa as to how he shall feed his prisoners, by telling him that it is the business of every bishop to support those of his diocese, and that any one who refuses to do so is to be coerced with excommunication and the secular arm. This was a mere *brutum*{155} *fulmen*, and in 1376 he endeavored to secure a share in the confiscations, but King Charles refused to divide them, though in 1378 he at last agreed to give the inquisitors a yearly stipend for their own support, similar to that paid to their brethren at Toulouse.[172]

All other devices being exhausted, Gregory at last had recourse to the unfailing resource of the curia—an indulgence. There is something so appallingly grotesque in tearing honest, industrious folk from their homes by the thousand, in thrusting them into dungeons to rot and starve, and then evading the cost of feeding them by presenting them to the faithful as objects of charity, that the proclamation which Gregory issued August 15, 1370, is perhaps the most shameless monument of a shameless age—

"To all the faithful in Christ: As the help of prisoners is counted among pious works, it befits the piety of the faithful to mercifully assist the incarcerated of all kinds who suffer from poverty. As we learn that our beloved son, the Inquisitor François Borelli, has imprisoned for safe-keeping or punishment many heretics and those defamed for heresy, who in consequence of their poverty cannot be sustained in prison unless the pious liberality of the faithful shall assist them as a work of charity; and as we wish that these prisoners shall not starve, but shall have time for repentance in the said prisons; now, in order that the faithful in Christ may through devotion lend a helping hand, we admonish, ask, and exhort you all, enjoining it on you in remission of your sins, that from the goods which God has given you, you bestow pious alms and grateful charity for the food of these prisoners, so that they may be sustained by your help, and you, through this and other good works inspired by God, may attain eternal blessedness!"[173]

Imagination refuses to picture the horrors of the economically constructed jails where these unfortunates were crowded to wear out their dreary lives, while their jailers vainly begged for the miserable pittance that should prolong their agonies. Yet so far was Gregory from being satisfied with victims in number far beyond his ability to keep, that, December 28, 1375, he bitterly scolded the officials of Dauphiné for the negligent manner in which they obeyed the king's commands to aid the inquisitors—a complaint which he reiterated May 18, 1376. From some expressions in these letters it is permissible to assume that this whole inhuman{156} business had shocked even the dull sensibilities of that age of violence. Yet in spite of all that had been accomplished the heretics remained obstinate, and in 1377 Gregory indignantly chronicles their increase, while reproaching the inquisitors with their slackness in performing the duties for which they had been appointed.[174]

What effect on the future of the Waldenses a continuance of Gregory's remorseless energy would have wrought can only be matter of conjecture. He died March 27, 1378, and the Great Schism which speedily followed gave the heretics some relief, during which they continued to increase, although in 1380 Clement VII. renewed the commission of Borel, whose activity was unabated until 1393, and his victims were numbered by the hundred. A good many conversions rewarded his labors, and the converts were allowed to retain their property on payment of a certain sum of money, as shown by a list made out in 1385. In 1393 he is said to have burned a hundred and fifty at Grenoble in a single day. San Vicente Ferrer was a missionary of a different stamp, and his self-devoted labors for several years in the Waldensian valleys won over numerous converts. His memory is still cherished there, and the village of Puy-Saint-Vincent, with a chapel dedicated to him, shows that his kindly ministrations were not altogether lost.[175]

The Waldenses by this time were substantially the only heretics with whom the Church had to deal outside of Germany. The French version of the *Schwabenspiegel*, or South German municipal code, made for the Romande speaking provinces of the empire, is assignable to the closing years of the century, and it attests the predominance of Waldensianism in its chapter on heresy, by translating the *Käezer* (Catharus) of the original by *vaudois*. Even "Leschandus" (Childeric III.) is said to have been dethroned by Pope Zachary because he was a protector of vaudois. That at this period the Inquisition had become inoperative in those regions where it had once been so busy is proved by the episcopal tribunals being alone referred to as having cognizance of such cases—the{157} heretic is to be accused to his bishop, who is to have him examined by experts.[176]

How completely the Waldenses dropped out of sight in the struggles of the Great Schism is seen in a bull of Alexander V., in 1409, to Frère Pons Feugeyron, whose enormous district extended from Marseilles to Lyons and from Beaucaire to the Val d'Aosta. This comprehended the whole district which François Borel and Vicente Ferrer found swarming with heretics. The inquisitor is urged to use his utmost endeavors against the schismatic followers of Benedict XIII. and Gregory XII., against the increasing numbers of sorcerers, against apostate Jews and the Talmud, but not a word is said about Waldenses. They seem to have been completely forgotten.[177]

After the Church had reorganized itself at the Council of Constance it had leisure to look after the interests of the faith, although its energies were mostly monopolized by the Hussite troubles. In 1417 we hear of Catharine Sauve, an anchorite, burned at Montpellier for Waldensian doctrines by the deputy-inquisitor, Frère Raymond Cabasse, assisted by the Bishop of Maguelonne. The absence of persecution had by no means been caused by a diminution in the number of heretics. In 1432 the Council of Bourges complained that the Waldenses of Dauphiné had taxed themselves to send money to the Hussites, whom they recognized as brethren; and there were plenty of them to be found by any one who took the trouble to look after them. On August 23, of this same year, we have a letter from Frère Pierre Fabri, Inquisitor of Embrun, to the Council of Basle, excusing himself for not immediately obeying a summons to attend it on the ground of his indescribable poverty, and of his preoccupations in persecuting the Waldenses. In spite of the great executions which he had already made, he describes them as flourishing as numerously as ever in the valleys of Freyssinières, Argentière, and Pute, which had been almost depopulated by the ferocious raids of François Borel. He now has in his dungeons of Embrun and Briançon six relapsed heretics, who have revealed to him the names of more than five hundred others whom he is about to seize, and whose trials will be a work of time,{158} but as soon as he can absent himself without prejudice to the faith his first duty will be to attend the council. Evidently the harvest was abundant and the reapers were few.[178]

In 1441 the Inquisitor of Provence, Jean Voyle, made some effort at persecution, but apparently with little result, and the Waldensian churches seem to have enjoyed a long respite, for the terrible episode of the so-called Vaudois of Arras, in 1460, as we shall see hereafter, was merely a delirium of witchcraft. In France, so completely had the Waldenses monopolized the field of misbelief in the public mind that sorcery became popularly known as *vauderie* and witches as *vaudoises*. Accordingly, when, in 1465, at Lille, five "Poor Men of Lyons" were tried, and four of them recanted and one was burned, it was necessary to find some other name for them, and they were designated as Turelupins.[179]

It is not until 1475 that we find the inquisitors again at work in their old hunting-ground among the valleys around the headwaters of the Durance. The Waldenses had quietly multiplied again. They held their conventicles undisturbed, they dared openly to preach their abhorred faith, and their missionary zeal was rewarded with abundant conversions. Worse than all, when the bishops and inquisitors sought to repress them in the accustomed manner, they appealed to the royal court, which was so untrue to its duty that it granted them letters of protection and they waxed more insolent than ever. In vain Sixtus IV. sent special commissions armed with full powers to put an end to this disgraceful state of things. Men at this time in France recked little of papal authority, and the commissioners found themselves scorned. Sixtus, therefore, July 1, 1475, addressed an earnest remonstrance to Louis XI. The king was surely ignorant of the acts of his representatives; he would hasten to disavow them and lend the{159} whole power of the State, as of old, to the support of the Inquisition.[180]

The correspondence which ensued would doubtless be interesting reading if it were accessible. Its purport, however, can readily be discerned in the Ordonnance of May 18, 1478, which marks in the most emphatic manner the supremacy which the State had obtained over the Church. The king assumed that his subjects of Dauphiné were all good Catholics. In a studied tone of contemptuous insolence he alludes to the old Mendicants (*vieux mendiens*) styling themselves inquisitors, who vex the faithful with accusations of heresy and harass them with prosecutions in the royal and ecclesiastical courts for purposes of extortion or to secure the confiscation of their property. He therefore forbids his officers to aid in making such confiscations, decrees that the heirs shall be reinstated in all cases that have occurred, and in order to put a stop to the frauds and abuses of the inquisitors he strictly enjoins that for the future they shall not be permitted to prosecute the inhabitants in any manner.[181]

Such was the outcome of the efforts which, for two hundred and fifty years, the Church had unremittingly made to obtain despotic control over the human mind. For far less than such defiance it had destroyed Raymond of Toulouse and the civilization of Languedoc. It had built up the monarchy with the spoils of heresy, and now the monarchy cuffed it and bade it bury its Inquisition out of the sight of decent men. This put an end for a time to the labors of the Inquisition against the Waldenses of Dauphiné, but the troubles of the latter were by no means over. The death of Louis, in 1483, deprived them of their protector, and the Italian policy of Charles VIII. rendered him less indifferent to the wishes of the Holy See. At the request of the Archbishop of Embrun, Innocent VIII. ordered the persecutions renewed. The Franciscan Inquisitor, Jean Veyleti, whose excesses had caused the appeal to the throne in 1475, was soon again at work, and had the satisfaction of burning both consuls of Freyssinières. Though the Waldenses had represented themselves to Louis XI. as faithful Catholics, the ancient errors were readily brought to{160} light by the efficient means of torture. Though they believed in transubstantiation, they denied that it could be effected by sinful priests. Their *barbes*, or pastors, were ordained, and administered absolution after confession, but the pope, the bishops, and the priests had lost that power. They denied the existence of purgatory, the utility of prayers for the dead, the intercession of saints, the power of the Virgin, and the obligation of keeping any feast-days save Sunday. Wearied with their stubbornness, the archbishop, in June and July, 1486, summoned them either to leave the country or to come forward and submit, and as they did neither he excommunicated them. This was equally ineffective, and he appealed again to Innocent VIII., who resolved to end the heresy with a decisive blow. Accordingly, in 1488, a crusade on a large scale was organized in both Dauphiné and Savoy. The papal commissioner, Alberto de" Capitanei, obtained the assistance of the Parlement of Grenoble, and a force was raised under the command of Hugues de La Palu, Comte de Vanax, to attack them on every side. The attack was delayed by legal formalities, during which they were urged to submission, but refused, saying that their faith was pure and that they would die rather than abandon it. At length, in March, 1489, the crusaders advanced. The valley of Pragelato was the first assailed, and, after a few days, was reduced to the alternative of death or abjuration, when fifteen obstinate heretics were burned. In Val Cluson and Freyssinières the resistance was more stubborn and there was considerable carnage, which so frightened the inhabitants of Argentière that they submitted peaceably. In Val Louise the people took refuge in the cavern of Aigue Fraide, which they imagined inaccessible, but La Palu succeeded in reaching it, and built fires in the mouth, suffocating the unhappy refugees. This, and the confiscations which followed, divided between Charles VIII. and the Archbishop of Embrun, gave a fatal blow to Waldensianism in the valleys. To prevent its resuscitation the legate left behind him François Ploireri as Inquisitor of Provence, who continued to harass the people with citations and pronounced condemnations for contumacy, burning an occasional *barbe* and confiscating the property of relapsed and hardened heretics.[182]{161}

With a new king, in the person of Louis XII., there came a new phase in the affairs of the Waldenses. A conference was held in Paris before the royal chancellor, where envoys from Freyssinières met Rostain, the new Archbishop of Embrun, and deputies of the Parlement of Grenoble. It was resolved to send to the spot papal and royal commissioners, with power to determine the status of the so-called heretics. They went to Freyssinières and examined witnesses, who satisfied them that the population were good Catholics, in spite of the urgent assertions of the archbishop that they were notorious heretics. All the excommunications were removed, which put an end to the prosecutions. On October 12, 1502, Louis XII. confirmed the decision, and Alexander VI., to whose son, Cæsar Borgia, Louis had given the Duchy of Valentinois, embracing the territory in question, was not disposed to run counter to the royal wishes. The Waldenses were, however, unable to loosen the grip of the Archbishop of Embrun on the property which he had confiscated, in spite of positive orders for its restoration from the king, but at least they were allowed, under the guise of Catholicism, to worship God after their own fashion, until the crowding pressure of the Reformation forced them to a merger with the Calvinists. In the Briançonnais, in spite of occasional burnings, heresy continued to spread until, in 1514, Antoine d'Estaing, Bishop of Angoulême, was sent thither, when the measures he adopted, vigorously enforced by the secular authorities, put an end to it in a few years.[183]{162}

54

CHAPTER III.

THE SPANISH PENINSULA.

THE kingdom of Aragon, stretching across both sides of the Pyrenees, with a population kindred in blood and speech to that of Mediterranean France, was particularly liable to inroads of heresy from the latter. The Counts of Barcelona had been Carlovingian vassals, and even owned a shadowy allegiance to the first Capetians. We have seen how ready were Pedro II. and his successors to aid in resisting Frankish encroachments, even at the cost of encouraging heresy, and it was inevitable that schismatic missions should be established in populous centres such as Barcelona, and that heretics, when hard-pressed, should seek refuge in the mountains of Cerdaña and Urgel. In spite of this, however, heresy never obtained to the west of the Pyrenees the foothold which it enjoyed to the east. Its manifestations there were only spasmodic, and were suppressed with effort comparatively slender.

It is somewhat remarkable that we hear nothing specifically of the Cathari in Aragon proper. Matthew Paris, indeed, tells a wild tale of how, in 1234, they were so numerous in the parts of Spain that they decreed the abrogation of Christianity, and raised a large army with which they burned churches and spared neither age nor sex, until Gregory IX. ordered a crusade against them throughout western Europe, when in a stricken field they were all cut off to a man; but this may safely be set down to the imagination of some pilgrim returning from Compostella and desiring to repay a night's hospitality at St. Alban's. In the enumeration of Rainerio Saccone, about 1250, there is no mention of any Catharan organization west of the Pyrenees. That many Cathari existed in Aragon there can be no doubt, but they are never described as such, and the only heretics of whom we hear by name are *los encabats*—the Insabbatati or Waldenses. It will be remembered that it was against these that the savage edicts of Alonso II.{163} and Pedro II. were directed, towards the close of the twelfth century.[184]

After this, for a while, persecution seems to have slept. The sympathies and ambition of King Pedro were enlisted with Raymond of Toulouse, and after his fall at Muret, during the minority of Jayme I., the Aragonese probably awaited the results of the Albigensian war with feelings enlisted in favor of their race rather than of orthodoxy. As it drew to a close, however, Don Jayme, in 1226, issued an edict prohibiting all heretics from entering his kingdom, doubtless moved thereunto by the numbers who sought escape from the crusade of Louis VIII., and he followed this, in 1228, with another, depriving heretics, with their receivers, fautors, and defenders, of the public peace. The next step, we are told by the chroniclers of the Inquisition, was taken in consequence of the urgency of Raymond of Pennaforte, the Dominican confessor of the young king, who prevailed on him to obtain from Gregory IX. inquisitors to purge his land. This is based on the bull *Declinante*, addressed, May 26, 1232, to Esparrago, Archbishop of Tarragona, and his suffragans, instructing them to make inquest in their dioceses after heretics, either personally or by Dominicans or other fitting persons, and to punish such as might be found, according to the statutes recently issued by him and by Annibaldo, Senator of Rome. This doubtless gave an impulse to what followed, but as yet there was no thought of a papal or Dominican Inquisition, or of adopting foreign legislation. In the following year, 1233, Don Jayme returned from Tarragona, with the advice of his assembled prelates, a statute on the subject, showing that the matter was regarded as pertaining to the State rather than to the Church. Seigneurs who protected heretics in their lands forfeited them to the lord, or, if allodial, to the king. Houses of heretics, if allodial, were to be torn down; if held in fief, forfeited to the lord. All defamed or suspected of heresy were declared ineligible to office. That the innocent might not suffer with the guilty, no one was to be punished as a heretic or believer except by his bishop or such ecclesiastic as had authority to determine his guilt. Bishops were ordered, when it might seem expedient to them in{164} places suspected of heresy, to appoint a priest or clerk, while the king or his bailli would appoint two or three laymen, whose duty it should be to investigate heretics, and, taking precautions against their escape, to report them to the bishop or to the royal officials, or to the lord of the place. In this incongruous mixture of clerical and lay elements there may, it is true, be discovered the germ of an Inquisition, but one of a character very different from that which was at this time taking shape at Toulouse. The subordinate position of these so-called inquisitors is seen in the provision that any negligence in the performance of their functions was punishable, in the case of a clerk, by the loss of his benefice, in that of a layman, by a pecuniary mulct.[185]

To what extent this crude expedient was put in practice we have no means of knowing, but probably some attempts were made which only proved its inefficiency. Esparrago died soon afterwards and was succeeded in the archiepiscopal seat of Tarragona by Guillen Mongriu, whose vigorous and martial temperament was illustrated by his conquest of the island of Iviza. Mongriu speedily found that the domestic Inquisition would not work, and applied for the solution of some doubts to Gregory, who sent him, April 30, 1235, a code of instructions drawn up by Raymond of Pennaforte. About this time we find the first record of active work in persecution, which illustrates the absence of all formal inquisitorial procedure. Robert, Count of Rosellon, was one of the great feudatories of the crown of Aragon. He seems to have been involved, as most nobles were, in some disputes as to fiefs and tithes with the Bishop of Elne, whose diocese was in his territories. The bishop accused him of being the chief of the heretics of the region and of using his castles as a refuge for them. All this was very likely true—at least the bishop had no difficulty in finding witnesses to prove it, when Robert obediently abjured, but subsequently relapsed. Don Jayme accordingly had him arrested and imprisoned, but Robert managed to escape and shut himself in one of his inaccessible mountain strongholds. His position,{165} however, was desperate, and his lands liable to confiscation; he therefore expressed to Gregory IX. his desire to return to the bosom of the Church, and offered to serve with his followers against the Saracen as long as the pope might designate. Gregory therefore wrote, February 8, 1237, to Raymond of Pennaforte, that if the count would for three years with his subjects assist in the conquest of Valencia, and give sufficient security that in case of relapse his territories should be forfeited to the crown, he could be absolved. On hearing this the good bishop hastened to the papal court and declared that if Robert was absolved he and his witnesses would be exposed to the imminent peril of death, and that heresy would triumph in his diocese; but, on receiving assurances that his fiefs and tithes would be taken care of, he quieted down and offered no further opposition.[186]

Under the impulsion of Gregory and of Raymond of Pennaforte, Dominican inquisitors had at last been resorted to, and in this year, 1237, we first become cognizant of them. In right of his wife Ermessende, Roger Bernard the Great of Foix was Vizconde of Castelbo, a fief held of the Bishop of Urgel, with whom he had had a bitter war. He gave Castelbo to his son Roger, who, by the advice of his father, in 1237, allowed the Inquisition free scope there, placing the castle in the hands of Ramon Fulco, Vizconde of Cardona, in the name of the Archbishop of Tarragona and the bishops assembled at the Council of Lerida. That council thereupon appointed a number of inquisitors, including Dominicans and Franciscans, who made a descent on Castelbo. It had long been noted as a nest of Catharans. In 1225, under the protection of Arnaldo, then lord of the place, perfected heretics publicly preached their doctrines there. In 1234 we hear of a heretic of Mirepoix going thither to receive the *consolamentum* on his death-bed. The inquisitors, therefore, had no difficulty in finding victims. They ordered two houses to be destroyed, exhumed and burned the bones of eighteen persons, condemned as heretics, and carried off as prisoners some forty-five men and women, condemned fifteen who fled, and were undecided about sundry others. Still, the Bishop of Urgel was not satisfied, and he gratified his rancor by condemning and excommunicating Roger{166} Bernard as a defender of heretics, and it was not until 1240 that the latter, through the intervention of the Archbishop of Tarragona, and by submitting, abjuring heresy, and swearing to perform any penance assigned to him, procured from the bishop absolution and a certificate that he recognized him *"per bon et per leyal e per Catholich."*[187]

In 1238 the Inquisition of Aragon may be said to be founded. In April of that year Gregory IX. wrote to the Franciscan Minister and Dominican Prior of Aragon deploring the spread of heresy through the whole kingdom, so that heretics no longer seek secrecy, but openly combat the Church, to the destruction of its liberties; and though this may be an exaggeration, we know from a confession before the Inquisition of Toulouse that there were enough scattered through the land to afford shelter to the wandering Catharan missionaries. Gregory, therefore, placed in the hands of the Mendicants the sword of the Word of God, which was not to be restrained from blood. They were instructed to make diligent inquisition against heresy and its abettors, proceeding in accordance with the statutes which he had issued, and calling in when necessary the aid of the secular arm. At the same time he made a similar provision for Navarre, which was likewise said to be swarming with heretics, by commissioning as inquisitors the Franciscan Guardian of Pamplona and the Dominican Pedro de Leodegaria. As an independent institution the Inquisition of Navarre seems never to have advanced beyond an embryonic condition. In 1246 we find Innocent IV. writing to the Franciscan Minister there to publish that Grimaldo de la Mota, a citizen of Pamplona, is not to be aspersed as a heretic because while in Lombardy he had eaten and drunk with suspected persons, but this is the only evidence of vitality that I have met with, and Navarre was subsequently incorporated into the Inquisition of Aragon.[188]

In Aragon the institution gradually took shape. Berenger de Palau, Bishop of Barcelona, was busily engaged in organizing it{167} throughout his diocese at the time of his death in 1241, and the vicar, who replaced him while the see was vacant, completed it. In 1242 Pedro Arbalate, who had succeeded Guillen Mongriu as archbishop, with the assistance of Raymond of Pennaforte, held the Council of Tarragona to settle the details of procedure. Under the guidance of so eminent a canonist, the code drawn up by the council showed a thorough knowledge of the principles guiding the Church in its dealings with heretics, and long continued to be referred to as an authority not only in Spain, but in France. At the same time its careful definitions, which render it especially interesting to us, indicate that it was prepared for the instruction of a Church which as yet practically knew nothing of the principles of persecution firmly established elsewhere. It was probably under the impulse derived from these movements that active persecution was resumed at Castelbo, which does not seem to have been purified by the raid of 1237. This time the heretics were not as patient as before, and resorted to poison, with which they succeeded in taking off Fray Ponce de Blanes, or de Espira, the inquisitor, who had made himself peculiarly obnoxious by his vigorous pursuit of heresy for several years. This aroused all the martial instincts of the retired archbishop, Guillen Mongriu, who assembled some troops, besieged and took the castle, burned many of the heretics, and imprisoned the rest for life. An organized effort was made to extend the Inquisition throughout the kingdom, and the parish priests were individually summoned to lend it all the aid in their power. Urgel seems to have been the headquarters of the sectaries, for subsequently we hear of their sharp persecution there by the Dominican inquisitor, Bernardo Travesser, and of his martyrdom by them. As usual, both he and Ponce de Blanes shone forth in miracles, and have remained an object of worship in the Church of Urgel, though in 1262 the latter was translated to Montpellier, where he lies magnificently entombed.[189]

Still, the progress of organization seems to have been exceedingly slow. In 1244 a case decided by Innocent IV. shows a complete absence of any effective system. The Bishop of Elne and a{168} Dominican friar, acting as inquisitors, had condemned Ramon de Malleolis and Helena his wife as heretics. By some means they succeeded in appealing to Gregory IX., who referred the matter to the Archdeacon of Besalu and the Sacristan of Girona. These acquitted the culprits and restored them to their possessions; but the case was carried back to Rome, and Innocent finally confirmed the first sentence of conviction. Again, in 1248, a letter from Innocent IV. to the Bishop of Lerida, instructing him as to the treatment in his diocese of heretics who voluntarily return to the Church, presupposes the absence of inquisitors and absolute ignorance as to the fundamental principles in force. The power conferred the same year on the Dominican Provincial of Spain to appoint inquisitors seems to have remained unused. The efforts of Archbishop Mongriu and Raymond of Pennaforte had spent themselves apparently without permanent results. King Jayme grew dissatisfied, and, in 1254, urgently demanded a fresh effort of Innocent IV. This time the pope concluded, at Jayme's suggestion, to place the matter entirely in Dominican hands; but so little had been done in the way of general organization that he confided the choice of inquisitors to the priors of Barcelona, Lerida, Perpignan, and Elne, each one to act within his own diocese, unless, indeed, there are inquisitors already in function under papal commissions—a clause which shows the confusion existing at the time. Innocent further felt it necessary to report this action to the Archbishops of Tarragona and Narbonne, and to call upon them to assist the new appointees. This device does not seem to have worked satisfactorily. At that time the whole peninsula constituted but one Dominican province, and, in 1262, Urban IV. again adopted definitely the plan, in general use elsewhere, of empowering the provincial to appoint the inquisitors—now limited to two. A few days before he had sent to those of Aragon a bull defining their powers and procedure, and a copy of this was enclosed to the provincial for his guidance. This long remained the basis of organization; but after the division of the province into two, by the General Chapter of Cologne in 1301, the Aragonese chafed under their subordination to the Provincial of Spain, whose territories consisted only of Castile, Leon, and Portugal. The struggle was protracted, but the Inquisition of Aragon at last achieved independence in 1351, when Fray Nicholas Roselli, the Provincial of{169} Aragon, obtained from Clement VI. the power of appointing and removing the inquisitors of the kingdom.[190]

Meanwhile the inquisitors had not been inactive. Fray Pedro de Cadreyta rendered himself especially conspicuous, and as usual Urgel is the prominent scene of activity. In conjunction with his colleague, Fray Pedro de Tonenes, and Arnaldo, Bishop of Barcelona, he rendered final judgment, January 11, 1257, against the memory of Ramon, Count of Urgel, as a relapsed heretic who had abjured before the Bishop of Urgel, and whose bones were to be exhumed; but, with unusual lenity, the widow, Timborosa, and the son, Guillen, were admitted to reconciliation and not deprived of their estates. Twelve years later, in 1269, we find Cadreyta, together with another colleague, Fray Guillen de Colonico, and Abril, Bishop of Urgel, condemning the memory of Arnaldo, Vizconde de Castelbo, and of his daughter Ermessende, whom we know as the heretic wife of Roger Bernard the Great of Foix. They had both been dead more than thirty years, and her grandson, Roger Bernard III. of Foix, who had inherited the Vizcondado of Castelbo, was duly cited to defend his ancestors; but if he made the attempt, it was vain, and their bones were ordered to be exhumed. It is not likely that these sturdy champions of the faith confined their attention to the dead, though the only execution we happen to hear of at this period is that of Berenguer de Amoros, burned in 1263. That the living, indeed, were objects of fierce persecution is rendered more than probable by the martyrdom of Cadreyta, who was stoned to death by the exasperated populace of Urgel, and who thus furnished another saint for local cult.[191]

During the remainder of the century we hear little more of the Inquisition of Aragon, but the action of the Council of Tarragona, in 1291, would seem to show that it was neither active nor much respected. Otherwise the council would scarce have felt called upon to order the punishment of heretics who deny a future existence, and, further, that all detractors of the Catholic faith ought{170} to be punished as they deserve, to teach them reverence and fear. Still more significant is the injunction on parish priests to receive kindly and aid efficiently the beloved Dominican inquisitors, who are laboring for the extirpation of heresy.[192]

With the opening of the fourteenth century there would appear to be an increase of vigor. In 1302 Fray Bernardo celebrated several *autos de fé*, in which a number of heretics were abandoned to the secular arm. In 1304 Fray Domingo Peregrino had an *auto* in which we are told that those who were not burned were banished, with the assent of King Jayme II.—one of the rare instances of this punishment in the annals of the Inquisition. In 1314 Fray Bernardo Puigcercos was so fortunate as to discover a number of heretics, of whom he burned some and exiled others. To Juan de Longerio, in 1317, belongs the doubtful honor of condemning the works of Arnaldo de Vilanova. The names of Arnaldo Burguete, Guillen de Costa, and Leonardo de Puycerda have also reached us, as successful inquisitors, but their recorded labors were principally directed against the Spiritual Franciscans, and will be more particularly noted hereafter. The Aragonese seem not to have relished the methods of the Inquisition, for in 1325 the Cortes, with the assent of King Jayme II., prohibited for the future the use of the inquisitorial process and of torture, as violations of the Fueros. Whether or not this was intended to apply to the ecclesiastical as well as to the secular courts it is impossible now to tell, but, if it were, it had no permanent result, as we learn from the detailed instructions of Eymerich fifty years later. About the middle of the century, the merits of the Inquisitor Nicholas Roselli earned him the cardinalate. It is true that when the energetic action of the Inquisitor Jean Dumoulin, in 1344, drove the Waldenses from Toulouse to seek refuge beyond the Pyrenees, Clement VI. wrote earnestly to the kings and prelates of Aragon and Navarre to aid the Inquisition in destroying the fugitives, but there is no trace of any corresponding result.[193]

To Roselli, however, belongs the credit of raising a question{171} which inflamed to a white heat the traditional antagonism of the two great Mendicant Orders. It is worth brief attention as an illustration of the nicety to which doctrinal theology had attained under the combined influence of scholastic subtlety in raising questions, and inquisitorial enforcement of implicit obedience in the minutest articles of faith. In 1351 the Franciscan Guardian of Barcelona, in a public sermon, stated that the blood shed by Christ in the Passion lost its divinity, was sundered from the Logos, and remained on earth. The question was a novel one and a trifle difficult of demonstration, but its raising gave Roselli a chance to inflict a blow on the hated Franciscans, and he referred it to Rome. The answer met his most ardent anticipations. The Cardinal of Sabina, by order of Clement VI., wrote that the pope had heard the proposition with horror; he had convened an assembly of theologians in which he himself argued against it, when it was condemned, and the inquisitors everywhere were ordered to proceed against all audacious enough to uphold it. Roselli's triumph was complete, and the unfortunate guardian was obliged to retract his speculations in the pulpit where he had promulgated them. The Franciscans were restless under this rebuff, which they construed as directed against their Order. In spite of the papal decision the question remained an open one in the schools, where it was eagerly debated on both sides. The Franciscans argued, with provoking reasonableness, that the blood of Christ might well be believed to remain on earth, seeing that the foreskin severed in the Circumcision was preserved in the Lateran Church and reverenced as a relic under the very eyes of pope and cardinal, and that portions of the blood and water which flowed in the Crucifixion were exhibited to the faithful at Mantua, Bruges, and elsewhere. After the lapse of a century, the Franciscan, Jean Bretonelle, professor of theology in the University of Paris, in 1448 brought the matter before the faculty, stating that it was causing discussion at Rochelle and other places. A commission of theologians was appointed, which, after due debate, rendered a solemn decision that it was not repugnant to the faith to believe that the blood shed at the Passion remained on earth. Thus encouraged, the Franciscans grew bolder.

The Observantine Franciscan, Giacomo da Monteprandone, better known as della Marca, was one of the most prominent{172} ecclesiastics of the fifteenth century. His matchless eloquence, his rigid austerity, his superhuman vigor, and his unquenchable zeal for the extermination of heresy well earned the beatification conferred on him after death; and since 1417 he had been known as a hammer of heretics. He held a commission as universal inquisitor which clothed him with power throughout Christendom, and the heretics in every corner of Italy, in Bohemia, Hungary, Bosnia, and Dalmatia, had learned with cause to tremble at his name. It required no little nerve to assail such a man, and yet when, April 18, 1462, at Brescia, he publicly preached the forbidden doctrine, the Dominican Inquisitor, Giacomo da Brescia, lost no time in calling him to account. First a courteous note expressed disbelief in the report of the sermon and asked a disclaimer; but on the Observantine adhering to the doctrine, a formal summons followed, citing him to appear for trial on the next day. The two Orders had thus fairly locked horns. The Bishop of Brescia interfered and obtained a withdrawal of the summons, but the question had to be fought out before the pope. The bitterness of feeling may be judged by the complaint of the inquisitor that his opponent had so excited the people of Brescia against him and the Dominicans that but for prompt measures many of them would have been slain; while, from Milan to Verona, every Dominican pulpit resounded with denunciations of Giacomo della Marca as a heretic.

The politic Pius II. feared to quarrel with either Order, and had a tortuous path to tread. To the Dominicans he furnished an authenticated copy of the decision of Clement VI. To Giacomo della Marca he wrote that this had been done because he could not refuse it, and not to give it authority. It had not been issued by Clement, but only in his name, and the question was still an open one. Giacomo might rest in peace in the conviction that the pope had full confidence in his zeal and orthodoxy, and that his calumniators should be silenced. On May 31 he issued commands that all discussions of the question should cease, and that both sides should send their most learned brethren to an assembly which he would hold in September for exhaustive debate and final decision. This he hoped would put an end to the matter, while skilful postponement of the conference would allow it to die out; but he miscalculated the enmity of the rival Orders. The{173} quarrel raged more fiercely than ever. The Franciscans declared that the inquisitor who started it would be deprived of his office and mastership in theology. Pius thereupon soothed him by assuring him that he had only done his duty, and that he had nothing to fear.

The conference had become an inevitable evil, and Pius found himself obliged to allow it to meet in December, 1463. Each side selected three champions, and for three days, in the presence of the pope and sacred college, they argued the point with such ardent vehemence that, in spite of the bitter winter weather, they were bathed in sweat. Then others took part and the question was debated pro and con. The Franciscans put in evidence the blood of Christ exhibited for the veneration of the faithful in many shrines, and to the foreskin which was in the Lateran and also in the royal chapel of France. They also appealed to the cuttings of Christ's hair and beard, the parings of his nails, and all his excretions—did these remain on earth or were they divine and carried to heaven? To these arguments the Dominican reply is a curious exhibition of special pleading and sophistry; but as no one could allege a single text of Scripture bearing upon the question, neither side could claim the victory. The good Bishop of Brescia, who had at first played the part of peacemaker, consistently presented a written argument in which he proved that the pope ought not to settle the question because such a determination would, firstly, be doubtful; secondly, superfluous; and, thirdly, perilous. This wise utterance was probably inspired, for Pius reserved his decision, and, August 1, 1464, only eight days before his death, issued a bull in which he recited how the faithful had been scandalized by the quarrel between the two Orders, and, therefore, he forbade further discussion on the subject until the Holy See should finally decide it. The Dominicans were emphatically prohibited from denouncing the Franciscans as heretics on account of it, and any infraction of his commands was punishable by *ipso facto* excommunication supplemented with harsh imprisonment. He tells us himself that after the public discussion the cardinals debated the matter for several days. The majority inclined to the Dominicans and he agreed with them, but the preaching of the Franciscans was necessary for the crusade against the Turks which he proposed to lead in person, and it was impolitic{174} to offend them, so he postponed the decision. Mutterings of discussion, without open quarrel, have since then occasionally occurred between the Orders, but the popes have never seen fit to issue a definite decision on the subject, and the momentous question started by Roselli remains still unsettled—a pitfall for unwary feet.{194}

In 1356 Roselli was created Cardinal of S. Sisto, and was succeeded after a short interval by Nicolas Eymerich, the most noteworthy man of whom the Aragonese Inquisition can boast, although after more than thirty years of service he ended his days in disgrace and exile. Trained in varied learning, and incessant in industry, of his numerous works but one has had the honors of print—his "Directorium Inquisitorum," in which, for the first time, he systematized the procedure of his beloved institution, giving the principles and details which should guide the inquisitor in all his acts. The book remained an authority to the last, and formed the basis of almost all subsequent compilations. Eymerich's conception of the model inquisitor was lofty. He must be fully acquainted with all the intricacies of doctrine, and with all the aberrations of heresy—not only those which are current among the common people, but the recondite speculations of the schools, Averrhoism and Aristotelian errors, and the beliefs of Saracen and Tartar. At a time when the Inquisition was declining and falling into contempt, he boldly insisted on its most extreme prerogatives as an imprescriptible privilege. If he assumed that the heretic had but one right—that of choosing between submission and the stake—he was in this but the conscientious exponent of his age, and his writings are instinct with the conviction that the work of the inquisitor is the salvation of souls.

From Eymerich's lament over the difficulty of providing for the expenses of an institution so necessary to the Church, it is evident that the kings of Aragon had not felt it their duty to support the Holy Office, while the bishops, he tells us, were as firm as their brethren in other lands in evading the responsibility{175} which by right was incumbent on them. The confiscations, he adds, amounted to little or nothing, for heretics were poor folk—Waldenses, Fraticelli, and the like. In fact, so far as we can gather, the sum of Eymerich's activity during his long career is so small that it shows how little was left of heresy by this time. Occasional Fraticelli and Waldenses and renegade Jews or Saracens were all that rewarded the inquisitor, with every now and then some harmless lunatic whose extravagance unfortunately took a religious turn, or some over-subtle speculator on the intricacies of dogmatic theology. Thus, early in his career, about 1360, Eymerich had the satisfaction of burning as a relapsed heretic a certain Nicholas of Calabria, who persisted in asserting that his teacher, Martin Gonsalvo of Cuenca, was the Son of God, who would live forever, would convert the world, and at the Day of Judgment would pray for all the dead and liberate them from hell. In 1371 he had the further gratification of silencing, by a decision of Gregory XI., a Franciscan, Pedro Bonageta. The exact relation between the physical matter of the consecrated host and the body of Christ under certain circumstances had long been a source of disputation in the Church, and Fray Pedro taught that if it fell into the mud or other unclean place, or if it were gnawed by a mouse, the body of Christ flew to heaven and the wafer became simple bread; and so also when it was ground under the teeth of the recipient, before he swallowed it. Gregory did not venture to pronounce this heretical, but he forbade its public enunciation. About the same time Eymerich had a good deal of trouble with Fray Ramon de Tarraga, a Jew turned Dominican, whose numerous philosophical writings savored of heresy. After he had been kept in prison for a couple of years, Gregory ordered him to have a speedy trial, and threatened Eymerich with punishment for contumacy if his commands were disobeyed. Ramon must have had powerful friends in the Order whom Eymerich feared to provoke, for six months later Gregory wrote again, saying that if Ramon could not be punished according to the law in Aragon, he must be sent to the papal court under good guard with all the papers of the process duly sealed. In fact, the Inquisition was not established for the trial of Dominicans. At the same time another Jew, Astruchio de Piera, held by Eymerich on an accusation of sorcery and the invocation of demons, was claimed as justiciable{176} by the civil power, and was sequestrated until Gregory ordered his delivery to the inquisitor, who forced him to abjure and imprisoned him for life. Somewhat earlier was a certain Bartolo Janevisio, of Majorca, who indulged in some apocalyptic writing about Antichrist, and was forced, in 1361, by Eymerich to recant, while his book was publicly burned. More practical, from a political point of view, was Eymerich's doctrine that all who lent assistance to the Saracens were punishable by the Inquisition as fautors of heresy, but this seems to have remained a theoretical assertion which brought no business to the Holy Office. We shall see hereafter how he fared in seeking the condemnation of Raymond Lulli's writings, and need only say here that the result was his suspension from office, to be succeeded by his capital enemy Bernardo Ermengaudi, in 1386, and that after the succession to the throne, in 1387, of Juan I., who was bitterly hostile to him, he was twice proscribed and exiled, and was denounced by the king as an obstinate fool, an enemy of the faith inspired by Satan, anointed with the poison of infidelity, together with other unflattering qualifications. He did not succeed better when in his rash zeal he assailed the holy San Vicente Ferrer for saying in a sermon that Judas Iscariot had a true and salutary repentance; that, being unable to reach Christ and obtain forgiveness owing to the crowd, he hanged himself and was pardoned in heaven. When the case was drawing to a conclusion, Pedro de Luna, then Cardinal of Aragon, took Vicente under his protection and made him his confessor, and, after his election in 1394 as Avignonese pope, under the name of Benedict XIII., he forced Eymerich to surrender the papers, which he unceremoniously burned. The next inquisitor, Bernardo Puig, is said to have been earnest and successful, punishing many heretics and confuting many heresies. In Valencia, about 1390, there was a case in which Pedro de Ceplanes, priest of Cella, read in his church a formal declaration that there were three natures in Christ—divine, spiritual, and human. A merchant of the town loudly contradicted it, and a tumult arose. The inquisitor of Valencia promptly arrested the too ingenious theologian, who only escaped the stake by public recantation and condemnation to perpetual imprisonment; but he broke jail and fled to the Balearic Isles, interjecting an appeal to the Holy See.[195]{177}

The creation, in 1262, of the kingdom of Majorca, comprising the Balearic Isles, Rosellon, and Cerdaña, by Jayme I. of Aragon, for the benefit of his younger son Jayme, seemed to render a separate inquisition requisite for the new realm. At what time it was established is uncertain, the earliest inquisitor of Majorca on record being Fr. Ramon Durfort, whose name occurs as a witness on a charter of 1332, and he continued to occupy the position until 1343, when he was elected Provincial of Toulouse. From that time, at least, there is a succession of inquisitors, and the forcible reunion in 1348, by Pedro IV., of the outlying provinces to the crown of Aragon did not effect a consolidation of the tribunals. As the Inquisition declined in dignity and importance, indeed, it seems to have sought a remedy in multiplying and localizing its offices. In 1413 Benedict XIII. (who was still recognized as pope in Aragon) made a further division by separating the counties of Rosellon and Cerdaña from the Balearic Isles, Fray Bernardo Pages retaining the former, and Guillen Sagarra obtaining the latter. Both of these were energetic men who celebrated a number of *autos de fé*, in which numerous heretics were reconciled or burned. Sagarra was succeeded by Bernardo Moyl, and the latter by Antonio Murta, who was confirmed in 1420, when Martin V. approved of the changes made. At the same time Martin, at the request of the king and of the consuls of Valencia, erected that province also into a separate Inquisition. The Provincial of Aragon appointed Fray Andrea Ros to fill the position; he was confirmed in 1433 by Eugenius IV., but was removed without cause assigned the next year by the same pope, although we are told that he inflexibly persecuted the "Bohemians" or "Wickliffites" with fire and sword. His successors, Domingo Corts and Antonio de Cremona, earned equal laurels in suppressing Waldenses.[196]

A case occurring in 1423 would seem to indicate that the Inquisition had lost much of the terror which had rendered it formidable.{178} Fray Pedro Salazo, Inquisitor of Rosellon and Cerdaña, threw in prison on charges of heresy a hermit named Pedro Freserii, who enjoyed great reputation for sanctity among the people. The accused declared that the witnesses were personal enemies, and that he was ready to purge himself before a proper judge, and his friends lodged an appeal with Martin V. The pope referred the matter, with power to decide without appeal, to Bernardo, Abbot of the Benedictine Monastery of Arles, in the diocese of Elne. Bernardo deputed the case to a canon of the church of Elne, who acquitted the accused without awaiting the result of another appeal to the pope interjected by the inquisitor; and Martin finally sent the matter to the Ordinary of Narbonne, with power to summon all parties before him and decide the case definitely. The whole transaction shows a singular want of respect for the functions of the Inquisition.[197]

Even more significant is a complaint made in 1456 to Calixtus III. by Fray Mateo de Rapica, a later inquisitor of Rosellon and Cerdaña. Certain neophytes, or converted Jews, persisted in Judaic practices, such as eating meat in Lent and forcing their Christian servants to do likewise. When Fray Mateo and Juan, Bishop of Elne, prosecuted them, they were so far from submitting that they published a defamatory libel upon the inquisitor, and, with the aid of certain laymen, afflicted him with injuries and expenses. Finding himself powerless, he appealed to the pope, who ordered the Archbishop and Official of Narbonne to intervene and decide the matter. The same spirit, in even a more aggravated form, was exhibited in a case already referred to, when, in 1458, Fray Miguel, the Inquisitor of Aragon, was maltreated and thrown in prison for nine months by some nobles and high officials of the kingdom, whom he had offended in obeying the instructions sent to him by Nicholas V.[198]

Yet, as against the poor and friendless, the Inquisition retained its power. Wickliffitism—as it had become the fashion to designate Waldensianism—had continued to spread, and about 1440 numbers of its sectaries were discovered, of whom some were reconciled, and more were burned as obstinate heretics by Miguel Ferriz,{179} Inquisitor of Aragon, and Martin Trilles of Valencia. Possibly among these was an unfortunate woman, Leonor, wife of Doctor Jayme de Liminanna, of whom, about this time, we hear that she refused to perform the penance assigned to her by the Inquisition of Cartagena, and that she was consequently abandoned to the secular arm. The post of inquisitor continued to be sought for. To multiply it, Catalonia was separated from Aragon by Nicholas V. shortly after his accession in 1447. In 1459 another division took place, the diocese of Barcelona being erected into an independent tribunal by Martiale Auribelli, Dominican General Master, for the benefit of Fray Juan Conde, counsellor and confessor of the infant Carlos, Prince of Viane. The new incumbent, however, had not a peaceful time. It was probably the Inquisitor of Catalonia, objecting to the fractioning of his district, who obtained from Pius II., in 1461, a brief annulling the division, on the ground that one inquisitor had always sufficed. Fray Juan resisted and incurred excommunication, but the influence of his royal patron was sufficient to obtain from Pius, October 13, 1461, another bull restoring him to his position and absolving him from the excommunication. In 1479 a squabble occurring at Valencia shows that the office possessed attractions worth contending for. The Provincial of Aragon had removed Fray Jayme Borell and appointed Juan Marquez in his stead. Borell carried the tale of his woes to Sixtus IV., who commanded the General Master to replace him and retain him in peaceful possession.[199]

Ferdinand the Catholic succeeded to the throne of Aragon in 1479, as he had already done, in 1474, to that of Castile by right of his wife Isabella. Even before the organizing of the new Inquisition in Aragon, in 1483, it is probable that the influence of Ferdinand had done much to restore the power of the institution. In 1482, on the eve of the change, we find the Inquisition of Aragon acting with renewed vigor and boldness, under the Dominican, Juan de Epila. A number of cases are recorded of this period, including the prosecution of the father and mother of Felipe de Clemente, Prothonotary of the kingdom. As a preparatory step to placing the dominions of the crown of Aragon under Torquemada{180} as Inquisitor-general, it was requisite to get rid of Cristobal Gualvez, who had been Inquisitor of Valencia since 1452, and who had disgraced his office by his crimes. Sixtus IV. had a special enmity to him, and, in ordering his deposition, stigmatized him as an impudent and impious man, whose unexampled excesses were worthy of severe chastisement; and when Sixtus, in 1483, extended Torquemada's authority over the whole of Spain, with power to nominate deputies, he excepted "that son of iniquity, Cristobal Gualvez," who had been interdicted from the office in consequence of his demerits, and whom he even deprived of the function of preaching.[200]

The great kingdom of Castile and Leon, embracing the major portion of the Spanish peninsula, never enjoyed the blessing of the mediæval Inquisition. It was more independent of Rome than any other monarchy of the period. Lordly prelates, turbulent nobles, and cities jealous of their liberties allowed scant opportunity for the centralization of power in the crown. The people were rude and uncultured, and not much given to vain theological speculation. Their superfluous energy, moreover, found ample occupation in the task of winning back the land from the Saracen. The large population of Jews and of conquered Moors gave them peculiar problems to deal with which would have been complicated rather than solved by the methods of the Inquisition, until the union of Aragon and Castile under Ferdinand and Isabella, followed by the conquest of Granada, enabled those monarchs to undertake seriously the business, attractive both to statecraft and to fanaticism, of compelling uniformity of faith.

It is true that the Dominican legend relates how Dominic returned from Rome to Spain as Inquisitor-general, on the errand of establishing there the Inquisition for the purpose of punishing the renegade converted Jews and Moors; how he was warmly seconded by San Fernando III.; how he organized the Inquisition throughout the land, celebrating himself the first *auto de fé* at{181} Burgos, where three hundred apostates were burned, and the second *auto* in the presence of the saintly king, who himself carried on his shoulders fagots for the burning of his subjects, and the pertinacious wretches defiantly rejoiced in the flames which were consuming them; how, after this, he established the Inquisition in Aragon, whence he journeyed to Paris and organized it throughout France; how, in 1220, he sent Conrad of Marburg as inquisitor to Germany, and in 1221 finished his labors by founding it in all the parts of Italy. All this can rank in historical value with the veracious statement of an old chronicler—a compatriot of the Pied Piper of Hamelin—that St. Boniface was an inquisitor, and that, with the support of Pepin le Bref, he burned many heretics. Detailed lists, moreover, are given of the successive inquisitors-general of the Peninsula—Frailes Suero Gomes, B. Gil, Pedro de Huesca, Arnaldo Segarra, Garcia de Valcos, etc., but these are simply the Dominican provincials of Spain, who were empowered by the popes to appoint inquisitors, and whose exercise of that power did not extend beyond Aragon. Even Paramo, although he tries to prove that there were inquisitors nominally in Castile, is forced to admit that practically there was no Inquisition there.[201]

Yet, even in the distant city of Leon, Catharism had obtained a foothold. Bishop Rodrigo, who died in 1232, expelled a number of Cathari, on his attention being called to them by their circulating a story to excite hatred of the priesthood, relating how a poor woman placed a candle on the altar in honor of the Virgin, and on her leaving it a priest took it for his own use. The following night the Virgin appeared to her votary and cast burning wax into her eyes, saying, "Take the wages of your service. As soon as you went away a priest carried off the candle; as you would have been rewarded had the candle been consumed on my altar, so you must bear the punishment, since your carelessness gave me the light only for a moment." This diabolical story, says Lucas of Tuy, an eye-witness, so affected the minds of the simple that the devotion of offering candles ceased, and it required two genuine miracles to restore the faith of the people. During the interval{182} between the death of Bishop Rodrigo, in March, 1232, and the election of his successor, Arnaldo, in August, 1234, the heretics had ample opportunity to work their wicked will. A Catharan named Arnaldo had been burned, about 1218, in a place in the suburbs used for depositing filth. There was a spring there which the heretics colored red, and proclaimed that it had miraculously been turned to blood. Many of them, simulating blindness, lameness, and demoniacal possession, were carried there and pretended to be cured, after which they dug up the heretic's bones and declared them to be those of a holy martyr. The people were fired with enthusiasm, erected a chapel,

61

and worshipped the relics with the utmost ardor. In vain the clergy and the friars endeavored to stem the tide; the people denounced them as heretics, and despised the excommunication with which the neighboring bishops visited the adoration of the new saint; while the real heretics made many converts by secretly relating how the affair had been managed, and pointing it out as a sample of the manufacture of saints and miracles. God visited the sacrilege with a drouth of ten months, which was not broken until Lucas, at the risk of his life, destroyed the heretic chapel; and when the rains came there was a revulsion of feeling which enabled him to expel the heretics. All this would seem to indicate that the heretics were numerous and organized; it certainly shows that there was no machinery for their suppression; but after the elevation of Lucas to the see of Tuy, in 1239, we hear no more of heretics or of persecutions. The whole affair, apparently, was a sporadic manifestation, probably of some band of fugitives from Languedoc, who disappeared and left no following.[202]

If what Lucas tells us be true, that ecclesiastics frequently joined in and enjoyed the ridicule with which heretics derided the sacraments and the clergy, the Spanish Church was not likely to give much aid to the introduction of the Inquisition. How little its methods were understood appears in the fact that when, in 1236, San Fernando III. found some heretics at Palencia, he proceeded to brand them in the face, which brought them to reason and led them to seek absolution. No one seemed to know{183} what to do with them, so Gregory IX. was applied to, and he authorized the Bishop of Palencia to reconcile them. There is probably no truth in the statement of some historians that the king, on several occasions, was obliged to levy from his subjects a tribute of wood with which to burn the unrepentant, and the story only serves to show how utterly vague have been the current conceptions of the period.[203]

We reach firmer ground with the codes known as El Fuero Real and Las Siete Partidas, the first issued by Alonso the Wise, in 1255, and the second about ten years later. By this time the Inquisition was at its height. It was thoroughly organized, and wherever it existed the business of suppressing heresy was exclusively in its hands. Yet not only does Alonso take no count of it, but in his regulation by secular law of the relations between the heretic and the Church he shows how completely, up to this period, Spain had remained outside of the great movements of the twelfth and thirteenth centuries. Heresy, it is true, is one of the matters pertaining to the ecclesiastical tribunals, and any one can accuse a heretic before his bishop or vicar. If the accused is found not to believe as the Church teaches, effort is to be made to convert him, and if he returns to the faith he is to be pardoned. If he proves obstinate, he is to be handed over to the secular judge. Then, however, his fate is decided without reference to the laws which the Church had endeavored to introduce throughout Christendom. If the culprit had received the *consolamentum*, or is a believer observing the rites, or one of those who deny the future life, he is to be burned; but if a believer not observing the rites, he is to be banished or imprisoned until he returns to the faith. Any one learning heresy, but not yet a believer, is fined ten pounds of gold to the fisc, or, if unable to pay, to receive fifty lashes in public. In the case of those who die in heresy or are executed, their estates pass to Catholic descendants, or, in default of these, to the next of kin; if without such kindred, the property of laymen goes to the fisc, of ecclesiastics, to the Church, if claimed within a year, after which it inures to the fisc. Children disinherited for heresy recover their portions, but not the{184} mesne profits, on recantation. No one, after condemnation for heresy, can hold office, inherit property, make a will, execute a sale, or give testimony. The house where a wandering heretic missionary is sheltered is forfeited to the Church, if inhabited by the owner; if rented, the offending tenant is fined ten pounds of gold or publicly scourged. A *rico home* or noble sheltering heretics in his lands or castles, and persisting after a year's excommunication, forfeits the land or castle to the king; and if a non-noble his body and property are at the king's pleasure. The Christian who turns Jew or Moslem is legally a heretic, and is to be burned, as well as one who brings up a child in the forbidden faith. Prosecutions of the dead, however, are humanely limited to five years after decease.[204]

All this shows that Alonso and his counsellors recognized the duty of the State to preserve the purity of the faith, but that they considered it wholly an affair of the State, in which the Church had no voice beyond ascertaining the guilt of the accused. All the voluminous and minute legislation of Gregory IX., Innocent IV., and Alexander IV. was wholly disregarded—the canon law had no currency in Castile, which regulated such matters to suit its own needs. That in this respect the popular needs were met is shown by the Ordenamiento de Alcalà, issued in 1348, which is silent on the subject of heresy. Apparently no change was deemed necessary in the provisions of the Partidas, which were then for the first time confirmed by the popular assembly. Under such legislation it follows as a matter of course that the Dominican provincial had no inquisitors to appoint, except in Aragon, under the bull of Urban IV. in 1262.

Castile continued unvexed by the Inquisition, and persecution for heresy was almost unknown. In 1316 Bernard Gui, of Toulouse, discovered in his district some of the dreaded sectaries known as Dolcinists or Pseudo-Apostoli, who fled to Spain to escape his energetic pursuit. May 1, 1316, he wrote to all the prelates and friars of Spain describing their characteristics and urging their apprehension and punishment. Had there been an Inquisition there he would have addressed himself to it. From remote Compostella{185} he received an answer, written by Archbishop Rodrigo, March 6, 1317, announcing that five persons answering to the description had been captured there and were held in chains, and asking for instructions as to the mode of trying them and the punishment to be inflicted in case they are found guilty, "for all this is heretofore unaccustomed in our parts." Evidently there was no Inquisition in Castile and Leon to which to apply, and even the provisions of the

Partidas were unknown, though of all places in the kingdom Compostella must have been the one most familiar with the outer world and with heretics, from the stream of penitents continually sent thither as pilgrims.[205]

In 1401 Boniface IX. made a demonstration by appointing the provincial, Vicente de Lisboa, inquisitor over all Spain, directing that his expenses should be paid by the bishops, and that no superior of his Order could remove him. The only heresy specifically alluded to in the bull is the idolatrous worship of plants, trees, stones, and altars—apparently superstitious relics of paganism which indicate the condition of religion and culture in the Peninsula. Boniface's action could hardly have been taken with any expectation of result, as Spain rendered obedience to Benedict XIII., the Antipope of Avignon, and it was probably only a move in the political game of the Great Schism. Whatever the motive, however, the effort was fruitless, for Fray Vicente was already dead in the odor of sanctity at the date of the bull. On learning this, Boniface returned to the charge, February 1, 1402, by empowering forever thereafter the Dominican Provincial of Spain to appoint and remove inquisitors, or to act as such himself, with all the privileges and powers accorded to the office by the canons. Inoperative as this remained, it at least had the advantage of supplying to the Spanish historians an unbroken line of inquisitors-general to be catalogued. About the same time King Henry III. increased the penalties of heresy by decreeing confiscation to the royal treasury of one-half of the possessions of heretics condemned by the ecclesiastical judges.[206]{186}

This, perhaps, technically justifies Alonso Tostado, Bishop of Avila, who soon afterwards alludes to inquisitors in Spain investigating those defamed for heresy, and it explains the remarks of Sixtus IV. when, in January, 1482, he confirmed the two inquisitors appointed at Seville by Ferdinand and Isabella at the commencement of their reforms, and forbade their naming more, for the reason that the appointees of the Dominican provincial were sufficient. In spite of all this, the Spanish Inquisition was simply potential, not existent. When, in 1453, Alonso de Almarzo, Abbot of the great Benedictine foundation of Antealtares of Compostella, with his accomplices, was tried for selling throughout Spain and Portugal indulgences warranted to release the souls of the damned from hell, for counterfeiting the papal Agnus Dei, for forging and altering papal letters, and for persuading Jewish converts to apostatize, had there been an Inquisition it would promptly have taken cognizance of the culprits; but in place of this the case was referred to Nicolas V., who instructed the Bishop of Tarazona to proceed against them. A few years later Alonso de Espina, about 1460, sorrowfully admits the absence of all persecution of heresy. Bishops and inquisitors and preachers ought all to resist the heretics, but there is no one to do it. "No one investigates the errors of heretics. The ravening wolves, O Lord, have gained admittance to thy flock, for the shepherds are few. There are many hirelings, and because they are hirelings they care only for shearing, not for feeding the sheep!" and he draws a deplorable picture of the Spanish Church, distracted with heretics, Jews, and Saracens. Soon after this, in 1464, the Cortes assembled at Medina turned its attention to the subject and complained of the great number of "*malos cristianos e sospechosos en la fe*," but the national aversion to the papal Inquisition still manifested itself, and its introduction was not suggested. The archbishops and bishops were requested to set on foot a rigid investigation after heretics, and King Henry IV. was asked to lend them aid, so that every suspected place might be thoroughly searched, and offenders brought to light, imprisoned, and punished. It was represented to the king that this would be to his advantage, as the confiscations would inure to the royal treasury, and he graciously expressed his assent; but the effort was resultless.[207]{187}

For the most part the orthodoxy of Spain had been vexed only with a few Fraticelli and Waldenses, not numerous enough to call for active repression. The main trouble lay in the multitudes of Jews and Moors who, under the law, were entitled to toleration, but whom popular fanaticism had forced to conversion in great numbers, and whose purity of faith was justly liable to suspicion. Hereafter I hope to have the opportunity of showing that from both the religious and the political standpoint of the age the measures taken by Ferdinand and Isabella were by no means without justification, however mistaken they were both in morals and in policy, and however unfortunate in their ultimate results. At present it suffices to point out this condition of affairs to explain the dissatisfaction which was widely prevalent and the demand for an efficient remedy.

At the same time even Spain was not wholly unmoved by the spirit of unrest and inquiry which marked the second half of the fifteenth century, sapping the foundations of tradition and rejecting the claims of sacerdotalism. About 1460 we learn from Alonso de Espina that many were beginning to deny the efficacy of oral confession, and this point could not have been reached without calling in question many other doctrines and observances which the Church taught to be necessary to salvation. At length these innovators grew so bold that Pedro de Osma, a professor in the great University of Salamanca, ventured to promulgate their obnoxious opinions in print. Oral confession, he asserted, was of human, not of divine precept, and was unnecessary for the forgiveness of sins; no papal indulgence could insure the living from the fires of purgatory; the papacy could err, and had no power to dispense with the statutes of the Church. Had there been any machinery of persecution at hand, short work would have been made with so bold a heretic, but the authorities were so much at a loss what to do with him that they applied to Sixtus IV., who sent a commission to Alonso Carrillo, Archbishop of Toledo, the dignitary next in rank to the king, to try him. In 1479 a council was assembled for the purpose at Alcalà, consisting of fifty-two of the best theologians in Spain, besides a number of canon lawyers.{188} Pedro was summoned to appear, and on his failing to do so his doctrine was condemned as heretical, and he was sentenced—not to the stake for contumacy, but to recant publicly in the pulpit. He submitted and did so, and we are told in the official report of the proceedings that all the faithful burst into tears at this signal manifestation of the conquering hand of God. Pedro died peacefully in the bosom of the Church during the next year, 1480, and Sixtus IV., in confirming the action of the council, ordered the archbishop to prosecute as heretics any of his followers who would not imitate his obedience.[208]

Evidently some more efficient and less cumbrous method was requisite if the population of reunited Spain was to enjoy the blessing of uniformity in faith. It did not take long for the piety of Isabella and the policy of Ferdinand to discover appropriate means.

In Portugal, Affonso II., at the commencement of his reign, in 1211, had manifested his zeal by inducing his Cortes to adopt severe laws for the repression of heresy; but when Sueiro Gomes, the first Dominican Provincial of Spain, endeavored to introduce in his kingdom inquisitors of the order, Affonso refused to admit them, and successfully insisted that heretics should be tried as heretofore by the ordinary episcopal courts. This rebuff sufficed for nearly a century and a half, and there must have been considerable freedom of thought, for, about 1325, Alvaro Pelayo gives a long list of the errors publicly defended in the schools of Lisbon by Thomas Scotus, a renegade friar. Their nature may be appreciated from his Averrhoistic assertion that there had been three deceivers—Moses who deceived the Jews, Christ the Christians, and Mahomet the Saracens. He seems to have enjoyed immunity until he declared that St. Antony of Padua kept concubines, when the Franciscan prior had him incarcerated, and his trial followed. At last, by a bull, dated January 17, 1376, Gregory XI. authorized Agapito Colonna, Bishop of Lisbon, to appoint, for this time only, a Franciscan inquisitor, as heresies were known to be spreading,{189} and there were no inquisitors in the kingdom. The nominee was to receive an annual salary of two hundred gold florins assessed upon all the dioceses in the proportion of their contributions to the apostolic chamber. Under this authority Agapito appointed the first Portuguese inquisitor, Martino Vasquez. From what we have seen elsewhere we may reasonably doubt his success in collecting his stipend; but, small as his receipts may have been, they were the equivalent of his service, for no trace of any labors performed by him remains.[209]

The Great Schism commenced in 1378, and as Portugal acknowledged Urban VI. while Spain adhered to the antipope Clement VII., the Dominican province of Spain divided itself, the Portuguese choosing a vicar-general, and finally a provincial, Gonçalo, in 1418, when Martin V. legalized the separation. This perhaps explains why Martino Vasquez was succeeded by another Franciscan. In 1394 Rodrigo de Cintra, calling himself Inquisitor of Portugal and Algarve, applied to Boniface IX. for confirmation, which was graciously accorded to him. Apparently the revenues of the office were nil, for the privilege was granted to him of residing with one associate at will in any Franciscan convent, which was bound to minister to his necessities, the same as to any other master of theology. Rodrigo was preacher to King João I., who requested this favor of Boniface, and his career, like that of his predecessor, is a blank. He was followed by a Dominican, Vicente de Lisboa, who had been Provincial of Spain at the time of the disruption, when he returned to Portugal and became confessor of Dom João. The king, in 1399, requested of Boniface his appointment as inquisitor, which was duly granted; and, as we have seen, in 1401, the pope endeavored to extend his jurisdiction over Castile and Leon. No trace of his inquisitorial activity exists. After his death, in 1401, there appears to have been an interval. The office apparently was regarded as a perquisite of the royal chapel for those who would condescend to accept it. The next appointment of which we hear is that of another confessor of Dom João, in 1413, this time a Franciscan, Affonso de Alprão, of whose doings no record has been preserved. When,{190} in 1418, the kingdom was reorganized as an independent Dominican province, the earnest annalists of the Inquisition assume that under the bull of Boniface IX., in 1402, each successive provincial was likewise an inquisitor-general, and the lists of these worthies are laboriously paraded as such, until the founding of the New Inquisition in 1531. No acts of theirs in such capacity, however, are recorded. The Holy Office continued dormant, without even a titular official, until, in the early years of the sixteenth century, Dom Manoel, stimulated by the example of his Castilian neighbors, and feeling solicitude as to the status of the New Christians, or converts from Judaism and Islam, bethought him of its revival. Although he had the Dominican provincial at hand, no purpose of utilizing him in this manner seems to have been entertained. The king applied to the pope and obtained the appointment of a Franciscan, Henrique de Coimbra, but there is no trace of his activity.[210]

The New Inquisition of Spain was a model which the smaller kingdom would naturally be expected to adopt, and in fact, to ardent Catholics, there might well seem to be a necessity for such an institution in view of the problems arising from the large influx of New Christians flying from Spanish persecution. Dom Manoel, indeed, at one time entertained so seriously the idea of establishing the Spanish Inquisition in his dominions that, in 1515, he ordered his ambassador at Rome, D. Miguel da Silva, to obtain from Leo X. the same privileges as those which had been conceded to Castile, but from some cause the project was abandoned. His son, Dom João III., who succeeded him in 1521, was a weak-minded fanatic, and it is only singular that the introduction of the Inquisition on the Spanish model was delayed for still ten years. The struggle which took place over the measure belongs, however, to a period beyond our present limits.[211]{191}

CHAPTER IV.

ITALY.

64

IN France we have seen the stubbornness of heresy in alliance with feudalism resisting the encroachments of monarchy. In Italy we meet with different and more complicated conditions, which gave additional stimulus to antagonism against the established Church, and rendered its suppression a work of much greater detail. Here heresy and politics are so inextricably intermingled that at times differentiation becomes virtually impossible, and the fate of heretics depends more on political vicissitudes than even on the zeal of men like St. Peter Martyr, or Rainerio Saccone.

For centuries the normal condition of Italy was not far removed from anarchy. Spasmodic attempts of the empire to make good its traditional claim to overlordship were met by the steady policy of the papacy to extend its temporal power over the Peninsula. During the century occupied by the reigns of the Hohenstaufens (1152-1254), when the empire seemed nearest to accomplishing its ends, the popes sought to erect a rampart by stimulating the attempts of the cities to establish their independence and form self-governing republics, and it thus created for itself a party in all of them. North of the Patrimony of St. Peter the soil of Italy thus became fractioned into petty states under institutions more or less democratic. For the most part they were torn with savage internal feuds between factions which, as Guelf or Ghibelline, hoisted the banner of pope or kaiser as an excuse for tearing each other to pieces. As a rule, they were involved in constant war with each other. Occasionally, indeed, some overmastering necessity might bring about a temporary union, as when the Lombard League, in 1177, broke the Barbarossa's power on the field of Legnano, but, in general, the chronicles of that dismal period are a confused mass of murderous strife inside and outside the gates of every town. {192}

Heresy could scarce ask conditions more favorable for its spread. The Church, worldly to the core, was immersed in temporal cares and pleasures, and during the strife between Alexander III. and the four antipopes successively set up by Frederic I.—Victor, Pascal, Calixtus, and Innocent—the enforcement of orthodoxy was out of the question. After the triumph of the papacy, stringent decrees, as we have seen, were issued by Lucius III., and edicts were promulgated by Henry VI. in 1194, and by Otho IV. in 1210, but they were practically inefficient. When every town was divided against itself heresy could bargain for toleration by holding the balance of power, and was frequently able, by throwing its weight on one side or the other, to obtain a share in the government. The larger struggles of city against city and of pope against emperor afforded a still wider field for the exercise of this diplomatic ability, of which full advantage was taken. When the formulas of persecution became defined under Honorius III., Gregory IX., and Frederic II., and fautorship was made equivalent to heresy, the factions and the nobles who tolerated or protected heretics became involved in the common anathema, and whole communities were stigmatized as given over to false idols. Yet although Ghibelline and heretic were frequently held by the popes to be almost convertible terms, there was in reality no test capable of universal application. Traditional hostility to the empire rendered Milan an intensely Guelf community, and yet it was everywhere recognized as the greatest centre of heresy.

Though heresy was by no means so universal as the papal anathemas would indicate, yet heretics were quite numerous enough to possess political importance, and to have some justification for their hopes of eventually becoming dominant. Little concealment was deemed necessary. When Otho IV. was in Rome for his coronation in 1209, under the vigilant rule of Innocent III., the ecclesiastics who accompanied him were scandalized at finding schools where Manichæan doctrines were openly taught, apparently without interference. The earlier Dominican persecutors are represented as constantly holding public disputations with heretics in the most populous cities of Italy, and the miracles related of them were mostly occasioned by the taunts and challenges of heretics. Otho, at Ferrara, in 1210, was obliged to order the magistrates to put to the ban the Cathari who refused, at the {193} instance of the bishop, to return to the Church, and also those who publicly supported them.[212]

Although Stephen of Bourbon relates that a converted heretic informed him that in Milan there were no less than seventeen heterodox sects which bitterly disputed with each other, yet they can, as in France, be reduced to two main classes—Cathari, or Patarins, and Waldenses. The Cathari, it will be remembered, made their appearance in the first half of the eleventh century, at Monforte, in Lombardy, and they had continued to multiply since then. About the middle of the thirteenth century Rainerio Saccone gives us an enumeration of their churches. In Lombardy and the Marches there were about five hundred perfected Cathari of the Albanensian sect, more than fifteen hundred Concorrezenses, and about two hundred Bajolenses. The Church of Vicenza reckoned about a hundred; there were as many in Florence and Spoleto, and in addition about one hundred and fifty refugees from France in Lombardy. As he estimates the total number, from Constantinople to the Pyrenees, at four thousand, with a countless congregation of believers, it will be seen that nearly two thirds of the whole number were concentrated in northern Italy, chiefly in Lombardy, and that they constituted a notable portion of the population.[213]

Lombardy, in fact, was the centre whence Catharism was propagated throughout Europe. We have seen above how for more than half a century it served as a refuge to the persecuted saints of Languedoc, and as a source whence to draw missionaries and teachers. About 1240 a certain Yvo of Narbonne was falsely accused of heresy and fled to Italy, where he was received as a martyr, and had full opportunity of penetrating into the secrets of the sectaries. In a letter to Géraud, Archbishop of Bordeaux, he describes their thorough organization throughout Italy, with ramifications extending into all the neighboring lands. From all the cities of Lombardy and Tuscany their youth were sent to Paris to perfect themselves in logic and theology, so as to be able

65

successfully to defend their errors. Catharan merchants{194} frequented fairs and obtained entrance into houses where they lost no opportunity of scattering the seed of false doctrine. Full of zeal and courage, the Catharan believed his faith to be the religion of the future, and his ardor courted martyrdom in the effort to spread it everywhere. Milan was the headquarters whither every year delegates were sent from the churches throughout Christendom, bringing contributions for the support of the central organization, and receiving instructions as to the symbol, changed every twelvemonth, whereby the wandering Patarin could recognize the houses of his brethren and safely claim hospitality. It was in vain that, in 1212, Innocent III. warned the heretical city of the fate of Languedoc, and threatened to send a similar crusade for its extirpation. Fortunately for the Lombards he had no one to summon to their destruction, for Germany, however desirous of conquering Italy, was too distracted for such an enterprise, and the popes dreaded imperial domination quite as much as heresy. There was bitter irony in the reply of Frederic II., when, in 1236, he was subduing the rebellious Lombards, and he answered the clamor of Gregory IX., who called upon him to transfer his arms to Syria, by pointing out that the Milanese were much worse than Saracens, and their subjugation much more important.[214]

We have no means of obtaining an approximate estimate of the Waldenses, but in some districts they must have been almost as numerous as the Cathari. The remains of the Arnaldistæ and Umiliati had eagerly welcomed the missionaries of the Poor Men of Lyons, and had not only adopted their tenets, but had pushed them to a further development in antagonism to Rome. As early as 1206 we see Innocent III. alluding to Umiliati and Poor Men of Lyons as synonymous expressions, and endeavoring with little success to effect their expulsion from Faenza, where they were spreading and infecting the people. In Milan they had built a school where they publicly taught their doctrines; this was at length torn down by a zealous archbishop, and when, in 1209, Durán de Huesca sought to bring them back to the fold, a hundred or more of them consented to be reconciled if the building{195} were restored to them. Evidently they had little to dread from active persecution, and subsequent letters of Innocent show them to be still flourishing there. The Waldenses who were burned at Strassburg in 1212 admitted that their chief resided in Milan, and that they were in the habit of collecting money and remitting it to him.[215]

It was, however, in the valleys of the Cottian Alps, to which they spread from Dauphiné, that they settled themselves most firmly. In those inhospitable regions, till then almost uninhabited, their marvellous and self-denying industry occupied every spot where incessant labor could support life. There they rapidly increased and filled the valleys of Luserna, Angrogna, San Martino, and Perosa. In 1210 Giacomo di Carisio, Bishop of Turin, alarmed at the constant growth of this heresy in his diocese, applied to Otho IV. for aid in its suppression, but the emperor in reply merely ordered him to use severity in their punishment and expulsion. Authority for this he already had in abundance under the canons, but he lacked the physical force to render it effective, and the imperial rescript went for naught. This shows that the local suzerains took no measures to enforce persecution, and the heretics continued to increase. The immediate sovereign of the district most deeply infected was the Abbey of Ripaille, which found itself unable to control them, and made over its temporal rights to Tommaso I., Count of Savoy. He issued an edict, to which I have already referred, imposing a fine of ten sols for giving refuge to heretics, which proved altogether ineffective. Thus, in the absence of efficient repression, were established those Alpine communities whose tenacity of belief supplied through centuries an unfailing succession of humble martyrs, and who ennobled human nature by their marvellous example of constancy and endurance.[216]{196}

Although the Lombard Waldenses admitted their descent from the Poor Men of Lyons, their more rapid development gave rise to differences, and in 1218 a conference was held at Bergamo between delegates of both parties. This did not succeed in removing the points of dissidence, and about 1230 the Lombards sent to the brethren in Germany a statement of the discussion and of their views. It is not our province to enter into these minute details of faith and Church government, but the affair is worth alluding to as illustrating the flourishing condition of the Church, the practical toleration which it enjoyed, and the active communication which existed between its organizations throughout Europe.[217]

The aggressiveness of the heretics, the favor shown them by the people, and the impossibility of any systematic suppression by the Church under existing political conditions are well exhibited in the troubles which commenced at Piacenza in 1204. There the heretics were strong enough to provoke a quarrel between the authorities and Bishop Grimerio, which resulted in either the withdrawal or the expulsion of the prelate and all the clergy. The exiles transferred themselves to Cremona, but in 1205 that city likewise quarrelled with its pastors, and the wanderers were again driven forth, to find a refuge in Castell'' Arquato. For three years and a half Piacenza remained without an orthodox priest, and deprived of all the observances and consolations of religion. So weak was the hold of the Church upon the people that this deprivation was acquiesced in with the utmost indifference. In October, 1206, Innocent III. sent three Apostolic Visitors to effect a reconciliation, with a threat of dividing the diocese and apportioning it among the neighboring sees, but the citizens cared nothing for this, and refused the terms demanded, which required them to compensate their bishop for the damage inflicted on him. After some six months wasted in fruitless negotiations the Visitors departed, and it was not till July, 1207, that another commission, offering more favorable conditions, succeeded in effecting a reconciliation{197} which enabled the clergy to return from exile. About the same period Innocent found himself obliged to use persuasion and argument in the endeavor to urge the people of Treviso to expel their heretics. So far from threatening them, he begged them to have faith that their bishop would reform the excesses of the clergy whose evil example had disturbed them. It is easy thus to understand the exulting confidence with which the heretics anticipated the eventual triumph of their creeds, and the despair which led Abbot Joachim of Flora, in expounding the Apocalypse, to see in them the locusts with the power of scorpions who issue from the bottomless pit at the sounding of the fifth trumpet (Rev. IX. 3, 4). These heretics are the Antichrist; they are to grow in power and their king is already chosen, that king of the locusts "whose name in the Hebrew tongue is Abaddon, but in the Greek tongue hath his name Apollyon" (Rev. IX. 11). Resistance to them will be in vain; they are to unite with the Saracens, with whom, in 1195, he says they are already entering into negotiations.[218]

When Honorius III., in 1220, obtained from Frederic II. the ferocious coronation-edict against heresy, he may well have imagined that the way was open for its immediate suppression. If so, he was not long in discovering his mistake. Whatever professions Frederic might make, or whatever rigor he might exercise in his Sicilian dominions, it was no part of his policy to estrange the Ghibelline leaders, or to strengthen the Guelfic factions in the turbulent little republics which he sought to reduce to subjection. His whole reign was an internecine conflict, open or concealed, with Rome, and he was too much of a free-thinker to have any scruples as to the sources whence he could draw strength for himself or annoyance for his enemy. In central and upper Italy, therefore, his laws were for the most part virtually a dead letter. Already, in 1221, Ezzelin da Romano, the most powerful Ghibelline in the March of Treviso, was complained of for the protection which he afforded to heretics, and his continuing to do so to the end shows that he found it to be good policy. When, in 1227,{198} Ingheramo da Macerata, the late podestà of Rimini, was persecuted by the citizens because he had delivered for burning as heretics some of their daughters and sisters, and because he had wished to inscribe on their statute-books the constitutions of Frederic, it was not to the emperor that he applied for protection, but to Honorius III.[219]

Something more than imperial edicts was plainly necessary, and Honorius, in casting around for methods to check the spread of heresy, appointed, in 1224, the Bishops of Brescia and Modena as commissioners with special powers to exterminate the heretics of Lombardy—as inquisitors, in fact, this being one of the steps which gradually led to the establishment of the Inquisition, the usefulness of the Dominicans in this respect not having yet been divined. The Bishop of Modena, however, undertook a mission to convert the pagans of Prussia, and the Bishop of Rimini was substituted in his place. The prelates commenced with Brescia itself, whose prelate doubtless knew where to strike. They ordered the tearing down of certain houses where heretical preachers had been accustomed to hold forth. At once an armed insurrection broke out. The perennial factions of the city took sides. Several churches were burned, and the heretics parodied from them the anathema by casting lighted torches from the windows, and solemnly excommunicating all members of the Church of Rome. It was not until after a severe and prolonged conflict that the Catholics obtained the upper hand, and then the terms prescribed by Honorius were so mild as to indicate that it was not deemed politic to drive the defeated party to despair. All excommunicates were required to apply personally for absolution to the Holy See. The fortified houses of the lords of Gambara, of Ugona, of the Oriani, of the sons of Botatio, who had been the leader in the troubles, were ordered to be razed to the ground, never to be rebuilt, while other strongholds, which had been defended against the Catholics, were to be cut down one-third or one-half. Benificed clerks who were children of heretics or of fautors were to be suspended for three years or more as their individual participation in the troubles might indicate. A levy of three hundred and thirty lire was ordered on the clergy of Lombardy and the Trivigiana{199} to recompense the Catholics for the losses endured in contending with the heretics. So unaccustomed as yet were the Lombards to persecution that even these conditions were deemed too harsh. The city of Milan interceded, and finally even the authorities of Brescia itself urged that moderation would be conducive to peace; and, May 1, 1226, Honorius authorized the bishops to use their discretion in diminishing the penalties. When, however, the Dominican Guala was elected Bishop of Brescia in 1230, he speedily succeeded in introducing in the local statutes the law of Frederic, of March, 1224, which decreed for heretics the stake or loss of the tongue, and he forced the podestà to swear to its execution.[220]

Gregory IX. was a man of sterner temper than Honorius, and, despite his octogenary age, his advent to the pontificate, in 1227, was the signal for unrelenting war on heresy. Within three weeks of his accession peace was signed, under the auspices of the papacy, between Frederic II. and the Lombard League, with provisions for the suppression of heresy. Gregory immediately, in the most imperious fashion, summoned the Lombards to perform their duty. Hitherto, he told them, all their pretended efforts had been fraudulent. No enforcement of the imperial constitutions had been attempted. If the heretics had at any time been driven away, it was with a secret understanding that they would be allowed to return and dwell in peace. If fines had been inflicted, the money had been covertly refunded. If statutes had been enacted, there was always a reservation by which they were rendered ineffective. Thus heresy had grown and strengthened while the liberties of the Church had been subverted. Heretics had been permitted to preach their doctrines publicly, while ecclesiastics had been outlawed and imprisoned. All this must cease, the provisions of the treaty of peace must be enforced, and, if they continued in their evil courses, the Holy See would find means to coerce them in their perversity.[221]

These were brave words, though the political condition of Lombardy rendered them ineffective. Nearer home, however, Gregory had fairer opportunity of enforcing his will, and we have{200} already seen how promptly he recognized the utility of the Order of Dominic and laid the foundations of the Inquisition by his tentative action in Florence. While this was taking shape his zeal was stimulated by the discovery, in 1231, that in Rome itself heresy had become so bold that it ventured to assert itself openly, and that many priests and other ecclesiastics had been converted. Probably the first *auto de fé* on record was that held by the Senator Annibaldo at the portal of Santa Maria Maggiore, when these unfortunates were burned or condemned to perpetual prison, and Gregory took advantage of the occasion to issue the decretal which became the basis of inquisitorial procedure, and to procure the enactment of severe secular laws in the name of the senator. The details I have already given (Vol. I. p. 325), and they need not be repeated here; but Gregory did not content himself with what he thus accomplished in Rome. His aid just then was desirable to Frederic II. in his Lombard complications, and to Gregory's urgency may doubtless be attributed the severe legislation of the Sicilian Constitutions, issued about this time, and the Ravenna decrees of 1232. Shortly afterwards, indeed, we find Frederic writing to him that they are like father and son; that they should sharpen the spiritual and temporal swords respectively committed to them against heretics and rebels, without wasting effort on sophistry, for if time be spent in disputation nature will succumb to disease. It is not probable that Gregory counted much on the zeal of the emperor, but he sent the edict of Annibaldo to Milan, with instructions that it be adopted and enforced there. Already, in 1228, his legate, Goffredo, Cardinal of San Marco, had obtained of the Milanese the enactment of a law by which the houses of heretics were to be destroyed, and the secular authorities were required to put to death within ten days all who were condemned by the Church; but thus far no executions seem to have taken place under it.{222}

It was now that Gregory, seeing the futility of all efforts thus far save those which the Dominicans were making in Florence,{201} hit upon the final and successful experiment of confiding to the Order the suppression of heresy as part of their regular duties. A fresh impulse was felt all along the line. The Church suddenly found that it could count upon an unexpected reserve of enthusiasm, boundless and exhaustless, despising danger and reckless of consequences, which in the end could hardly fail to triumph. A new class of men now appears upon the scene—San Piero Martire, Giovanni da Vicenza, Rolando da Cremona, Rainerio Saccone—worthy to rank with their brethren in Languedoc, who devoted themselves to what they held to be their duty with a singleness of purpose which must command respect, however repulsive their labors may seem to us. On one hand these men had an easier task than their Western colleagues, for they had not to contend with the jealousy, or submit to the control, of the bishops. The independence of the Italian episcopate had been broken down in the eleventh century. Besides, the bishops naturally belonged to the Guelfic faction, and welcomed any allies who promised to aid them in crushing the antagonistic party in their turbulent cities. On the other hand, the political dissensions which raged everywhere with savage ferocity increased enormously the difficulties and dangers of the task.

In Italy, as in France, the organization of the Inquisition was gradual. It advanced step by step, the earlier proceedings, as we have seen both in Florence and Toulouse, being characterized by little regularity. As the tribunal by degrees assumed shape, a definite code of procedure was established which was virtually the same everywhere, except with regard to the power of confiscation, the application of the profits of persecution, and the acquittal of the innocent. To these attention has already been called, and they need not detain us further. The problems which the founders of the Inquisition had to meet in Italy, and the methods in which these were met, can best be illustrated by a rapid glance at what remains to us of the careers of some of the earnest men who undertook the apparently hopeless task.

The earliest name I have met with bearing the title of Inquisitor of Lombardy is that of a Frà Alberico in 1232. The Cardinal Legate Goffredo, whom we have seen busy in Milan, undertook to quiet civil strife in Bergamo, with the consent of all factions, by appointing as podestà Pier Torriani of Milan; and at the same{202} time he seized the opportunity to make a raid on heretics, a number of whom he cast into prison. No sooner was his back turned than the citizens refused to receive his podestà, elected in his place a certain R. di Madello, and, what was worse, set at liberty the captive heretics. Thereupon the legate placed the city under interdict, which brought the people to their senses, and they agreed to stand to the mandate of the Church. Gregory accordingly, November 3, 1232, instructed Alberico, as Inquisitor of Lombardy, to reconcile the city on condition that the people refund to Pier Torriani all his expenses and give sufficient security to exterminate heresy. Here we see how intimate were the relations between politics and heresy, and what difficulties the alliance threw in the way of persecution.{223}

Frà Rolando da Cremona we have already met as professor in the inchoate University of Toulouse, and we have seen how rigid and unbending was his zeal. Hardly had he quitted Langueduc when we find him, in 1233, already actively at work in the congenial duty of suppressing heresy at Piacenza. The twenty-five years which had elapsed since the Piacenzans had shown themselves so indifferent to their spiritual privileges had not greatly increased their respect for orthodoxy. Rolando assembled them, preached to them, and then ordered the podestà to expel the heretics. The result did not correspond to his expectations. With the connivance of the podestà, the heretics and their friends arose and made a general onslaught on the clergy, including the bishop and the friars, in which a monk of San Sabino was slain and Rolando and some of his comrades were wounded.

The Dominicans carried Rolando half-dead from the city, which was placed under interdict by the bishop. Then a revulsion of feeling occurred; Rolando was asked to return, and full satisfaction was promised. He prudently kept away, but ordered the imprisonment of the podestà and twenty-four others till the pleasure of the pope should be known. Gregory took advantage of the opportunity by sending thither the Archdeacon of Novara, with instructions to place the city under control of the orthodox party, taking ample security that the heretics should be suppressed; but this arrangement did not please the citizens, who rose again and liberated the {203} prisoners. Sharp as was this experience, it did not dull the edge of Rolando's zeal, for the next year we find him at work in the Milanese, where he received rough treatment at the hands of Lantelmo, a noble who sheltered heretics in his castle near Lodi. For this Lantelmo was condemned to be led through the streets, stripped and with a halter around his neck, to Rolando's presence, and there to accept such penance as the friar, at command of the pope, might enjoin on him. A month later we hear of his seizing two Florentine merchants, Feriabente and Capso, with all their goods. They evidently were persons of importance, for Gregory ordered their release in view of having received bail for them in the enormous sum of two thousand silver marks.[224]

During this transition period, while the Inquisition was slowly taking shape, one of the most notable of the Dominicans engaged in the work of persecution was Giovanni Schio da Vicenza. I have alluded in a previous chapter to his marvellous career as a pacificator, and it may perhaps not be unjust to assume that his motive in employing his unequalled eloquence in harmonizing discordant factions was not only the Christian desire for peace, but also to remove the obstruction to persecution caused by perpetual strife, for in almost all these movements we may trace the connection between heresy and politics. After his wonderful success at Bologna, Gregory urged him to undertake a similar mission to Florence, where constant civic war was accompanied by recrudescence of heresy. In spite of the efforts of the embryonic Inquisition there, heresy was undisguised, and the ministers of Christ were openly opposed and ridiculed. Gregory assumed that Giovanni acted under the direct inspiration of the Holy Ghost, and did not venture to send him orders, but only requests. He was, like all his colleagues, popularly regarded as a thaumaturgist, and {204} stories were told of his crossing rivers dry-shod, and causing vultures to descend from on high at his simple command. The Bolognese were so loath to part with him that they used gentle violence to retain him, and only let him go after Gregory had ordered their city laid under interdict, and had threatened to deprive of its episcopal dignity any place which should detain him against his will. After completely succeeding in his mission to Florence he was despatched on a similar one to Lombardy. The League, which had been so efficient an instrument in curbing the imperial power, was breaking up. Fears were entertained that Frederic would soon return from Germany with an army, and a portion of the Lombard cities and nobles were disposed to invite him. Some countervailing influence was required, and nothing more effective than Giovanni's eloquence could be resorted to. At Padua, Treviso, Conigliano, Ceneda, Oderzo, Belluno, and Feltre he preached on the text "Blessed are the feet of the bearers of peace" with such effect that even the terrible Ezzelin da Romano is said to have twice burst into tears. The whole land was pacified, save the ancestral quarrel between Ezzelin and the counts of Campo San Piero, which unpardonable wrongs had rendered implacable. After a visit to Mantua, the apostle of peace went to Verona, then besieged by an army of Mantuans, Bolognese, Brescians, and Faenzans, where he persuaded the assailants to withdraw, and the Veronese, in gratitude, proclaimed him podestà by acclamation. He promptly made use of the position to burn in the market-place some sixty heretics of both sexes, belonging to the noblest families of the city. Then he summoned to a great assembly in a plain hard by all the confederate cities and nobles. Obedient to his call there came the Patriarch of Aquileia, the Bishops of Mantua, Brescia, Bologna, Modena, Reggio, Treviso, Vicenza, Padua, and Ceneda, Ezzelin da Romano, the Marquis of Este, who was Lord of Mantua, the Count of San Bonifacio, who ruled Ferrara, and delegates from all the cities, with their carrochi. The multitude was diversely estimated at from forty thousand to five hundred thousand souls, who were wrought by his eloquence to the utmost enthusiasm of mutual forgiveness. After denouncing as rebels and enemies of the Church all who adhered to Frederic or invited him to Italy, Giovanni induced his auditors to swear to accept such settlement of their quarrels as he should {205} dictate, and when he announced the terms they unanimously signed the treaty.[225]

So great became his reputation that Gregory IX. was seriously disturbed at a report that Giovanni contemplated making himself pope. A consistory was assembled to consider the advisability of excommunicating him, and that step would have been taken had not the Bishop of Modena sworn upon a missal that he had once seen an angel descend from heaven while Giovanni was speaking, and place a golden cross upon his brow. A confidential mission was sent to Bologna to investigate his career there, which returned with authentic accounts of numberless miracles performed by him, among them no less than ten resuscitations of the dead. So holy a man could not well be thrust from the pale of the Church, and the project was abandoned.[226]

Meanwhile he had visited his native place, Vicenza, on invitation of the bishop, and had so impressed the people that they gave him their statutes to revise at his pleasure, and proclaimed him duke, marquis, and count of the city—titles which belonged to the bishop, who also offered to make over the episcopate to him. As at Verona, he used his power to burn a number of heretics. During his absence at Verona, Uguccione Pileo, an enemy of the Schia family, induced the people to revolt, when Giovanni hastened back and suppressed the rebellion, putting to death, with torture, a number of citizens, who are charitably supposed to have been heretics. Uguccione brought up reinforcements; a fierce battle was fought in the streets, and Giovanni was worsted and taken prisoner. A letter of condolence, addressed to him in prison, by Gregory, under date of September 22, 1233, serves to fix the date of this, and to show how powerless was the papacy to protect its agents in the fierce dissensions of the period. Giovanni was obliged to ransom himself and return to Verona, and thence to Bologna. The peace which he had effected was of short duration. The chronic wars broke out afresh, and Giovanni, at the instance of Gregory, came again to pacify them. In this he succeeded, but no sooner was his back turned than hostilities were renewed.{206} Gregory made a third attempt, through the Bishops of Reggio and Treviso, who induced the warring factions to lay down their arms for a while; but the main object, of presenting a united front and keeping Frederic out of Italy, was lost, Ezzelin and a number of the cities urged his coming, and the decisive victory of Cortenuova, in November, 1237, dissolved the Lombard League which had so long held the empire in check, and made him master of Lombardy.[227]

During all this time Gregory had been untiring in his efforts to subdue heresy in Lombardy, undeterred by the disheartening lack of result. All his legates to that province were duly instructed to regard this as one of their chief duties. In May, 1236, he had even attempted to establish there a rudimentary Inquisition, but, in the existing condition of the land, even he could hardly have expected to accomplish anything. Frederic came with professions that the extirpation of heresy was one of the motives impelling him to the enterprise; and when Gregory reproached him with suppressing the preaching of the friars and thus favoring heresy, he astutely retorted, with a reference to Giovanni, by alluding to those who, under pretext of making war on heresy, were busy in establishing themselves as potentates, and were taking castles as security from those suspect in faith. Gregory, in reply, could only disclaim all responsibility for the acts of the adventurous friar. Yet Gregory himself, when it suited his Lombard policy, did not hesitate to relax his severity against the heretics, and it became a popular cry in Germany that he had been bribed with their gold.[228]

For some years Giovanni Schio led a comparatively quiet existence in Bologna, but in 1247, by which time the Inquisition was fairly taking shape, Innocent IV. appointed him perpetual inquisitor throughout Lombardy, arming him with full powers and releasing him from all subjection or accountability to the Dominican general or provincial. In the existing condition of the north of Italy the commission was virtually inoperative, and its only interest{207} lies in its terms, which show that up to this time there was no organized Inquisition there. We hear nothing further of his activity, even after the death of Frederic, in 1250, until, in 1256, the long-delayed crusade was undertaken against Ezzelin da Romano. By his fiery eloquence he raised in Bologna a considerable force of crusaders, at whose head he marched against the tyrant of the Trevisan, but, disgusted with the quarrels of the leaders, he returned to Bologna before the final catastrophe, and he is supposed to have perished, in 1265, in the crusade against Manfred, when there was a contingent of ten thousand Bolognese in the army of Charles of Anjou.[229]

Yet the most noteworthy in all respects of the dauntless zealots who fought the seemingly desperate battle against heresy was Piero da Verona, better known as St. Peter Martyr. Born at Verona in 1203 or 1206, of a heretic family, his legend relates that he was divinely led to recognize their errors. When a schoolboy of only seven years of age his uncle chanced to ask him what he learned, and he repeated the orthodox creed. His uncle thereupon told him he must not say that God created the heaven and the earth, for he was not the creator of the visible universe; but the child, filled with the Holy Ghost, overcame his elder in argument, who thereupon urged the parents to remove him from school, but the father, who hoped to see him become a leader of the sect, allowed him to complete his education. His orthodox zeal grew with his growth, and in 1221 he entered the Dominican Order. His confessor testified that he never committed a mortal sin, and the bull of his canonization bears emphatic evidence to his humility, his meek obedience, his sweet benignity, his exhaustless compassion, his unfailing patience, his wonderful charity, his passionate supplications to God for martyrdom, and the innumerable miracles which illustrated his life.[230]

Before the Dominicans were armed with the power of persecution Piero earnestly devoted himself to the original function of the Order, that of controverting heresy, and preaching against heretics. In this the success of the young apostle was marvellously aided by his thaumaturgic development. At Ravenna,{208} Mantua, Venice, Milan, and other places, numerous wonders are related of his performance. Thus, at Cesena, the success of his efforts at conversion irritated the heretics, who, on one occasion, interrupted his preaching in the public square by volleys of filth and stones discharged from a house near by. He several times mildly entreated them to desist, but in vain, when, inspired by divine wrath, he launched a terrible imprecation against them. Instantly the house crumbled in ruin, burying the sacrilegious wretches, nor could it be rebuilt until long afterwards.[231]

When the Dominicans were charged with the duty of persecution his earnest zeal naturally caused him to be selected as one of the earliest laborers. In 1233 he was sent to Milan, where, thus far, all the efforts of papal missives and legates had proved ineffectual to rouse the authorities and the citizens to undertake the holy work. The laws which, in 1228, Cardinal Goffredo had inscribed on the statute-book had remained a dead letter. All this was changed when Piero da Verona made his influence felt. Not only did he cause Gregory's legislation of 1231 to be adopted in the municipal law, but he stimulated the podestà, Oldrado da Tresseno, and the archbishop, Enrico da Settala, to work in earnest. A number of heretics were burned, who were probably the first victims of fanaticism which Milan had seen since the time of the Cathari of Monforte. So strong was the impression made by these executions that they earned for the podestà Oldrado the honor of an equestrian portrait in bas-relief, with the inscription, "*Qui solium struxit, Catharos ut debuit uxit,*" which is still to be seen adorning the wall of the Sala del Consiglio, now the Archivio pubblico. It fared worse with the archbishop, who was rendered so unpopular that he was banished, for which the magistracy was duly excommunicated; but he, too, had posthumous reward, for his tomb bore the legend *"instituto inquisitore jugulavit hæreses."* Piero likewise founded in Milan a company, or association, for the suppression of heresy, which was taken under immediate papal protection—the model of that which ten years later did such bloody work in Florence. We may safely assume that his fiery activity continued unabated, though we hear nothing of him until 1242, when we again find him in Milan so vigorously at work that{209}he is said to have caused a sedition which nearly ruined the city.[232]

Two years later we meet him fighting heresy in Florence. That city, it will be remembered, was the subject of the earliest inquisitorial experiments, Frà Giovanni di Salerno, Prior of Santa Maria Novella, having been commissioned to prosecute heretics in 1228, and being succeeded after his death, in 1230, by Frà Aldobrandini Cavalcante, and about 1241 by Frà Ruggieri Calcagni. The first two of these accomplished little, being, in fact, rather preachers than inquisitors. The heretics were protected by the Ghibelline faction and the partisans of Frederic II., and heresy, far from decreasing, spread rapidly in spite of occasional burnings. When the Catharan Bishop Paternon fled, his position was successively held by three others, Torsello, Brunnetto, and Giacopo da Montefiascone. Many of the most powerful families were heretics or open defenders of heresy—the Baroni, Pulci, Cipriani, Cavalcanti, Saraceni, and Malpresa. The Baroni built a stronghold at San Gaggio, beyond the walls, which served as a refuge for the Perfected, and there were plenty of houses in the town where they could hold their conventicles in safety. The Cipriani had two palaces, one at Mugnone and the other in Florence, where troops of Cathari assembled under the leadership of a heresiarch named Marchisiano, and there were great schools at Poggibonsi, Pian di Cascia, and Ponte a Sieve.[233]

The whole of central Italy, in fact, was almost as deeply infected with heresy as Lombardy, and little had as yet been done to purify it. That as late as 1235 no comprehensive attempt had been made to establish the Inquisition is shown by a papal brief addressed in that year to the Dominicans of Viterbo, empowering them, in all the dioceses of Tuscany, Viterbo, Orta, Balneoreggio, Castro, Soano, Amerino, and Narni, to absolve heretics not publicly defamed for heresy, who should spontaneously accuse themselves, provided the bishops assented and sufficient bail were given; and the bishops were ordered to co-operate. Heretics not thus voluntarily confessing were to be dealt with according to the papal statutes.{210} At Viterbo dwelt Giovanni da Benevento, who was called the pope of the heretics, but it was not until Gregory went thither in 1237 and undertook the task of purifying the place himself that any efficient action was taken; he condemned Giovanni and many other heretics, and ordered the palaces of some of the noblest families of the city to be torn down, as having afforded refuge to heretics. At the same time the Bishop of Padua was urged to persevere in the good work, and at Parma the Knights of Jesus Christ were instituted with the same object by Jordan, the Dominican general. All this indicates the commencement of systematic operations, and the pressure grew stronger year by year. Under the energetic management of Ruggieri Calcagni the Florentine Inquisition rapidly took shape and executions became frequent, while in the confessions of the accused allusions are made to heretics burned elsewhere, showing that persecution was becoming active wherever political conditions rendered it possible. Thus in a confession of 1244 there is a reference to two, Maffeo and Martello, burned not long before at Pisa.[234]

In Florence Frà Ruggieri's vigor was reducing the heretics to desperation. Each trial revealed fresh names, and as the circle spread the prosecutions became more numerous and terrible. The Signoria was coerced by papal letters to enforce the citations of the inquisitor, and as the prisoners multiplied and their depositions were taken, fully a third of the citizens, including many nobles, were found to be involved. Excited by the magnitude of the developments, Ruggieri determined to strike at the chiefs, and, invoking the aid of the Priors of the Arts, he seized a number of them and condemned to the stake those who proved contumacious. The time had evidently come when they must choose between open resistance and destruction. The Baroni assembled their followers, broke open the jails, and carried off the prisoners, who were distributed through various strongholds in the Florentine territory, where they continued to preach and spread their doctrines.

Matters were rapidly approaching a crisis. On the one hand it was impossible for so large a body as the heretics to permit themselves to be slaughtered in detail with impunity, to say nothing{211} of the spoliation and gratification of private feuds which could not fail to involve the innocent with the guilty in a persecution of such extent so recklessly pursued. On the other hand, the persecutors were maddened with excitement and with the prospects of at last triumphing over the adversaries who had so long defied them. Innocent IV. wrote pressingly to the Signoria commanding energetic support for the inquisitor, and he summoned from Lombardy Piero da Verona to lend his aid in the approaching struggle. Towards the end of 1244 Piero hastened to the conflict, and his eloquence drew such crowds that the Piazza di Santa Maria Novella had to be enlarged to accommodate the multitude. He utilized the enthusiasm by enrolling the orthodox nobles in a guard to protect the Dominicans, and formed a military order under the name of the Società de" Capitani di Santa Maria, uniformed in a white doublet with a red cross, and these led the organization known as the Compagnia della Fede, sworn to defend the Inquisition at all hazards, under privileges granted by the Holy See. Thus encouraged and supported, Ruggieri pushed forward the trials, and numbers of victims were burned. This was a challenge which the heretics could only decline under pain of annihilation. They likewise organized under the lead of the Baroni, and it was not difficult to persuade the podestà, Ser Pace di Pesannola of Bergamo, recently appointed by Frederic II., that the interest of his master required him to protect them. Thus the perennial quarrel between the Church and the empire filled the streets of Florence with bloodshed under the banners of orthodoxy and heterodoxy.

Ruggieri provoked the conflict without flinching. He cited the Baroni before him, and when they contemptuously refused to appear he procured a special mandate from Innocent IV. This they obeyed with the utmost docility, about August 1, 1245, swearing to stand to the mandates of the Church, and depositing one thousand lire as security; but when they understood that he was about to render sentence against them, they appealed to the podestà. Ser Pace thereupon sent his officers, August 12, to Ruggieri, ordering him to annul the proceedings as contrary to the mandate of the emperor, to return the money taken as bail, and, in case of contumacy, to appear the next day before the podestà under penalty of a thousand marks. Ruggieri's only notice of this was a {212} summons the next day to Ser Pace to appear before the Inquisition as suspect of heresy and fautorship, under pain of forfeiture of office. The fervid rhetoric of Frà Piero poured oil upon the flames, and the city found itself divided into two factions, not unequally matched and eager to fly at each other. Taking advantage of the assembling of the faithful in the churches on a feast-day, the podestà sounded the tocsin, and many unarmed Catholics are said to have been slaughtered before the altars. Then on St. Bartholomew's day (August 24) Ruggieri and Bishop Ardingho, in the Piazza di S. Maria Novella, publicly read a sentence condemning the Baroni, confiscating their possessions, and ordering their castles and palaces to be destroyed, which naturally led to a bloody collision between the factions. Piero then placed himself at the head of the Compagnia della Fede, carrying a standard like the other captains, among whom the de" Rossi were the most conspicuous. Under his leadership two murderous battles were fought, one at the Croce al Trebbio and the other in the Piazza di S. Felicità, in both of which the heretics were utterly routed. Monuments still mark the scene of these victories; and, until recent times, the banner which San Piero gave to the de" Rossi was still carried by the Compagnia di San Piero Martire on the celebration of his birthday, April 29, while the one which he bore himself is preserved among the relics of Santa Maria Novella and is publicly displayed on his feast-day.

Thus was destroyed in Florence the power of the heretics and of the Ghibellines. Ruggieri, for his steadfast courage, was rewarded, before the close of 1245, with the bishopric of Castro, and was succeeded as inquisitor by San Piero himself, whose indefatigable zeal allowed the heretics no rest. Many of them, recognizing the futility of further resistance, abandoned their errors; others fled, and when Piero left Florence he could boast that heresy was conquered and the Inquisition established on an impregnable basis; though Rainerio's estimate of the Florentine Cathari, some years later, shows that it still had an ample harvest to reward its labors.[235] {213}

While Ruggieri, in the summer of 1245, was precipitating the conflict in Florence, Innocent IV., in the Council of Lyons, was passing sentence of dethronement on Frederic II. and trying to find some aspirant hardy enough to accept the imperial crown. Frederic laughed the sentence to scorn and easily disposed of his would-be competitors, but he was obliged to struggle hard to maintain his Italian possessions, and his death, December 13, 1250, relieved the papacy from the most formidable antagonist which its ambitious designs had ever encountered. Skilled equally in the arts of war and peace, untiring in activity, dismayed by no reverses, intellectually far in advance of his age, and encumbered with few scruples, Frederic's brilliant abilities and indomitable courage had been the one obstacle in the papal path towards domination over Italy and the foundation on that basis of a universal theocratic monarchy. His son, Conrad IV., a youth of twenty-one, was scarce to be dreaded in comparison, though Innocent cautiously waited for a while in Lyons before venturing into Italy. After reaching Genoa, June 8, 1251, he addressed to Piero da Verona and Viviano da Bergamo a brief which shows that the intervening six months had not sufficed to dull the sense of rejoicing at the death of his great opponent, and that no more time was to be lost in taking full advantage of the opportunity. A dithyrambic burst of exultation is followed by the declaration that thanks to God for this inestimable mercy are to be rendered not so much in words as in deeds, and of these the most acceptable is the purification of the faith. Frederic's favor towards heretics had long impeded the operations of the Inquisition throughout Italy, and now that he is removed it is to be put into action everywhere with all possible vigor. Inquisitors are to be sent into all parts of Lombardy; Piero and Viviano are ordered to proceed forthwith to Cremona, armed with all necessary powers; rulers who do not zealously assist them will be coerced with the spiritual sword, and, if this proves insufficient, Christendom will be aroused to destroy them in a crusade. This bull was followed by a rapid succession of others addressed to the Dominican provincials and to potentates, ordering strenuous co-operation, and the {214} inscription in all local statutes of the constitutions of the dead emperor and of the popes—bulls issued in such haste that, June 13, 1252, the pope was obliged to explain that the blunders and omissions arising from the hurried work of the scribes are not to invalidate them. The whole was crowned, May 15, 1252, by the issue of the bull *Ad extirpanda*, of which I have given an abstract in a former chapter. This sought to render the civil power completely subservient to the Inquisition, and prescribed the extirpation of heresy as the chief duty of the State.[236]

Innocent's mandate probably found Piero at the convent of San Giovanni in Canali at Piacenza, of which he was prior in 1250, and where his austerities so impressed his brethren that they begged his friend, Matteo da Correggio, pretor of the city, to induce him to moderate them, lest the flesh which he so persistently macerated should give way under the ardent spirit within. If, in fact, we are to believe the statement that he habitually never

72

broke his fast before sunset, and that he passed most of the night in prayer, restricting his sleep to the least that was compatible with life, his career becomes easily intelligible. Deficiency of nourishment, replaced by unceasing and unnatural nervous exaltation, must have rendered him virtually an irresponsible being.[237]

We have no details of what he accomplished as inquisitor at Cremona, or at Milan to which he was afterwards transferred. It is presumable, however, that his relentless activity fully responded to the expectations of those who had selected him as the fittest instrument to take advantage, in the headquarters of heresy, of the unexpected opportunity to visit the now defenceless heretics with the wrath of God. Within nine months after he had been summoned to action he had already become such an object of terror that in despair a plot was laid for his assassination. The matter was intrusted to Stefano Confalioniero, a noble of Aliate, and the hire of the assassins, twenty-five lire, was furnished by Guidotto Sachella. The week before Easter (March 23-30), 1252, Stefano proposed the murder to Manfredo Clitoro of Giussano, who agreed to do it, and associated with him Carino da Balsamo. At the same time Giacopo della Chiusa undertook to go to Pavia{215} to slay Rainerio Saccone, and made the journey, but failed to accomplish his mission. The other conspirators were more successful. Frà Piero at that time was Prior of Como, and went thither to pass his Easter. He was obliged to return to Milan on Low Sunday, April 7, as on that day expired the term of fifteen days which he had assigned to a contumacious heretic. During Easter week Stefano, with Manfredo and Carino, went to Como and awaited Piero's departure. It shows the fearlessness and the austerity of the man that he set out on foot, April 7, though weakened with a quartain fever, and accompanied only by a single friar, Domenico. Manfredo and Carino followed them as far as Barlassina, and set upon them in a lonely spot. Carino acted as executioner, laying open Piero's head with a single blow, mortally wounding Domenico, and then, finding that Piero still breathed, plunging a dagger in his breast. Some passing travellers carried the body of the martyr to the convent of San Sempliciano, while Domenico was conveyed to Meda, where he died five days afterwards. As for the conspirators, I have already alluded to the strange delay which postponed for forty-three years the final sentence of Stefano Confalioniero, and to the repentance and beatification of Carino, who became St. Acerinus. Daniele da Giussano, another of the confederates, also repented and entered the Dominican Order. Giacopo della Chiusa seems to have escaped, and Manfredo and a certain Tommaso were captured and confessed. Manfredo admitted that he had been concerned in the murder of two other inquisitors, Frà Pier di Bracciano and Frà Catalano, both Franciscans, at Ombraida in Lombardy. He was simply ordered to present himself to the pope for judgment, but in place of obeying he very naturally fled, and there is no record of his subsequent fate. No one seems to have been put to death, and common report asserted that the assassins found a safe refuge among the Waldenses of the Alpine valleys, which is not improbable.[238]{216}

In fact, the Church made much shrewder use of the martyrdom than the exaction of vulgar vengeance. Its whole machinery was set to work at once to impress the populations with the sanctity of the martyr. Miracles multiplied around him. When the General Chapter of the Order assembled at Bologna in May, Innocent wrote to them in terms of the most extravagant hyperbole respecting him, and urged them to fresh exertions in the cause of Christ. By August 31, he ordered the commencement of proceedings of canonization, and before a year had elapsed, March 25, 1253, the bull of canonization was issued—I believe the most speedy creation of a saint on record. It would be difficult to exaggerate the cult which developed itself around the martyr. Before the century was out, Giacopo di Voragine compared his martyrdom with that of Christ, establishing many similitudes between them, and he assures us that the disappearance of heresy in the Milanese was owing to the merits of the saint—indeed, already, in the bull of canonization it is asserted that many heretics had been converted by his death and miracles. It is true that when, in 1291, Frà Tommaso d'Aversa, a Dominican of Naples, in a sermon on the feast of San Piero dared to compare his wounds with the stigmata of St. Francis—saying that the former were the signs of the living God and not of the dead, while the latter were those of the dead God and not of the living—it is true that the expression was thought to savor of blasphemy. The existing pope, Nicholas IV., chanced to be a Franciscan, so Tommaso was summoned before him, forced to confess, and was sent back to his provincial with orders to subject him to a punishment that would prevent a repetition of the sacrilege. Yet successive popes encouraged the cult of San Piero until Sixtus V., in 1586, designated him as the second head of the Inquisition after St. Dominic, and as its first martyr, and in 1588 granted plenary indulgence to all who should visit for devotion the Dominican churches on the days of St. Dominic, Peter Martyr, and Catharine of Siena. In the seventeenth century an enthusiastic Spaniard declared that he was crowned with three crowns, "*como Emperador de Martyres.*" In 1373, Gregory XI. granted permission to erect a small oratory on the spot of{217} the murder, which grew to be a magnificent church with a splendid convent, through the offerings of the innumerable pilgrims who flocked thither. The authenticity of the martyr's sanctity was proved when, in 1340, eighty-seven years after death, the body was translated to a tomb of marvellous workmanship, and was found in a perfect state of preservation; and when the sepulchre was opened in 1736 it was still found uncorrupted, with wounds corresponding exactly to those described in the annals.[239]

The enthusiasm excited by the career of San Piero was turned to practical account by the organization in most of the Italian cities of *Crocesegnati*, composed of the principal cavaliers, who swore to defend and assist the inquisitors at peril of their lives, and to devote person and property to the extermination of heretics, for which service they received plenary remission of all their sins. These associations were wont to assemble on the feast of San Piero in the Dominican churches, which were the seats of the Inquisition, and hold aloft their drawn swords during the reading of the Gospel, in testimony of their readiness to crush heresy with force. They continued to exist until the last century, and Frà Pier-Tommaso Campana, who was inquisitor at Crema, relates with pride how, in 1738, he presided over such a ceremony in Milan. The Crocesegnati, moreover, furnished material support to the inquisitors, {218} supplying them when necessary with both men and money for the performance of their functions. In fact, they were subject to excommunication if they refused to give money when called upon by the inquisitor. It can readily be conceived how greatly the effectiveness of the Inquisition was increased by such an organization.[240]

If the heretics had hoped to strike their persecutors with terror they were short-sighted. The fanaticism of the Order of Dominic furnished an unfailing supply of men eager for the crown of martyrdom and unsparing in their efforts to earn it. Hardly were the splendid obsequies of San Piero completed when his place was occupied by Guido da Sesto and Rainerio Saccone da Vicenza. The latter had been high in the Catharan Church, when, divinely illuminated as to his errors, he was converted and expiated his past life by entering the strict Dominican Order. It was possibly in his favor that in 1246 Innocent IV. authorized the Dominican prior at Milan to admit repentant heretics into the Order without requiring the year's novitiate that was imposed on Catholics. Thoroughly acquainted with all the secrets of heresy, he could render invaluable aid in persecuting his old associates, whom he pursued with all the ruthless bigotry of an apostate. He was speedily made an inquisitor, and earned an enviable reputation among the faithful by his vigor and success in exterminating heresy. The fact that, as we have seen, he was singled out with San Piero by the conspirators to be slain shows how thoroughly he had earned the hate of the persecuted. We know nothing of the details of the attempt upon his life save that Giacopo della Chiusa returned from Pavia with his errand unaccomplished. Rainerio was at once transferred to Milan as the man best fitted to replace the martyr, and he justified the selection by the unbending firmness with which he vindicated the authority of his office. It was still a novelty in Lombardy, and a man of his keen intelligence, strength of purpose, and self-devotion was required to organize it and establish it among a recalcitrant population.[241]{219}

Heretics, in fact, were more numerous than ever in Lombardy, for the active work carried on in Languedoc by Bernard de Caux and his colleagues had caused a wholesale emigration. Until the death of Frederic, Lombardy was regarded as a secure haven; colonies established themselves there, and even after the Lombard Inquisition was thoroughly organized the persecuted wretches continued for half a century to seek refuge there, nor do we often hear of their being detected.[242] All of Rainerio's resolution and energy were required for the work before him. In the March of Treviso, Ezzelin da Romano, whose influence extended far to the west, continued openly to protect heresy, and even in Lombardy the hopes excited by Frederic's death threatened to prove fallacious. In 1253, when Conrad IV. passed through Treviso to recover possession of his Sicilian kingdom, he appointed as his Lombard vicar-general Uberto Pallavicino, who soon became as obnoxious to the Church as Ezzelin himself; and, though Conrad died in 1254, and Innocent IV. seized Naples as a forfeited fief of the Church, Pallavicino's power continued to increase, and he soon established relations with Manfred, Frederic's illegitimate son, who wrested Naples from the papacy and became the chief of the Ghibelline faction. Even more threatening was the revulsion of feeling in Milan itself, when its ardent Guelfism was changed to indifference by Innocent's indiscreet assertion of certain ecclesiastical immunities which touched the pride of the citizens. The heads of the hydra might well seem indestructible.

One of Rainerio's first enterprises, in 1253, was summoning Egidio, Count of Cortenuova, before his tribunal, as a fautor and defender of heresy. The castle of Cortenuova, near Bergamo, had been razed as a nest of heretics, and its reconstruction prohibited, but the count had seized the castle of Mongano, which was claimed by the Bishop of Cremona, and had converted it into a den of heretics, who enjoyed immunity under his protection. He disdained to obey the citation and was duly excommunicated. He paid no attention to this, and on March 23, 1254, Innocent IV. ordered the authorities of Milan, under pain of ecclesiastical censures, to take the castle by force and deliver its inmates to the inquisitors for trial. The count, however, was in close alliance with {220} Pallavicino, "that enemy of God and the Church," and the Milanese appear to have had no appetite for the enterprise at the time. Mongano continued to be a place of refuge for the persecuted until 1269, when the Milanese were at last stimulated to undertake the siege, and on capturing it handed it over to the Dominicans.[243]

Better success awaited Rainerio's efforts with Roberto Patta da Giussano, a Milanese noble who for twenty years had been one of the most conspicuous defenders of heresy in Lombardy. At his castle of Gatta he publicly maintained heretic bishops, allowing them to build houses, and establish schools whence they spread their pernicious doctrines through the land. They had also there a cemetery where, among others, were buried their bishops, Nazario and Desiderio. The place was notorious, and it is related of San Piero-Martire, as an instance of his prophetic gifts, that once when passing it he had foretold its destruction and the exhumation of the heretic bones. Roberto had been cited by the archbishop and had abjured heresy, but no effective measures had been ventured upon to coerce him from his evil ways, and the heretics of Gatta had continued to enjoy his protection. It was otherwise when, in 1254, Rainerio and Guido summoned him again. On his failing to appear they summarily condemned him as a heretic, declared his property confiscated and his descendants subject to the usual disabilities. Roberto saw that the new officials were not to be trifled with. The prospects of the Ghibellines at the moment were apparently hopeless. He hastened to make his peace, binding himself to submit

74

to any terms which the pope might dictate; and Innocent doubtless deemed himself merciful when, August 19, 1254, he ordered the castle of Gatta and all the heretic houses to be destroyed by fire, the bones in the cemetery to be dug up and burned, and the count to perform such salutary penance as Rainerio might prescribe.[244]

The papal power was now at its height. Conrad IV. had died May 20, 1254, not without suspicion of poison; Innocent IV. had seized his Sicilian kingdoms, and for a brief space, until Manfred's romantic adventures and victory of Foggia, he might well imagine{221} himself on the eve of becoming the undisputed temporal as well as spiritual head of Italy. Every effort was made to perfect the Inquisition and to render it efficient both as a political instrument and as a means of bringing about the long-desired uniformity of belief. On March 8 Innocent had taken an important step in its organization by ordering the Franciscan Minister of Rome to appoint friars of his Order as inquisitors in all the provinces south of Lombardy. On May 20 he reissued his bull *Ad extirpanda*; on the 22d he sent the constitutions of Frederic II. to all the Italian rulers, with orders to incorporate them in the local statutes, and informed them that the Mendicants were instructed to coerce them in case of disobedience. On the 29th he proceeded to reorganize the Lombard Inquisition by instructing the provincial to appoint four inquisitors whose power should extend from Bologna and Ferrara to Genoa. Under this impulsion and the restless energy of Rainerio no time was lost in extending the institution in every direction save where Ghibelline potentates such as Ezzelin and Uberto prevented its introduction. We chance to have an illustration of the process in the records of the little republic of Asti, on the confines of Savoy. It is recited that in 1254 two inquisitors, Frà Giovanni da Torino and Frà Paulo da Milano, with their associates, appeared before the council of the republic and announced to them that the pope enjoined them to admit the Inquisition within their territories. Thereupon the Astigiani made answer that they were ready to obey the pontiff, but they had no laws providing for persecution and it would be necessary to frame one. Accordingly an *ordenamento* was drawn up prescribing obedience to the constitutions of Innocent IV. and Frederic II., and it was forthwith added to the local statutes. Similar action was doubtless taking place in every quarter where the people had thus far remained in ignorance of the new doctrine that the suppression of heresy was the first duty of the government.[245]

The death of Innocent IV., December 7, 1254, whether it was the result of Dominican litanies or of mortification at Manfred's{222} success, made no difference in the energy with which the progress of the Inquisition was pushed. The accession of Alexander IV. was signalized by a succession of bulls repeating and enforcing the regulations of his predecessor, and urging prelates and inquisitors to increased activity. To overcome the resistance of such cities as were slack in the duty of capturing and delivering all who were designated for arrest by the inquisitors, the latter were empowered to punish such delinquency with the heavy fine of two hundred silver marks. Under this impulsion Rainerio assembled the people of Milan, August 1, 1255, in the Piazza del Duomo, read to them his commission, and gave them notice that, although he had hitherto acted with great mildness, the time had passed for trifling. Many citizens, he said, openly derided the Inquisition in the public streets; others caused scandal by opposing and molesting it. He therefore gave three formal warnings, attested by a notarial instrument duly witnessed, that all who should continue to indulge in detraction or should in any way impede the Inquisition were excommunicate as fautors of heresy, and would be prosecuted to such penalties as their audacity deserved.[246]

As the Inquisition warmed to its work, the four inquisitors provided for Lombardy by Innocent IV. proved insufficient, and, March 20, 1256, Alexander IV. ordered the provincial to increase the number to eight. He appears to have been somewhat dilatory in obedience, for in 1260 he was sharply reminded of the command and enjoined no longer to postpone its fulfilment. Possibly the delay may have arisen from the fact that in January, 1257, Rainerio had risen to the position of supreme inquisitor over the whole of Lombardy and the Marches of Genoa and Treviso, with power to appoint deputies. He thus was doubtless practically emancipated from the control of the provincial, and was able to supply any deficiency in the working force with those who were absolutely dependent upon himself. In March, 1256, the prelates had been required in the most urgent terms to render all aid and support to the inquisitors; and in January, 1257, this was emphasized by informing them that those who manifested neglect should not escape punishment, while those who showed themselves{223} zealous would find the Holy See benignant to them in their "opportunities." The significance of this is not to be mistaken, and it would be difficult to set limits to the power thus concentrated in the hands of the ex-Catharan.[247]

Territorially, however, his authority was circumscribed by the possessions of Uberto and Ezzelin, within which no inquisitor dared venture. In this very year, 1257, Piacenza, which had fallen under control of Uberto, was placed in such complete hostility to the Church that it was deprived of its episcopate, and its bishop, Alberto, was transferred to Ferrara. In Vicenza, which was ruled by Ezzelin, matters were even worse. There the heretics had a recognized chief named Piero Gallo, of the Borgo di San Piero, whose name was adopted by them as a rallying cry, to which the Catholics responded with "*viva Volpe!*"—a member of the family of Volpe being the leader of their faction; and so thoroughly did this become encrusted in the habits of the people that we are told in the seventeenth century that the cry of the citizens of the Borgo (then corruptly called Porsampiero) was still "*viva Gallo!*" while that of the dwellers in the Piazza and Porta Nuova was "*viva Volpe!*" Ezzelin would permit no persecution, and when the blessed Bortolamio di Breganze, one of the immediate disciples of St. Dominic, was made Bishop of Vicenza, in 1256, he was reduced to seeking conversions by persuasion. After preaching for a while with little effect he had a public discussion with Piero Gallo, and so impressed him by argument that the heretic was converted. We may reasonably doubt the assertion that Ezzelin's displeasure at this feat was the cause of Bortolamio's banishment from his see, but, whatever was the motive, he was consoled by Alexander IV., who sent him as nuncio to England. During his absence, in 1258, his archdeacon, Bernardo Nicelli, was bolder, and made a capture of importance in the person of the Catharan Bishop, Viviano Bogolo. He endeavored to convert his prisoner, but his powers of persuasion were insufficient, and Ezzelin interfered and set the heretic at liberty.[248]

So long as these Ghibelline chiefs retained power it was evident{224} that the foothold of heresy was secure, and that the hopes based on the death of Frederic II. were not destined to fruition. Every motive had long conspired to render the Church eager for the destruction of Ezzelin, who was its most dreaded antagonist, and every expedient had been tried to reduce him to subjection. As far back as 1221 Gregory IX., then legate in Lombardy, had extorted from him assurances of his hatred of heresy. In 1231 his sons, Ezzelin and Alberico, were at the papal court expressing horror at his crimes and promising to deliver him up for trial as a heretic if he would not reform, in order to escape the disinheritance which they would otherwise incur under Frederic's laws. They pledged themselves, moreover, to deliver to him letters from Gregory, dated September 1, in which he was bitterly reproached for his protection of heretics, and told that if he would humbly acknowledge his errors and expel all heretics from his lands he might come within two months to the Holy See, prepared to obey implicitly all commands laid upon him; otherwise heaven and earth would be invoked against him, his lands should be abandoned to seizure, and he, who was already a scandal and a horror to men, should become an eternal opprobrium.[249]

Whether the sons dutifully presented to their father this portentous epistle does not appear, nor is it of any importance save as showing how Ezzelin was already regarded as the mainstay of heresy, and how habitually zeal for the faith was made to cover the ambitious political designs of the Church. Ezzelin's courage never wavered, and his adventurous career was pursued with scarce a check. When Frederic II. overcame the resistance of Lombardy, he gave, in 1238, his natural daughter Selvaggia to Ezzelin in marriage and created him imperial vicar. The unanimous testimony of the ecclesiastical chroniclers represents him as a monster whose crimes almost transcend the capacity for evil of human nature, but the unrelieved blackness of the picture defeats the object of the painter. Possibly he may have been among the worst of the Italian despots of the time, when faithlessness and contempt for human suffering were the rule, but the long unbroken success which attended him shows that he must have had qualities which attached men to him, and the report that he was{225} twice moved to tears by the eloquence of Frà Giovanni Schio indicates a degree of sensibility impossible in one utterly depraved. In fact, the anecdote related by Benvenuto da Imola, that he carried on his back his sister's lover Sordello to and from the place of assignation, and then gave the frightened troubadour a friendly warning, presupposes a character wholly at variance with that currently attributed to him. Some of the stories circulated to excite odium against him are so absurdly exaggerated as to cast doubt upon all the accusations of the papalist writers.[250]

Gregory's letters of September 1, 1231, were simply a ruse. So far was he from awaiting the two months" delay for Ezzelin to present himself, that three days later, on September 4, he executed his threat by ordering the Bishops of Reggio, Modena, Brescia, and Mantua to offer Ezzelin's lands to the spoiler, and to preach the cross against him, with the same indulgences as for the Holy Land. This proved a failure, and when Frà Giovanni Schio was sent on his mission of peace, in 1233, Ezzelin's absolution was included in the general pacification, though he had not abandoned the protection of heresy, which had been the ostensible reason for assailing him. While Frederic was at peace with the Church, Ezzelin appears to have been let alone; and when the quarrel broke out afresh, after the emperor's subjugation of Lombardy, Ezzelin was again attacked. Frederic's excommunication of April 7, 1239, was followed, November 20, by that of Ezzelin. This time there is no mention of fautorship of heresy, but only of his encroachments on the church of Treviso and of his remaining under excommunication for more than three years. A month is given to him to submit, after which he is to be proceeded against as a heretic, for the Church had already discovered the convenience of treating disobedience as heresy. Nothing came of this, and in 1244 Innocent IV. resolved to see whether the Inquisition could not be used to better effect. Frà Rolando da Cremona, whose dauntless energy we have witnessed, was commissioned to make inquest on him as on one suspected and publicly defamed for heresy{226} by reason of his association with heretics; and as the accused was "terrible and powerful," the inquisitor was empowered to publish the legal citations in any place where he could do so in safety. The result of this trial *in absentia* was conclusive. It was found that he was the son of a heretic, that his kinsmen were heretics, that under his protection heresy had spread throughout the March of Treviso, and it was decided that he did not believe in the faith of Christ, and must be held suspect of heresy. In March, 1248, Innocent pronounced his condemnation as a manifest heretic to receive the reward of damnation incurred by damned heretics, but promised him that he would learn the abundant clemency of the Church if he would present himself in person by the next Ascension day (May 28). The wary old chief did not allow his curiosity as to the extent of papal clemency to overcome his caution, and abstained from placing his person in Innocent's power. He sent envoys, however, who offered to purge him of the suspicion of heresy by swearing to his orthodoxy; but Innocent held that he must appear in person, and offered him a safe-conduct in coming and going. There was no security promised in staying, however, and

Ezzelin was cautious. The term allowed him passed away, and he was duly excommunicated. After two years more he was notified that unless he appeared by August 1, 1250, he would be subjected to the statutes against heresy. The obdurate sinner was equally unmoved by this, and in June, 1251, the Bishop of Treviso and the Dominican Prior of Mantua were ordered to summon him personally again to appear by a given time, offering him ample security for his safety: if he disobeyed, his subjects of Treviso were commanded to coerce him, and if this failed a crusade was to be preached against him.[251]

To a pope desirous of extending his temporal sway it was exceedingly convenient to condemn his political opponents for heresy, and exceedingly economical to pay for their subjugation by lavishing the treasures of salvation. Thus, in April, 1253, Innocent IV., as an episode in his quarrel with Brancaleone, Senator of Rome, ordered the Dominicans of the Roman province to preach{227} a crusade, with Holy-Land indulgences, against the so-called heretics of Tuscany. Preparations were similarly made, on a larger scale, to crush those of Lombardy, where heresy was described as being more rampant and aggressive than ever. For two years a succession of bulls was issued directing all prelates, and especially the inquisitors, to preach the cross against them, with a most liberal assortment of indulgences. In one of these absolution was actually offered to those who held property wrongfully acquired, provided they contributed its value in aid of the crusade, thus deliberately rendering the Church an accomplice in robbery. In another, all persons or communities neglecting to aid the crusade were ordered to be prosecuted by the inquisitors as fautors of heresy. As a formal preliminary, Ezzelin was again cited, April 9, 1254, to present himself for judgment by the next Ascension day (May 21), failing which he was sentenced as a manifest heretic, to be dealt with as such. In all these proceedings the curious travesty of an inquisitorial trial shows us the influence which the Inquisition was already exercising on the minds of churchmen, and the employment of inquisitors proves how useful the institution was becoming as a factor in advancing the power of the Holy See.[252]

The Neapolitan conquest and the death of Innocent IV. postponed the organization of the crusade, but at length, in June, 1256, it set out from Venice under the leadership of the Legate Filippo, Archbishop-elect of Ravenna. The capture by assault of Padua, Ezzelin's most important city, was an encouraging commencement of the campaign, but the seven-days" sack, to which the unfortunate town was abandoned, showed that the soldiers of the cross were determined to make the most of the indulgences which they had earned. Under its incompetent captain the crusade dragged on without further result, in spite of reiterated bulls offering salvation, until, in 1258, the legate was utterly routed near Brescia and captured, together with his astrologer, the Dominican Everard. Brescia fell into Ezzelin's hands, who, more powerful than ever, entertained designs upon Milan, where he had relations with the Ghibelline faction. When all danger seemed to him past,{228} however, there was a sudden revulsion of fortune. The Ghibelline chiefs of Lombardy, Uberto Pallavicino and Buoso di Dovara, lords of Cremona, had been in alliance with him; they had aided in the capture of Brescia, with the understanding that they were to share in its possession, but he had monopolized the conquest, and they were resolved on revenge. June 11, 1259, they signed a treaty against Ezzelin with the Milanese and with Azzo d'Este, the head of the Lombard Guelfs. Ezzelin took the field with a heavy force, hoping to gain possession of Milan through the intelligences which he had within the walls, but on the march he was attacked by Uberto, Buoso, and Azzo, who by skilful strategy dispersed his troops and captured him, grievously wounded. His savage pride would not brook this degradation: he tore the bandages from his wound, refused all aid, and died in a few days.[253]

No greater service could have been rendered to the Church than that performed by Uberto, who had been in field and council the soul of the alliance that destroyed the dreaded Ezzelin and threw open, after thirty years of fruitless effort, the March of Treviso to the Inquisition. Some show of favor in return for such services would not have been amiss; would perhaps, indeed, have been wise, as it might have won over the powerful Ghibelline chief. In the treaty of June 11, however, the allies had alluded to Manfred as King of Sicily, and had pledged themselves to labor for his reconciliation with the pope. No service, especially after it had become irrevocable, could overbalance this recognition of the hated son of Frederic. Uberto, Buoso, and the Cremonese had been absolved from excommunication when they entered the alliance, but Alexander IV. wrote, December 13, 1259,{229} to his legate in Lombardy that the absolution was worthless because it had not been administered by a Dominican or a Franciscan, who alone were empowered to grant it; if, however, the allies would repudiate Manfred and give sufficient security to obey the mandates of the Church and to restore all Church property, they might still be absolved.[254]

Apparently Alexander's head had been turned by the triumph over Ezzelin, but he knew little of the man whom he thus treated with such supercilious ingratitude. By intrigues with the Torriani and other powerful nobles of Milan, Uberto created for himself a party in that city, and in 1260 he procured his election as podestà for five years. Rainerio Saccone vainly endeavored to prevent a consummation so deplorable. He assembled the citizens, denounced Uberto as vehemently suspected of heresy and as a manifest defender of heretics, and threatened that if it was persisted in he would ring all the church bells, and summon the people and clergy and Crocesegnati to oppose it by force. Unfortunately the citizens did not take in good part this somewhat insolent interference of a stranger with their internal affairs; or, as Alexander IV. describes it, "this wholesome counsel given in the spirit of humility and kindness." In wrath they assembled and rushed to the Dominican convent, where they gave Rainerio the alternative of leaving the city or faring worse. He chose the wiser alternative and departed.[255]

It was in vain that Alexander, in the bull detailing these griefs, ordered Rainerio and the other inquisitors to prosecute the guilty parties. It was in vain also that he approved, October 14, 1260, the statutes of an association of Defenders of the Faith recently formed in Milan in honor of Jesus Christ, the Blessed Virgin, St. John the Baptist, and St. Peter Martyr, whose members pledged themselves to give assistance, armed or otherwise, to the Inquisition in its labors for the extermination of heresy. Uberto was now the most powerful man in Lombardy, and wherever his influence extended he prohibited inquisitors from performing their functions. Heretics were safe under his rule, and they flocked to his territories from other parts of Lombardy and from Languedoc{230} and Provence. One of his confidential servitors was a certain Berenger, who had been condemned for heresy. Alexander lost no time in repeating with him the comedy of an inquisitorial trial, which we have seen performed with Ezzelin. December 9, 1260, he addressed instructions to the inquisitors of Lombardy to cite him, from some safe place, to the papal presence within two months, offering him a safe-conduct for coming (but not for going), when if he can prove his innocence he will be admitted to swear obedience to the papal mandates. If he does not appear, he is to be proceeded against inquisitorially.[256]

Uberto cared as little as Ezzelin for the impotent papal thunder, and quietly went on strengthening his position and adding city after city to his dominions, in spite of Alexander's instructions to Rainerio and his inquisitors to act vigorously and to preach a crusade. Between his success in the north, and the daily extending influence of Manfred's wise and vigorous rule in the south, it looked for a while as though the ambitious designs of the papacy were permanently crushed, and that the Italian Inquisition might come to an untimely end. Inquisitors were no longer able to move around in safety, even in the Roman province, and prelates and cities were ordered to provide them with a sufficient guard in all their journeys. An indication of the popular feeling is afforded by the action taken in 1264 by the people of Bergamo, greatly to the indignation of the Roman curia, to defend themselves against the arbitrary methods of inquisitorial procedure. They enacted that any one cited or excommunicated for heresy or fautorship might take an oath before the prosecutor or bishop that he held the faith of the Church of Rome in all its details, and then another oath before the podestà binding himself to pay one hundred sols every time that he deviated from it; after this he could not be cited outside of the city, and was eligible to any municipal office within it, while the magistrates were to defend him at the public expense against any such citation or excommunication. Yet outside of Uberto's territories and influence the business of the Inquisition in Lombardy went steadily on. In 1265 and 1266 Clement IV. is found issuing instructions as to the duties and appointment of inquisitors as vigorously as though there were no{231} impediments to their functions. It seemed only a question of time, however, when the districts yet open should be closed to them.[257]

There have been few revolutions more pregnant with results than that which occurred when the popes, renouncing the hope of acquiring for themselves the kingdom of Sicily, and vainly tempting Edmond, son of Henry III. of England, succeeded in arousing the ambition of Charles of Anjou, and caused a crusade to be preached everywhere in his behalf. The papacy fully recognized the supreme importance of the issue, and staked everything upon it. The treasures of salvation were poured forth with unstinted hand, and plenary indulgences were given to all who would contribute a fourth of their income or a tenth of their property. The temporal treasury of the Church was drawn upon with equal liberality. Three years" tithe of all ecclesiastical revenues in France and Flanders were granted to Charles, and when all this proved insufficient, Clement IV. sacrificed the property of the Roman churches without hesitation. An effort to raise one hundred thousand livres by pledging it brought in only thirty thousand, and then he pawned for fifty thousand more the plate and jewels of the Holy See. He could truly answer Charles's increasing demands for money to support his naked and starving crusaders by declaring that he had done all he could, and that he was completely exhausted—he had no mountains and rivers of gold, and could not turn earth and stones into coin. So utter was his penury that the cardinals were reduced to living at the expense of the monasteries; and when the Abbot of Casa Dei complained of the number quartered on him, he was told that he would be relieved of the Cardinal of Ostia, but that he must support the rest. More permanent relief, however, was found at the expense of the foreigner by assigning to{232} them revenues on churches abroad on the liberal scale of three hundred marks a year apiece.[258]

Vainly Pallavicino sought to prevent the passage of the crusaders through Lombardy. The fate of Italy—one may almost say of the papacy—was decided, February 26, 1266, on the plain of Benevento, where Guelf and Ghibelline from all portions of the Peninsula faced each other. Had Charles been defeated it would have fared ill with the Holy See. Europe had looked with aversion on the prostitution of its spiritual power to advance its temporal interests, and success alone could serve as a justification, in an age when men looked on the battle ordeal as recording the judgment of God. In the previous August, Clement had despairingly answered Charles's demands for money by declaring that he had none and could get none—that England was hostile, that Germany was almost openly in revolt, that France groaned and complained, that Spain scarce sufficed for her internal necessities, and that Italy did not furnish her own share of expenses. After the battle, however, he could exultingly write, in May, to Cardinal Ottoboni of San Adriano, his legate in England, that "Charles of Anjou holds in peace the whole kingdom of that pestilent man, obtaining his putrid body, his wife, his children, and his treasure," adding that already the Mark of Ancona had returned to obedience, that Florence, Siena, Pistoja, and

Pisa had submitted, that envoys had come from Uberto and Piacenza, and that others were expected from Cremona and Genoa; and on June 1 he announced the submission of Uberto and of Piacenza and Cremona.[259]

Although one by one Pallavicino's cities revolted from him in the general terror, his submission was only to gain time, and in 1267 he risked another cast of the die by joining in the invitation to Italy of the young Conradin, but the defeat and capture of that prince at Tagliacozza, in August, 1268, followed by his barbarous execution in October, extinguished the house of Suabia and the hopes of the Ghibellines. Charles of Anjou was master of Italy; he was created imperial vicar in Tuscany; even in the{233} north we find him this year appointing Adalberto de" Gamberti as podestà in Piacenza. Before the close of 1268 Pallavicino died, broken with age and in utter misery, while besieged in his castle of Gusaliggio by the Piacenzans and Parmesans. For a presumed heretic he made a good end, surrounded by Dominicans and Franciscans, confessing his sins and receiving the viaticum, so that, as a pious chronicler observes, we may humbly believe that his soul was saved. Despite the calumnies of the papalists, he left the reputation of a man of sterling worth, of lofty aims, and of great capacity. As for Rainerio Saccone, the last glimpse we have of him is in July, 1262, when Urban IV. orders him to come with all possible speed for consultation on a matter of moment, defraying, from the proceeds of the confiscations, all expenses for horses and other necessaries on the journey. His expulsion from Milan had evidently not diminished his importance.[260]

Under these circumstances, the long interregnum of nearly three years, which occurred after the death of Clement IV., in 1268, made little difference. Henceforth there was to be no refuge for heresy. The Inquisition could be organized everywhere, and could perform its functions unhampered. By this time, too, its powers, its duties, and its mode of procedure had become thoroughly defined and universally recognized, and neither prelate nor potentate dared to call them in question. As already stated, in 1254, Innocent IV. had divided the Peninsula between the two Orders, giving Genoa and Lombardy to the Dominicans, and central and southern Italy to the Franciscans. To the provinces of Rome and Tuscany were allotted two inquisitors each, while for that of St. Francis, or Spoleto, one was deemed sufficient, but in 1261 each inquisitor was furnished with two assistants, and the provincials were instructed to appoint as many more as might be asked for, so that the holy work might be prosecuted with full vigor. Lombardy, as we have seen, had eight inquisitors, and when the Dominicans divided that province, in 1304, the number was increased to ten, seven being assigned to Upper and three to Lower Lombardy. For a while the March of Treviso and Romagnola{234} were intrusted to the Franciscans, but, as stated above (Vol. I. p. 477), their extortions were so unendurable that, in 1302, Boniface VIII. transferred these districts to the Dominicans, without thereby relieving the people.[261]

No time had been lost in enforcing unity of belief in the territories redeemed from Ghibelline control. As early as February, 1259, the Franciscan Minister of Bologna was ordered to appoint two friars as inquisitors in Romagnola. At Vicenza, no sooner was quiet restored after the death of Ezzelin than Frà Giovanni Schio was sent thither to remove the excommunication incurred by the people in consequence of their subjection to Ezzelin. The ceremony was symbolic of the scourging inflicted on penitents. The podestà and council assembled at the usual place of meeting, whence they marched in pairs to the cathedral. At the south portal stood Giovanni with seven priests, and as the magistrates entered they touched each one lightly with rods, after which the rites of absolution were solemnly performed. The exiled bishop, Bortolamio, on his return from England had tarried with St. Louis, whose confessor he had been in Palestine, where he had served as papal legate during the saintly king's crusade. As soon as he heard of the death of Ezzelin he hastened homeward, bearing with him the priceless treasures of a thorn of the crown and a piece of the cross which St. Louis had bestowed upon him in parting. At once he commenced to build the great Dominican church and convent of the Santa Corona. The site chosen was on the most elevated spot in the city, known as the Colle, and among the buildings destroyed to give place for it was the church of Santa Croce, which had been occupied by the heretics as their place of assembly and worship. We are told that the presence of the relics worked the miracle of relieving the city of its three leading sins—avarice, heresy, and discord. As for heresy, the miracle lay in the unlooked-for conversion of the chief heretic of the district, Gieremia, known as the Archbishop of the Mark, who, with his son Alticlero, made public recantation. The heretic bishop, Viviano Bogolo, fled to Pavia, where he was recognized and burned. His two deacons, Olderico da Marola and Tolomeo, with eight others,{235} probably Perfects, were obstinate, and were promptly burned. These examples were sufficient. The "credentes" furnished no further martyrs, and heresy, at least in its outward manifestation, was extinguished.[262]

In some places, unblessed with such wonder-working relics, however, the Inquisition had much greater trouble in establishing orthodoxy. In Piacenza it is said to have found the burning of twenty-eight wagon loads of heretics necessary. At Sermione for sixteen years the inhabitants defiantly refused to allow persecution. Though Catholic themselves, they continued to afford protection to heretics, who naturally flocked thither as one refuge after another was rendered unsafe by the zeal of the inquisitors. It was in vain that Frà Timedeo, the inquisitor, obtained evidence by sending there a female spy, named Costanza da Bergamo, who pretended to be a heretic, received the *consolamentum*, and was then unreservedly admitted to their secrets. At last the scandal of such ungodly toleration became unendurable, and the Bishop of Verona prevailed upon Mastino and Alberto della Scala of Verona, and Pinamonte de" Bonacolsi of Mantua, to reduce Sermione to obedience. It was obliged to submit in 1276, delivering up no less than one hundred and seventy-four perfected heretics, and humbly asking to be restored to Catholic unity, with a pledge to stand to the mandates of the Church. Frà Filippo Bonaccorso, the Inquisitor of Treviso, applied to John XXI. for instructions as to the treatment of the penitent community. The pope was a humane and cultured man who cared more for poetry than theology, and he was disposed to be lenient with repentant sinners. He instructed Frà Filippo to remove the interdict if the town would appoint a syndic to abjure heresy in its name, and to swear in future to seize all heretics and deliver them to the Inquisition, any infraction of the oath to work a renewal, *ipso facto*, of the interdict. Every inhabitant was then to appear personally before the inquisitor, and make full confession of everything relating to heresy, to abjure, and to accept such penance as might be assigned—all infamous penalties, disabilities, imprisonment, and confiscation being mercifully excluded. Full records were to be kept of{236} each case, and any withholding of the truth or subsequent relapse was to expose the delinquent to the full rigor of the law. Obstinate heretics were to be dealt with according to the canons, and of these there were found seventy, whom Frà Filippo duly condemned, and had the satisfaction of seeing burned. To insure the future purity of the faith, in 1278 a Franciscan convent was built at Sermione with the proceeds of a fine of four thousand lire levied upon Verona as one of the conditions of removing the interdict incurred by its upholding the cause of the unfortunate Conradin; and in 1289 Ezzelin's castle of Illasio was given to some of the nobles who had been conspicuous in the reduction of Sermione, as a reward for their service, and to stimulate them in the future to continue their support of the Inquisition.[263]

Thus heresy, deprived of all protection, was gradually stamped out, and the Inquisition established its power in every corner of the land. How that power was abused to oppress the faithful with ingeniously devised schemes of extortion we have already seen. In fact, in the territories which had once been Ghibelline, it was impossible for any man, no matter how rigid his orthodoxy, to be safe from prosecution if he chanced to provoke the ill-will of the officials, or possessed wealth to excite their cupidity. So successful had the Church been in confounding political opposition with heresy that the mere fact of having adhered of necessity to Ezzelin during the period of his unquestioned domination long continued sufficient to justify prosecution for heresy, entailing the desirable result of confiscation. When Ezzelin's generation passed away, the memory of the dead was assailed and the descendants were disinherited. In all this there was no pretence of errors of faith, but the men to whom the Church intrusted the awful powers of the Inquisition seemed implacably determined to erase from the land every trace of those who had once dared to resist its authority. At last, in 1304, the authorities of Vicenza appealed to Benedict XI. no longer to allow the few survivors of Ezzelin's party and their descendants to be thus cruelly wronged, and the pope graciously granted their petition. By this time the empire was but a shadow; Ghibellinism represented no living force that{237} the papacy could reasonably dread, and its persecution had long been merely the gratification of greed or malice.[264]

The triumph of the Inquisition had not been effected wholly without resistance. In 1277 Frà Corrado Pagano undertook a raid against the heretics of the Valtelline. It was, doubtless, organized on an extended scale, for he took with him two associates and two notaries. This would indicate that heretics were numerous; the event showed that they did not lack protectors, for Corrado da Venosta, one of the most powerful nobles of the region, cut short the enterprise by slaughtering the whole party, on St. Stephen's day, December 26. Pagano had been a most zealous persecutor of heresy, and when his body was brought to Como it lay there for eight days before interment, with wounds freshly bleeding, showing that he was a martyr of God, and justifying the title bestowed on him by his Dominican brethren of St. Pagano of Como. His relics are still preserved there and are the objects of a local cult. Nicholas III. made every effort to avenge the murder, even invoking the assistance of Rodolf of Hapsburg, and his joy was extreme when, in November, 1279, the podestà and people of Bergamo succeeded in capturing Corrado and his accomplices. He at once ordered their delivery, under safe escort, to the inquisitors, Anselmo da Alessandria, Daniele da Giussano, and Guidone da Coconate, who were instructed to inflict a punishment sufficient to intimidate others from imitating their wickedness, and all the potentates of Lombardy were commanded to co-operate in their safe conveyance.[265]

The same year that justice was thus vindicated, a popular ebullition in Parma shows how slender was the hold which the Inquisition possessed on the people. Frà Florio had been diligent in the exercise of his functions, and we are told that he had burned innumerable heretics, when, in 1279, he chanced at Parma to have before him a woman guilty of relapse. It was a matter of course to condemn her to relaxation, and she was duly burned. In place of being piously impressed by the spectacle the Parmesans were{238}inspired by Satan to indignation which expressed itself by sacking the Dominican convent, destroying the records of the Inquisition, and maltreating the friars so that one of them died within a few days. The Dominicans thereupon abandoned the ungrateful city, marching out in solemn procession. The magistrates showed singular indifference as to punishing this misdeed, and when summoned by the Cardinal Legate of Ostia, the representatives who presented themselves lacked the necessary authority, so that, after vainly waiting for satisfaction, he laid an interdict upon the city. This was not removed till 1282, and even then the guilty were not punished. In 1285 we find Honorius IV. taking up the matter afresh and summoning the Parmesans to send delegates to him within a month to receive sentence; what that sentence was does not appear, but in 1287 the humbled citizens petitioned the Dominicans to return, received them with great honor, and voted them one thousand lire, in annual instalments of two hundred lire, wherewith to build a church. So stubborn was the opposition elsewhere to the Inquisition and its ways, that in 1287 the Provincial Council of Milan still deemed it necessary to decree that any member of a municipal government in any city within the province who should urge measures favoring heretics should be deemed suspect of heresy, and should forfeit any fiefs or benefices held of the Church.[266]

Even in the Patrimony of St. Peter resistance was not wholly at an end. In 1254, when the papacy was triumphant, Innocent IV. urged the inquisitors of Orvieto and Anagni to take advantage of the propitious time and act with the utmost vigor. In 1258 Alexander IV. sounded the alarm that heresy was increasing even in Rome itself, and he pressingly urged increased activity on the inquisitors and greater zeal in their support by the bishops. Their efforts were not wholly successful. Twenty years later a knight named Pandolfo still made his stronghold of Castro Siriani, near Anagni, a receptacle of heretics. Frà Sinibaldo di Lago, the inquisitor{239} of the Roman province, made various ineffectual attempts to prosecute him, and in 1278 Nicholas III. sent his notary, Master Benedict, with offers of pardon in return for obedience, but the heretics were obdurate, and Nicholas was forced to order Orso Orsini, Marshal of the Church in Tuscany, to levy troops and give Frà Sinibaldo armed assistance sufficient to enable him to coerce them to penitence. A similar enterprise against the Viterbian noble, Capello di Chia, in 1260, has already been described (Vol. I. p. 342). In this case the zeal of the Viterbians, who levied an army to assist the inquisitor, must have had some political motive, for their city was of evil repute in the matter of heresy. In 1265, encouraged by the assistance of Manfred, the people had risen against the Inquisition and had only been subdued after a bloody fight in which two friars were slain. In 1279 Nicholas expresses his regret that although, while he had been inquisitor-general, he had labored strenuously to purge Viterbo of heresy, his labors had been unsuccessful. Heretics were still concealed there, and the whole city was infected. Frà Sinibaldo was therefore ordered to go thither to make a thorough inquisition of the place.[267]

Earnest and unsparing as were the labors of the inquisitors, it seemed impossible to eradicate heresy. Its open manifestations were readily suppressed when the Ghibelline chiefs who protected it were destroyed, but in secret it still flourished and maintained its organization. In the inquest held on the memory of Armanno Pongilupo of Ferrara there is a good deal of testimony which shows not only the activity and success of the Inquisition of that city, but the continued existence of heresy throughout the whole region. There are allusions to numerous heretics in Vicenza, Bergamo, Rimini, and Verona. In the latter city a lady-in-waiting of the Marchesa d'Este, named Spera, was burned in 1270, and about the same time there were two Catharan bishops there, Alberto and Bonaventura Belesmagra. In 1273 Lorenzo was Bishop of Sermione, and Giovanni da Casaletto was Bishop of Mantua. There was a secret organization extending through all the Italian cities, with visitors and *filii majores* performing their rounds, and messengers{240} were constantly passing to and fro, elaborate arrangements being made for secreting them. Those who were in prison were kept supplied with necessaries by their brethren at large, who never knew at what moment they might be incarcerated. From the sentences of Bernard Gui we know that until the fourteenth century was fairly advanced the Cathari of Languedoc still looked to Italy as to a haven of refuge; that pilgrims thither had no trouble in finding their fellow-believers in Lombardy, in Tuscany, and in the kingdom of Sicily; that when the French churches were broken up those who sought to be admitted to the circle of the Perfect, or to renew their *consolamentum*, resorted to Lombardy, where they could always find ministers authorized to perform the rites. When Amiel de Perles had forfeited his ordination a conference was held in which it was determined that he should be sent with an associate to "the Ancient of the Heretics," Bernard Audoyn de Montaigu, in Lombardy for reconciliation; and on another occasion we hear of Bernard himself visiting Toulouse on business connected with the propagation of the faith.[268]

How difficult, indeed, was the task of the inquisitor in detecting heresy under the mask of orthodoxy is curiously illustrated by the case of Armanno Pongilupo himself. In Ferrara heretics were numerous. Armanno's parents were both Cathari; he was a "*consolatus*" and his wife a "*consolata.*" In 1254 he was detected and imprisoned; he confessed and abjured, and was released. From his Catharan bishop he received absolution for his oath of abjuration, and was received back into the sect. From this time until his death, in 1269, he was unceasingly engaged in propagating Catharan doctrines and in ministering to the wants of his less fortunate brethren in the clutches of the Inquisition, which was exceedingly active and successful. Meanwhile be preserved an exterior of the strictest Catholicism; he was regular in attendance at the altar and confessional, and wholly devoted to piety and good works. He died in the odor of sanctity, was buried in the cathedral, and immediately he began to work miracles. He was soon reverenced as a saint. A magnificent tomb arose over his remains, an altar was erected, and, as the miraculous manifestations of his{241} sanctity multiplied, his chapel became filled with images and ex-votos, to the no little profit of the church fortunate enough to possess him. Adored as a saint in the popular cult, there came a general demand for his canonization, in which the pride of the city was warmly enlisted, but which was steadfastly opposed by the Inquisition. In the confessions of heretics before it the name of Armanno constantly recurred as that of one of the most active and trusted members of the sect, and ample evidence accumulated as to his unrepentant heresy. Then arose a curious conflict, waged on both sides with unremitting vigor for thirty-two years. Hardly had the remains been committed to honorable sepulture in the cathedral when Frà Aldobrandini, the inquisitor who had tried him in 1254, ordered the archpriest and chapter to exhume and burn the corpse, and on their refusal excommunicated them and placed the cathedral under interdict. From this they appealed to Gregory X. and set to work to gather the evidence for canonization. For this purpose at different times five several inquests were held and superabundant testimony was forthcoming as to the success with which his suffrage was invoked, how the sick were healed, the blind made to see, and the halt to walk, while numerous priests bore emphatic witness to his pre-eminent piety during life. Gregory and Aldobrandini passed away leaving the matter unsettled. Frà Florio, the next inquisitor, sent to Rome expressly to urge Honorius IV. to come to a decision, but Honorius died without concluding the matter. On the accession of Boniface VIII., in 1294, Frà Guido da Vicenza, then inquisitor, again visited Rome to procure a termination of the affair. Still the contending forces were too evenly balanced for either to win. At length the Lord of Ferrara, Azzo X., interposed, for the contest between the inquisitor and the secular clergy seriously threatened the peace of the city. In 1300 Boniface appointed a commission to make a thorough investigation, with power to decide finally, and in 1301 sentence was rendered to the effect that Armanno had died a relapsed heretic; that no one should believe him to be anything but a heretic; that his bones should be exhumed and burned, the sarcophagus containing them and the altar erected before it be destroyed; that all statues, images, ex-votos, and other offerings set up in his honor in the cathedral and other Ferrarese churches should be removed within ten days; and that all his property, real and personal, was{242} confiscated to the Inquisition, any sales or conveyances made of them during the thirty-two years which had elapsed since his death being void. Frà Guido's triumph was complete, and on the death of the Bishop of Ferrara, in 1303, he was rewarded with the episcopate. Extraordinary as this case may seem, it was not unique. At Brescia a heresiarch named Guido Lacha was long adored as a saint by the people until the imposture was detected by the Inquisition, which caused his bones to be dug up and burned.[269]

This was the period of the greatest power and activity of the Inquisition, and the extent of its perfected organization is shown in a document of 1302, wherein Frà Guido da Tusis, Inquisitor of Romagnola, publishes in the communal council of Rimini the names of thirty-nine officials whom he has selected as his assistants. The expenses of such a body could not have been light, and to defray them there must have been a constant stream of fines and confiscations pouring into the inquisitorial treasury, showing an abundant harvest of heresy and active work in its suppression.[270] It was probably between 1320 and 1330 that was produced the treatise of Zanghino Ugolini, so often quoted above. Frà Donato da Sant'' Agata had been appointed Inquisitor of Romagnola, and the learned jurisconsult of Rimini drew up for his instruction a summary of the rules governing inquisitorial procedure, which is one of the clearest and best manuals of practice that we possess.

A singular episode of lenity occurred not long before, which is not to be passed over, although inexplicable in itself and unproductive of consequences. Its importance, indeed, lies in the evidence which it affords that the extreme severity of the laws against heresy was recognized as really unnecessary, since its relaxation in favor of a single community as a matter of favor would otherwise have been a crime against the faith. In February, 1286, Honorius IV., in consideration of the fidelity manifested by the people of{243} Tuscany to the Roman Church, and especially to him before his elevation, relieved them individually and universally from the penalties for heresy, including all disabilities decreed by his predecessors and by Frederic II., whether incurred by their own errors or by those of their ancestors. Catholic children of heretic parents were thus *ipso facto* restored to all privileges and were no longer liable to disinheritance. In the case of existing heretics it was necessary for them to appear before the inquisitors within a time to be named by the latter—excepting absentees in foreign lands, to whom a term of five months was allowed—to abjure heresy and receive penance, which was to be a secret one, involving neither humiliation, disability, or loss of property. Cases of relapse, however, were to be treated with all the rigor of the law. As this bull abrogated in Tuscany the constitutions of Frederic II., it required confirmation by Rodolph of Hapsburg, which was duly procured. For a while this extraordinary privilege seems to have been observed, for, in 1289, Nicholas IV., when anathematizing heretics and stimulating the zeal of inquisitors throughout Genoa, Lombardy, Romagnola, Naples, and Sicily, pointedly omits Tuscany from his enumeration. In time, however, it was either repealed or disregarded. No case could come more completely within its purview than that already referred to of Gherardo of Florence, dying prior to 1250 and prosecuted in 1313. His numerous children and grandchildren were good Catholics, and yet they were all disinherited and subjected to the canonical disabilities.[271]

Together with this exhibition of papal indulgence may be classed the occasional interference of the Holy See to moderate the rigor of the canons, or to repress the undue zeal of an inquisitor, when the sufferer had influence or money enough to attract the papal attention. It is pleasant to record three instances of this kind on the part of the despotic Boniface VIII., when, in 1297, he declared that Rainerio Gatti, a noble of Viterbo, and his sons had been prosecuted by the inquisitors on perjured testimony, wherefore the process was to be annulled and the accused and their heirs relieved from all stain of heresy; when, in 1298, he ordered the Inquisition to restore to the innocent children of a heretic{244} the property confiscated by Frà Andrea the inquisitor, and when he ordered Frà Adamo da Como, the inquisitor of the Roman province, to desist from molesting Giovanni Ferraloco, a citizen of Orvieto, whom his predecessors, Angelo da Rieti and Leonardo da Tivoli, had declared absolved from heresy. This Frà Adamo apparently rendered his office a terror to the innocent. May 8, 1293, we find him compelling Pierre d'Aragon, a gentleman of Carcassonne who chanced to be in Rome, to give him security in the heavy sum of one hundred marks to present himself within three months to the Inquisition of Carcassonne and obey its mandates. Pierre accordingly appeared before Bertrand de Clermont on June 19, and was closely examined, and then again on August 16, but nothing was discovered against him. Whether or not he recovered his one hundred marks from Frà Adamo does not appear, but the incident affords an illustration at once of the perfected organization of the Holy Office, and of the dangers which surrounded travellers in the countries where it flourished.[272]

The Inquisition was thus thoroughly established and at work in northern and central Italy, and heresy was gradually disappearing before its remorseless and incessant energy. To escape it many had fled to Sardinia, but in 1258 that island was added to the inquisitorial province of Tuscany, and inquisitors were sent thither to track the fugitives in their retreats.[273] There were two regions, however, Venice and the Two Sicilies, which thus far we have not considered, as they were in some sort independent of the movement which we have traced in the rest of the Peninsula.

Naples, like the other portions of southern Europe, had been exposed to the infection of heresy. At an early period missionaries from Bulgaria had penetrated the passes of the southern Apennines, and, in that motley population of Greek and Saracen and Norman, proselytes had not been lacking. The Norman kings, usually at enmity with the Holy See, had not cared to inquire too closely into the orthodoxy of their subjects, and had they done so the independence of the feudal baronage would have rendered{245} minute perquisition by no means easy. The allusions of the Abbot Joachim of Flora to the Cathari indicate that their existence and doctrines were familiar facts in Calabria, though as Rainerio makes no allusion to any Catharan church in Italy south of Florence it is presumable that the sectaries were widely scattered and unorganized. In 1235, when the Dominican convent in Naples was broken into by a mob and several of the friars were grievously wounded, Gregory IX. attributed the violence to friends of heretics.[274]

Frederic II., however much at times his policy might lead him to proclaim ferocious edicts of persecution, and even spasmodically to enforce them, had no convictions of his own to render him persistent in persecution, and his lifelong contest with the papacy gave him, secretly at least, a fellow-feeling with all who resisted the supremacy of the Holy See, whether in temporal or spiritual concerns. Occasional attacks such as that under the auspices of the Archbishop of Reggio, in 1231, or the form of secular inquisition which he instituted in 1233, had little permanent effect. Cathari driven from Languedoc, who perhaps found even Lombardy insecure, were tolerably sure of refuge in the wild and secluded valleys of Calabria and the Abruzzi, lying aside from the great routes of travel. The domination in Naples of Innocent IV. was too brief for the organization of any systematized persecution, and when Manfred reconquered the kingdom, although he seems to have felt his position too precarious to risk open toleration, and, under pressure from Jayme of Aragon, he ordered Bishop Vivian of Toulouse and his disciples, who had settled in Apulia, to leave his dominions, yet he went no further in active measures of repression.[275]

Charles of Anjou came as a crusader and as the champion of the Church. Scarce was his undisputed domination assured by the execution of Conradin, October 20, 1268, than we see him zealously employed in establishing the Inquisition throughout the kingdom. Numerous royal letters of 1269 show it actively at work, and manifest the solicitude of the king that the stipends and{246} the expenses of the inquisitors should be provided for, and that every assistance should be rendered by the public officials. Each inquisitor was furnished with a letter which placed all the forces of the State at his unreserved command. The Neapolitan Inquisition was fully manned. There was one inquisitor for Bari and the Capitanata, one for Otranto, and one for the Terra di Lavoro and the Abruzzi; and in 1271 one was added for Calabria and one for Sicily. Most of them were Dominicans, but we meet with at least one Franciscan, Frà Benvenuto. Yet no buildings or prisons seem to have been provided for them. The royal jails were placed at their disposal, and the keepers were instructed to torture prisoners on requisition from the inquisitors. Even as late as 1305 this arrangement appears to be in force.[276]

Charles's zeal did not confine itself to thus organizing and promoting the Inquisition. He supplemented its labors by instituting raids on heretics conducted under his own auspices. Thus, although there was an inquisitor for the Abruzzi, we find him, December 13, 1269, sending thither the Cavaliere Berardo da Rajano with instructions to investigate and seize heretics and their fautors. The utmost diligence was enjoined on him, and the local officials were ordered to assist him in every way, but there is no allusion to his mission being in co-operation with the inquisitor. Another significant manifestation of Charles's devotion is seen in his founding, in 1274, and richly endowing for the Dominicans the splendid church of San Piero Martire in Naples, and stimulating his nobles to follow his example in showering wealth upon it. Yet fifty years afterwards, in 1324, the building was still incomplete for lack of funds, when King Robert aided the construction with fifty ounces of gold, which he ordered the inquisitors to pay out of the royal third of the confiscations coming into their hands. This is interesting as showing how, in Naples, the profitable side of persecution was wholly under the control of the Holy Office.[277] {247}

Few details have been preserved to us of the activity of the Inquisition in Naples. We know that heretics continued to exist there, but the wild and mountainous character of much of the country doubtless afforded them abundant opportunities of safe asylum. Already, in August, 1269, a letter of Charles ordering the seizure of sixty-eight heretics designated by Frà Benvenuto shows that the work was being energetically prosecuted, and in another letter of March 14, 1270, there is an allusion to three others whom Frà Matteo di Caetellamare had recently caused to be burned in Benevento. The inquisitors of Languedoc, moreover, made haste, as early as 1269, to send agents to Naples to hunt the refugees whom their severity had driven there, and Charles ordered every assistance to be rendered to them, which, perhaps, explains the success of Frà Benvenuto. Yet the perpetual necessity for royal interposition leads to the inference that the Inquisition was not nearly so effective in Naples as it proved in Languedoc and Lombardy. The royal authority seems to be required at every turn, partly because the king allowed little independent initiative to the inquisitors, and partly, perhaps, because the local officials did not lend as hearty a co-operation as they might have done. Thus the Neapolitan Inquisition, even under the Angevines, seems never to have attained the compact and effective organization of which we have seen the results elsewhere, though Charles II. was an eager persecutor who stimulated the zeal of his inquisitors, and his son Robert earned the name of the Pious. In 1305 we shall see Frà Tommaso di Aversa active in persecuting the Spiritual Franciscans, and in 1311, King Robert, at the instance of Frà Matteo da Ponza, ordered that all newly converted Jews should live scattered among Christians, so as not to be tempted back to Judaism.[278]

The ineffectiveness of the Neapolitan Inquisition is seen in the comparative security which attended an organized immigration of Waldenses from the valleys of the Cottian Alps. It was probably about 1315 that Zanino del Poggio, a Milanese noble, led forth the first band from Savoy, under specified guarantees of lands and privileges, after the intending emigrants had received the report of deputies sent in advance to survey the promised refuge. Fresh{248} bands came to join them and a group of villages sprang up—Guardia Piemontese, or Borgo degli Oltremontani, Argentina, La Rocca, Vaccarizzo, and San Vincenzo in Calabria, while in Apulia there were Monteleone, Montanto, Faito, La Cella, and Matta. These were regularly visited by the "barbes," or missionary pastors, who spent their lives wandering around among the scattered churches, administering the consolations of religion and watching over the purity of the faith. The fierce persecutions conducted by François Borel led to further emigration on an enlarged scale, which naturally sought the Neapolitan territories as a haven of rest, until Apulia came to be regarded as the headquarters of the sect. That considerable bodies of heretics could thus establish themselves and flourish argues great negligence on the part of the Inquisition. In fact, its recognized inefficiency was shown as early as 1326, when John XXII. was in pursuit of some Fraticelli who had fled to Calabria; instead of calling upon the inquisitors he applied to King Robert and to the Duke of Calabria to capture them and hand them over to the episcopal tribunals.[279]

When, as the result of the Sicilian Vespers in 1282, the Island of Sicily passed into the hands of Pedro III. of Aragon, it was placed in the bitterest antagonism towards the Holy See, and no active persecution is to be looked for. In fact, in 1285, Martin IV., in ordering a crusade preached against Pedro, gives as one of the four reasons alleged in justification that heresy was multiplying in the island, and that inquisitors were prevented from visiting it. It was not till 1302 that Boniface VIII. was brought to accept the accomplished fact, and to acknowledge Frederic of Aragon as King of Trinacria. The Inquisition soon followed. In 1304 we find Benedict XI. ordering Frederic to receive and give all due assistance to Frà Tommaso di Aversa the inquisitor, and all other inquisitors who may be sent thither. The pope, however,{249} did not erect it into a separate tribunal, but instructed the Holy Office of the mainland that its jurisdiction extended over both sides of the Faro. Yet the introduction of the Inquisition in the island was nominal rather than real except, as we shall see, with regard to the Templars, and Sicily long remained a safe refuge for the persecuted Fraticelli. Doubtless Arnaldo de Vilanova contributed to this by the picture which he presented to Frederic of the inquisitors of the day. They were a diabolical pest, trafficking in their offices, converting themselves into demons, never edifying the faithful, but rather making them infidels, as they abandoned themselves to hatred, greed, and lust, with no one to condemn them or to repress their fury. When, in 1328, the Archbishop of Palermo arrested a Fraticello, appeal was at once made to Frederic, and John XXII. wrote to the archbishop urgently commanding that the sect be extirpated, showing apparently that there was no Inquisition then at work.[280]

The Republic of Venice was always a law unto itself. Though forming part of the March of Treviso, its predominant interests in the thirteenth century lay to the east of the Adriatic, and it did not become a formidable power on the mainland until the acquisition of Treviso in 1339. That of Padua, in 1405, followed by Verona, Vicenza, Feltre, Belluno, and Brescia, greatly increased its strength, and in 1448 it wrenched Bergamo from the dukes of Milan. Thus its policy with regard to the Inquisition eventually controlled the whole of the March of Treviso, and a considerable portion of Lombardy.

That policy held at bay in all things the pretensions of the Holy See, and looked with extreme suspicion on whatever might give the popes an excuse for interference with either the domestic policy or the foreign enterprises of the Signoria. Fairly orthodox, though not bigoted, Venice held aloof from the strife between Guelf and Ghibelline, and was not involved in the anathemas lavished upon Ezzelin da Romano. Venice, in fact, was the basis of operations in the crusade against him, and it was a Venetian who{250} led the expedition up the Brenta which captured Padua. Yet the republic made no haste to join in the movement for the extermination of heresy so energetically pushed by Gregory IX. and his successors. The Constitutions of Frederic II. were never inscribed in its statute-books. In 1229 the official oath of the Doge Giacopo Tiepoli, which, as is customary, contains the criminal code of the day, embodies no allusion to heresy or its suppression, and the same is true of the criminal statute of 1232 published by the same doge.[281]

It was about this time that the Inquisition was developed with all the aggressive energy of which Gregory IX. was capable, but it found no foothold in Venice. Yet the duty to punish heresy was at length recognized, though the civil authorities would abate no jot of their right to control the administration of justice in spiritual as well as in temporal matters. The official oath taken in 1249 by the Doge Marino Morosini contains a promise that certain upright and discreet and Catholic men shall be appointed, with the advice of the Council, to inquire after heretics. All heretics, moreover, who shall be delivered to the secular arm by the Archbishop of Grado or other bishops of the Venetian territories shall be duly burned, under the advice of the Council, or of a majority of its members. Thus a kind of secular Inquisition was established to search after heretics. The ancient jurisdiction of the episcopal courts was alone recognized, but the judgment of the bishops was subject to revision by the Council before the death-penalty could be inflicted.[282]

This could by no means be satisfactory to the papacy, and when the death of Frederic II. led to an immediate effort to extend the Inquisition through the territories hitherto closed to it, Venice was not forgotten. By a bull of June 11, 1251, Innocent IV. ordered the Frati Vicenzo of Milan, and Giovanni of Vercelli, to proceed to Venice and persecute heretics there with the same powers as those exercised by inquisitors elsewhere in Lombardy. Whether the good friars made the attempt to exercise these powers is questionable; if they did so, their ill-success is unquestionable. There is a document of 1256 which contains an oath to pursue {251} heretics and to denounce them, not to the ecclesiastical tribunals, but to the doge or to the magistrates—an oath presumably administered to the secular inquisitors established in 1249. The same document contains a clause which indicates that the death-penalty threatened in 1249 had already been abrogated. It classes Cathari and usurers together: it alludes to the punishment decreed for those convicted of relapse into either sin, and shows that this was not capital, by providing that if the convict is a foreigner he shall be banished from Venice, but if a citizen he shall not be banished. Yet the death-penalty seems to have been restored soon afterwards, for, in 1275, the oath of Giacomo Contarini is the same as that of 1249, with the unimportant addition that the judgment of an episcopal vicar during the vacancy of a see can be substituted for that of a bishop.[283]

As the pressure of the Inquisition extended throughout Lombardy and the Marches, the persecuted heretics naturally sought a refuge in Venetian territory, where supervision was so much more negligent. It was in vain that about 1286 Frà Filippo of Mantua, the Inquisitor of Treviso, was sent by Honorius IV. with a summons to the republic to inscribe in its laws the constitutions against heresy of Frederic and of the popes. Although the example of the other cities of the Marca Trivigiana was urged, and Venice was repeatedly required to do the same, obedience was persistently refused. At length, in 1288, Nicholas IV. lost patience with this persistent contumacy. He peremptorily ordered the Signoria to adopt the imperial and papal laws, and commanded that the doge should swear not only not to impede the Inquisitor of Treviso in his duties, but to assist him. In default of obedience he threatened to proceed against the city both spiritually and temporally.[284]

The position of the republic was already indefensible under the public law of the period. It was so administering its own laws as to afford an asylum to a class universally proscribed, and it was refusing to allow the Church to apply the only remedy deemed appropriate to this crying evil. It therefore yielded to {252} the inevitable, but in a manner to preserve its own autonomy and independence. It absolutely refused to incorporate in its own statutes the papal and imperial laws, but, August 4, 1289, it empowered the doge, Giovanni Dandolo, to give assistance to the inquisitor, when called upon, without referring each case to the Senate. A further wise provision decreed that all fines and confiscations should inure to the State, which in turn undertook to defray the expenses of the Holy Office. These were not light, as, in addition to the cost of making arrests and maintaining prisoners, the inquisitor received the liberal salary of twelve ducats a month. For this purpose the proceeds of the corn-tax were set aside, and the money was deposited with the Provveditore delle Viare, who disbursed it on the requisition of the inquisitor. This compromise was accepted by Nicholas IV., August 28, 1288, and was duly embodied in the official oath of the next doge, Piero Gradenigo. Thus, while the inquisitor had full opportunity of suppressing heresy, the temptation to abuse his office for purposes of extortion was reduced to a minimum, and the State, by retaining in its hands all the financial portion of the business, was able at any time to exercise control.[285]

The Inquisition was unaccustomed to submit to control, and soon chafed under these limitations. Already, in 1292, Nicholas IV. complained to Piero Gradenigo that the terms of the agreement were not carried out. The inquisitors, Bonagiunta of Mantua and Giuliano of Padua, reported that the papal and imperial laws against heresy were not enforced, and that under the arrangement for expenditures they were unable to employ a force of familiars sufficient to detect and seize the heretics. Heresy consequently, they said, continued to flourish in Venetian territory, for all of which Nicholas bitterly scolded the doge, and demanded such changes as should remove these scandals, but without effect. The Signoria, apparently, had not seen fit to abolish the office of secular inquisitors provided by the legislation of 1249. These were three in number, and were known as the *"tre Savi dell" eresia,"* or *"assistenti."* It was hardly possible that a duplicate organization {253} such as this could work without clashing. The situation became intolerable, and in 1301 Frà Antonio, the Inquisitor of Treviso, resolved to put an end to it. He notified the three Savi, Tommaso Viaro, Marino Zorzi, and Lorenzo Segico, to recognize no superior save himself. Their submission not being forthcoming, he proceeded to Venice, and addressed to the Doge Gradenigo a monition ordering him, under pain of excommunication, to swear to obey all the papal constitutions on heresy. Gradenigo refused, alleging that this would be a violation of his oath of office; the inquisitor withdrew his monition, and matters remained as before. Whatever hopes had been entertained that the entering wedge would enable the Inquisition to establish itself without restriction were foiled by the steadfastness of the republic. The three Savi continued their functions and, perhaps, even enlarged them; it had become customary for them to be selected from among the senators, and they acted in conjunction with the inquisitor in all cases coming within his jurisdiction. As Venice extended her conquests on the mainland, in all cities under her domination the *rettori* or governors performed this function, and their participation was required in all prosecutions for heresy, not only by the inquisitor, but by the bishops.[286]

In Italy, as in France, the history of the Inquisition during the fourteenth and fifteenth centuries is one of decadence. It is true that in Italy it had not to contend with the consolidation of power in the hands of a monarch, but the Captivity of Avignon and the debasement of the papacy under the influence of the French court, co-operating with the rise of the cities in wealth and culture, conduced to the same result; while the Great Schism, followed by the Councils of Constance and Basle, tended to emancipate the minds of men and foster independence. During the fourteenth century much of the inquisitorial activity was devoted to the new heresy of the Fraticelli, which will be referred to hereafter when we come to consider that remarkable religious movement. That movement, indeed, was the chief exception to the {254} decay in spiritual enthusiasm which diminished at once the veneration which the Inquisition inspired and the opposition of heterodoxy which constituted its *raison d" être*. As heretics grew fewer and poorer its usefulness decreased, its means of impressing the popular imagination disappeared, and its rewards grew less and less.

As regards the Cathari, the Inquisition had done its work too well. Unceasing and unsparing repression gradually annihilated the sect which, during the first half of the thirteenth century, seemed almost able to dispute with Rome the possession of Italy on equal terms. Yet when we see that the Waldenses, exposed to the same merciless rigor, were not extinguished, we recognize that some other factor besides mere persecution was at work to obliterate a belief which once enjoyed so potent an influence on the human mind that thousands for its sake went joyfully to a dreadful death. The secret must be looked for in the hopeless pessimism of the faith itself. There was in it nothing to encourage and strengthen man in the battle of life. Manes had robbed the elder Mazdeism of its vitality when he assigned to the Evil Principle complete dominion over Nature and the visible universe, and when he adopted the Sankhya philosophy, which teaches that existence is an evil, while death is an emancipation for those who have earned spiritual immortality, and a mere renewal of the same hated existence for all who have not risen to the height of the austerest maceration. As civilization slowly advanced, as the midnight of the Dark Ages began to yield to the approaching dawn of modern ideas, as the hopelessness of humanity grew less abject, the Manichæan theory grew less attractive. The world was gradually awakening to new aims and new possibilities; it was outgrowing the dreary philosophy of pessimism, and was unconsciously preparing for the yet unknown future in which man was to regard Nature not as an enemy, but as a teacher. Catharism had no possibility of development, and in that lay its doom.

The simple and earnest faith of the Waldenses, on the other hand, inculcated helpfulness and hopefulness, patience under tribulation, and an abiding trust in the watchful care of the Heavenly Father. The arduous toil of the artisan or husbandman was blessed in the consciousness of the performance of a duty. The virtues which form the basis of all Christian society—industry,{255} charity, self-abnegation, sobriety, chastity, thrift—were stimulated and cultivated, and man was taught that his fate, here and hereafter, depended on himself, and not on the ministration or mediation of his fellow-creatures, alive or dead. It was a faith which fitted man for the environment in which he had been placed by his Creator, and it was capable of adaptation to the infinite vicissitudes of human progress. Accordingly, it had proportionate vitality. Rooted out in one place, it grew in another. It responded too nearly to the needs and aspirations of multitudes ever to be wholly blotted out. There was always a propitious soil for its scattered seeds, and its resistance of inertia in the end proved too much for even the persistent energy of its destroyers.

Yet in Italy the Cathari lasted long after they had disappeared from France. Driven from the plains of Lombardy and central Italy, they took refuge in places less accessible. In 1340 we hear of them in Corsica, when Gerald, the Franciscan general, sent his friars thither, who succeeded in exterminating them for a time. In 1369 we again find Franciscans, under Frà Mondino da Bologna, zealously at work there, and earnestly supported by Gregory XI. In 1372 and 1373 Gregory wrote to the Bishops of Marrana and Ajaccio, and to Frà Gabriele da Montalcino, urging renewed activity, and, with singular lenity, authorizing them to remit the death-penalty in cases of single relapse. These hunted refugees were mostly in the forests and mountains, and to subdue them a chain of spiritual forts was established, in the shape of Franciscan houses. As late as 1397 a certain Frà Francesco was sent to Corsica in the double capacity of papal nuncio and inquisitor.[287]

On the mainland, in spite of the vigilance of the Inquisition, Cathari continued to exist in Piedmont. In 1388 Frà Antonio Secco of Savigliano had the good-fortune to lay hands on one of the active members of the sect, Giacomo Bech of Chieri, near Turin. The report of his examination before the inquisitor and the Bishop of Turin, which has been printed by Sig. Girolamo Amati, gives full details of the condition of the sect. After his tongue had been loosened by repeated applications of torture, his confession{256} shows that it was numerous in the vicinage, and that it comprised members of many noble families—the Patrizi, Bertoni, Petiti, Narro, and ancestors of Balbi and Cavour. Although in Italy, as in France, the name of Waldenses had become applicable to all heretics, and they were commonly designated by this name, they retained the moderated dualism of the Lombard Cathari. Satan fell from heaven, created the visible universe, and will finally return to glory. The law of Moses was dictated by him, and Moses was the greatest of sinners. Human souls are fallen demons, who transmigrate into other human bodies, or into those of animals, until released by death-bed *consolamentum*. The purity of the faith was maintained by occasional intercourse with its headquarters in Bosnia. Giacomo Bech was converted by a Slavonian missionary, in conjunction with Jocerino de' Balbi and Piero Patrizi, and the latter gave him ten florins and sent him to Bosnia to perfect himself in the doctrines, though he was compelled by ill-fortune at sea to return without accomplishing his pilgrimage. Forty years before one of the Balbi had gone thither for the same purpose; in 1360 a Narro and a Benso, Piero Patrizi himself in 1377, and Berardo Rascherio in 1380. Evidently the little community of Chieri maintained active relations with the heads of the Church. In 1370 Bech had fallen into the hands of the inquisitor, Frà Tommaso da Casacho, had been forced to confess, and had been released after abjuration in reward for his betraying his fellow-disciples.[288]

Frà Antonio's labors had been already rewarded by the discovery of another sect of Cathari in the valleys to the west and northwest of Turin. Their heresiarch was Martino del Prete, and the community of Chieri had vainly endeavored to win them over to unity. In Pignerol, Frà Antonio had, in November, 1387, arrested a suspected heretic named Antonio Galosna, who passed for a Franciscan Tertiary. The Inquisition in those parts was greatly dependent upon the secular authorities, and the Count of Savoy, Amadeo VII., was not disposed to second it with zeal. When Galosna at first denied, Antonio succeeded in having him tortured till he promised to tell everything if released from torture, and accordingly the next day he made confession; but Giovanni{257} di Brayda, the chamberlain of Amadeo, and Antonio da Valencia, the Judge of Pignerol, promised him that if he would retract they would effect his deliverance. The Castellan of Pignerol, in whose charge he was, also offered to liberate him on receiving five florins for himself and seventy more for necessary expenses; but, although Galosna pledged all his property to raise the sum, this device seems to have failed. On December 29 he was brought before the count himself, after being warned by di Brayda that if he confirmed his confession he should be hanged. He accordingly retracted it, but was not liberated, and a month later, in the presence of the count and the inquisitor, he repeated that his confession had been extorted by violence. Apparently he was made the subject of a prolonged debate between State and Church, in which the latter triumphed, for on May 29 we find him in the possession of the Bishop of Turin and of the inquisitor, undergoing examination in the castle of Dross, near Turin.[289]

He proved a mine of information well worth the repeated interrogatories which extended from May 29 to July 10, for he had been a member of the sect for twenty-five years and a wandering missionary for fifteen, and was familiar with all the congregations, which appear to have been numerous, some in the neighborhood of Turin, but mostly in the lower Alpine valleys between Pignerol and Susa. Though he repeatedly alludes to the sectaries as Vaudois, they had no affinity with the Waldenses, and it is observable that he makes no reference to their existence in any of the distinctive Waldensian valleys, such as Angrogna, Perosa, or San Martino. They were mostly poor folk—peasants, servants, muleteers, innkeepers, mechanics, and artisans, and the chiefs of their "synagogues" were generally of this class, although occasionally a clerk, a canon, a notary, or other educated person is enumerated among the members. What were their precise distinctive tenets it is not easy to define with accuracy. Galosna's rough handling had evidently rendered him eager to satisfy the credulity of his examiners, and the imaginative character of some of his revelations casts a doubt on the truthfulness of them all. The applicant for initiation had to drink a beverage, foul of aspect, made with the excrement of a toad kept for the purpose; taken{258} in excess it was apt to prove fatal, and its power was such that whoso once partook of it could never thereafter abandon the sect. Martino del Prete, the chief heresiarch, had a black cat as large as a lamb, which he declared to be the best friend he had on earth. We may safely set down the accounts of the sexual abominations which succeeded religious services in the conventicles, when the lights were extinguished, as worthy of equal credence. Contradictions in the repeated statements of the doctrines taught show that Galosna's imagination served him better than his memory in his prolonged examinations. He was told that in joining the sect he would secure salvation in glory with God the Father, and yet he declares that the sect rejected immortality, and held that the soul died with the body—and again, that there was no purgatory, but only heaven and hell hereafter. They believed, moreover, in God the Father who created the heavens, but they worshipped the Great Dragon, the creator of the world, who fought God and the angels, and was more powerful than he on earth. Christ was not the Son of God, but of Joseph, and was worthy of no special reverence. Altogether the account is hopelessly confused, but we can discern the dualism of a bastard Catharism, and allusions are made to the *consolamentum* and the sacrament of bread. Like Jacopo Bech, Galosna had already abjured in the hands of Frà Tommaso da Casacho. Both were therefore relapsed; there was no mercy for them, and on September 5, 1388, they were abandoned to the secular arm in Turin and necessarily burned. Unfortunately the record ends here, and we have no details as to the rich harvest which Frà Antonio must have reaped from the ample information obtained from his victims as to the scattered members of the sects.[290]

Notwithstanding these evidences of vitality, Catharism was rapidly dying out. The latest definite reference to it, west of the Adriatic, occurs in 1403, when San Vicente Ferrer, the great Spanish revivalist, undertook a peaceful mission in the remote valleys which no Catholic priest had dared to visit for thirty years, when he found and converted a number of Cathari dwelling among the Waldenses. He regarded as a form of Manichæism the worship{259} of the rising sun which he found habitual among the peasants of the diocese of Lausanne, and some such survival of nature-worship was probably not infrequent, for a penitent of Frà Antonio Secco, in 1387, speaks of adoring the sun and moon on bended knees. Yet there would seem to be a remnant of Catharism lingering among the Waldenses of the Savoy valleys as late as 1451, when Filippo Regis was tried by the Inquisition.[291]

Italian Waldensianism continued to flourish in the mountain fastnesses of Piedmont, where the endless struggle with parsimonious nature fostered the hardier virtues. Thence, as we have seen, were emigrants and even colonies sent out, as persecution scattered the faithful or as population outgrew the narrow means of subsistence. The kindlier climate and less aggressive Inquisition of Naples finally rendered the southern colonies the headquarters of the sect, with which constant intercommunication was kept up. In 1387 we are told that the chief pontiff resided in Apulia and that the Waldensian community at Barge in Piedmont was presided over by two Apulians. A century later the mother communities in the Cottian Alps still looked to southern Italy as to the centre of their Church.[292]

In 1292 we hear of persecutions in the Val Perosa, and again in 1312 there were burnings of obstinate heretics in the valleys, but these efforts effected little, for in 1332 a brief of John XXII. describes the Waldensian church of the diocese of Turin as being in a most flourishing condition. The heretics were so numerous that they disdained concealment, holding assemblies in public in which as many as five hundred would be gathered together. When Frà Giovanni Alberto, the Inquisitor of Turin, had recently made an effort to repress them, they boldly rose in arms. On the public square of Angrogna they slew the parish priest Guillelmo, whom they suspected of furnishing information, and Alberto himself they besieged in a castle where he had taken refuge, so that he was glad to escape with his life, leaving the land abandoned to{260} heresy. For twenty years and more one of their principal chiefs had been a man named Pier Martino, known also as Giuliano or Martino Pastrae, who chanced in his wandering missions to fall into the hands of Jean de Bades, the Inquisitor of Provence. The pope thereupon orders the latter to deliver his prisoner to Frà Alberto, who will be able to extract from him information of the utmost value in tracking and seizing his fellow-religionists—information, as the pope suggests, which will justify the use of torture. Doubtless this lucky capture enabled Frà Alberto to lay hands on a number of outlying heretics, though he probably did not again venture his person in the populous communities which had shown so sturdy a readiness in self-protection.[293]

Persecution continued, and in 1354 we chance to hear of an order issued by Giacomo, Prince of Piedmont, to the Counts of Luserna, to imprison a number of Waldenses recently discovered in Luserna and the neighboring valleys. The order was issued at the instance of Pietro di Ruffia, Inquisitor of Piedmont, who paid for his zeal with his life, being shortly afterwards slain at Susa. In 1363 and 1364 Urban V. made another attempt to reduce the heretics to obedience. The infected district was exposed to attack on both sides, for the jurisdiction of the Inquisitor of Provence extended over the Tarantaise. Frère Jean Richard of Marseilles was directed to assail them from the west, while the inquisitor and the Bishop of Turin were busy on the east. Amadeo of Savoy was requested to co-operate with the Seneschal of Provence, and this combined assault resulted in a number of captures and trials. It was doubtless the mingled despair and thirst for revenge excited by this that led to many Waldenses joining in the rising of the Jacquerie in Savoy in 1365—a rising which was suppressed with the customary merciless cruelty by the King of Navarre and Wenzel of Brabant. In spite of these efforts at repression a letter written by them in 1368, to their German brethren, would seem to show that they were still regarded as the leaders of the sect.[294]{261}

Gregory XI. was especially zealous in the warfare with heresy, and we have already seen how earnest were his efforts in 1375 to suppress the Waldenses of Provence and Dauphiné. Those of Piedmont had rendered themselves peculiarly obnoxious. Frà Antonio Pavo had recently gone to "Bricarax," a place deeply infected with heresy, to preach against them—his sermon, of course, including a summons before his tribunal—when in place of humbly submitting, a dozen of them, incited by the Evil One, had set upon him as he left the church and had slain him. Another inquisitor, probably Pietro di Ruffia, had met the same fate in the Dominican cloister at Susa, on the day of the Purification of the Virgin (February 2). Such misdeeds demanded exemplary chastisement, and Gregory's exhortations to Charles V. of France were accompanied with the strongest urgency on Amadeo VI. of Savoy to clear his land of brambles. We have seen how successful were the labors of the Nuncio, Antonio Bishop of Massa, and the Inquisitor of Provence, François Borel. They did not confine their energies to the French valleys. The Waldenses of the Val di Susa were exposed to the most pitiless persecution; on a Christmas night Borel with an armed force attacked Pragelato, putting to the sword all whom he could reach. The wretches who escaped perished of hunger and cold, including, it is said, fifty women with children at the breast.[295]

It may be hoped that this holocaust satisfied the manes of the murdered inquisitors, for they seem to have received no other satisfaction. A succession of inquisitors—Piero di Castelmonte, Ruffino di Terdona, Tommaso da Casacho, and Michele Grassi, undaunted by the fate of their predecessors, wasted their energies on the Piedmontese Waldenses without reducing them to subjection. The pitiless forays of Borel drove the poor wretches from their native valleys, and they poured over into Piedmont. Amadeo VII., who succeeded his father in 1383, seems to have given the Inquisition but slender support, and it had little encouragement in its efforts to subdue the stubborn mountaineers. The fragmentary records of Frà Antonio Secco, who undertook the work in the spring of 1387, show how fruitless was the endeavor to co-operate{262} with the ruthless proselytism of Borel. It is true that he caught Isabel Ferreria, the wife of Giovanni Gabriele, one of the murderers of Antonio Pavo, and had the satisfaction of torturing her, but he could get no evidence against her, and could only learn

88

that her husband had died in 1386. Some other suspects he tortured and penanced with crosses: apparently he had no prisons at his disposal in which to incarcerate them. Accusations and denunciations poured in to him by the hundred, showing that the land was alive with heretics, but he was powerless to inflict on them punishment that would make an impression. One of his first cases had been a certain Lorenzo Bandoria, who had abjured before Antonio Pavo, and who under torture confessed to continued heresy. Here was a clear case of relapse, and accordingly, on March 31, he was abandoned to the secular arm and all his property declared confiscated to the Inquisition. This proved a mere *brutum fulmen*, for on May 6 Frà Antonio was obliged to issue a mandate to Ugonetto Bruno, Lord of Ozasco, ordering him, under pain of a hundred marks, to capture Lorenzo and present him before the tribunal the next day, while the treasurer of Ozasco was required, under threat of excommunication, to appear at the same time with an inventory of all the convict's property. As Lorenzo had been handed over to the Castellan of Pignerol for execution, it is evident that the officials refused to carry out the sentences of the inquisitor, nor does this new effort appear to have had any better result. Many of his citations were disregarded, and when, on May 19, he ordered the lords of Ozasco to arrest three heretics under penalty of a hundred marks, no attention seems to have been paid to the command. This insubordination increased, and as the season advanced we observe that when an accused refuses to confess, the dread entry "the lord inquisitor is not content" is not followed by the customary torture, but that the culprit is mercifully dismissed under bail. One case gave Frà Antonio infinite disgust. On June 27 he cited Giacomo Do and Sanzio Margarit of Sangano; they did not appear, but on August 6 he found them in Turin and seized them. For fifteen days he kept them in chains, when they broke jail, but by the help of God he caught them again and carried them to the castle of Avegliana, where they remained ten days. He had been unable to get them tortured, and they would not confess without it; the magistrates{263} of Avegliana appealed to Count Amadeo, who ordered them released, and Frà Antonio records the unwillingness with which he obeyed the command. He endeavored to turn his stay in Avegliana to account by publishing the customary monition for all persons to come forward and confess their own heresy or denounce those who were suspect. For nine days he waited, but not a soul appeared to accuse himself or his neighbors, and he departed, grieved at heart over the obduracy of the people, for it was common fame that there were many heretics there and in the neighborhood, especially at Coazze and Valgione. The final blow came when in December he issued a summons to all the officials of Val Perosa, one of the recognized Waldensian valleys, reciting that their land was full of heretics and that they must appear before him in Pignerol to purge themselves and their communities of this infamy. They did not obey, but through the intervention of the Piedmontese Chancellor, Giovanni di Brayda, and other courtiers, they agreed to pay Count Amadeo five hundred florins a year, for which he was to prevent the inquisitor from visiting Val Perosa, and they were to be exempted from obeying his citations. This was too much to endure, and Frà Antonio shook the dust of Pignerol from his feet for the more promising chase of the Cathari near Turin, first denouncing the officials of Val Perosa as having incurred excommunication and the penalties of contumacy, the only result of which was to draw upon his head the wrath of Count Amadeo. It does not appear that he had any better success in endeavoring to obtain for his Inquisition the confiscations of the people of Pragelato condemned by the Provençal inquisitor, François Borel. By a special privilege of Clement VII. the latter's jurisdiction had been extended over some of the Piedmontese valleys, and though Frà Antonio might abandon the persons of the heretics to his Franciscan rival, he was resolved, if he could, to retain their property. These mishaps of Frà Antonio have an interest, not only as a rare instance of difficulties thrown into the path of the Inquisition, but as explaining why the fierce persecutions of Borel had so little effect in diminishing Waldensianism.[296]{264} Pragelato, however, suffered more severely in 1400 when, about Christmas, it was attacked by an armed force from Susa. The inhabitants who escaped death or capture took refuge on the mountain-tops of the Val San Martino, where many perished from exposure in the inclement season; and the survivors, on returning after the departure of the troops, found their dwellings dismantled. This cold-blooded cruelty shocked even Boniface IX., who ordered the inquisitor in charge of the foray to moderate his zeal in future.[297]

Vicente Ferrer's visit of 1403 was of a more peaceful nature, but it is not likely that the conversions of which he boasted were more permanent than those which his eloquence effected with the Moors and Jews of his native land, where they eagerly clamored for baptism under the persuasion of massacre.[298]

During the Great Schism persecution slackened, but already, in 1416, fresh decrees were issued against the Waldenses. Our knowledge of details is but fragmentary at best, and it is impossible to construct a complete history of the conflict between them and the Inquisition, but we may fairly infer that the latter was at least spasmodically active. A petition addressed to the Duke of Savoy by the lords of Luserna recites that the inhabitants of the valley were in full rebellion, owing to repeated persecution; the document is without date, but must be posterior to 1417, when Sigismund erected the county into a duchy. Again, we know that, between 1440 and 1450, Frà Bertrando Piero, vicar of the inquisitor, in one raid burned at Coni twenty-two relapsed heretics, and confiscated their property. This happens to be alluded to in a memorial{265} addressed in 1457 to Calixtus III., by the people of the neighboring village of Bernez, who proceed to relate that after this exploit Frà Bertrando visited their town in company with his principal, Frà Ludovico da Soncino, and commenced an inquisition there, but abandoned it, to the scandal of the people, without concluding the trials. Then Felix V. (Amadeo of Savoy) sent the Abbot of San-Piero of Savigliano to complete the unfinished business, who

89

acquitted a number of the accused. Then recently there had come a new inquisitor who took up the cases again and molested those who had been discharged, whereupon they petitioned the pope that he be restrained from further proceedings until two experts in theology be appointed as assessors by the Bishop of Mondovi and the Abbot of Savigliano. The presentation of such a request shows how much the Inquisition had lost of its power of inspiring awe, and this is emphasized by the action of Calixtus in ordering the Bishop of Turin and the inquisitor to associate with themselves two experts and proceed with the cases. It indicates, moreover, that little rest was allowed to the Waldenses. While this affair was dragging its slow length along, Nicholas V., in 1453, addressed to the Bishops of Turin and Nice and to the Inquisitor Giacomo di Buronzo, a bull reciting that Giacomo had found in the Valley of Luserna a majority of the inhabitants infected with heresy, many of them having relapsed repeatedly. Unable to convert them, he had placed an interdict on the valley; the people had repented and begged for readmission to the Church, wherefore Nicholas orders the removal of the interdict, and that penitents, whether relapsed or not, be pardoned and restored to all their civil rights—a degree of lenity which indicates that sterner measures at the time were clearly inexpedient.[299]

In 1475 a more serious war of extermination was commenced against them under the Duchess Yolande, Regent of Savoy, in conjunction with the simultaneous action of the Inquisition in Dauphiné. By an edict of January 23, 1476, all the officials in the infected districts were placed at the disposition of the Inquisition, and the podestà of Luserna was cited to appear on February 10, to answer for his conduct, in refusing, at the instance of the Inquisitor{266} Andrea di Aquapendente, to make proclamation that none of the converts of Giacomo di Buronzo should be permitted to effect sales greater in amount than one florin, and that all sales which had been made by them were void, for they had relapsed, were endeavoring to emigrate, and to dispose of their property, which was legally confiscated. Louis XI., who stopped the persecution, as we have seen, so unceremoniously in his own dominions, felt interest enough in the matter to extend protection over the unfortunates in his sister's territories, and his word had power sufficient to dampen the zeal of the duchess, who was wholly dependent on him after the misfortunes of Charles the Bold. Sixtus IV. was much scandalized by this. He had sent a special papal commissioner to speed the holy work, and he wrote pressingly to Louis, assuming that the royal letters of protection must have been surreptitiously obtained. He instructed the Bishop of Turin to go, if possible, in person to Louis and to make every effort to exterminate the heretics, who dared openly to propagate their doctrines and make converts, to the ruin of immortal souls. The death of Louis, in 1483, deprived the Waldenses of their protector, and persecution recommenced. An order of Duke Carlo I., in 1484, to inquire into the violences committed by the people of Angrogna, Villaro, and Bobbio because their lords endeavored to suppress their heresies, shows how soon and how bitterly the struggle broke out afresh. The heretics scattered through the towns of Piedmont were mercilessly dealt with by the inquisitors, but those who inhabited the mountain valleys were safe, except from assault by overwhelming forces. In April, 1487, Innocent VIII. recites how the inquisitor-general, Frà Blasio di Monreale, had gone to the infected district, and had vainly sought by earnest exhortations to induce the heretics to abandon their errors; how they had contemptuously defied his censures, had continued openly to preach and make converts, had attacked his house, slain his familiar, and pillaged his goods. More strenuous efforts were evidently requisite, and Innocent appointed Alberto de" Capitanei, Archdeacon of Cremona, as papal nuncio and commissioner to Piedmont and Dauphiné, with instructions to coerce the people to receive Frà Blasio, and permit the free exercise of his office, and to crush the heretics like venomous serpents. To this end Alberto was empowered to preach a crusade with plenary indulgences,{267} and to deprive of their office and dignities all, whether ecclesiastics or laymen, who refused to obey his commands. From February to May, 1488, he duly issued his citations to the heretics, and as they were contumacious, he condemned them accordingly and abandoned them in mass to the secular arm. Meanwhile a force estimated at eighteen thousand crusaders had been raised in France and Piedmont, which advanced in four columns so as to block every avenue of escape. The slaughter in Val Louise has already been alluded to. The Val d'Angrogna was more fortunate, and in the attack upon it the crusading army was virtually annihilated. This victory earned for the Waldenses a respite, and in 1490 Carlo I. invited them to a conference at Pignerol, where he granted them peace and confirmed their privileges. In 1498 they were visited by Lucas of Prague and Thomas Germanus, envoys of the *Unitas Fratrum* of Bohemia. Through these they addressed a letter to the Bohemian King Ladislas and his nobles, boasting that they did not frequent the Catholic churches, fiercely denouncing the vices of the priesthood, and arguing that the benediction of such men was rather a malediction. Evidently the spirit of the persecuted saints was unbroken, and it was soon after put to the test in the valley of the Po, where whole villages were found to consist of Waldenses. Marguerite de Foix, Marchioness of Saluces, put troops at the command of the Inquisitor Angelo Ricciardino, who had found his ordinary machinery baffled. The villages of Pravillelm, Beitoneto, and Oncino were raided; most of the inhabitants succeeded in escaping to Luserna, but some were captured, and five were sentenced to be burned, March 24, 1510. A heavy snow-storm delayed the execution, and during the ensuing night the prisoners broke jail and joined their comrades. The inquisitor, however, was not to be balked of his exhibition, and replaced the fugitives with three prisoners to whom he had promised pardon in consideration of the fulness of their confessions, and who were duly burned. The deserted villages were confiscated and made over to good Catholics, but the refugees at intervals descended on them, slaying and spoiling without mercy, till no one dared to dwell there. Finally the bigoted marchioness yielded, and for a round sum of money, in 1512, permitted the exiles to return and dwell in peace. The triumph of toleration thus won by the sword was but local and temporary.{268} In Savoy, the statutes published in 1513 contain all the time-honored provisions for the suppression of heresy, with instructions to all public officials to aid in every way the Inquisition, whose expenses are to be defrayed out of the confiscations. Continued persecution was thus provided for, nor was it averted when, in 1530, the Waldenses opened negotiations with the Protestants of Switzerland, resulting in their final incorporation with the Calvinists.[300]

These incessant ravages naturally led to emigration on an extended scale, which, as we have seen, mostly turned itself to Calabria and Apulia, where the brethren had dwelt in comparative peace for nearly two centuries. A large portion of the population of Freyssinières, for instance, expatriated themselves and settled in the valley of Volturara. The Inquisition was virtually extinct in the kingdom of Naples during the fifteenth century, and the heretics had earned toleration by a decent reserve. They attended mass occasionally, allowed their children to be baptized by the priests, and, what was more important, they paid their tithes with exemplary regularity—tithes which grew satisfactorily under the incessant industry of the God-fearing husbandmen. The mountain valleys which had been almost a desert became smiling with corn-fields and pastures, orchards and vine-yards. The nobles on whose lands they had settled under formal agreements gave willing protection to those who contributed so greatly to their revenues. When the independence of the feudatories was lost under the growing royal power of the House of Aragon, the heretics sought and obtained, in 1497, from King Frederic, the confirmation by the crown of the agreements with the nobles, and thus felt assured of continued toleration. They were visited every two years by the travelling pastors, or *barbes*, who came in pairs, an elder, known as the *reggitore*, and a younger, the *coadiutore*, journeying with some pretence of occupation, finding in every city the secret band of believers whom it was their{269} mission to comfort and keep steadfast in the faith, and from whom they made collections which they reported to the General Assembly or Council. Between Pignerol and Calabria they counted twenty-five days" journey along the western coast, returning by the eastern to Venice. Everywhere they met friends acquainted with their secret passwords, and in spite of ecclesiastical vigilance there existed throughout Italy a subterranean network of heresy disguised under outward conformity. In 1497 the envoys from the Bohemian Brethren, Lucas and Thomas, found in Rome itself one of their faith, whom they bitterly reproached for concealing his belief. In Calabria, in 1530, it was estimated that they numbered ten thousand souls, in Venetia, six thousand. The fate of these poor creatures, after generations of peaceful existence which might well seem destined to be perpetual, belongs to a period beyond our present limits, but the fact that they could thus prosper and increase shows how rusty had grown the machinery of the Inquisition, and how incapable had become its officials.[301]

It only remains for us to note cursorily such indications as have reached us of the activity and condition of the Inquisition in the several provinces of Italy during the fourteenth and fifteenth centuries. In Savoy, as we have seen, the bitter contest with the Waldenses kept it in fair working condition, while it was gradually falling into desuetude elsewhere, although in Lombardy it still, for a while, maintained its terrors. We have a somewhat vague description of its sleepless vigilance in 1318, in pursuing certain heretics who are described as Lollards—whether Begghards or Waldenses does not appear, but probably the latter, as we are told that when concealment became impossible the men escaped to Bohemia, leaving some women with children at the breast, whereupon the women were burned, and the children given to good Catholics to be brought up in the faith. In 1344 we hear of a great popular excitement, caused by the belief that a number of victims of the Inquisition had suffered unjustly. Matters went so far that the Imperial Vicar, Lucchino Visconti, asked Clement VI. to order an{270}investigation, which was duly held, though we do not know the result. It was possibly the feeling thus aroused which led, in 1346, to the murder in the Milanese of a Franciscan inquisitor conspicuous for his persecuting zeal. The perpetual troubles during the century between the Holy See and the Visconti cannot but have greatly interfered with the efficiency of persecution. In the collected statutes of the Dukes of Milan from 1343 to 1495 there is no allusion of any kind to the Inquisition, or to the punishment of heretics. There is, however, on record a decree of 1388 placing the civil officials at the service of the Inquisition, but it enforces the conditions of the Clementines, which require episcopal consent to the use of torture and harsh prison, and to the final sentence. It moreover threatens inquisitors with punishment for using their office to extort money or gratify malice; and it further significantly commands them not to abuse the privilege of armed familiars, or to unnecessarily multiply their officials. How the political passions of the time hindered the functions of the Holy Office is seen in the case of Frà Ubertino di Carleone, a bustling Franciscan, subsequently Bishop of Lipari, who, about 1360, was accused of heresy by the Inquisitor of Piacenza. He at once proclaimed that his Ghibellinism was the motive of the prosecution, and aroused the factions of the city to a tumult, under cover of which he escaped.[302]

Inquisitors, indeed, continued to be regularly appointed, and to perform such of their functions as they could, but the decline in their usefulness is shown by one of the earliest acts of Martin V., in 1417, before leaving Constance, in commissioning the Observantine Franciscan, Giovanni da Capistrano, as a special inquisitor against the heretics of Mantua. From this time, in fact, when any effective effort against heresy was called for, the regular machinery of the Inquisition was no longer relied upon. It seems to have been regarded as effete for all the purposes for which it had been instituted, and special appointments were necessary of men devoted to the work, such as Capistrano and his friend Giacomo{271} della Marca. Just as the inquisitorial jurisdiction had superseded the episcopal, so now both were overslaughed as insufficient. Thus, in 1457, when a new heresy sprang up in Brescia and Bergamo concerning Christ, the Virgin, and the Church Militant, infecting both clergy and laity, and including suspicion of sorcery, Calixtus III. ordered his nuncio in those parts, Master Bernardo del Bosco, to seize the heretics and try them, with even more than the privileges of an inquisitor, for he was empowered to proceed to final judgment and execution without appeal, leaving it to his discretion whether he should call for advice upon the inquisitors and episcopal ordinaries. Two years later, in the case of Zanino da Solcia, to which I shall recur hereafter, the sentence was rendered by the Lombard inquisitor, Frà Jacopo da Brescia, but the examination took place in the presence of Master Bernardo del Bosco, who moreover received the abjuration of Zanino, and the sentence was sent to Pius II. and was modified by him. The diminution of popular respect for the Inquisition was still further manifested in 1459, by the doubts publicly expressed of the validity of the bulls of Innocent IV. and Alexander IV. authorizing inquisitors to preach crusades against heretics and to prosecute for heresy all persons and communities impeding them, so that Calixtus III. was obliged to reissue the authorization.[303]

A curious case occurring about this time illustrates the growing indifference felt in Lombardy for the Inquisition. In Milan, about 1440, a learned mathematician, named Amadeo de" Landi, was accused of heresy before the inquisitors. During the progress of his trial he was, to the great damage of his reputation, denounced as a heretic by sundry friars in their sermons, and among others by Bernardino of Siena, the saintly head of the Observantines. The Inquisition pronounced him a good Catholic and discharged him, but those who had slandered him offered no reparation. The acquittal by the Inquisition apparently did not outweigh the denunciations of Bernardino, and Amadeo appealed to Eugenius IV., who referred the matter to Giuseppe di Brippo, with power to enforce his decision with censures. Giuseppe summoned the detractors to appear on a certain day, and on their failing to{272} present themselves condemned Bernardino to make public retraction under pain of excommunication. Bernardino paid no heed to this, and on his death in 1444, when immediate efforts were made for his canonization, Amadeo raised great scandal by proclaiming that he had died in mortal sin as an excommunicate. This gratified the jealousy of the conventual branch of the Franciscans and many of the secular clergy, who spread the scandal far and wide. By this time, however, the Observantines were too influential for such an assault upon their revered vicar-general to be successful; and in 1447 they obtained from Nicholas V. a bull in which he annulled all the proceedings of Giuseppe, ordered every record of them to be destroyed, imposed silence on the unlucky Amadeo, declared Bernardino to have acted righteously throughout, and forbade all clerks, friars, and others from indulging in further detraction concerning him. I may add that the opposition of the Conventuals was powerful enough to postpone until 1450 the canonization of San Bernardino, and a humorous incident in the struggle may be worth mention. When the blessed Tommaso of Florence died at Rieti in 1447, and immediately began to coruscate in miracles, Capistrano hurried thither and forbade him to display further his thaumaturgic powers until Bernardino should be canonized—and Tommaso meekly obeyed.[304]

Yet, shorn as the Inquisition had become of real effectiveness for its avowed functions, the office continued to be sought, doubtless because it conferred a certain measure of importance, and possibly because it afforded opportunity of illicit gains. Inquisitors were regularly appointed, and the custom grew up in Lombardy that in each city where a tribunal existed vacancies were filled on the nomination of the prior of the local Dominican convent with the assent of discreet brethren, whereupon the General Master of the Order issued the commission. In 1500 this was modified by giving the Vicar-general of Lombardy power to reject or ratify the nomination. The subordinate position to which the inquisitorial office had fallen is illustrated in the last decade of the fifteenth century by Frà Antonio da Brescia, who was inquisitor of his native place, and who was claimed as an ornament of the Dominican Order, but his eulogist has nothing to say as to his persecuting{273} heretics, while praising his pulpit labors in many of the Italian cities.[305]

In Venice, as we have seen, the Inquisition never succeeded in shaking off the trammels of state supervision and interference. In what spirit the State regarded its relations with the Holy Office was exhibited in 1356, when Frà Michele da Pisa, the Inquisitor of Treviso, imprisoned some Jewish converts who had apostatized. This was strictly within his functions, but the secular officials interposed, forbade his proceeding to try his prisoners, seized his familiars, and tortured them on the charge of pilfering the property of the accused. These high-handed measures provoked the liveliest indignation on the part of Innocent VI., but the republic stood firm, and nothing seems to have been gained. In the correspondence which ensued, moreover, there are allusions to former troubles which show that this was by no means the first time that Frà Michele's labors had been impeded by the secular power. Sometimes, indeed, the Signoria completely ignored the Inquisition. In 1365 a case in which a prisoner had blasphemed the Virgin was brought before the Great Council, which ordered him to be tried by the vicar of the Bishop of Castello, and on conviction to be banished, thus prescribing the punishment, and recognizing only the episcopal jurisdiction.[306]

In 1373 Venice was honored with the appointment of a special inquisitor, Frà Ludovico da San-Martino, while Frà Niccolò Mucio of Venice was made Inquisitor of Treviso. This led to some debate about their partition of the great Patriarchate of Aquileia, which extended from the province of Spalatro to that of Milan. The Patriarchate of Grado (which was not transferred to Venice till 1451) was adjudged to Ludovico, together with the see of Jesol. This latter place, though close to Venice, was then, we are told, in ruins, with a roofless cathedral serving as a place of refuge for heretics, who there felt safe from persecution. This partition did not improve the position of the inquisitor, whose importance was reduced to a minimum. He seems, in fact, to be regarded only as{274} a functionary of the state police. In 1412 the Great Council orders him, April 17, to put an end to the performance of divine service by a Greek priest named Michael, whose celebrations attract great crowds, and also to banish him, taking care to so manage the affair that the interposition of the council may not be suspected; and a month later, May 26, the order of banishment is revoked, but the prohibition of celebration is maintained. In all his proper functions the inquisitor was overslaughed and disregarded. In 1422 the Council of Ten appointed a commission to examine some Franciscans charged with sacrificing to demons and other abominable practices, and a month later they sent to Martin V., requesting powers to terminate the matter, in view of the immunities enjoyed by the Mendicants. When, in the following year, 1423, the Senate withdrew the pecuniary provision with which the State had always defrayed the expenses of the Inquisition, they marked their sense of its inutility and their indifference to its power. This may possibly have led to the reunion of the districts of Venice and Treviso, for, in 1433 and 1434, we find single inquisitors appointed to both. In the latter year the lack of power of the incumbent, Frà Luca Cioni, is shown by the fact that when he desired to proceed against Ruggieri da Bertona, accused of heresy, he was forced to get Eugenius IV. to order the Bishop of Castello (Venice) to assist him. A further recognition of the inefficiency of the Inquisition is seen in the sending of Frà Giovanni da Capistrano to Venice in 1437, when the Jesuats were accused of heresy, and he acquitted them, and again, about 1450, when heretical notions spread there concerning the origin and nature of the soul, which he suppressed.[307]

Allusion has been made in a former chapter to the limitation imposed in 1450 by the Council of Ten on the number of armed familiars whom the inquisitor might retain, reducing them to four, and in 1451 increasing them to twelve, with instructions to the police to see that they were really engaged in the duties of the Holy Office. In so large and populous a district this sufficiently{275} shows how purely nominal were the functions of the Inquisition, and how close was the supervision exercised by the State. Yet inquisitors continued to be appointed, but when they attempted to exercise any independent jurisdiction we have seen, in the case of the sorcerers of 1521, that even the most energetic interference of Leo X. could not induce the Signoria to waive its right of final decision.[308]

In Mantua, which formed part of the Patriarchate of Aquileia, we hear, in 1494, of an inquisitor who, for lack of heresies to suppress, assailed the *monts de piété*, or public pawning establishments, and all who favored them. These institutions were founded about this period as a charitable work for the purpose of rescuing the poor from the exactions of the usurers and the Jews. Frà Bernardino da Feltre, a celebrated Observantine Franciscan, made this a special object of his mission-work in the Italian cities, and on his coming to Mantua he completely silenced his adversaries. The decline of visible heresy at this period, in fact, is illustrated in the very diffuse account which Luke Wadding gives, year after year, of Bernardino's triumphant progress throughout Italy to call the people to repentance, when cities eagerly disputed with each other the blessing of his presence. In all this there is no allusion to any attacks by him on heresy; had there been any to assail, his burning zeal would not have suffered it to enjoy impunity.[309]

In Tuscany the growing insubordination felt towards the Inquisition was manifested at Siena, in 1340, by the enactment of laws checking some of its abuses. Frà Simone Filippo, the inquisitor, complained to Benedict XII., who at once pronounced them null and void, and ordered them erased from the statute-book. The relations between the Holy Office and the people at this period, however, are more significantly displayed in a series of events occurring at Florence, of which the details chance to have been{276}preserved. In Tuscany the triumph of orthodoxy had been complete. A sermon of Frà Giordano da Rivalto, in 1304, asserts that heresy was virtually exterminated: scarce any heretics remained, and they were in strict hiding. This is confirmed by Villani, who tells us that, by the middle of the century, there were no heretics in Florence. This is doubtless too absolute an assertion, but the existence of a few scattered Waldenses and Fraticelli offered scant excuse for such an establishment as the inquisitor was accustomed to maintain. In 1337 the papal nuncio, Bertrand, Archbishop of Embrun, took the incumbent of the office severely to task for the abuse of appointing an excessive number of assistants, and ordered him in future to restrict himself to four counsellors and assessors, two notaries, two jailers, and twelve ministers or familiars. This was by no means a small or inexpensive body of officials; the Inquisition's share of confiscations from the few poverty-stricken heretics who could occasionally be picked up evidently was insufficient to maintain such a corps, and means, either fair or foul, must be found to render the income of the office adequate to the wants of those who depended upon it for their fortunes. How this was done, on the one hand by cheating the papal camera, and on the other by extorting money on false charges of heresy and by selling to bravoes licenses to carry arms, has already been pointed out. The former device was one which, when detected, was difficult to condone, and its discovery caused, in the commencement of 1344, a sudden vacancy in the Florentine Inquisition. The republic was in the habit of suggesting names to the Franciscan General for appointment, and sometimes its requests were respected. In the present case it asked, February 26, that the Tuscan inquisitor, Frà Giovanni da Casale, be permitted to exercise his functions within the city, but the suggestion was unheeded, and in March the post was given to Frà Piero di Aquila.[310]

93

Frà Piero was a distinguished member of the Franciscan Order. But two months earlier he had been appointed chaplain to Queen Joanna of Naples, and his Commentaries on the Sentences of Peter Lombard were highly esteemed, receiving, in 1480, the{277} honor of an edition printed at Speier. A man so gifted was warmly welcomed, and the republic thanked the Franciscan General for the selection. I have already detailed how he fell into the same courses as his predecessor in cheating the papal camera, how he was prosecuted for this, and for what the republic officially denounced as "*estorsioni nefande*" committed on the people, and how, within two years after his appointment, he was a fugitive, not daring to stand trial. There is another phase of his activity, however, which is worth recounting in some detail, as it illustrates perfectly how useful an instrument was the Inquisition in carrying out the wishes of the Roman curia in matters wholly disconnected with the purity of the faith.[311]

The Cardinal of Santa Sabina, while visiting various courts in the capacity of papal legate, had had occasion to collect large sums. In charity to him we may assume, what doubtless was the truth, that the money belonged to the pope, although it stood in the cardinal's name on the books of his bankers, the great Florentine company of the Acciajuoli. In receiving it the members of the company had bound themselves jointly and severally for its repayment, agreeing to subject themselves to the judgment of the Court of Auditors of the Apostolic Chamber. In 1343 there was due the cardinal some twelve thousand florins, which the Acciajuoli were unable to pay. A commercial and financial crisis had paralyzed the commerce and industries of the city. Its bankers had advanced vast sums to Edward III. of England and to Robert the Good of Naples, and clamored in vain for repayment. The Lombard war had exhausted the public treasury and the whole community was bankrupt. Not only the Acciajuoli, but the Bardi, the Peruzzi, and other great banking-houses closed their doors, and ruin stared the Florentines in the face. There was at least one creditor, however, who was resolved to have his money.[312]

On October 9, 1343, Clement VI. wrote to the republic, stating the claim of the cardinal and ordering the Signoria to compel{278} the Acciajuoli to pay it. Under the circumstances this was clearly impossible, but judgment against the debtors had been rendered by the auditors of the papal camera. This was enough to bring the affair within the sphere of spiritual jurisdiction, and authority was sent to the inquisitor to execute the sentence, calling in the aid of the secular arm, and, if necessary, laying an interdict on the city. The matter dragged on until, November 23, 1345, Frà Piero appeared before the Gonfaloniero and the Priors of the Arts, and summoned them to imprison the debtors until payment, under pain of excommunication and interdict; whereupon the magistrates responded that, out of reverence for the pope and respect for the inquisitor and to oblige the cardinal, they would lend the aid of the secular arm. Still the money was not forthcoming, and although such assets of the Acciajuoli as could be seized were delivered to Frà Piero, and security was given for the balance, he held the whole community responsible for the debt of a few of the citizens. The discussion became angry, and when the inquisitor, in violation of a law of the republic, committed the indiscretion of arresting Salvestro Baroncelli, a member of the bankrupt company, as he was leaving the palace of the Priors of the Arts, his three familiars who had committed the offence were, in compliance with a savage statute, punished with banishment and the loss of the right hand.

All this did not extract the money from the bankrupts, and Frà Piero laid the city under interdict, but both the clergy and people refused to observe it. The churches remained open and the rites of religion continued to be celebrated, leading to a fresh series of prosecutions against the bishop and priests. Inside the walls the Florentines might disregard the censures of the Church, but a commercial community could not afford to be cut off from intercourse with the world. Her citizens and their goods were scattered in every trade-centre in Christendom, and were virtually outlawed by the interdict. This was the reason alleged by the priors when, June 14, 1346, they humbled their pride and sent commissioners to Clement authorized to bind the republic to pay the debt of the Acciajuoli to the cardinal, not exceeding seven thousand florins, in eight months. Their submission was graciously received, and, February 28, 1347, the pope ordered the interdict removed, cautiously providing, however, for its *ipso facto*{279} renewal in case the obligation for six thousand six hundred florins was not met at maturity.[313]

Meanwhile another scene of the comedy was developing itself. In its contest with Frà Piero the republic had not stood solely on the defensive. Piero, papal nuncio at Lucca, who had in charge the prosecutions against the inquisitors for embezzling the sums due to the camera, had appointed as his deputy in Florence, Niccolò, Abbot of Santa Maria, who proceeded against Frà Piero on that charge, to which the Signoria added the accusation, sustained by abundant testimony, of extorting from citizens large sums of money by fraudulent prosecutions for heresy. By March 10, 1346, the Signoria was asking the appointment of Frà Michele di Lapo as his successor. Frà Piero was a fugitive, and refused to return and stand his trial when legally cited and tendered a safe-conduct. After due delay, in 1347, the Abate Niccolò, being armed with papal authority, declared him in default and contumacious, and then proceeded to excommunicate him. The excommunication was published in all the churches of Florence, and Frà Piero was thus cut off from the faithful and abandoned to Satan. He could afford to regard all this with calm philosophy. His success in collecting the cardinal's money entitled him to reward, and the booty of seven thousand florins which he had personally carried off from Florence as the results of his two years" inquisitorial career, could doubtless be used to advantage. While Niccolò was vainly citing him, he was promoted, February 12, 1347, to the episcopate of Sant-Angeli de" Lombardi, and his excommunication was answered, June 29, 1348, by his translation to the presumably preferable see of Trivento. All that the

94

Florentines could do was to petition repeatedly that in future inquisitors should be selected from among their own citizens, who would be less likely than strangers to be guilty of extortions and scandals. Their request was respected at{280} least in 1354, when a Florentine, Frà Bernardo de" Guastoni, was appointed Inquisitor of Tuscany.[314]

This was not likely to be effective, and the Signoria made a more promising effort at self-protection by passing various laws imitated from those adopted not long before at Perugia. To limit the abuse of selling licenses to bear arms, the inquisitor, as we have seen, was restricted to employing six armed familiars. Moreover, it was decreed that no citizen could be arrested without the participation of the podestà, who was required to seize all persons designated to him by the bishop—the inquisitor not being alluded to—which would seem to leave small opportunity for independent action by the latter, especially as he was deprived of his private jail and was ordered to send all prisoners to the public prison. He was further prohibited from inflicting pecuniary punishments, and all whom he condemned as heretics were to be burned. This was revolutionary in a high degree, and did not tend to harmonize the relations between the republic and the papacy. The desperate quarrel between them which arose in 1375 was caused by political questions, but it was embittered by troubles arising from the Inquisition, especially as a demand made by Innocent VI., in 1355, for a revision of their statutes remained unheeded. In 1372 efforts were made to obtain the removal of Frà Tolomeo da Siena, the Inquisitor of Tuscany, who was exceedingly unpopular, but Gregory XI. expressed the fullest confidence in him and ordered him to be protected by the Vicar-general, Filippo, Bishop of Sabina. Yet the pope probably yielded, for I find in 1373 that Frà Piero di Ser Lippo, who had already served as Tuscan inquisitor in 1371, was again appointed to replace a certain Frà Andrea di Ricco. With some intervals Frà Piero served until at least 1384, and he proved no more disposed than his predecessors to yield to the resistance which the methods of the Inquisition inevitably provoked in the free Italian cities. Pistoia had followed the example of Florence in endeavoring to protect its citizens by municipal statutes, and in 1375 it was duly placed under interdict and its citizens were excommunicated. At the same time{281} Frà Piero complained of Florence as impeding the free action of the Inquisition, and Gregory at once ordered the Signoria to abrogate the obnoxious statutes. No attention was paid to these commands by Florence, and when the rupture came the Florentine mob expressed its feelings by destroying the inquisitorial prison and driving the inquisitor from the city. It was also alleged that in the disturbances a monk named Niccolò was tortured and buried alive. These misdeeds, although denied by the Signoria, were alleged as a justification of the terrible bull of March 31, 1376, fulminated against Florence by Gregory. In this he not only excommunicated and interdicted the city, but specially outlawed the citizens, exposing their property wherever found to seizure, and their persons to slavery. This shocking abuse was the direct outgrowth of the long series of legislation against heresy, and was sanctioned by the public law of the period; everywhere throughout Christendom the goods of Florentines were seized and the merchants were glad to beg their way home, stripped of all they possessed. Not all were so fortunate, as some pious monarchs, like Edward III., in addition reduced them to servitude. No commercial community could long endure a contest waged after this fashion, and, as before, Florence was compelled to submit. In the peace signed July 28, 1378, the republic agreed to annul all laws restricting the Inquisition and interfering with the liberties of the Church, and it authorized a papal commissioner to expunge them from the statute-book. The Great Schism, however, weakened for a time the aggressive energy of the papacy, and much of the obnoxious legislation reappears in the revised code of 1415.[315]

The career of Tommasino da Foligno, who died in 1377, has{282} interest for us, not only as illustrating the activity of the Inquisition of the period, but also from the curious parallelism which it affords with that of Savonarola. He is one of the prophets, like St. Birgitta of Sweden, St. Catharine of Siena, and the Friends of God in the Rhinelands, who were called forth by the untold miseries then afflicting mankind. A tertiary of St. Francis, he had practised for three years the greatest austerities as an anchorite, when God summoned him forth to preach repentance to the warring factions whose savage quarrels filled every city in the land with wretchedness. Like the other contemporary prophets, he spared neither clerk nor layman; and his bitter animadversions at Perugia on the evil life of Gerald, Abbot of Marmoutiers, papal vicar for the States of the Church, may perhaps account for his subsequent rough handling by the Inquisition. Gifted with miraculous power, as well as with the spirit of prophecy, he wandered from town to town, proclaiming the wrath of God, and foretelling misfortunes which, in the existing state of society, were almost sure to come to pass. To convince the incredulous at Siena, on a midsummer day he predicted a frost for the morrow. When it duly came he was accused of sorcery, seized by the Inquisition, and tortured nearly to death, but he was discharged when a miracle established his innocence and healed the wounds of the torture-chamber. After an intermediate pilgrimage to far-off Compostella, his preaching at Florence excited so much antagonism that again he was arrested by the Inquisition, cast into a dungeon, and kept three days without food or drink, to be finally discharged as insane. After his death at Foligno, unsuccessful attempts were made to procure his canonization, and he long remained an object of local veneration and worship.[316]

During the fifteenth century the Inquisition in central Italy subsided into the same unimportance that we have witnessed elsewhere. The effect of the Great Schism in reducing the respect felt for the papacy was especially felt in Italy, and the papal officials lost nearly all power of enforcing obedience, although the Inquisition at Pisa, when it was strengthened by the presence of the council held there in 1409, took its revenge on a man named Andreani, whom it burned for the crime of habitually and publicly{283} ridiculing it. When the schism was healed at Constance, one of the earliest efforts of Martin V. was directed against the Fraticelli, whose increase in the Roman province he especially deprecated. In his bull on the subject, November 14, 1418, he complained that when inquisitors endeavored to exercise their office against the heretics the latter would claim the jurisdiction of some temporal lord and then threaten and insult their persecutors, so that the latter were afraid to perform their functions. Martin's only remedy was practically to supersede the inquisitors by special appointments, and this naturally sank the institution to a deeper degradation. Thus in 1424, when there were three Fraticelli to be tried in Florence, Martin placed the matter in the hands of Frà Leonardo, a Dominican professor of theology. Still the office of inquisitor continued to be sought and appointments to be made with more or less regularity, from motives which can easily be conjectured; but of activity against heresy there is scarce a trace. How unimportant its functions had become in Bologna may be gathered from the fact that in 1461 the inquisitor, Gabriele of Barcelona, was sent to Rome by his superiors to teach theology in the convent of Minerva, when Pius II. authorized him to appoint a vicar to discharge his duties during his absence. Ten years afterwards the Bolognese inquisitor, Frà Simone da Novara, was fortunate enough to lay hands on a man named Guizardo da Sassuolo, who was suspected of heresy. So completely were such proceedings forgotten that he felt obliged to apply for instructions to Paul II., who congratulated him on the capture, ordered him to proceed according to the canons, and desired the episcopal vicar to co-operate. Heretics evidently had grown scarce, and the inquisitorial functions had fallen into desuetude.[317]

In Rome, when there really was a heresiarch to condemn, there{284} was no Inquisition at hand to perform the duty. In the proceedings against Luther there is no trace of its intervention. The bull *Exsurge Domine*, June 15, 1520, contains no allusion to his doctrines having been examined by it; when they were publicly condemned, June 12, 1521, the ceremony was performed by the Bishop of Ascoli, Auditor of the Rota, and Silvestro Prierias, Master of the Sacred Palace, while the sentence which consigned his effigy and his books to the flames was pronounced by Frà Cipriano, professor in the College of Sacred Theology. It was perhaps the most momentous *auto de fé* that has ever been celebrated, but the Inquisition can boast of no participation in it.[318]

In the Two Sicilies the Inquisition dragged on a moribund existence. Letters of King Robert in 1334 and 1335 and of Joanna I. in 1342 and 1343 show that inquisitors continued to be appointed and to receive the royal exequatur, but they were limited to making fifty arrests each, and record of these was required to be entered in the royal courts; they had no jails, and the royal officials received their prisoners and tortured them when called upon. The Jews appear to be the main object of inquisitorial activity, and this can only have been halting, for in 1344 Clement VI. orders his legate at Naples, Aymerico, Cardinal of S. Martino, to punish condignly all apostate Jews, as though there were no Inquisition at work there. Yet in 1362 there were three inquisitors in Naples, Francesco da Messina, Angelo Cicerello da Monopoli, and Ludovico da Napoli, who took part in the trial of the rebellious Luigi di Durazzo. Still, when efforts were to be made against the Fraticelli, Urban V., in 1368, deemed it necessary to send a special inquisitor, Frà Simone del Pozzo, to Naples. Although his jurisdiction extended over the island of Sicily, Gregory XI., in 1372, when informed that the relics of the Fraticelli were venerated there as those of saints, ordered the prelates to put a stop to it, as though he had no inquisitor to call upon. Yet Frà Simone was there in that year, and had a theological disputation with Frà Niccolò di Girgenti, a learned Franciscan who had been provincial of his Order. The question turned upon some scholastic subtleties respecting the three persons of the Trinity, and as each disputant{285} claimed the victory, Simone proceeded to settle the matter by secretly prosecuting his antagonist for heresy. Niccolò got wind of this and at once appealed to Rome, before the Archbishop of Palermo, demanding his *apostoli*—an appeal which Simone pronounced frivolous. The revelations made by Niccolò as to his antagonists present a most dismal picture of the internal condition of the Church at the time, although Frà Simone's learning and ascetic life won him the popular reputation of a saint, and he obtained the bishopric of Catania, becoming an important political personage. In 1373 Frederic III. issued letters to all the royal officials ordering them to lend all aid to him and to his familiars, and the Inquisition seems to have been firmly established, with prisons of its own. In 1375 we find Gregory applying to the king for the confiscations, and procuring from the revenues of Palermo an appropriation of twelve ounces of gold, to be applied to the extermination of heresy. In this recrudescence of persecution the Jews appear to have been the principal victims. They appealed to Frederic, who in the same year, 1375, issued letters severely blaming the inquisitors and ordering that in future their prisoners should be confined only in the royal jails; that civil judges should assist in their decisions, and that an appeal should lie to the High Court. This was imposing serious limitations on inquisitorial jurisdiction, but no reclamation against it appears to have been made. In Naples, letters of Charles III., issued in 1382 to Frà Domenico di Astragola and Frà Leonardo di Napoli, show that inquisitors continued to be appointed. In 1389 Boniface IX. seems to unite Naples with Sicily by appointing Frà Antonio Traverso di Aversa as inquisitor on both sides of the Faro; but in 1391 another brief of the same pope alludes to the Inquisition of Sicily having become vacant by the death of Frà Francesco da Messina, and as there is customarily but one inquisitor there he fills the vacancy by the appointment of Frà Simone da Amatore. Frà Simone had a somewhat stormy career. Already, in 1392, he was replaced by Frà Giuliano di Mileto, afterwards Bishop of Cefalù, but seems to have regained his position, for in

1393 he was obliged by King Martin to refund moneys extorted from some Jews whom he had prosecuted for holding illicit relations with Christian women, and was told not to interfere with matters beyond his jurisdiction. Engaging in treasonable{286} intrigues, he was driven from the island, and in 1397 we find him acting as papal legate and provincial in Germany. In 1400 he obtained his pardon from King Martin, and was allowed to reside in Syracuse, but was strictly forbidden from exercising the office of inquisitor. Meanwhile, in 1395, we hear of Guglielmo di Girgenti as inquisitor, and in 1397, of Matteo di Catania, a sentence by whom in that year, fining a Jew and his wife in forty ounces, was confirmed by the king, showing that the Inquisition continued to be subordinated to the civil power. Frà Matteo was inquisitor on both sides of the Faro, for a royal letter of 1399 describes him as such, and orders obedience rendered to his vicar, while another of 1403 shows that he still retained the position. A royal decree of 1402 specially provides for Jews an appeal to the king from all inquisitorial sentences, thus continuing what had long been the practice. In 1415 royal letters confirming the appointment of Frà Antonio de Pontecorona, others of 1427 in favor of Frà Benedetto da Perino, and of 1446, in favor of Frà Andrea de la Pascena, show that the organization was maintained, but all sentences were required to be transmitted to the viceroy, who submitted them to a royal judge before they were valid. Thus, in 1451, King Alfonso confirmed a fine of ten thousand florins, levied upon the Jews as a punishment for their usuries and other offences.[319]

On the mainland we have seen proof of the decay of the Inquisition in the undisturbed growth of the Waldensian communities, and the complete breaking-down of its machinery is fairly illustrated in 1427, when Joanna II. undertook to enforce certain measures against the Jews of her kingdom. Had there been an effective and organized Inquisition she would have required no better instrument for her purpose; and it could only have been the absence of this that led her to call in the indefatigable persecutor, Frà Giovanni da Capistrano, to whom she issued a commission to coerce the Jews to abandon usury and to wear the sign Tau, as provided by law. He was empowered to decree such punishments{287} as he might deem fit, which were to be mercilessly inflicted by all judges and other officials, and he was moreover to constrain, under pain of confiscation, the Jews to surrender to him for cancellation all letters and privileges granted to them by former monarchs. Yet there was still a simulacrum of the Inquisition maintained, for in the following year, 1428, we find Martin V. confirming the appointment of Frà Niccolò di Camisio as Inquisitor of Benevento, Bari, and the Capitanata.[320]

Whatever vitality the Inquisition retained was still more reduced when, in 1442, the House of Aragon obtained the throne of Naples. Giannone tells us that the Aragonese princes rarely admitted inquisitors, and, when they did so, required minute reports as to their every official act, never permitting any conviction without the participation of the secular magistrates, followed by royal confirmation, as we have seen to have been the case in Sicily. When, in 1449, Nicholas V. appointed Frà Matteo da Reggio as inquisitor to exterminate the apostate Jews who were said to be numerous throughout the kingdom, the terms employed would seem to indicate that for some time the Inquisition had been practically extinct, although but two years before he had given a commission to Frà Giovanni da Napoli, and although subsequent inquisitors were occasionally appointed.[321]

In Sicily, however, in 1451, the Inquisition obtained fresh vitality by means of an ingenious device. Frà Enrico Lugardi, Inquisitor of Palermo, produced a most impudent forgery in the shape of a long and elaborate privilege purporting to have been issued by the Emperor Frederic II. in 1224, ordering all his Sicilian subjects to give aid and comfort to the "inquisitors of heretical pravity," and stating that, as it was unfitting that all confiscations should inure to the royal fisc without rewarding the inquisitors for their toils and perils, the confiscations henceforth should be divided equally between the fisc, the Inquisition, and the Holy See; moreover, all Jews and infidels were required once a year{288} to supply inquisitors and their attendants, when in prosecution of their duty, with all necessaries for man and beast. Though the fraudulent character of this document was conspicuous on its face, to say nothing of a blunder in the regnal year of its date, the age was not a critical one; Frà Enrico seems to have had no trouble in inducing King Alonso to confirm it, and it was subsequently confirmed again in 1477 by Ferdinand and Isabella. The privileges which it conferred were substantial, and gave fresh importance to the Inquisition, although its judgments were still subjected to revision by the civil power. When, in 1474, famine led Sixtus IV. to request of the Viceroy Ximenes the shipment of a large supply of corn from Sicily to Rome, he wrote to the inquisitor, Frà Salvo di Cassetta, ordering him to strain every nerve to secure the granting of the favor. The inquisitor at that time was evidently a personage of influence, for Frà Salvo in fact was also confessor of the viceroy. The central tribunal of the Inquisition sat in Palermo, and there were three commissioners or deputies in charge of the three "valleys" of the island.[322]

Ferdinand the Catholic, in founding the New Spanish Inquisition, obtained for his grand inquisitor the power of nominating deputies in all the dependencies of Castile and Aragon. About 1487 Fray Antonio de la Peña was sent to Sicily in that capacity, who speedily organized the Holy Office on its new basis throughout the island; and in 1492 an edict of banishment was issued against the Jews, who, as of old, were the chief objects of persecution. On the mainland there was more trouble. When, in 1503, Ferdinand acquired the kingdom of Naples, the Great Captain, Gonsalvo of Cordova, finding the people excited with the fear that the Spanish Inquisition might be introduced, made a solemn compact that no inquisitors should be sent thither. The old rules were kept in force; no one was allowed to be arrested without a special royal warrant, and no inquisitor could exercise any functions without the confirmation of his commission by the royal{289} representative.

Notwithstanding this, in 1504, Diego Deza, the Spanish inquisitor-general, sent to Naples an inquisitor and a receiver of confiscated property, with royal letters ordering them to have free exercise of their authority, but Gonsalvo, who knew by how slender a tenure the new dynasty held the allegiance of the people, seems not to have admitted them. Under the excuse that the Jews and New Christians expelled from Spain found refuge in Naples, the attempt was again made in 1510, and Andres Palacio was sent there as inquisitor, but the populace rose in arms and made demonstrations so threatening that even Ferdinand's fanaticism was forced to give way. The movements of the French in the north of Italy were disquieting, the loyalty of the Neapolitans was not to be relied upon, and the inquisitor was withdrawn with a promise that no further effort would be made to force upon the people the dreaded tribunal. Even Julius II. recognized the necessity of this and assented to the understanding. The Calabrian and Apulian Waldenses thus had a respite until the progress of the Reformation in Italy aroused the Church to renewed efforts and to a complete reorganization of its machinery of persecution.[323]{290}

CHAPTER V.

THE SLAVIC CATHARI.

WHEN Innocent III. found himself confronted with the alarming progress of the Catharan heresy, his vigilant activity did not confine itself to Italy and Languedoc. The home of the belief lay to the east of the Adriatic among the Slavic races. Thence came the missionaries who never ceased to stimulate the zeal of their converts, and every motive of piety and of policy led him to combat the error at its source. Thus the field of battle stretched from the Balkans to the Pyrenees along a front of over a thousand miles, and the result might have been doubtful but for the concentration of moral and material forces resulting from the centralized theocracy founded by Hildebrand.

The contest in the regions south of Hungary is instructive as an illustration of the unconquerable persistence of Rome in conducting for centuries an apparently resultless struggle, undeterred by defeat, taking advantage of every opening for a renewal of the strife, and using for its ends the ambition of monarchs and the self-sacrificing devotion of zealots. A condensed review of the rapid vicissitudes of such a contest is therefore not out of place, although the scene of action lay too far from the centres of European life to have decisive influence upon the development of European thought and belief, except as it served as a refuge for the persecuted and a centre of orthodoxy to which neophytes could be sent.

The vast regions east of the Adriatic scarce paid more than a nominal spiritual allegiance to Rome. A savage and turbulent population, conquered by Hungary towards the end of the eleventh century, and always endeavoring to throw off the yoke, was Christian in little more than name. Such Christianity as it boasted, moreover, was not Latin. The national ritual was Slavic, in spite of its prohibition by Gregory VII., and the Roman observance was detested, from its foreign origin, as the badge of subjugation.{291}The few Latin prelates and priests and monks were encamped amid a hostile population to whom they were strangers in language and manners, and the dissoluteness of their lives gave them no opportunity of acquiring a moral influence that might disarm national and race antipathies. Under such circumstances there was nothing to hinder the spread of Catharism, and when the devastating wars of the Hungarians came to be dignified as crusades for the extermination of heresy, heresy might well claim to be identified with patriotism. From the Danube to Macedonia, and from the Adriatic to the Euxine, the Catharan Church was well organized, divided into dioceses with their bishops, and actively engaged in mission work. Its most flourishing province was Bosnia, where, at the end of the twelfth century, it counted some ten thousand devoted partisans. Culin, the Ban who held it under the suzerainty of Hungary, was a Catharan, and so were his wife and the rest of his family. Even Catholic prelates were suspected, not without cause, of leaning secretly to the heretic belief.[324]

The earliest interference with heresy occurs at the end of the twelfth century, when the Archbishop of Spalatro, doubtless under impulsion from Innocent, drove out a number of Cathari from Trieste and Spalatro. They found ready refuge in Bosnia, where Culin welcomed them. Vulcan, King of Dalmatia, who had designs upon Bosnia, in 1199 represented to Innocent the deplorable prevalence of heresy there, and suggested that Emeric, King of Hungary, should be urged to expel the heretics. Innocent thereupon wrote to Emeric, sending him the severe papal decretal against the Patarins of Viterbo as a guide for his action, and ordering him to cleanse his territories of heresy and to confiscate all heretical property. Culin seems to have taken the initiative by attacking Hungary, but at the same time he tried to make his peace with Rome by asserting that the alleged heretics were good Catholics. He sent some of them, with two of his prelates, to Innocent for examination, and asked for legates to investigate the matter on the spot. In 1202 the pope accordingly ordered his chaplain, Giovanni da Casemario, and the Archbishop of Spalatro, to{292} proceed to Bosnia, where, if they found any heretics, including the Ban himself, they were to be prosecuted according to the rigor of the canons. Giovanni successfully accomplished this mission in 1203. He reported to Innocent a pledge given by the Cathari to adopt the Latin faith, while, to insure the maintenance of religion, he recommended the erection of three or four additional bishoprics in the territory of the Ban, which were ten days" journey in extent and which yet had but one see, of which the incumbent was dead. At the same time King Emeric wrote that Giovanni had brought to him the leaders of the heretics, and he had found them converted to orthodoxy. Culin's son had likewise presented himself, and had entered into bonds of one thousand marks, to be forfeited in case he should hereafter protect heretics within his dominions. The triumph of the Church seemed assured, especially when, in the same year, Calo Johannes, the Emperor of the Bulgarians, applied to Innocent to have cardinals sent to crown him, and professed himself in all things obedient to the Holy See.[325]

All such hopes proved fallacious. With the development of the Albigensian troubles the attention of Innocent was directed from the Slavs. The conversions made under pressure were but temporary. The metropolitan of the province, Arringer, Archbishop of Ragusa, filled the vacant see of Bosnia with a Catharan, and, dying himself soon after, his episcopal city became a nest of heretics. The few Catholic priests scattered through the region abandoned their posts, and Catholicism grew virtually almost extinct. In 1221 it is said that in the whole of Bosnia there was not a single orthodox preacher to be heard. Equally disheartening was the course of affairs among the Bulgarians. After Calo Johannes had been crowned by a legate from Rome, his quarrels with the Latin Emperors of Constantinople led to a breach, and in the wide territories under his dominion the Cathari had full liberty of conscience.[326]

At length the papal attention was again directed to this deplorable state of affairs. In 1221 Honorius III. sent his chaplain, Master Aconcio, as legate to Hungary, with orders to arouse the king and the prelates to a sense of their obligation to exterminate{293} the heretics who were thus openly defiant. On his way the legate paused at Ragusa to superintend the election of an orthodox archbishop, after which he ordered all Dalmatia and Croatia to join in a crusade, but no one followed him, and he went alone to Bosnia, where he died the same year. Better results were promised by the ambition of Ugolin, Archbishop of Kalocsa, who desired to extend his province; he proposed to Andreas II. of Hungary that he would lead a crusade at his own cost, and king and pope promised him all the territories which he should clear of heretics, but Ugolin overrated his powers, and adopted the expedient of subsidizing with two hundred silver marks the ruler of Syrmia, Prince John, son of Margaret, widow of the Emperor Isaac Angelus. John took the money without performing his promise, though reminded of it by Honorius in 1227. Relieved from apprehension, the Bosnians deposed their Ban Stephen and replaced him with a Catharan, Ninoslav, one of the most notable personages in Bosnian history, who maintained himself from 1232 to 1250.[327]

The scale at length seemed to turn with the advent on the scene of the Mendicant Orders, full of the irrepressible enthusiasm, the disregard of toil and hardship, and the thirst for martyrdom of which we have already seen so many examples. Behind them now, moreover, was Gregory IX., the implacable and indefatigable persecutor of heresy, who urged them forward unceasingly. The Dominicans were first upon the ground. As early as 1221 the Order formed establishments in Hungary, developing its proselyting energy from that centre, and thus taking the heretics in flank. The Dominican legend relates that the Inquisition was founded in Hungary by Friar Jackzo (St. Hyacinth), an early member of the Order, who died in 1257, and that it could soon boast of two martyred inquisitors, Friar Nicholas, who was flayed alive, and Friar John, who was lapidated by the heretics. In 1233 we hear of the massacre of ninety Dominican missionaries among the Cumans, and it was perhaps somewhat earlier than this that thirty-two were drowned by the Bosnian heretics, whom they were seeking to convert; but Dominican ardor was only inflamed by such incidents.{294} Preparations were made for systematic work. In 1232 Gregory ordered his legate in Hungary, Giacopo, Bishop of Palestrina, to convert the Bosnians. King Andreas gave the Banate to his son Coloman, Duke of Croatia and Dalmatia, and ordered him to assist. Results soon followed. The Catholic Bishop of Bosnia was himself infected with heresy, and excused himself on the ground that he had ignorantly supposed the Cathari to be orthodox. The Archbishop of Ragusa was cognizant of this, and had paid no attention to it, so Giacopo transferred Bosnia to Kalocsa—a transfer, however, which was for the present inoperative. More important was the conversion of Ninoslav, who abandoned the religion of his fathers in order to avert the attacks of Coloman, which were rapidly dismembering his territories. He was effusively welcomed by Gregory; he gave money to the Dominicans for the building of a cathedral; many of his magnates followed his example, and his kinsman, Uban Prijesda, handed his son to the Dominicans as a hostage for the sincerity of his conversion. Gregory was overjoyed at this apparent success. In 1233 he ordered the boy restored to his father; he took Bosnia under the special protection of the Holy See, and ordered Coloman to defend Ninoslav from the attacks of disaffected heretics; he deposed the heretic bishop, and instructed his legate to divide the territory into two or three sees, appointing proper incumbents. The latter measure was not carried out, however, and a German Dominican, John of Wildeshausen, was consecrated Bishop of all Bosnia.[328]

The Legate Giacopo returned to Hungary satisfied that the land was converted, but success proved fleeting. Either Ninoslav's conversion was feigned or he was unable to control his heretic subjects, for in the next year, 1234, we find Gregory complaining that heresy was increasing and rendering Bosnia a desert of the faith, a nest of dragons and a home of ostriches. In conjunction with Andreas he ordered a crusade, and Coloman was instructed to attack the heretics. The Carthusian Prior of St. Bartholomew was sent thither to preach it with Holy Land indulgences, and by the end of 1234 Coloman laid Bosnia waste with fire and sword.{295} Ninoslav threw himself heart and soul with the Cathari, and the struggle was bloody and prolonged. The Legate Giacopo induced Bela IV. to take an oath to extirpate all heretics from every land under his jurisdiction, and the Franciscans hastened to take a hand in the good work. They commenced with the city of Zara, but the Archbishop of Zara, instead of seconding their labors, impeded them, which earned for him the emphatic rebuke of Gregory. Indeed, from the account which Yvo of Narbonne gives about this time of the Cathari of the maritime districts, they could not have been much disturbed by these proceedings.[329]

In 1235 the crusaders were unlucky. Bishop John lost all hope of recovering his see and asked Gregory to relieve him of it, as the labors of war were too severe for him; but Gregory reproved his faintheartedness, telling him that if he disliked war the love of God should urge him on.[330] In 1236 the aspect of affairs improved, probably because Bela IV. had replaced Andreas on the throne of Hungary, and because the crusaders were energetically aided by Sebislav, Duke of Usora, the son of the former Ban Stephen, who hoped to recover the succession. He was rewarded by Gregory calling him a lily among thorns and the sole representative of orthodoxy among the Bosnian chiefs, who were all heretics. At last, in 1237, Coloman triumphed, but heresy was not eradicated, in spite of his efforts through the following years. In fulfilment of his request, Gregory ordered the consecration of the Dominican Ponsa as Bishop of Bosnia, and soon afterwards appointed Ponsa as legate for three years in order that he might exterminate the remnant of heresy. It must have been a tolerably large remnant, for in the same breath he promised the protection of the Holy See to all who would take the cross to extirpate it. In 1239 the Provincial Prior of Hungary was ordered to send to the heretic districts a number of friars, powerful in speech and action,{296} to consummate the work. Ponsa, though bishop and legate, had no revenues and no resources, so Gregory ordered paid over to him the moneys collected from crusaders in redemption of vows, and the sum which Ninoslav, during his interval of orthodoxy, had given to found a cathedral. By the end of 1239 heresy seemed to be exterminated, but scarce had Coloman and his crusaders left the land when his work was undone and heresy was as vigorous as ever. In 1240 Ninoslav appears again as Ban, visiting Ragusa with a splendid retinue to renew the old treaty of trade and alliance. King Bela's energies, in fact, were just then turned in another direction, for Assan, the Bulgarian prince, had declared in favor of the Greeks; his people therefore were denounced as heretics and schismatics, and Bela was stimulated to undertake a crusade against him, for which, as usual, Holy Land indulgences were promised. It was hard to make head at once against so many enemies of the faith, and in the confusion the Cathari of Bosnia had a respite. Still more important for them as a preventive of persecution was the Tartar invasion which, in 1241, reduced Hungary to a desert. In the bloody day of Flusse Sajo the Hungarian army was destroyed, Bela barely escaped with his life, and Coloman was slain. The respite was but temporary, however, for in 1244 Bela again overran Bosnia. Ninoslav made his peace and the heretics were persecuted, until 1246, when Hungary was involved in war with Austria, and promptly they rose again with Ninoslav at their head.[331]

All these endeavors to diffuse the blessings of Christianity had not been made without bloodshed. We have few details of these obscure struggles in a land little removed from barbarism, but there is one document extant which shows that the Albigensian crusades, with all their horrors, had been repeated to no purpose. In 1247 Innocent IV., in making over the see of Bosnia to the Archbishop of Kalocsa, alludes to the labors performed by him and his predecessors in the effort to redeem it from heresy. They had meritoriously devastated the greater part of the land; they had carried away into captivity many thousands of heretics, with great effusion of blood, and no little slaughter of their own men{297} and waste of their substance. In spite of these sacrifices, as the churches and castles which they had built were not strong enough to resist siege, the land could not be retained in the faith; it had wholly relapsed into heresy, and there was no hope of its voluntary redemption. The church of Kalocsa had been thoroughly exhausted, and it was now rewarded by placing the recalcitrant region under its jurisdiction, in the expectation that some future crusade might be more fortunate. Innocent IV. had, a few months earlier, ordered Bela to undertake a decisive struggle with the Cathari, but Ninoslav appealed to him, protesting that he had been since his conversion a faithful son of the Church, and had only accepted the aid of the heretics because it was necessary to preserve the independence of the Banate. Moved by this, Innocent instructed the Archbishop of Kalocsa to abstain from further persecution. He ordered an investigation into the faith and actions of Ninoslav, and gave permission to use the Glagolitic writing and the Slavic tongue in the celebration of Catholic service, recognizing that this would remove an obstacle to the propagation of the faith. Ninoslav's last years were peaceful, but after his death, about 1250, there were civil wars stimulated by the antagonism between Catharan and Catholic. He was succeeded by Prijesda, who had remained Catholic since his conversion in 1233. Under pretence of supporting Prijesda, Bela intervened, and by 1254 he had again reduced Bosnia to subjection, leading, doubtless, to active persecution of heresy, although the transfer of the see of Bosnia to Kalocsa was not carried into effect.[332]

It was about this time that Rainerio Saccone gives us his computation of the Perfects in many of the Catharan churches. In Constantinople there were two churches, a Latin and a Greek, the former comprising fifty Perfects. The latter, together with those of Bulgaria, Roumania, Slavonia, and Dalmatia, he estimates at about five hundred. This would indicate a very large number of believers, and shows how unfruitful had been the labors and the wars which had continued for more than a generation. In fact, although Bela's long reign lasted until 1270, he failed utterly in his efforts to extirpate heresy. On the contrary, the Cathari grew{298} ever stronger and the Church sank lower and lower. Even the Bosnian bishops dared no longer to remain in their see, but resided in Djakovar. So little reverence was there felt in those regions for the Holy See that so near as Trieste, when, in 1264, two Dominicans commissioned to preach the crusade against the Turks endeavored to perform their duty, the dean and canons hustled them violently out of the church, and would not even allow them to address the crowd in the public square, while the archdeacon publicly declared that any one who listened to them was excommunicate.[333]

Things grew worse with the accession, in 1272, of Bela's grandson, Ladislas IV., known as the Cuman, from his mother Elizabeth, a member of that pagan tribe. Ladislas lived with the Cumans and shared their religion until his contempt for the Holy See manifested itself in the most offensive manner. The papal legate, Filippo, Bishop of Fermo, had called a council to meet at Buda, when Ladislas ordered the magistrates of the city not to permit the entrance of any prelates, or the supplying of any food to the legate, who was thus forced to depart ignominiously. This called down upon him the anger of Rodolph of Hapsburg and of Charles of Anjou, and he was fain, in 1280, to make reparation, not only by a humble apology and a grant of one hundred marks per annum for the founding of a hospital, but by adopting and publishing as the law of the land all the papal statutes against heresy, and swearing to enforce them vigorously, while his mother Elizabeth did the same as Duchess of Bosnia. Something was gained by this, and still more, when, in 1282, Ladislas appointed as ruler of Bosnia his brother-in-law, Stephen Dragutin, the exiled King of Servia. The latter, although a Greek, persecuted the Cathari; and when, about 1290, he was converted to Catholicism, his zeal increased, He sent to Rome Marino, Bishop of Antivari, to report the predominance of heresy and to ask for aid. Nicholas IV. promptly responded by commissioning a legate to Andreas III., the new King of Hungary, to preach a crusade, and the Emperor Rodolph was ordered to assist, but the effort was bootless. Equally vain was his command to the Franciscan Minister of Slavonia to select{299} two friars acquainted with the language, and send them to Bosnia to extirpate heresy. The request at the same time made to Stephen to support them with the secular arm shows that the missionaries were in fact inquisitors. Unluckily, Nicholas in his zeal also employed Dominicans in the business. Inspired by the traditional hatred between the Orders, the inquisitors, or missionaries, employed all their energies in quarrelling with each other, and became objects of ridicule instead of terror to the heretics.[334]

In 1298 Boniface VIII. undertook finally to organize the Inquisition in the Franciscan province of Slavonia, which comprised all the territory south of Hungary, from the Danube to Macedonia. The provincial minister was ordered to appoint two friars as inquisitors for this immense region, and was intrusted as usual with the power of removing and replacing them. This slender organization he endeavored to supplement by ordering the Archbishop of Kalocsa to preach a crusade, but there was no response, and the proposed Inquisition effected nothing. When Stephen Dragutin died, in 1314, Bosnia was conquered by Mladen Subić, son of the Ban of Croatia, under whom it was virtually independent of Hungary. Mladen made some show of persecuting heresy—at least when he had a request to make at Avignon—but as the vast majority of his subjects were Cathari, whose support was absolutely necessary to him, it is safe to say that he made no serious effort. In 1319 John XXII. describes the condition of Bosnia as deplorable. There were no Catholic ecclesiastics, no reverence for the sacraments; communion was not administered, and in many places the rite of baptism was not even known or understood. When such a pontiff as John felt obliged to appeal to Mladen himself to put an end to this reproach, it shows that he had no means of effective coercion at hand.[335]

Mladen was overthrown by Stephen Kostromanić, and when he fled to Hungary, Charles Robert cast him in prison, leaving undisturbed possession to Stephen, who styled himself Ban by the grace of God. Stephen, in 1322, seems to have abandoned Catholicism, joining either the Greeks or the Cathari, but in spite of this{300} affairs commenced to look more favorable. Hungary began to emerge from the disorders and disasters which had so long crippled it, and King Charles Robert was inclined to listen to exhortations as to his duty towards the Bosnian heretics. In 1323, therefore, John XXII. made another attempt, sending Frà Fabiano thither and ordering Charles Robert and Stephen to give him effective support. The latter was obdurate, though the former seems to have manifested some zeal, if one may believe the praises bestowed on him in 1327 by John. Fabiano was indefatigable, but his duty proved no easy one. At the very outset he met with unexpected resistance in a city so near at hand as Trieste. When he endeavored there to enforce the decrees against heresy, and to arouse the people to a sense of their duty, the bells were rung, a mob was assembled, he was dragged from the pulpit and beaten, the leaders in the disturbance being two canons of the Cathedral, Michele da Padua, and Raimondo da Cremona, who were promptly ordered by the pope to be prosecuted as suspects of heresy. Hardly had he settled this question when he was involved in a controversy with the rival Dominicans, whom he found to be poaching on his preserves. A zealous Dominican, Matteo of Agram, by suppressing the fact that Slavonia was Franciscan territory, had obtained from John letters authorizing the Dominican provincial to appoint inquisitors, commissioned to preach a crusade with Holy Land indulgences, and these inquisitors had been urgently recommended by the pope to the King of Hungary and other potentates. It was impossible that the Orders could co-operate in harmony, and Fabiano made haste to represent to John the trap into which he had been led. The pope was now at the height of his controversy with the greater part of the Franciscans over the question of poverty, and it was impolitic to give just grounds of complaint to those who remained faithful; he therefore promptly recalled the letters given to the Dominicans, and scolded them roundly for deceiving him. Even yet it seemed impossible for Fabiano to penetrate beyond the borders of his district, or to work without impediment, for in 1329 he was occupied with prosecuting for heresy the Abbot of SS. Cosmas and Damiani of Zara and one of his monks, when John, the Archbishop of Zara, intervened forcibly and stopped the proceedings. The difficulties thrown in Fabiano's way must have been great, for he felt compelled to visit

Avignon {301} for their removal, but his usual ill-luck accompanied him. The contest between the papacy on the one side, and the Visconti and Louis of Bavaria on the other, rendered parts of Lombardy unsafe for papalists, and a son of Belial named Franceschino da Pavia had no scruple in laying hands on the inquisitor and despoiling him of his horses, books, and papers. During all this time the Inquisition must have been at a standstill, but at last Fabiano overcame all obstacles. In 1330 he returned to the scene of action; Charles Robert and Stephen lent him their assistance, and the work of suppressing the Cathari commenced under favorable auspices, and by the methods which we have seen so successful elsewhere. The condition of the Bosnian Church may be guessed from the fear felt by John XXII. that the bishops would be heretics, leading him, in 1331, to reserve their appointment to the Holy See. Yet on the death of Bishop Peter, in 1334, the chapter elected a successor, and Charles Robert endeavored to force a layman on the Church, causing a disgraceful quarrel which was not settled until Benedict XII., in 1336, pronounced in favor of the candidate of the chapter.[336]

The spiritual condition of the Slavs at this period is indicated by an occurrence in 1331 nearer home. The Venetian inquisitor, Frà Francesco Chioggia, in visiting his district, found in the province of Aquileia innumerable Slavs who worshipped a tree and fountain. Apparently they were impervious to his exhortations, and he had no means at the moment to enforce obedience. He was obliged to preach against them, in Friuli, a crusade with Holy Land indulgences. He thus raised an armed force with which he cut down the tree and choked up the fountain; unfortunately, we have no record of the fate of the nature-worshippers.[337]

Benedict XII. was as earnest as his predecessor. Yet even Dalmatia was still full of heresy, for in 1335 be felt obliged to write to the Archbishop of Zara and the Bishops of Trau and Zegna, ordering them to use every means for the extermination of heretics, and to give efficient support to the inquisitors. The Dalmatian prelates, it is true, prevailed upon the magistrates of Spalatro and Trau to {302} enact laws against heresy, but these were not enforced. A century had passed since the Inquisition was founded, and yet the duties of persecution had not even then been learned on the shores of the Adriatic. The work seemed further than ever from accomplishment. The Cathari continued to multiply under the avowed protection of Stephen and his magnates. A gleam of light appeared, however, when, in 1337, the Croatian Count Nelipić, a bitter enemy of Stephen, offered his services to Benedict, who joyfully accepted them, and summoned all the Croatian barons to range themselves under his banner in aid of the pious labors of Fabiano and his colleagues. War ensued between Bosnia and Croatia, of the details of which we know little, except that it brought no advantage to the faith, until it threatened to spread.[338]

Stephen's position, in fact, was becoming precarious. To the east was Stephen Dusan the Great, who styled himself Emperor of Servia, Greece, and Bulgaria, and who had shown himself unfriendly since the union of Herzegovina with Bosnia. To the north was Charles Robert, who was preparing to take part in the war. It is true that the Venetians, desirous to keep Hungary away from their Adriatic possessions, were ready to form an alliance with Stephen, but the odds against him were too great. He probably intimated a readiness to submit, for when, in 1339, Benedict sent the Franciscan General Gherardo as legate to Hungary, Charles Robert convoyed him to the Bosnian frontier, where Stephen received him with all honor, and said that he was not averse to extirpating the Cathari, but feared that in case of persecution they would call in Stephen Dusan. If liberally supported by the pope and King of Hungary he would run the risk. In 1340 Benedict promised him the help of all Catholics, and he allowed himself to be converted, an example followed by many of the magnates. It was quite time, for Catholicism had virtually disappeared from Bosnia, where the churches were mostly abandoned and torn down. Gherardo hastened to follow up his advantage by sending missionaries and inquisitors into Bosnia. That there was no place there, however, for the methods of the Inquisition, and that persuasion, not force, was required, is seen by the legends which recount how {303} one of these inquisitors, Fray Juan de Aragon, made numerous converts, after a long and bitter disputation in an heretical assembly, by standing unhurt on a blazing pyre; and how one of his disciples, John, repeated the experience, remaining in the flames while one might chant the Miserere. These miracles, we are told, were very effective, and the stories show that nothing else could have been so. Stephen remained true to his promises, and the Catholic Church commenced to revive. A bull of Clement VI., in 1344, recites that, deceived by the falsehoods of the Franciscan General Gherardo, he had ordered the Bosnian tithes paid over to the friars on the pretext of rebuilding the churches, but on the representation of Laurence, Bishop of Bosnia, that they belonged to him and that he had no other source of support, he is in future to receive them. At the instance of Clement, in 1345, Stephen consented to allow the return of Valentine, Bishop of Makarska, who for twenty years had been an exile from his see, and the next year a third bishopric, that of Duvno, was erected. The Catharan magnates were restless, however, and when Dusan the Great, in 1350, invaded Bosnia many of them joined him, but their prospects became worse when peace followed in 1351, and when, in 1353, shortly before his death, Stephen married his only child to Louis of Hungary, a zealous Catholic who had succeeded his father, Charles Robert, in 1342.[339]

Stephen Kostromanić was succeeded by his young nephew, Stephen Tvrtko, under the regency of his mother, Helena. Under such circumstances, dissatisfied and insubordinate Catharan magnates had ample opportunity to produce confusion. Of this full advantage was taken by Louis of Hungary as soon as the death of Dusan the Great, in 1355, relieved him from that formidable antagonist. The Dominicans hastened, in 1356, to obtain from Innocent VI. a confirmation of the letters of John XXII., of 1327, authorizing them to preach a crusade against the heretics with Holy Land indulgences. Louis seized Herzegovina as a dower for his wife Elisabeth, reduced Stephen Tvrtko to the position of a vassal, and forced him to swear to extirpate the Cathari. Not content with this he proceeded to stir up rebellion among the magnates, producing{304} great confusion, during which the Cathari regained their position. Then, in 1360, Innocent VI. conferred on Peter, Bishop of Bosnia, full powers as papal inquisitor, and also ordered a new crusade, which served as a pretext to Louis for a fresh invasion. Nothing was accomplished by this; but in 1365 the Cathari, irritated at Tvrtko's efforts to suppress them, drove him and his mother from Bosnia. Louis furnished him with troops, and asked Urban V. to send two thousand Franciscans to convert the heretics. After a desperate struggle Tvrtko regained the throne. His brother, Stephen Vuk, who had aided the rebels, fled to Ragusa and embraced Catholicism, after which, in 1368, he appealed for aid to Urban V., representing that his heretic brother had disinherited him on account of his persecuting heretics. Urban accordingly urged Louis to protect the orthodox Vuk, and to force Tvrtko to abandon his errors, but nothing came of it. Whether Tvrtko was Catharan or Catholic does not clearly appear. Probably he was indifferent to all but his personal interests, and was ready to follow whatever policy promised to serve his ambition, and his success shows that he must have had the support of his subjects, who were nearly all Cathari. Although, in 1368, Urban V. congratulated Louis of Hungary on the success of his arms, aided by the friars, in bringing into the fold many thousand heretics and schismatics, Louis himself, in 1372, reported that Christianity was established in but few places; in some the two faiths were commingled, but for the most part all the inhabitants were Cathari. It was in vain that Gregory XI. endeavored to found Franciscan houses as missionary centres; the Bosnians would not be weaned from their creed. Had Tvrtko followed a policy of persecution he could not have accomplished the conquests which, for a brief period, shed lustre on the Bosnian name. He extended his sway over a large part of Servia and over Croatia and Dalmatia, and when, in 1376, he assumed the title of king, there was no one to dispute it. After his death, in 1391, the magnates asserted virtual independence under a succession of royal puppets—Stephen Dabisa, his young son, under the regency of his widow, Helena, and then Stephen Ostoja. The most powerful man in Bosnia was the Vojvode Hrvoje Vukcić, who ruled the north, and next to him was his kinsman Sandalj Hranić who dominated the south. Both of these men were Cathari, and so was the king, Stephen,{305} Ostoja, and all his family. Catholicism almost disappeared, and Catharism was the religion of the State. It was organized under a Djed (grandfather), or chief, with twelve Ucitelji, or teachers, of whom the first was the Gost, or visitor, the deputy and successor of the Djed, and the second was known as the Starac, or elder.[340]

These were state officials, and we see them occasionally acting in an official capacity. Thus, when, in 1404, the Vojvode Paul Klesić, who had been exiled, was recalled, it was the Djed Radomjer who sent Catharan envoys to Ragusa to bring him home, and who wrote to the Doge of Ragusa on the subject. Klesić was a Catharan, and his residence in Ragusa, as well as that of many similar Catharan exiles, shows that persecution had grown obsolete even on the coast of the Adriatic. In spite of his Catharism, Hrvoje Vukcić was made by Ladislas of Naples, Duke of Spalatro and lord of some of the Dalmatian islands, thus making Catharism dominant along the shore. In the troubles which ended in the deposition of Stephen Ostoja and the election of Stephen Tvrtko II. a "Congregation of the Bosnian Lords" was held in 1404, in which, among those present, are enumerated the Djed and several of his Ucitelji, but no mention is made of any Catholic bishop. Toleration seemed to have established itself. The Great Schism gave the Holy See abundant preoccupation, and missionary efforts are no longer heard of, until the Emperor Sigismund, as King of Hungary, bethought himself of re-establishing his claim over Bosnia. Two armies sent in 1405 were unsuccessful, but in 1407 Gregory XII. aided him with a bull summoning Christendom to a{306} crusade against the Turks, the apostate Allans, and the Manichæans. Under these auspices, in 1408, he led a force of sixty thousand Hungarians and Poles into Bosnia, defeated and captured Tvrtko II., and recovered Croatia and Dalmatia, but the Bosnians were obstinate, and replaced Ostoja on the throne. Another expedition, in 1410-1411, drove Ostoja to the south, and Sigismund, for a while, retained possession of Bosnia, but when, in 1415, he released Tvrtko II. and sent him to Bosnia as king, a civil war immediately ensued. Tvrtko at first was successful, supported with a large Hungarian army, but Ostoja called the Turks to his assistance, and in a decisive battle the Hungarians were defeated. The Turks penetrated to Cillei in the Steyermark, devastating and plundering everywhere, and on their return carried with them thousands of Christian captives.[341]

This shows the new factor which had injected itself into the already tangled problem. In 1389 the fatal day of the Amselfeld had thrown open the whole Balkan peninsula to the Turks, who since then had been steadily winning their way. In 1392 we hear of their first incursion in southern Bosnia, after which they had constantly taken a greater part in the affairs of the Banate. The condition of the country was that of savage and perpetual civil war. There was no royal power capable of enforcing order, and the magnates were engaged in tearing each other to pieces. Devoid of all sentiment of nationality, no one had any scruple in calling in the aid of the infidel, in paying allegiance to him, or in subsidizing him to prevent his joining the opposite party. It was the same with Catholic, Catharan, and Greek. No sense of the ever-approaching danger served to make them abandon their internecine quarrels, and if a temporary petty advantage was to be gained there was no hesitation in aiding the Turk to a farther advance. The only wonder is that the progress of the Moslem conquest was so slow; there can be little doubt that it could have been arrested by united effort, and it may be questioned whether the rule of Islam was not, after all, an improvement on the state of virtual anarchy which it replaced. To the peasantry it offered itself rather as a deliverance. When, in 1461, Stephen Tomasević ascended the throne, in his appeal for aid to Pius II. he describes{307} the Turks as treating the peasants kindly, promising them freedom, and thus winning them over, and he adds that the magnates cannot defend their castles when thus abandoned by the peasants.[342]

As regards the Cathari, the Turkish advance produced two contrary effects. On the one hand there was the danger that persecution would drive them to seek protection from the enemy. On the other hand there was absolute need of assistance from Christendom, which could only be obtained by submission to Rome, and obedience to her demands for their extermination. Both of these influences worked to the destruction of Bosnia, for when toleration was practised aid was withheld, and when at last persecution was established as a policy the Cathari welcomed the invader, and contributed to the subjugation of the kingdom.

In 1420 Stephen Tvrtko II. reappeared upon the scene, and the next year he was acknowledged. There followed a breathing-space, for the Turkish general Isaac was defeated and killed during an incursion into Hungary, and Mahomet I., involved in strife with Mustapha, had no leisure to repair the disaster. This did not last long, however, for in 1424 the sons of Ostoja endeavored, with Turkish help, to win back their father's throne, the only result of which was a war ending with the surrender of a portion of Bosnian territory to Murad II. Again, in 1433, when Tvrtko was fighting with the Servian despot, George Branković, he was suddenly called to the south to withstand a Turkish inroad invited by Radivoj, one of the sons of Ostoja, and this was immediately followed by the rising of Sandalj Hranić, the powerful magnate of Herzegovina, who drove Tvrtko to seek refuge with Sigismund. His absence lasted three years, during which the wildest confusion reigned in Bosnia, the Turks being constantly called in to participate with one side or the other.[343]

Meanwhile the rise of the Observantine Franciscans was restoring to the Church some of its old missionary fervor, and furnishing it with the necessary self-devoted agents. In spite of the preoccupations arising from the contest between Eugenius IV. and the Council of Basle, an effort was made to win back Bosnia to the faith. If anything could accomplish this there might be{308} hope from the fierce and inexhaustible enthusiasm of the Observantine Friar, the Blessed Giacomo della Marca, who had already given evidence of ruthless efficiency as inquisitor of the Italian Fraticelli. In 1432 he was accordingly sent with full powers to reform the Franciscan Order in Slavonia, and to turn its whole energies to missionary work. Under this impulsion we are told that conversions were numerous from Bosnia to Wallachia, and Eugenius IV. stimulated rivalry by also setting the Dominicans at work. In 1434 Giacomo was driven out, but was sent back the next year, and distinguished himself by redoubled ardor and success, attributed, according to his biographers, partly to his miraculous powers. Alarmed at his progress, the wicked queen sent four assassins to despatch him, when he extended his arms and bade them do whatever God would permit, whereupon they became rigid and suffered agonies until he prayed for their release. Indignant at this attempt, he bearded the king and queen in full court, and his boldness gained him so many converts that the king became alarmed for his throne. A sorcerer was accordingly employed to slay the intrepid inquisitor, but Giacomo promptly rendered the man speechless for life. Some heretics then sawed through the supports of a platform where he was preaching. It fell, but he escaped, and to this day, says the legend, the posterity of the perpetrators have all been born halt and lame. These proofs of divine favor led to numerous conversions, but he became involved in quarrels with the Catholic clergy, caused, we are told, by envy, and they excommunicated him, so that he was obliged to seek absolution from the pope. His triumphant career was cut short by a summons from the Emperor Sigismund to assist in the pacification of the Hussite troubles, and his field of action was transferred to regions farther north, where we shall meet him hereafter. Even there, however, he did not forget his Bosnian enemies, for at Stuhlweissenburg, on meeting the legates of the Council of Basle, he at once asked them to exert their influence on Sigismund. Though King Stephen, he said, was an unbaptized heretic who would not allow his subjects to be baptized, a command from the emperor would be sufficient to compel him to yield. Giacomo, moreover, had left behind him worthy disciples from among the natives. One of these, the Blessed Angelo of Verbosa, shone also by miraculous gifts. On one occasion the{309} heretics gave him poison to drink, but on making the sign of the cross above the cup it became innocuous, which brought him many converts.[344]

This legendary extravagance has some foundation in fact. A bull of Eugenius IV., in 1437, speaks of sixteen Franciscan churches and monasteries destroyed by the Turks within two years, and another grants to the friars who remained certain privileges in hearing confessions, which show that they had been active, and had been winning their way. Giacomo's influence at Stuhlweissenburg is, moreover, indicated by his inducing Sigismund to compel Stephen Tvrtko to undergo baptism, and to issue from that place, in January, 1436, an edict taking the Franciscans under his protection, and permitting them to spread Catholicism throughout Bosnia. In reward for this Sigismund aided his return to his kingdom, which he found possessed partly by Servia, partly by the Turks, and wholly devastated. For what he could obtain of this ruined land he had to render allegiance to Murad II., and to pay him a yearly tribute of twenty-five thousand ducats. Wretched as was this simulacrum of royalty, it was incompatible with the favor which he had been compelled to show to Catholicism. Southern Bosnia by this time was independent under Stephen Vukčić, nephew and successor of Sandalj; as a Catharan, he

104

was regarded throughout Bosnia as the defender of the national faith, and, in alliance with Murad II., he overthrew Stephen Tvrtko II.[345]

In 1444 another king was elected in the person of Stephen Thomas Ostojić, a younger natural son of Ostoja, who had carefully kept himself in obscurity with a low-born Catharan wife, to whom he had been married with the Catharan ceremony—a fact which subsequently served as an excuse for a divorce. Almost the first question which the new king had to decide was whether he would adhere to his religion or cast his fortunes with Catholicism. The Church had not relaxed its efforts to win over the fragments remaining[310] of Bosnia, in spite of the fact that it was only aiding the designs of the Turks by adding to confusion and discord. In 1437 the vacancy left by Giacomo della Marca had been filled by the appointment of Frà Niccolò of Trau, and since 1439 Tommaso, Bishop of Lesina, had been in Bosnia as papal legate, busily engaged in furthering the interests of Catholicism. He had failed in an effort to convert Stephen Vukcić, but the advent of a new king was an incentive to further exertions. Eugenius promptly appointed the Observantine Vicar of Bosnia, Fabiano of Bacs, and his successors perpetual inquisitors over the Slavonic lands, and instructed the Bishop of Lesina to promise Stephen Thomas the recognition of his election if he would embrace the true faith. The position was a difficult one. All his magnates, with the exception of Peter Vojsalić, were Catharans, and to offend them would be to invite Turkish intervention, while, so long as he held aloof from Christendom, he could expect no aid from the West. Doubtless promises that could not be fulfilled were made to him in plenty, for he concluded to cast his fortunes with Catholicism, but he abstained from receiving the crown offered to him by Eugenius for fear of offending his Catharan subjects. He permitted the erection of two new bishoprics, he was duly baptized, and he labored long and earnestly to induce his subjects to follow his example. Nearly all his magnates did so, but Stephen Vukcić was a conspicuous exception, and the common people were not so easily moved. Even the king himself did not dare to omit the customary "adoration" of the Perfects, for which he was duly excommunicated by the inquisitor, but the pope recognized the difficulty of his position, and wisely gave him a dispensation for associating with heretics.[346]

Although many Catholic churches were built, the legate reported, on a visit to Rome, that the land was too full of heresy for other cure than the sword. The king's position was too insecure for him to venture on persecution, which would infallibly have led to a revolt. In a grant, in 1446, of certain towns to Count Paul Dragisić and his brothers, who were zealous Cathari,[311] it is provided that, in case of their committing treason, the gift is not to be resumed without a previous investigation "by the Lord Djed and the Bosnian Church and good Bosnians." The Franciscans complained of his lukewarmness to Nicholas V., when he justified himself on the plea of necessity; he longed, he said, for the time when he could offer to his subjects the alternative of death or conversion, but as yet the heretics were too numerous and powerful and his position too precarious. Nicholas calmed the Franciscans, and they eagerly awaited the good time to come.[347]

The defeat, in 1448, of John Hunyady, in a three days" battle on the historic Amselfeld, led, in 1449, to a seven years" peace between him and Murad II., in which Bosnia was included. Peace with Servia followed, and, thus relieved from the fear of foreign aggression, Stephen Thomas was summoned to perform his promises. Before the papal representatives he was obliged to give a solemn pledge to John Hunyady that he would strike heresy with a crushing blow. Nicholas V., who had sent the Bishop of Lesina back as legate, ordered him to preach a crusade with Holy Land indulgences, and active efforts were made in the good work. Early in 1451 the Bishop of Lesina sent most encouraging reports of the result. Many of the nobles had sought conversion; the king in every way helped the Franciscans, and had founded several houses for them; wherever these houses existed the heretics melted away like wax before the fire, and if a sufficient supply of friars could be had heresy would be extirpated. Not quite so rose-colored was the statement of a Dominican, Frà Giovanni of Ragusa, that in Bosnia and Servia there were very few monks and priests, so that the people were wholly untrained in the faith. Unmindful of the danger of conjoining the two Orders, Nicholas sent him thither with some of his brethren on missionary work, and at the same time despatched the Franciscan Eugenio Somma to Albania, Bulgaria, and Servia in the double capacity of nuncio and inquisitor.[348]

The good Bishop of Lesina had been over-sanguine. In the[312] first pressure of persecution forty heads of the Catharan Church, with great numbers of the laity, sought refuge with Stephen Vukcić, who proceeded to attack the Catholics of Ragusa, while many others fled to Servia and to the Turks, and appealed to them for help. Those who remained prepared for resistance, and a bloody religious war broke out, of which George Branković of Servia took advantage to renew the war suspended in 1449. This was more than Stephen Thomas could endure; he was forced to abandon persecution and to call for help. John Hunyady was enraged at his weakness, and ordered him to make peace with Servia. He appealed to Nicholas V., who remonstrated with Hunyady, when the latter retorted that Stephen Thomas was false to his promises, and, in place of exterminating the heretics, was protecting them, to the scandal of all Christendom.[349]

On the fall of Constantinople, in May, 1453, Stephen Thomas promptly sent envoys to Mahomet II. to tender his allegiance. In the ever-deepening menace of the Turks persecution could hardly be resumed with activity, but the popes occasionally gave him a portion of the moneys raised for the crusade, and the Cathari were humiliated and proscribed as far as could be ventured upon, and constituted a discontented and dangerous element of the population. In 1459 we find the king protesting to Pius II. that he persecuted the Cathari roundly, and asking for more bishops; and one of his latest acts was to send the Bishop of Nona to the pope with three Catharan magnates—George Kucinić, Stojsav Tvrtković, and Radovan Viencinić—that they might be converted. It seems incredible that any one should covet a throne so precarious, and yet, in 1461, while Stephen Thomas was battling with the Croatian magnates, he was murdered by his son, Stephen Thomasević, and his brother Radivoj. The crown which Stephen Thomasević thus won by a parricide was a crown of thorns. To the north Matthias Corvinus of Hungary was estranged and unforgiving; to the west was Croatia, with which he was at war; in the south Stephen Vukcić was his enemy; while on the east lay Servia, now a Turkish pashalic, from which Mahomet II. only awaited the fitting moment to reduce Bosnia to a like condition. Thus surrounded by foes, the internal condition of the land was {313} not reassuring, for it was full of secret or open Cathari, who longed for help or revenge, no matter whence it might come.[350]

The new king recognized that his only hope lay in obtaining aid from Christendom, to earn which he labored energetically to strengthen the Catholic Church in his dominions, but, in the fatal perverseness of the time, this only precipitated his downfall. From Pius II. he obtained only barren instructions to the legate, Lorenzo, Abbot of Spalatro, to collect money and crusaders. From Matthias Corvinus he purchased an alliance by a heavy payment, by surrendering some castles, and by breaking off relations with the Turks and ceasing to pay them tribute. In all this he estranged still further his heretic subjects and drew upon his head the vengeance of Mahomet II. Many Cathari, driven from Bosnia, had found refuge in Moslem territory; others, especially nobles, forced to pretend conversion, maintained constant relations with the Turks, kept them advised of all that occurred, and were eager to aid them, in hopes of revenge. The news of the treaty with Matthias Corvinus was speedily conveyed to Mahomet, who, to test its truth, sent an envoy to demand the tribute. King Stephen took him to the treasury, showed him the money, and refused to deliver it, saying that he needed it for self-defence, or that it would support him in exile if driven from the kingdom, and he paid no heed to the envoy's warning that treasure withheld in defiance of pledges would bring him no luck.[351]

Defiance such as this left nothing to hope for from the Turk, but preoccupations in Wallachia kept Mahomet busy during 1462, and he postponed his revenge till the following year. It shows the blindness of Rome to the situation and the unflagging persistency of the determination to secure uniformity of faith, that during this respite Pius II. sent learned friars to Bosnia with instructions that the best mode of overcoming heresy was to promote study. The instructions were excellent, but sadly misplaced. Through the winter and spring of 1463 Mahomet was preparing the final blow by massing one hundred and fifty thousand men at Adrianople. To throw Stephen Thomasevic off of his guard, his request for a fifteen years" truce was granted, and his envoys, returning {314} with this welcome news, were followed, after an interval of four days, by the Turkish host. The land was found defenceless, and no resistance was offered till the invaders reached the royal castle of Bobovac, a stronghold capable of prolonged defence. Its commandant, however, was Count Radak, a Catharan who had been forced to conversion, and on the third day he surrendered on a promise of reward. When he claimed this, Mahomet, reproaching him with his treason, had him promptly beheaded, and tradition still points out on the road to Sutiska the rock Radakovica, where the traitor met his end. The capitulation of Bobovac cast terror throughout the land. Resistance was no longer thought of, and the only alternatives were flight or submission. The king hurried towards the Croatian frontier, with Mahomet Pasha at his heels, and was compelled at Kljuć to surrender on promise of life and freedom, but, in spite of this, he was put to death, after being utilized to order all commandants of cities and castles to surrender them. Within eight days more than seventy towns fell into the hands of the Turks, and by the middle of June all Bosnia was in their possession. Then Mahomet turned southward to overrun the territories of Stephen Vukcić, but the mountains of Herzegovina were bravely defended by the Cathari, and by the end of June the Turkish host took its way homeward, carrying with it one hundred thousand prisoners and thirty thousand youths to be converted into Janissaries.[352]

Thus abandoned by Christendom, except to hasten the end through perpetually inflaming religious strife, Bosnia was conquered without a struggle, while Herzegovina held out for twenty years longer. How easily the catastrophe might have been averted is seen in the fact that before the year 1463 was out Matthias Corvinus had reconquered a large portion of the territory so easily won, which was held until the Hungarian power was broken on the disastrous field of Mohacs in 1526. In the Turkish lands the Cathari for the most part embraced Mahometanism, and the sect which had so stubbornly endured the vicissitudes of more than a thousand years disappeared in obscurity. The Christians had the resource of flight, which they embraced, commencing an emigration which continued until the middle of the eighteenth {315} century. This was rather to escape oppression than persecution, for the Turks permitted them the exercise of their religion. When the blessed Angelo of Verbosa, the disciple of Giacomo della Marca, persuaded his fellow-believers to leave the country, Mahomet sent for him and menacingly asked him his reasons. "To worship God elsewhere," he boldly replied, and so eloquently pleaded his cause that the Turk ordered the Christians to be unmolested, and gave Angelo permission to preach. Thenceforth the Franciscans were the refuge and support of the Christians up to modern times, though they had many cruelties to endure at the hands of the barbarous conquerors.[353] {316}

CHAPTER VI.

GERMANY.

IN 1209 Henry of Veringen, Bishop of Strassburg, accompanied Otho IV. on his coronation expedition to Rome. We have seen (p. 192) how some of the ecclesiastics in the emperor's train were scandalized by the almost open toleration of heretics in the papal city; possibly recriminations may have passed between the German and the Italian prelates, and the former may have been recommended to look more sharply after the orthodoxy of their own dioceses. Be this as it may, Bishop Henry is said to have carried home with him some theologians eager to punish aberrations from the faith, and a little investigation showed to his horror that his land was full of misbelievers. A searching inquest was organized, and he soon had five hundred prisoners representing all classes of society. He was a humane man, as the times went, and he sincerely sought their conversion, to which end he set on foot disputations, but his clergy were no match for the sectaries in knowledge of Scripture, and the faith gained little by the attempt. Recourse to stronger measures was evidently requisite, and he announced that all who were obstinate should be burned. This brought most of them to their senses; heretic books and writings were eagerly surrendered, and the converts abjured. About a hundred of them, however, under the persuasion of their leader, a priest of Strassburg named John, were obdurate, including twelve priests, twenty-three women, and a number of nobles. So ignorant were the episcopal officials of the method of proceeding against heretics that they were utterly at a loss how to convict these recusants; some form of trial seems to have been thought necessary, and resort was had to the old expedient of the red-hot iron ordeal. The heretics protested against it as a manifest tempting of God, but their objections were unavailing; those who denied their heresy were subjected to it, and naturally but few escaped.{317} One of them, named Reinhold, appealed to Innocent III. against this form of trial, and the pope promptly responded by forbidding its further use in such matters, although we are told by contemporaries that its efficacy was abundantly proved by miracles. One of the heretics who repented at the last moment was divinely cured of his burn and was discharged. Returning home rejoicing, his wife upbraided him with his weakness, and under her reproof he relapsed. Immediately the burn reappeared, and a similar one was developed on the hand of the wife, inflicting such agony that neither could restrain their screams. Fearing to betray themselves, they rushed to the woods, where they yelled like wild beasts; this led to their speedy discovery, and before the ashes of their confederates were yet cold they both shared the same fate. More fortunate was one of a number of heretics convicted in this manner at Cambrai about the same time. On his way to the stake he listened to the exhortations of a priest and commenced to repent and confess. As he did so his hand began to heal, and when he received absolution there was no trace left of the burn. Then the priest called attention to him, pronouncing him innocent, and on the evidence of his uninjured hand he was discharged. At Strassburg there were eighty obstinate ones, whose heresy was proved by the ordeal. They were all burned the same day in a ditch beyond the walls, and in the sixteenth century the hollow was still known to the citizens as the Ketzergrube. The property of the condemned was duly confiscated and was divided between the magistrates and those who had labored so successfully in vindicating the faith.[354]{318}

It is not to be supposed that Strassburg was a solitary centre of heresy, and that this was the only case of contemporary persecution. Fragmentary allusions to the detection and punishment of misbelief in other places during the next few years show that the population of the Rhinelands was deeply infected, and that when the ignorance and sloth of the clergy permitted detection, heretics were ruthlessly exterminated. The event at Strassburg, however, happens to have been reported with a fulness of detail which invests it with peculiar importance as revealing the methods of the episcopal inquisition of the period, and the nature of existing religious dissidence.[355]

The Cathari appear to have virtually disappeared from Germany, where their foothold, at best, had been precarious. German soil seems to have been unpropitious to this essentially Southern growth. On the other hand, Waldenses were numerous, together with sectaries known as Ortlibenses or Ordibarii.

We have already seen how rapidly Waldensianism extended from Burgundy to Franche Comté and Lorraine, and how, in 1199, Innocent III., after vainly endeavoring to persuade the Waldenses of Metz to surrender their vernacular Scriptures, had sent thither the Abbot of Citeaux and two other abbots to repress their zeal. The abbots duly performed their mission, preached to the misguided zealots, and burned all such copies of the forbidden books as they could lay their hands on, though it is fair to presume, from the silence of the chronicler, that no human victims expiated at the stake their unlawful studies. The consequence of this misplaced lenity was the emboldenment of the heretics. Some years later when Bishop Bertrand was preaching in the cathedral he saw two whom he recognized, and pointed them out, saying, "I see among you missionaries of the Devil; there they are, who in my presence at Montpellier were condemned for heresy and cast out." The unabashed Waldenses, with a companion, replied to him with insults, and, leaving the church, gathered a crowd, to whom they preached their doctrines. The bishop was powerless to silence them, for, when he attempted to use force, he found them{319} protected by some of the most influential citizens of the town, and they were able to disseminate their pestiferous opinions in safety. Here, as in many other places, quarrels between the people and the bishop paralyzed the arm of the Church, and the Waldenses for many years continued to infect the city.[356]

It cannot, therefore, surprise us that nearly all the heretics burned at Strassburg in 1212 belonged to this sect. From their writings and confessions a list of three hundred errors was compiled, afterwards condensed into seventeen, and these were read before them to the people while they were on their way to the place of execution. Priest John, their leader, admitted the correctness of all save one alleging promiscuous sexual intercourse, which he indignantly denied. Those which he admitted show how rapidly their doctrines were developing to their logical conclusions, and how impassable was the gulf which already separated them from the Church. All the holy orders were rejected, and this already led to the abolition of sacerdotal celibacy; disbelief in purgatory was definitely adopted, with its consequences as to prayers and masses for the dead, and there had already been invented, before St. Francis and his followers, the dogma that Christ and his disciples held no property.[357]

The Ortlibenses or Ordibarii, who were also represented among the victims of Strassburg, demand a somewhat more detailed consideration than their immediate importance would seem to justify, because, although comparatively few in numbers, they present the earliest indication of a peculiar tendency in German free thought which we shall find reproduce itself in many forms, and constitute, with almost unconquerable stubbornness, the principal enemy with which the Inquisition had to deal.

Early in the century Maître David de Dinant, a schoolman of Paris, whose subtlety of argumentation rendered him a favorite with Innocent III., had indulged in dangerous speculations derived{320} from the Aristotelian philosophy, as transmitted through the Arab commentators, adulterated with neo-Platonic elements, which transmuted the theism of the Greek into a kind of mystic pantheism. These speculations were carried still further by his fellow-schoolman, Amauri de Bène, a favorite of the heir-apparent, Prince Louis. His views were condemned by the university in 1204; he appealed to the Holy See, but was compelled to abjure in 1207, when he is said to have died of mortification. He had disciples, however, who propagated his doctrines in secret. They were mostly men of education and intelligence, theologians of the university and priests, except a certain goldsmith named Guillaume, who was esteemed as the prophet of the little sect. It was impossible that bold speculations of this nature should remain stationary, and the theoretical premises of David and Amauri were carried to unexpected conclusions in the effort to reduce them into a system for proselytism among the people. Amauri had taught that God was the essence of all creatures, and, as light could not be seen of itself, but only in the air, so God was invisible except in his creatures. The inevitable deduction from this was that after death all beings would return to God, and in him be unified in eternal rest. This swept away the doctrines of future retribution, purgatory, and hell, and, as the Amaurians did not fail to point out, the innumerable observances through which the Church controlled the consciences and the wealth of men through its power over the keys and the treasury of salvation. As this was destructive to the ecclesiastical system, so was the doctrine equally subversive of morality, which taught that such was the virtue of love and charity that whatever was done in their behalf could be no sin, and, further, that any one filled with the Holy Ghost was impeccable, no matter what crime he might commit, because that Spirit, which is God, cannot sin, nor can man, who is nothing of himself, so long as the Spirit of God is in him.[358]

There was in these utterances an irresistible attraction to{321} minds prone to mystic exaltation. Even the orthodox Cæsarius of Heisterbach argues that much is permitted to the saints which is forbidden to sinners; where is the Spirit of God, there is liberty—have charity, and do what thou pleasest.[359] When the fatal word had once been spoken, it could not be hushed to silence, and, in spite of the most persistent and unsparing efforts of repression, these dangerous heights of superhuman spirituality continued to be the goal of men dissatisfied with the limitations of frail humanity, down to the time of Molinos and the Illuminati, and the influence of the doctrine is to be traced in the reveries of Madame Guyon and the Quietists.

Yet the Amaurian heresy was speedily crushed in its place of origin. In his proselyting zeal, Guillaume the goldsmith, in 1210, approached a certain Maître Raoul de Nemours, who feigned readiness of conviction, and reported the matter to Pierre, Bishop of Paris, and Maître Robert de Curzon, the papal supervisor of preaching in France. By their advice he pretended conversion and accompanied the Amaurians on a missionary tour which lasted for three months and extended as far as Langres. We learn something of the habits of the sectaries when we are told that to keep up the deception he would pretend to be wrapped in ecstasy, with face upturned to heaven, and on recovering himself would relate the visions which had been vouchsafed to him, though he successfully evaded the requests that he should preach the new doctrines in public. When fully informed as to all details, he communicated with the authorities, and arrests were made. A council of bishops was convened in Paris which found no difficulty in condemning all concerned; those who were in orders were degraded, and they were all handed over to the secular authorities. There were as yet no laws defining the punishment of heresy, so their fate was postponed until the return of the king, who was then absent. The result was that four of the leaders were imprisoned for life and ten were burned, who met their fate with unshrinking calmness. The simple folk of both sexes who had been seduced into following them were mercifully spared. A few executions took place elsewhere, such as that of one of the heresiarchs, Maître Godin, who was tried and burned at Amiens; the remains of Amauri{322} were exhumed and exposed to the dogs, after which his bones were scattered in the fields; the writings of the enthusiasts were forbidden to be read; the study of natural science in the university was suspended for three years, and the works of Aristotle, which had given rise to the heresy, were publicly burned.[360]

The doctrine of impeccability was likely to give loosened rein to human passion in those whose spiritual exaltation did not lift them above the weakness of the flesh, and there may be truth in the accusations current against the Amaurians, that the disciples of both sexes abandoned themselves to scandalous license, under the pretext of yielding to the demands of Christian love. Yet the popular designation of Papelards bestowed on the sectaries show that they at least preserved an exterior of sanctity and devotion, and that they prudently abstained from putting into practice their theories of the uselessness of the sacraments and of all external cult.

The heresy was thus crushed in its birthplace, where we hear no more of it except that there were teachers of it in Dauphiné, where they were confounded with the Waldenses, and that in 1225 Honorius III. ordered the destruction of the Periphyseos of Erigena, which was thought to have given rise to Amauri's speculations. The seed, however, was widely scattered, to bear fruit in foreign soil. The University of Paris drew together eager searchers after knowledge from every country in Europe, and it could not be difficult for the Amaurians to find among those from abroad converts who would prove useful missionaries. In 1215, Robert de Curzon includes the works of a certain Maurice the Spaniard in his condemnation of those of David and Amauri. Another disciple is said to have been Ortlieb of Strassburg, the teacher of the sectaries known by his name whose fate we have seen at Strassburg. That the heresy was known not to be extinguished{323} is shown by the fact that in 1215 the great Council of Lateran still deemed it necessary to utter a formal condemnation of the doctrines of Amauri, which it stigmatized as crazy rather than heretical.[361]

We know little of the faith originally professed by the Brethren of the Free Spirit, as the followers of Ortlieb called themselves. The principal account we have of their doctrines in the thirteenth century concerns itself much more with the results in denying the efficacy of sacerdotal observances than with the principles which led to those results; but there are indications of pantheism in the assertion of the eternity of the uncreated universe, in the promise of eternal life to all, while denying the resurrection of the flesh, and in the mystic representation of the Trinity by three members of the sect. No immorality is attributed to them; nay, the severest continence was prescribed by them, even in marriage; the only generation of children permitted was spiritual, through conversion, while homicide, lying, and oaths were strictly forbidden. It is quite probable that in Alsace the prevalence of Waldensianism and the sympathies born of common proscription may have considerably modified the opinions of the disciples of Ortlieb. They were by no means exterminated in the persecutions of 1212, and we hear of further pursuit against them in 1216, extending as far as Thurgau, in Switzerland. About the middle of the century they are described as prevailing in Suabia, especially in the neighborhood of Nördlingen and Oettingen, and Albertus Magnus thought them of sufficient importance to draw up an elaborate list of their errors.[362]

It was not long before another consequence, especially shocking to the faithful, was drawn from the fruitful premises of pantheism. If God was the essence of all creatures, Satan himself could not be excepted; if all were to be eventually reunited in God, Satan and his angels could not be condemned to eternal perdition.{324} So infinite were the conclusions which flowed from the bold assumptions of the Amaurians, that those who accepted their views inevitably diverged in the applications, as they attributed greater or less importance to one series of propositions or another. There were some who took special interest in this theory as to Satan, and as their utterances were peculiarly exasperating to the orthodox, they were designated as a separate sect under the name of Luciferans. Of these we hear much but see little. Their doctrines were exaggerated into devil-worship, and they were included in the list of heretics to be periodically anathematized with a zeal which attributed to them vastly greater importance than their scanty numbers deserved. Probably this was because they were peculiarly well adapted to serve as a stimulus for a healthy popular abhorrence of heresy. The most extravagant and repulsive stories were circulated as to their hideous rites, which gradually took shape under the current superstitions as to witchcraft, which they aided to formulate and render concrete. At the period under consideration they formed the basis of the wildest and most ferocious epidemic of persecution that the world had yet seen.

The first indication we have of this tendency occurs in the case of Henry Minneke, Provost of the Cistercian nunnery of Neuwerke in Goslar, which is further of interest as showing how utterly, at the close of the first quarter of the thirteenth century, Germany was destitute of any inquisitorial machinery, and how ignorant were her prelates as yet of inquisitorial procedure. In 1222 Minneke was accused before his bishop, the fanatic Conrad von Reisenberg of Hildesheim, of certain heretical opinions. An assembly of prelates was held at Goslar, which took testimony of his nuns, and found him guilty. He was simply ordered to teach his doctrines no longer. When he disobeyed he was summoned before Bishop Conrad, who examined him for three days and sentenced him to return to his Premonstratensian monastery, and ordered the nuns to elect another provost. To this, again, he paid no attention, probably considering that his immunities as a monk exempted him from episcopal jurisdiction, and the bishop seems to have had no resource but to implore the intervention of Honorius III. When the pope ordered the sentence executed, the nuns interjected an appeal back to him and to the emperor. Both appeals were rejected; Minneke was declared a diseased member of the{325} Church, fit only to be cut off, and the nuns were told that they should rejoice in being liberated from his influence. Still he remained firm, and the bishop was obliged to consult the Cardinal-legate, Cinthio of Porto, before he ventured to throw the indomitable heretic into prison. From his jail, Minneke himself appealed to the pope, asserting that he had been condemned unheard, praying for an examination, and offering to submit to incarceration for life if he should refuse to recant any erroneous opinions of which he might be convicted. Honorius thereupon, in May, 1224, ordered Bishop Conrad to bring his prisoner before the legate and an assembly of prelates for a final hearing and judgment. About October I, at Bardewick, Cinthio met an assembly of the bishops of North Germany, where it was decided that Minneke was convicted of having encouraged the nuns to regard him as greater than any other born of woman; he had on many points relaxed the severe Cistercian discipline; in his sermons he had declared that the Holy Ghost was the Father of the Son, and had so exalted the state of virginity as to represent marriage as a sin; in a vision he had seen Satan praying to be forgiven, and he had asserted that in heaven there was a woman greater than the Virgin, whose name was Wisdom. Still another synod, held at Hildesheim, October 22, was requisite to conclude the matter. Minneke was brought before it, was convicted of his errors, and degraded from the priesthood, but even yet Bishop Conrad was so little sure of his authority that the sentence was published under the seal of the legate. The culprit was handed over to the secular authorities, and was duly burned in 1225. The prominence accorded to this assertion, that Satan desired forgiveness, is shown by his being stigmatized as a Manichæan and a Luciferan.[363]

This case has a further interest for us, inasmuch as one of the participators in the final judgment was a man who filled all Germany with his fame, and who was the most perfect embodiment of the pure fanaticism of his time—Conrad of Marburg. Though a secular priest and holding himself aloof from both Mendicant Orders,[364] Conrad steeped himself in the severest poverty and gained{326} his bread by beggary. Though he could have aspired to any dignity in the Church, which reverenced him as its greatest apostle, and though for years all the benefices of Thuringia were placed by the Landgrave Louis at his absolute disposal, he never accepted a single preferment. Devoted solely to the work of the Lord, his fiery soul and unrelaxing energies were directed with absolute singleness of purpose to advancing the kingdom of heaven upon earth, according to the light which was in him.[365]

Stern in temper and narrow in mind, his bigotry was ardent to the pitch of insanity. What were his conceptions of the duty of man to his Creator and how his conscience led him to abuse unlimited authority can best be judged by his course as spiritual director of St. Elizabeth of Thuringia. The daughter of Andreas of Hungary, born in 1207, married in 1221, at the age of thirteen, to Louis of Thuringia, one of the most powerful of German princes, a mother at fourteen, a widow at twenty, and dying of self-inflicted{327} austerities in her twenty-fourth year, Elizabeth was the rarest type of womanly gentleness and self-abnegation, of all Christian virtues and spiritual aspirations. When but eighteen years of age she placed herself under Conrad's direction, and he proceeded to discipline this heavenly spirit with a ferocity worthy of a demon. Such implicit obedience did he exact that on one occasion when he had sent for her to hear him preach, and she was unable to do so on account of an unexpected visit from her sister-in-law, the Margravine of Misnia, he angrily declared that he would leave her. She went to him the next day and entreated for pardon; on his continuing obdurate, she and her maidens, whom he blamed for the matter, cast themselves at his feet, when he caused them all to be stripped to their shifts and soundly scourged. It is no wonder that he inspired her with such terror that she was wont to say "If I so much dread a mortal man, how is God to be rightly dreaded?" After the death of Louis, whom she tenderly loved, and when his brother Henry despoiled her and drove her out, penniless, with her children, she submitted with patient resignation and earned her living by beggary; and when he was forced to compound for her dower-rights with money, she made haste to distribute it in charity. Under the influence of the diseased pietism inculcated by Conrad, she abandoned her children to God and devoted herself to succoring casual outcasts and lepers; and the depth of her humility was shown when scandal made busy with her fame in consequence of her relations with Conrad. On being warned of this and counselled to greater prudence, she brought forth the bloody scourge which she used, and said, "This is the love the holy man bears to me. I thank God, who has deigned to accept this final oblation from me. I have sacrificed everything—station, wealth, beauty—and have made myself a beggar, intending only to preserve the adornment of womanly modesty; if God chooses to take this also, I hold it to be a special grace." It was this spirit, so self-abased and humble, that Conrad's brutal fanaticism sought systematically to break, contradicting her of set purpose in all things, and demanding of her every possible sacrifice. Merely to add to her afflictions he drove away, one by one, the faithful serving-women who idolized her, finally expelling Guda, who had been her loved companion since infancy in Hungary; as they themselves said,{328} "He did this with a good intention, because he feared our influence in recalling her past splendors, and he wished to deprive her of all human comfort that she might rely wholly on God." When she disobeyed his orders he used to beat her and strike her, which she endured with pleasure, in memory of the blows inflicted on Christ. Once he sent for her to come to him at Oldenburg to determine whether he would put her into an extremely rigid convent there. The nuns asked him to let her visit them, and he gave her permission, expecting that she would decline in view of the excommunication hanging over all intruders on the sacred precincts. Supposing, however, that she had leave, she went, and while her woman Irmengard stood outside, received the key, and opened the door. For this Conrad made them both lie down, and ordered his faithful comrade, Friar Gerhard, to beat them with a heavy rod, so that they bore the marks of the flogging for weeks. Well might, in the next century, the mysterious Friend of God in the Oberland, when speaking of St. Elizabeth, remark that she had abandoned herself, in place of to God, to a man far inferior to herself in natural aptitudes as well as in the gifts of divine grace.[366]

The significance of all this lies not only in the coarse violence of Conrad's methods, which regarded torture, mental and physical, as the most efficient aid to salvation, but also in the arrogance of the nature which could, without a shadow of hesitation, assume the position of an avenging God punishing humanity for its weakness and sin. When a man of such a temper was inflamed with the most fiery fanaticism, was armed with irresponsible power, and believed himself to be engaged in a direct conflict with Satan, his mad enthusiasm could lead only to a catastrophe. For the evil which he wrought it would be unjust to hold him responsible. The crime lay with those who could coolly select such an instrument, work up his crazy zeal to the highest pitch, and then let him loose to wreak his blind wrath upon defenceless populations.

Conrad had long been a man of mark, and his qualities were well known to those who made use of him. His burning eloquence was adapted to move the passions of the people, and as early as 1214 he had been honored with a commission to preach in Germany{329} the crusade which was one of the objects for which the great Council of Lateran was assembled. From this time on his activity was unabated, and there is probably truth in the assertion that he took part in the occasional persecutions of heresy which are reported, though no details have reached us. His mission as preacher brought him into direct relations with Rome, and his success in inducing thousands to take the cross gave him high repute with the curia, doubtless enhanced by the disinterestedness which asked for no reward. He gradually came to be employed as a representative in matters of importance, and his unwearied energy rendered him increasingly useful. In 1220 he was intrusted with the duty of compelling, by the censures of the Church, the Emperor Frederic to fulfil his long-delayed vow of leading an expedition to the Holy Land, and he was further made chief of the business of preaching in its behalf, by being empowered to commission assistants throughout Germany. In these letters he is addressed as "*Scholasticus*" or head of the church schools in Mainz, showing that he then held that dignity. In 1227 still greater evidence was given of the confidence reposed in him. In March of that year Gregory XI. had mounted the papal throne with full resolve to crush the rising powers of heresy, and, if possible, to deprive it of its excuse for existence in the corruptions of the church establishment. We have seen how, on June 20, 1227, he tried the experiment in Florence of creating a kind of inquisition, with a Dominican to exercise its functions. In Germany there seems to have been no one but Conrad on whom to rely. June 12, eight days before the commission issued to Giovanni di Salerno, Gregory wrote to Conrad commending highly the diligence with which he was tracking and pursuing heretics—a diligence of which, unfortunately, all details are lost to us. In order that his labors might be more efficacious, Conrad was directed and empowered to nominate whomsoever he might see fit as his assistants, and with them to inquire energetically after all who were infected with heresy, so that the extirpation of the tares from the fields of the Lord might proceed with due authority. Though the Inquisition was scarce as yet even a prospective conception, this was in effect an informal commission as inquisitor-general for Germany, and it is probably no injustice to Gregory to suggest that one of the motives prompting it was the desire to substitute papal authority for the episcopal{330} jurisdiction under which the local and spasmodic persecutions had hitherto been carried on.[367]

Eight days later, on June 20, another commission was sent to Conrad, which increased enormously his power and influence. The German Church was as corrupt and depraved as its neighbors, and all efforts to purify it had thus far proved failures. In 1225 the Cardinal-legate Cinthio had assembled a great national council at Mainz, which had solemnly adopted an elaborate series of searching canons of reformation, that proved as bootless as all similar efforts before or since. Something more was wanted, and the sternly implacable virtue of Conrad seemed to point him out as the fitting instrument for burning out the incurable cancer which was consuming the vitals of the German Church. Gregory, whose residence beyond the Alps as legate had rendered him familiar with its condition, describes its priesthood as abandoned to lasciviousness, gluttony, and all manner of filthy living, like cattle putrescing in their own dung; as committing habitually wickedness which laymen would abhor, corrupting the people by their evil example, and causing the name of the Lord to be blasphemed. To remedy these deplorable evils, he now commissioned Conrad as reformer, with full powers to enforce the regulations of the cardinal-legate, and the monasteries were especially designated as objects for his regenerating hand.[368]

Armed with almost illimitable powers, Conrad was now the foremost German ecclesiastic of the time, and we may well understand the admiration of Theodoric of Thuringia, who declares that he shone like a star throughout all Germany. Yet at this time his ill-balanced impulsiveness was concentrating his energies on the torturing of St. Elizabeth. There is no trace of his exercising his inquisitorial functions, and the only record of his activity as a reformer is his reorganizing the nunnery of Nordhausen by the simple expedient of expelling the nuns, who all led ungodly lives. Yet his services as a persecutor never were more needed. The excommunication of the Emperor Frederic, on September 29 of the same year, for temporarily abandoning his crusade, had set{331} Church and State fairly by the ears, and had inspired the heretics with fresh hopes. Everywhere their missionary activity redoubled, and the land was said to be full of them. In each diocese they had a bishop to whom they gave the name of the regular incumbent, and they pretended to have a pope whom they called Gregory, so that, under examination, they could swear that they held the faith of the bishop and of Pope Gregory. In 1229 the Waldenses were again discovered in Strassburg, and for several years persecution continued there, resulting in burning many obstinate heretics and penancing those who yielded.[369]

111

Local measures such as these were manifestly insufficient, and thus far all efforts at a comprehensive system of persecution had failed. In 1231 Gregory was busily occupied in organizing some more efficient method, and Germany was not forgotten. The Roman statutes of Annibaldo and the papal edicts of that year, to which frequent allusion has been made above, were sent to the Teutonic prelates, June 20, with letters blaming them for their lukewarmness and lenity, and ordering them to put vigorously into force the new edicts. Yet already there had been sufficient persecution to occasion the necessity of settling the novel questions arising from the confiscations, and the Diet of Worms, on June 2 of the same year, had decided that the allodial lands and the movables should go to the heirs, the fiefs to the lord, and in case of serfs the personalty to the master, thus excluding the Church and the persecutors from any share. Under Gregory's earnest impulsion the sluggishness of the bishops was somewhat stimulated. The Archbishop of Trèves made a perquisition through his city, and found three schools of heretics in full activity. He called a synod for the trial of those who were captured, and had the satisfaction of burning three men, and a woman named Leuchardis, who had borne the reputation of exceeding holiness, but who was found, upon examination, to belong to the dreaded sect of Luciferans, deploring the fall of Satan as unjustly banished from heaven.[370]{332}

Still the results did not correspond to Gregory's desires. In October of the same year (1231) he sought to spur Conrad on to a discharge of his duty by praising in the most exalted terms his activity and success in exterminating heretics, and by exhorting him, with the same wealth of exaggeration, to redoubled energy. The need of earnest work was more pressing than ever. The Archbishops of Trèves and Mainz had reported that an apostle of heresy had been sowing tares through all the land, so that not only the cities, but the towns and hamlets, were infected. Many heresiarchs, moreover, each in his own appointed district, were laboring to overthrow the Church. Conrad was therefore given full discretionary powers; he was not even required to hear the cases, but only to pronounce judgment, which was to be final and without appeal—justice to those suspect of heresy being, apparently, of no moment. He was authorized to command the aid of the secular arm, to excommunicate protectors of heresy, and to lay interdict on whole districts. The recent decrees of the Holy See were referred to as his guide, and heretics who would abjure were to have the benefit of absolution, care being taken that they should have no further opportunity of mischief—a delicate expression for condemning them to lifelong incarceration. When Conrad received these extensive powers he was so dangerously ill that his life was despaired of, and before he had fairly recovered St. Elizabeth died, November 29, 1231. Harsh as was his nature, her loss affected him severely, and for a considerable time his energies were concentrated on fruitless efforts for her canonization. In intervals of leisure, however, he exercised his powers on such heretics as were unlucky enough to be within easy reach. In Marburg itself many suspects were seized, including knights, priests, and persons of condition, of whom some recanted and the rest were burned. On one excursion to Erfurt, moreover, in 1232, he took the opportunity to burn four more victims.[371]

Results so far below what might reasonably have been expected could not but be disappointing in the extreme to Gregory.{333} One expedient remained—to try whether among the Dominicans there might not be found men able and willing to devote themselves fearlessly and exclusively to the holy work. Between the end of 1231 and that of 1232, therefore, commissions were sent to various Dominican establishments empowering their officials to undertake the work. The treaty of Ceperano, in 1230, had restored peace between the empire and the papacy, and Frederic's aid was successfully invoked to give the imperial sanction to the new experiment. From Ravenna, in March, 1232, he issued a constitution addressed to all the prelates and potentates of the empire, ordering their efficient co-operation in the extirpation of heresy, and taking under the special imperial protection all the Mendicants deputed by the pope for that purpose. The secular authorities were commanded to arrest all who should be designated to them by the inquisitors, to hold them safely until condemnation, and to put to a dreadful death those convicted of heresy or fautorship, or to imprison for life such as should recant and abjure. Relapse was punishable with the death-penalty, and descendants to the second generation were declared incapable of holding fiefs or public office.[372]

Here were laws provided and ministers for their enforcement, and the business of vindicating the faith might at last be expected to prosper. If Conrad was remiss, others would be found enthusiastically ready for the work. So it proved. Suddenly there appeared on the scene a Dominican named Conrad Tors, said to be a convert from heresy, who, without special commission, commenced to clear the land of error. He carried with him a layman named John, one-eyed and one-handed, of thoroughly disreputable character, who boasted that he could recognize a heretic at sight. Apparently with little more evidence than this, Conrad Tors raided from town to town, condemning his victims wholesale, and those whom he delivered to the magistrates they were compelled by popular excitement to burn. Soon, however, a revulsion of feeling took place, and then the Dominican shrewdly enlisted the support of the nobles by directing his attacks against the more wealthy, and holding out the prospect of extensive confiscations to be divided. When remonstrated with he is{334} said to have replied, "I would burn a hundred innocent if there was one guilty among them." Stimulated by this shining example, many Dominicans and Franciscans joined him, and became his eager assistants in the work.[373]

Whether, as reported, Conrad Tors, to strengthen himself, sought out Conrad of Marburg and persuaded him to take part in the good work, or whether the latter, scenting the battle from afar, was aroused from his torpor and rushed eagerly to the fray, cannot positively be determined. This much is certain, that at length he came forward, and not only lent the weight of his great name to the proceedings, but urged them to a crueller and wider development with all his vehemence of character and implacable severity.

The heresy of which the miserable victims of this onslaught were accused was not Waldensian, but Luciferan. Its hideous rites were described in full detail by Master Conrad to Pope Gregory, and are worth repeating as illustrating the superstitions concerning witchcraft which, for centuries, worked such cruel wrong in every corner of Europe. Indeed, it seemed inevitable that such embroideries should be added by inquisitorial craft or popular credulity to the tenets of heretics, for, on the first emergence of Catharism at Orleans in 1022, very similar stories were told of the infernal rites of the heretics, which are repeated by Walter Mapes in the latter half of the twelfth century.[374] That Conrad obtained these wild fictions in endless duplication from those who stood before his judgment-seat there need be no reasonable doubt. The reports of witch-trials in later times are too numerous and authentic for us to question the readiness of self-accusation of those who saw no other means of escape, or their eagerness to propitiate their judge by responding to every incriminating suggestion, and telling him what they found him desirous of hearing. Crude as were Conrad's methods, the inquisitorial process proved its universal effectiveness by their producing confessions as surely as the more elaborate refinements invented by his successors, although he had not the advantage of the use of torture.{335}

According to these revelations, when a novice is received into the sect and first attends the assembly, there appears to him a toad, which he kisses either on the posteriors or on the mouth; in the latter case it deposits something in his mouth. Occasionally it has the aspect of a goose or of a duck, and sometimes it is as large as an oven. Then there comes to him a man of wonderful paleness, with the blackest of eyes, and so thin that he is naught but skin and bone. Him the novice likewise kisses, finding him ice-cold, and with that kiss all remembrance of the Catholic faith vanishes from his heart. Then all sit down to a feast, after which, from a statue which is always present, there descends a black cat, as large as a dog, with the tail bent back. She comes down backwards and her posteriors are kissed, first by the novice, then by the master of the assembly, and finally by all who are worthy and perfect, while those who are imperfect and feel themselves unworthy receive peace from the master. Then each resumes his place, songs are sung, and the master says to his next neighbor, "What does this teach?" The answer is, "The highest peace," and another adds, "And that we must obey." All lights are then extinguished and indiscriminate intercourse takes place, after which the candles are relighted, each one takes his seat, and from a dark corner appears a man shining like the sun in his upper half, while from the hips down he is black like the cat. He illuminates the whole place, and the master, taking a fragment of the novice's garment, hands it to him, saying, "Master, I give this to thee which has been given to me." To this the shining man replies, "Thou hast served me well, thou wilt serve me more and better. I leave to thy care what thou hast given me," and then he disappears. Each year at Easter they receive the host, carry it home in their mouths, and spit it out into a cesspool to show their contempt for the Redeemer. They hold that God unjustly and treacherously cast Satan into hell; the latter is the Creator, who in the end will overcome God, when they expect eternal bliss with him. That which is pleasing to God is to be avoided, and that which he hates is to be cherished.

This transparent tissue of inventions was apparently doubted by no one, and it excited almost to insanity the credulous old man who filled the papal chair. He replies that he is drunk with wormwood, and in fact his letters read like the ravings of a madman.{336} "If against such men the earth should rise up, and the stars of heaven reveal their iniquity, so that not only men, but the elements, should unite in their destruction, wiping them from the face of the earth without sparing sex or age, and rendering them an eternal opprobrium for the nations, it would not be a sufficient and worthy punishment of their crimes." If they cannot be converted, the strongest remedies must be used. Fire and steel must be applied to wounds incurable by milder applications. Conrad was instructed forthwith to preach a crusade against them, and the bishop of the province, the emperor, and his son, King Henry, were ordered to exert all their powers for the extirpation of the wretches.[375]

The means which Master Conrad took to obtain these avowals from his victims were simple in the extreme. The processes of the Inquisition had not yet been formulated, and the unlimited powers with which he was clothed enabled his impatient temper to reach the desired goal by the shortest possible course. As officially reported, after the bursting of the bubble, to Gregory by his own penitentiary, the Dominican Bernard, and the Archbishop of Mainz, the accused was allowed simply the option of confessing what was demanded of him, and receiving penance, or of being burned for denial—which, in fact, was the essence of the inquisitorial process, reduced to its simplest terms. Conrad had no prisons at his disposal for the incarceration of penitents, and the infliction of wearing crosses seems to have been unknown to him, so he devised the penance of shaving the head as a mark of humiliation for his converts, who were moreover, of course, obliged to give the names of all whom they had seen in the hideous nocturnal assemblies.

At the outset he had fallen into the hands of a designing woman, a vagrant about twenty years old who had quarrelled with her relations, and who, coming by chance to Bingen, and observing what was going on, saw her opportunity of revenge. She pretended to be of the sect, that her husband had been burned, that she wished to perish likewise, but added that if the Master would believe her she would reveal the names of the guilty. Conrad{337} eagerly swallowed the bait, and sent her with his assistants to Clavelt, whence she came, where she caused the burning of her kindred. Then there was a certain Amfrid, who finally confessed that he had led Conrad to condemn a number of innocent men. Creatures of this kind were sure not to be lacking, and it was even said that cunning heretics caused themselves to be accused, and accepted penance, for the purpose of incriminating Catholics, and thus rendering the whole proceeding odious. As no one had the slightest opportunity of defence, some steadfast men preferred to be burned and thus earn salvation, rather than to confess to lies and falsely accuse others. The weaker ones who saved their lives, when pressed to name their accomplices, would often say, "I know not whom to accuse: tell me the names of those you suspect;" or, when interrogated about individuals, would evasively reply, "They were as I was; they were in the assemblies as I was," which was apparently sufficient. "Thus," proceeds the official report to the pope, "brother accused brother, the wife the husband, and the master the servant. Others gave money to the shaven penitents in order to learn from them methods of evasion and escape, and there arose a confusion unknown for ages. I, the archbishop, first by myself and afterwards with the two archbishops of Trèves and Cologne, warned Master Conrad to proceed in so great a matter with more moderation and discretion, but he refused."[376]{338}

From this last fact we gather that the prelates of the land, while not interfering effectively to protect their people, had, at least, taken no part in the insane persecution which was raging. Conrad had found plenty of assistants among the Dominicans and Franciscans, but the secular hierarchy had held aloof. In vain had Gregory, in October, 1232, written to them and to the princes, telling them that the heretics who formerly lay in hiding were now coming forward openly, like war-horses harnessed for battle, publicly preaching their errors and seeking the perdition of the simple and ignorant. Faith was rare in Germany, he said, and, therefore, he ordered them to make vigorous inquisition throughout their lands, seizing all heretics and suspects, and proceeding against them in accordance with the papal decrees of 1231. The appeal fell upon deaf ears. The bishops seem to have been thoroughly disturbed by the encroachments which the papacy was making on their independence through the new agencies which it was bringing into play. The Mendicant Orders were already a sufficiently dangerous factor, and now came these new inquisitors, armed with papal commissions, superseding their time-honored jurisdiction in every spot within their dioceses. It is no wonder that they felt alarmed, and that they held aloof. The German prelates were great secular princes, combining civil and spiritual authority. The three electoral archbishops—Mainz, Trèves, and Cologne—stood on a level as temporal lords with the most powerful princes of the empire, and the wide extent of many of the dioceses rendered the bishops scarcely less formidable. They were always suffering from the greed of the Roman curia, and were perpetually involved in struggles to resist its encroachments. Frederic II., indeed, by his constitutions of 1232, had increased their secular authority by rendering them absolute masters of the episcopal cities, whose municipal rights and liberties he abolished, but at the same time he had given, as we have seen, the imperial sanction to the papal Inquisition, and had rendered it everywhere supreme. It is no wonder that they felt aggrieved and alarmed, that they withheld their co-operation as far as they{339} safely could, and that well-grounded jealousy would lead them to seize the first safe opportunity of crushing the intruding upstarts.[377]

Fortunately for the German people, Conrad's blind recklessness was not long in affording them the desired chance. Beginning with the lowly and helpless, his operations had rapidly advanced to the higher classes. In his eyes the meanest peasant and the loftiest noble were on an equality, and he was as prompt to assail the one as the other, but his witnesses at first had not dared to accuse the high-born and powerful. It is quite possible, indeed, that, as the persecution became more dreadful, some of them may have felt that the surest mode of bringing on a crisis was to involve the magnates of the land. Rumors were spread impugning the faith of the Counts of Aneberg, Lotz, and Sayn. Conrad eagerly directed his interrogatories to obtaining evidence against them, and summoned them to appear before him. Count Sayn was an especially notable prey, as he was one of the most powerful nobles of the diocese, whose extensive possessions were guarded by castles renowned for strength, and whose reputation was that of a stern and cruel man. The crime of which he was accused was that of riding on a crab, and open defiance was expected from him. Sigfried, the Archbishop of Mainz, to make a show of obedience to the papal commands, had called a provincial council to assemble March 13, 1233. When it met, it deplored the prevalence of heresy, from which scarce a village in the land was free; it prayed the prelates to labor zealously for the suppression of the evil, commanded them to enforce in their respective dioceses the recent decrees of the pope and of the emperor, which were to be read and explained in the local synods, so that the heretics might be frightened to conversion; it deprecated the practice of seizing the property of suspects before their guilt was determined; it ordered the bishops to provide prisons for coiners and incorrigible clerks, without alluding to the imprisonment of heretics, although Gregory, but a few weeks before, had specially ordered them to employ perpetual incarceration in all cases of relapse; it endeavored to maintain episcopal jurisdiction by enacting that inquisitors must obtain letters from the bishop before{340} exercising their powers in any diocese; finally, it anticipated the resistance of Count Sayn and the other inculpated nobles, by directing that if any magnate, relying upon the strength of his castles and the support of his subjects, should refuse to appear after three citations, his bishop should preach a crusade against him with indulgences, and he should be manfully assailed.[378]

Thus, while ostensibly obeying the commands of the pope and emperor, the action of the bishops was practically directed to limiting the powers of the inquisitors. As for the threat of a crusade, its significance is seen in the steps actually taken in the case of Count Sayn. That shrewd noble saw that he could rely upon episcopal protection if he could promise the bishops efficient support, and he had sufficient interest with King Henry to induce him to join with Sigfried of Mainz in calling a council for July 25, to consider his case. The king and his princes attended the assembly as well as the prelates, so that it was rather an imperial diet than an ecclesiastical council. The count asserted his innocence and offered to prove it by conjurators. Conrad, who was present, found his position suddenly changed. The assembly was, in reality, a national protest against the supremacy of the papal Inquisition, and the inquisitor, in place of being a judge armed with absolute jurisdiction, was merely a prosecutor. He presented his witnesses, but in that august presence the hearts of some of them failed, and they withdrew; others felt emboldened to declare that they had been forced to accuse the count in order to save their own lives, and those who persisted were easily shown to be personal enemies of the accused. The whole assemblage seemed inspired with a common desire to put an end to Conrad's arbitrary proceedings, and the prosecution broke down totally. King Henry alone, perhaps already meditating his rebellion against his father, and anxious not to offend either the nobles or the papacy, desired to postpone the matter for further consideration. The count pressed earnestly for immediate judgment, but the Archbishop of Trèves interposed— "My lord, the king wishes the case postponed;" then turning to the people,{341} "I announce to you that Count Sayn departs from here unconvicted, and as a good Catholic," Master Conrad sullenly muttered, "If he had been convicted it would have been different," and withdrew. The count finally agreed to allow the matter to be referred to Rome, and ecclesiastics of distinction were appointed to lay the proceedings before the Holy See for final decision.[379]

Maddened by his defeat, Conrad at once proceeded to preach in the streets of Mainz a crusade against some nobles who had been summoned and who had not appeared. To this both the archbishop and the king objected, and he was forced to desist. With his usual impulsiveness he then abruptly determined to quit an ungrateful world, and to live henceforth in retirement at Marburg. The king and archbishop offered him an armed escort, but he would accept nothing save letters of surety, and with these he departed to meet his fate. Those against whom his crusade had been preached lay in wait for him near Marburg and despatched him, July 31, regardless of his entreaties for mercy. His faithful follower, Friar Gerhard, refused the opportunity offered him to escape, threw himself on the body of his beloved master, and perished with him. The scene of the murder is supposed to be Kappeln on the Lahnsberg, where a chapel was erected to commemorate it. The body was carried to Marburg and buried by the side of St. Elizabeth, and when the latter was translated to the magnificent Elizabethskirche, his bones were likewise carried thither.[380]

The immediate reputation which Conrad left behind him is shown by the vision, related by a contemporary, which indicated that he was hopelessly damned. Modern ecclesiastics, however, take a more favorable view of his career, and even the amiable Alban Butler describes him as a virtuous and enlightened priest, who rendered great service by his preaching, and whose fervor, disinterestedness, and love of poverty and austerity rendered him a model for his contemporaries. Yet, unaccountably, the Church has not yet proceeded to his vindication as a martyred saint, and{342} has neglected to place him alongside of those kindred spirits, St. Peter Martyr and St. Pedro Arbues.[381]

With Conrad's withdrawal from the Council of Mainz the proceedings of which he had been the mainspring came to an end at once. "Thus," says a contemporary ecclesiastic, "ceased this storm, the most dangerous persecution of the faithful since the days of Constantius the Heretic and Julian the Apostate. People once more began to breathe. Count Sayn was a wall for the mansion of the Lord, lest this madness should rage further, enveloping guilty and innocent alike, bishops and princes, religious and Catholics, like peasants and heretics." The murderers evidently felt that they had nothing to dread from public opinion, for they voluntarily came forward and offered to submit themselves to the judgment of the Church as regards the heresy whereof Conrad had accused them, and to the secular tribunals as regards the homicide, agreeing to present themselves for examination at a diet of the empire which was ordered for February, 1234, at Frankfort.[382]

Gregory, who in June had been ordering a crusade preached against the heretics, and had been stimulating prince and prelate to a yet more ferocious persecution, was moved to regret when the envoy of the assembly of Mainz, Conrad, the "Scholasticus" of Speier, presented letters from the king and bishops describing the arbitrary methods of his inquisitor. He ordered letters drawn up prescribing a more regular form of trial for heretics; but before the envoy had permission to depart, there arrived the originator of the trouble, Conrad Tors, with the pitiful tale of the Master's martyrdom. At this news the emotional pope could not contain his wrath. The letters just written were recalled and torn up, and the unlucky envoy was threatened with the deprivation of all his benefices. Under the remonstrances of the Sacred College, however, Gregory's ire subsided sufficiently to allow him to renew the letters and to enable the envoy to depart unscathed. The pope solaced himself, however, with pouring out his grief at full length in letters to the German prelates. The death of Conrad was a thunderclap which had shaken the walls of the Christian{343} sanctuary. No words were strong enough to describe the transcendant merits and services of the martyr, and no punishment could be invented too severe for the murderers. The bishops were roundly rated for their indifference in the matter, and were ordered to take immediate and effective measures. The Dominican provincial, Conrad, was commanded, in conjunction with the bishops, to carry on the Inquisition vigorously, and to preach a crusade against the heretics.[383]

In spite of this furious grief and wrath the German prelates maintained a most provoking calmness. The fanatic Conrad, Bishop of Hildesheim, it is true, preached a crusade as ordered by the pope, and under his impulsion the Landgrave, Conrad of Thuringia, zealously purged his land of heretics, and completely destroyed all their assemblies, levelling to the ground Willnsdorf, which was reckoned their chief abiding-place; while his brother, Henry Raspe, and Hartmann, Count of Kiburg (Zurich), took the cross under the same auspices, and received, in consequence, papal protection for their dominions. Even this measure of activity, however, was regarded unfavorably in Germany, and there was no response to the cry for vengeance. The Diet of Frankfort duly assembled February 2, 1234, and the first business recorded was an accusation brought by King Henry himself against the Bishop of Hildesheim for having preached the crusade; it was treated as an offence, and though he was pardoned by unanimous request, the recalcitrance against the papal tendencies was none the less significant. Then the memory of the martyred Conrad was arraigned, and this, as a matter of faith, was discussed by the ecclesiastics separately. There were twenty-five archbishops and bishops present, who were almost unanimous in condemning him, while the Bishop of Hildesheim and a Dominican named Otto strenuously defended him. One of the prelates exclaimed that Master Conrad ought to be dug up and burned as a heretic; but no conclusion seems to have been reached, for the proceedings were interrupted by the introduction of a procession of those whom he had shaved in penance the preceding year, who marched in with a cross at their head, and complained of his cruelty with dolorous {344} cries, when a tumult arose from which his defenders were glad to escape with their lives. On the following Monday the solemn purgation of Count Sayn took place in the field of judgment beyond the walls. Eight bishops, twelve Cistercian and three Benedictine abbots, twelve Franciscan and three Dominican friars, who, with many other clerks and numerous nobles, took part in his oath of denial, show how emphatically the German hierarchy desired to disclaim all sympathy with Conrad's acts. Count Solms, whom Conrad had forced to confession, went through the same ceremony, declaring with tears in his eyes that the fear of death alone had compelled him to admit himself guilty. The diet then proceeded to legislate for the future, and its slender enunciation on the subject of heresy can have carried little comfort to the wrathful Gregory. It simply commanded that all who exercised judicial functions should use every effort to purge the land of heresy, but at the same time it cautioned them to prefer justice to unjust persecution.[384]

Two months later, April 2, 1234, a council was held at Mainz for final action. Count Sayn and others who had been accused were subjected to a form of examination, were declared innocent, and were restored to reputation and to their possessions. Conrad's unlucky witnesses who had been forced to commit perjury were ordered to undergo a penance of seven years; those who had accused the innocent were maliciously sent to the pope for the imposition of penance, and he was, in the same spirit, asked what should be done about those whom Conrad had unjustly burned. As for the murderers, they were simply excommunicated.[385]

All this was a direct challenge to the Holy See, but Gregory prudently delayed action. He was involved in troubles with the Romans which rendered inadvisable any trial of strength with the united Teutonic Church. He sent his penitentiary, Bernard, who made an investigation on the spot, and, in conjunction with Archbishop Sigfried, furnished him with a report to which we are indebted for most of our knowledge of the affair. On receiving this, {345} Gregory expressed his regret that he had intrusted to Master Conrad the enormous powers which had led to a result so lamentable. Still his decision was delayed. Towards the end of the year 1234 he appealed earnestly to the German bishops for aid in his quarrel with the Romans, which continued until he made peace with them in April, 1235. His hands were now free, but it was not until July that he trusted himself to express his indignation. Then he scolded most vehemently the Council of Mainz for daring, in the absence of any defenders of the faith, to absolve those whom Conrad had prosecuted, and for sending to him for absolution the murderers, without having first exacted of them full satisfaction for their detestable crime. His sentence upon them is that they shall join the crusade to Palestine when it sets sail the following March, giving good security to insure their obedience, and meanwhile they shall visit all the greater churches in the region of the crime, bare-footed and naked, except drawers, with a halter around the neck, and a rod in the hand, and, when the affluence of people is the greatest, cause themselves to be scourged by all the priests, while they chant the penitential psalms, and publicly confess their guilt. After this they may be absolved.[386]

It is satisfactory to know that the immediate author of the troubles met with the fate which he deserved. Conrad Tors, on his return from Rome, endeavored to resume his interrupted labors, but the temper of the people had changed, and the victims were no longer unresisting. At Strassburg he summoned the Junker Heinz von Müllenheim, who unceremoniously settled the accusation by slaying him. His assistant, the one-eyed John, met an even more ignominious fate, for he was recognized at Freiburg and hanged.[387] {346}

Thus ended this terrible drama, which left an impression of horror on the souls of the German people not easily effaced. The number of Conrad's victims can only be guessed at. Some chroniclers vaguely speak of them as innumerable, and one asserts that a thousand unfortunates were burned. Although this is probably an exaggeration, for the period of Conrad's insane activity cannot have exceeded a twelvemonth, yet the number must have been considerable to produce so profound an impression on a generation which was by no means susceptible.[388]

One good result there undoubtedly was. The universal detestation excited by Conrad's crazy fanaticism rendered it comparatively easy for the bishops to maintain the jurisdiction which they had assumed, and to keep the Inquisition confined within narrow limits. For a time this was doubtless facilitated by the open quarrels between Frederic II. and the papacy, but even after his death, during the Great Interregnum and the reigns of emperors who were more or less dependent upon the Holy See, more than a century was to pass away before the popes, who were so zealously organizing and strengthening it elsewhere, made a serious effort to establish the Inquisition in Germany. We hear of no endeavors on their part, we meet with no appointments or commissions of German inquisitors. It seems to have been tacitly understood that the institution was unfitted for German soil until a period when it had fairly entered into decadence in the lands where its growth was the rankest.

The excitement of Conrad of Marburg's exploits was naturally succeeded by a reaction. In 1233 the murder of Bishop Berthold of Coire, attributed to heretics, shows how far persecution spread, accompanied by a dangerous tendency to resistance. Throughout 1234 both Dominicans and Franciscans are reported as busy, with the result of numerous burnings; but the lesson taught by the attitude of the German prelates was not lost, and in 1235 the magistrates of Strassburg enjoined on them to seek conversions by preaching, and not to burn people without at least giving them a hearing. The languor and reaction continued. We have seen{347} from the complaints of the Count of Salins, in 1248, and the fruitless efforts of Innocent IV. to establish the Inquisition in Besançon, that the western borders of Germany were full of Waldenses who had little to dread. At the same period there was a demonstration in the neighborhood of Halle which may be reasonably regarded as Waldensian. The papacy had succeeded in raising a rival to Frederic in the person of William of Holland, and a crusade was on foot in his favor against Conrad, Frederic's son. The imperialists would naturally regard with favor the Waldensian doctrines denying the power of the keys and the obedience due to interdicts, and they might not object further to the tenet that sinful priests cannot administer the sacraments. Such were the dogmas attributed to the heretics of Halle, who came boldly forward in 1248, were eagerly listened to by the nobles, and were favored by King Conrad, but they speedily disappeared from sight in the changeful circumstances of that tumultuous time.[389]

We have much more distinct indications of the existence both of heresy and of the Inquisition in the writings of David of Augsburg, and of the author now generally known as the Passauer Anonymus. The date of the latter is not absolutely certain, but it cannot vary much from 1260. His field of action was the extensive diocese of Passau, stretching from the Iser to the Leitha, and from Bohemia to Styria, embracing eastern Bavaria and northern Austria. His instructions seem to take for granted the existence of an organized Inquisition with its fully developed code of procedure, but his description of the prevalence of Waldensianism would indicate that it was almost inoperative. He tells us that he had often been concerned in the inquisition and examination of the "schools," or communities, of Waldenses, of which there were forty-one in the diocese, ten of them being in the single town of Clamme, where the heretics slew the parish priest without any one being punished for it. There were also forty-one Waldensian churches, organized under a bishop residing in Empenbach, and there was a school for lepers at Newenhoffen. All this shows a prosperous growth of heresy little disturbed by persecution. It is observable that the places enumerated as the seats of these churches are{348} mostly insignificant villages, the larger towns appear to be avoided, and the heretics belong to the humbler classes—mostly peasants and mechanics. Their wonderful familiarity with Scripture and their self-devoted earnestness in making converts have already been alluded to. From the writer's long description of the tenets of the Ordibarii and Ortlibenses it is evident that they formed a fair proportion of the heretics with whom the inquisitor had to deal, and their belief that the Day of Judgment would come when the pope and the emperor should be converted to their sect, indicates the hopefulness of a faith that is growing and spreading. Soon afterwards we hear of Waldenses captured in the diocese of Ratisbon, and their continued activity, in spite of persecution, through all the south German regions.[390]

There was little on the part of the Inquisition or the bishops to prevent the growth and spread of heresy. During the Interregnum, in 1261, a council of Mainz seems suddenly to have awakened to a sense of neglected duty in the premises; it vigorously anathematized all heretics after the fashion customary in the papal bulls, and it strictly commanded the bishops of the province to labor zealously for the extermination of heresy in their respective dioceses, enforcing, with regard to the persons and property of heretics, the papal constitutions and the statutes of a former provincial council. There is here no sign of the existence of a papal Inquisition, and the episcopal activity which was threatened appears to have lain dormant, though the action of the council would seem to show that heretics were numerous enough to attract attention. It is true that, in the chancery of Rodolph of Hapsburg, whose reign extended from 1273 to 1292, there was a formula for acknowledging and confirming the papal commissions presented by inquisitors, showing that this must, at least occasionally, have been done. The emperor calls God to witness that his chief object in accepting the crown was to be able to defend the faith; he alludes to the exercise of inquisitorial jurisdiction over the descendants of heretics as well as over heretics themselves, but he carefully inserts a saving clause to the effect that the accused{349} must be legitimately proved guilty and be properly condemned. If, however, inquisitors presented themselves to obtain this recognition of their powers, they have left no visible traces of the results of their activity.[391]

In the codes which embody the customs current in mediæval Germany there is no recognition whatever of the existence of such a body as the Inquisition. The Sachsenspiegel, which contains the municipal law of the northern provinces, provides, it is true, the punishment of burning for those convicted of unbelief, poisoning, or sorcery, but says nothing as to the manner of trial; and the rule enunciated that no houses shall be destroyed except when rape is committed in them, or a violated woman is carried into them, shows that the demolition of the residences and refuges of heretics was unknown within its jurisdiction. The code throughout is singularly disregardful of ecclesiastical pretensions, and richly earned the papal anathema bestowed upon it when its practical working happened to attract the attention of the Roman curia.[392]

The Schwabenspiegel, or code in force in southern Germany, is much more complaisant to the Church, but it knows of no jurisdiction over heretics save that of the bishops. It admits that an emperor rendering himself suspect in the faith can be put under ban by the pope. It provides death by fire for the heretic. It directs that when heretics are known to exist, the ecclesiastical courts shall inquire about them and proceed against them. If convicted, the secular judge shall seize them and doom them according to law. If he neglects or refuses he is to be excommunicated by the bishop, and his suzerain shall inflict on him the penalty of heresy. If a secular prince does not punish heresy he is to be excommunicated by the episcopal court; if he remains under the censure for a year the bishop is to report him to the pope, who shall deprive him of his rank and honors, and the emperor is{350} bound to execute his sentence by stripping him of all his possessions, feudal and allodial. All this shows ample readiness to accept the received ecclesiastical law of the period as to heresy, but utter ignorance of the inquisitorial process is revealed in the provision which inflicts the *talio* on whoever accuses another of certain crimes, including heresy, without being able to convict him. When the accuser had to accept the chances of the stake, prosecutions were not apt to be common.[393]

Towards the close of the thirteenth century and the opening of the fourteenth, attention was aroused to the dangerous tendencies of certain forms of belief lurking among some semi-religious bodies which had long enjoyed the favor of the pious and the protection of the Church, known by the names of Beguines, Beghards, Lollards, Cellites, etc. Infinite learned trifling has been wasted in imagining derivations for these appellations. The Beguines and Beghards themselves assert their descent from St. Begga, mother of Pepin of Landen, who built a Benedictine nunnery at Andennes. Another root has been sought in Lambert-le-Bègue, or the Stammerer, a priest of St. Christopher at Liège, about 1180, who became prominent by denouncing the simony of the canons of the cathedral. Prebends were openly placed for sale in the hands of a butcher named Udelin, who acted as broker, and when Lambert aroused the people to a sense of this wickedness, the bishop arrested him as a disturber, and the clergy assailed him and tore him with their nails. His connection with the Beguines arose from his affording them shelter in his house at St. Christopher, which has remained until modern times the largest and richest Beguinage of the province. The soundest opinion, however, would seem to be that both Beghard and Beguine are derived from the old German word*beggan*, signifying either to beg or to pray, while Lollard is traced to *lullen*, to mutter prayers.[394]{351}

The motives were numerous which impelled multitudes to desire a religious life without assuming the awful and irrevocable vows that cut them off absolutely from the world. This was especially the case among women who chanced to be deprived of their natural guardians and who sought in those wild ages the protection which the Church alone could confer. Thus associations were formed, originally of women, who simply promised chastity and obedience while they lived in common, who assisted either by labor or beggary in providing for the common support, who were assiduous in their religious observances, and who performed such duties of hospitality and of caring for the sick as their opportunities would allow. The Netherlands were the native seat of this fruitful idea, and as early as 1065 there is a charter extant given by a convent of Beguines at Vilvorde, near Brussels. The drain of the crusades on the male population increased enormously the number of women deprived of support and protection, and gave a corresponding stimulus to the growth of the Beguinages. In time men came to form similar associations, and soon Germany, France, and Italy became filled with them. To this contributed in no small degree the insane laudation of poverty by the Franciscans and the merit conceded to a life of beggary by the immense popularity of the Mendicant Orders. To{352} earn a livelihood by beggary was in itself an approach to sanctity, as we have seen in the case of Conrad of Marburg and St. Elizabeth. About 1230 a certain Willem Cornelis, of Antwerp, gave up a prebend and devoted himself to teaching the pre-eminent virtue of poverty. He carried the received doctrine on the subject, however, to lengths too extravagant, for he held that poverty consumed all sin, as fire ate up rust, and that a harlot, if poor, was better than a just and continent rich man; and though he was honorably buried in the church of the Virgin Mary, yet when, four years later, these opinions came to be known, Bishop Nicholas of Cambrai caused his bones to be exhumed and burned.[395]

Extremes such as this show us the prevailing tendencies of the age, and it is necessary to appreciate these tendencies in order to understand how Europe came to tolerate the hordes of holy beggars, either wandering or living in communities, who covered the face of the land, and drained the people of their substance. Of the two classes the wanderers were the most dangerous, but in both there was the germ of future trouble, although the settled Beguines approached very nearly the Tertiaries of the Mendicants. Indeed, they frequently placed themselves under the direction of Dominicans or Franciscans, and eventually those who survived the vicissitudes of persecution mostly merged into the Tertiaries of either one Order or the other.

The rapid growth of these communities in the thirteenth century is easily explicable. Not only did they respond to the spiritual demands of the age, but they enjoyed the most exalted patronage. In Flanders the counts seem never wearied of assisting them. Gregory IX. and his successors took their institution under the special protection of the Holy See. St. Louis provided them with houses in Paris and other cities, and left them abundant legacies in his will, in which he was imitated by his sons. Under such encouragement their numbers increased enormously. In Paris there were multitudes. About 1240 they were estimated at two thousand in Cologne and its vicinity, and there were as many in the single Beguinageof Nivelle, in Brabant. Philippe de

Montmirail,{353} a pious knight who devoted himself to good works, is said to have been instrumental in providing for five thousand Beguines throughout Europe. The great Beguinage of Ghent, founded in 1234, by the Countesses of Flanders, Jeanne and Marguerite, is described in the seventeenth century as resembling a small town, surrounded with wall and fosse, containing open squares, conventual houses, dwellings, infirmary, church, and cemetery, inhabited by eight hundred or a thousand women, the younger living in the convents, the older in separate houses. They were tied by no permanent vows and were free to depart and marry at any time, but so long as they were inmates they were bound to obey the Grand Mistress. The guardianship of the establishment was hereditary in the House of Flanders, and it was under the supervision of the Dominican prior of Ghent. How large was the space that Beguinism occupied in public estimation in the thirteenth century is shown by Philippe Mousket, who calls Conrad of Marburg a Beguine, *"uns bégins mestre serrmonnière."*[396]

Those who thus lived in communities could be subjected to wholesome supervision and established rules, but it was otherwise with those who maintained an independent existence, either in one spot or wandering from place to place, sometimes supporting themselves by labor, but more frequently by beggary. Their customary persistent cry through the streets—*"'Brod durch Gott{354}'"*—became a shibboleth unpleasantly familiar to the inhabitants of the German cities, which the Church repeatedly and ineffectually endeavored to suppress. A circumstance occurring about 1240 illustrates their reputation for superior sanctity and the advantages derivable from it. A certain Sibylla of Marsal near Metz, we are told, seeing how many women under the name of Beguines flourished in the appearance of religion, and under the guidance of the Dominicans, thought fit to imitate them. Assiduous attendance at matins and mass gained her the repute of peculiar holiness. Then she pretended to fast and live on celestial food, she had ecstasies and visions, and deceived the whole region, not excepting the Bishop of Metz himself. The Beguines who had hailed her as a saintly sister were excessively mortified when an accident revealed the imposture; the people were so enraged that some wanted to burn her and others to bury her alive, but the bishop shut her up in a convent, *in pace*, where, naturally enough, she soon died.[397]

The Church was not long in recognizing the danger inherent in these practices when withdrawn from close supervision. On the one hand there was simulated piety, like that of Sibylla of Marsal, on the other the far more serious opportunity of indulgence in unlawful speculation. In 1250 and the following years the Beguines of Cologne repeatedly sought the protection of papal legates against the oppression of both clergy and laity. Already, in 1259, a council of Mainz strongly reproved the pestiferous sect of Beghards and Beguttæ (Beguines), who wandered through the streets crying *"Broth durch Gott,"* preaching in caverns and other secret places, and given to various practices disapproved by the Church. All priests were ordered to warn them to abandon these customs, and to expel from their parishes those who were obstinate. In 1267 the Council of Trèves forbade their preaching in the streets on account of the heresies which they disseminated. In 1287 a council of Liège deprived all who did not live in the Beguinages of the right to wear the peculiar habit and enjoy the privileges of Beguines. In Suabia, about the same period, some members of communities of Beghards and Beguines sought to persuade the rest that they could better serve God "in freedom of spirit," when the bishops proceeded to abolish all such associations, and some of them asked to adopt the rule of St. Augustin.[398]

All this points to the adoption, by the followers of Ortlieb, who called themselves Brethren of the Free Spirit, of the habit and appellation of the Beghards and Beguines, and the gradual invasion among the latter of the doctrines derived from Amaury.{355}Comparatively few of the Lollards, Beghards, or Beguines were contaminated with these heresies, but they all had to share the responsibility, and the communities of both sexes, who led the most regular lives and were inspired with the purest orthodoxy, were exposed to unnumbered tribulations for lack of a distinctive appellation. When heretics regarded as peculiarly obnoxious were anathematized as Beghards and Beguines, it was impossible for those who bore the name, without sharing the errors, to escape the common responsibility. It became even worse when John XXII. plunged into a quarrel with the Spiritual Franciscans, drove them into open rebellion, and persecuted the new heresy which he had thus created with all the unsparing wrath of his vindictive nature. In France the Tertiary Franciscans were popularly known as Beguines, and this became the appellation customarily bestowed on these Spiritual heretics, and adopted by the Avignonese popes to designate them. Not only has this led to much confusion on the part of heresiologists, but its effect, for a time, on the fortunes of the virtuous and orthodox Beguines of both sexes was most disastrous. The heretic Beghards, it is true, adopted for themselves the title of Brethren of the Free Spirit; the rebellious Franciscans insisted that they were the only legitimate representatives of the Order, and, at most, assumed the term of Spirituals, in order to distinguish themselves from their carnal-minded conventual brethren; but the authorities were long in admitting these distinctions, and, in the eyes of the Church at large, the condemnation of Beghards and Beguines covered all alike.

We have here to do only with the Brethren of the Free Spirit, whose doctrines, as we have seen, were derived from the speculations of the Amaurians carried to Germany by Ortlieb of Strassburg. Descriptions of their errors have reached us from so many sources, covering so long a period, with so general a consensus in fundamentals, that there can be little doubt as to the main principles of their faith. In a sect extending over so wide a reach of territory, and stubbornly maintaining itself through so many generations, there must necessarily have existed subdivisions, as one heresiarch or another pushed his speculations in some direction further than his fellows, and founded a special school whose aberrations there was no central authority to control. Many of{356} the peculiarly repulsive extravagances attributed to them, however, may safely be ascribed to keen-witted schoolmen engaged in trying individual heretics, and forcing them to admit consequences logically but unexpectedly deduced from their admitted premises. There was no little intellectual activity in the sect, and their tracts and books of devotion, written in the vernacular, were widely distributed, and largely relied upon as means of missionary effort. These, of course, have wholly disappeared, and we are left to gather their doctrines from the condemnations passed upon them.

The foundation of their creed was pantheism. God is everything that is. There is as much of the divinity in a louse as in a man or in any other creature. All emanates from him and returns to him. As the soul thus reverts to God after death, there is neither purgatory nor hell, and all external cult is useless. Thus at one blow was destroyed the efficacy of all sacerdotal observances and of the sacraments. Of the latter, indeed, no terms were severe enough to express their contempt, and they were sometimes in the habit of saying that the Eucharist tasted to them like dung. Man being thus God by nature, has in him all that is divine, and each one may say that he himself created the universe. One of the accusations brought against Master Eckart was that he had declared that his little finger created the world. Nay, more, man can so unite himself with God that he can do whatever God does; he thus needs no God; he is impeccable, and whatever he does is without sin. In this state of perfection he grieves at nothing, he rejoices at nothing, he is free from all virtue and all virtuous actions. No one is bound to labor for his bread; as all things are in common, each one may take what his necessities or desires may prompt.[399]

The practical deductions from these doctrines were not only destructive to the Church, but dangerous to the moral and social order. The lofty mysticism of the teachers might preserve them{357} from the evil results which flowed from the presumption of impeccability. In their austere stoicism they condemned all sexual indulgence save that of which the sole object was the procurement of offspring. They taught that a woman in marrying should deeply deplore the loss of her virginity, and that no one was perfect in whom promiscuous nakedness could awaken either shame or passion. That tests of this kind were not infrequent, the history of ill-regulated enthusiasm, from the time of the early Christians, will not permit us to doubt, and the Beghards succeeded so well in subduing the senses that a hostile controversialist can only suggest Satanic influence, well known to demonologists for its refrigerating power, as an explanation of their wonderful self-control under such temptation. Yet this rare exaltation of austerity was not possible to all natures. It was easy for him who had not risen superior to the allurements of the senses to imagine himself perfected, impeccable, and entitled to gratify his passions. St. Paul, in arguing against the bondage of the Old Law, had furnished texts which, when cited apart from their contexts, could be and were alleged in justification: "For the law of the spirit of life in Christ Jesus hath made me free from the law of sin and death" (Rom. VIII. 2)—"The law is not made for a righteous man" (1 Tim.I. 9)—"But if ye be led of the Spirit ye are not under the law" (Galat. V. 18)—and the Brethren of the Free Spirit claimed freedom from all the trammels of the law. Such a doctrine was attractive to those who desired excuse and opportunity for license, and the evidence is too abundant and confirmatory for us to doubt that, at least in some cases, the sectaries abandoned themselves to the grossest sensuality. It is noteworthy that, in order to describe the divine internal light which they enjoyed, they invented for themselves the term Illuminism, which for more than three centuries continued to be of most serious import.[400]

As a branch of the sect may be reckoned the Luciferans, who have been repeatedly alluded to above. Pantheism, of course, included{358} Satan as an emanation from God, who in due time would be restored to union with the Godhead, and it was not difficult to assume that his fallen state was an injustice. In 1312 Luciferans were discovered at Krems, in the diocese of Passau, whose bishop, Bernhard, together with Conrad, Archbishop of Salzburg, and Frederic, Duke of Austria, undertook their extirpation with the aid of the Dominican Inquisition, which seems to have maintained some foothold in those regions. The persecution lasted until 1315, but the sect was not exterminated, and reappeared repeatedly in after-years. It is reported to have been thoroughly organized, with twelve "apostles" who travelled annually throughout Germany, making converts and confirming the believers in the faith. All the ceremonies of external worship were rejected, but they did not enjoy the impeccability of Illuminism, for two of their ministers were held to enter paradise every year, where they received from Enoch and Elias the power of absolving their followers, and this power they communicated to others in each community. Those who were detected proved obdurate; they were deaf to all persuasion, and met their death in the flames with the utmost cheerfulness. One of the apostles, who was burned at Vienna, stated, under torture, that there were eight thousand of them scattered throughout Bohemia, Austria, and Thuringia, besides numbers elsewhere. Bohemia was especially infected with these errors, and Trithemius, in the opening years of the sixteenth century, states that there were still thousands of them in that kingdom. This is doubtless an exaggeration, if not a complete mistake, but they were again discovered in Austria in 1338 and 1395, and many of them were burned.[401]

The tendency to mysticism which found its complete expression in the Brethren of the Free Spirit influenced greatly the development of German religious thought in channels which, although assumedly orthodox, trenched narrowly upon heresy. If, as Altmeyer argues, a period of tribulation leads to the predominance of sentiment over intellect, to the yearning for direct intercourse between the soul and the Divine Essence, which is the supreme aim of the mystic, the Germany of the fourteenth century had troubles{359} enough to justify the development of mysticism. Yet it is rather a question of the mental characteristics of a race than of external circumstances. Bonaventura was the father of the mystics, yet he founded no sect at home; France, in the hundred years" war with England, had ample experience of trial, and yet mysticism never flourished on her soil. In Germany, however, the mystic tendency of religious sentiment during the fourteenth century is the most marked spiritual phenomenon of the period. Few names in the first quarter of the century were more respected than that of Master Eckart, who stood high in the ranks of the great Dominican Order. I have already (Vol. I., p. 360) related how he fell under suspicion of participating in the errors of the Beghards, how his brethren vainly strove to save him, and how the Archbishop of Cologne won a decided victory over the feeble and unorganized Dominican Inquisition by vindicating the subjection of a Dominican to his episcopal Inquisition. If the twenty-eight articles finally condemned by John XXII. as heretical be correctly extracted from Eckart's teachings, there can be no doubt that he was deeply infected with the pantheistic speculations of the Brethren of the Free Spirit, that he admitted the common divinity of man and God, and shared in the dangerous deductions which proved that sin and virtue were the same in the eyes of God. To a hierarchy founded on sacerdotalism, moreover, nothing could be more revolutionary than the rejection of external cult, which was the necessary conclusion from the doctrine that there is no virtue in external acts, but that only the internal operations of the soul are of moment; that no man should regret the commission of sin, or ask anything of God.[402]

The importance of Eckart's views lies not so much in his own immediate influence as in that of his disciples. He was the founder of the school of German mystics, through whom the speculations{360} of Amauri of Bene, in various dilutions, made a deep impression on the religious development of the fourteenth and fifteenth centuries. All the leaders in the remarkable association known as the "Friends of God" drew, directly or indirectly, their inspiration from Master Eckart, and all, to a greater or less extent, reveal their affinity to the Brethren of the Free Spirit, although they succeeded in keeping technically within the limits of orthodoxy.

John of Rysbroek, humane and gentle as he was, regarded the Brethren of the Free Spirit with such horror that he deemed them worthy of the stake. Yet, though he avoided their pantheism, he taught, like them, the supreme end of existence in the absorption of the individual into the infinite substance of God; moreover, the Perfect, inflamed by divine love, are dead to themselves and to the world, and are thus incapable of sin. It is no wonder that Gerson regarded as dangerous these doctrines, so nearly akin to those of the Beghards, and though Rysbroek might hesitate to draw from them the conclusions inevitable to hardier thinkers, they were sufficient to render unsuccessful the attempt made, in 1624, to canonize him, in spite of the incontestable miracles wrought at his tomb. His most distinguished disciple was Gerard Groot, who partially outgrew the metaphysical subtleties of his teacher and turned his energies to the more practical directions out of which sprang the Brethren of the Common Life. Groot was equally severe upon the corruption of the clergy and the errors of the heretics. When the introduction of the Inquisition into Germany drove the Brethren of the Free Spirit to find new places of refuge, some of them came to Holland, where the prevalence of pantheistic mysticism gave opportunity of spreading their doctrines. Groot's own views sufficiently resembled theirs to render their bolder speculations doubly offensive to him, and he sought to repress them with especial zeal. The convent of Augustinian Hermits at Dordrecht had the reputation of being tainted with the heresy, and Groot was eager to detect and punish it. Bartholomew, one of the Augustinians, was particularly suspected, and Groot proposed to follow him secretly with a notary and take down his words. In this, or some other way, evidence was obtained; there was no Inquisition in Holland, and Groot procured his citation before Florent, Bishop of Utrecht, about the year 1380. The case was beard before the episcopal vicar; Bartholomew denied{361} the expressions attributed to him and was let off with an injunction to publicly repeat the denial in Kampen and Zwolle, where he was said to have uttered his heresies. This unexpected lenity excited the indignation of Groot, who had sufficient influence to induce Bishop Florent to take up the case again and try it personally. Bartholomew endeavored to escape his persecutor by appearing a day in advance of the one set for his trial, but word was sent to Groot, who threw himself into a wagon, and by travelling all night reached Utrecht in time. On this occasion he was successful; Bartholomew was condemned as a heretic, abjured, and was sentenced to wear crosses in the form of scissors. The Augustinians did not lack friends, and they retaliated on those who had busied themselves in the matter. The magistrates of Kampen prosecuted some women who had served as witnesses and fined them, and they also banished for ten years Werner Keynkamp, a friend of Groot, who subsequently was thrice prior of houses of Brethren of the Common Life. Groot himself did not escape, for soon afterwards Bishop Florent, for the purpose of silencing him, issued an order withdrawing all commissions to preach. Groot then endeavored to procure from Urban VI. papal commissions as preacher and inquisitor, and sent to Rome ten florins to pay for the bulls. Fortunately for his fame, he died, in 1384, before the return of his messenger, and Holland was spared the effects of his inconsiderate zeal, inflamed by strife and armed with the irresponsible power of the Inquisition. In his gentler capacity he left his mantle to Florent Radewyns, under whom were developed the communities of the Common Life. These spread rapidly throughout the Netherlands and Germany, and though occasionally the subject of inquisitorial persecution, they were covered by the decision of Martin V., when Matthew Grabon, at the Council of Constance, endeavored to procure the condemnation of the Beguines, of which more anon. After this they flourished without opposition, supporting themselves by disseminating culture, as educators and copiers of manuscripts. After the Reformation the communities rapidly died out, although the house of Emmerich, near Düsseldorf, remained to be closed by

Napoleon, in 1811, and the four brethren then ejected from it continued to observe the rules, till the last one, Gerard Mulder, died at Zevenaar, March 15, 1854. One branch of the brethren, however, {362} adopted the Rule of the canons-regular of St. Augustin. Their convent of Windesheim became the model which was universally followed, and the order had the honor of training two such men as Thomas-à-Kempis and Erasmus. The Imitation of Christ is the final exquisite flower of the moderated mysticism of John of Rysbroek. Brought down to practical life, this mysticism contributed largely to the spiritual movement which culminated in the Reformation, for it taught the superfluity of external works and the dependence of the individual on himself alone for salvation. In this the Brethren of the Common Life were active. To them dogma became less important than the interior discipline which should fit men to be really children of God. Preaching among the people and teaching in the schools, such brethren as Henry Harphius, John Brugman, Denis Van Leeuwen, Jon Van Goch, and John Wessel of Groningen, were unwittingly undermining the power of the hierarchy, although they virtually escaped all imputation of heresy and danger of persecution.[403]

Less lasting, though more noticeable at the time, was the association of Friends of God, which formed itself in the upper Rhinelands. The most prominent disciple of Master Eckart was John Tauler, who retained enough of his master's doctrines to render him amenable to the charge of heresy had there been in those days a German Inquisition in working order. That he escaped prosecution is the most conclusive evidence that the machinery of persecution was thoroughly out of gear. In the heights of his illuminated quietism all the personality of the devotee was lost in the abyss of Divinity. No human tongue could describe the resignation to God in which the whole being is merged so that it lost all sense of power of its own. No priestly ministrant or mediator was required. The individual could bring his soul into relations with the Godhead so intimate that it was virtually lost in the Divine Essence, and he could become so thoroughly under the influence of the Holy Ghost that he was, so to speak, inspired, and {363} his acts were the acts of the Third Person of the Trinity. All this was possible for the layman without sacerdotal observance. Man was answerable for himself to himself alone, and could make himself at one with God without the intervention of the priest.[404]

Great as was Tauler's renown as the foremost preacher of his day, he bowed as a little child before the mysterious layman known as the Friend of God in the Oberland. In the full strength of mature manhood, when at least fifty years of age and when all Strassburg was hanging on his words, a stranger sought his presence and probed to the bottom his secret weaknesses. He was a Pharisee, proud of his learning and his skill in scholastic theology; before he could be fit for the guidance of souls he must cast off all reliance on his own strength and become as an infant relying on God alone. Overcome by the mystic power of his visitor, the doctor of theology subdued his pride, and in obedience to the command of the stranger, who never revealed his name, Tauler for two years abstained from preaching and from hearing confessions. From this struggle with himself he emerged a new man, and formed one of the remarkable band of Friends of God whom the nameless stranger was engaged in selecting and uniting.[405]

This association was not numerous, for only rare souls could rise to the altitude in which they would surely wish only what God wishes and dislike what God dislikes; but its adepts were scattered from the Netherlands to Genoa, and from the Rhinelands to Hungary. Terrible were the struggles and spiritual conflicts, {364} the alternations of hope and despair, of ravishing ecstasies and hideous temptations, with which God tried the neophyte who sought to ascend into the serene atmosphere of mystic illuminism—struggles and conflicts which form a strangely resembling prototype of those which for long years tested the steadfastness of John Bunyan. When at length the initiation was safely endured, God drew them to him, he illuminated their souls so that they became one with him; they were gods by grace, even as he is God by nature. Then they were in a condition of absolute sinlessness, and could enjoy the assurance that it would continue during life, so that at death they would ascend at once to heaven with no preliminary purgatory.[406]

In many of their tenets and practices there is a strange reverberation of Hinduism, all the stranger that there can be no possible connection between them, unless perchance there may be some elements derived from mystic Arabic Aristotelianism, which so strongly influenced scholastic thought.[407] As the old Brahmanic *tapas*, or austere meditation, enabled man to acquire a share of the divine nature, so the interior exercises of the Friends of God assimilated man to the Divinity, and the miraculous powers which they acquired find their prototypes in the Rishis and Rahats. The self-inflicted barbarities of the Yoga system were emulated in the efforts necessary to subdue the rebellious flesh; Rulman Merswin, for instance, used to scourge himself with wires and then rub salt into the wounds. The religious ecstasies of the Friends of God were the counterpart of the Samadhi or beatific insensibility of the Hindu; and the supreme good which they set before themselves was the same as that of the Sankhya school—the renunciation of the will and the freedom from all passions and desires, even that of salvation. Yet these resemblances were modified by the Christian sense of the omnipotence and omnipresence of God, and by the more practical character of the Western mind, which did not send its votaries into the jungle and forest, but ordered them, if laymen, to continue their worldly life; if rich, they were not to despoil themselves, but to employ their riches in good works, and to discharge their duties to man as well as to God. Rulman Merswin {365} was a banker, and continued in active business while founding the community of the Grün Wöhrd and writing the treatises which were the support and the comfort of the faithful. Yet the chief of them all and his immediate disciples founded a hermitage in the wilderness, where they devoted themselves to propitiating the wrath of God. The unutterable wickedness of man called for divine vengeance.

Earthquakes, pestilence, famine, had been disregarded warnings, and only the intercession of the Friends of God had obtained repeated reprieves. The Great Schism, in 1378, was a new and still greater calamity, and in 1379 an angel messenger informed them that the final punishment was postponed for a year, after which they must not ask for further delay. Still, in 1380, thirteen of them were mysteriously called to assemble in a "divine diet," to which an angel brought a letter informing them that, at the prayer of the Virgin, God had granted a respite of three years provided they would constitute themselves "prisoners of God," living the life of recluses in absolute silence, broken only two days in the week from noon to eve, and then only to ask for necessaries or to give spiritual counsel. To this they assented, and not long afterwards they disappear from view.[408]

The Friends of God are noteworthy not only as a significant development of the spiritual tendencies of the age, but they have a peculiar interest for us from their relations with the Church on the one hand and with the Brethren of the Free Spirit on the other. They were an outgrowth of the latter, though they avoided the deplorable moral extravagances of the parent sect. The "Ninth Rock," which was the supreme height of ascetic illuminism of the Beghards, reappears in the same sense in the most notable of Rulman Merswin's works, attributed until recently to Henry Suso. It is no wonder that Nider confounded the Friends of God with the Beghards, though Merswin's "Baner Buechelin" was written for the purpose of denouncing the errors of the latter. In much, as we have seen, they differed from the current doctrines of the Church, carrying their aberrations further than those which in the seventeenth century were so severely repressed in Molinos and the Illuminati. To these they added special errors of their own. Many Jews and Moslems, they said, were saved, for God abandons{366} none who seek him, and though they cannot enjoy Christian baptism, God himself baptizes them spiritually in the sufferings of the death-agony. In the same spirit they refused to denounce the heretic to human justice for fear of anticipating divine justice; they could tolerate him in the temporal world as long as God saw fit to do so. Yet they had one saving principle which preserved them from the temporal and spiritual consequences of their errors, giving us a valuable insight into the relations between the Church and heresy. While denouncing in the strongest language the corruptions and worldliness of the establishment, they professed the most implicit obedience to Rome, and much could be overlooked or pardoned so long as the supremacy of the Holy See was not called in question. When, in June, 1377, the Friend of God in the Oberland was inspired to visit, with a comrade, Gregory XI., and warn him of the dangers which threatened Christendom, they spoke to him with the utmost freedom, and though he at first was angered, he finally recognized in them the envoys of the Holy Ghost and honored them greatly, urging them to resume their abandoned design of founding a great institution of their order. Gregory was relentless in the extermination of Waldenses, Beghards, and the remnants of the Cathari, but he saw nothing to object to in the mysticism and illuminism of his visitors. He did not even take offence when they threatened him with death within the twelvemonth if he did not reform the Church. In effect he died March 28, 1378; but, if we may believe Gerson, his dying regrets were not that he had neglected these warnings, but that by too credulously listening to the visions of male and female prophets he had paved the way for the Great Schism, which he foresaw would break out when he was removed from the scene.[409]

After this hasty review of the more orthodox developments of mysticism we may return to the history of the Brethren of the Free Spirit, who maintained the pantheistic doctrine in all its crudity, and did not shrink from its legitimate deductions. Towards{367} the close of the thirteenth century the transcendent merits of beggary, so long acknowledged, began to be questioned. In 1274 the Council of Lyons endeavored to suppress the unauthorized mendicant associations. In 1286 Honorius IV. condemned the Segarellists, and some ten years later the persecution, by Boniface VIII., of the Celestines and stricter Franciscans showed that poverty was no longer to be regarded as the supreme virtue. About the same time he issued a bull ordering the active persecution of some heretics, whose teaching that perfection required men and women to go naked and not to labor with the hands would seem to identify them with the Brethren of the Free Spirit. The same feeling manifested itself contemporaneously in Germany. The first instance of actual persecution recorded is a curt notice that, in 1290, the Franciscan lector at Colmar caused to be arrested two Beghards and two Beguines, and several others at Basle whom he considered to be heretics. Two years later the Provincial Council of Mainz, held at Aschaffenburg, emphatically repeated the condemnation of the Beghards and Beguines, expressed by the previous council of 1259, and this was again repeated by another council of Mainz in 1310, while other canons regulating the recognized communities of Beguines show that the distinction was clearly drawn between those who led a settled life under supervision and the wandering beggars who preached in caverns and disseminated doctrines little understood, but regarded with suspicion.[410]

It was Henry von Virnenburg, Archbishop of Cologne, however, who commenced the war against them which was to last so long. Elected in 1306, he immediately assembled a provincial council, of which the first two canons are devoted to them with an amplitude proving how important they were becoming. They wore a long tabard and tunics with cowls distinguishing them from the people at large; they had the hardihood to engage in public disputation with the Franciscans and Dominicans, and the obstinacy to refuse to be overcome in argument, and, what was worse, their persistent beggary was so successful that it sensibly diminished the alms which were the support of the authorized{368} Mendicants. All this shows the absence of any papal inquisition and an enjoyment of practical toleration unknown outside of the boundaries of Germany, but it may be assumed that the Beghards did not publicly reveal their more dangerous and repulsive doctrines, for the enumeration of their errors by the council presents them in a very moderate form. Still, the archbishop pronounced them excommunicated heretics, to be suppressed by the secular arm unless they recanted within fifteen days. A month was given them to abandon their garments and mode of life, after which they were to earn their bread by honest labor. This was well-intentioned legislation, but it seems to have remained wholly inoperative. The Beghards continued to assail the Mendicants with such ardor and success that the Franciscans, who were crippled by the death of their lector in 1305, applied for succor to their general, Gonsalvo. The necessity must have been pressing, for in 1308 he sent to their assistance the greatest schoolman of the Order, Duns Scotus. He was received with the enthusiasm which his eminence merited, but, unfortunately, he died in November of the same year, and the Beghards were able to continue their proselytism without efficient opposition.[411]

About this time their missionary labors seem to have become particularly active and to have attracted wide attention. We have seen how, in 1310, the Beguine, Marguerite Porete of Hainault, was burned in Paris, and bore her martyrdom with unshrinking firmness. In the same year occurred the Council of Mainz already referred to, and also a council of Trèves, in which their unauthorized exposition of Scripture was denounced, and all parish priests were required to summon them to abandon their evil ways within a fortnight, under pain of excommunication. In 1309 we hear of certain wandering hypocrites called Lollards, who, throughout Hainault and Brabant, had considerable success in obtaining converts among noble ladies.[412]

This missionary fervor seems to have attracted attention to the sect, leading to special condemnation under the authority of the{369} General Council of Vienne, which was assembled in November, 1311. The heresy had evidently been studied with some care, for the first tolerably complete account which we have of its doctrines is embodied in the canon proscribing it. Bishops and inquisitors were ordered to perform their office diligently in tracking all who entertained it, and seeing that they were duly punished unless they would freely abjure. Unfortunately, Clement's zeal was not satisfied with this. The pious women who lived in communities under the name of Beguines were not easily distinguishable from the heretical wanderers. In another canon, therefore, the Beguinages are described as infected with those who dispute about the Trinity and the Divine Essence and disseminate opinions contrary to the faith. These establishments are therefore abolished. At the same time there was evidently a feeling that this was inflicting a wrong, and the canon ends with the contradictory declaration that faithful women, either vowing chastity or not, may live together in houses and devote themselves to penitence and the service of God. There was a lamentable lack of clearness about this which left it for the local prelates to interpret their duty according to their wishes.[413]

The Clementines, or book of canon law containing these provisions, was not issued during Clement's life, and it was not until November, 1317, that his successor, John XXII., gave them legal force by their authoritative publication. Apparently the bishops waited for this, for during the interim we hear nothing of persecution, until August, 1317, just before the issue of the Clementines, when John of Zurich, Bishop of Strasbourg, suddenly took the matter up. He did not act under the canons of Vienne, but under those of 1310 adopted by the Council of Mainz, of which province he was a suffragan; but an allusion to the penalties decreed by the Holy See shows that the action at Vienne was known. The Beghards apparently had sought no concealment, for he threatened with excommunication all who should not within three days lay aside the distinguishing garments of the sect, and their fearless publicity is further shown by the bishop's confiscating the houses in which their assemblies were held, and forbidding any one to read or listen to or possess their hymns and writings, which {370}were to be delivered up for burning within fifteen days. The fact that among them were many clerks in holy orders, monks, married folks, and others, shows that their opinions were widely held among those who were not mere wandering beggars—the latter probably being merely the missionaries who made converts and administered to the spiritual needs of the faithful. John of Zurich was not content with merely threatening. He made a visitation of his diocese, in which he found many of the sectaries. He organized an Inquisition of learned theologians, by whom they were tried; those who recanted were sentenced to wear crosses—the first authentic record in Germany of the use of this penance, so long since established elsewhere—and those who were obstinate he handed over to the secular arm to be burned. These active proceedings may be regarded as the first regular exercise of the episcopal Inquisition on German soil. Multitudes of Beghards fled from the diocese, and in June, 1318, the bishop had the satisfaction of reporting his success to his fellow-suffragans and urging them to follow his example. Yet this persecution, if sharp, was transitory, for in 1319 we find him again issuing letters to his clergy, saying that the Clementines had been enforced elsewhere, but not in the diocese of Strasbourg. All incumbents are ordered, under pain of suspension, to require the Beguines to lay aside their vestments within fifteen days and to conform to the usages of the Church. If any refuse, the inquisitors will be instructed to inquire into their faith.[414]{371}

Meanwhile the publication of the Clementines had produced results not corresponding exactly to the intentions of Clement. The canon directed against the heretics received little attention, and five years elapse before we hear of any serious persecutions under it. The heretics were poor; there were no spoils to tempt episcopal officials to the thankless labor of tracking them and trying them, and few of the bishops had the zeal of John of Zurich to divert them from their temporal cares and pleasures. The Beguinages, however, were an easy prey; there was property to be confiscated in reward of intelligent activity. Besides, many of the establishments were under the supervision of the Mendicant Orders, and were virtually or absolutely Tertiary houses, the destruction of which gratified the inextinguishable jealousy between the secular clergy and the Orders; the struggle between John XXII. and the Franciscans, moreover, was commencing, and the Tertiaries of the latter, who were popularly known as Beguines in France, were fair game. The bishops for the most part, therefore, neglected the saving clause of the canon respecting the Beguinages, and construed literally and pitilessly the orders for their abolition. So eager were they to gratify their vindictiveness against the Mendicants that, when these interfered to save their Tertiaries, they were excommunicated as fautors and defenders of heresy. Thus arose a persecution which, though bloodless, was most deplorable. All through France and Germany and Italy the poor creatures were turned adrift upon the world, without means of support. Those who could, found husbands; many were driven to a life of prostitution, others, doubtless, perished of want and exposure. Even the quasi-conventual dress to which they were accustomed was proscribed, and they were forced to wear gay colors under pain of excommunication. In the history of the Church there have been many more cruel persecutions, but few which in suddenness and extent have caused greater misery, and none, we are safe to say, so wanton, causeless, and lacking even the shadow of justification. The impression made on the popular{372} mind is seen in the current report that on his death-bed Clement bitterly repented of three things—that he had poisoned the Emperor Henry VII. and that he had destroyed the Orders of the Templars and of the Beguines.[415]

The Church had declared, in the great Council of Lateran, that no congregations should be allowed to exist save under some approved rule. The Beguines had gradually, almost unconsciously, grown up in practical contravention of this canon. The solution of their present difficulties lay in attaching themselves to some recognized Order, and John XXII., in 1319, recognizing the mischief wrought by the heedless legislation of Vienne, promised exemption from further persecution of those who would become Mendicant Tertiaries. Large numbers of them sought this refuge, though their adhesion was more nominal than real. They preserved their self-government, their habits of labor, and their ownership of individual property. In a bull of December 31, 1320, and others of later date, John drew the distinction between those who lived piously and obediently in their houses, and those who wandered around disputing on matters of faith. The former, he is told, amount to two hundred thousand in Germany alone, and he bitterly reproached the bishops who were disturbing them on account of the comparatively small number whose misconduct had drawn forth the misinterpreted condemnation of Clement. They are in future to be left in peace. This, at least, put an end, in 1321, to the persecution of those of Strassburg.[416]

The innocent Beguines thus obtained a breathing-space, and the gaps in their ranks were soon filled up. The obnoxious members, however, felt the effects of the Clementine canon as severely as the habitual sloth and indifference of the German prelates in such matters would permit. Archbishop Henry, of Cologne, was{373} one of the few who manifested an active interest in the matter, and his exertions were rewarded with considerable success. The Lollards and Beghards no longer ventured to show themselves publicly, and in the absence of organized machinery it was not easy to detect them, but in 1322 the archbishop had the good fortune to capture the most formidable heresiarch of the region. Walter, known as the Lollard, was a Hollander, and was the most active and successful of the Beghard missionaries. He was not an educated man, and was ignorant of Latin, but he had a keen intelligence and ready eloquence, indefatigable enthusiasm and persuasiveness. His proselyting labors were facilitated by his numerous writings in the vernacular, which were eagerly circulated from hand to hand. He had been busy in Mainz, where he had numerous disciples, and came from there to Cologne, where he chanced to fall into the archbishop's hands. He made no secret of his belief, refused to abjure, and welcomed death in the service of his faith. The severest tortures were vainly employed to force him to reveal the names of his fellow-believers; his constancy was unalterable, and he perished in the flames with serene cheerfulness.[417]

The episcopal Inquisition was not as efficient as the zeal of the archbishop might wish, but, such as it was, it pursued its labors with indifferent success. In 1323 we hear of a priest detected in heresy, who was duly degraded and burned. In 1325 greater results followed the accidental discovery of an assembly of Beghards. The story told is the legend common to other places, of a husband, whose suspicions were aroused, tracking his wife to the nocturnal conventicle and witnessing the sensual orgies which were popularly believed to be customary in such places. The episcopal Inquisition was rewarded with a large number of culprits, whose trial was speedy and sure. Those who would not abjure, about fifty in number, were put to death—some at the stake, and some drowned in the Rhine, a novel punishment for heresy, which shows how uncertain as yet were the dealings with heretics in Germany. It is quite probable that some of these poor creatures may have sought to shield their errors under the reputation of the great Dominican preacher, Master Eckart, and thus{374} brought upon him the prosecution which worried him to death. It is possible, also, that pursuit of this higher game may have diverted the archbishop from the chase of the humbler quarry, for we hear of no further victims in the next few years, though we are told that the heresy was by no means suppressed.[418]

Archbishop Henry died in 1331 without further success, so far as the records show, and his successor Waleran, Count of Juliers, took up the cause in more systematic fashion. He endeavored to organize a permanent episcopal Inquisition by appointing a commissioner whose duty it was to inquire after heretics, and who had power to reconcile and absolve those who should recant—in fact, an inquisitor under another name. The success of this attempt did not correspond to its deserts. In March, 1335, Waleran was obliged to announce that the evil had greatly increased in both the city and diocese, and he called upon all his prelates and clergy to assist his Inquisition by rigidly enforcing the statutes of Archbishop Henry. This was as ineffective as the

125

previous measures. The heretics were so bold that they openly wore the garments of the sect and followed its practices; nay, more, the inquisitor was either so negligent or so corrupt that he gave absolutions without requiring conformity. In October of the same year, therefore, the archbishop issued another pastoral epistle, in which he pronounced all such absolutions void, and deplored the constant spread of the heresy.[419]

The zeal of the Archbishops of Cologne was not without imitators. Throughout Westphalia, Bishops Ludwig of Munster, Gottfrid of Osnabruck, Gottfrid of Minden, and Bernhard of Paderborn had been active in eradicating the heresy within their dioceses. In 1335 Bishop Berthold of Strassburg made a spasmodic effort to enforce the Clementines, and in the same year there were some victims burned in Metz. The Magdeburg Archbishop Otto was of more tolerant temper. In 1336 a number of "Brethren of the Lofty Spirit" were detected in his city, who did not hesitate, under examination, to admit their belief, which to{375} pious ears sounded like the most horrible blasphemy; yet he liberated them after a few days" confinement on their simply recanting their errors verbally. In this same year, however, we have the first instance of a papal inquisitor at work in north Germany. Friar Jordan, an Augustinian eremite, held a commission as inquisitor in both sections of Saxony. He was not well versed in the inquisitorial process, for when at Angermünde in the Uckermark he came upon a nest of Luciferans, he humanely offered them the opportunity of canonical purgation. Fourteen of them failed to procure the requisite number of conjurators, and were duly burned. From Angermünde Friar Jordan seems to have hastened to Erfurt, where he was present at the trial of a Beghard named Constantine, though the proceedings were carried on by the vicar of the Archbishop of Mainz. There was no desire to punish the heretic, who bore a good reputation and was useful as a writer of manuscripts. He asserted himself to be the Son of God, and that he would arise three days after death, so there was ample ground for the endeavor humanely made by his judges to prove him insane. A long respite was given him for this purpose, but he persistently declared his sanity, refused all attempts at conversion, and perished in the flames.[420]

When the effort was made to find heretics there seems to have been plenty of them to reward the search. In this same year, 1336, we hear of the discovery in Austria of a numerous sect who, from the description, were probably Luciferans. The rites of their nocturnal subterranean assemblies bear a considerable resemblance to those revealed by the penitents of Conrad of Marburg, showing how the tradition was handed down to the outbreak of witchcraft. We are told that they had contaminated innumerable souls, but they were exterminated by the free use of the stake and other cruel torments. The next year, in Brandenburg, many simple folk were seduced into demonolatry by three evil spirits who personated the Trinity; and though these were driven off by a Franciscan with the host, the dupes persisted in their error, and preferred burning to recantation. Even divested of its supernatural{376} embroidery, the heresy, probably Luciferan, must have been one which excited enthusiasm in its followers, for at the place of execution they declared that the flames lighted to consume them were golden chariots to carry them to heaven. Another instance of Luciferanism occurred at Salzburg, in 1340, when a priest named Rudolph, in the cathedral, cast to the ground the cup containing the blood of Christ, a sacrilege which he had previously committed at Halle. Under examination, he denied transubstantiation, and asserted the final salvation of Satan and his angels. He was obstinate to the last, and consequently was burned.[421]

The Brethren of the Free Spirit had by no means been suppressed. In 1339 three aged heresiarchs of the sect were captured at Constance and tried by the bishop. Disgusting practices of sensuality were proved against them, and they described their abhorrence of the rites of the Church in the most revolting terms. Their constancy held good until they were brought to the place of execution, when it failed them; they recanted, and were sentenced to imprisonment for life in a dungeon on bread and water. In 1342, at Würzburg, two more were forced to recantation. Persecution, however, was spasmodic, and in many places toleration practically existed. Thus, in Suabia, in 1347, we are told that the heresy of the Beghards spread without let or hindrance. It was impossible to eradicate it, even had there been efforts made to suppress it, which there were not, and it would eventually have overturned the Church had there not finally arisen theologians able and willing to combat it.[422]

About this period flourished Conrad of Montpellier, a canon of Ratisbon, one of the most learned men of the day, who wrote a tract against the sect. In spite of the condemnation uttered by the Council of Vienne, he says it continues to increase and multiply, as there are no prelates found to oppose it. The heretics are mostly ignorant peasants and mechanics, who wander around wearing the distinctive garments of the sect, which are also frequently used as a disguise by Waldenses. They seek hospitality of{377} the Beguines, whom they corrupt by persuading them that man, through piety, can become the equal of Christ. At Ratisbon, Conrad met one of these, who was not suffered to enjoy security, for the bishop arrested him, and, on his obstinately maintaining his errors, cast him in a dungeon, where he perished. Another, named John of Mechlin, preached his heresy publicly through upper Germany, where his eloquence gained him crowds of followers, including nobles and ecclesiastics, though Conrad declares that, on arguing with him, he proved to be utterly ignorant. There would appear to have been equal toleration in the Netherlands, for about this period, at Brussels, a woman named Blomaert, who wrote several treatises on the Spirit of Liberty and on Love, was reverenced as something more than human, and when she went to take the Eucharist she was said by her disciples to be attended by two seraphim. She vanquished the most learned theologians, until John of Rysbroek succeeded in confuting her.[423]

Since the disputed election of Louis of Bavaria, in 1314, the relations between the empire and the papacy had been strained. The victory of Mühldorf, in 1322, which assured to Louis the sovereignty, had been followed, in 1323, by an open rupture with John XXII., after which the strife had been internecine. Each declared his enemy a heretic who had forfeited all rights, and the interdicts which John showered over Germany had been met by Louis with cruel persecution of all ecclesiastics obeying them, wherever he could enforce his power.[424] Such a state of affairs had not{378} been favorable for the persecution of heresy; it may, partially at least, explain the immunity enjoyed in so many places by heretics, and the impossibility of introducing the Inquisition in any form of general organization. Though the papacy assumed that the imperial throne was vacant, and asserted that, during such vacancy, the government of the empire devolved upon the pope, these pretensions could not practically be made good. With the death of Louis, in 1347, and the recognition of his rival, Charles IV.—the "priest's emperor"—Rome might fairly hope that all obstacles would be removed; that the opposition of the episcopate to the Inquisition would be broken down, and that the field would be open for a persistent and systematic persecution, which would soon relieve Germany of the reproach of toleration. When Clement VI., in 1348, could paternally reprove the young emperor for lack of dignity in the fashion of his garments, which were too short and too tight for his imperial station, the youth could surely be relied upon to obey whatever instructions might be sent him with regard to the suppression of heresy. The same year saw the appointment of John Schandeland, doctor of the Dominican house at Strassburg, as papal inquisitor for all Germany.[425]

Scarcely, however, had the pope and emperor felt their positions assured, and preparations had been thus made to take advantage of the situation, when a catastrophe supervened which defied all human calculation. The weary fourteenth century was nearing the end of its first half when Europe was scourged with a calamity which might well seem to fulfil all that apocalyptic prophets{379} had threatened of the vengeance of God on the sins of man. In 1347 the plague known as the Black Death invaded Europe from the East, making leisurely progress during 1348 and 1349 through France, Spain, Hungary, Germany, and England. No corner of Europe was spared, and on the high seas it is said that vessels with rich cargoes were found floating, of which the crews had perished to the last man. Doubtless there are exaggerations in the contemporary reports which assert that two thirds or three quarters or five sixths of the inhabitants of Europe fell victims to the pest; but Boccaccio, as an eye-witness, tells us that the mortality within the walls of Florence from March to July, 1348, amounted to one hundred thousand souls; that in the fields the harvests lay ungathered; that in the city palaces were tenantless and unguarded; that parents forsook children and children parents. In Avignon the mortality was estimated at one hundred thousand; Clement VI. shut himself up in his apartments in the sacred palace, where he built large fires to ward off the pestilence, and would allow none to approach him. In Paris fifty thousand were said to have perished; in St. Denis sixteen thousand; in Strassburg sixteen thousand. That these figures, though vague, are not improbable, is shown by the case of Béziers, where, in 1348, Mascaro, who was chosen *escudier* to fill a vacancy, records in his diary that all the consuls were carried off, all their *escudiers* or assistants, and all the *clavars* or tax-collectors, and that out of every thousand inhabitants only a hundred escaped. As though Nature did not cause sufficient misery, man contributed his share by an uprising against the Jews. They were accused of causing the plague by poisoning the waters and the pastures, and the blind wrath of the population did not stop to consider that they drank from the same wells as the Christians, and suffered with them in the pestilence. From the Atlantic to Hungary they were tortured and slain with sword and fire. At Erfurt three thousand are said to have perished, and in Bavaria the number was computed at twelve thousand.[426]{380}

It was not only by the massacre of the Jews that the people sought to placate the wrath of God. The gregarious enthusiasm of which we have seen so many instances was by no means extinct. In 1320 France had seen another assemblage of the Pastoureaux, when the dumb population arose, armed only with banners, for the conquest of the Holy Land, and an innumerable multitude wandered over the land, peaceably at first, but subsequently showing their devotion by attacking the Jews, and finally manifesting their antagonism to the hierarchy by plundering the ecclesiastics and the churches, until they were dispersed with the sword and put out of the way with the halter. In 1334 the great Dominican preacher, Venturino da Bergamo, roused the population of Lombardy to so keen a sense of the necessity of propitiating God that he organized a pilgrimage to Rome for the sake of obtaining pardons, variously estimated as consisting of from ten thousand to three millions of penitents. Clothed in white, with black cloaks{381} bearing on one side a white dove and olive-branch, and on the other a white cross, they marched peaceably in bands to the holy city, though when Venturino went to John XXII., in Avignon, to get the pardons for his followers, he was accused of heresy, and had to undergo a trial by the Inquisition.[427]

Such being the popular tendencies of the age, it is no wonder that the profound emotions caused by the fearful scourge of the Black Death found relief in a gregarious outburst of penitence. Germany had suffered less than the rest of Europe, only one fourth of the population being estimated as perishing, but the religious sensibilities of the people had been stirred by the interdicts against Louis of Bavaria, and the pestilence had been preceded by earthquakes, which were portents of horror. It well might seem that God, wearied with man's wickedness, was about to put an end to the human race, and that only some extraordinary effort of propitiation could avert his wrath. In this state of mental tension it needed but a touch to send an impulse through the whole population. Suddenly, in the spring of 1349, the land was covered with bands of Flagellants, like those whom we have seen nearly a century before, expiating their sins by public scourging. Some said that the example was set in Hungary; others attributed it to different places, but it responded so thoroughly to the vague longings of the people, and it spread so rapidly, that it seemed to be the result of a universal consentaneous impulse. All the proceedings, at least at first, were conducted decently and in order. The Flagellants marched in bands of moderate size, each under a leader and two lieutenants. Beggary was strictly{382} prohibited, and no one was admitted to fellowship who would not promise obedience to the captain, and who had not money to defray his own expenses, estimated at four pfennige per diem, though the hospitality universally offered in the towns through which they passed was freely accepted to the extent of lodging and meals; but two nights were never to be spent in the same place. Monks and priests, nobles and peasants, women and children were marshalled together in common contrition to placate an offended God. They chanted rude hymns—

"Nü tretent herzu die bussen wellen.
Fliehen wir die heissen hellen.
Lucifer ist ein bose geselle," etc.—

and scourged themselves at stated times, the men stripping to the waist and using a scourge knotted with four iron points, so lustily laid on that an eye-witness says that he had seen two jerks requisite to disengage the point from the flesh. They taught that this exercise, continued for thirty-three days and a half, washed from the soul all taint of sin, and rendered the penitent pure as at birth.

From Poland to the Rhine the processions of Flagellants met with little opposition, except in a few towns, such as Erfurt, where the magistrates prohibited their entrance, and in the province of Magdeburg, where Archbishop Otho suppressed them. They spread through Holland and Flanders, but when they invaded France, Philippe de Valois interfered, and they penetrated no farther than Troyes. The guardians of public order, indeed, could not look without dread upon such a popular demonstration, which by organization might become dangerous. When the Flagellants of Strassburg proposed to form a permanent confraternity, Charles IV., who was in that city, peremptorily forbade it. Already dangerous characters were attracted to the wandering bands; in many places their zeal had led to the merciless persecution of the Jews, and there were not lacking symptoms of a significant antagonism to the Church, manifesting itself in attacks upon ecclesiastics and clerical property. The Church, in fact, looked askance upon a religious manifestation not of her prescription, and her susceptibilities were not soothed by the daily reading, amid the flagellation, of a letter brought by an angel to the Church of St.{383}Peter, in Jerusalem, relating that God, incensed at the non-observance of Sundays and Fridays, had scourged Christendom, and would have destroyed the world but for the intercession of the angels and the Virgin. This was accompanied by a message that general flagellation for thirty-three and a half days would cause him to lay aside his wrath. There was danger, indeed, of open antagonism and insubordination. The Mendicants, who endeavored to discourage this independent popular penitence, incurred the bitterest hostility, which had no scruple in finding expression. At Tournay the orator of the Flagellants denounced them as scorpions and antichrists, and on the borders of Misnia two Dominicans, who endeavored to reason with a band of Flagellants, were set upon with stones; one had sufficient agility to escape, but the other was lapidated to death.[428]

When in Basle about a hundred of the principal citizens organized themselves into a confraternity, and made a flagellating pilgrimage to Avignon, they excited great admiration among the citizens, and most of the cardinals were disposed to think highly of the new penitential discipline. Clement VI. penetrated deeper below the surface, and recognized the danger to the Church of allowing irregular and independent manifestations of zeal, and of permitting unauthorized associations and congregations to form themselves. Moreover, what was to become of the most serviceable and profitable function of the Holy See in administering the treasures of salvation, if men could cleanse themselves of sin by self-prescribed and self-inflicted penance? The movement bore within it the germ of revolution, as threatening and as dangerous as that of the Poor Men of Lyons, or of any of the sects which had thus far been successfully combated, and self-preservation required its prompt suppression at any cost. From the standpoint of worldly wisdom this reasoning was unanswerable, but members{384} of the Sacred College were obstinate. They prevailed upon Clement not to execute his first intention of casting the Flagellants into prison, and the discussion on the policy to be pursued must have been protracted, for it was not until October 20, 1349, that the papal bull of condemnation was issued. This took the ground that it was a disregard of the power of the keys and a contempt of Church discipline for these new and unauthorized associations to wear distinctive garments, to form assemblies governed by self-dictated statutes, and performing acts contrary to received observances. Allusion was made to the cruelties exercised on the Jews, and the invasion of ecclesiastical property and jurisdiction. All prelates were ordered to suppress them forthwith; those who refused obedience were to be imprisoned until further orders, and the aid of the secular arm was to be called upon if necessary.[429]

Clement was correct in his anticipation of the effects of the new discipline on the minds of the faithful. When the subject came up for discussion at the Council of Constance, in 1417, and San Vicente Ferrer was inclined to regard it with favor, his lofty reputation and his services in procuring the abandonment of Peter of Luna (Benedict XIII.) by Spain rendered it impossible not to treat him with respect, but Gerson took him delicately to task and wrote a tract to show the evils resulting from the practice. Experience, he said, had shown that the members of the sect of Flagellants were led to look with contempt on sacramental confession and the sacrament of penitence, for they exalted their peculiar form of penance, not only over that prescribed by the

128

Church, but even over martyrdom, because they shed their own blood, while the blood of martyrs was shed by others. This led directly to insubordination and to destroying the reverence due to the Church, and was the fruitful parent of heresy. From some of his allusions, indeed, we may gather that it frequently caused collisions between the people and the priesthood, in which the latter were apt to be roughly handled.[430]

This shows how inefficient had been Clement's prohibition, and how obstinately the practice had maintained itself until it had{385} risen to the rank of a new heresy. When his bull was received by the German prelates they fully comprehended the dangers which it sought to avert, and addressed themselves vigorously to its enforcement. The Flagellants were denounced from the pulpit as an impious sect, condemned by the Holy See. Those who would humbly return to the Church would be received to mercy, while the obdurate would be made to experience the full rigor of the canons. This thinned the ranks considerably, but there were enough of persistent ones to furnish a new harvest of martyrs. Many were executed, or exposed to various forms of torment, and not a few rotted to death in the dungeons in which they were thrown. Even ecclesiastics could not be prevented from adhering to the obnoxious sect. William of Gennep, Archbishop of Cologne, in a provincial council excommunicated all clerks who joined the Flagellants; yet this was so completely disregarded that in his vernal synod of 1353 he was obliged to order all deans and rectors of churches to assemble their chapters, read his letters, and make provision for the public excommunication by name of all the disobedient, to be followed within a fortnight by their suspension. We shall see hereafter with what persistent obstinacy the outbreak of flagellation recurred from time to time, and how it was regarded as heresy, pure and simple, by the Church. Meanwhile, it is not to be doubted that the Brethren of the Free Spirit took full advantage of the excitement prevailing in men's minds, and of the upturning which resulted, both spiritually and socially. When the bands of Flagellants first made their appearance they were joined in many places, we are told, by the heretics known as Lollards, Beghards, and Cellites. Involved in common persecution, they grew to have common interests, and they became too intimately associated together not to lend each other mutual support.[431]

Thus far the faith had not gained the advantage which had naturally been expected to follow the undisputed domination of the pious Charles IV. At the end of 1352 Innocent VI. ascended the papal throne and promptly repeated the attempt to introduce the papal Inquisition in Germany by renewing, in July, 1353, the commission{386} as inquisitor of Friar John Schandeland, and writing earnestly to the German prelates to lend him all assistance. The pestiferous madness of the Beghards, he said, was blazing forth afresh, and efforts were requisite for its suppression. As in their dioceses the Inquisition had no prisons of its own, they were required to give it the free use of the episcopal jails. We are told in general terms that Friar John was energetic and successful, but no records remain to prove his activity or its results, and it is fair to conclude that the bishops, as usual, gave him the cold shoulder. There is no proof even that he was concerned in the condemnation of the Beghard heresiarch Berthold von Rohrback, who in 1356 expiated his heresy in the flames. Berthold had previously been caught in Würzburg, and had recanted through dread of the stake. He ought to have been imprisoned for life, but the German spiritual courts, as usual, were unversed in the penalties for heresy, and he was allowed to go free, when he secretly made his way to Speier. There he was successful in propagating his doctrines until he was again arrested. As a relapsed heretic, under the rules of the Inquisition, there was no mercy for him, but the rules were imperfectly understood in Germany, and again he was treated more leniently than the canons allowed, and was offered reconciliation. This time his courage did not fail him. "My faith," he said, "is the gift of God, and I neither ought nor wish to reject his grace." That Innocent's attempt to introduce the Inquisition proved a failure may be gathered from the action of William of Gennep, in his vernal synod of Cologne in 1357. While deploring the increase of the pernicious sect of Beghards, which threatens to infect his whole city and diocese, he makes no allusion whatever to the papal Inquisition and the canons. The measures of his predecessors are referred to, in accordance with which all parish priests are directed to proceed against the heretics, under threat of prosecution for remissness, and excommunication is pronounced against those who aid the Beghards with alms.[432]

Undeterred by ill-success the effort was renewed. From a MS. sentence of June 6, 1366, printed by Mosheim, we learn that the Dominican, Henry de Agro, was at that time commissioned as{387} inquisitor of the province of Mainz and the diocese of Bamberg and Basle, the latter of which belonged to the province of Besançon. He was conducting an active inquisition in the diocese of Strassburg, whose bishop, John of Luxemburg, had gratified episcopal jealousy by not allowing him to perform his office independently, but had adjoined to him his vicar, Tristram, who acted in the matter not simply as representing the bishop in the sentence, but as co-inquisitor. According to the rules of the Inquisition, the judgment was rendered in an assembly of experts. The victim in this case was a woman, Metza von Westhoven, a Beguine, who had been tried and who had abjured in the persecution under Bishop John of Zurich, nearly half a century before. As a relapsed heretic there was no pardon for her, and she was duly relaxed.[433]

Thus far whatever hopes might have been based upon the zeal of Charles IV. had not been realized. He seems to have taken no part in the efforts of the papacy, and without the imperial exequatur the commissions issued to inquisitors had but moderate chance of enjoying the respect and obedience of the prelates. In 1367 Urban V. returned to the work by commissioning two inquisitors for Germany, the Dominicans Louis of Willenberg and Walter Kerlinger, with powers to appoint vicars. The Beghards were the only heretics alluded to as the object of their labors; prelates and magistrates were ordered to lend their efficient assistance and to place all prisons at their disposal until the German Inquisition should have such places of its own. This was the most comprehensive measure as yet taken for the organization of the Holy Office in Germany, and it proved the entering wedge, though at first Charles IV. does not seem to have responded. The choice of inquisitors was shrewd. Of Friar Louis we hear little, but Friar Walter (variously named Kerling, Kerlinger, Krelinger, and Keslinger) was a man of influence, a chaplain and favorite of the emperor, who had the temper of a persecutor and the opportunity and ambition to magnify his office. In 1369 he became Dominican Provincial of Saxony, and continued to perform the duplicate functions until his death, in 1373. He lost no time in getting to work, for in 1368 we hear of a Beghard burned in Erfurt, and{388} to his unwearied exertions is generally attributed the temporary suppression of the sect.[434]

Still there was at first no appearance of any hearty support from either the spiritual or temporal potentates of Germany, and without this the business of persecution could only languish. When, however, the emperor made his Italian expedition, in 1368, the opportunity was utilized to arouse him to a sense of his neglected duties. It was rare indeed for an emperor to have the cordial support of the papacy, and we may reasonably assume that Charles was made to see that through their union the Inquisition might be rendered serviceable to both in breaking down the independence of the great prince-bishops. Thus it happened that when that institution was falling into desuetude in the lands of its birth, it was for the first time regularly organized in Germany and given a substantive existence. From Lucca, on June 9 and 10, 1369, the emperor issued two edicts which excel all previous legislation in the unexampled support accorded to inquisitors—the extravagance of their provisions probably furnishing a measure of the opposition to be overcome. All prelates, princes, and magistrates are ordered to expel and treat as outlaws the sect of Beghards and Beguines, commonly known as *Wilge Armen* or *Conventschwestern*, who beg with the vainly prohibited formula "*Brod durch Gott!*" At the command of Walter Kerlinger and his vicars or other inquisitors, all who give alms to the proscribed class shall be arrested and so punished as to serve as a terror to others. With special significance the prelates are addressed and commanded to use their powers for the extermination of heresy; in the strongest language, and under threats of condign punishment to be visited on them in person and on their temporalities, they are ordered to obey with zeal the commands of Friar Kerlinger, his vicars, and all other inquisitors as to the arrest and safekeeping of heretics; they are to render all possible aid to the inquisitors, to receive and treat them kindly and courteously, and furnish them with guards in their movements. Moreover, all inquisitors are taken under the special imperial favor and protection. All the powers, privileges, liberties, and immunities granted to them by preceding emperors or by the{389} rulers of any other land are conferred upon them, and confirmed, notwithstanding any laws or customs to the contrary. To enforce these privileges, two dukes (Saxony and Brunswick), two counts (Schwartzenberg and Nassau), and two knights (Hanstein and Witzeleyeven) are appointed conservators and guardians, with instructions to act whenever complaint is made to them by the inquisitors. They shall see that one third of the confiscations of heretic Beghards and Beguines are handed over to the Inquisition, and shall proceed directly and fearlessly, without appeal, against any one impeding or molesting it in any manner, making examples of them, both in person and property. Any contravention of the edict shall entail a mulct of one hundred marks, one half payable to the fisc and one half to the party injured. Besides this, any one impeding or molesting any of the inquisitors or their agents, directly or indirectly, openly or secretly, is declared punishable with confiscation of all property for the benefit of the imperial treasury, and deprivation of all honors, dignities, privileges, and immunities.[435]

These portentous edicts provided for the *personnel* of the Inquisition and the exercise of its powers, but to render it a permanent institution there were still lacking houses in which it could hold its tribunals, and prisons in which to keep its captives. The imperial resources were not adequate to this, and nothing was to be expected from the piety of princes and prelates. Somebody must be despoiled for its benefit—somebody too defenceless to resist, yet possessed of property sufficient to be tempting. These conditions were exactly filled by the orthodox Beghards and Beguines, who, since their temporary persecution after the publication of the Clementines, had continued to prosper and to enjoy the donations of the pious. They were accordingly marked as the victims, and, a week after the issue of the edicts just described, another was published in which these poor creatures are described as cultivating a sacrilegious poverty, which they assert to be the most perfect form of life, and their communities, if left undisturbed, will become seminaries of error. Moreover, the Inquisition has no house, domicile, or strong tower for the detention of the accused and for the perpetual incarceration of those who abjure, whereby{390} many heretics remain unpunished and the seed of evil is scattered. Therefore the houses of the Beghards are given to the Inquisition to be converted into prisons; those of the Beguines are ordered to be sold and the proceeds divided into thirds, one part being assigned to repairing roads and the walls of the towns, another to be given to inquisitors, to be expended on pious uses, among which is included the maintenance of prisoners. But three days" notice is given to the victims prior to expulsion from their homes.[436]

If the Inquisition could have been permanently established in Germany this unscrupulous measure would have accomplished the object. What between the imperial favor and Kerlinger's energy it at last had a fair start. The last edict alludes to two additional inquisitors whom Kerlinger was authorized to appoint and to his successful labors, by which the heretic Brethren of the Free Spirit had been completely destroyed in the provinces of Magdeburg and Bremen, and in Thuringia, Hesse, Saxony, and elsewhere. Probably this is exaggerated, but we learn from other sources that Kerlinger was zealously active and that his labors were rewarded with success. In Magdeburg and Erfurt he burned a number of heretics and forced the rest to outward conformity or to flight. We hear of him at Nordhausen in 1369, where he captured forty Beghards; of these seven were obdurate and were burned, and the rest abjured and accepted penance. This is probably a fair example of his work, and we may believe Gregory XI. when, in 1372, he says that the Inquisition had destroyed heresy and heretics in the central provinces and driven them to the outlying districts of Brabant, Holland, Stettin, Breslau, and Silesia, where they are gathered in such multitudes that they hope to be able to maintain themselves; wherefore he earnestly calls upon the prelates and nobles to bring the good work to an end by efficiently supporting the Holy Office in its final labors. Apparently Kerlinger had not been anxious to divide his authority by exercising his power to appoint two additional colleagues, and Gregory now intervened to relieve him of this duty and place the German Inquisition on a{391} permanent footing by assimilating its organization to that of the institution elsewhere. He increased the number of Inquisitors to five and placed their appointment and removal in the hands of the Dominican master and provincial, or either of them. Kerlinger and Louis, however, were to remain as two of the five, and no power, whether imperial or episcopal, should have authority to interfere with the free exercise of their functions.[437]

A further extension of the power of the Inquisition granted by Charles IV. was of no great importance at the time, but has the highest interest to us as the first indication of what was to come. A leading feature of the Beghard propaganda was the circulation among the laity of written tracts and devotional works. Composed in the vernacular, they reached a class which was not wholly illiterate and yet was unable to profit by the orthodox works of which Latin was the customary vehicle. For the suppression of this effective method of missionary work the Inquisition was intrusted with a censorship of literature, to which further reference will be made hereafter. Less interesting to us, but probably more important at the time, was the permission granted to the inquisitors to appoint notaries. It will be remembered how jealously these appointments were guarded, and this concession was evidently looked upon as a special favor. The inquisitors apparently had been trammelled by the lack of notaries, and they were now authorized to appoint one in each diocese, and to replace him when removed by death or disability.[438]

As regards the seizure of the Beguinages, it was ruthlessly carried out by Kerlinger. Those of Mühlhausen had been very flourishing, and on February 16, 1370, four of them were delivered by him to the magistrates to be converted to public uses—probably the city's share of the plunder. It would seem, however, that obstacles were thrown in his way. The jealousy of the bishops was not likely to look with favor upon this permanent establishment of the Inquisition in their dioceses, with prisons and landed property that would render it independent. Mosheim{392} judiciously suggests that as these houses were benevolent gifts for pious uses the bishops could assert them to be under their jurisdiction and not subject to an imperial edict; nobles and citizens, moreover, had been trained to regard their inoffensive inmates with favor, and were not eager to share in the spoils. Whatever may have been their motives, Kerlinger could not have found the way open to the general confiscation that he desired. In 1371 he was obliged to petition Gregory XI., reciting the existence of heretics called Beghards and Beguines, and the imperial edict confiscating their conventicles, the confirmation of which he desired. There was nothing to lead Gregory to suppose that there was in this anything but the well-understood confiscation of heretical property, and he willingly gave the desired confirmation.[439]

Thus, after a desultory struggle lasting for nearly a century and a half, the Inquisition finally established itself in Germany as an organized body. For a while, at least, the office of inquisitor was kept regularly filled as vacancies occurred. When Kerlinger died, in 1373, his successor in the Provincialate of Saxony, Hermann Hetstede, is qualified as being an inquisitor, and the same title is given to Henry Albert, who followed Hetstede in 1376. The Holy Office seems to have been almost exclusively in Dominican hands, and we rarely hear of its functions as performed by Franciscans. The good work proceeded apace. In 1372 Kerlinger had a heretic of higher rank than usual to deal with in the person of Albert, Bishop of Halberstadt, who publicly taught fatalistic doctrines—possibly some form of predestination such as Wickliff was commencing to formulate. This resulted in a great decrease in pious works, for it struck at the root of the invocation of saints, masses for the dead, and liberality to the clergy, and the consequences threatened to be so serious that Gregory XI. ordered Kerlinger, together with Hervord, Provost of Erfurt, and an Augustinian named Rodolph, to force the bishop to an abjuration, and in case of disobedience to transmit him to the papal court for judgment. In the same year Gregory recounts with much satisfaction the success of the inquisitors in driving the Beghards{393} out of central and northern Germany; he stimulated the emperor to support their labors with fresh zeal, and sent encyclicals to the princes, prelates, and magistrates, commanding them to use every effort to render the work complete, by exterminating the heretics in the regions where they had taken refuge. Early in the next year he commissioned the Dominican, John of Boland, an imperial chaplain, as inquisitor in the dioceses of Trèves, Cologne, and Liège, the Beghards and Beguines being the objects specially indicated; and Charles hastened to invest him with all the powers specified in his letters of 1369, ordering the Dukes of Luxembourg, Limburg, Brabant, and Juliers, the Princes of Mons and Cleves, and the Counts of La Marck, Kirchberg, and Spanheim to serve as conservators and guardians of the edict.[440]

Although the Brethren of the Free Spirit were the chief objects of all this inquisitorial activity, the Flagellants were not neglected. In 1361 a demonstration of these enthusiasts in far-off Naples awakened the solicitude of Innocent VI. In 1369 we hear of an outbreak of women coming from Hungary, which was summarily suppressed in Saxony. In 1372 Flagellants reappeared in various parts of Germany, asserting the peculiar efficacy of their penance as replacing the sacraments of the Church, so that Gregory XI. felt it necessary to direct the inquisitors to exterminate them. In 1373 and 1374 this irrepressible tendency took a new shape, known as the Dancing Mania, which broke out at the consecration of a church in Aix-la-Chapelle. Bands of both sexes, mostly consisting of poor and simple folk, poured into Flanders from the Rhinelands, dancing and singing as though possessed by the Furies. Under intense spiritual excitement the performer would leap and dance until he fell to earth with convulsions, when his comrades would revive him by jumping upon him, or a cloth which he wore, tied around the belly, would be tightly twisted with a stick. This was generally looked upon as a kind of demoniacal possession until a multitude of these dancers assembled at Herestal and consulted together as to the best plan for slaying all the priests, canons, and clergy of Liège, when the madness was{394} recognized as no longer harmless. Still it spread over a large portion of Germany and lasted for several years. Though not in itself a heresy, it led in some places to heretical opinions on the sacraments, for it was popularly explained by attributing it to defective baptism, caused by the universal practice among priests of keeping concubines.[441]

Scarce had the Inquisition been fairly organized and had settled to its work, when its arbitrary proceedings awakened active opposition. As the heretic Beghards and Beguines were the principal objects of its activity, and the orthodox ones of its cupidity, the sufferings of the latter speedily awoke compassion which found expression in terms so decided that Gregory XI. could not refuse to listen. Accordingly, in April, 1374, he wrote to the Archbishops of Mainz, Trèves, and Cologne, reciting these complaints and ordering a report about the life and conversation of the persons concerned, who should be protected and cherished if innocent, and be punished if guilty. At least from Cologne and Worms, probably from the other prelates, came answers that the persecuted communities were composed of faithful Catholics. In Cologne the magistrates intervened and complained energetically to the pope that a Dominican inquisitor was vexing the poor folk, and they asked that his proceedings be stopped. The victims, they said, were people of little culture, who were interrogated with questions so difficult that the most skilful theologians could scarce answer them, while their edifying lives had led the clergy to protect them against the threats of the Inquisition. Proceedings were thus checked, but still the peculiar garments which the devotees had always worn furnished an excuse for continued persecution, and another appeal was made to Gregory, to which he responded in December, 1377, by ordering the prelates not to permit their molestation on this account so long as they were good Catholics and obedient to the ecclesiastical authorities. The German bishops were thus fully armed with papal authority to restrict the operations of the inquisitors, and those who, like Bishop Lambert{395} of Strassburg, were themselves disposed to persecution, did not dare to proceed further. The regular communities of Beghards and Beguines were assured of toleration, and if the heretical Brethren of the Free Spirit managed to share in this immunity, it probably did not give the prelates much concern.[442]

All this was discouraging to the zeal of inquisitors whose institution had hardly yet taken root in the land, but worse was still to follow. In 1378 died both Gregory XI. and Charles IV. The election of Urban VI. gave rise to the Great Schism, and Wenceslas, the son and successor of Charles, was notoriously indifferent to the interest of religion as represented by the Church. Thus deprived of its two indispensable supporters, the Inquisition could not make head against episcopal jealousy. In 1381 there could have been no inquisitors in the extensive dioceses of Ratisbon, Bamberg, and Misnia, for we find the Archbishop of Prague as papal legate ordering the bishops to appoint them, and threatening to do so himself in case of disobedience. Still the Inquisition did not entirely pretermit its labors. In 1392 we hear of a papal inquisitor named Martin who travelled through Suabia to Würzburg, finding in the latter place a number of peasants and simple folk belonging to the sect of Flagellants and Beghards. They had not in them the stuff of martyrs, and accepted the penance imposed upon them of joining in a crusade then preaching against the Turks—the first time for nearly a century that we meet with this penalty. Then Martin went to Erfurt—always a heretical centre—where he came upon numerous heretics of the same kind. Some of these were obstinate and were duly burned, others accepted penance, and the rest sought safety in flight. The following year there was burned at Cologne, by the papal inquisitor, Albert, a leading Beghard known as Martin of Mainz, a former Benedictine monk and a disciple of the celebrated Nicholas of Basle; and in his trial there are allusions to others of the sect executed not long before at Heidelberg.[443]

About this period, after a long interval, we again become cognizant{396} of the existence of Waldenses. The Beghards had succeeded in concentrating upon themselves the attention of the papal and episcopal inquisitions, and the followers of Peter Waldo had remained unnoticed, doubtless owing their safety to outward conformity, though by absenting themselves from their parishes about the Easter tide they sometimes managed to escape taking communion for five or six years in succession. Thus laboring quietly and peacefully, preaching by night in cellars, mills, stables, and other retired places, they gained numerous converts among the peasants and artisans, who saw in the sanctity of their lives, as sadly admitted by the so-called Peter of Pilichdorf, the strongest contrast with the scandalous license of the clergy.[444] Thus they multiplied in secret until all Germany was full of them, including the closely-related sect of Winkelers. About 1390 they were discovered in Mainz, where for a hundred years they had lurked undisturbed. The Archbishop, Conrad II., kept the matter in his{397} own hands. In 1392 he issued a commission, as episcopal inquisitors, to Frederic, Bishop of Toul, Nicholas of Saulheim, the Dean of St. Stephen, and John Wasmod, of Homburg, a priest of the cathedral, to

132

whom the papal inquisitor could adjoin himself if he so chose. These inquisitors were armed with full authority to arrest, try, torture, sentence, and abandon to the secular arm all heretics, and were instructed to proceed in accordance with the practice of the Inquisition. They zealously discharged their duty. A number of Waldenses were already in the episcopal prison, and they made diligent perquisition after the rest. By free use of torture they obtained the necessary avowals and evidence. Those who were obstinate were handed over to the secular arm, and an *auto de fé* celebrated at Bingen in 1392, where six-and-thirty wretches were burned, proved that the papal Inquisition itself could not have been more effective. A little tract on the examination of Waldenses, evidently written on this occasion, shows that the inquisitorial process was fairly well understood, and that the episcopal officials had not much to learn from their rivals.[445]{398} and Saxony are represented. The author of the tract which passes under the name of Peter of Pilichdorf, who took an energetic part both with the pen and in action in suppressing this suddenly discovered heresy, informs us, in 1395, that the Netherlands, Westphalia, Prussia, and Poland were not infected with it, while Thuringia, Misnia, Bohemia, Moravia, Austria, and Hungary numbered their heretics by thousands. Curiously enough, in this list he omits Pomerania, where, along the Baltic regions, the Waldenses were thickly scattered from Stettin to Königsberg. The heresy had been deeply rooted there for at least a century, and the local priesthood seem to have borne no ill-will to the harmless sectaries, who conformed outwardly to the orthodox observances. Even when in confession intimations of the heresy escaped, as sometimes happened, they were wisely and mercifully overlooked. Yet there is evidence of previous persecution in the confession of Sophia Myndekin, of Fleit, who said that she had been fifty years in the sect, that her husband had been burned at Angermünde, and that she had only escaped on account of pregnancy, while all their little property was confiscated. They were poor folk, mostly peasants and laborers, and though there are occasional allusions in the trials to men of gentle blood, the tenets of the sect excluded all who owed feudal military service, war and bloodshed being strictly forbidden. They were visited yearly by their ministers, some of whom were mechanics, and others learned men skilled in Holy Writ, probably from Bohemia, who preached, heard confessions, and granted absolution, the utmost secrecy being observed in these ministrations. Moreover, collections were made and remitted to the headquarters of the sect, showing that they formed part of the great Waldensian organization.[446]

They had long been unmolested when one of their ministers, known as Brother Klaus, who had visited them in 1391 and had heard many confessions, apparently became frightened at the movement against them. He apostatized, and seems to have betrayed the names of his penitents. The Church made haste to secure the fruits of his repentance. Brother Peter, Provincial of {399} the Celestinian Order, was appointed papal inquisitor, and early in 1393 he came to Stettin armed with full powers from the Archbishop of Prague and the Bishops of Lebus and Camin to represent them. He issued citations, both general ones from the pulpits of the infected region, and special summonses to individuals. This naturally caused great excitement, and some of the suspects fled; in Klein-Wurbiser, indeed, there was a faint demonstration made against the inquisitorial apparitors, but there was no resistance, and the great majority submitted to the inevitable. Friar Peter, as customary, was lenient with those who spontaneously confessed and abjured; all took the oaths, including that of persecuting heresy and heretics, with only an occasional manifestation of hesitancy. Torture seems to have been unnecessary; there was no exhibition of obstinacy, and no burnings. They were condemned to wear crosses and perform other penance, and when, as was usually the case, their parents had died in the sect, they were required to indicate the place of burial, presumably for exhumation. From January, 1393, until February, 1394, Friar Peter was engaged in this work. One of his registers, comprising four hundred and forty-three cases, was in the hands of Flacius Illyricus, fragments of which have recently been discovered and described by Herr Wattenbach.[447]

From Pomerania, Friar Peter hastened to the south, where he found Waldenses as numerous, and less inclined to submission. He has left a brief memorial of his labors, written in 1395, in which he expresses his fears that the heresy would become dominant, as the Waldenses were resorting to force, and were employing arson and homicide to intimidate the orthodox. His only evidence of this, however, is that on September 8, those of Steyer, to punish the parish priest for receiving the inquisitors in his house, burned his barn, and affixed to the town gates, by night, a warning in the shape of a half-burned brand and a bloody knife. This offence was cruelly avenged, for in 1397, at Steyer, more than a hundred Waldenses of either sex were burned. In this relentless persecution the case of a child of ten condemned to wear crosses shows how unsparing were the tribunals, while others in which the culprits {400} were burned for relapse, having already abjured before the inquisitor, Henry of Olmütz, indicate that this was not the first effort made to exterminate the heresy. How extended it was, and how vigorous its repression, may be gathered from the pseudo Peter of Pilichdorf, who tells us that from Thuringia to Moravia a thousand converts were made in two years, and that the inquisitors who were busy in Austria and Hungary expected soon to have a thousand more.[448]

About the year 1400, in Strassburg, there was active persecution against a sect known as Winkelers, who were discovered to have four assemblies in the city, and others in Mainz and Hagenau. In their confessions they alluded to their comrades in many other places, such as Nordlingen, Ratisbon, Augsburg, Tischengen, Soleure, Berne, Weissenberg, Speier, Holzhausen, Schwäbisch-Wörth, Friedberg, and Vienna. Although, strictly speaking, not Waldenses, they had so many traits in common that the distinction is rather one of organization than of faith. In 1374 one of their number returned to the Church, and the fear of his betraying the little community led to his deliberate murder, the assassins being paid, and undergoing penance to obtain absolution. Some years later the inquisitor, John Arnoldi, was threatened with similar vengeance and left the city. In the final persecution some thirty families were put on trial, while many succeeded in remaining concealed. There was but one noble among them, Blumstein, who abjured, and who, some twenty years later, is found filling important civic posts. Though reference is made in one of the trials to members of the sect who had been burned at Ratisbon, those of Strassburg were more fortunate. The inquisitor, Böckeln, is said to have received bribes for assigning private penance to some of the guilty; and though the Dominicans demanded the burning of the heretics, the magistrates interceded with the episcopal official, and banishment was the severest penalty inflicted. Torture, however, had been freely used in obtaining confessions. After this, nothing more is heard in Strassburg of either Winkelers or Waldenses until the burning of Frederic Reiser in 1458.[449]{401}

There evidently was ample work for the Inquisition in Germany, but it seems to have been more anxious to repair its defeat in the contest with the Beghards than to operate against the Waldenses. In the general excitement on the subject of heresy it was not difficult to render the Beghards objects of renewed suspicion and persecution. To some extent the bishops and most of the inquisitors joined in this, but the suspects had friends among the prelates, who wrote, towards the close of 1393, to Boniface IX., eulogizing their piety, obedience, and good works, and asking protection for them. To this Boniface responded, January 7, 1394, in a brief addressed to the German prelates, ordering them to investigate whether these persons are contaminated with the errors condemned by Clement V. and John XXII., and whether they follow any reproved religious Order; if not, they are to be efficiently protected. An exemplified copy of this brief, given by the Archbishop of Magdeburg, October 20, 1396, shows that it continued to be used and was relied upon in the troubles which followed, soon after, through a sudden change of policy by Boniface. The Inquisition did not remain passive under this interference with its operations. It represented to Boniface that for a hundred years heresies had lurked under the outward fair-seeming of the Beghards and Beguines, in consequence of which, almost every year, obstinate heretics had been burned in the different cities of the empire, and that their suppression was impeded by certain papal constitutions which were urged in their protection. Boniface was easily moved to reversing his recent action, and by a bull of January 31, 1395, he restored to vigor the decrees of Urban V., Gregory XI., and Charles IV., under which he ordered the Inquisition to prosecute earnestly the Beghards, Lollards, and *Zwestriones*. This gave full power to molest the orthodox associations as well as the heretic Brethren of the Free Spirit, and a severe storm of persecution burst over them. Even some of the bishops joined in this, as appears from a synod held in Magdeburg about this time, which ordered the priests to excommunicate and expel them. Yet this again aroused their friends, and Boniface was induced to reissue his bull with an addition which, like the contradictory provisions of the Clementines, shows the perplexity caused by the admixture of orthodoxy and heresy among the Beguines. After repeating his commands for their suppression, he adds that there{402} are pious organizations known as Beghards, Lollards, and *Zwestriones*, which shall be permitted to wear their vestments, to beg, and to continue their mode of life, excommunication being threatened against any inquisitor who shall molest them, unless they have been convicted by the ordinaries of the diocese.[450]

This left the matter very much to the discretion of the local authorities, but the spirit of persecution was fairly revived, and the Inquisition made haste to fortify its position. Under pretext that the bulls of Gregory XI. were becoming worn by age and use, it procured their renewal from Boniface IX., in 1395, though the pope is careful to express that he grants no new privileges. In 1399 it succeeded in having the number of inquisitors increased to six for the Dominican province of Saxony alone, on the plea that its wide extent and populous cities rendered the existing force insufficient. This was not without reason, for the province embraced the great archiepiscopal districts of Mainz, Cologne, Magdeburg, and Bremen, to which were added Rügen and Camin. Camin belonged to the province of Gnesen, and Rügen formed part of the diocese of Roskild, which was suffragan to the metropolitan of Lünden in Sweden, thus furnishing the only instance of inquisitorial jurisdiction in any region that can be called Scandinavian, save a barren attempt made, in 1421, under the stimulus of the Hussite troubles. A few weeks later Boniface issued another bull, ordering the prelates and secular rulers of Germany to give all aid and protection to Friar Eylard Schöneveld and other inquisitors, and especially to lend the use of their prisons, as the Inquisition in those parts is said to have none of its own, which shows that Kerlinger's scheme of obtaining them from the property of the Beghards had not proved a success. Eylard set vigorously to work in the lands adjoining the Baltic, which from their remoteness had probably escaped his predecessors. At Lubec, in 1402, he procured the arrest of a Dolcinist named Wilhelm by the municipal officials, showing that he had no familiars of his own; the accused was examined several times in the presence of numerous clerks, monks, and laymen, showing that the secrecy of the inquisitorial process was unknown or unobserved, and he was finally burned.{403} He had a comrade named Bernhard, who fled to Wismar, whither Schöneveld followed him and had him burned in 1403. The same year he seized a priest at Stralsund, who rejected all solicitations to abjure, and was burned as a persistent heretic; and at Rostock he condemned for heresy a woman who drove away with the bitterest reproaches her son, a Cistercian monk, when he urged her to recant, and who likewise perished in the flames.[451]

About this period heresy appears to have had also to contend with a reaction on the part of the secular authorities. When, in 1400, the Flagellants made a demonstration in the Low Countries, the magistrates of Maestricht expelled them, and when the people took their side the energetic interference of the Bishop of Liège put an end to the insubordination; besides, the Sire de Perweis threw a band of Flagellants into his dungeons and

Tongres closed its gates upon them, so that the epidemic was checked. With the year 1400 the comparative peace which the Beguines had enjoyed for some fifteen years came to an end. Their most dreaded enemy was the Dominican, John of Mühlberg, whose purity of life and energy in battling with the moral and spiritual errors of his time won him a wide reputation throughout Germany, so that when he died in exile, driven from Basle by the clergy whom his attacks had embittered, he was long regarded by the people as a saint and a martyr. About 1400 he stirred up in Basle a struggle with the Beguines, which for ten years kept the city in an uproar. Primarily an episode in the hostility between the Dominicans and Franciscans, it extended to the clergy and magistrates, and finally to the citizens at large. In 1405 the Beguines were expelled, but the Franciscans obtained from the papacy bulls ordering their restoration, and the retraction of all that had been said against them. At last, in 1411, Bishop Humbert and the town council, excited by a fiery sermon of John Pastoris, abolished the associations, which were forced to abandon their living in common and their vestments, or to leave the place. The city of Berne followed this example, and the magistrates of Strassburg took the same course, when some of the Beguines adopted the former alternative and {404} some the latter. Many of these took refuge secretly at Mainz. They were discovered, and the archbishop, John II., holding them to be heretics, ordered them to be prosecuted. The matter was intrusted to Master Henry von Stein, who set vigorously about it. The refugees from Strassburg, mostly women, were thrown into prison; we also hear of a nun who was likewise incarcerated, and of a youth from Rotenburg, who was mounted on a hogshead in the public square, and in the presence of the populace was obliged to accept the penance of crosses, in an *auto de fé* much less impressive than those which Bernard Gui was wont to celebrate.[452]

It was not long before this that the Brethren of the Free Spirit were deprived of their greatest leader, Nicholas of Basle. As a wandering missionary he had for many years been engaged in propagating the doctrines of the sect, and had gained many proselytes.{405} The Inquisition had been eagerly on his track, but he was shrewd and crafty, and had eluded its pursuit. Forced, probably about 1397, to fly to Vienna with two of his disciples, John and James, they were discovered and seized. The celebrated Henry of Hesse (Langenstein) undertook their conversion, and flattered himself that he had succeeded, but they all relapsed and were burned. As Peter, the Celestinian abbot, was at this time Inquisitor of Passau, he probably had the satisfaction of ridding the Church of this dangerous heresiarch, whose belief in his own divine inspiration was such that he considered his will to be equal to that of God.

Not long after a similar martyrdom occurred at Constance, where a Beghard, named Burgin, had founded a sect of extreme austerity. Captured with his disciples by the bishop, he would not abandon his doctrines, and was duly relaxed. Gerson's numerous allusions to the Turelupins and Beghards show that at this period the sect was attracting much attention and was regarded as seductively dangerous. With all his tendency to mysticism, Gerson could recognize the peril incurred by those whom he describes as deceived through too great a desire to reach the sweetness of God, and who mistake the delirium of their own hearts for divine promptings: thus disregarding the law of Christ, they follow their own inclinations without submitting to rule, and are precipitated into guilt by their own presumption. He was especially averse to the spiritual intimacy between the sexes, where devotion screened the precipice on the brink of which they stood. Mary of Valenciennes, he says, was especially to be avoided on this account, for she applied what is set forth about the divine fruition to the passions seething in her own soul, and she argues that he who reaches the perfection of divine love is released from the observance of all precepts. Thus the Brethren of the Free Spirit were practically the same in the fifteenth century as in the times of Ortlieb and Amauri.[453]

Giles Cantor, who founded in Brussels the sect which styled itself Men of Intelligence, was probably a disciple of Mary of Valenciennes, {406} and the name was adopted merely to cover its affiliation with the proscribed Brethren of the Free Spirit. Its doctrines were substantially the same in their mystic pantheism and illuminism; and their practical application is seen in the story that on one occasion Giles was moved by the spirit to go naked for some miles when carrying provision to a poor person. So open a manifestation would have insured his prosecution had there been any machinery for persecution in efficient condition in Brabant; but he was allowed to propagate his doctrines in peace until he died. He was succeeded in the leadership of the sect by a Carmelite known as William of Hilderniss, and at length it attracted, in 1411, the attention of Cardinal Peter d'Ailly, Bishop of Cambrai. Fortunately for William, the bishop chose to direct the proceedings himself, and they show complete disregard of inquisitorial methods. He appointed special commissioners, who made an inquisition; both the names and the testimony of the witnesses were submitted to William, who made what defence he could. In rendering judgment d'Ailly called in the Dominican Prior of St. Quentin, who was inquisitor of the district of Cambrai, and the sentence was as irregular as the proceedings. William had no desire for martyrdom, and abjured the heresy; he was required to purge himself with six compurgators, after which he was to undergo the penance of three years" confinement in a castle of the bishop's, while if he failed in his purgation he was to be imprisoned in a convent of his order during the archbishop's pleasure—a most curious and illogical medley. He succeeded in finding the requisite number of compurgators, but though he disappeared from the scene his sect was by no means extinguished, and we hear of the persecution of a heresiarch as late as 1428.[454]

That Clement VI. did not err when he foresaw the dangerous errors lurking under the devotion of the Flagellants was demonstrated in 1414. The sect still existed, and its crude theories as to the efficacy of

135

flagellation had gradually been developed into an antisacerdotal heresy of the most uncompromising character. A certain Conrad Schmidt was the constructive heresiarch who gave to its belief an organized completeness, and his death made{407} no diminution of the zeal of his disciples, nor did the failure of his prophecy of the end of the world in 1309. The curious connection between the Flagellants and the Beghards is indicated by the fact that these Flagellant Brethren, or Brethren of the Cross, as they styled themselves, regarded Conrad as the incarnation of Enoch, and a certain Beghard, who had been burned at Erfurt about 1364, as Elias—an angel having brought their souls from heaven and infused them into Schmidt and this Beghard while yet in the womb. Schmidt was to preside at the approaching Day of Judgment, which was constantly believed to be at hand, Antichrist being the pope and the priests, whose reign was drawing to an end.

When, in 1343, the letter commanding flagellation, to which I have already alluded, was brought by an angel and laid on the altar of St. Peter, God withdrew all spiritual power from the Church and bestowed it on the Brethren of the Cross. Since then all sacraments had lost their virtue, and to partake of them was mortal sin. Baptism had been replaced by that of the blood drawn by the scourge; the sacrament of matrimony only defiled marriage; the Eucharist was but a device by which the priests sold a morsel of bread for a penny—if they believed it to be the body of Christ they were worse than Judas, who got thirty pieces of silver for it; flagellation replaced them all. Oaths were a mortal sin, but to avoid betraying the sect the faithful could take them and receive the sacraments, and then expiate it by flagellation. The growth of such a belief and the mingled contempt and hatred manifested for the clergy prove that to the people the Church was as much a stranger and an oppressor as it had been in the twelfth century. It had learned nothing, and was as far from Christ as ever.

Conrad Schmidt had promulgated his errors in Thuringia, where his sectaries were discovered, in 1414, at Sangerhausen. Thither sped the inquisitor Schöneveld—called Henry by the chroniclers, but probably the same as the Eylard, whom we have seen at work some years before on the shores of the Baltic. The princes of Thuringia and Misnia were ordered to assist him, and they were eager to share in the suppression of a heresy which threatened to revolutionize the social order. The proceedings must have been more energetic than regular. Torture must have{408} been freely used to gather into the net so many victims; nor can a patient hearing have been given to the accused. Their shrift was short, and before Schöneveld had left the scene of action he had caused the burning of ninety-one at Sangerhausen, forty-four in the neighboring town of Winkel, and many more in other villages. Yet such was the persistence of the heresy that even this wholesale slaughter did not suffice for its suppression. Two years later, in 1416, its remains were discovered, and again Schöneveld was sent for. He examined the accused. To those who abjured he assigned penances, and handed over the obstinate to the secular arm. His assizes must have been hurried, for he did not stay to witness the execution of those whom he had condemned, and after his departure the princes gathered all together, both penitents and impenitents, some three hundred in number, and burned the whole of them in one day. This terrible example produced the profound impression that was desired, and hereafter the sect of Flagellants may be regarded as unimportant. Some discussion, as we have seen, took place the next year at the Council of Constance, when San Vicente Ferrer expressed his approbation of this form of discipline, and Gerson mildly urged its dangers; but when, in 1434, a certain Bishop Andreas specified, among the objects of the Council of Basle, the suppression of the heresies of the Hussites, Waldenses, Fraticelli, Wickliffites, the Manichæans of Bosnia, the Beghards, and the schismatic Greeks, there is no allusion in the enumeration to Flagellants. Yet the causes which had given rise to the heresy continued in full force and it was still cherished in secret. In 1453 and 1454 Brethren of the Cross were again discovered in Thuringia, and the Inquisition was speedily at work to reclaim them. Besides the errors propagated by Conrad Schmidt, it was not difficult to extort from the accused the customary confessions of foul sexual excesses committed in dark subterranean conventicles, and even of Luciferan doctrines, teaching that in time Satan would regain his place in heaven and expel Christ; though when we hear that they alleged the evil lives of the clergy as the cause of their misbelief we may reasonably doubt the accuracy of these reports. Aschersleben, Sondershausen, and Sangerhausen were the centres of the sect, and at the latter place, in 1454, twenty-two men and women were burned as obstinate{409}heretics. In 1481 a few were punished in Anhalt, and the sect gradually disappeared.[455]

The case of the Beghards and Beguines came before the Council of Constance in several shapes. To guard themselves from the incessant molestations to which they were exposed they had, to a large extent, affiliated themselves, nominally at least, as Tertiaries, to the Mendicant Orders, chiefly to the Franciscan, whose scapular they adopted. In a project of reform, carefully prepared for action by the council, this is strongly denounced; they are said to live in forests and in cities, free from subjection, indulging in indecent habits, not without suspicion of heresy, and though able of body and fit to earn their livelihood by labor, they subsist on alms, to the prejudice of the poor and miserable. It was therefore proposed to forbid the wearing of the scapular by all who were not bound by vows to the Orders and subjected to the Rules. It was also pronounced necessary to make frequent visitations of their communities on account of the peculiarities of their life, and magistrates and nobles were to be ordered not to interfere with such wholesome supervision under pain of interdict. It was possibly to meet this attack that numerous testimonial letters from the clergy and magistrates of Germany certifying to the orthodoxy, piety, and usefulness of the associations were sent to Martin V., who submitted them to Angelo, Cardinal of SS. Peter and Marcellus, and received from him a favorable report. Towards the close of the council, in 1418, a more formidable assault was made upon them by Matthew Grabon, a Dominican of Wismar, who {410} laid before Martin V. twenty-four articles to prove that all such associations outside of the approved religious orders ought to be abolished. To accomplish this, after the approved style of scholastic logic, he was obliged to assert such absurd general principles as that it was equivalent to suicide, and therefore a mortal sin, for any secular person to give away his property in charity, and that the pope had no power to grant a dispensation in such cases. Grabon's propositions and conclusions were referred to Antonio, Cardinal of Verona, who submitted them to Cardinal Peter d'Ailly and Chancellor Gerson. The former reported that the paper was heretical and should be burned, while the jurists should be called upon to decide what ought to be done to its writer. The latter, that the doctrine was pestiferous and blasphemous, and that its author, if obstinate, should be arrested. Grabon was glad to escape by publicly abjuring some of his articles as heretical, others as erroneous, and others as scandalous and offensive to pious ears. The triumph of the Beguines was decisive, and they might at last hope for a respite from persecution. The associations increased and flourished accordingly, and under their shelter the Brethren of the Free Spirit continued to propagate their heresy.[456]

From this time forward the attention of the Church was mainly directed to Hussitism, the most formidable enemy that it had encountered since the Catharism of the twelfth century. This will be considered in a following chapter, and meanwhile I need only say that its secret but threatening progress throughout Germany called for active means of repression and led to more thorough organization of the Inquisition. The bull of Martin V., issued February 22, 1418, against Wickliffites and Hussites, is addressed not only to prelates but to inquisitors commissioned in the dioceses and cities of Salzburg, Prague, Gnesen, Olmütz, Litomysl, Bamberg, Misnia, Passau, Breslau, Ratisbon, Cracow, Posen, and Neutra. While of course this is not to be taken literally, as though there were an organized tribunal of the Holy Office in each of these places, still it indicates that in the districts infected or exposed to infection the Church was arming itself with its {411} most effective weapons. The growing danger, moreover, was leading the bishops to abandon somewhat their traditional jealousy. In this same year, 1418, the council of the great province of Salzburg not only urged the bishops to extirpate heresy and to enforce the canons against the secular powers neglecting their duty in this respect, but commanded all princes and potentates to seize and imprison all who were designated as suspect of heresy by the prelates and the inquisitors. Thus at last the episcopate recognized the Inquisition and came to its support.[457]

Yet the attention of the persecutors was not so exclusively directed to the Hussites as to allow the Brethren of the Free Spirit to escape, and in their zeal they continued to molest the orthodox Beguines in spite of the action of Martin V. at Constance. In 1431 Eugenius IV. found himself obliged to intervene for their protection. In a bull, addressed to the German prelates, he recites the favorable action of his predecessors and the troubles to which, in spite of this, they were exposed by the inquisitors. Those who wander around without fixed habitations he orders to be compelled to dwell in the houses of the confraternity, and those who reside quietly and piously are to be efficiently protected. This bull affords perhaps the only instance in which the episcopal power is rendered superior to the Inquisition, for the bishops are authorized to enforce its provisions by the censures of the Church, without appeal, even if those who interfere with the Beguines enjoy special immunities, thus subjecting the inquisitors to excommunication by the prelates. This stretch of papal power exasperated Doctor Felix Hemmerlin, Cantor of Zurich, who detested the Beguines. He wrote several bitter tracts against them, and explained the favor shown them by Eugenius by irreverently stating that the pope had himself been once a Beghard at Padua. In one of his numerous assaults upon them, written probably about 1436, he alludes to several recent cases within a limited region, which would indicate that in spite of the papal protection of the Beguines, the Brethren of the Free Spirit were actively persecuted, and that, if the statistics of the whole empire could be procured, the number of victims would be found not small. Thus in Zurich a certain {412} Burchard and his disciples were tried and penanced with crosses; but they were subsequently found to be relapsed and were all burned. At Uri, Charles and his followers were similarly burned. At Constance Henry de Tierra was forced to abjure. At Ulm, John and a numerous company were subjected to public penance. In Würtemberg there was a great heresiarch punished, whose conviction was only secured after infinite pains. Then from Bohemia there come Beghards every year who seduce a countless number to heresy in Berne and Soleure. This leads one to think that Hemmerlin, in his passion, may confound Hussites with Beghards, and this is confirmed by his assertion that there is in Upper Germany no heresy save that introduced by the foxes of this pernicious sect. Nider, in fact, writing immediately after the Council of Basle had effected a settlement with the Hussites, when, for a time at least, in Germany they were no longer considered enemies of the Church, declares that heretics were few and powerless, skulking in concealment and not to be dreaded, although he had, in describing the errors of the Brethren of the Free Spirit, stated that they were still by no means uncommon in Suabia. It was evidently a member of this sect whom he describes as seeing at Ratisbon when proceeding with the Archdeacon of Barcelona on a mission from the Council of Basle to the Hussites. She was a young woman of spotless character, who made no effort to propagate her faith, but she could not be induced to recant. The archdeacon advised that she be tortured to break her spirit, which was done without success and without forcing her to name her confederates; but when Nider visited her in her cell during the evening, he found her exhausted with suffering, and he readily brought her to acknowledge her error, after which she made a public recantation. This shows us that there could have been no Inquisition in Ratisbon, and that the local authorities had even lost the memory of inquisitorial proceedings.[458]

137

In 1446 the Council of Würzburg found it necessary to repeat the canon of that of Mainz in 1310, ordering the expulsion of all wandering Beghards using the old cry of *"Brod durch Gott"* and preaching in caverns and secret places, showing the maintenance{413} of the traditional customs and also the absence of more active persecution. In 1453 Nicholas V. formally adjoined them to the Mendicant Orders as Tertiaries. Some of them obeyed and formed a distinct class, known as Zepperenses, from their principal house at Zepper. They diminished greatly in number, however, and in 1650 Innocent X. united them with the Tertiaries of Italy, under the General Master residing in Lombardy. The female portion of the associations, which became distinctively known as Beguines, were more fortunate. They were able to preserve their identity and their communities, which remain flourishing to the present day, especially in the Netherlands, where in 1857 the great Beguinage of Ghent contained six hundred Beguines and two hundred locataires or boarders.[459]

Still there remained a considerable number both of heretic Brethren of the Free Spirit and of orthodox Beghards of both sexes who recalcitrated of being thus brought under rule and deprived of their accustomed independence. Thus it is related of Bernhard, who was elected Abbot of Hirsau in 1460, that among other reforms he ejected all the Beguines from their house at Altburg, on account of their impurity of life, and replaced them with Dominican Tertiaries. This aroused the hostility of the Beghards who dwelt in hermitages in the forest of Hirsau, and they conspired against the abbot, but only to their own detriment. In 1463 the Synod of Constance complains of the unlawful wearing of the Franciscan scapular by Lollards and Beguines; all who do so are required to prove their right or to lay it aside, and able-bodied Lollards are ordered to live by honest labor and not by beggary. This latter practice was ineradicable, however, and twenty years later another synod was compelled to repeat the command. In 1491 a synod of Bamberg refers to the provisions of the Clementines against the Beguines as though their enforcement was still called for; and Friar John of Moravia, who died at Brünn in 1492, is warmly praised as a fierce and indefatigable persecutor of Hussites and Beghards. These insubordinate religionists continued to exist under almost constant persecution, until the Reformation,{414} when they served as one of the elements which contributed to the spread of Lutheranism.[460]

It was impossible that Hussitism should triumph in Bohemia without awakening an echo throughout Germany, or that the Hussites should abstain from missionary and proselyting efforts, but the spread of the heresy through the Teutonic populations was sternly and successfully repressed. In 1423 the Council of Siena, under the presidency of papal legates, showed itself fully alive to the danger. It sharply reproved both inquisitors and episcopal ordinaries for the supineness which alone could explain the threatening spread of heresy. They were urged to constant and unsparing vigilance under pain of four months' suspension from entering a church and such other punishment as might seem opportune. They were further ordered to curse the heretics with bell, book, and candle every Sunday in all the principal churches. Holy Land indulgences were offered to all who would assist them in capturing heretics, as well as to rulers who, unable to capture them, should at least expel them from their territories. The earnest tone of the council reflects the alarm that was everywhere felt, and it unquestionably led to renewed exertions, though only a few instances of successful activity chance to be recorded. Thus, in 1420, a priest, known as Henry Grünfeld, who had embraced Hussite doctrines, was burned at Ratisbon, where likewise, in 1423, another priest named Henry Rathgeber met the same fate. In 1424 a priest named John Drändorf suffered at Worms, and in 1426 Peter Turman was burned at Speier. Even after the Council of Basle had recognized the Hussites as orthodox, and under the Compactata they enjoyed toleration in states where they held temporal authority, they were still persecuted as heretics elsewhere. About 1450 John Müller ventured to preach Hussite doctrines throughout Franconia, where he met with much acceptance and gained a numerous following, but he was forced to fly, and one hundred and thirty of his disciples were seized and carried to Würzburg. There they were persuaded to recant by the Abbot John of Grumbach and Master Anthony, a preacher of the cathedral.{415} More tragic was the fate of Frederic Reiser, a Suabian, educated in Waldensianism. Under the guise of a merchant he had served as a preacher among the Waldensian churches which maintained a secret existence throughout Germany. At Heilsbronn he was captured in a Hussite raid, when, carried to Mount Tabor, he recognized the practical identity of the faiths and received ordination at the hands of the Taborite Bishop Nicholas. He labored to bring about a union of the churches, and wandered as a missionary through Germany, Bohemia, and Switzerland. Finally he settled at Strassburg, which was always a heretic centre, and gathered a community of disciples around him. He called himself "Frederic, by the grace of God bishop of the faithful in the Roman Church who spurn the Donation of Constantine." He was detected in 1458 and arrested with his followers. Under torture he confessed all that was required of him, only to withdraw it when removed from the torture-chamber. The burgomaster, Hans Drachenfels, and the civic magistracy earnestly opposed his execution, but they were obliged to yield, and he was burned, together with his faithful servant, Anna Weiler, an old woman of Nürnberg.[461]

Reiser had been specially successful with the descendants of the Pomeranian Waldenses who, as we have seen, abjured before the inquisitor Peter in 1393. They appear to have by no means abandoned their heresy, and were easily brought to the modifications which assimilated them to the Hussites--.the adoption of bishops, priests, and deacons, the communion in both elements, and the honoring of Wickliff, Huss, and Jerome of Prague. In this same year, 1458, a tailor of Selchow, named Matthew Hagen, was arrested with three disciples and carried to Berlin for trial by order of the Elector Frederic II. He had been ordained as a priest in Bohemia by Reiser, and had returned to propagate the doctrines of the sect and administer its sacraments. His followers weakened and abjured, but he remained steadfast, and was abandoned to the secular arm. To root out the sect, Dr. John Canneman, {416}who had tried Hagen, was sent to Angermünde as episcopal inquisitor; he found many sectaries but no obstinacy, for they willingly submitted and abjured.[462]

There was, in fact, enough in common between the doctrines of the more radical Hussites and those of the Waldenses to bring the sects eventually together. The Waldenses had by no means been extirpated, and when, in 1467, the remnant of the Taborites known as the Bohemian Brethren opened communication with them, the envoys sent had no difficulty in finding them on the confines between Austria and Moravia, where they had existed for more than two centuries. They had a bishop named Stephen, who speedily called in another bishop to perform the rite of ordination for the Brethren, showing that the heretic communities were numerous and well organized. The negotiations unfortunately attracted attention, and the Church made short work of those on whom it could lay its hands. Bishop Stephen was burned at Vienna and the flock was scattered, many of them finding refuge in Moravia. Others fled as far as Brandenburg, where already there were flourishing Waldensian communities. These were soon afterwards discovered, and steel, fire, and water were unsparingly used for their destruction, without blotting them out. A portion of those who escaped emigrated to Bohemia, where they were gladly received by the Bohemian Brethren and incorporated into their societies. The close association thus formed between the Brethren and the Waldenses resulted in a virtual coalescence which gave rise to a new word in the nomenclature of heresy. When, in 1479, Sixtus IV. confirmed Friar Thomas Gognati as Inquisitor of Vienna, he urged him to put forth every exertion to suppress the Hussites and Nicolinistæ. These latter, who took their name from Nicholas of Silesia, were evidently Bohemian Brethren who adhered to the extreme doctrine common to both sects, that nothing could justify putting a human being to death. Thus the struggle continued, and though the danger was averted which had once seemed threatening, of the widespread adoption of Hussite theories, there remained concealed enough Hussite and Waldensian hostility to Rome to serve as a nucleus of discontent and to give sufficient support to revolt when a man was found, {417} like Luther, bold enough to clothe in words the convictions which thousands were secretly nursing.[463]

Signs, indeed, were not wanting in the fifteenth century or the inevitable rupture of the sixteenth. Prominent among those who boldly defied the power of Rome was Gregory of Heimburg, whom Ullman well designates as the citizen-Luther of the fifteenth century. He first comes into view at the Council of Basle, in the service of Æneas Sylvius, who was then one of the foremost advocates of the reforming party, and he remained steadfast to the principles which his patron bartered for the papacy. A forerunner of the Humanists, he labored to diffuse classical culture, and with his admiration for the ancients he had, like Marsiglio of Padua, imbibed the imperial theory of the relations between Church and State. With tongue and pen inspired by dauntless courage he was indefatigable to the last in maintaining the rights of the empire and the supremacy of general councils. The power of the keys, he taught, had been granted to the apostles collectively; these were represented by general councils, and the monopoly in the hands of the pope was a usurpation. His free expression of opinion infallibly brought him into collision with his early patron, and the antagonism was sharpened when Pius II. convoked the assembly of princes at Mantua to provide for a new crusade. Gregory, who was there as counsellor of the princes, boldly declared that this was only a scheme to augment the papal power and drain all Germany of money. When Nicholas of Cusa, a time-server like Pius, was appointed Bishop of Brixen and claimed property and rights regarded by Sigismund of Austria as belonging to himself, Sigismund, under Gregory's advice, arrested the bishop. Thereupon Pius, in June, 1460, laid Sigismund's territories under interdict, and induced the Swiss to attack him. Gregory drew up an appeal to a general council, which Sigismund issued, although Pius had forbidden such appeals, and he further had the hardihood to prove by Scripture, the fathers, and history, that the Church was subject to the State. It was no wonder that Gregory shared his master's excommunication. In October, 1460, he was declared a heretic, and all the faithful were ordered to seize his property{418} and punish him. To this he responded in vigorous appeals and replications, couched in the most insolent and contemptuous language towards both Pius and Nicholas. In October, 1461, Pius sent Friar Martin of Rotenburg to preach the faith and preserve the faithful from the errors of Sigismund and his heresiarch Gregory, and, professing to believe that Martin was in personal danger, he offered an indulgence of two years and eighty days to all who would render him assistance in his need. He also ordered the magistrates of Nürnburg to seize Gregory's property and expel him or deliver him up for punishment. We next find Gregory aiding Diether, Archbishop of Cologne, in his quarrel with Pius over the unprecedented and extortionate demand of the Holy See for annates; but Diether resigned, Sigismund made his peace, and Gregory was abandoned to his excommunication, even the city of Nürnburg withdrawing its protection. He then took refuge in Bohemia with George Podiebrad, whom he served efficiently as a controversialist, earning a special denunciation as a heretic of the worst type from Paul II., in 1469; but Podiebrad died in 1471. Gregory then went to Saxony, where Duke Albert protected him and effected his reconciliation with Sixtus IV. He was absolved at Easter, 1472, only to die in the following August, after spending a quarter of a century in ceaseless combat with the papacy.[464]

If Gregory of Heimburg embodies the revolt of the ruling classes against Rome, Hans of Niklaushausen shows us the restless spirit of opposition to sacerdotalism which was spreading among the lower strata of society. Hans Böheim was a wandering drummer or fifer from Bohemia, who chanced to settle at

Niklaushausen, near Würzburg. He doubtless brought with him the revolutionary ideas of the Hussites, and he seems to have entered into an alliance with the parish priest and a Mendicant Friar or Beghard. He began to have revelations from the Virgin which suited so exactly the popular wishes that crowds speedily began to assemble to listen to him. She instructed him to announce to her people that Christ could no longer endure the pride, the avarice,{419}and the lust of the priesthood, and that the world would be destroyed in consequence of their wickedness, unless they promptly showed signs of amendment. Tithes and tribute should be purely voluntary, tolls and customs dues were to be abolished, and game was no longer to be preserved. As the fame of these revelations spread, crowds flocked to hear the inspired teacher, from the Rhinelands, Bavaria, Thuringia, Saxony, and Misnia, so that at times he addressed an audience of twenty thousand to thirty thousand souls. So great was the reverence felt for him that those who could touch him deemed themselves sanctified, and fragments of his garments were treasured as relics, so that his clothes were rent in pieces whenever he appeared, and a new suit was requisite daily. That no one doubted the truth of the Virgin's denunciations of the clergy shows the nature of the popular estimation of the Church, for the vast crowds who came eagerly to listen were by no means composed of the dangerous elements of society. They were peaceful and orderly; men and women slept in the neighboring fields and woods and caves without fear of robbery or violence; they had money to spend, moreover, for the offerings of gold and silver, jewels, garments, and wax were large—large enough, indeed, to tempt the greed of the potentates, for after the downfall of Hans the spoils were divided between the Count of Wertheim, suzerain of Niklaushausen, the Bishop of Würzburg, and his metropolitan, the Archbishop of Mainz. The latter used a portion of his plunder in building a citadel near Mainz, the destruction of which soon afterwards by fire was generally regarded as indicating the displeasure of the Virgin.

Bishop Rudolph of Würzburg repeatedly forbade the pilgrimage to Niklaushausen, but in vain, and at length he was led to take more decided steps. The great festivity of the region was the feast of St. Kilian, the martyr of Würzburg, falling on July 8. On the Sunday previous, July 6, 1476, Hans significantly told his audience to return the following Saturday armed, but to leave their women and children at home. Matters were evidently approaching a crisis, and the bishop did not wait for the result, but sent a party of guards, who seized Hans and conveyed him to a neighboring stronghold. The next day about six thousand of his deluded followers, including many women and children, set out for the castle, without arms, believing that its walls would fall at{420} their demand. They refused to disperse when summoned, but were readily scattered by a sally of men-at-arms, supported by a discharge from the cannon of the castle, in which many were slain. Hans was easily forced by torture to confess the falsity of his revelations and the deceits by which he and his confederates had stimulated the excitement by false miracles; but his confession did not avail him, and he was condemned to be burned. At the place of execution his followers expected divine interference, and to prevent enchantment the executioner shaved him from head to foot. He walked resolutely to the stake, singing a hymn, but his fortitude gave way and he shrieked in agony as the flames reached him. To prevent his ashes from being treasured as relics, they were carefully collected and cast into the river. The priest and Beghard who had served as his confederates sought safety in flight, but were caught and confessed, after which they were discharged; but two peasants—one who had suggested the advance upon the castle and one who had wounded the horse of one of the guards who captured Hans—were beheaded.[465]

If Gregory of Heimburg and Hans of Niklaushausen represent the antagonism to Rome which pervaded the laity from the highest to the lowest, John von Ruchrath of Wesel indicates that even in the Church the same spirit was not wanting. One of the most eminent theologians and preachers of whom Germany could boast, celebrated in the schools as the "Light of the World" and the "Master of Contradictions," he was a hardy and somewhat violent disputant, who in his sermons had no scruple in presenting his opinions in the most offensive shape. Like Luther, of whom he was the true precursor, he commenced by an assault upon indulgences, moved thereto by the Jubilee of 1450, when pious Europe precipitated itself upon Rome to take heaven by assault. Step by step he advanced to strip the Church of its powers, and was led to reject the authority of tradition and the fathers, recurring to Scripture as the sole basis of authority. He even banished from the creed the word "*Filioque*," and his predestinarian views deprived the Church of all the treasures of salvation. How little he recked of the feelings of those whose faith he assailed is seen in his remark that if fasting was instituted by St. Peter, it was probably to obtain a better market for his fish.{421}

It shows how rusty had become the machinery of persecution and the latitude allowed to free speech that John of Wesel was permitted so long, without interference, to ripen into a heresiarch and to disseminate from the pulpit and professorial chair these opinions, as dangerous as any emitted by Waldenses, Wickliffites, or Hussites. In fact, but for the bitter quarrel between the Realists and Nominalists, which filled the scholastic world with strife, it is probable that he would have been unmolested to the end and enabled to close his days in peace. He was a leader of the Nominalists, and the Dominican Thomists of Mainz were resolved to silence him. The Archbishop of Mainz was Diether of Isenburg, who had been forced to abandon his see in 1463, but had resumed it in 1475 on the death of his competitor, Adolph of Nassau; he did not wish another conflict with Rome, to which he was exposed in consequence of his public denunciations of the papal auctions of the archiepiscopal pallium; he was threatened with this unless he would surrender John of Wesel as a victim, and he yielded to the pressure in 1479.

In the great province of Mainz there was no inquisitor; trial by the regular episcopal officials would be of uncertain result; and as there was a Dominican inquisitor at Cologne, in the person of Friar Gerhard von Elten, he was sent for. He came, accompanied by Friar Jacob Sprenger, not yet an inquisitor, but whom we shall see hereafter in that capacity busy in burning witches. With him came the theologians from the universities of Heidelberg and Cologne, who were to sit as experts and assessors, and so carefully were they selected that one of the Heidelberg doctors, to whom we are indebted for an account of the proceedings, tells us that among them all there was but one Nominalist. He evidently regards the whole matter as an incident in the scholastic strife, and says that the accused would have been acquitted had he been allowed counsel and had he not been so harshly treated.

The proceedings are a curious travesty of the inquisitorial process, which show that, however much its forms had been forgotten, the principle was rigidly maintained of treating the accused as guilty in advance. There was no secrecy attempted; everything was conducted in an assembly consisting of laymen as well as ecclesiastics, prominent among whom we recognize the Count of Wertheim, fresh from the plunder of Hans of Niklaushausen.{422} After a preliminary meeting, when the assembly convened for business, February 8, 1479, the inquisitor von Elten presided, with Archbishop Diether under him, and opened the proceedings by suggesting that two or three friends of the accused should warn him to repent of his errors and beg for mercy, in which case he should have mercy, but otherwise not. A deputation was thereupon despatched, but their mission was not speedily performed; the inquisitor chafed at the delay, and began blustering and threatening. A high official was sent to hurry the matter, but at that moment John of Wesel entered, pallid, bent with age, leaning on his staff, and supported by two Franciscans. He was made to sit on the floor; von Elten repeated to him the message, and when he attempted to defend himself he was cut short, badgered and threatened, until he was brought to sue for pardon. After this he was put through a long and exhausting examination, and was finally remanded until the next day. A commission consisting principally of the Cologne and Heidelberg doctors was appointed to determine what should be done with him. The next day he was again brought out and examined afresh, when he endeavored to defend his views. "If all men renounce Christ," he said, "I will still worship him and be a Christian," to which von Elten retorted, "So say all heretics, even when at the stake." Finally it was resolved that three doctors should be deputed, piously to exhort him to abandon his errors. As in the case of Huss, it was not his death that was wanted, but his humiliation.

On the 10th the deputies labored with him. "If Christ were here," he told them, "and were treated like me, you would condemn him as a heretic—but he would get the better of you with his subtlety." At length he was persuaded to acknowledge that his views were erroneous, on the deputies agreeing to take the responsibility on their own consciences. He had long been sick when the trial was commenced, all assistance was withheld from him; age, weakness, and the dark and filthy dungeon from which he had vainly begged to be relieved broke down his powers of resistance, and he submitted. He publicly recanted and abjured, his books were burned before his face, and he was sentenced to imprisonment for life in the Augustinian monastery of Mainz. He did not long survive his mortification and misery, for he died in 1481. The trial excited great interest among the scholars{423} of Germany, who were shocked at this treatment of a man so eminent and distinguished. Yet his writings survived him and proved greatly encouraging to the early Reformers. Melanchthon enumerates him among those who by their works kept up the continuity of the Church of Christ.[466]

It is evident from this case that the Inquisition, though not extinct in Germany, was not in working order, and that even where it existed nominally a special effort was requisite to make it function. Still we hear occasionally of the appointment of inquisitors, and from the career of Sprenger we know that their labors could be fruitfully directed to the extirpation of witchcraft. Sorcery, indeed, had become the most threatening heresy of the time, and other spiritual aberrations were attracting little attention. In the elaborate statutes issued by the Synod of Bamberg, in 1491, the section devoted to heresy dwells at much length on the details of witchcraft and magic, and mentions only one other doctrinal error—the vitiation of sacraments in polluted hands—and it directs that all who neglect to denounce heretics are to be themselves treated as accomplices, but it makes no allusion to the Inquisition. Still there is an occasional manifestation showing that inquisitors existed and sometimes exercised their powers. I shall hereafter have occasion to refer to the case of Herman of Ryswick, who was condemned and abjured in 1499, escaped from prison, and was burned as a relapsed by the inquisitor at The Hague, in 1512, and only allude to it here as an evidence of continued inquisitorial activity.[467]

The persecution of John Reuchlin, like that of John of Wesel, sprang from scholastic antagonisms, but its development shows how completely, during the interval, the inquisitorial power had wasted away. Reuchlin was a pupil of John Wessel of Groningen; as the leader of the Humanists, and the foremost representative in Germany of the new learning, he was involved in bitter controversy with the Dominicans, who, as traditional Thomists, were ready to do battle to the death for scholasticism. The ferocious{424} jocularity with which Sebastian Brandt dilates, in his most finished Latinity, upon the torture and burning of four Dominicans at Berne, in 1509, for frauds committed in the controversy over the Immaculate Conception, indicates the temper which animated the hostile parties, even as its lighter aspect is seen in the unsparing satire of Erasmus and of the *Epistolæ Obscurorum Virorum*. When, therefore, Reuchlin stood forward to protect Jews and Jewish literature against the assaults of the renegade Pfefferkorn, the opportunity to destroy him was eagerly seized. In 1513 a Dominican inquisitor, the Prior Jacob von Hochstraten, came from Cologne to Mainz on an errand precisely similar to that of his predecessor von Elten. Unlike John of Wesel, however, Reuchlin felt that he could safely appeal to Rome, where Leo X. was himself a man of culture and a Humanist. Leo was well disposed, and commissioned the Bishop of Speier to decide the question, which was in itself a direct blow at the inquisitorial power. Still more contemptuously damaging was the bishop's judgment. Reuchlin was declared free of all suspicion of heresy, the prosecution was pronounced frivolous, and the costs were put upon Hochstraten, with a threat of excommunication for disobedience. This was confirmed at Rome, in 1415, where silence was imposed on Reuchlin's accusers under a penalty of three thousand marks. The Humanists celebrated their victory with savage rejoicing. Eleutherius Bizenus printed a tract summoning, in rugged hexameters, all Germany to assist in the triumph of Reuchlin, in which Hochstraten—that thief, who as accuser and judge persecutes the innocent—marches in chains, with his hands tied behind his back, while Pfefferkorn, with ears and nose cut off, is dragged by a hook through his heels, face downwards, until his features lose the semblance of humanity. The Dominicans are characterized as worse than Turks, and more worthy to be resisted, and the author wonders what unjust pope and cowardly emperor had enabled them to impose their yoke on the land. These were brave words, but premature. The quarrel had attracted the attention of all Europe, the Dominican Order itself and all it represented were on trial, and it could not afford to submit to defeat. Hochstraten hastened to Rome; the Dominicans of the great University of Cologne did not hesitate to say that if the pope maintained the sentence they would appeal to the future council, they would refuse to abide by{425} his decision, they would pronounce him to be no pope and organize a schism, and much more, which shows upon what a slender tenure the papacy held the allegiance of its Janissaries. Leo cowered before the storm which he had provoked, and in 1416 he issued a mandate superseding the sentence, but the spirit of insubordination was growing strong in Germany, and Franz von Sickingen, the free-lance, compelled its observance. As the Lutheran revolt grew more threatening, however, the support of the Dominicans became more and more indispensable, and in 1420 Leo settled the matter by setting aside the decision of the Bishop of Speier, imposing silence on Reuchlin, and laying all the costs on him. Hochstraten, moreover, was restored to his office.[468]

The reparation came too late to render the Inquisition of any service, now that its efficiency was more sorely needed than ever before. Had it existed in Germany in good working order, Luther's career would have been short. When, October 31, 1517, he nailed his propositions concerning indulgences on the church-door of Wittenberg, and publicly defended them, an inquisitor such as Bernard Gui would have speedily silenced him, either destroying his influence by forcing him to a public recantation, or handing him over to be burned if he proved obstinate. Hundreds of hardy thinkers had been thus served, and the few who had been found stout enough to withstand the methods of the Holy Office had perished. Fortunately, as we have seen, the Inquisition never had struck root in German soil, and now it was thoroughly discredited and useless. Hochstraten's hands were tied; Doctor John Eck, inquisitor for Bavaria and Franconia, was himself a Humanist, who could argue and threaten, but could not act.

In France the University had taken the place of the almost forgotten Inquisition, repressing all aberrations of faith, while a centralized monarchy had rendered—at least until the Concordat of Francis I.—the national Church in a great degree independent of the papacy. In Germany there was no national Church; there was subjection to Rome which was growing unendurable for{426} financial reasons, but there was nothing to take the place of the Inquisition, and a latitude of speech had become customary which was tolerated so long as the revenues of St. Peter were not interfered with. This perhaps explains why the significance of Luther's revolt was better appreciated at Rome than on the spot. After he had been formally declared a heretic by the Auditor-general of the Apostolic Chamber at the instance of the promoter fiscal, the legate, Cardinal Caietano, wrote that he could terminate the matter himself, and that it was rather a trifling affair to be brought before the pope. He did not fulfil his instructions to arrest Luther and tell him that if he would appear before the Holy See, to excuse himself, he would be treated with undeserved clemency. After the scandal had been growing for a twelvemonth, Leo again wrote to Caietano to summon Doctor Martin before him, and, after diligent examination, to condemn or absolve him as might prove requisite. It was now too late. Insubordination had spread, and rebellion was organizing itself. Before these last instructions reached Caietano, Luther came in answer to a previous summons, but, though he professed himself in all things an obedient son of the Church, he practically manifested an ominous independence, and was conveyed away unharmed. The legate trusted to his powers as a disputant rather than to force; and had he attempted the latter, he had no machinery at hand to frustrate the instructions given by the Augsburg magistrates for Luther's protection. In the paralysis of persecution the inevitable revolution went forward.[469]{427}

<h2 style="text-align:center">CHAPTER VII.</h2>

<h3 style="text-align:center">BOHEMIA.</h3>

THERE is no historical foundation for the legend that Peter Waldo's missionary labors carried him into Bohemia, where he died, but there can be no question that the Waldensian heresy found a foothold among the Czechs at a comparatively early date. Bohemia formed part of the great archiepiscopal province of Mainz, whose metropolitan could exercise but an ineffective supervision over a district so distant. The supremacy of Rome pressed lightly on its turbulent ecclesiastics. In the last decade of the twelfth century a papal legate, Cardinal Pietro, sent thither to levy a tithe for the recovery of the Holy Land, was scandalized to find that the law of

142

celibacy was unknown to the secular priesthood; he did not venture to force it on those already in orders, and his efforts to make postulants take the vow of continence provoked a tumult which required severe measures of suppression. In a Church thus partially independent the abuses which stimulated revolt elsewhere might perhaps be absent, but the field for missionary labor lay open and unguarded.[470]

We have seen how the Inquisitor of Passau, about the middle of the thirteenth century, describes the flourishing condition of the Waldensian churches in Austria, along the borders of Bohemia and Moravia, and the intense zeal of propagandism which animated their members. Close to the west, moreover, they were to be found in the diocese of Ratisbon. That the heresy should cross the boundary line was inevitable, and it ran little risk of detection and persecution by a worldly and slothful priesthood, until it gained strength enough to declare itself openly. The alarm was first sounded by Innocent IV. in 1245, who summoned the prelates {428} of Hungary to intervene, as those of Bohemia apparently were not to be depended upon, and there was evidently no inquisitorial machinery which could be employed. Innocent describes the heresy as established so firmly and widely that it embraced not only the simple folk, but also princes and magnates, and it was so elaborately organized that it had a chief who was reverenced as pope. These are all declared excommunicate, their lands confiscated for the benefit of the first occupant, and any who shall relapse after recantation are to be abandoned to the secular arm without a hearing, in accordance with the canons.[471]

We have no means of knowing whether any action was taken in consequence of this decree, but if efforts were made they did not succeed in eradicating the heresy. In 1257 King Premysl Otokar II. applied to Alexander IV. for aid in its suppression, as it continued to spread, and to this request was due the first introduction of the Inquisition in Bohemia. Two Franciscans, Lambert the German and Bartholomew lector in Brünn, received the papal commission as inquisitors throughout Bohemia and Moravia. It is fair to assume that they did their duty, but no traces of their activity have reached us, nor is there any evidence that their places were filled when they died or retired. The Inquisition may be considered as non-existent, and when, after a long interval, we again hear of persecution, it is in a shape that shows that the Bishop of Prague, like his metropolitan of Mainz, was not disposed to invite papal encroachments on his jurisdiction. In 1301 a synod of Prague deplored the spread of heresy and ordered every one cognizant of it to give information to the episcopal inquisitors, from which we may infer that heretics were active, that they had been little disturbed, and that the elaborate legislation {429} elsewhere in force for the detection and punishment of heresy was virtually unknown in Bohemia.[472]

In 1318 John of Drasic, the Bishop of Prague, was summoned to Avignon by John XXII. to answer accusations brought against him by Frederic of Schönberg, Canon of Wyschehrad, as a fautor of heresy. The complaint set forth that heretics were so numerous that they had an archbishop and seven bishops, each of whom had three hundred disciples. The description of their faith would seem to indicate that there were both Waldenses and Luciferans—the latter forming part of the sect which we have seen described about this time as flourishing in Austria, where they are said to have been introduced by missionaries from Bohemia—and that their doctrines have been commingled. They are described as considering oaths unlawful; confession and absolution could be administered indifferently by layman or priest; rebaptism was allowed; the divine unity and the resurrection of the dead were denied; Jesus had only a phantasmic body; and Lucifer was expected finally to reign. Of course there were also the customary accusations of sexual excesses committed in nocturnal assemblies held in caverns, which only proves that there was sufficient dread of persecution to prevent the congregations from meeting openly. The good bishop, it appears, only permitted these wretches to be arraigned by his inquisitors after repeated pressure from John of Luxemburg, the king. Fourteen of them were convicted and handed over to the secular arm, but the bishop interfered, to the great disgust of the king, and forcibly released them, except a physician named Richard, who was imprisoned; the bishop, moreover, discharged the inquisitors, who evidently were his own officials and not papal appointees. These were serious offences on the part of a prelate, and he expiated his lenity by a confinement of several years in Avignon. Possibly his hostility to the Franciscans may have rendered him an object of attack.[473]

Papal attention being thus called to the existence of heresy in {430} the east of Europe, and to the inefficiency of the local machinery for its extermination, steps were immediately taken for the introduction of the Inquisition. In 1318 John XXII. commissioned the Dominican Peregrine of Oppolza and the Franciscan Nicholas of Cracow as inquisitors in the dioceses of Cracow and Breslau, while Bohemia and Poland were intrusted to the Dominican Colda and the Franciscan Hartmann. As usual, the secular and ecclesiastical powers were commanded to afford them assistance whenever called upon. Poland, doubtless, was as much in need as Bohemia of inquisitorial supervision, for John Muscata, the Bishop of Cracow, was as negligent as his brother of Prague, and drew upon himself in 1319 severe reprehension from John XXII. for the sloth and neglect which had rendered heresy bold and aggressive in his diocese. This does not seem to have accomplished much, for in 1327 John found himself obliged to order the Dominican Provincial of Poland to appoint inquisitors to stem the flood of heresy which was infecting the people from regions farther west. Germany and Bohemia apparently were sending missionaries, whose labors met with much acceptance among the people. King Ladislas was especially asked to lend his aid to the inquisitors; he promptly responded by ordering the governors of his cities to support them with the civil power, and their vigorous action was rewarded with abundant success.[474]

Among these heretics there may have been Brethren of the Free Spirit, but they were probably for the most part Waldenses, who at this time had a thoroughly organized Church in Bohemia, whence emissaries were sent to Moravia, Saxony, Silesia, and Poland. They regarded Lombardy as their headquarters, to which they sent their youth for instruction, together with moneys collected for the support of the parent Church. All this could not be concealed from the vigilance of the inquisitors appointed by John XXII. No doubt active measures of repression were carried out with little intermission, though chance has only preserved an indication of inquisitorial proceedings about the year 1330. Saaz and Laun are mentioned as the cities in which heresy was most prevalent. With the open rupture between the papacy and Louis{431} of Bavaria its repression became more difficult, although Bohemia under John of Luxembourg remained faithful to the Holy See. Heretics increased in Prague and its neighborhood; after a brief period of activity the Inquisition seems to have disappeared; John of Drasic, whose tolerance we have seen, was still Bishop of Prague, and fresh efforts were necessary. In 1335 Benedict XII. accordingly appointed the Franciscan Peter Naczeracz as inquisitor in the diocese of Olmütz and the Dominican Gall of Neuburg for that of Prague. As usual, all prelates were commanded to lend their aid, and King John was specially reminded that he held the temporal sword for the purpose of subduing the enemies of the faith. His son, the future Emperor Charles IV., at that time in charge of the kingdom, was similarly appealed to.[475]

In the subject province of Silesia, about the same period, a bold heresiarch known as John of Pirna made a deep impression. He was probably a Fraticello, as he taught that the pope was Antichrist and Rome the Whore of Babylon and a synagogue of Satan. In Breslau the magistrates and people espoused his doctrines, which were openly preached in the streets. Breslau was ecclesiastically subject to Poland, and in 1341 John of Schweidnitz was commissioned from Cracow as inquisitor to suppress the growing heresy. The people, however, arose, drove out their bishop and slew the inquisitor, for which they were subsequently subjected to humiliating penance, and John of Pirna's bones were exhumed and burned. The unsatisfied vengeance of Heaven added to their punishment by a conflagration which destroyed nearly the whole city, during which a pious woman saw an angel with a drawn sword casting fiery coals among the houses.[476]

Bohemia and its subject provinces were thus thoroughly infected with heresy, mostly Waldensian, when several changes took place which increased the prominence of the kingdom and stimulated vastly its intellectual activity. In 1344 Prague was separated from its far-off metropolis of Mainz and was erected into an archbishopric, for which the piety of Charles, then Margrave of Bohemia, provided a zealous and enlightened prelate in{432} the person of Arnest of Pardubitz. Two years later, in 1346, Charles was elected King of the Romans by the Electors of Trèves and Cologne in opposition to Louis of Bavaria, as the supporter of the papacy; and a month later he succeeded to the throne of Bohemia through the knightly death of the blind King John at Crécy. Still more influential and far-reaching in its results was the founding in 1347 of the University of Prague, to which the combined favor of pope and emperor gave immediate lustre. Archbishop Arnest assumed its chancellorship, learned schoolmen filled its chairs; students flocked to it from every quarter, and it soon rivalled in numbers and reputation its elder sisters of Oxford, Paris, and Bologna.[477]

During the latter half of the century, Bohemia, under these auspices, was one of the most flourishing kingdoms of Europe. Its mines of the precious metals gave it wealth; the freedom enjoyed by its peasantry raised them mentally and morally above the level of the serfs of other lands; culture and enlightenment were diffused from its university. It was renowned throughout the Continent for the splendor of its churches, which in size and number were nowhere exceeded. At the monastery of Königsaal, where the Bohemian kings lay buried, around the walls of the garden the whole of the Scriptures, from Genesis to Revelations, was engraved, with letters enlarging in size with their distance from the ground, so that all could be easily read. In the bitter struggles of after generations the reign of King Charles was fondly looked back upon as the golden age of Bohemia. Wealth and culture, however, were accompanied with corruption. Nowhere were the clergy more worldly and depraved. Concubinage was well-nigh universal, and simony pervaded the Church in all its ranks, the sacraments were sold and penitence compounded for. All the abuses for which clerical immunity furnished opportunity nourished, and the land was overrun by vagrants whose tonsure gave them charter to rob and brawl, and dice and drink. The influences from above which moulded the Bohemian Church may be estimated from a single instance. In 1344 Clement VI. wrote to Arnest, then simple Bishop of Prague,{433} calling attention to the numerous cases in his diocese wherein preferment had been procured for minors either by force or simony. The horror which the good pope expresses at this abuse is significantly illustrated by his having not long before issued dispensations to five members of one family in France, aged respectively seven, eight, nine, ten, and eleven years, to hold canonries and other benefices. Apparently the Bohemians had not taken the proper means to obtain the sanction of the curia for such infraction of the canons, so Clement ordered Arnest to dispossess the incumbents in all such cases, and to impose due penance on them. But he was also instructed, in conjunction with the papal collector, to force them to compound with the papal camera for all the revenues which they had thus illegally received, and after they had undergone this squeezing process he was authorized to reinstate them.[478]

Such unblushing exhibitions of rapacious simony did not tend either to the purity of the Bohemian Church, or to enhance its respect for the Holy See, especially as the frequently recurring papal exactions strained to the last degree the relations between the papacy and the German churches. When, in 1354, Innocent VI., to carry on his Italian wars, suddenly demanded a tenth of all the ecclesiastical revenues of the empire, it threw, for several years, the whole German Church into an uproar of rage and indignation. Some prelates refused to pay, and, when legal proceedings were commenced against them, formulated appeals which were contemptuously rejected as frivolous. The Bishops of Camin and Brandenburg were only compelled to yield by the direct threat of excommunication. Others pleaded poverty, and were mockingly reminded of the large sums which they had succeeded in exacting from their miserable subjects; others made the best bargain they could, and compounded for yearly payments; others banded together and formed associations mutually pledged to resist{434} to the last. Frederic, Bishop of Ratisbon, took the audacious step of seizing the papal collector and conveying him away to a convenient castle. An ambush was laid for the Bishop of Cavaillon, the papal nuncio charged with the business, and his life, and that of his assistant, Henry, Archdeacon of Liége, were only saved by the active interposition of William, Archbishop of Cologne. When, in 1372, the levy was repeated by Gregory XI., the same spirit of resistance was aroused. The clergy of Mainz bound themselves to each other in a solemn engagement not to pay it, and Frederic, Archbishop of Cologne, promised his clergy to give them all the assistance he safely could in their refusal to submit. Trifling incidents such as these afford us a valuable insight into the complex relations between the Holy See and the churches of Christendom. On the one hand, there was the superstitious awe generated by five centuries of unquestioned domination as the representative of Christ, and there was, moreover, the dread of the material consequences of unsuccessful revolt. On the other, there was the indignation born of lawless oppression ever exciting to rebellion, and the clear-sighted recognition of the venality and corruption which rendered the Roman curia a source of contagion for all Europe. There was ample inflammable material, which the increasing friction might at any moment kindle into flame.[479]

Bohemia was peculiarly dangerous soil, for it was thoroughly interpenetrated with the leaven of heresy. We hear nothing of papal inquisitors after those commissioned by Benedict XII. in 1335, and it is presumable that for a while the heretics had peace. Archbishop Arnest, however, soon after his accession, set resolutely to work to purify the morals of his Church and to uproot heresy. He held synods frequently, he instituted a body of Correctors whose duty it was to visit all portions of the province and punish all transgressions, and he organized an episcopal Inquisition for the purpose of tracking out and suppressing heresy. In the fragmentary remains of his synodal acts, the frequency and earnestness with which this latter duty is insisted upon serve as a measure of its importance, and of the numbers of those who had{435} forsaken the Church. In the earliest synod whose proceedings have reached us the first place is given to this subject; the archdeacons were directed to make diligent perquisition in their respective districts, both personally and through the deans and parish priests, without exciting suspicion, and all who were found guilty or suspect of heresy were to be forthwith denounced to the archbishop or the inquisitor. Similar instructions were issued in 1355; and after Arnest's death, in 1364, his successor, John Ocko, was equally vigilant, as appears from the acts of his synods in 1366 and 1371. The neighborhood of Pisek was especially contaminated, and from the acts of the Consistory of 1381 it appears that a priest named Johl, of Pisek, could not be ordained because both his father and grandfather had been heretics. What was this heresy that thus descended from generation to generation is not stated, but it was doubtless Waldensian. In this same year Archbishop John, as papal legate for his own province and for the dioceses of Ratisbon, Bamberg, and Misnia, held a council at Prague, in which he mournfully described the spread of the Waldenses and Sarabites—the latter probably Beghards. He sharply reproved the bishops who, through sloth or parsimony, had not appointed inquisitors, and threatened that if they did not do so forthwith, he would do it himself. When, ten years later, the Church took the alarm and acted vigorously, the Waldenses of Brandenburg, who were prosecuted, declared that their teachers came from Bohemia.[480]

In all this activity for the suppression of heresy it is worthy of note that the episcopal Inquisition alone is referred to. In fact there was no papal Inquisition in Bohemia. The bull of Gregory XI., in 1372, ordering the appointment of five inquisitors for Germany, confines their jurisdiction to the provinces of Cologne, Mainz, Utrecht, Magdeburg, Salzburg, and Bremen, and pointedly omits that of Prague, although the zeal of Charles IV. might have been expected to secure the blessings of the institution for his hereditary realm.[481] This is the more curious, moreover,{436} since the intellectual movement started by the University of Prague was producing a number of men distinguished not only for learning and piety, but for their bold attacks on the corruptions of the Church, and their questioning of some of its most profitable dogmas. The appearance of these precursors of Huss is one of the most remarkable indications of the tendencies of the age in Bohemia, and shows how the Waldensian spirit of revolt had unconsciously spread among the population.

Conrad of Waldhausen, who died in 1369, is reckoned the earliest of these. He maintained strict orthodoxy, but his denunciation in his sermons of the vices of the clergy, and especially of the Mendicants, created a deep sensation. More prominent in every way was Milicz of Kremsier, who, in 1363, resigned the office of private secretary to the emperor, the function of Corrector intrusted to him by Archbishop Arnest, and several rich preferments, in order to devote himself exclusively to preaching. His sermons in Czech, German, and Latin were filled with audacious attacks on the sins and crimes of clergy and laity, and the evils of the time led him to prophesy the advent of Antichrist between 1365 and 1367. In the latter year he went to Rome in order to lay before Urban V. his views on the present and future of the Church. While awaiting Urban's advent from Avignon, he affixed on the portal of St. Peter's an announcement of a sermon on the subject, which led the Inquisition to throw him into prison, but in October, on the arrival of the pope, he was released and treated with distinction. On his return to Prague he preached with greater violence than ever. To get rid of him the priesthood accused him to the emperor and archbishop, but in vain. Then they formulated twelve articles of accusation against him to the pope, and obtained, in January, 1374, from Gregory XI., bulls denouncing him as a persistent heresiarch who had filled all Bohemia, Poland, Silesia, and the neighboring lands with his errors. According to them, he taught not only that Antichrist had come, that the Church was extinct, that pope, cardinals, bishops and prelates showed no light of truth, but he permitted to his followers the unlimited gratification of their passions. Milicz undauntedly pursued his course until an inquisitorial prosecution was commenced against him, when he appealed to the pope. In Lent, 1374, he went to Avignon, where he readily proved his{437} innocence, and on May 21 was admitted to preach before the cardinals, but he died June 29, before the formal decision of his case was published. It is highly probable that he was a Joachite—one of those who, as we shall see hereafter, reverenced the memory and believed in the apocalyptic prophecies of the Abbot Joachim of Flora.[482]

The spirit of indignation and disquiet did not confine itself to denunciations of clerical abuses. Men were growing bolder, and began to question some of the cherished dogmas which gave rise to those abuses. In the synod of 1384 one of the subjects discussed was whether the saints were cognizant of the prayers addressed to them, and whether the worshipper was benefited by their suffrages—the mere raising of such a question showing how dangerously bold had become the spirit of inquiry. The man who most fitly represented this tendency was Mathias of Janow, whom the Archbishop John of Jenzenstein utilized in his efforts to reform the incurable disorders of the clergy. Mathias was led to trace the troubles to their causes, and to teach heresies from the consequences of which even the protection of the archbishop could not wholly defend him. In the synod of 1389 he was forced to make public recantation of his errors in holding that the images of Christ and the saints gave rise to idolatry, and that they ought to be banished from the churches and burned; that relics were of no service, and the intercession of saints was useless; while his teaching that every one should be urged to take communion daily foreshadowed the eucharistic troubles which play so large a part in the Hussite excitement. Yet he was allowed to escape with six months" suspension from preaching and hearing confessions outside of his own parochial church, a mistaken lenity which he repaid by continuing to teach the same errors more audaciously than ever, and even urging that the laity be admitted to communion in both elements. Mathias was not alone in his heterodoxy, for in the same synod of 1389 a priest named Andreas was obliged to revoke the same heresy respecting images, and another named Jacob was suspended from preaching for ten years for a still more offensive expression of similar beliefs, with the addition{438} that suffrages for the dead were useless, that the Virgin could not help her devotees, and that the archbishop had erred in granting an indulgence to those who adored her image, and that the utterances of the holy doctors of the Church are not to be received.[483]

Other earnest men who prepared the way for what was to follow were Henry of Oyta, Thomas of Stitny, John of Stekno, and Matthew of Cracow. Step by step the progress of free thought advanced, and when, in 1393, a papal indulgence was preached in Prague, Wenceslas Rohle, pastor of St. Martin's in the Altstadt, ventured to denounce it as a fraud, though only under his breath, for fear of the Pharisees. All this, it is evident, could only be favorable to the growth of Waldensianism, as is seen in the activity of the sectaries. It was missionaries from Bohemia who founded the communities in Brandenburg and Pomerania; and, as we have seen, a well-informed writer, in 1395, asserts that they were numbered by thousands in Thuringia, Misnia, Bohemia, Moravia, Austria, and Hungary, notwithstanding that a thousand of them had been converted within two years in the districts extending from Thuringia to Moravia.[484]

While Bohemia was thus the scene of an agitation the outcome of which no man could foretell, a similar movement was running a still more rapid course in England, which was destined to exercise a decisive influence on the result. The assaults of John Wickliff were the most serious danger encountered by the hierarchy since the Hildebrandine theocracy had been established. For the first time a trained scholastic intellect of remarkable force and clearness, informed with all the philosophy and theology of the schools, was led to question the domination which the Church had acquired over the life, here and hereafter, of its members. It was not the poor peasant or artisan who found the Scriptures in contradiction to the teaching of the pulpit and the confessional, and with the practical examples set by the sacerdotal class; but it was a man who stood in learning and argumentative power on{439} a level with the foremost schoolmen of the Middle Ages; who could quote not only Christ and the apostles, but the fathers and doctors of the Church, the decretals and the canons, Aristotle and his commentators; who could weave all these into the dialectics so dear to students and masters of theology, and who could frame a system of philosophy suited to the intellectual wants of the age. It is true that William of Ockham had been bold in his attacks on the overgrown papal system, but he was a partisan of Louis of Bavaria, and, with Marsiglio of Padua, his aim had merely been to set the State above the Church. With the subjection of the empire to the papacy the works of both had perished and their labors had been forgotten. The infidelity of the Averrhoists had never taken root among the people, and had been wisely treated by the Church with the leniency of contempt. It was the secret of Wickliff's influence that he had worked out his conclusions in single-hearted efforts to search for truth; his views developed gradually as he was led from one point to another; he spared neither prince nor prelate; he labored to instruct the poor more zealously perhaps than to influence the great, and men of all ranks, from the peasant to the schoolman, recognized in him a leader who sought to make them better, stronger, more valiant in the struggle with Apollyon. It is no wonder that his work proved not merely ephemeral; that his fame as a heresiarch filled all the schools and became everywhere synonymous with rebellion against the sacerdotal system; that simple Waldenses in Spain and Germany became thereafter known as Wickliffites. Yet the endurance of his teachings was due to his Bohemian disciples; at home, after a brief period of rapid development, they were virtually crushed out by the combined power of Church and State.

As the heresy of Huss was in nearly all details copied from his master, Wickliff, it is necessary, in order to understand the nature of the Hussite movement, to cast a brief glance at the views of the English reformer. About four years after his death, in 1388 and 1389, twenty-five articles of accusation were brought against his followers, whose reply gives, in the most vigorous English, a summary of his tenets. Few documents of the period are more interesting as a picture of the worldliness and corruption of the Church, and of the wrathful indignation aroused by the hideous contrast between the teaching of Christ and the lives of those who{440} claimed to represent him. It is observable that the only purely speculative error admitted is that concerning the Eucharist; all the others relate to the doctrines which gave to the Church control over the souls and purses of the faithful, or to the abuses arising from the worldly and sensual character of the clergy. It was an essentially practical reform, inspired for the most part with rare common-sense and with wonderfully little exaggeration, considering the magnitude of the evils which pressed so heavily upon Christendom.

The document in question shows the Wickliffite belief to be that the popes of the period were Antichrist; all the hierarchy, from the pope down, were accursed by reason of their greed, their simony, their cruelty, their lust of power, and their evil lives. Unless they give satisfaction "thai schul be depper dampned then Judas Scarioth." The pope was not to be obeyed, his decretals were naught, and his excommunication and that of his bishops were to be disregarded. The indulgences so freely proffered in return for money or for the services of crusaders in slaying Christians were false and fraudulent. Yet the power of the keys in pious hands was not denied—"Certes, as holy prestis of lyvynge and cunnynge of holy writte han keyes of heven and bene vicaris of Jesus Crist, so viciouse prestis, unkonnynge of holy writte, ful of pride and covetise, han keyes of helle and bene vicaris of Sathanas." Though auricular confession might be useful, it was not necessary, for men should trust in Christ. Image-worship was unlawful, and representations of the Trinity were forbidden—"Hit semes that this offrynge ymages is a sotile cast of Antichriste and his clerkis for to drawe almes fro pore men.... Certis, these ymages of hemselfe may do nouther gode nor yvel to mennis soules, but thai myghtten warme a man's body in colde if thai were sette upon a fire." The invocation of saints was useless; the best of them could do nothing but what God ordained, and many of those customarily invoked were in hell, for in modern times sinners stood a better chance of canonization than holy men. It was the same with their feast-days; those of the apostles and early saints might be observed, but not the rest. Song was not to be used in divine service, and prayer was as efficient anywhere as in church, for the churches were not holy-{441}-"all suche chirches bene gretely poluted and cursud of God, nomely for sellynge of leccherie and fals swering upon bokus. Sithen tho chirches bene dunnus of thefis and habitacionis of fendis." Ecclesiastics must not live in luxury and pomp, but as poor men "gyvynge ensaumple of holynes by ther conversacion." The Church must be deprived of all its temporalities, and whatever was necessary for the support of its members must be held in common. Tithes and offerings were not to be given to sinful priests; it was simony for a priest to receive payment for his spiritual ministrations, though he might sell his labor in honest vocations, such as teaching and the binding of books, and though no one was forbidden to make an oblation at mass, provided he did not seek to obtain more than his share in the sacrifice. All parish priests and vicars who did not perform their functions were to be removed, and especially all who were non-resident. All priests and deacons, moreover, were to preach zealously, for which no special license or commission was required.

All these tenets of which they were accused the Wickliffites admitted and defended in the most incisive fashion, but there were two articles which they denied. Wickliff's teaching so closely resembled that of the Waldenses that it was natural that the orthodox should attribute to him the two Waldensian errors which regarded all oaths as unlawful, and held that priests in mortal sin could not administer the sacraments. To the former, his followers replied that, though they rejected all unnecessary swearing, they admitted that "If hit be nedeful for to swere for a spedful treuthe men mowe wele swere as God did in the olde lawe." As to the latter, they said that the sinful priest can give sacraments efficient to those who worthily receive them, though he receive damnation unto himself. The prominence of the Fraticelli also suggested the imputation that the Wickliffites believed the entire renunciation of property to be essential to salvation; but this they denied, saying that a man might make lawful gains and hold them, but that he must use them well.{485}

All these antisacerdotal teachings flowed directly from the{442} resoluteness with which Wickliff carried out to its logical conclusion the Augustinian doctrine of predestination, thus necessarily striking at the root of all human mediation, the suffrages of the saints, justification by works, and all the machinery of the Church for the purchase and sale of salvation. In this, as in the rest, Huss followed him, though the distinction between his principles and the orthodox ones of the Thomists and other schoolmen was too subtle to render this point one which the Church could easily condemn.{486}

The one serious speculative error of Wickliff lay in his effort to reconcile the mystery of the Eucharist with the stubborn fact that after consecration the bread remained bread and the wine continued to be wine. He did not deny conversion into the body and blood of Christ; they were really present in the sacrifice, but his reason refused to acknowledge transubstantiation, and he invented a theory of the remanence of the substance coexisting with the divine elements. Into these dangerous subtleties Huss refused to follow his master. It was the one point on which he declined to accept the reasoning of the Englishman, and yet, as we shall see, it served as a principal excuse for hurrying him to the stake.

Wickliff's career as a heresiarch was unexampled, and its peculiarities serve to explain much that would otherwise be incomprehensible in the growth and tolerance of his doctrines in Bohemia, and in the simplicity with which Huss refused to believe that he could himself be regarded as a heretic. Although, as early as 1377, the assistance which Wickliff rendered to Edward III. in diminishing the papal revenues moved Gregory XI. to command his immediate prosecution as a heretic, yet the political situation was such as to render ineffectual all efforts to carry out these instructions; he was never even excommunicated, and was allowed to die peacefully in his rectory of Lutterworth on the last day of the year 1384. No further action was taken by Rome until the question of his heresy was raised in Prague. Although, in 1409, {443} Alexander V. ordered Archbishop Zbinco not to permit his errors to be taught or his books to be read, yet when, in 1410, John XXIII. referred his writings to a commission of four cardinals, who convoked an assembly of theologians for their examination, a majority decided that Archbishop Zbinko had not been justified in burning them. It was not until the Council of Rome, in 1413, that there was a formal and authoritative condemnation pronounced, and it was left for the Council of Constance, in 1415, to proclaim Wickliff as a heresiarch, to order his bones exhumed, and to define his errors with the authority of the Church Universal. Huss might well, to the last, believe in the authenticity of the spurious letters of the University of Oxford, brought to Prague about 1403, in which Wickliff was declared perfectly orthodox, and might conscientiously assert that his books continued to be read and taught there.[487]

The marriage of Anne of Luxemburg, sister of Wenceslas of Bohemia, to Richard II., in 1382, led to considerable intercourse between the kingdoms until her death, in 1394. Many Bohemians visited England during the excitement caused by Wickliff's controversies, and his writings were carried to Prague, where they found great acceptance. Huss tells us that about 1390 they commenced to be read in the University of Prague, and that they continued thenceforth to be studied. No orthodox Bohemian had hitherto ventured as far as the daring Englishman, but there were many who had entered on the same path, to say nothing of the secret Waldensian heretics, and the general feeling excited throughout Germany by the reckless simony and sale of indulgences which marked the later years of Boniface IX. Thus the movement which had been in progress since the middle of the century received a fresh impulsion from the circumstances under which the works of Wickliff were perused and scattered abroad in innumerable copies. All of his treatises were eagerly sought for. A MS. in the Hofbliothek of Vienna gives a catalogue of ninety of them which {444} were known in Bohemia, and it is to those regions that we must look for the remains of his voluminous labors, the greater part of which were successfully suppressed at home. In time he came to be reverenced as the fifth Evangelist, and a fragment of stone from his tomb was venerated at Prague as a relic. Still more suggestive of his commanding influence is the fidelity with which Huss followed his reasoning, and oftentimes the arrangement, and even the words, of his treatises.[488]

John of Husinec, commonly known as Huss, who became the leading exponent and protomartyr of Wickliffitism in Bohemia, is supposed to have been born in 1369, of parents whose poverty forced him to earn his own livelihood. In 1393 he obtained the degree of bachelor of arts; in 1394 that of bachelor of theology; in 1396 that of master of arts; but the doctorate he never attained, though in 1398 he was already lecturing in the university; in 1401 he was dean of the philosophical faculty, and rector in 1402. Curiously enough, he embraced the Realist philosophy, and won great applause in his combats with the Nominalists. So little promise did his early years give of his career as a reformer that, in 1392, he spent his last four groschen for an indulgence, when he had only dry crusts for food. In 1400 he was ordained as priest, and two years later he was appointed preacher to the Bethlehem chapel, where his earnest eloquence soon rendered him the spiritual leader of the people. The study of Wickliff's writings, begun shortly after this, quickened his appreciation of the evils of a corrupted Church, and when Archbishop Zbinco of Hasenburg, shortly after his consecration in 1403, appointed him as preacher to the annual synods, Huss improved the opportunity to address to the assembled clergy a series of terrible invectives against their worldliness and filthiness of living, which excited general popular hatred and contempt for them. After one of peculiar vigor, in October, 1407, the clamor among the ecclesiastics grew so strong that they presented a formal complaint against him to Archbishop Zbinco, and he was deprived of the position. {445} By this time he was recognized as the leader in the effort to purify the Church, and to reduce it to its ancient simplicity, with such men as Stephen Palecz, Stanislas of Znaim, John of Jessinetz, Jerome of Prague, and many others eminent for learning and piety as his collaborators. To some of these he was inferior in intellectual gifts, but his fearless temper, his unbending rectitude, his blameless life, and his kindly nature won for him the affectionate veneration of the people and rendered him its idol.[489]

Discussion grew hot and passions became embittered. Old jealousies and hatreds between the Teutonic and Czech races contributed to render the religious quarrel unappeasable. The vices and oppression of the clergy had alienated from them popular respect, and the fiery diatribes of the Bethlehem chapel were listened to eagerly, while the Wickliffite doctrines, which taught the baselessness of the whole sacerdotal system, were welcomed as a revelation, and spread rapidly through all classes. King Wenceslas was inclined to give them such support as his indolence and self-indulgence would permit, and his queen, Sophia, was even more favorably disposed. Yet the clergy and their friends could not submit quietly to the spoliation of their privileges and wealth, although the Great Schism, in weakening the influence of the Roman curia, rendered its support less efficient. Preachers who assailed their vices were thrown into prison as heretics and were exiled, and the writings of Wickliff, which formed the key of the position, were fiercely assaulted and desperately defended. The weak point in them was the substitution of remanence for transubstantiation; and although this was discarded by Huss and his followers, it served as an unguarded point through which the whole position might be carried. The synod of 1405 asserted the doctrine of transubstantiation in its most absolute shape; any one teaching otherwise was pronounced a heretic, and was ordered to be reported to the archbishop for punishment. In 1406 this was {446} repeated in a still more threatening form, showing that the Wickliffite views had obstinate defenders; as, indeed, is to be seen by a tract of Thomas of Stitny, written in 1400. Already, in 1403, a series of forty-five articles extracted from Wickliff's works was formally condemned by the university. Around these the battle raged with fury; the condemnation was repeated in 1408, and in 1410 Archbishop Zbinco solemnly burned in the courtyard of his palace two hundred of the forbidden books, while the populace revenged itself by singing through the streets rude rhymes, in which the prelate is said to have burned books which he could not read; for his ignorance was notorious, and he was reported to have first acquired the alphabet after his elevation.[490]

In the strife between rival popes it suited the policy of King Wenceslas, in 1408, to maintain neutrality, and he induced the university to send envoys to the cardinals who had renounced allegiance to both Benedict XIII. and Gregory XII. In this mission were included Stephen Palecz and Stanislas of Znaim, but the whole party fell, in Bologna, into the hands of Balthasar Cossa, the papal legate (afterwards John XXIII.), who threw them all in prison as suspect of heresy, and it required no little effort to secure their release. This adventure cooled the zeal of Stephen and Stanislas; they gradually changed sides, and from the warmest friends of Huss they became, as we shall see, his most dangerous and implacable enemies.[491]

In this affair the university had not seconded the wishes of the king with the alacrity which he had expected, and Huss took advantage of the royal displeasure to effect a revolution in that institution, which had hitherto proved the chief obstacle in the progress of reform. It was divided, in the ordinary manner, into four "nations." As each of these nations had a vote, the Bohemians constantly found themselves outnumbered by the foreigners.{447} It was now proposed to adopt the constitution of the University of Paris, where the French nation had three votes, and all the foreign nations collectively but one. The vacillation of Wenceslas delayed decision, but in January, 1409, he signed the decree which ordered the change. The German students and professors bound themselves by a vow to procure the revocation of the decree or to leave the university. Failing in the former alternative, they abandoned the city in vast numbers, founding the University of Leipsic, and spreading throughout Europe the report that Bohemia was a nest of heretics. The dyke was broken down, and the flood of Wickliffitism poured over the land with little to check its progress. In vain did Alexander V. and John XXIII. command Archbishop Zbinco to suppress the heresy, and in vain did the struggling prelate hold assemblies and issue comminatory decrees. The tide bore all before it, and Zbinco at last, in 1411, abandoned his ungrateful see to appeal to Wenceslas's brother Sigismund, then recently elected King of the Romans, but died on the journey.[492]

This removed the last obstacle. The new archbishop, Albik of Unicow, previously physician to Wenceslas, was old and weak, and more given to accumulating money than to defending the faith. He was said to carry the key of his wine-cellar himself, to have only a wretched old crone for a cook, and to sell habitually all presents made to him. Thoroughly unfitted for the crisis, he resigned in 1413, and was succeeded by Conrad of Vechta, who, after some hesitation, cast his lot with the followers of Huss. Yet, during these troubles, the papal Inquisition seems to have been established in Prague, and, strangely enough, to have seen nothing in the Hussite movement to call for its interference, though it could act against Waldenses and other recognized heretics. When, in 1408, the king ordered Archbishop Zbinco to make a thorough perquisition after heresy, Nicholas of Vilemonic, known as Abraham, priest of the Church of the Holy Spirit in Prague, was tried before the inquisitors Moritz and Jaroslav for Waldensianism, and was thrown into prison for asserting that he could preach under authority from Christ without that of the archbishop. {448} Huss interposed in his favor, but his liberation was postponed through his refusal to repeat, on the Gospels, an oath which he had already sworn by God. One of the accusations brought against Huss at Constance was the favor which he showed to Waldensian and other heretics; and yet, when he was about to depart on his fateful journey to Constance, the papal inquisitor Nicholas, Bishop of Nazareth, gave him a formal certificate, attested by a notarial act, to the effect that he had long known him intimately, and had never heard an heretical expression from him, and that no one had ever accused him of heresy before the tribunal. The Hussite and Waldensian movements were too nearly akin for Huss not to sympathize with the acknowledged heretics, and in the virtual spiritual anarchy of these tumultuous years Waldensian influence must have made itself more and more felt, and the sectaries must have been emboldened to show themselves ever more openly.[493]

Everything thus conspired to accelerate the progress of the revolution. Huss, who had hitherto, for the most part, confined himself to assaults upon the local ecclesiastical establishment, began to direct his attacks at the papacy itself, and in the writings of Wickliff he found ample store of arguments, which he used with great effect. He also made use of another of Wickliff's methods by the employment of itinerant priests. This was peculiarly well adapted to accomplish the object in view, for the Bohemians were given to listening to sermons, and the unlicensed preaching for which the negligence of the established clergy gave opportunity had been a frequent source of complaint since the year 1371. The repetition of the prohibitions shows their ineffectiveness; the popular craving for spiritual instruction, which the Church could have turned to such good account, was abandoned to the agitators; the people flocked in crowds to hear them, in spite of priestly anathemas, and the great mass of the nation, from nobles to peasants, eagerly adopted the new doctrines, and were prepared to support them to the death.[494]

Matters were rapidly tending to an open rupture with Rome.[449] In 1410 John XXIII., soon after his accession, referred to Cardinal Otto Colonna the complaints which came to Rome against Huss. On September 20 Colonna summoned him to appear in person. He sent deputies, who appealed from the cardinal to the pope, but they were thrown into prison and severely handled; and while the appeal was pending, in February, 1411, Colonna excommunicated him. On March 15 the excommunication was published in all the churches of Prague save two; the people stood by Huss, and an interdict was extended over the city, which was generally disregarded, and Huss continued to preach. While affairs were in this threatening position a new cause of trouble led to an explosion. Just as Wickliff had been stirred to fresh hostility against the papacy by the crusade which, under orders from Urban VI., the Bishop of Norwich had preached against France for its support of the rival pope Clement VII.; just as Luther was to be aroused from his obscurity by the indulgence-selling of Tetzel when Leo X. wanted money, so the Bohemians were stimulated to active opposition when John XXIII., towards the close of 1411, proclaimed a crusade with Holy Land indulgences against Ladislas of Naples, who upheld the claims of Gregory XII. Stephen Palecz, till then associated with Huss, was dean of the theological faculty. His experience of the Bolognese prison rendered him timorous about withstanding John XXIII., and he declared that there was no authority to prevent the publication of the indulgence. Huss was bolder, and a controversy arose between them which converted their former friendship into an enmity destined to bear bitter fruits. June 16, 1412, he held in the Carolinum a disputation which was a very powerful and eloquent attack upon the power of the keys, which lay at the foundation of the whole papal system. Absolution was dependent on the subjective condition of the penitent; as many popes who concede indulgences are damned, how can they defend their pardons before God? the sellers of indulgences are thieves, who take by cunning lies that which they cannot seize by violence; the pope and the whole Church Militant often err, and an unjust papal excommunication is to be disregarded. This was followed by other tracts and sermons which aroused popular enthusiasm to a lofty pitch. Wenceslas Tiem, the Dean of Passau, to whom the preaching of the crusade in Bohemia was confided, farmed out the indulgences to the[450] highest bidders, and their sale to the people was accompanied by the usual scandals, which were well calculated to excite indignation.[495]

A few days after the disputation a crowd led by Wok of Waldstein, a favorite of King Wenceslas, carried the papal bulls of indulgence to the pillory and publicly burned them. The well-known legend attributes to Jerome of Prague a leading part in this, and relates that the bulls were strung around the neck of a strumpet mounted on a cart, who solicited the favor of the mob with lascivious gestures. No punishment was inflicted on the participants, and Wok of Waldstein continued to enjoy the royal favor. The defiance of the pope was complete, and the temper of the people was shown on July 12, when in three several churches three young mechanics named Martin, John, and Stanislas, interrupted the preachers proclaiming the indulgences, and declared them to be a lie. They were arrested and beheaded in spite of Huss's intercession; many others were imprisoned, and some were exposed to torture. Then the people assumed a threatening aspect; the three who had been executed were reverenced as martyrs; tumults occurred, and the prisoners were released. Soon afterwards a Carmelite was begging at the doors of his church with an array of relics displayed upon a table, with the indulgences attached to them to excite the liberality of the pious. A disciple of Huss denounced the affair as a fraud and kicked over the table, and when he was seized by the friars a band of armed men broke into the house and released him, not without bloodshed.[496]

John XXIII. could not avoid taking up the gage of battle thus thrown down. The Bohemian clergy appealed to him piteously, representing the oppression to which they were subjected, and stating that many of them had been slain. He promptly responded. The major excommunication, to be published in all its awful solemnity in Prague, was pronounced against Huss; the Bethlehem chapel was ordered to be levelled with the earth; his[451] followers were excommunicated, and all who would not within thirty days abjure heresy were summoned to answer in person before the Roman curia. In spite of this Huss continued to preach, and when an attempt was made to arrest him in the pulpit the threatening aspect of the congregation prevented its execution. He appealed to a general council, and then to God, in a protest which, in lofty terms, asserted the nullity of the sentence pronounced against him. In his treatise "De Ecclesia," which followed not long after, he attacked the papacy in unmeasured language borrowed from Wickliff. The pope is not a pope and a true successor of Peter unless he imitates Peter; a pope given to avarice is the vicar of Judas Iscariot. So of the cardinals; if they enter save by the door of Christ they are thieves and robbers. Yet the clergy, for the most part gladly, obeyed the bull of excommunication, and Huss's presence in Prague led to a cessation of all church observances; divine service was suspended, the new-born were not baptized, and the dead lay unburied. At the request of the king, to relieve the situation of its tension, Huss left Prague and retired to Kosi hradek, whence he directed the movements of his adherents in the city and busied himself in active controversial writing, the chief product of which was the "De Ecclesia," which was publicly read in the Bethlehem chapel on July 8, 1413.[497]

150

King Wenceslas had vainly tried to bring about a pacification of the troubles in which passions were daily growing wilder, complicated by the race hatred between Teuton and Czech. A confused series of disputations and conferences and controversial tracts occupied the first half of the year 1413, which only embittered those who took part in them and rendered harmony more distant than ever. In fact there was no possible middle term, no compromise in which the disputants could unite. It was no longer a question of reforming the morals of the clergy, as to the necessity of which all were agreed. The controversy had drifted to the causes of clerical corruption, springing, as Wickliff and Huss and their disciples clearly saw, from the very principles on which the whole structure of Latin Christianity was based. Either the{452} power of the keys was a truth vital to the salvation of mankind, or it was a lie cunningly invented and boldly utilized to gratify the lust of power and the greed of avarice. Between these two antagonistic postulates dialectic subtlety was powerless to frame a project of reconciliation, and argument only hardened each side in its belief. One or the other must triumph utterly, and force alone could decide the controversy. Wearied at last with his unavailing efforts, Wenceslas finally cut the matter short by banishing the leaders of the conservatives, Stephen Palecz, Stanislas of Znaim, Peter of Znaim, and John Elias. Stanislas retired to Moravia, where, after incredible industry in controversial writing, he died on the road to the Council of Constance; Stephen survived him and revenged them both.[498]

Huss and his adherents were now masters of the field; and though he abstained from returning to Prague, except an occasional visit incognito, until his departure for Constance, he could truly say, when he stood up in the council to meet his accusers, "I came hither of my own free will. Had I refused to come neither the king nor the emperor could have forced me, so numerous are the Bohemian lords who love me and who would have afforded me protection." And when the Cardinal Peter d'Ailly indignantly exclaimed, "See the impudence of the man," and a murmur ran around the whole assembly, John of Chlum calmly arose and said, "He speaks the truth, for though I have little power compared with others in Bohemia, I could easily defend him for a year against the whole strength of both monarchs. Judge, then, how much more could they whose forces are greater and whose castles are stronger than mine."[499]

While thus in Bohemia the upholders of the old order of things were silenced and reformation in the morals of the clergy was enforced with no gentle hand, the news spread around Christendom that the long-desired general council was to be convoked at last for the settlement of the Great Schism, the reformation of the Church from its head downwards, and the suppression of heresy.{453} Many strivings had there been to effect this, but the policy of the Italian popes, as at Pisa, had thus far successfully eluded the dreaded decision. The pressure grew, however, until it became overwhelming. With the rival vicars of Christ each showering perdition upon the adherents of the others, the spiritual condition of the faithful was most anxious and a solution of the tremendous question was the most pressing necessity for all who believed what the Latin Church had assiduously taught for a thousand years. The politics of Europe, moreover, were hopelessly complicated by the strife, and no peace was to be expected while so dangerous an element of discord continued to exist. This was especially the case in Germany, where independent princes and prelates each selected for himself the pope of his preference, leading to bitter and intricate quarrels. Second only in importance to this was the reform of the abuses and corruption, the venality and license of the clergy, which made themselves felt everywhere, from the courts of the pontiffs to the meanest hamlet. Heresy likewise was to be met and suppressed, for though England could deal single-handed with the Lollardry within her shores, the aspect of matters in Bohemia was threatening, and Sigismund, the emperor-elect, as the heir of his childless brother Wenceslas, was deeply concerned in the pacification of the kingdom. In vain John XXIII. endeavored to have the council held in Italy, where he could control it. The nations insisted on some place where the free parliament of Christendom could convene unshackled and debate unchecked. Sigismund selected the episcopal city of Constance; John, hard pressed by Ladislas of Naples and driven from Rome, was forced to yield, and, December 9, 1413, issued his bull convoking the assemblage for the first of the following November. Not only were all prelates and religious corporations ordered to be represented, but all princes and rulers were commanded to be there in person or by deputy. Imperial letters from Sigismund, which accompanied the bull, gave assurance that the powers of State and Church would be combined to reach the result desired by all.[500]{454}

No such assemblage had been seen in Christendom since Innocent III., two centuries before, in the plenitude of his power, had summoned the representatives of Latin Christianity to sit with him in the Lateran. The later council might boast fewer mitred heads than the earlier, but it was a far more important body. Called primarily to sit in judgment on the claims of rival popes, its mere convocation was a recognition of its supremacy over the successor of Peter. From its decision there could be no appeal, and the questions to be submitted to it were far more weighty than those which had tasked the consciences of the Lateran fathers. From every part of Europe the Church sent its best and worthiest to take counsel together in this crisis of its fate—men like Chancellor Gerson and Cardinal Peter d'Ailly of Cambrai, as earnest for reform and as sensible of existing wrongs as Wickliff or Huss themselves. The universities poured forth their ablest doctors of theology and canon law. Princes and potentates were there in person or by their representatives, and crowds of every rank in life, from the noble to the juggler. The mere magnitude of the assemblage produced a powerful effect on the minds of all contemporaries, and the wildest estimates were current of the numbers present. One chronicler assures us that there were, besides members of the council, sixty thousand five hundred persons present, of whom sixteen thousand were of gentle blood, from knights and squires up to princes. The same authority informs us that there were four hundred and fifty public women, but an official census of the council, carefully taken, reports that the number was not less than seven hundred, and even *succubi* were popularly said to have joined in the nefarious trade. Thus the strength and the weakness, the virtue and the vice of the fifteenth century were gathered together to find relief as best they might for the troubles which threatened to overwhelm the Church. After many doubts and much hesitation John XXIII. fulfilled his promise to be present, relying upon his stores of gold to win a triumph over his adversaries and over the council itself.[501]

It was inevitable that Huss should tempt his fate at Constance.{455} To both Sigismund and Wenceslas it was of the utmost importance that some authoritative decision should put an end to the strife within the Bohemian Church. The reformers had always professed their desire to submit their demands to a free general council, and Huss himself had appealed to such a council from the papal sentence of excommunication. To hesitate now would be to abandon his life's work, to admit that he dared not face the assembled piety and learning of the Church, and to confess himself a heretic. The host of adversaries in the Bohemian clergy whom his bitter invectives had inflamed and whose preferment had been forfeited through the agitation which he had led would surely be there to blacken him and to misrepresent his cause, and all would be lost if he were not present to defend it in person. They had long jeered him for not daring to present himself to the Holy See in obedience to its summons, and had pronounced blasphemous his appeal to Christ from its excommunication. To hesitate to submit his cause to the council would give his adversaries an inestimable advantage. Besides, incredible as it may seem in view of the violence of his assaults upon the doctrine which rendered the high places in the hierarchy profitable, and his persistent denial of the validity of his excommunication, he believed himself to be in full communion with the Church, that he would find the council in sympathy with his views, and that certain sermons which he had prepared would, when delivered before the assembled prelates, be efficient in bringing about the reforms which he advocated. In his singleness of mind he could not comprehend that men who had thundered as vehemently as himself against current abuses and corruptions, but who had not dared to assail the principles from which those evils sprang, would shrink back aghast from his bolder doctrinal aberrations, and would regard him as a heretic subject to the inquisitorial rule prescribing the naked alternative of recantation or the stake.[502]{456}

When, therefore, the imperial and royal wishes for his presence at Constance were signified to him, with a promise of safe-conduct and full security, he willingly assented, and so anxious was he to be present at the opening of the council that he did not even wait for the promised safe-conduct, which reached him only after his arrival there. That some discussion took place among his friends as to the danger to be incurred there can be no doubt. Jerome of Prague, when on his trial, asserted that he had persuaded Huss to go, and Huss in one of his letters from prison alludes to the warnings which he had received. He himself was evidently not wholly without misgivings. A sealed letter left with his disciple, Master Martin, not to be opened till news should be received of his death, alludes to the persecution which he had suffered for restraining the inordinate lives of the clergy, and his expectation that it would soon reach its consummation. He makes disposition of his slender effects—his gray gown, his white gown, and sixty grossi, which comprise the whole of his worldly gear—and expresses his remorse for the time wasted before his ordination, when he used to play chess to the loss of his own temper and that of others. The unaffected simplicity and pure-heartedness of the man shine like a divine light through the brief words of his last request. A letter in the vernacular to his disciples also announces his fear that his enemies may seek in the council to take his life by false testimony. He asks the prayers of his friends that he may have eloquence to uphold the truth and constancy to endure to the last. Still, he did not wholly neglect precautions. Not only did he procure from the inquisitor Nicholas, Bishop of Nazareth, the certificate of his orthodoxy already alluded to, but he posted, August 26, throughout Prague a notice in Latin and Bohemian that he would appear before the archbishop, then holding a convocation of the Bohemian clergy, and challenged all who impugned his faith to come forward and accuse him either there or at Constance, asserting his readiness to submit to the punishment of heresy in case he was convicted, but that accusers who failed should be subjected to the talio. When John of Jessinetz, his representative, presented himself the next day at the door of the convocation, he was refused admission on the pretext that the body was deliberating on national affairs, and he was told to come back another time. In the assembly of nobles, however, Huss obtained an audience of the archbishop,{457} who was also papal legate, and who declared that he knew of nothing to render Huss guilty except that he ought to purge himself of the excommunication. Of this a certified notarial instrument was sent to Sigismund by Huss with the statement that under the imperial safe-conduct he was ready to go to Constance to defend publicly the faith for which he was prepared, if necessary, to die.[503]

Huss set out, October 11, 1414, under the escort and protection of John and Henry of Chlum and Wenceslas of Duba, all his friends, and delegated for the purpose by Sigismund. The cavalcade consisted of more than thirty horse and two carriages. It was preceded, a day in advance, by the Bishop of Lubec, who announced that Huss was being carried in chains to Constance, and warned the people not to look at him, as he could read men's minds. Already his name had filled all Germany, and this advertisement was an additional incentive for crowds to gather and gaze on him as he passed. His reception served to foster the fatal illusions which he nursed. Everywhere, he wrote to his friends, he was treated as an honored guest and not as an excommunicate; no interdict was proclaimed where he stopped to rest, and he held discussions with magistrates and ecclesiastics. In all cities he posted notices on the church-doors that he was on his way to Constance to defend his faith, and that any one who desired to assail it was invited to do so before the council. On reaching Nuremburg, October 19, in place of deflecting to seek King Sigismund and obtain the promised safe-conduct, he proceeded direct to Constance, while Wenceslas of Duba went to the court and brought the document to him there a few days after his arrival. It was dated October 18.[504]

On November 2 Huss reached Constance, to be greeted by a crowd of twelve thousand men assembled to look upon the dreaded reforming heretic. The council had not yet been opened. On the 10th a letter from one of the party states that as yet no ambassadors from any of the kings had arrived, and though John{458} XXIII. was there with his cardinals, no representatives from his rivals, Gregory XII. and Benedict XIII., had presented themselves. What to do with the Bohemian Wickliffite was a problem which puzzled pope and cardinal, and after much discussion it was determined to suspend his excommunication, and permit him to frequent the churches freely, at the same time requesting him not to be present at the solemnities of the council, lest it might lead to disorder. Considerable apprehension, moreover, was felt as to a sermon to the clergy which he was understood to propose delivering. Huss himself was utterly blind as to the position which he occupied. On November 4, the day before the council was opened, he wrote to his friends at home that overtures had been made to him to settle matters quietly, but that he expected to win a great victory after a great fight. On the 16th he mentioned that when the pope was celebrating mass every one but himself had assigned to him some function in the ceremony, and he characterized the omission as neglect, evidently considering that his position entitled him to recognition and distinction.[505]

He knew that his opponents had not been idle, but he did not fear them. He had been preceded in Constance by two of his bitterest enemies—Michael of Deutschbrod, known as de Causis, and Wenceslas Tiem, Dean of Passau—and these, in a few days, were reinforced by a more formidable antagonist, Stephen Palecz, fully equipped with most dangerous extracts from Huss's writings. Wenceslas Tiem had been the bearer to Prague of the bull offering indulgences for the crusade against Ladislas of Naples, and his profitable trade had been broken up by Huss. Michael de Causis had been priest of the Church of St. Adalbert in the Neustadt of Prague; he had gained the confidence of King Wenceslas by pretending that he could render profitable some abandoned gold-mines near Iglau, and the king had intrusted him with a considerable sum of money for the purpose. After working a few days at the mines he decamped to Rome with the funds, which enabled him to purchase a commission as papal procurator "de causis fidei," whence his appellation. He had already, in 1412, sent to Rome charges against Huss, which the latter pronounced to be lies. The day after Huss's arrival in Constance, Michael posted{459} on the church-doors that he would accuse him to the council as an excommunicate and suspect of heresy, but Huss treated the matter very lightly, and adopted the advice of his friends to take no notice of it until the arrival of Sigismund, who was not expected until Christmas. Meanwhile Huss himself gave ample cause for adverse comment. So perfect was his sense of innocence and security that he could not be content with prudent obscurity. Almost immediately on his arrival he began to celebrate mass in his lodgings. This attracted the people in crowds, and was necessarily a cause of scandal. Otto, Bishop of Constance, sent John Tenger, his vicar, and Conrad Helye, his official, to request Huss to cease, as he had long been under papal excommunication; but he refused, saying that he did not consider himself excommunicated, and that he would celebrate mass as often as he pleased. Although thus defied, the bishop, to avoid disturbance, contented himself with forbidding the people from attendance. Soon after this Huss placed himself, with some provisions, in a covered forage-wagon which was to be sent for hay. When the knights who were responsible for him could not find him, Henry of Lastenbock (Chlum) rushed to the burgomaster and demanded that he be searched for. The city was in an uproar; the gates were closed, horse and foot were sent in every direction to find him, and the circumstance was easily magnified into an attempt to escape.[506]

The sturdy Bohemian was evidently a troublesome subject to deal with. In the eyes of the faithful it was quite scandal enough to see at liberty a priest who had openly defied a papal excommunication, and had defended the recognized errors of Wickliff; there was, moreover, every probability that he would carry out his audacious design of preaching to the clergy a sermon in which the vices of the papal court and the shortcomings of the whole ecclesiastical body would be pitilessly and eloquently exposed, and it would be proved from Scripture that the whole system had no warrant in the law of Christ. The path which the pope and his cardinals had to tread in managing the council was likely to{460} be tortuous and thorny enough without this additional element of disturbance and turbulence. It was far safer to disarm him at once, to anticipate his attacks by treating him legally as one accused of heresy and awaiting trial. Stephen Palecz and Michael de Causis, and a crowd of other Bohemian doctors and priests whom Huss had roughly handled, had already furnished ample material for his indictment, and in the inquisitorial process the first step was to make sure that the accused should not escape. Even had the case been one in which bail could be taken, Huss had the whole kingdom of Bohemia at his back; bail to any amount would be furnished and forfeited, and, once safe at home, he would have laughed to scorn a condemnation for contumacy. Such might reasonably be the arguments of the cardinals when the resolve was taken to arrest him, but the execution of the design was either inexcusably insidious, or the manifestation of irresolution which reached its conclusion only by degrees. On November 28 the cardinals, in consistory with the pope, sent to Huss's lodgings the Bishops of Augsburg and Trent, with Henry of Ulm, the burgomaster of Constance, to summon him at once before them to defend his faith. The envoys greeted him kindly, and though both he and John of Chlum protested that the summons was a violation of the safe-conduct, he immediately consented to go, although he said he had come to Constance to appear openly in the council, and not secretly before the cardinals. He added that he could not be imprisoned because he had a safe-conduct. John of Chlum and some friends accompanied him to the palace occupied by the pope. When the cardinals told him he was accused of disseminating many heresies, he replied that he would rather die than be convicted of a single one; he had come with alacrity to Constance, and if he was found in error he would willingly abjure. To this the cardinals said, "You have answered well." No further examination was had, but John XXIII., whose policy was to embroil the council with Sigismund, took occasion to ask John of Chlum whether Huss had an imperial safe-conduct, to which Chlum replied, "Holy father, you know that he has." Again the pope asked the question and received the same answer, but none of the cardinals requested to see the document. When the morning session was over, guards were placed over Huss and John of Chlum. The weary afternoon wore away in suspense, while the cardinals{461} held another session in which Stephen Palecz and Michael de Causis were busy. The tedium of detention was only broken by a simple-looking Franciscan, who accosted Huss and asked for instruction on the subject of transubstantiation, and, on being satisfactorily answered, inquired about the union of humanity and divinity in Christ. Huss recognized that he was no simple inquirer, for he had asked the most difficult question in theology; he declined further colloquy, and on the retiring of the friar was informed by the guards that he was Master Didaco, renowned as the subtlest theologian of Lombardy. About nightfall John of Chlum was allowed to depart, while Huss was detained, and soon after Stephen and Michael came exultingly and told him that he was now in their power, and should not escape till he had paid the last penny. He was taken under guard to the house of the precentor of the cathedral, in charge of the Bishop of Lausanne, regent of the apostolic chamber, and after eight days was transferred to the Dominican convent on the Rhine. Here he was confined in a cell adjoining the latrines, where a fever soon caused his life to be despaired of. His sudden death would have been a most untoward event, and the pope sent his own physicians to restore him. It was in vain that his friends in Prague procured from Archbishop Conrad a declaration affirming that he had never found Huss to vary from the faith in a single word. His fate had already been virtually decided.[507]

John of Chlum's first thought on regaining his liberty was to hasten to the pope and to expostulate with him. When the safe-conduct had reached Constance, Chlum had at once exhibited it to John XXIII., who is reported to have declared, on reading it, that if his own brother had been slain by Huss the latter should be safe while in Constance so far as he was concerned. Now he disclaimed all responsibility and threw the blame on the cardinals.[508]{462} This question as to the safe-conduct and its violation has been the subject of so warm a discussion, and it illustrates so completely a phase of the relations between the Church and heretics, that its brief consideration here is not out of place.

The imperial safe-conduct issued to Huss was in the ordinary form, without limitation or condition. It was addressed to all the princes and subjects of the empire, ecclesiastical and secular, and to all nobles and magistrates and officials, informing them that Huss was taken into the protection of the king and of the empire, and ordering that he be permitted to pass, remain, and return without impediment, and that all help which he might require should be extended to him. Thus it was not a simple *viaticum* for protection during the journey from Bohemia, and it was not so regarded by any one. That it was intended as a safeguard during the council and the return home is shown by its issue, October 18, after Huss's departure from Prague, and its reaching him in Constance after his arrival there. That his imprisonment was at once looked upon as a gross violation of the imperial pledge is seen in the protests which John of Chlum affixed to the church doors on December 15, probably as soon as Sigismund could be heard from, and again on the 24th, when the king was near Constance and was to arrive the next day. This paper recited that Huss had come under the imperial protection and safe-conduct to answer in public audience all who might question his faith. That, in the absence of Sigismund, who would not have permitted it, and in contempt of his safe-conduct, Huss had been thrown into prison. That the imperial ambassadors had vainly demanded his release, and that when Sigismund comes he should plainly make known to all men his grief and indignation at this violation of the imperial pledge.[509]

The suggestion that the safe-conduct was a mere passport designedly insufficient to protect Huss is a recent discovery which would not have been left to the ingenuity of modern times if it could have been alleged during the warm debate which raged over the question at Constance. That nobody thought of it then is sufficient{463} proof that such an excuse is untenable. Such an assertion would have been all-sufficient when, May 13, 1415, the Bohemians in Constance presented a memorial to the council in which they referred to the treatment of Huss as a violation of the safe-conduct. Yet in its answer the council had no thought of making such an allegation, while at the same time Sigismund's services in the quarrel with John XXIII. were too recent, and still too necessary, for the good fathers to inflict on him the disgrace of publicly declaring that they had righteously overruled his attempt to protect a heretic. They therefore had recourse to a lie manufactured for the occasion, by asserting, in spite of the notorious existence of the safe-conduct in Constance at the time of Huss's arrest, that witnesses worthy of credit had proved that it had not been procured until fifteen days after that occurrence, and therefore that no public faith had been violated in the proceedings. This argument, which Sigismund himself asserted to be false in the public session of June 7, is an admission that the public faith was violated. A single fact such as this outweighs all the special pleadings of modern apologists.[510]{464}

Sigismund at first fully justified the confidence reposed in him by Huss and John of Chlum. He made no attempt to say that his letters were not intended to protect Huss from prosecution, but treated them as having been wrongfully violated. As soon as he had heard of the arrest he had ordered Huss's release with a threat to break open the prisons in case of refusal. On his arrival at Constance, on Christmas Day, his indignation was boundless and there was consequently great excitement. He protested that he would leave Constance, and, in fact, made a show of doing so; he even threatened to withdraw the imperial protection from the council, but was plainly told by the cardinals that they would themselves break it up unless he yielded. The hopes of Christendom had been raised to too high a pitch as to the results expected from the assemblage for him to venture on such a risk. Naturally faithless, his insistence was a matter of pride, and self-interest easily won the day. We have better materials for estimating his character than that of any other prince of the century, and from first to last we find fully justified the opinion of his contemporaries{465} that he was wholly unworthy of trust. During the long negotiations between the Council of Basle and the Hussites, in which he took part, we see him endeavoring impartially to deceive both sides, making solemn engagements with no intention of fulfilling them, and regarded by all parties as utterly devoid of honor. Unfortunate in war and chronically impecunious, he was ever ready to adopt any temporary expedient to evade a difficulty, and to sacrifice his plighted word to obtain an advantage.[511]

It cost him little, therefore, to withdraw from the assertion of his own honor, and the matter was so speedily arranged that when on January 1, 1415, the council formally asked him that free course of justice be allowed in the case of Huss, in spite of the pretext of safe-conduct, he at once issued a decree declaring the council free in all matters of faith and capable of proceeding against all who were defamed for heresy; moreover, he pledged himself to set at naught the threats which were freely uttered of defending Huss at all hazards. Yet the discussion still continued during January, and the pressure on him from Bohemia was so strong that for a while he still fluctuated irresolutely, but, April 8, he formally revoked all letters of safe-conduct. Huss himself had no hesitation in declaring that he had been betrayed and that Sigismund had promised his safe return. His friends took the same position. In February an assembly of the magnates of Bohemia and Moravia, gathered at Mezeritz, sent an address to Sigismund pointing out in language more forcible than courtly the disgrace and humiliation attendant upon the disregard of the imperial faith. Again, in May, after{466} the flight of John XXIII. had inspired new hopes as to the action of the council, two similar assemblages held at Brünn and Prague approached him with even stronger representations. It was all in vain. Sigismund had finally taken his position, and he redeemed his hesitation with great show of zeal. When, on June 7, Huss had his second hearing before the council, Sigismund thanked the prelates for their consideration for him as shown in their leniency to Huss, whom he sternly advised to submit, for he could look for no human help; "We will never protect you in your errors and pertinacity. Rather, indeed, than do so we will prepare the fire for you with our own hands." In the final session of July 6, Huss declared, "I came freely to the council under the public faith promised by the emperor, here present, that I should be free from all constraint, to bear witness to my innocence and to answer for my faith to all who call it in question." With this he fixed his eyes on Sigismund, who blushed deeply. The impression made in Bohemia by Sigismund's calculated faithlessness was ineffaceable. When, in 1433, the legates of the Council of Basle sought to throw the responsibility of the result at Constance on the false witnesses, John Rokyzana pertinently asked them how, if the council was inspired by the Holy Ghost, it could have been misled by perjurers, and he alluded to the violation of the safe-conduct in terms showing that it had been neither forgotten nor forgiven. This had been practically manifested a year earlier, in September, 1432, when the Council of Basle was eager to have Hussite deputies come to it, and the Bohemians would not stir without the most exaggerated provisions to guarantee their safety. Three safe-conducts had been furnished them—one from Sigismund, one from the council, and one from the city of Eger, but they still required others, from the city of Basle, the Margrave of Brandenburg, and the Counts Palatine Dukes of Bavaria, one of whom was the protector of the council. These were very different from that which had satisfied the simplicity of Huss. Thus Frederic of Brandenburg and John of Bavaria pledged themselves to furnish sufficient troops to conduct the Bohemians safely to Basle, to guard them while there, and to bring them back to any designated place in Bohemia. The princes, moreover, guaranteed the safe-conducts of Sigismund and the council, and agreed to forfeit honors and lands, to be entered upon and taken in possession by the Bohemians{467} in case of any unredressed violation of the pledge. These precautions were superfluous, for the envoys had at their back the terrible Bohemian levies which could enforce respect for plighted faith; but when reconciliation had taken place and Sigismund was seated on the throne of his fathers, his guarantees were again regarded as valueless. In April, 1437, he urged John Rokyzana to visit the council, and on the latter alleging fear that he might be treated as was Huss at Constance, the emperor was greatly moved and exclaimed, "Do you think that for you or for this city I would do aught against mine honor? I have given a safe-conduct and so also has the council;" but Rokyzana was not to be tempted by this appeal to the forfeited imperial honor, and steadfastly refused to go.[512]

The explanation of the controversy over the violation of the safe-conduct is perfectly simple. Germany and especially Bohemia knew so little about the Inquisition and the systematic persecution of heresy that surprise and indignation were excited by the application to the case of Huss of the recognized principles of the canon law. The council could not have done otherwise than it did without surrendering those principles. To allow a heresiarch who had become conspicuous to all Christendom, like Huss, to evade the punishment due to his crimes on so flimsy a pretext as that of his having confided himself to them on a promise of safety to which the public faith was pledged, would have seemed to the most conscientious jurists of the council the most absurd of solecisms. In point of fact, the best men who were there—the Gersons, the Peter d'Aillys, the Zabarellas—were as unflinching as the worst creatures of the curia. It had been, as we have seen, too long a principle of inquisitorial practice that the heretic had no rights,{468} and that the man accused of heresy by sufficient witnesses was to be treated as a heretic until he could clear himself, for any one to hesitate about putting it in force in this case. When Sigismund complained that he was dishonored by the imprisonment of Huss, the canonists of the council promptly assured him, in the words of a contemporary orthodox burgher of Constance, that "it could not and might not be in any law that a heretic could enjoy a safe-conduct," and though this was prejudging the case, we have seen how customary that was in all inquisitorial trials. These words Sigismund himself virtually repeated in his address to Huss in the session of June 7: "Many say that we cannot, under the law, protect a heretic or one suspect of heresy." When Huss's execution aroused the wildest indignation throughout Bohemia, expressed to the council in missives of scant courtesy, the council asserted its position in a decree formally adopted September 23, 1415, that no safe-conduct from any secular potentate could work prejudice to the Catholic faith, or could prevent any competent tribunal from trying, judging, and condemning a heretic or suspected heretic, even though, if trusting to the safe-conduct, he had come to the place of judgment and would not have come without it. So thoroughly did the council cause this to be recognized that, in 1432, in the Convention of Eger, stipulating the bases of negotiation between the Hussites and the Council of Basle, it was expressly agreed that no canons or decretals should be alleged to derogate, infringe, or annul the safe-conducts under which the Bohemian envoys were to appear before the council.[513]{469}

The trial of Huss has been the subject of much indignant eloquence. It is the most conspicuous instance of an inquisitorial{470} process on record, and to those unacquainted with the system of procedure which had grown up in the development of the Holy Office, its practical denial of justice has seemed a wilful perversity on the part of the council, while the sublimely pathetic figure of the sufferer has necessarily awakened the warmest sympathy. Yet, in fact, the only deviations of the council from the ordinary course of such affairs were special marks of lenity towards the accused. He was not subjected to the torture, as in the customary practice in such cases he should have been, and, at the instance of Sigismund, he was thrice permitted to appear before the whole body and defend himself in public session. When, therefore, we see how inevitable was his condemnation, how he could have saved himself only at the cost of burdening his soul with perjury and converting his remaining years into a living lie, we obtain a measure of the infamy of the system, and can in some degree estimate the innumerable wrongs inflicted on countless thousands of obscure and forgotten victims. In this aspect the trial is worthy of examination, for though it presents no novel points of procedure, except the concessions made to Huss, it affords an instructive example of the manner in which the inquisitorial process described in preceding chapters was practically applied.

The case against Huss was rendered stronger, almost at the outset, by the action of his friends at home. It must have been shortly after his arrival in Constance that Jacobel of Mies, who had{471} succeeded Michael de Causis in the Church of St. Adalbert, commenced to administer communion in both elements to the laity, and thus gave rise to the most distinguishing and obstinate feature of Bohemian heresy. Zeal for the Eucharist had long been a marked peculiarity of religious devotion in Bohemia. The synod of 1390 promised an indulgence of forty days to all who bent the knee on the elevation of the host; and the frequent partaking of the sacrament was repeatedly and strenuously urged by those who have been classed as the precursors of Huss. Mathias of Janow had even ventured to recommend that the cup should be restored to the laity, but the question had never reappeared during the stormy years in which Huss and his friends had been battling for the Wickliffite doctrines. According to Æneas Sylvius, a certain Peter of Dresden, infected with Waldensian errors, had left Prague with the other Germans in 1409, but was driven from home on account of his heresy and took refuge again in Prague, where he supported himself as a teacher of children. He it was who suggested to Jacobel the return to the ancient practice of the Church; the heretics, delighted to find a question in which they were clearly in the right, eagerly embraced it. The custom spread to the churches of St. Michael, St. Martin, the Bethlehem Chapel, and elsewhere, in spite of the opposition of King Wenceslas and Archbishop Conrad, who vainly threatened secular punishments and ecclesiastical interdicts. Huss was speedily communicated with. He approved of the custom, as indeed he could not well help doing, and his tract in its favor, when conveyed to the disciples, gave a fresh impetus to the movement. It was in vain that on June 15, 1415, the council condemned the use of the cup by the laity, pronounced heretics all priests so administering the sacrament, ordered them to be handed over to the secular arm, and commanded all prelates and inquisitors to prosecute as heretics those who denied the propriety of communion in one element. For more than a century the Utraquists, or Calixtins, as they called themselves, were the ruling party in Bohemia. The consciousness of being in the wrong and of having to justify itself by all manner of trivial excuses rendered the council additionally eager to crush the insubordination of which Huss was the representative. [514]{472}

We have seen that Huss was arrested November 28, 1414. Michael de Causis, Stephen Palecz, and others of his enemies had{473} presented formal articles of accusation against him. These, drawn up in the name of Michael, accused him of maintaining the remanence of the substance in the Eucharist after consecration, of

156

asserting{474} the vitiation of the sacraments in the hands of sinful priests and denying the power of the keys under the same conditions, of holding that the Church should have no temporal possessions, of{475} disregarding excommunication, of granting the cup to the laity, of defending the forty-five condemned articles of Wickliff, of exciting the people against the clergy, so that if he were allowed to return to Prague there would be a persecution such as had not been seen since the days of Constantine, and of other errors and offences. This was more than sufficient to justify his trial, and the process was commenced without delay by the appointment, December 1, of commissioners to examine him. These commissioners were, in fact, inquisitors, and the council at large served as the assembly of experts in which, as it will be remembered, final assent was given to the judgment. One of the commissioners at least, Bernardo, Bishop of Città di Castello, was already familiar with the matter, for only the year before, as papal nuncio in Poland, he had assisted in driving away Jerome of Prague. In addition to the articles of Michael de Causis there was a kind of indictment against Huss presented to the commissioners by the procurators and promoters of the council, reciting the troubles at Prague, his excommunication, and his teaching of Wickliffite heresies.[515]

At first the proceedings were pushed with a vigor which seemed to promise a speedy termination of the case. As soon as Huss recovered from his first sickness there was submitted to him a series of forty-two errors extracted from his writings by Palecz. To these he replied *seriatim* in writing, explaining the false constructions which he asserted had been placed on some passages, defending some, and limiting and conditioning others. As he was denied the use of books, even of the treatises which were the source of the charges, these answers manifest a wonderful retentiveness of memory and quickness and clearness of intellect. Sometimes he was visited in his prison by the commissioners and personally interrogated. A Carthusian, writing from Constance, May 19, relates that the day before he had been present at such an examination and had never seen so bold and audacious a scoundrel or one who could so cautiously conceal the truth. On the{476} other hand, we have his own account of one of these interviews. The commissioners were accompanied by Michael and Stephen to prompt them. Each article was read to him and he was asked if such was his belief; he replied, explaining the sense in which he held it. Then he would be asked if he would defend it, and he would answer no, but that he would stand to the decision of the council. Nothing could well seem more submissive or more orthodox, and under any other system of jurisprudence conviction might well appear impossible. Heresy, however, as we have seen, was a crime; once committed, even through ignorance, a simple return to the Church was not enough; belief in the errors must be admitted and then abjured, before the criminal could be considered as penitent and entitled to the substitution of perpetual imprisonment for the death-penalty. Huss was condemned on heresies which he had not held rather than those which he had taught.[516]

Thousands of miserable wretches had been convicted on a tithe of the evidence now brought against him. Stephen Palecz, a man of the highest repute, swore before the commissioners that since the birth of Christ there had been no more dangerous heretics than Wickliff and Huss, and that all who customarily attended the sermons of the latter believed in the remanence of the substance of bread in the Eucharist. What Palecz testified there were scores of others to substantiate and amplify. Witnesses were there in abundance to prove that he believed in the remanence of the bread, that the sacraments were vitiated in the hands of sinful priests, that indulgences were of no avail, that the Church of Rome was the synagogue of Satan, that heresy was to be overcome by disputation and not by force, that a papal excommunication was to be disregarded. Many of these errors he indignantly denied having entertained, but it was in vain. In vain he wrote out in prison, as early as March 5, 1415, his tract, "*De Sacramento Corporis et Sanguinis,*" in which he declared that full transubstantiation took place; that God worked the miracle irrespective of the merits of the celebrant; that the body and blood of Christ were both in the bread and in the wine, and that he had taught this doctrine since 1401, before he was a priest. In{477} vain, shortly before his execution, his devotion burst forth in a hymn in which he exclaimed:

"O quam sanctus panis iste,
Tu es solus Jesu Christe,
Caro, cibus, sacramentum,
Quo non majus est inventum!"

In vain during his public audience of June 8 he disputed earnestly in favor of the same belief. The witnesses swore to the contrary. He had no right to call rebutting testimony, and could only appeal to God and his conscience. He was proved a heretic who must confess and abjure or be burned.[517]

His only possible line of defence, as has been shown above (Vol. I. p. 446) would have lain in disabling the witnesses for mortal enmity—for enmity such as would lead them to seek his life—and even this would not have been available against the errors which the commissioners had extracted, falsely, as he asserted, from his writings. As regards the witnesses, the commissioners made an unusual concession to him when, during his sickness in December, some fifteen of them were taken to his cell that he might see them sworn. Some of them, it is said, declared that they knew nothing; others were bitterly hostile to him. To this extent he knew some of the names, and others he was acquainted with because they were attached to depositions taken in advance at Prague for Michael de Causis, which by some means had fallen into the hands of Huss before he started for Constance. Some of these names, probably on this account, were attached to the article on the subject of remanence presented in the hearing of June 7, but in the final sentence no names are mentioned; the witnesses to each article are designated simply by titles, such as a canon of Prague, a priest of Litomysl, a master of arts, a doctor of theology, etc., and when Huss asked the name of one of them it was refused. This was strictly in accordance with rule.[518]{478}

Yet the hostility of those who testified against him was notorious. At the place of execution he declared that he was convicted of errors which he did not entertain, on the evidence of false witnesses. The Bohemians in Constance, in their memorial of May 31, 1415, to the council, declared that the testimony against him was given by those who were his mortal enemies. At one time he or his friends thought of disabling them on this account, but when he asked the commissioners to permit him to employ an advocate who could take the necessary exceptions to the evidence, although they at first assented they finally refused, saying that it was against the law for any one to defend a suspected heretic. This, as we have seen, was strictly true, and if the maintenance of the rule may seem harsh, we must remember on the other hand that the friends of Huss were allowed unexampled liberty in working in his behalf. Their repeated memorials to the council and their efforts with Sigismund made them guilty of the crime of fautorship, and if there had been any disposition to enforce the law they could have been reduced to instant silence and have been grievously punished.[519]

It had not taken long to secure evidence more than ample for Huss's conviction, and if his burning had been the object desired it might have been speedily accomplished. We have seen, however, how much the Inquisition preferred a penitent convert to a cremated heretic, and in this case, perhaps more than in any other on record, confession and submission were supremely desirable. Huss, as a self-confessed heresiarch, would be deprived of all importance, and his disciples might be expected to follow his example: as a martyr, there was no predicting whether the result would be terror or exasperation. The milder customary methods of the Inquisition were therefore brought to bear to break down his stubborn obstinacy by procrastination, solitude, and despair. Had his judges desired to be harsh they could have had recourse to torture, which was the ordinary mode of dealing with similar cases. In this they would have been fully justified by law and custom. The less violent but equally efficient device of prolonged starvation could likewise have been employed, but was mercifully forborne.{479} Yet the slower but not less wearing torture of indefinite imprisonment was not spared him. He was kept in the Dominican convent until March 24. Although his petition to be allowed to see his friends was refused, they were permitted to furnish him with writing materials, and he employed his enforced leisure in composing a number of tracts which, written without the aid of books, show his extensive and accurate acquaintance with Scripture and the Fathers. His sweet temper won the good-will of all who were brought in contact with him, and he gratefully alludes to the kindness with which he was treated both by his guards and by the clerks of the papal chamber. The winning nature of the man, as well as the gold of his friends, probably explains the correspondence which at this period he was able to maintain with them, though all communication with him was forbidden. Letters were conveyed back and forth clandestinely, sometimes carried in food, in spite of the vigilance of his enemies. Michael de Causis hovered around the gate, saying, "By the grace of God we shall burn that heretic who has cost me so many florins," and procuring that the wives of the guards, whom he suspected as letter-carriers, should be excluded. All this ceased when the quarrel between pope and council culminated. On March 20 John XXIII. secretly fled from Constance, when the guards placed over Huss delivered the keys to Sigismund and followed their master. The council then handed Huss over to the custody of the Bishop of Constance, who carried him in chains by night to the castle of Gottlieben, some miles from the city across the Rhine. His friends had requested that he should have a more airy prison, and the request was more than granted, for he was now confined in a room at the top of a tall tower. Though his feet were fettered he was able to move about during the day, but at night his arm was chained to the wall. As escape was impossible, the confinement was evidently intended to be punitive. Here he was completely isolated from all intercourse with his fellow-beings and left to his own dreary introspection. Disease added to the harshness of his prison. From the foul Dominican cell to the windy turret-room of Gottlieben, he was exposed to every variety of unwholesome conditions. Stone, an affection hitherto unknown to him, tormented him greatly. Toothache and headache combined to increase his sufferings. On one occasion{480} a severe attack of fever, accompanied by excessive vomiting, so prostrated him that his guards carried him out of his cell thinking him about to die. Yet throughout all his letters from prison the beautiful patience of the man shines forth. For the enemies who were pursuing him to the death there is only forgiveness; for the trials with which God has seen fit to test his servant there is only submission. He overflows with gratitude for the steadfast affection of his friends, and sends touching requests of remembrance to them all; he teaches charity and gently points out the way to moral and spiritual improvement. There is neither the pride of martyrdom nor the desire for retribution; all is pious resignation and love and humility. Since Christ, no man has left behind him a more affecting example of the true Christian spirit than John Huss, while fearlessly awaiting the time when he should suffer for what he believed to be truth. He was one of the chosen few who exalt and glorify humanity. Yet he was but human, and the final victory was not won without the agony of self-conquest; while at times he comforted himself with dreams that God would not suffer him to perish, but that like Daniel and Jonah and Susannah he would be rescued when all help seemed vain.[520]

Hope seemed justified when the rupture occurred between the pope and the council. No sooner was Huss made aware of the flight of John XXIII. than he begged his friends to see Sigismund instantly and procure his liberation. The answer was his transfer to the tower of Gottlieben. When the pope was brought back a prisoner to the same castle of Gottlieben, and the council proceeded to try and condemn him as a simonist and dilapidator who was ruining the Church, while his personal vices and crimes, unfit for description, were a scandal to Christendom, such confirmation of all that the Wickliffites had urged might well seem to justifiy the expectation that Huss would be released with honor. John XXIII., however, with the wisdom of the children of the world, essayed no defence; he confessed all that was laid to his{481} charge, submitted to the council, and was eventually, after a few years of imprisonment, rewarded by Martin V. with the lofty post of Dean of the Sacred College. Huss, with the constancy of the children of light, refused to perjure himself by confession, and there could be no escape for him.[521]

The council had been assembled to reform the Church, and was performing its duty in its own way, but nothing could be further from the thoughts of its most zealous members than the revolutionary reform of Wickliff and Huss, which would reduce the Church to apostolic poverty and deprive it of all temporal power. Besides the doctrinal errors, attested by abundant witnesses, there was ample material in Huss's writings to prove him a most dangerous enemy of the whole ecclesiastical system. He had written his tract "*De Ablatione Bonorum*" in defence of one of the forty-five condemned Wickliffite articles which asserted that the temporal lord could at will deprive of their temporalities ecclesiastics who were habitual delinquents. His tract "*De Decimis*" defended another of the articles, contending that no one in mortal sin could be a temporal lord, a prelate, or a bishop. John Gerson, one of the leading members of the council, had, as Chancellor of the University of Paris, before coming to Constance, drawn up a series of twenty such dangerous errors, extracted from Huss's treatise "*De Ecclesia*," and had urged Archbishop Conrad of Prague to extirpate the Wickliffite heresy by calling in the secular arm. Huss, in his deductions from the Wickliffite doctrines of predestination, had overthrown the very foundations of the hierarchical system. Among the cardinals in the council, Ottone Colonna had fulminated the papal excommunication which Huss had disregarded; Zabarella and Brancazio had been actively concerned in the proceedings against him before the curia—all of these and many others were thoroughly familiar with his revolutionary doctrines. What was to become of the theocracy founded by Hildebrand if such teachings were to pass unreproved, if their assertor was to be allowed to defend them and was only to be adjudged a heretic when overcome in scholastic disputation? The whole structure of sacerdotalism would be undermined and the whole body of canon law{482} would be disregarded if so monstrous a proposition should be conceded. To the fathers of the council nothing could well seem more preposterous. Then Michael de Causis had intercepted a letter, written by Huss from prison, in which the ministers of the council were alluded to as the servants of Antichrist, and when this was brought to him by the commissioners he acknowledged its authenticity. Besides all this, he had remained under excommunication for suspicion of heresy during long years, during which he had constantly performed divine service, and he had called the pope an Antichrist whose anathema was to be disregarded. This of itself, as we have seen, constituted him a self-convicted heretic.[522]

It thus was idle to suppose that the council, because it had deposed John XXIII., would set free so contumacious a heretic, whose very virtues only rendered him the more dangerous. The inquisitorial process must go on to the end. Even during the bitterest and most doubtful portion of the contest, before the pope had been brought back to Constance, the successive steps of the trial received due attention. On April 17 four new commissioners were appointed to replace the previous ones, whose commissions from the pope were held to have expired, and the new commission was expressly granted power to proceed to final sentence. The only doubt arising was whether the condemnation of Wickliff, with which the case of Huss was inextricably related, should be uttered in the name of the pope or in that of the council, and its publication, May 4, in the latter form, showed that the assembly had no hesitation as to its duty in stamping out the heresy of the master and of the disciple. The active measures also, which during this period were taken against Jerome of Prague, were an indication not to be mistaken of the purposes of the council. Yet how little the friends of Huss understood the real position of affairs, and how false hopes had been excited by the rupture with the pope, is seen in their efforts at this juncture to press the trial to a conclusion. Under the procrastinating policy of the Inquisition it is quite possible that Huss would have been left to his solitary musings for a time indefinitely longer, in hopes that his resolution{483} would at last give way, but for the efforts of his friends, who hoped to secure his release. On May 13 they presented a memorial complaining of his treatment, imprisoned in irons and perishing of hunger and thirst, without trial or conviction, in violation of the safe-conduct and of the pledged faith of the empire. They also remonstrated against the stories which were circulated to prejudice the case, that in Bohemia the blood of Christ was carried around in bottles, and that cobblers heard confession and celebrated mass. On May 16 the council replied to the effect that as far back as 1411 Huss had had a hearing before the Holy See and had been excommunicated, and had since then not only proved himself a heretic, but a heresiarch, by remaining under excommunication and preaching forbidden doctrines, even in Constance itself. As for the safe-conduct, we have seen how it was pretended to have been procured after the arrest. This elusive answer might have shown how the case was already prejudged by those who were to decide it; yet again, on May 18, the Bohemians presented a rejoinder urging promptitude. It was fully expected in Constance that a session would be held on the 22d, at which Huss would be condemned; but about this time attention was engrossed by the trial of John XXIII., who was at length deposed, May 29, and notified of his deposition on the 31st. Sigismund was now preparing for the voyage to Spain, which was expected to take place in June, and if anything was to be done with Huss before his departure further delay was inadmissible. Probably the Bohemians imagined that in some indefinable way he would yet save their leader. On May 31, therefore, they presented another memorial, reiterating their complaints about the safe-conduct and asking for a speedy public hearing. Sigismund entered during the discussion and strenuously urged the public audience, which was finally promised. Huss's friends further urged that he should be brought from his prison and be allowed a few days to recover from his harsh incarceration, and a show was made of complying with the request. On the same day John of Chlum had the satisfaction of forwarding to Gottlieben an order for the transmission of Huss to Constance. The next day, June 1, a special deputation from the council followed and presented to him the thirty articles which had been proved against him. They reported that he submitted himself to the council; but{484} he maintained that he only agreed to do so on such points as he could be proved to have taught erroneously. At last he was brought to Constance in chains and confined in the Franciscan convent.[523]

In the routine of the inquisitorial process there was no necessity for further parley with the accused. The articles of heresy were proved against him, and if he continued obstinately to deny them delivery to the secular arm was a matter of course. There had been no intention of permitting such an innovation on the regular procedure as a public audience, but Sigismund could see, if the council could not, that its denial would have a most unfortunate influence on public opinion in Bohemia, where, in the prevailing ignorance as to the inquisitorial rules, it would be claimed that the council was afraid to face their champion and was forced to condemn him unheard. It could, in reality, have no influence on the result, for the case was already virtually decided, but Huss's friends could not recognize this, and an attempt was made, without success, to speculate on their eagerness, by a demand for two thousand florins to defray the alleged expenses. The audiences which followed were thus wholly irregular, and may be briefly dismissed as in no sense entitled to the importance which has commonly been ascribed to them.[524]

On June 5 a congregation of the council was held in the Franciscan convent. At first the intention was to carry out the ordinary inquisitorial procedure by considering, in the absence of Huss, the articles proved against him, but Peter Mladenowic hastened to John of Chlum and Wenceslas of Duba, who forthwith appealed to Sigismund. The latter at once sent the Palsgrave Louis and Frederic Burggrave of Nuremberg to the council, with orders that nothing should be done until Huss was present and his books were before them for verification. At length, therefore, he had the long-desired opportunity of meeting his adversaries, and defending himself in public debate. The books from which his errors had been extracted were laid before him—his treatise{485} "De Ecclesia" and his tracts against Stephen Palecz and Stanislaus of Znaim—and he acknowledged them to be his. The articles were taken up in succession. He was required to answer to each a simple yea or nay, and when he desired to explain anything a scene of indescribable confusion arose. When he asked to be taught wherein he had erred he was told that he must first recant his heresies, which was strictly in accordance with the law. The day wore away in the discussion, and it had to be renewed on the 7th, and again on the 8th—Sigismund being present on these latter occasions. Huss defended himself gallantly, with wonderful quickness of thought and dialectical skill, but nothing could be more unlike the free debate which he had deluded himself into anticipating when he left Prague. Although the Cardinal of Ostia, who presided, endeavored to show fairness, the assembly at times became a howling mob with shouts of "Burn him! Burn him!" Interruptions were incessant, he was baited on all sides with questions, and frequently his replies were drowned in clamor. As a judicial act it was a mockery, but it served the purpose desired by Sigismund, and the Church had shown itself not afraid of public discussion with the heresiarch. At the end of the third day of this tumultuous wrangling Huss was exhausted almost to fainting. The night before toothache had deprived him of sleep, an attack of fever supervened, and six months of harsh imprisonment had left him little physical endurance. The proceedings terminated with the cardinals urging him to recant and promising him merciful treatment if he would throw himself upon the mercy of the council. He asked for another hearing, saying that he would submit if his arguments and authorities were insufficient. To this Cardinal Peter d'Ailly replied that the unanimous decision of the doctors was that he must confess his error in publishing the articles ascribed to him, he must swear never in future to believe or teach them, and must recant them publicly. Huss begged the council for the love of God not to force him to wrong his conscience, for abjuration meant the renunciation of an error previously entertained, and many of those brought against him he had never held. Sigismund asked him why he could not renounce errors which he said had been ascribed to him through perjury, and Huss had to explain to him the technical meaning of abjuration. One member of the council even objected to the accused being admitted to recantation,{486} because he was not to be trusted, but this would have been wholly illegal. Even in the case of relapse the heretic always had a right to confess and recant, and the council was not to be betrayed into so manifest a denial of justice. It was impossible, in such a crowd of eager persecutors, to maintain the legal forms in all strictness, and there followed a number of volunteer accusations by individuals, on which an irregular discussion could not be repressed. Finally, as Huss was withdrawn, John of Chlum succeeded in giving him a friendly grasp of the hand and a word of sympathy. To the forlorn and despised heretic that touch and voice were a solace which nerved him for the yet harder trials of the succeeding weeks.[525]

His conscientious endurance was now to be tested to the uttermost. The wise general policy of the Inquisition, which preferred a confessed penitent to a martyr, was specially applicable in this case, for though Sigismund and the council underestimated the Bohemian fervor and obstinacy, the dullest could see that Huss confessing to having taught heresy and humbly seeking reconciliation would dispirit his followers, while no one could guess the extent of the conflagration which might spread from his pyre. Accordingly efforts were

160

redoubled to induce him to confess and recant. Sigismund had prepared the way by assuring him during the public audience that no mercy would be shown him and that persistent denial would bring him to the stake, while he was not notified that behind the bland promises of mercy for submission there lay a sentence, which, while expressing joy at his humbly seeking absolution, pronounced him to be pernicious, scandalous, and seditious, and condemned him to degradation from the priesthood and to perpetual imprisonment. The council could do no otherwise, for this, as we have seen, was the punishment provided by the canons for repentant heretics, and yet in estimating the{487} noble firmness of Huss we must bear in mind that no intimation of it seems to have been made to him.[526]

The obstacle in the way of Huss's abjuration lay not so much in the heresies which he had taught, as in those which he had not taught. On legal testimony his judges had found him guilty of all, but the worst of them, such as the remanence of the substance and the vitiation of the sacraments in polluted hands, he denied energetically ever to have held or expressed. Many of the errors extracted from his works, moreover, he repudiated, asserting that the passages had been garbled and perverted. In the eye of the law this denial was mere contumacy which only aggravated his guilt. The first condition of reconciliation was confessing under oath that he was guilty of having held these errors and then abjuring them. This was committing perjury to God in the most solemn fashion, and to a tender conscience like that of Huss it was worse than death. From this dilemma there was no escape. On the one hand lay the legal system, contrived with Satanic ingenuity and unalterable; on the other lay the purity of character which led Huss to reject without hesitation all the specious subterfuges suggested to beguile him.[527]

For a month the struggle continued, and no human soul ever bore itself with loftier fortitude or sweeter or humbler charity. He asked for a confessor, and intimated that he would prefer Stephen Palecz, the enemy who had hounded him to the death. Palecz came and heard his confession, and then urged him to abjure, saying that he ought not to mind the humiliation. "The humiliation of condemnation and burning is greater," replied Huss, "how then can I fear humiliation? But advise me: what would you do if you knew for certain that you did not hold the errors imputed to you? Would you abjure?" Palecz burst into tears and could only stammer, "It is difficult." He wept again freely when Huss begged his pardon for harsh words used in the heat of strife, and especially for calling him a falsifier. Another confessor was sent{488} to him, who listened to him kindly and gave him absolution without insisting on preliminary abjuration, which was a most irregular concession—indeed, almost incredible. Many others were allowed to visit him in the hope of persuading him to confess and recant. One learned doctor urged his submission, saying, "If the council told me I had but one eye, I would confess it to be so, though I know I have two," but Huss was impervious to such example. An Englishman adduced the precedent of the English doctors who had, without exception, abjured the heresies of Wickliff when required to do so; but when Huss offered to swear that he had never held or taught the heresies imputed to him, and that he would never hold or teach them, his baffled advisers withdrew.[528]

The most formidable effort, however, was of an official character. At the final hearing of June 8, Cardinal Zabarella had promised him that a recantation in a form strictly limited would be submitted to him, and the promise was fulfilled in a paper skilfully drawn up, so as to satisfy his scruples. It represented him as protesting anew that much had been imputed to him which he had never believed, but that nevertheless he submitted himself in everything to the correction and orders of the council in abjuring, revoking, and retracting, and in accepting whatever merciful penance the council might prescribe for his salvation. Carefully as this was phrased to elude the difficulty, Huss rejected it without hesitation. In some matters, he said, he would be denying the truth, in others he would be perjuring himself. It were better to die than to fall into the hands of the Lord in the effort to escape momentary suffering. Then one of the fathers of the council—supposed to be the Cardinal of Ostia, the highest in rank of the Sacred College—addressed him as his "dearest and most cherished brother," with the most honeyed persuasiveness, begging him not to confide too absolutely in his own judgment. In making the abjuration it will not be he that condemns truth, but the council; as for perjury, if perjury there be, it will fall on the heads of those who exact it. Yet Huss was not to be enticed with such allurements; he could not quiet his conscience with casuistry such as this, and he deliberately chose death. In daily expectation of the dreadful sentence, he quietly put his simple affairs in order. Peter{489} Mladenowic, the notary, had rendered him zealous service and was to be paid out of his sixty grossi. His little debts were to be settled, and his books, apparently his only other property, were to be distributed. Kind remembrances were sent to his numerous friends, and they were told if they had learned any good of him to hold fast to it; if they had seen in him aught reprehensible to cast it aside. It was not that he was insensible, for he describes in moving terms the mental conflicts and agony which he endured in his hopeless prison, expecting each day to be led forth to an agonizing death, but the spirit rose superior to the flesh and remained victor in the struggle. Solicitous to retain the good opinion of his disciples, he managed to transmit to them, on June 18, a copy of the articles proved against him, together with a report of what his defence had been. Of those drawn from his writings he retracted none, although many he declared to be false and garbled. Those alleged against him by witnesses he mostly asserted to be lies, and he pathetically concluded, "It only remains for me to abjure and revoke and undergo fearful penance or to burn. May the Father, Son, and Holy Ghost grant me the spirit of wisdom and fortitude to persevere to the end and to escape the snares of Satan!"[529]

In hope of his weakening, the end was postponed until the approaching departure of Sigismund rendered further delay impossible. Yet effort was not abandoned till the last. On July 1 a deputation of prelates endeavored to persuade him that he could reasonably recant, but he handed them a written confession calling God to witness that he had never taught many of the articles; as for the rest, if there were error in them he detested it, but he could not abjure any of them. Puzzled by his unexpected tenacity of purpose, and earnestly desirous of avoiding the catastrophe, a final and unprecedented concession was agreed upon. On July 5 Zabarella and Peter d'Ailly sent for him and offered to let him deny the heresies proved by witnesses if he would abjure those extracted from his books. This was, in fact, an abandonment of all inquisitorial precedent, but Huss had persistently declared that[490] most of the latter were fraudulently drawn, so as to attribute to him errors which he had never held, and he was immovable. As a last resource, later in the same day, Sigismund sent his friends John of Chlum and Wenceslas of Duba, with four bishops, to ask him whether he would persevere or recant, but his answer was as firm as ever. To the friendly adjuration of John of Chlum he replied with tears that he would willingly revoke anything in which he could be proved to have erred. The bishops pronounced him obstinate in error and left him.[530]

Thus the extraordinary efforts of the council to save itself and him were vain, and nothing remained but the inevitable final act of the tragedy. The next day, July 6, saw the most gorgeous *auto de fé* on record. The cathedral of Constance was crowded with Sigismund and his nobles, the great officers of the empire with their insignia, the prelates in their splendid robes. While mass was sung, Huss, as an excommunicate, was kept waiting at the door; when brought in he was placed on an elevated bench by a table on which stood a coffer containing priestly vestments. After some preliminaries, including a sermon by the Bishop of Lodi, in which he assured Sigismund that the events of that day would confer on him immortal glory, the articles of which Huss was convicted were recited. In vain he protested that he believed in transubstantiation and in the validity of the sacrament in polluted hands. He was ordered to hold his tongue, and on his persisting the beadles were told to silence him, but in spite of this he continued to utter protests. The sentence was then read in the name of the council, condemning him both for his written errors and those which had been proved by witnesses. He was declared a pertinacious and incorrigible heretic who did not desire to return to the Church; his books were ordered to be burned, and himself to be degraded from the priesthood and abandoned to the secular[491] court. Seven bishops arrayed him in priestly garb and warned him to recant while yet there was time. He turned to the crowd, and with broken voice declared that he could not confess the errors which he had never entertained, lest he should lie to God, when the bishops interrupted him, crying that they had waited long enough, for he was obstinate in his heresy. He was degraded in the usual manner, stripped of his sacerdotal vestments, his fingers scraped; but when the tonsure was to be disposed of an absurd quarrel arose among the bishops as to whether the head should be shaved with a razor or the tonsure be destroyed with scissors. Scissors won the day, and a cross was cut in his hair. Then on his head was placed a conical paper cap, a cubit in height, adorned with painted devils and the inscription, "This is the heresiarch." In accordance with the universal custom no proceedings by the secular authorities were regarded as necessary. As soon as the ecclesiastical court had pronounced him a heretic and handed him over, the laws against heresy operated of themselves. Sigismund, it is true, might have delayed the execution for six days, but this would have been so unusual as to have excited most unfavorable comment. There had already been afforded ample opportunity for resipiscence, and the convict could always still recant up to the lighting of the fagots. Nothing could reasonably be hoped from further postponement, and Sigismund's approaching departure counselled promptitude. He therefore briefly ordered the Palsgrave Louis to take charge of the culprit and to do to him as to a heretic. Louis called to Hans Hazen, the imperial vogt of Constance, "Vogt, take him as judged of both of us and burn him as a heretic." Then he was led forth, and the council calmly turned to other business, unconscious that it had performed the most momentous act of the century.[531]

The place of execution was a meadow near the river, to which he was conducted by two thousand armed men, with Palsgrave Louis[492] at their head, and a vast crowd, including many nobles, prelates, and cardinals. The route followed was circuitous, in order that he might be carried past the episcopal palace, in front of which his books were burning, whereat he smiled. Pity from man there was none to look for, but he sought comfort on high, repeating to himself, "Christ Jesus, Son of the living God, have mercy upon me!" and when he came in sight of the stake he fell on his knees and prayed. He was asked if he wished to confess, and said that he would gladly do so if there were space. A wide circle was formed, and Ulrich Schorand, who, according to custom, had been providently empowered to take advantage of any final weakening, came forward, saying, "Dear sir and master, if you will recant your unbelief of heresy, for which you must suffer, I will willingly hear your confession; but if you will not, you know right well that, according to canon law, no one can administer the sacrament to a heretic." To this Huss answered, "It is not necessary: I am no mortal sinner." His paper crown fell off and he smiled as his guards replaced it. He desired to take leave of his keepers, and when they were brought to him he thanked them for their kindness, saying that they had been to him rather brothers than jailers. Then he commenced to address the crowd in German, telling them that he suffered for errors which he did not hold, sworn to by perjured witnesses; but this could not be permitted, and he was cut short. When bound to the stake and two cartloads of fagots and straw were piled up around him the palsgrave and vogt for the last time adjured him to abjure. Even yet he could have saved himself, but he only repeated that he had been convicted by false witnesses of errors never entertained by him. They clapped their hands and then withdrew, and the executioners applied the fire. Twice Huss was heard to exclaim, "Christ Jesus, Son of the living God, have mercy upon me!" then a wind springing up and blowing the flames and smoke into his face checked further utterance, but his head was seen to shake and his lips to move while one might twice or thrice recite a paternoster. The tragedy was over; the sorely-tried soul had escaped from its tormentors, and the bitterest enemies of the reformer could not refuse to him the praise that no philosopher of old had faced death with more composure than he had shown in his dreadful extremity. No faltering of the voice had betrayed an internal {493} struggle. Palsgrave Louis, seeing Huss's mantle on the arm of one of the executioners, ordered it thrown into the flames lest it should be reverenced as a relic, and promised the man to compensate him. With the same view the body was carefully reduced to ashes and thrown into the Rhine, and even the earth around the stake was dug up and carted off; yet the Bohemians long hovered around the spot and carried home fragments of the neighboring clay, which they reverenced as relics of their martyr. The next day thanks were returned to God, in a solemn procession in which figured Sigismund and his queen, the princes and nobles, nineteen cardinals, two patriarchs, seventy-seven bishops, and all the clergy of the council. A few days later Sigismund, who had delayed his departure for Spain to see the matter concluded, left Constance, feeling that his work was done.[532]

The long-continued teaching of the Church, that persistent heresy was the one crime for which there could be no pardon or excuse, seemed to deprive even the wisest and purest of all power of reasoning where it was concerned. There was no hesitation in admitting that the pestilent heresy of the Hussites was caused by the simoniacal corruptions of the Roman curia, whereby many Christian souls were led to eternal perdition, and that it could not be eradicated until a thorough reformation was effected. Yet in place of drawing from this the necessary deduction, the feeling of the council is reflected by its historian in the blasphemous representation of Christ as recording with satisfaction the hideous details of the execution, and as saying that the wicked soul of the heretic commenced in temporal flame the torment which it would suffer through eternity in hell. The trial, in fact, had been conducted in accordance with the universally received practice in such cases, the only exceptions being in favor of the accused. If the result was inevitable, it was the fault of the system and not of the judges, and their consciences might well feel satisfied.[533] {494}

Great was the disgust of the orthodox when they learned that this pious view of the matter was not entertained in Prague, and it required the most positive assurances of eye-witnesses to make them believe the incredible fact that, from king to peasant in Bohemia, there was practical unanimity in the belief that he who had been condemned and executed as a heretic was a martyr; that the popular songs sung in the streets represented him as one who had shed his blood for Christ, and that he was inserted in the calendar of saints, with his feast on July 6, the day of his execution. The good fathers, however, were not long in finding, from indubitable evidence, that they had made a grave mistake as to the Bohemian temper, and that they had only succeeded in inflaming the disease which they had sought to eradicate. As soon as the defiance excited in Bohemia could be learned in Constance, the council made haste to write, July 26, to the authorities there, protesting that Huss and Jerome of Prague had been treated with all tenderness, that the persistent heresy of the former had forced his delivery to the secular court for judgment, and that all similar heretics would be treated in the same manner. The Bohemians were exhorted to justify, by similar persecution, the good opinion of their orthodoxy which the council had formed from the report of the Bishop of Litomysl, whose popular name of Iron John sufficiently indicates his inflexibility. This good opinion was not sustained when a protest was received from the barons of Bohemia and Moravia, hastily drawn up as soon as the news of the execution had reached them—a protest which the council promptly ordered to be burned. Its letter of July 26 led to the convocation of a national assembly, in which an address was framed and received the signatures of nearly five hundred barons, knights, and gentlemen. In this they asserted their belief in Huss's purity and orthodoxy; that he had unjustly been put to death without confession or lawful conviction; that Jerome they supposed had shared the same fate; that the defamation of the kingdom for heresy was the work of liars, and that any one who {495} asserted it, saving Sigismund, lied in his throat, was the vilest of traitors and the worst of heretics, and as such they would prosecute him before the future pope. A more dangerous symptom of rebellion was a pledge signed by the magnates, agreeing that all priests should be allowed to preach freely the truths of Scripture, that no bishop should be permitted to interfere with them unless they taught errors, and that no excommunications or interdicts from abroad should be received or observed.[534]

This was firing at long range with no result but mutual exacerbation, and it was probably the stimulus of Bohemian disaffection which led the council about this time to act vigorously in the case of Jerome of Prague, whom the Bohemian nobles had erroneously believed to have shared the fate of Huss.

Jerome of Prague stands before us as one of those meteoric natures which would be dismissed by the student as half mythical, if the substantial facts which are on record did not fix the details of his career with an exactness leaving no room for doubt. Born at Prague, his early training was received at a time when men's minds were beginning to waver in the confusion of the Great Schism, and under the impulsion of the Wickliffite writings. About the year 1400 he was brought under the influence of Huss, and thereafter he continued to be the steadfast adherent and supporter of the great protestant against the corruptions of the Church. Already, at Paris, Cologne, Heidelberg, and Cracow—at all of which he had been decorated with the honors of the universities— he had disturbed the philosophic calm of the schools with his subtleties on the theory of universals; at Paris, indeed, the disturbance had gone so far that John Gerson, the chancellor of the university, had driven him forth, perhaps retaining a grudge which explains his zeal in the prosecution of his old antagonist. His restless spirit left scarce a region of the known civilized world unvisited. At Oxford, attracted by the reputation of Wickliff, he{496} had copied with his own hand the Dialogus and the Trialogus, and had carried those outpourings of revolt to Prague, where they added fresh fuel to the rapidly rising fires of Bohemian insubordination. On a second visit he had been seized as a heretic, and had escaped through the intervention of the University of Prague. In Palestine he had trodden in the footsteps of the Saviour and had bent in reverence at the Holy Sepulchre. In Lithuania he had sought to convert the heathen. In Russia he had endeavored to win over the schismatic Greek. In Poland and Hungary he had scattered the doctrines of Wickliff and Huss. Driven out of Hungary, in 1410, he was arrested and thrown in prison in Vienna, by the papal inquisitor and episcopal official, for teaching Hussitism and infecting with it the university of that city. His trial was commenced and a day was set for its hearing, prior to which he was allowed his liberty on his oath not to leave the city, under pain of excommunication. Claiming that an extorted oath was of no force, he escaped, and from Olmütz wrote a free-and-easy letter to the Bishop of Passau, suggesting that the prosecutors and witnesses may be sent to Prague, where the trial can be finished. The excommunication, indeed, followed him to Prague, but in the tumultuous condition of Bohemia it gave him no trouble, though the University of Vienna wrote to the University of Prague that by remaining more than a year under the excommunication he had incurred the guilt of heresy, for which he ought to be condemned; and meanwhile the converts whom he had made in Vienna continued to give occupation to the Inquisition, and the university which interfered in their behalf incurred the suspicion of heresy. In the stirring events which followed, his restless and aggressive spirit would not allow him to be inactive, and the popular impression of his reckless audacity is shown in the story of his hanging the papal bulls of indulgence around the neck of a strumpet and carrying her to the place where they were to be burned. In 1413 he again visited Poland, where in a short time he succeeded in causing an unprecedented excitement, and was speedily sent back to Prague. His whole life had been spent in intellectual digladiation, from his youthful philosophic contests to the maturer struggles with the overwhelming forces of the hierarchy. A layman, not in holy orders and unfurnished with priestly gown and tonsure, he had preached to admiring crowds{497} of Majjars, Poles, and Czechs; nor was he wholly unskilled in the use of the arms of the flesh. On his trial he admitted that he had once been drawn into a quarrel with some monks in a monastery, when two of them attacked him with swords, and he defended himself successfully with a weapon hastily snatched from the hand of a bystander. His enemies, indeed, accused him of having, on another occasion, drawn a dagger on a Dominican friar, and of having been only prevented by force from stabbing him to the death. All of his contemporaries bear testimony to his wonderful powers. His commanding presence, his glittering eyes, his sable hair and flowing beard, his deep and impressive voice, his persuasive accents, enabled him to throw his influence over all with whom he came in contact; while his miraculous stores of learning, his unmatched readiness, and the subtlety of his intellect, rendered him an enemy of the Church only one degree less dangerous than the steadfast and irreproachable Huss.[535]

Jerome had watched from Prague the fate of his friend with daily increasing anxiety, and when the rupture between pope and council seemed to promise immunity for the opponents of hierarchical corruption he could not resist the temptation to aid in his rescue, and to assist in what appeared to be the approaching overthrow of the evils which he had so long combated. April 4, 1415, he came secretly to Constance, but speedily found how groundless were his hopes and how dangerous was the atmosphere of the place. Christann of Prachaticz, one of Huss's chief disciples, had recently ventured to visit Constance, had been arrested, and articles of accusation had been presented against him, when on the intervention of the Bohemian ambassadors he had been liberated under oath to present himself when summoned—an oath which he had forfeited by promptly escaping to Bohemia. Jerome contented himself with posting a notice on the walls affirming the orthodoxy of Huss; he withdrew at once to Ueberlingen and asked for a safe-conduct. The response was ambiguous, but, like a moth hovering around the fatal candle-flame, he returned to Constance, where, April 7, he affixed another notice on the church{498} doors addressed to Sigismund and the council. It stated that he had come of his own free will to answer all accusations of heresy, and if convicted he was ready to endure the penalty, but he asked a safe-conduct in coming and going, and if incarcerated or treated with violence during his stay the council would be committing injustice of which he could not suspect so many learned and wise men. This senseless bravado is only to be explained by his erratic temperament, and it did not prevent him from taking precautions as to his safety. He suddenly changed his mind, and on April 9, after obtaining from the Bohemians at Constance testimonial letters, he escaped from the city, none too soon, for the officials were in search of his lodgings, which they discovered a few days after at the Gutjar, in St. Paul Street, where in his haste he had left behind him the significant memento of a sword. This time he no longer trifled with fate, but travelled rapidly towards Bohemia. At Hirsau, however, his impetuous temper led him into a discussion in which he stigmatized the council as a synagogue of Satan. He was seized April 24, and the papers found upon him betrayed him. John of Bavaria threw him into the castle of Sulzbach, notified the council of his capture, and in obedience to its commands he was forthwith carried thither in chains.[536]

Meanwhile the council had responded to his appeal by publishing, April 18, a formal inquisitorial citation summoning him, as a suspected and defamed heretic, the suppression of whom was its chief duty, to appear for trial within fifteen days, in default of which he would be proceeded against in contumacy. A safe-conduct was offered him, but it was expressly declared subject to the exigencies of the faith. Unaware of his capture, on May 2 a new citation was published and his trial as contumacious was ordered, and this was repeated on the 4th. On May 24 his captors brought him to the city loaded with chains, and took him to the Franciscan convent, where a tumultuous congregation of the council greeted his arrival. Here Gerson gratified his rancor against his old opponent, loudly berating him for having taught falsely at Paris, Heidelberg, and Cologne, and the rectors of the two latter{499} universities corroborated the accusations. His replies were sharp and ready, but were drowned in the roar of fresh charges, mingled with shouts of "Burn him! Burn him!" Thence he was carried to a dungeon in the Cemetery of St. Paul, where he was chained hand and foot to a bench too high for him to sit on, and for two days he was fed on bread and water, until his friends ascertained his place of imprisonment and made interest with the jailer to give him better food. He soon fell dangerously sick and asked for a confessor, after which he was less rigorously fettered, but he never left the prison except for audience and execution.[537]

Stephen Palecz, Michael de Causis, and the rest were ready with their accusations, nor could there be difficulty in accumulating a mass of testimony sufficient to convict twenty such men as Jerome. His trial proceeded according to the regular inquisitorial process, the commissioners finding him much more learned and skilful than Huss; but, brilliant as was his defence when under examination, his nervous temperament unfitted him to bear, like Huss, the long-protracted agony. Sometimes with dialectic subtlety he turned his examiners to ridicule, at others he vacillated between obduracy and submission. Finally he weakened under the strain, while the rebellious attitude of the Bohemians doubtless led the council to increase the pressure. On September 11 he was brought before the assembly, where he read a long and elaborate recantation. Huss's sweetness of temper, he said, had attracted him, and his earnest exposition of Scripture truths had led him to believe that such a man could not teach heresy. He could not believe that the thirty articles condemned by the council were really Huss's, until he had obtained a book in Huss's own hand-writing, and on comparing them article by article he found them to be so. He therefore spontaneously and of free will condemned them, some of them as heretical, others as erroneous, others as scandalous. He also condemned the forty-five articles of Wickliff; he submitted himself wholly to the council, he condemned whatever it condemned, and he asked for fitting penance to be assigned him. He did not even shrink from a deeper degradation. He wrote to Bohemia that Huss had been justly executed, that he{500} had become convinced of his friend's errors and could not defend them.[538]

This was not a strictly formal abjuration such as was customarily required of prisoners of the Inquisition, yet it might have sufficed. It was read before a private congregation of the council, and some more public humiliation was needed. At the next general session, therefore, September 23, Jerome was placed in the pulpit, where he repeated his recantation, with an explanation of an expression in it, adding a recantation of his theory of Universals, and winding up by a solemn oath of abjuration in which he invoked an eternal anathema on all who wandered from the faith and on himself if he should do so. He had been told that he would not be allowed to return to Bohemia, but might select some Swabian monastery in which to reside, on condition that he should write home, over his hand and seal, that his teaching and that of Huss were false and not to be followed. This he promised to do, as, indeed, he had already done, but he was remanded to his prison, though his treatment was somewhat less harsh than before.[539]

Had the council been wise, it would have treated him as leniently as possible. A dishonored apostate, his power of evil was gone, and generosity would have been policy. The canons, however, prescribed harsh prison for converted heretics, whose conversion was always regarded as doubtful, and the assembled fathers were too bigoted to be wise. The zealots converted the apostate to a martyr, whose steadfast constancy redeemed his temporary weakness, and regained for him the forfeited influence over the imagination of his disciples.

His remorse was not long in showing itself. Stephen Palecz, Michael de Causis, and his other enemies who were still hovering around his prison, soon got wind of his self-accusation. John{501} Gerson, whose hostility seems to have been insatiable, readily made himself their mouthpiece, and in a learned dissertation on the essentials of revocations called the attention of the council, October 29, to the unsatisfactory character of that of Jerome. Some Carmelites, apparently arriving from Prague, furnished new accusations, and demands were made that he be required to answer additional articles. Some of the Cardinals, Zabarella, Pierre d'Ailly, Giordano Orsini, Antonio da Aquileia, on the other hand, labored with the council to procure his liberation, but on being actively opposed by the Germans and Bohemians and accused of receiving bribes from the heretics and King Wenceslas, they abandoned the hopeless defence. Accordingly, February 24, 1416, a new commission was appointed to hold an inquisition on him. The whole ground was gone over again in examining him, from the Wickliffite heresies to his exciting rebellion in Prague and contumaciously enduring the excommunication incurred in Vienna. April 27 the commissioners made their report, and the *Promotor Hæreticæ Pravitatis*, or prosecutor for heresy, accompanied it with a long indictment enumerating his offences. Jerome, resolved on death, had recovered his audacity; he not only, in spite of his recantation, denied that he was a heretic, but complained of unjust imprisonment and claimed to be indemnified for expenses and damages. His marvellous dialectical dexterity had evidently nonplussed the slower intellects of his examiners, who had found themselves unable to cope with his subtlety, for the council was asked, in conclusion, to diminish the diet on which he was described as feasting gluttonously, and by judicious starvation, the proper torment of heretics, to bring him to submission. Moreover, authority was asked to use torture and to force him to answer definitely yes or no to all questions as to his belief. If then he continues contumaciously to deny what has been or may be proved against him, he is to be handed over to the secular arm, in accordance with the canon law, as a pertinacious and incorrigible heretic. Thus with Jerome, as with Huss, the invariable principle of inquisitorial procedure was applied, that the denial of heretical opinions was simply an evidence and an aggravation of guilt.[540]{502}

In this case, more than in that of Huss, the council seems to have taken upon itself the part of an inquisitorial tribunal, with its commissioners simply as examiners to take testimony, possibly because Jerome had refused to accept them as judges on account of enmity towards him. There is no evidence that it consented to the superfluous infamy of torturing, or even of starving its victim. The commissioners were left to their own devices as to extracting a confession, and May 9 they made another report of the whole case from beginning to end, for what object is not apparent, unless to demonstrate their helplessness. Having thus wearied them out, Jerome finally promised to answer categorically before the council. Perhaps it was curiosity to hear him, perhaps the precedent set in the case of Huss weighed with the fathers. The concession was made to him, and at a general session held May 23 he was brought in and the oath was offered to him. He refused to take it, saying that he would do so if he would be allowed to speak freely, but if he was only to say yes or no he would not. As the articles were read over he remained silent as to a portion, while to the rest he answered affirmatively or negatively, occasionally making a distinction, and answering with admirable readiness the clamors and interruptions which assailed him from all sides. The day wore away in this, and the completion of the hearing was adjourned till the 26th. Again the same scene occurred till the series of articles was exhausted, when the chief of the commissioners, John, Patriarch of Constantinople, summed up, saying that Jerome was convicted of fourfold heresy; but as he had repeatedly asked to be heard he should be allowed to speak, in order to silence absurd reflections on the council; moreover, if he was prepared to confess and repent, he still would be received to mercy, but if obdurate, justice must take its course.[541]

Of the scene which followed we have a vivid account in a letter to Leonardo Aretino from Poggio Bracciolini, who attended the council as apostolic secretary. Poggio had already been profoundly impressed with the quickness and readiness of a man who for three hundred and forty days had lain in the filth and squalor of a noisome dungeon, but now he breaks forth in unqualified admiration-{503}-"He stood fearless, undaunted, not merely despising death, but longing for it, like another Cato. O man worthy of eternal remembrance among men! If he held beliefs contrary to the rules of the Church I do not praise him, but I admire his learning, his knowledge of so many things, his eloquence, and the subtlety of his answers." In the midst of that turbulent and noisy crowd, his eloquence was so great that Poggio evidently thinks he would have been acquitted had he not courted death.[542]

His address was a most skilful vindication, gliding with seemingly careless negligence over the dangerous spots in his career—for his whole life had been made the subject of indictment—and giving most plausible explanations of that which could not be suppressed, as though the Bohemian troubles had been solely due to political differences. As for his recantation, his judges had promised him kindly treatment if he would throw himself on the mercy of the council. He was but a man, with a human dread of a dreadful death by fire; he had weakly yielded to persuasion, he had abjured, he had written to Bohemia as required, he had condemned the teaching of John Huss. Here he rose to the full height of his manly and self-devoted eloquence. Huss was a just and holy man, to whom he would cleave to the last; no sin that he had ever committed so weighed upon his conscience as his cowardly abjuration, which now he solemnly revoked. Wickliff had written with a profounder truth than any man before him, and dread of the stake alone could have induced him to condemn such a master, saving only the doctrine on the sacrament, of which he could not approve. Then he burst forth into a ringing invective on the vices of the clergy, and especially of the Roman curia, which had stimulated Wickliff and Huss to their efforts for reform. The good fathers of the council might be stunned for a moment by the fierce self-sacrifice of the man who thus deliberately threw away his life, but they soon recovered themselves, and quietly assigned the following Saturday for his definite sentence. Although, as a self-confessed relapsed, he was entitled to no further consideration, they proposed, with unusual mercy, to give him four days to reconsider and repent, but he had been addressing an audience far beyond the narrow walls of the Cathedral of Constance, and his words were seeds which sprouted forth in armed warriors.[543]

On May 30 the final acts of the tragedy were hurried through;{504} the council assembled early, and by ten o'clock Jerome was at the stake. After the mass, the Bishop of Lodi preached a sermon. He had been selected to perform the same office at the condemnation of Huss, and the brutality of his triumph over the unfortunate prisoner on this occasion even exceeded his former effort. The charity and tenderness with which Jerome had been treated ought to have softened his heart, even had the recollection of his crimes failed to do so. A comparison was drawn between the favor shown him and the severity customary with suspected heretics. "You were not tortured—I wish you had been, for it would have forced you to vomit forth all your errors; such treatment would have opened your eyes, which guilt had closed." The nobles present were called upon to mark how Huss and Jerome, two base-born men, plebeians of the lowest rank and unknown origin, had dared to trouble the noble kingdom of Bohemia, and what evils had sprung from the presumption of those two peasants. Then Jerome in a few dignified sentences replied, asserting his conscientiousness and deploring his condemnation of Wickliff and Huss. Cardinal Zabarella, he said, was winning him over when his judges were changed and he would not plead to new ones. His abjuration was read to him; he acknowledged it; he said it had been extorted by the dread of fire. Then the prosecutor asked for a definite sentence in writing against him, and the head commissioner, John of Constantinople, read a long one condemning him as a supporter of Wickliff and Huss, and ending with the declaration that he was a relapsed heretic and anathematized excommunicate. To this the council unanimously responded "*Placet.*" There was no pretence of asking mercy for him. He was handed over to the secular power with a command that it should do its duty under the sentence rendered. Not being in orders, there was no ceremony of degradation to be performed, but a tall paper crown with painted devils was brought. He tossed his cap among the prelates and put on the crown, saying, "Our Lord Jesus Christ, when about to die for me, wore a crown of thorns. In place of that, I gladly bear this for his sake," and with this he was hurried off to execution on the same spot where Huss had suffered.[544]{505}

The details of the execution were much the same, except that Jerome was stripped and a cloth tied around his loins. He sang the Creed and a litany, and when his voice could no longer be heard in the flames his lips were still seen to move as though praying to himself; after his beard was burned off, a blister the size of an egg was seen to form itself, showing that he still was alive, and his agony was unusually prolonged, through his extraordinary strength and vitality. One eye-witness says that he shrieked awfully, but other unfriendly witnesses declare that he continued praying till his voice was checked by the fire, and Poggio, who was present, was much impressed with his cheerful courage to the last. When bound to the stake, the executioner offered to light the fire from behind, where he could not see it, but he refused: "Come forward," he said, "and light the fire where I can see it. Had I feared this, I would not have been here." Æneas Sylvius likewise couples him with Huss for the unsurpassed constancy of his death. After it was over, his bedding, shoes, cap, and all his personal effects were brought from his dungeon and thrown upon the pile, that no relic of him might be left, and the ashes were cast into the Rhine.[545]

It only remained to secure the submission of John of Chlum, the courageous defender of Huss. He had remained in Constance and was in the power of the council. What means were adopted for his abasement do not appear, but, on July 1, he swore to maintain the faith, admitted that Huss and Jerome had suffered justly, and desired letters of his declaration to be made, that he might send them to Bohemia.[546]{506}

CHAPTER VIII.

THE HUSSITES.

THE Council of Constance, after eighteen months of labor, had disposed of Huss and Jerome. The methods employed had been the only ones known to the Church, the only ones possible to the council. Two centuries earlier the corruptions of the Church were recognized as the cause and excuse of the revolt of the Albigenses and Waldenses, but the revolt was ruthlessly put down without an effective effort to remove the cause. Now again unchecked corruption had produced another revolt and the same policy was followed—to leave untouched the profitable abuses and punish those who refused to tolerate them, and who rejected the principles out of which such abuses inevitably sprang. The council could do no otherwise; the traditions of procedure established in the subjugation of the Albigenses and the succeeding heresies furnished the only precedent and machinery through which it could act. Again a religious revolt had been provoked, and again that revolt was nursed and intensified till its only recognized cure lay in the sword of the crusader.

The prelates and doctors assembled in Constance could not hesitate for a moment as to their duty. Canon law and inquisitorial practice had long established the principle that the only way to meet heresy—and opposition to the constituted authorities of the Church was heresy—was by force, as soon as argument was found ineffective. The disobedient son of the Church who would not submit was to be cast out, after due admonition, and casting out meant that he should have in this world a wholesome foretaste of the wrath to come, in order to serve as an edifying example. Accordingly the council addressed itself, as a matter of course, to the task of widening the breach with Bohemia, of consolidating and intensifying the indignation caused by the execution of Huss and Jerome, and to stigmatizing as{507} heresy the belief which was now professed by the majority of Bohemians.

The council had proposed to follow up the execution of Huss by an immediate application of inquisitorial methods to the whole Bohemian kingdom, but, at the instance of John, Bishop of Litomysl, it had commenced by the expedient of giving notice in its letter of July 26, 1415. This, as we have seen, only added to the exasperation of Bohemia, and on August 31 it issued to Bishop John letters commissioning him with inquisitorial powers to suppress all heresy in Bohemia; if he could not perform his office in safety elsewhere he was authorized to summon all suspect to his episcopal seat at Litomysl. Wenceslas dutifully issued to him a safe-conduct, but the irate Bohemians were already ravaging his territories, and he consulted prudence in not venturing his person there. The canons evidently could not be enforced amid a people so exasperated; so, on September 23, after listening to the recantation of Jerome, the council tried a further expedient, by a decree appointing John, Patriarch of Constantinople, and John, Bishop of Senlis, as commissioners (or, rather, inquisitors) to try all Hussite heretics. They were empowered to summon all heretics or suspects to appear before them in the Roman curia by public edict, to be posted in the places frequented by such heretics, or in the neighboring territories if it were dangerous to attempt it at the residences of the accused, and such edicts might be either general in character or special. This was strictly according to rule, and if the object had been to secure the legal condemnation *in absentia* of the mass of the Bohemian nation, it was well adapted for the purpose; but

167

as the nation was seething in revolt, and was venerating Huss and Jerome with as much ardor as was shown in Rome to St. Peter and St. Paul, its only effect was to strengthen the hands of the extremists. This was seen when, on December 30, 1415, an address was delivered to the council, signed by four hundred and fifty Bohemian nobles, reiterating their complaints of the execution of Huss, and withdrawing themselves from all obedience. This hardy challenge was accepted February 20, 1416, by citing all the signers and other supporters of Huss and Wickliff to appear before the council within fifty days and answer to the charge of heresy, in default of which they were to be proceeded against as contumacious. As it was not safe to serve this{508} citation on them personally, or, indeed, anywhere in Bohemia, it was ordered to be affixed on the church doors at Constance, Ratisbon, Vienna, and Passau. This was followed up with all the legal forms; the citations were affixed to the church doors, and record made in Constance May 5, in Passau May 3, in Vienna May 10, and in Ratisbon June 14, 21, and 24. On June 3 the offenders were declared to be in contumacy, and on September 4 the further prosecution of the matter was intrusted to John of Constantinople.[547]

Here the affair seems to have dropped, for it had long been evident that the inquisitorial methods were of no avail when the accused constituted the great body of a nation. As early as March 27, 1416, the council had, without waiting to see the result of its judicial proceedings, resolved to appeal to force, if yet there was sufficient zeal for orthodoxy in Bohemia to render such appeal successful. The fanatic John of Litomysl was armed with legatine powers, and despatched with letters to the lords of Hazemburg, John of Michaelsburg, and other barons known as opponents of the popular cause. The council recited in moving terms its patience and tenderness in dealing with Huss, who had perished merely through his own hardness of heart. In spite of this, his followers had addressed to the council libellous and defamatory letters, affording a spectacle at once horrible and ludicrous. Heresy is constantly spreading and contaminating the land, priests and monks are despoiled, expelled, beaten, and slain. The barons are therefore summoned, in conjunction with the legate, to banish and exterminate all these persecutors, regardless of friendship and kinship. Bishop John's mission was a failure, in spite of letters written by Sigismund, March 21 and 30, in which he thanked the Catholic nobles for their devotion, and warned the Hussite magnates that, if they persisted, Christendom would be banded against them in a crusade. The University of Prague responded, May 23, with a public declaration, certifying to the unblemished orthodoxy and supereminent merits of Huss. His whole life spent among them had been without a flaw; his learning and eloquence had{509} been equalled by his charity and humility; he was in all things a man of surpassing sanctity, who sought to restore the Church to its primitive virtue and simplicity. Jerome, also, whom the university seems to have supposed already executed, was similarly lauded for his learning and strict Catholic orthodoxy, and was declared to have in death triumphed gloriously over his enemies. In this the university represented with moderation the prevailing opinion in Bohemia. The more earnest disciples did not hesitate to declare that the Passion of Christ was the only martyrdom fit to be compared with that of Huss.[548]

There was evidently no middle term which could reconcile conflicting opinions so firmly entertained; and, as the Catholic nobles of Bohemia could not be stimulated to undertake a devastating civil war, the council naturally turned to Sigismund. In December, 1416, a doleful epistle was addressed to him, complaining that the execution of Huss and Jerome, in place of repressing heresy, had rendered it more violent than ever. As though men condemned to Satan by the Church were the chosen of God, the two heretics were venerated as saints and martyrs, their pictures shrined in the churches, and their names invoked in masses. The faithful clergy were driven out, and their lot rendered more miserable than that of Jews. The barons and nobles refuse obedience to the mandates of the council, and will not allow them to be published. Communion in both elements is taught to be necessary to salvation, and is everywhere practised. Sigismund is therefore requested to do his duty, and reduce by force these rebellious heretics. Sigismund replied that he had forwarded the document to Wenceslas, and that if the latter had not power to suppress the heretics he would assist him with all his force. Sigismund was in no position to undertake the task, but after waiting for nine months he saw an opportunity of attacking his brother, who had been utterly powerless to control the storm. In a circular letter of September 3, 1417, addressed to the faithful in Bohemia, he drew a moving picture of the excesses committed on the Bohemian clergy, compelled by Neronian tortures to abjure their faith. His{510} brother was suspected of favoring the heretics, as no one could conceive that such wickedness could be committed under so powerful a king without his connivance, and the council had decided to proceed against him, but had consented to delay at the instance of Sigismund, who for three years had been strenuously endeavoring to avert the prosecution. He warns every one, in conclusion, not to aid the heresy, but to exert themselves for its suppression.[549]

Shortly after this, November 11, 1417, the weary schism was closed by the election to the papacy of Martin V. Under the impulsion of a capable and resolute pontiff, who, as Cardinal Ottone Colonna, had, in 1411, condemned and excommunicated Huss, the reunited Church pressed eagerly forward to render the conflict inevitable. In February, 1418, the council published a series of twenty-four articles as its ultimatum. King Wenceslas must swear to suppress the heresy of Wickliff and Huss. Minute directions were given to restore the old order of things throughout Bohemia; priests and Catholics who had been driven out were to be reinstated and compensated; image and relic worship to be resumed, and the rites of the Church observed. All infected with heresy were to abjure it, while their leading doctors, John Jessenitz, Jacobel of Mies, Simon of Rokyzana, and six others, were to betake themselves to Rome for trial. Communion in both elements was to be specially abjured, and all who held the doctrines of Wickliff and Huss, or regarded Huss and Jerome as holy men, were to be burned as relapsed heretics; that is, without opportunity of recantation or hope of pardon. Finally, every one was required to lend assistance to the episcopal officials when called upon, under pain of punishment as fautors of heresy. It was simply the application of existing laws, as we have so many times already seen them brought to bear on offending communities. To enforce it, Sigismund promised to visit the rebellious region with four bishops and an inquisitor, and to burn all who would not recant.[550]

This was speedily followed, February 22, 1418, by a bull of{511} Martin V., addressed to the prelates and inquisitors, not only of Bohemia and Moravia, but of the surrounding territories, Passau, Salzburg, Ratisbon, Bamberg, Misnia, Silesia, and Poland. The pope expressed his grief and surprise that the heretics had not been brought to repentance by the miserable deaths of Huss and Jerome, but had been excited by the devil to yet greater sins. The prelates and inquisitors were ordered to track them out and deliver them to the secular arm; and such as proved themselves remiss in the work were to be removed, and replaced with more energetic successors. Secular potentates were commanded to seize and hold in chains all heretics, and to punish them duly when convicted, and a long series of instructions was given as to trials, penalties, and confiscations, in strict accordance with the inquisitorial practice which had so long been current. If this was intended to give countenance to Sigismund's promised expedition it proved useless, for the royal promise ended as Sigismund's were wont to do, and the next we hear of him is a letter of December, 1418, to Wenceslas, threatening that unlucky monarch with a crusade if he shall not suppress heresy.[551]

The glimpse into the condition of Bohemia afforded by these documents is, perhaps, somewhat highly colored, yet on the whole not incorrect. The kingdom was almost wholly withdrawn from obedience to the Church, although the German miners in the mountains of Kuttenberg were already slaying the native heretics. The Wickliffite doctrines adopted by Huss were triumphant, and the pressure of central authority being removed, men were naturally using the unaccustomed liberty to develop further and further the ruling hostility to the sacerdotal system. Utraquism, or communion in both elements, had been received with a frenzy of welcome which seems almost inexplicable; it aroused universal enthusiasm, which was only stimulated by the interdict pronounced on it by Archbishop Conrad, November 1, 1415, and repeated February 1, 1416. When, in 1417, the University of Prague issued a solemn declaration in its favor and pronounced void any human ordinance modifying the command of Christ and the custom of the early Church, it speedily became the distinguishing mark which separated the Hussite from the Catholic. Other innovations had{512} already been introduced, and it was impossible that all should agree on the bounds to be set between conservatism and progress. As early as 1416 Christann of Prachatitz remonstrated with Wenceslas Coranda for denying purgatory and the utility of prayers for the dead and the suffrages of saints, for refusing adoration to the Virgin, for casting out relics and images, for administering the Eucharist to newly-baptized infants, for discarding all rites and ceremonies, and reducing the Church to the simplicity of primitive times. Others taught that divine service could be celebrated anywhere as well as in consecrated churches; that baptism could be performed by laymen in ponds and running streams. Already there was forming the sect which, in carrying out the views of Wickliff, came to be known as Taborites. The more conservative element, which adopted the name of Calixtins, or Utraquists, satisfied with what had been acquired, endeavored to set bounds to the zeal which threatened to remove all the ancient landmarks. Parties were beginning to range themselves, and on January 25, 1417, probably not long before its declaration in favor of Utraquism, the University issued a letter reciting that there were frequent disputes as to the existence of purgatory and the use of benedictions and other church observances; to put an end to these it pronounced obligatory on all to believe in purgatory and in the utility of suffrages, prayers, and alms for the dead, of images of Christ and the saints, of incensing, aspersions, bell-ringing, the kiss of peace, of benediction of the holy font, salt, water, wax, fire, palms, eggs, cheese, and other eatables. Any one teaching otherwise was not to be listened to until he should prove the truth of his doctrine to the satisfaction of the University. In September, 1418, it was obliged to renew the declaration, with the addition of condemning the doctrines which pronounced against all oaths, judicial executions, and sacraments administered by sinful priests, showing that Waldensian tenets were making rapid progress among the Taborites.[552]

All this indicates the questions which were occupying men's minds and the differences which were establishing themselves.{513} Opinions were too strongly held, and mutual toleration was too little understood for peaceful discussion, and excitement daily grew higher, leading to tumults and bloodshed. In the spirit of unrest which was abroad, men and women of the more advanced views from all parts of the kingdom began assembling on a mountain near Bechin, to which they gave the name of Tabor, where they received the sacrament in both kinds. These assemblages were larger on feast days, and on the day of Mary Magdalen, July 22, 1419, the multitude was computed at forty thousand. Numbers gave courage, and there was even talk of deposing King Wenceslas and replacing him with Nicholas Lord of Hussinetz, whose popularity had been increased by his banishment for advocating their cause with the monarch. From this they were dissuaded by their chief spiritual leader, the priest Wenceslas Coranda, who pointed out that as the king was an indolent drunkard, permitting them to do what they liked, they would scarce benefit themselves by a change. The abandonment of this project, however, did not assure peace. On July 30 there was a tumult in the Neustadt of Prague; at command of the king, the authorities endeavored to prevent the progress of a procession bearing the sacrament; the people rose, and under the lead of John Ziska, whose fiery zeal and cool audacity were rapidly bringing him to the front, they rushed into the town-hall and cast out of the windows such of the magistrates as they found there, who were promptly slain by the mob below. The agitation and alarm caused by this affair brought on King Wenceslas an attack of paralysis, of which he died August 15.[553]

Feeble as had been the royal authority, it yet had served as a restraint upon the hostile sects eager to tear each other to pieces. With the death of the king the untamable passions burst forth. Two days afterwards the churches and convents were mobbed, the images and organs were broken, and those in which the cup had been refused to the laity were the objects of special vengeance. Priests and monks were taken prisoners, and within a few days the Dominican and Carthusian convents were burned. Queen Sophia endeavored, in vain, to maintain order with such of the{514} barons as remained loyal; civil war broke forth, until, on November 13, the queen concluded with the cities of Prague a truce to last until April 23, 1420, the queen promising to maintain the law of God and communion in both elements, while the citizens pledged themselves to refrain from image-breaking and the destruction of convents. Mutual exasperation, however, was too great to be restrained. Ziska came to Prague and destroyed churches and monasteries in the city and neighborhood; Queen Sophia laid siege to Pilsen; a neighborhood war broke out in which shocking cruelties were perpetrated on both sides; German miners of Caurzim and Kuttenberg threw into abandoned mines all the Calixtins on whom they could lay their hands, and some Bavarians who were coming to the assistance of Rackzo of Ryzmberg tied to a tree and burned the priest Naakvasa, a zealous Calixtin. Ziska was not behindhand in this, and in burning convents not infrequently allowed the monks to share the fate of their buildings. In the desultory war which raged everywhere both sides cut off the hands and feet of prisoners.[554]

Sigismund was now the lawful King of Bohemia, and he came to claim his inheritance. As a preliminary step he sent envoys to Prague offering to leave the use of the cup as it had been under Wenceslas, to call a general assembly of the nation, and after consultation to refer any questions to the Holy See. A meeting of the barons and clergy was held which agreed to accept the terms. On Christmas Day, 1419, he came to Brünn, and thither flocked the magnates and representatives of the cities to tender their allegiance. The envoys of Prague, it is true, persisted in using the cup, and there was an interdict in consequence placed on Brünn during their stay, but when he ordered them to remove the chains from the streets of Prague, and destroy the fortifications which they had raised against the castle, there was no refusal, and on their return, January 3, 1420, his commands were obeyed. His natural faithlessness soon showed itself. He changed all the castellans and officials who were favorable to the Hussites; the Catholics who had fled or been expelled returned and commenced to triumph over their enemies; and a royal edict was issued, in obedience{515} to the decrees of Constance, commanding all those in authority to exterminate the Wickliffites and Hussites and those who used the sacramental cup. Still, the kingdom made no sign of organized opposition to him, except that the provident Ziska and his followers, seeing the wrath to come, diligently set to work to fortify Mount Tabor. Strong by nature, it soon was made virtually impregnable, and for a generation it remained the stronghold of the extremists who became renowned throughout the world as Taborites. Mostly peasant-folk, they showed to the chivalry of Europe what could be done by freemen, animated by religious zeal and race hatred; their rustic wagons made a rampart which the most valiant knights learned not to assail; armed sometimes only with iron-shod flails, the hardy zealots did not hesitate to throw themselves upon the best-appointed troops, and often bore them down with the sheer weight of the attack. Wild and undisciplined, they were often cruel, but their fanatic courage rendered them a terror to all Germany.[555]

Nothing, probably, could have averted an eventual explosion; but, for the moment, it seemed that Sigismund was about to enter on peaceable possession of his kingdom, and any subsequent rebellion would have been attempted under great disadvantages. Suddenly, however, an act of inconsiderate and gratuitous fanaticism set all Bohemia aflame. Some trouble in Silesia had called Sigismund to Breslau, where he was joined by a papal legate armed by Martin V. with power to proclaim a crusade with Holy Land indulgences. John Krasa, a merchant of Prague, who chanced to be there, talked over boldly about the innocence of Huss; he was arrested, persisted in his faith, and was condemned by the legate and prelates who were with Sigismund to be dragged by the heels at a horse's tail to the place of execution and burned. While lying in prison he was joined by Nicholas of Bethlehem, a student of Prague, who had been sent by the city to Sigismund to offer to receive him if he would not interfere with the use of the cup to the laity. In place of listening to him he was tried as a heretic and thrown into prison to await the result. Krasa encouraged him to endure to the last, and both were brought forth on March{516} 15, 1420, to undergo the punishment. As the feet of Nicholas were about to be attached to the horse, his courage gave way and he recanted. Krasa was undaunted; the legate followed him, as he was dragged to the place of execution, exhorting him to repent, but in vain; he was attached half-dead to the stake and duly burned. Two days later, March 17, the legate proclaimed the crusade. The die was cast; the Church so willed it, and a new Albigensian war was inevitable.[556]

There was wavering no longer in Bohemia. The events at Breslau united all, with the exception of a few barons and such Germans as were left, in resistance against Sigismund. The preachers thundered against him as the Red Dragon of the Apocalypse. By April 3 the citizens of Utraquist Prague had bound themselves by a solemn oath with the Taborites to defend themselves against him to the last, and were busy in preparations to sustain a siege. Sigismund's forces were wholly inadequate for the conquest of a virtually united kingdom. After an advance to Kuttenberg he was forced to withdraw and await the assembling of the crusade, which took long to organize, and did not burst in its fury over Bohemia until the following year, 1421. It was on a scale to crush all resistance. In its mass of one hundred and fifty thousand men all Europe was represented, from Russia to Spain and from Sicily to England. The reunited Church aroused all Christendom to stamp out the revolt, and the treasures of salvation were poured lavishly forth to exterminate those who dared to maintain the innocence of Huss and Jerome, and to take the Eucharist as all Christians had done until within two hundred years. The war was waged with desperation. Five times during 1421 the crusaders invaded Bohemia, and five times they were beaten back disastrously. The gain to the faith was scarce perceptible, for Sigismund stripped the churches of all their precious ornaments, declaring that he was{517} not impelled by lack of reverence, but by a prudent desire to prevent their falling into the hands of the Hussites. Both sides perpetrated cruelties happily unknown save in the ferocity of religious wars. During the siege of Prague all Bohemians captured were burned as heretics whether they used the cup or not; and on July 19 the besieged demanded of the magistrates sixteen German prisoners, whom they took outside of the walls and burned in hogsheads in full sight of the invading army. We can estimate the mercilessness of the strife when it was reckoned among the good deeds of George, Bishop of Passau, who accompanied Albert of Austria, that by his intercession he saved the lives of many Bohemian captives.[557]

It is not our province to follow in detail this bloody struggle, in which for ten years the Hussites successfully defied all the forces that Martin and Sigismund could raise against them. When the crusaders came they presented a united front, but within the line of common defence they were torn with dissensions, bitter in proportion to their exaltation of religious feeling. The right of private judgment when once established, by admitting the doctrines of Wickliff and Huss, was not easily restrained, nor could it be expected that those who were persecuted would learn from persecution the lesson of tolerance. In the wild tumult, intellectual, moral, and social, which convulsed Bohemia, no doctrines were too extravagant to lack believers.

In 1418 it is related that forty Pikardi with their wives and children came to Prague, where they were hospitably received and cared for by Queen Sophia and other persons of rank. They had no priest, but one of their number used to read to them out of certain little books, and they took communion in one element. They vanish from view without leaving a trace of their influence, and were doubtless Beghards driven from their homes and seeking a refuge beyond the reach of orthodoxy. Yet their name remained, and was long used in Bohemia as a term of the bitterest contempt for those who denied transubstantiation. Subsequently, however, there was a more portentous demonstration of{518} the Brethren of the Free Spirit. A stranger, said to come from Flanders, whose name, "Pichardus," shows evidently that he was a Beghard, disseminated the doctrine of the Brethren, and among other things that nakedness was essential to purity, which we have seen was one of the extravagances of the sect. The practice was one which in a more settled state of society could not have been ventured on, but in Bohemia he found little difficulty in obtaining quite a large following of both sexes, with whom he settled on an island in the river Luznic, and dignified them with the name of Adamites. Perhaps they might have flourished undisturbed had not fanaticism, or possibly retaliation for aggression, led them to make a foray on the mainland and slay some two hundred peasants, whom they styled children of the devil. Ziska's attention being thus drawn to them, he captured the island and exterminated them. Fifty of them, men and women, were burned at Klokot, and those who escaped were hunted down and gradually shared the same fate, which they met with undaunted cheerfulness, laughing and singing as they went to the stake.[558]

In the sudden removal of ecclesiastical repression of free thought it was inevitable that unbalanced minds should riot in extravagant speculation. Among the zealots who subsequently developed into the sect of the Taborites there was at first a strong tendency to apocalyptic prophecy suited to the times. First, there was to be a period of unsparing vengeance, during which safety could be found only in five specified cities of refuge, after which would follow the second advent of Christ, and the reign of peace and love among the elect, and earth would become a paradise. At first, the destruction of the wicked was to be the work of God, but as passions became fiercer it was held to be the duty of the righteous to cut them off without sparing. These Chiliasts or Millenarians had for their leader Martin Huska, surnamed Loquis, on account of his eloquence, and numbered among them Coranda and other prominent Taborite priests. Waldensian influence is visible in some features of their faith, and they rendered themselves peculiarly obnoxious by the denial of transubstantiation.{519} For this they were exposed to pitiless persecution wherever their adversaries could exercise it. One of their leading members, a cobbler of Prague, named Wenceslas, was burned in a hogshead, July 23, 1421, for refusing to rise at the elevation of the host, and soon afterwards three priests shared the same fate because they refused to light candles before the sacrament. Martin Loquis himself was arrested in February of the same year, but was released at the intercession of the Taborites, and set out with a companion to seek Procopius in Moravia. At Chrudim, however, the travellers were arrested, and were burned at Hradisch after two months of torture vainly inflicted to wean them from their errors and force them to reveal the names of their associates. As a distinct sect the Chiliasts speedily disappear from view, but their members remained a portion of the Taborites, the development of whose opinions they profoundly influenced. In the delegation sent to Basle, in 1433, Peter of Zatce, who represented the Orphans, had been a Chiliast.[559]

Thus these minor sects vanished as parties organized themselves in a permanent form, and the Bohemian reformers are found divided into two camps—the moderates, known as Calixtins or Utraquists, from their chief characteristic, the administration of the cup to the laity, and the extremists, or Taborites.

171

The Calixtins virtually regarded the teachings of Huss and Jacobel of Mies, as a finality. When, after the death of Wenceslas, the necessity of some definite declaration of principles was felt, the University of Prague, on August 1, 1420, adopted, with but one dissenting voice, four articles which became for more than a century the distinguishing platform of their sect. As concisely enunciated by the University they appeared simple enough: I. Free preaching of the Word of God; II. Communion in both elements for the laity; III. The clergy to be deprived of all dominion over temporal possessions, and to be reduced to the evangelical life of Christ and the apostles; IV. All offences against divine law to be punished without exception of person or condition.{520}These four articles were speedily accepted by the strongly Calixtin community of Prague, and were proclaimed to the world in various forms which added to their completeness and rendered their purport definite. Any one was declared a heretic who did not accept the Apostles", Athanasian, and Nicene creeds, the seven sacraments of the Church, and the existence of purgatory. Offences against the law of God were declared to be worthy of death, both of the offender and those who connived at them, and were defined to be, among the people, fornication, banqueting, theft, homicide, perjury, lying, arts superfluous, deceitful, and superstitious, avarice, usury, etc.: among the clergy, simoniacal exactions, such as fees for administering the sacraments, for preaching, burying, bell-ringing, consecration of churches and altars, as well as the sale of preferment; also concubinage and fornication, quarrels, vexing and spoiling the people with frivolous citations, greedy exactions of tribute, etc.[560]

Upon this basis the Calixtin Church proceeded to organize itself in a council held at Prague in 1421. Four leading doctors, John of Przibram, Procopius of Pilsen, Jacobel of Mies, and John of Neuberg, were made supreme governors of the clergy throughout the kingdom, with absolute power of punishment. No one was to teach any new doctrine without first submitting it to them or to a provincial synod. Transubstantiation was emphatically affirmed as well as the seven sacraments. The daily use of the Eucharist was recommended to all, including infants and the sick. The canon of the mass was simplified and restored to primitive usage. Auricular confession was prescribed, as well as the use of the chrism and of holy water in baptism. Clerks were to be distinguished by tonsure, vestments, and conduct. Every priest was to possess a copy of the Scriptures, or at least of the New Testament, and stringent regulations were adopted for the preservation of priestly morality, including the prohibition of their protection by any layman after conviction.[561]

Thus the Calixtin Church kept as close as possible to the old{521} lines. It accepted all Catholic dogmas, even the power of the keys in sacramental penance, and only was a protest and revolt against the abuses which had grown out of the worldly aspirations of the clergy. It was a Puritan reform, and it founded a Puritan society. When, after the reconciliation effected at Basle, on the basis of the four articles, Sigismund, in 1436, held his court in Prague, the Bohemians speedily complained that the city was becoming a Sodom with dicing, tavern-haunting, and public women. It must have sounded strange to them to be coolly told by a Christian prelate, the Bishop of Coutances, who was the legate of the council empowered to enforce the settlement, that it would be well if public sins could be eradicated, but that strumpets must be tolerated to prevent greater evils.[562]

The Calixtins thus sought to keep themselves strictly within the pale of orthodoxy, and deemed themselves greatly injured and insulted by the appellation of heretic. After the reconciliation of 1436 one of their most constant causes of complaint was that they were still stigmatized as heretics, and that the Council of Basle would not issue letters proclaiming to Christendom that they were regarded as faithful sons of the Church. In 1464, after successive popes had repeatedly refused to ratify the pacification of Basle and had excommunicated as hardened heretics George Podiebrad and all who acknowledged him as king, when George sent an embassy to Louis XI. of France, Kostka of Postubitz, the envoy, and his attendants were more than once surprised and annoyed to find that the people of the towns through which they passed were disposed to regard them as heretics. The position of the Bohemian Calixtins was an anomalous one which has no parallel in the history of mediæval Christendom.[563]{522}

In the intellectual and spiritual excitement which stirred Bohemia to the depths, it was impossible that all earnest souls should thus pause on the threshold. The old Waldensian heretics, who had hailed the progress of Wickliffite and Hussite doctrines, would naturally seek to prevent the arrested development of the Calixtins from prevailing, and, as we have seen, there were plenty of zealots who were ready to throw aside all the theology of sacerdotalism. Under the energetic leadership of Ziska, Coranda, Nicholas of Pilgram, and other resolute men, the progressive elements were rapidly moulded into a powerful party, which after sloughing off impracticable enthusiasts presented itself with a definite creed and purpose, and became known as the Taborites. Of late years there has been an active controversy as to whether the Waldenses were the teachers or the disciples of the Taborites. Without denying that the fearless vigor of the latter lent added strength to the development of the former, I cannot but think that the secret Waldensianism of Bohemia had much to do both with the revolt of Huss and with the carrying out of that revolt to its logical consequences. Certain it is that there were close and friendly relations between Waldensian and Taborite, while the very name of the former was regarded by all other Bohemians as a term of reproach—in fact there was so much in common between Wickliffite and Waldensian doctrine that this could scarce be otherwise. I have already alluded to the contributions made to the Hussites in 1432 by the Waldensian churches of Dauphiné, and to the virtual coalescence of Hussitism and Waldensianism throughout Germany. When Procopius the Great, in 1433, was taking leave of the Council of Basle, he had the hardihood to inject into his address a good word for the Waldenses, saying that he had heard them well spoken

172

of for chastity, modesty, and similar virtues. Persecution in 1430 so thinned them out that they had neither bishop nor priests; Nicholas of Pilgram, the Taborite bishop, had enjoyed consecration in the Roman Church, and thus had the right to transmit the apostolic succession, and he, in 1433, in Prague consecrated for the Waldenses as bishops two of their number, Frederic the German, and John the Italian. When, in 1451, Æneas Sylvius passed a night in Mount Tabor, and wrote a picturesque description of what he observed, he states that while all heresies had a refuge there, the Waldenses were held in {523} chief honor as the vicars of Christ and enemies of the Holy See.[564]

When the Calixtins, in 1421, defined their position, the Taborites did the same. Various special Waldensian errors were attracting attention and obtaining currency among the people—the denial of purgatory, the vitiation of the sacrament in sinful hands, the absolute rejection of the death-punishment and of the oath— showing the influences at work. The position assumed by the Taborites was so strikingly similar to the beliefs ascribed in 1395 to the Waldenses in Austria by the Celestinian inquisitor, Peter, that it is impossible not to recognize the connection between them. While the Taborites accepted the four articles of the Calixtins they reduced the Church to a state of the utmost apostolic simplicity. Tradition was wholly thrown aside; all images were to be burned; there was no outward sign of distinction between layman and priest, the latter wearing beards, rejecting the tonsure, and using ordinary garments; all priests, moreover, were bishops, and could perform the rite of consecration; they baptized in running water, without the chrism, celebrated mass anywhere, reciting the simple words of consecration and the Paternoster in a loud voice and in the vernacular, administering the body in fragments of bread and the blood in any vessel which might be handy; all consecrations of sacred vessels, oil, and water was forbidden; purgatory, which Huss had accepted, was denied, and to manifest their contempt for the suffrages of the saints they ate more than usual on fast-days and saints"- days; auricular confession was derided—for venial sins confession to God sufficed, for mortal ones, public confession before the brethren, when the priest would assign a penalty commensurate with the offence. At the same time the rude and uncultured vigor of the Taborites led them to regard all human learning as a snare. Those who studied the liberal arts were regarded as heathen and as sinning against the Gospel, and all writings of the doctors, save what were expressly contained in the Bible, were to be destroyed.[565] {524}

What were their views with respect to the Lord's Supper cannot be stated with precision. Laurence of Brezowa, a Calixtin bitterly hostile to them, says that they consecrated the elements in a loud voice and in the vulgar tongue, that the people might be assured that they were receiving the real body and the real blood, which infers belief in transubstantiation. In 1431 Procopius the Great and other leaders of the Taborites issued a proclamation defining their position, in which they asserted their disbelief in purgatory, in the intercessory power of the Virgin and saints, in masses for the dead, in absolution through indulgences, etc., but said nothing against transubstantiation. When, in 1436, the legates of the Council of Basle complained of the non-observance of the Compactata, one of their grievances was that Bohemia still sheltered Wickliffites who believed in the remanence of the substance of the bread, but they said nothing about the existence of any worse form of belief. On the other hand, the Taborite Bishop, Nicholas of Pilgram, strongly asserted that Christ was only present spiritually, that no veneration was due to the consecrated elements, and that there was less idolatry in those who of old adored moles and bats and snakes than in Christians who worshipped the host, for those things at least had life. During the negotiations, in January, 1433, the legates of the council presented a series of twenty-eight articles, attributed to the Bohemians, and asked for definite answers, yea or nay. One of these was a denial of transubstantiation, and the Bohemians could never be induced to make the desired reply. Peter Chelcicky reproached the Taborites with concealing their belief on the subject, but it is probable that there was no absolute accord among them. The Chiliast leaven doubtless spread the denial of transubstantiation; others probably adopted the Wickliffite doctrine of remanence; others again may have preserved the orthodox faith, and all resented the appellation of Pikards, with which the Bohemians designated those who disbelieved in the absolute conversion of the elements. Certain it is that the question did not come up with any prominence {525} in the negotiations with the Council of Basle; and in the description which Æneas Sylvius gives, in 1451, of the Taborites of Mount Tabor he simply says that some of them are so foolish that they hold the doctrine of Berenger, that the body of Christ is only figuratively in the sacrament.[566]

It was impossible that harmony could be preserved between Taborite and Calixtin when there was so marked a divergence of religious conviction. They quarreled and held conferences and persecuted each other, but they presented a united front to the levies of crusaders which Europe repeatedly sent against them, and Sigismund's hope of reconquering the throne of his fathers grew more and more remote. The death of Ziska, in 1424, made little difference, save that his immediate followers organized themselves into a separate party under the name of Orphans, but continued in all things to co-operate with the Taborites. He was succeeded in the leadership by the warrior-priest Procopius Rasa, or the Great, whose military skill continued to hold banded Europe at bay. Hussitism, moreover, was spreading into the neighboring lands, especially to the south and east, requiring, as we shall see hereafter, the strenuous efforts of the Inquisition to eradicate it from Hungary and the Danubian provinces. In Poland its missionary efforts called forth an edict from King Ladislas V., April 6, 1424, ordering all his subjects to join in exterminating heretics; every Pole who returned from a sojourn in Bohemia was subjected to examination by the inquisitors or episcopal officials, and all who should not return by June 1 were declared heretics, their estates confiscated, and their children subjected to the customary

173

disabilities.{526}[567] The Church was completely baffled. It had triumphed over a similar revolt in Languedoc, and had shown the world, in characters of blood and fire, how it utilized its triumphs. It now had a different problem to solve. Force having failed, it was obliged to discover some formula of reconciliation which should not too nearly peril its claim to infallibility.

To do it justice, it did not yield without compulsion. Tired of standing on the defensive against assaults whose repetition seemed endless, Procopius, in 1427, adopted the policy of aggression. He would win peace by making the coterminous states feel the miseries of war, and in a series of relentlessly destructive raids, continued till 1432, he carried desolation into all the surrounding provinces. Thus in a foray of 1429, which cut a swath through Franconia, Saxony, and the Vogtland, over a hundred castles and fortified towns were captured, and an immense booty was carried back to Bohemia. Misnia, Lusatia, Silesia, Bavaria, Austria, and Hungary in turn felt the weight of the Hussite sword, while the prompt retirement of the invaders in every case showed that retaliation and not conquest was their object. It was no wonder that a general cry for peace went up among those who bore the brunt of the effort to reassert the papal supremacy.[568]

Meanwhile the Church was perplexed with another yet more vexatious question. Christendom never ceased to clamor for the reform of which it had been cheated at Constance. Skilful procrastination had wearied the reforming fathers, and they had consented, in 1418, to the dissolution of the council, hoping that the promises made in the election of Martin V. would be fulfilled. They took the precaution, however, to provide for an endless series of councils, which might be expected to resume and complete their unfinished work, and the plan which they laid out shows how deep-seated was the distrust entertained of the papacy. Another general council was ordered to be held in five years, then{527} one in seven years thereafter, and finally a perpetual succession at intervals of ten years, with careful provisions to nullify the expected evasions of the popes.[569]

As far as relates to Germany, Martin endeavored to perform the two duties for which he had been elected—the suppression of heresy and the reformation of the Church—by sending, in 1422, Cardinal Branda thither as legate. To accomplish the former object the legate was directed to preach another crusade, that of 1421 having ended so disastrously. As regards the latter feature of his mission, the papal commission and the decree issued in conformity with it by Branda describe the vices of the German clergy in terms quite as severe as those employed by Huss and his followers, and furnish a complete justification of the Bohemian revolt. The only wonder is that pope or kaiser could expect the populations to rest satisfied with the ministrations of men who assumed to be gifted with supernatural power and to speak in the name of the Redeemer, while steeped to the lips in every form of greed, uncleanness, and lust. The constitution which Branda issued to cure these evils only prescribed a repetition of remedies which had vainly been applied for centuries. It simply attacked the symptoms and not the cause of the disease, and it consequently remained inoperative.[570]

Five years had elapsed since the ending of the Council of Constance. Nothing had been accomplished to suppress heresy or reform the Church, and when in due time the Council of Siena assembled, in 1423, it remained to be seen whether the unfinished work of Constance could be completed. Under the presidency of four papal legates it was held that the attendance of prelates and princes was too small to permit the work of reformation to be undertaken, but it was sufficient to justify the council in confirming the promises made by Martin of forgiveness of sins for all who should assist in exterminating the heretics. All Christian princes were summoned to lend their aid in the good work without delay if they wished to escape divine vengeance and the penalties provided by law. All commerce of every kind with the heretics was forbidden, especially in victuals, cloth, arms, gunpowder, and lead; every one trading with them, or any prince permitting communication{528} with them over his lands was pronounced subject to the punishments decreed against heresy. Bohemia was to be isolated and starved into submission by a material blockade enforced by spiritual censures.[571]

As for reformation, it was found that all efforts seriously to consider it were skilfully blocked by the legates. This is not surprising, as the Church was to be reformed in its head as well as in its members, and the head was recognized as the chief source of infection. A project presented by the Gallican deputies described in indignant bitterness the abuses of the curia—the sale of preferments and dignities to the highest bidder, irrespective of fitness, with the consequent destruction of benefices and plunder of the people; the papal dispensations which enabled the most incongruous pluralities to be held by individuals, and the other devices whereby Rome was enriched at the cost of religion; the centralizing of all jurisdiction in Rome to the spoliation of the indigent who dwelt at a distance; the papal decrees which set aside the salutary regulations of general councils—showing how nugatory had been the reformatory regulations wherewith Martin, when elected, had parried the attacks of the Council of Constance. The disappointment of the Council of Siena at the baffling of its efforts was leading to a tension of feeling that grew dangerous. A French friar, Guillaume Joselme, preached a sermon in which he demonstrated that the pope was the servant and not the master of the Church. The legates denounced him as a heretic, and ordered the magistrates of Siena to arrest him, but they, unlike Sigismund, replied that they had given a safe-conduct to all the members of the council, and could not go behind it. Finally, finding that under the control of the papacy no reformatory action was possible, the attempt was made to shorten to two or three years the seven years" interval that was to elapse before the next council. All the several nations had agreed to it when its enactment was prevented by the legates suddenly dissolving the council, March 8, 1424, in spite of a protest intimating very plainly that they had prevented all reformatory legislation. The seven

174

years" interval was preserved, and the next council was indicated for Basle, in 1431. The reformers consoled themselves by pointing{529} out that, of the four papal representatives concerned in thus strangling the council, three died within a year, of terrible deaths, manifestly the divine vengeance on their wickedness. Martin made a show of supplementing this lack of performance by appointing a commission of three cardinals to carry on the work of reform, and requested all complaints and suggestions to be sent to them—a measure which was as profitless in result as it was intended to be. Equally illusory was a constitution issued shortly after, restraining the ostentation and extravagance of the cardinals, and prohibiting them from assuming the "protection" of any prince or potentate, or asking favors except for the poor or for their own retainers and kindred, thus reducing the importance of the Sacred College as a factor of the Holy See and exalting his own.[572]

The time fixed for the assembling of the Council of Basle, March, 1431, was rapidly drawing nigh without any action on the part of Martin looking to its convocation. He who owed his election to a general council was notorious for abhorring the very name of council. At length, on November 8, 1430, there appeared on the doors of the papal palace, and in the most conspicuous places in Rome, an anonymous notice, purporting to be issued by two Christian kings, reciting the necessity of holding a council in obedience to the decrees of Constance, and appending some conclusions of a threatening character, to the effect that if the pope and cardinals impede it, or even evade promoting it, they are to be held as fautors of heresy; that if the pope does not open the council himself or by his deputies, those who may be present will be compelled by divine law to withdraw obedience from him, and Christendom will be bound to obey them, and that they will be forced to proceed summarily to his deposition and that of the cardinals as fautors of heresy. It was evident that Christendom was determined to have the council, with the pope or without him, and Martin, after holding out till the last moment, was compelled to yield. He had appointed, January 11, 1431, Cardinal Giuliano Cesarini as legate to preach another crusade with plenary indulgences{530} against the Hussites, and to him he issued, February 1, a commission to open and preside at the council. One of those most earnest in bringing this about was the Cardinal of Siena. Had he been able to forecast the future he would have tempered his zeal. Within three weeks Martin was dead, and on March 3 the Cardinal of Siena was elected his successor, taking the name of Eugenius IV.[573]

Cardinal Giuliano went on his double mission and preached the fifth crusade against the Hussites. The Bohemian forays had stimulated Germany to an earnest effort to crush the troublesome rebels, and he found himself at the head of an army variously estimated at from eighty thousand to one hundred and thirty thousand men. The Bohemians applied to the Emperor Sigismund for a safe-conduct to Basle, offering to submit the questions at issue to debate on the basis of Scripture. This was refused, and they were told that they must agree to stand to the decisions of the council without limitation. They preferred the arbitrament of arms, and issued a protest to the Christian world in which, with coarse good sense, they defined their position, attacked the temporal power of the papacy, and ridiculed the indulgences issued for their subjugation. This document was received by the council on August 10, very nearly on the day on which, at Taas, the crusaders fled without striking a blow, on hearing the battle-hymn of the dreaded Hussite troops. As a military leader Cardinal Giuliano was evidently a failure, and it only remained for him to try peaceful measures. The German princes, alarmed and exhausted, showed evident signs of determination to come to terms with their unconquerable neighbors. It was a hard necessity, but there was no alternative, and on October 15 the council resolved to invite the Bohemians to a{531} conference and to give them a safe-conduct, although the letters were not forwarded until November 26.[574]

Meanwhile the inevitable quarrels between pope and council had broken out with bitterness. But three weeks after the invitation to the Bohemians had been despatched, on December 18, Eugenius took the extreme step of dissolving the council and calling another to be held in eighteen months at Bologna, where he would preside in person. At this action Germany was aghast. Sigismund remonstrated energetically, and the council, assured of his support, refused to obey. Cardinal Giuliano was won over and made himself its mouthpiece. He had had an opportunity of observing the condition of men's minds north of the Alps, and he knew to what a storm the bark of St. Peter would be exposed. It may safely be said that since the papacy became dominant over the Church few popes have received from a subordinate so vigorous a reproof as that in which Giuliano gave his reasons for disobedience, and it contains so vivid a picture of the times that a brief abstract of it cannot well be spared. Clerical wickedness, he says, in Germany is such that the laity are irritated to the last degree against the Church, wherefore it is greatly to be feared that if there is no reformation they will execute their public threats of rising, like the Hussites, against the clergy. This turpitude has given great audacity to the Bohemians and lends color to their heresy, and if the clergy cannot be reformed the suppression of this heresy would lead only to the breaking-out of another. The Bohemians have been invited to the council; they have replied and are expected to come. If the council is dissolved, what will the heretics say? Will not the Church confess herself defeated when she dares not await those whom she has invited? Will not the hand of God be seen in it? A host of warriors has fled before them, and now the Church universal flies! Behold, they cannot be overcome either by arms or arguments! Alas for the wretched clergy wherever they be! Will they not be deemed incorrigible and determined to live in their filth? So many councils have been held in our days from which no reformation has come! From this one the nations have expected some{532} fruit. If it be thus dissolved, we shall be said to laugh at God and man, and when there is no hope of our correction the laity will justly assail us, like the Hussites. Already there are reports of it, already they begin to spit forth the venom which is to destroy us. They will think to offer a welcome sacrifice to God when they slay or despoil us, who will then be odious both to God and man, and whereas now there is little respect for us, there will then be none. The council was some restraint upon them, but when they lose all hope they will persecute us publicly, and the whole blame will be thrown upon the Roman curia, which breaks up the assembly convened to effect reform. Latterly the city of Magdeburg has expelled her archbishop and clergy; the citizens march with wagons like the Bohemians, and are said to have sent for a Hussite captain, and they have, moreover, a league with many other communities of those parts. The people of Passau have driven out their bishop and are besieging one of his castles. Both cities are near to Bohemia, and if, as is to be feared, they unite they will have a following of many other towns. At Bamberg there is fierce discord between the citizens on the one side and the bishop and chapter on the other, which is especially dangerous by reason of the neighborhood of the heretics. If the council is dissolved these quarrels will increase, and many other communities will be drawn in.[575]

Making due allowance for inevitable rhetorical exaggeration this picture is a true one. Hussite ideas were rapidly spreading through Germany, and finding a congenial soil in the aversion born of incurable clerical corruption. About this time Felix Hemmerlin complains of the countless souls seduced to heresy by the emissaries who, every year, come from Bohemia to Berne and Soleure. Numerous executions of heretics are recorded at this period in Flanders, where persecution had been for centuries almost unknown, and we may be sure that Hussite missionaries were busily carrying on an equally successful propaganda elsewhere. If the hopes which were built on the council were destroyed, the{533} Church might well expect a general revolt. Sustained by the united support of Cismontane Christendom, the council resolutely went its way. Sigismund urged it to stand firm, and in November, 1432, he issued an imperial declaration that he would sustain it against all assailants. Eugenius held out until February, 1433, when he assented to its continuance, but in July he again dissolved it, and in September repeated the command. Then the council commenced active proceedings to arraign and try him, and in December he revoked these bulls. In the subsequent quarrel the council decreed his suspension in January, 1439, and his deposition in June, while the election of Amedeo of Savoy as Felix V. was confirmed in November of the same year.[576]

Into the details of the interminable negotiations which followed between the council and the Hussites it is not worth while to enter. The latter carried their point, and, in a conference held at Eger, May 18, 1439, it was agreed that the questions should be debated on the basis of the Scriptures and the writings of the early fathers. The four articles which were the common ground of Calixtins and Taborites were put forward as their demands, and to these they steadily adhered through all the dreary discussions in Basle, Prague, Brünn, Stuhlweissenberg, to the final conference of Iglau in July, 1436. The discussions were ofttimes hot and angry, and the good fathers of Basle were sometimes scandalized at the freedom of speech of the Bohemian delegates. When John of Ragusa alluded to the Hussites as heretics, John Rokyzana, one of the Calixtin delegates, indignantly denied it, and demanded that if any one accused them of heresy he should offer the *talio* and prove it. Procopius, who represented the Taborites, joined in and declared that he would not have come to Basle had he known that he would be thus insulted. Time and skill were required to pacify the Bohemians, and John of Ragusa and the Archbishop of Lyons were forced to apologize formally. On another occasion the Inquisitor Henry of Coblentz, a Dominican doctor, complained that Ulric of Znaim, a deputy of the Orphans, had said that monks were introduced by the devil. Ulric denied it, and Procopius intervened, saying that he had remarked to the{534} legate that if the bishops came from the apostles, and priests from the seventy-two disciples, the others could have had no other source but the devil. This sally raised a general laugh, which was increased when Rokyzana called to the inquisitor, "Doctor, make Dom Procopius provincial of your order." These trifles have their significance when compared with the shouts of "Burn him! Burn him!" which assailed Huss at Constance. In fact the Hussites were urged to incorporate themselves with the council, but they were too shrewd to fall into the snare.[577]

By unbending firmness the Bohemians carried their point, and secured the recognition of the four articles, which became celebrated in history as the Compactata—the Magna Charta of the Bohemian Church until swept away by the counter-Reformation. This was agreed to in Prague, November 26, 1433, and confirmed by mutual clasp of hands between the legates of the council and the deputies of the three Bohemian sects, but matters were by no means settled. The four articles were brief and simple declarations which admitted of unlimited diversity of construction. The dialecticians of the council had no difficulty in explaining them away, until they practically amounted to nothing; the Hussites, on the other side, with equal facility, expanded them to cover all that they could possibly wish to claim. Hardly was the handclasping over when it was found that the Bohemians asserted that the permission of communion in both elements meant that they were to continue to administer it to infants, and to force it proscriptively on every one—positions to which the council could by no means assent. This will serve as an illustration of the innumerable questions which kept the negotiators busy during yet thirty dreary months. So far, indeed, was the matter as yet from being settled, that, in April, 1434, the council levied a half-tithe on Christendom for a crusade against the Hussites, which enabled it to stimulate with liberal payments the zeal of the Bohemian Catholic nobles.[578]{535}

It is not likely that any results would have been reached but for events which at first seemed to threaten the continuance of the negotiations. The Taborites could only have consented to treat on the basis, so inadequate to them, of the four articles, in the confidence that the practical application would cover a vastly wider sphere. After the preliminary agreement of November 26, the construction assumed by the legates of the council made them draw back. The affair was reaching a conclusion, and it was necessary to have a definite understanding of that to which they were binding themselves. After the departure of the legates from Prague, in January, 1434, hot discussions arose between them and the Calixtins as to the continuance of the negotiations. There were political as well as religious differences between them. The Taborites were mostly peasants and poor folk; they wanted no nobles or gentlemen in their ranks, and seem to have had republican tendencies, as they desired to add to the four articles two others, providing for the independence of Bohemia and for the retention of all confiscated property. Both parties became exasperated, and flew to arms for a contest decisive as to their respective mastery. The Taborites had for some time been besieging Pilsen, a city which held out for Sigismund. Learning that their friends in the Neustadt of Prague had been slaughtered without distinction of age or sex, to the number, it is said, of twenty-two thousand, they raised the siege, May 9, to take vengeance on the city, but after a demonstration before it, they withdrew towards Moravia. Meanwhile the Calixtins had formed an alliance with the Catholic barons, who had been liberally subsidized by the council, and followed them with a formidable force. The shock came at Lipan, on Sunday, May 30. All day and night the battle raged, and until the third hour of Monday morning. When it was over, Procopius, Lupus, and thirteen thousand of the bravest Taborites lay dead upon the field, and the murderous nature of the strife is seen in the fact that but seven hundred prisoners were taken, though we may question the claim of the victors that the battle cost them but two hundred men, and we may hope that there is {536} exaggeration in the boast that they burned several thousand of those whom they subsequently captured. The power of the Taborites was utterly broken. It is true that they continued to hold Mount Tabor until finally crushed by George Podiebrad, in 1452; and that in the December following the battle their unconquerable spirit was again contemplating an appeal to arms, but after Lipan they were only a troublesome element of insubordination, and not a factor in the political situation. The congratulatory letters sent by some of the victors to Sigismund, and the effusive joy with which he communicated the news to the council, show that the victory was one for the Catholics. [579]

Even after the virtual elimination of the Taborites there were ample subjects of dispute, and at one time the prospect seemed so unpromising that preliminary arrangements were set on foot, in August, 1434, for organizing a new crusade on the proceeds of the half-tithe levied shortly before. One source of endless trouble sprang from the personal ambition of Rokyzana. Learned, able, a hardy disputant, and a skilled man of affairs, he had determined to be Archbishop of Prague, and this object he pursued with unalterable constancy. He bore a leading part in the negotiations, and made himself as conspicuous as possible, shifting his ground with dexterity, interposing objections and smoothing them as the interest of the moment might dictate. At first he endeavored to have a clause inserted that the people and the clergy should be empowered to elect an archbishop, who should be acknowledged and confirmed by the emperor and the pope. This being rejected, he procured of Sigismund a secret agreement that the election {537} should be held, and that the emperor would do all in his power to secure the confirmation by the pope, without cost for pallium, confirmation, or notarial fees. Although this, when discovered, was protested against by the legates of the council and refused by the council itself, he proceeded, in 1435, to obtain an election by the national assembly of Bohemia, to the great disgust of the orthodox, who reasonably dreaded this example of a return of the primitive methods of selecting prelates. Again Sigismund secretly accepted this, while the legates declared it to be invalid, and that, as an infraction of the Compactata, it must be annulled. On this question the whole negotiation was nearly wrecked, and it was only settled by Sigismund and his son-in-law and heir, Albert of Austria, promising to issue letters recognizing Rokyzana as archbishop, and to compel obedience to him as such. After this it required but a fortnight more of quarrelling to bring the matter to a termination, and signatures to the Compactata were duly exchanged July 5, 1436, amid general rejoicings. Sigismund, restored to the throne of his fathers, made a show of complying with his promise, by writing to the council a letter asking Rokyzana's confirmation, at the same time explaining to the legates that he considered the council ought to refuse, but that he did not wish to break with his new subjects too suddenly. Of course the confirmation never came, and although Rokyzana called God to witness that he did not wish the archbishopric, the policy of his long life was devoted to obtaining it. With all convenient speed Sigismund forgot the pledge to enforce obedience to him. His position became so dangerous that he secretly fled from Prague, June 16, 1437, and remained in exile until after the deaths of Sigismund and Albert, when he returned in 1440, and speedily became the most powerful man in Bohemia. This position he retained until his death, in 1471, administering the archbishopric, constantly seeking confirmation at the hands of successive popes, and subordinating the policy of the kingdom, internal and external, so far as he dared, to that object—not the least anomalous feature of the anomalous Calixtin Church. [580] {538}

A peace in which all parties distrusted each other and placed radically different interpretations on its conditions was not likely to heal dissensions so profound. The very day after the solemn ratification of the Compactata an ominous disturbance showed how superficial was the reconciliation. In the presence of an immense crowd, at the high altar of the church of Iglau, where the final conferences were held, the Bishop of Coutances, chief of the legation of the council, celebrated mass and returned thanks to God. After this the letters of agreement were read in Bohemian, and Rokyzana commented upon them in the same language, much to the discomfort of the legates. He had been celebrating mass at a side altar, and when the reading was finished he called out, "If any one wishes communion in both elements let him come to this altar and it will be given to him." The legates rushed over to him and twice forbade him, but he quietly disregarded them and administered the sacrament to eight or ten persons. The incident excited intense feeling on both sides. The Bohemians demanded that a church be assigned to them in Iglau where during their stay they could receive the sacrament in both kinds; the legates refused the request, although urged by the emperor, and finally, after threats of departure, the Bohemians were forced to content themselves with celebrating, as they had previously done, in private houses.[581]

When Sigismund was fairly seated on the throne, there followed an endless series of bickerings, as the rites and ceremonies and usages of the Roman Church were restored, supplanting the simpler worship which had prevailed for twenty years. Consecrations, confirmations, images, relics, holy water, benedictions, were one by one introduced—even the hated religious orders were surreptitiously smuggled in. The canonical hours and chants were renewed in the churches, and every effort was made to accustom the people to a resurrection of the old order of things. On Corpus Christi day, May 30, 1437, a gorgeous procession swept through the streets of Prague bearing the host on high; the legate, the Archbishop of Kalocsa, and the Bishop of Segnia headed it, and were dutifully followed by the emperor and empress, the nobles{539} and a mass of citizens. As a mute protest, Rokyzana met the splendid array, attended only by three priests, and bearing both host and cup. To the stern puritans who had so long struggled against the Scarlet Woman the imposing ceremony must have seemed a bitter mockery, for the Empress Barbara, who occupied a conspicuous position in the ranks, was a woman notorious for shameless licentiousness, and, moreover, was an avowed atheist, who disbelieved in the immortality of the soul.[582]

Within three weeks of this celebration, Rokyzana was a fugitive, seeking the protection of George Podiebrad at Hradecz, not without reason, if Æneas Sylvius is correct in saying that Sigismund was about to arrest him and punish him condignly. Then the process of reaction went on apace. Had Sigismund lived, he might have overcome all resistance, and reduced the land to obedience to Rome. His power was constantly growing. In March the surrender of the Taborite stronghold of Konigingrätz filled the Hussites with consternation. Not long after siege was laid to Zion, the fastness of John Rohacz, a powerful baron who had refused submission. He was finally captured in it, brought to Prague, and hanged in the presence of the emperor with sixty of his followers and a priest. Tradition relates that on that very day Sigismund was attacked with an ulcer which grew constantly worse and ended his days in December. Almost simultaneous with this was the decision by the Council of Basle on the question of communion in both elements, in which it skilfully evaded the inconsistency of the prohibition of the cup, and pronounced it to be the law of the Church, not to be modified without authority. As Albert of Austria, the son-in-law and successor of Sigismund, was a zealous Catholic prince, the council was emboldened in January, 1438, to issue an edict reciting and ordering the strict enforcement of the implacable bull of February 22, 1418, by Martin V., directed against the errors of Wickliff, Huss, and Jerome. This evidence of what they were to expect as the outcome of the Compactata gave the Taborites and the disaffected parties in Bohemia new energy. After a fruitless appeal to the council an alliance was made with Poland, whose boy-king, Casimir, was elected as a{540} competitor. Thus strengthened they offered effective resistance to Albert, who up to his sudden death, October 27, 1439, was unable to occupy the whole of his kingdom. Four months later, Ladislas, his posthumous son, was born, and a long minority, with its accompanying turbulence, enabled the Calixtins again to get the upper hand, over both the Taborites and the Catholics. In 1441 a council held at Kuttenberg organized the national Church on a Calixtin basis. Several conferences were held with the Taborites, and the points at issue were referred to the national diet held in January, 1444. Its emphatic decision in favor of the Calixtin doctrine broke up the Taborite organization. The cities still held by them surrendered one by one, and the members were scattered, for the most part joining the Calixtins. As a separate sect they may be said to have disappeared when, in 1452, George Podiebrad captured Mount Tabor and dispersed their remains.[583]

After the death of Albert what central authority there was in Bohemia was lodged in the hands of two governors, Ptacek representing the Calixtins, and Mainhard of Rosenberg, the victor of Lipan, the Catholics. In October, 1443, we hear of the Emperor Frederic III. as about starting for Bohemia where he expected to receive the regency, but his hopes were frustrated. Ptacek died in 1445, when the choice for his succession fell upon George Podiebrad, a powerful baron, who, though only twenty-four, had acquired a high reputation for military ability and sagacity. He was largely under the influence of Rokyzana, to whom doubtless his election was due. After a long interval, Rome again appeared upon the scene. Nicholas V., who ascended the papal throne in 1447, sent, in 1448, John, Cardinal of Sant" Angelo, to Prague as legate. The Bohemians earnestly urged him to ratify the Compactata and confirm Rokyzana as archbishop. He promised an answer, but finding the situation embarrassing, he secretly left Prague with Mainhard of Rosenberg. Popular indignation{541} enabled George by a *coup d"état*, in which there was considerable bloodshed, to render himself master of Prague and to cast Mainhard into prison, where he died soon after. George thus became the undisputed master of Bohemia. When Ladislas, in 1452, was recognized as king, George secured the regency, and when the young monarch died towards the close of 1457, at the early age of eighteen, George's coronation as king soon followed. Under him, until just before his death in 1471, Rokyzana's influence was almost unbounded.[584]

The situation of Bohemia, as a member of the Latin Church, was unprecedented. After the first break between Eugenius IV. and the Council of Basle the name of the pope disappears in the negotiations for the restoration of unity. These were carried on by both sides as though the conciliar authority was supreme, and the papal assent or confirmation was a matter of no moment, although a papal legate was present in January, 1436, at the conference at Stuhlweissenberg, where the matter was virtually settled. As the council drew to its weary end, powerless and discredited, the triumphant Eugenius was not disposed to recognize the validity of its acts or to ratify them gratuitously. The Bohemians alleged that he had confirmed the Compactata, but no positive evidence was forthcoming. To purchase the submission of Germany, in 1447, he had ratified a portion of the acts of the council, but the Compactata could not be included in his carefully. guarded decrees. On the accession of Nicholas V., in 1447, the Bohemians sent to him a deputation offering him allegiance, but we have seen how wary was the legate whom he despatched in return to Prague. It is true that to obtain the abdication of Felix V., Nicholas issued a bull, June 28, 1449, approving all the acts of the council which might strictly be held to confirm the Compactata, but the character of the bull shows that it had in view rather the material interests involved in benefices and preferment. Whatever doubt the Bohemians may have had as to the papal intentions towards them was speedily dissipated.[585]{542}

Rome, in fact, had never proposed to recognize the compromise made by the council. While the latter was busy in endeavoring to win back the Hussites, Eugenius IV. was laboring for their extermination by the usual methods, in such regions as he could reach. The relations between Bohemia and Hungary had long been close, and Hussitism had spread widely throughout the latter kingdom as well as in the Slavic territories to the south. As early as 1413 we hear complaints of Wickliffite doctrines carried into Croatia by students returning from the University of Prague. As Sigismund was King of Hungary, the Compactata were supposed to cover the Hungarian Hussites, and were published in Hungarian as well as in Bohemian, German, and Latin. We have seen, however, how false he was to his Bohemian subjects, and those of Hungary he cheerfully abandoned to Rome. Six weeks after the signature of the Compactata at Iglau, on August 22, 1436, Eugenius commissioned the indefatigable persecutor, Frà Giacomo della Marca, as Inquisitor of Hungary and Austria. He was already on the ground, for in January of that year we catch a glimpse of him as present in the conference at Stuhlweissenberg. Frà Giacomo lost no time. Before the close of the year he had traversed Hungary from end to end, with merciless severity. The Archbishop of Gran, the Chapter of Kalocsa, the Bishop of Waradein, were loud in his praises. Their dioceses, they said, had been infected with heretics so numerous that a rising was anticipated which would have exceeded in horror the Bohemian wars, but this holy man had exterminated them. The numbers whom he put to death are not enumerated, but they must have been considerable from the expressions employed, and from the terror inspired, for his associates declared that in this expedition he had received the submission of fifty-five thousand converts. As the Bishop of Waradein rapturously declared, had the Apostle Paul accompanied him{543} he could not have effected more. Earnestly the Bishops of Csanad and Transylvania appealed to him to visit their dioceses, which abounded in heretics; and as the latter prelate speaks of the Hussites having penetrated to his bishopric from Moldavia, it shows how widely the heresy had been diffused through southeastern Europe.[586]

Suddenly, in 1437, Frà Giacomo's career was interrupted. He had crushed the Fraticelli of Italy, the wild Cathari of Bosnia, and the fiercer Hussites of Hungary, but when he attacked the orthodox concubinary priests of Fünfkirchen, and strove to force them to abandon the illicit partners who were universally kept, they proved too strong for even his iron will and seasoned nerves, backed though he was by the power of pope and kaiser and the awful authority of the Inquisition. They raised such a storm at this attempted invasion of their accustomed privileges that he was obliged to abandon his work and fly for his life. He appealed to Eugenius, and Eugenius to Sigismund. The latter wrote to Henry, the Bishop of Fünfkirchen, peremptorily ordering him to recall Giacomo and give him every aid, and also to Giacomo, assuring him of support. Thus assailed, Bishop Henry gave instructions that Giacomo should be supplied with all necessaries, but the attempt to enforce chastity on the priesthood seems to have been abandoned. The customary penalty in Hungary for such offences was five marks, and the synods of Gran in 1450 and 1480 complain that the archdeacons not only keep these fines for themselves, but encourage the criminals in order to derive profit from them; in fact, they issued in Hungary, as in many other places, licenses to sin, which may, perhaps, explain the indignation caused by Giacomo's interference and its lack of success.[587]

He appears to have meddled no longer with the private lives of the orthodox clergy, but to have devoted his energies to the easier work of exterminating heretics. Early in 1437 we hear of him south of the Danube, where the Bishop of Sreim praised his effective work; by putting to death all who could not be converted, he had saved the diocese from a rising of the Hussites, in which{544} all the clergy would have been slain. Eugenius rewarded him by describing him as "a vigorous and most ruthless extirpator of heresy," and granting him the power of appointing subordinate inquisitors, thus rendering him an inquisitor-general in all the wide region confided to him. It was probably a result of the quarrel over the priestly concubines that led, in 1438, Simon of Bacska, Archdeacon of Fünfkirchen, to excommunicate him; but that official was speedily forced to withdraw the anathema by the Emperor Albert and the Archbishop of Gran. For a while his labors were interrupted by a call to attend the Council of Ferrara, held in 1438 by Eugenius IV., to offset the hostile assemblage at Basle, but he speedily returned to Hungary. It was doubtless owing to his efforts that in Poland the barons and cities entered into a solemn league and covenant to suppress heresy, April 25, 1438—just before Poland intervened in Bohemia to protect the Hussites from the Emperor Albert. In 1439 Giacomo's zeal received a check on the more immediate fields of his labors. In Sreim he delivered to the secular arm, as convicted heretics, a priest and three associates; their friends assembled in force, broke open the prison and carried off the culprits, and, what is difficult to understand, unless the heresy was merely concubinage, the Archbishop of Kalocsa, when appealed to, protected the criminals. Giacomo had recourse to the Emperor Albert, who wrote sharply to the archbishop in June; and this proving ineffectual, again in August. What was the result of the affair is not known, but Albert, as we have seen, died in October, to the great detriment of religion; and in 1440 Giacomo left Hungary on account of ill-health. He seems not to have been immediately replaced, and, in the absence of organized persecution, the tares speedily began to multiply again among the wheat. In January, 1444, Eugenius IV., deploring the spread of Hussitism throughout the Danubian regions, appointed the Observantine Vicar Fabiano of Bacs as inquisitor for the whole Slavonian vicariate, which included Hungary, with power to appoint inquisitors under him. These were authorized to act in complete independence of the local prelates; Holy Land indulgences were promised to all who would aid them, and excommunication, removable only by pope or inquisitor, against all withholding assistance. In July, 1446, Eugenius again alludes to the flourishing condition of Hussitism in Hungary and{545} Moldavia, in spite of the labors of the friars, and he recurs to the question which baffled Giacomo della Marca. Many parish priests, he says, in these regions not only keep concubines publicly, but teach that there is no sin in intercourse between unmarried persons; the question has been asked him whether this is heresy, justiciable by the Inquisition; this he answers in the affirmative, and authorizes Fabiano and his deputies to treat it as such. Apparently it was not the practice itself, but the justification of it, which was so heinous.[588]

If Rome was thus active in repressing Hussitism, and thus regardless of the Compactata while crippled by the quarrel with the fathers of Basle, it may readily be imagined that, after the abdication of Felix V. and the restoration of unquestioned supremacy, Nicholas V. was not disposed to respect the bargain made by the council or to regard the Calixtins in any light but that of heretics. It was in vain that the Bohemians proffered obedience if only the Compactata were confirmed, with a tacit condition that Rokyzana's claims to the archbishopric should be recognized. Ostensibly the sole difficulty in the way of reunion lay in the use of the cup by the laity and the communion of infants; save this there was by this time but little to distinguish the Calixtins from the rest of the Latin churches, although occasionally the question of the sequestrated church lands emerged into view. The papacy had taken its position, however, and it would have plunged all Christendom into war, as, in fact, it more than once attempted, rather than admit that the Council of Basle had been justified in purchasing peace by conceding communion in both elements. Behind this, however, was the question of Rokyzana's confirmation. Æneas Sylvius informs us that in 1451 he convinced George Podiebrad of the impossibility of effecting this, and secured a promise that the attempt should be abandoned, he pledging himself that if George would present the names of several suitable persons the pope would select one, and peace would then be established. This treated the Compactata as of minor importance, and was{546} doubtless wholly unauthorized. Neither George nor Rokyzana gave up their hopes; the effort was renewed again and again, now with the pope, now with the Emperor Frederic III., and now with the German Diet, but all to no purpose. Occasionally when there was an object to be gained hopes would be held out, only to be withdrawn. The papal emissaries represented Rokyzana to Rome as the most wicked and perfidious of heresiarchs, whose recognition would be the destruction of what remained of Catholicism in Bohemia, and there never was the slightest idea of confirming him.[589]

When the overthrow of Mainhard of Rosenberg and the concentration of power in the hands of George Podiebrad showed that no further hopes were to be built on the Catholic party in Bohemia, Nicholas V. fell back upon the old methods and resolved to try what could be done by a missionary inquisitor. He had at hand an instrument admirably fitted for the work. Giovanni da Capistrano, vicar-general of the Observantine Franciscans, had commenced his career as an inquisitor in 1417; he was now in his sixty-sixth year, vigorous and implacable as ever. Small and insignificant in appearance, shrivelled by austerities until he seemed{547} to consist only of skin and bone and nerves, he rarely tasted meat and allowed himself but four hours of sleep out of the twenty-four, the remainder being all too few for his restless and indefatigable activity. His saintly and self-denying life had gained him enviable powers as a thaumaturge, and his reputation as a preacher drew crowds to listen to his eloquence. In 1451 he was busy in exterminating the Fraticelli, but he suspended his bloody work at the call of Nicholas to undertake the conversion of the Hussites. Nothing was omitted that could contribute to the dramatic effect of his mission. Before assuming it he sought the divine assent by consulting the Virgin at Assisi, when the heavenly light diffused around him was a sign that his apostolate was confirmed; he accepted the enlarged powers which extended his inquisitorial commission to the Bohemian territories, and set forth. Everywhere on his road multitudes assembled to see and listen to the man of God, and everywhere his miraculous powers manifested the authenticity of his mission. At Brescia he addressed an assembly computed at one hundred and twenty thousand souls, and, though walls and trees were broken down by the masses of men gathered thickly upon them, not a human being was injured. At the crossing of the River Sile, near Treviso, the party, with true Observantine austerity, had no money to pay ferriage, and the surly ferryman refused free transportation; but Capistrano quietly took the habit of San Bernardino, which he carried with him, laid it upon the waters, and they shrank away till all had passed dry-shod, when they resumed their former volume. Thus heralded, his way through Venice and Vienna was a triumphal progress; crowds of sixty thousand or one hundred thousand to hear him preach were common; men came from a distance of five hundred miles to listen to him; at Vienna three hundred thousand were reckoned present; the sick were brought before him in thousands, and the miraculous cures which he wrought were computed by hundreds. The ecclesiastical machinery was evidently well-devised and effectively worked, and the desired impression was produced.[590]

In vain the emperor asked permission for him to visit Prague. Podiebrad and Rokyzana refused it peremptorily, and Capistrano's zeal for martyrdom was not sufficient to prompt him to disregard{548} their wishes. Furnished with imperial letters to the Catholic nobles and to their leader, Ulric Mainhard of Rosenberg, he turned in July to the safer region of Moravia, where presumably the influence of Podiebrad and Rokyzana was not so strong. Here his career indicates how little foundation there was for the persistent Catholic complaints of the proscriptive intolerance of the Calixtins. Though on Bohemian territory, Catholic and Hussite seem to have been dwelling together in mutual harmony; the Bishop of Olmütz was a Catholic, and no hindrance seems to have been experienced by Capistrano in his labors for the conversion of the so-called heretics. Beginning at Brünn, August 1, 1451, there is a register containing names and dates of more than eleven thousand conversions made by him up to May, 1452. Yet at the same time he was restricted to persuasion, and was not allowed to use inquisitorial methods. As his converts were voluntary, he smoothed the path of the repentant heretic, reconciling him to the Church with only the infliction of a salutary penance, and allowing him to retain all his possessions and dignities. Where the heretic was hardened, he was powerless, except through such miraculous power as he could wield. The situation was an anomalous one—unexampled, in fact, in the Middle Ages—of heretic and Catholic dwelling together in peace, the heretic in the ascendant, yet not only tolerating the Catholic, but allowing a man like Capistrano to wander through the land denouncing heretics and making conversions unmolested. To Capistrano the position was irritating in the extreme, insomuch as he was limited to the arts of persuasion, and was unable to enforce his arguments with the dungeon and the stake. This peculiar state of things is well illustrated by an adventure related of him at Breslau. Though Silesia had a Catholic bishop, it belonged to Bohemia, and mutual tolerance was established. In the summer of 1453 Capistrano came there and labored to convert the Hussites, but these sons of Belial, to ridicule his miraculous powers, placed a young man in a bier, carried him to where the inquisitor was preaching, and asked the latter to resuscitate the dead. Capistrano sternly replied, "Let him have his portion with the dead in eternity!" and went his way. Then the heretics said to the crowd, "We have holier men among us;" and one of them went to the coffin, calling to its inmate, "Peter, arise!" and then whispering, "It is time to get up;" but there{549} was no response, and the unfortunate youth was found to be really dead. Yet at this very time Capistrano had no difficulty in exercising his inquisitorial office pitilessly when the victims were unfortunate Jews. A country priest was said to have sold them eight consecrated hosts for use in their infernal rites. Capistrano seized those implicated, tortured them to confession, and burned them, while a woman who was implicated was torn with red-hot pincers. An old Jewess embraced Christianity, and soon afterwards was slain. The Jews were accused of the murder, and also of that of a Christian boy. Capistrano made another onslaught on them, and this time burned no less than forty-one. It is easy to gather from this incident what would have been the fate of the Hussites had he been able to wreak his will on them. Those of Moldavia and Poland, whither he despatched three of his associate inquisitors under Ladislas the Hungarian, probably felt the full rigor of the canons.[591]

During all this the Calixtin leaders had not been wholly indifferent. At the commencement of Capistrano's mission Rokyzana wrote to him in a friendly tone, remonstrating with him for condemning as a heresy the communion in both elements, which the Council of Basle had permitted to the Bohemians. Some correspondence ensued, in which Capistrano took high ground as to the use of the cup and the papal supremacy; there were negotiations for a conference, and at one time hopes were entertained of an accommodation. Capistrano, however, skilfully eluded a disputation on various pretexts, but really, as we learn from his confidential letter to the cardinal-legate, Nicholas of Cusa, because he knew that the Calixtins had on their side the weight of authority and tradition. Both parties gradually lost their temper and published against each other letters filled with scurrility. Having thus rendered amicable negotiations impossible, Capistrano could safely, in 1452, ask Podiebrad for a safe-conduct to Prague, and on its refusal summon him to render the aid and service due to him as apostolic commissioner and inquisitor.[592]

When the German princes assembled in the Diet of 1452 the{550} Bohemians addressed them, complaining that although they were living in peace and obedience to the Holy See, the provisions of the Compactata, which declared that no one should be stigmatized as a heretic for partaking in both elements, were violated by a friar named Capistrano, who, under the guise of an apostolic commissioner and inquisitor, was traversing their territories proclaiming that all Utraquists were heretics. The agreement which had cost so much blood was thus plainly infringed, and, notwithstanding their desire for peace, a persistence in this would revive all the old troubles. This was significant of strife, and Capistrano, on his side, was eagerly engaged in stimulating it. He wrote to the pope that certain propositions of accommodation entertained by the cardinal-legate were disgraceful, and spoke hopefully of negotiations which he was carrying on with the German princes for a new crusade against the Hussites. Nicholas of Cusa was effectually snubbed for daring to talk of conferences and terms of accommodation. He promptly threw himself on the other side and contributed his share towards provoking a fresh conflict, by issuing, in June, 1452, an encyclical to the Bohemians, in which he plainly told them that those who were not with the Church must be against it; that the Compactata must be thrown aside, as

181

they had not effected the union for which they were designed, and that nothing save pure and simple obedience to the Holy See could be entertained. To render the irritation complete needed only the exquisite insolence with which he assured them that the Church was too pious a mother to concede to her children what she knew to be injurious.[593]

Capistrano's busy mischief-making was bearing its fruits. The breach between Rome and Bohemia was constantly widening, and if the zeal of the German princes could be brought to correspond to the ardor of the missionary of strife, the horrors of the old Hussite wars might be hopefully looked for again. During the remainder of the year 1452 we find him travelling through Germany, probably with this charitable object, though at Leipsic he paused long enough for his eloquence to win for his rigid Order sixty professors and students.[594] His efforts to raise a crusade{551} against Bohemia, however, were frustrated by the capture of Constantinople in May, 1453. The immense impression which this produced throughout Christendom, the universal alarm at the progress of the Turk, and the necessity of defending Europe against his approach, speedily threw into the shade all minor questions. A new crusade was imperatively wanted, but it could not be wasted upon Bohemia and the Utraquists.

During the summer of 1453, as we have seen, Capistrano was tranquilly employing his enforced leisure in burning Jews at Breslau. Thence he went to Poland, where we find him at Cracow throwing into prison a physician, Master Paul, whom he suspected of being an emissary of Rokyzana. He applied again to Podiebrad for a safe-conduct to Prague, which was curtly refused on the ground that when it had been previously offered it had not been accepted, and that Ladislas did not want the peace of his kingdom disturbed. He left Cracow May 15, 1454, for Breslau and Olmütz, whence he still hoped to accomplish something within the charmed circle of Bohemia, into which he had not been allowed to penetrate. Rokyzana at this time was inspired with hopes that the terror of the Turk and the need for Christian unity would enable him to realize his dream of the archbishopric. He made the large concessions alluded to above on many of the points of dissidence, and used every effort with the emperor to procure through him the papal confirmation. A letter from Ladislas, of June 13, to the Bishop of Olmütz, asking him to restrain Capistrano from using such violent terms in denouncing Bohemians, as he was doing more harm than good, was evidently a move in the same game. Yet even the paramount interests of Christendom could not win for Rokyzana the coveted confirmation, although those interests soon diverted Capistrano's fiery energies from the heretic to the infidel.[595]

A brief and clear-cut letter of Æneas Sylvius to Capistrano, dated July 26, 1454, tells him to give up the dream of getting to Prague and go to Frankfort, where he will be useful. An assembly of princes had been held in Ratisbon, where a crusade had{552} been agreed upon, and Philip of Burgundy had consented to lead it. Final arrangements were to be made in Frankfort in October, and there Æneas Sylvius wanted the aid of Capistrano's tireless ardor. Their correspondence at this juncture shows the terror which existed lest Europe should be overrun; the confusion and uncertainty which prevailed, and the selfish differences which threatened to neutralize effort. At Frankfort their worst fears were realized. The zeal of the princes had cooled, and they declared the purpose of the pope and emperor was to steal their money and not to fight. They demanded that the business should be conducted by a general council which should at the same time repress the Holy See—in fact, both parties were selfishly endeavoring to turn the agony of Europe to account; the pope to raise money, and the princes to recover their independence. All that Æneas and Capistrano could obtain was a promise that at the Pentecost of 1455 they would meet the emperor and determine what could be done. In February and March, 1455, they began to assemble at Neuburg, near Vienna, where Podiebrad again used every effort to procure Rokyzana's confirmation. As for the crusade, the energies of Christendom seemed paralyzed by the petty jealousies and ambitions of its rulers. At last, under the unflagging eloquence of Æneas and Capistrano, things appeared to be taking shape, when the news was received of the death of Nicholas V. on March 22. Everything fell to pieces, and the princes departed, postponing action until the next year. It was a forcible example of the utility of the papacy, which supplied a common head to the discordant forces of the time.[596]

Capistrano's impetuous energies were now fairly enlisted in the strife with the Turk, and the Hussites had a respite. In fact, the situation was too alarming to permit of their persecution, and it is a remarkable instance of the unbending rigidity of Rome, that even in this perilous juncture the overtures and concessions of Podiebrad and Rokyzana availed them nothing.

Calixtus III. was elected April 8, with a speed which showed how dangerous a papal interregnum was considered. He at once{553} sent legates to preach the crusade throughout Europe, and commenced to build war-ships on the Tiber. The Hungarians, who were justly excited at the impending invasion of Mahomet II. begged Capistrano to come to them and use his eloquence. Calixtus gave him permission, confirmed all the powers conferred on him by Nicholas, and he undertook the task which was to complete his life's work. Yet even these new duties, which wrought his fiery soul to a higher tension than ever, did not wholly distract his attention from the hated Hussites. The juncture seemed favorable for a reconciliation, which every motive of policy dictated. Besides, Æneas Sylvius had just been promoted to the cardinalate, and that crafty diplomat had succeeded in making the Bohemians look upon him as their friend. They not only hoped to obtain the confirmation of the Compactata, but the cardinal's hat for Rokyzana. Hearing of this, Capistrano wrote, March 24, 1456, from Buda to Calixtus dissuading him in the most vigorous terms. The Hussites are the worst of mankind, fearing neither God nor man; the heart can scarce conceive the errors which they believe, or the abominations which they practise in secret. The Compactata are their sole bulwark; if these are confirmed, the Hussites, who abound secretly, not only in Bohemia but in Hungary, Transylvania, Moldavia, and the neighboring regions, will rise and declare themselves. The warning was sufficient and the overtures were rejected.[597]

Suddenly the news came that the dreaded Mahomet II. was advancing, and had laid siege to Belgrade. Ladislas, who was King of Hungary as well as of Bohemia, was at Buda-Pesth, and with his uncle, the Count of Cillei, on pretext of a hunting-excursion, basely fled to Austria. John Hunyady, Count of Transylvania, who had been regent of the kingdom, organized the Hungarian forces, with some German crusaders who had come to his assistance, while Capistrano marched with him as papal commander of the crusade. Glorious in the annals of Hungary is the victory of Belgrade. "With a flotilla of boats on the Danube, Hunyady, on July 14, 1456, cut his way into the town through the beleaguering forces. Furious were the attack and the defence until the 22d, when a fierce assault by the Turks was repulsed, and the besieged{554} followed the retreating enemy, burned one of their camps, spiking some of their cannon and carrying the rest back into the town, where they did good service during the rest of that memorable day. Mahomet gathered together his forces for a last desperate attempt, which was a failure, and during the night he fled, leaving twenty-four thousand men upon the field, and three hundred cannon. His army was utterly dispersed, and this disaster, aided by the heroic resistance of Scanderbeg in Albania, arrested the Turkish invasion and gave Europe a breathing-spell. It cost, however, the lives of the two heroes to whom it was due. The stench of the dead bodies sickened the army of the victors, and John Hunyady fell a victim, August 11, to the epidemic, which prevented the following up of the advantage. Capistrano had thrown himself into the work with all his self-forgetful enthusiasm. His eloquence had wrought the Christians up to the highest pitch of religious exaltation; the crusaders would obey no one but him, and his labors were incessant. He passed days without time for food, and nights without rest; for seventeen days, it is said, before the victory, he slept but seven hours in all. He was in his seventy-first year, with a frame weakened by habitual austerities, and when the strain was past exhausted nature paid the penalty. A slow fever set in, August 6, under which he wasted away, and died, October 23. He was perhaps the most perfect type which the age produced of the ideal son of the Church; a purely artificial creation, in which the weakness of humanity disappeared with some of its virtues, and the whole nature, with its rare powers, was concentrated in unselfish devotion to a mistaken purpose. Such men are the tools of the worldly and unscrupulous who know how to use them, and for forty years Capistrano had been thus employed to bring misery on his fellow-beings, unconscious of the evil which he wrought. Yet, as Æneas Sylvius shrewdly points out, there was one weak spot left in his nature. In the letters in which he and Hunyady described the victory of Belgrade neither chief gave credit to the other. As Æneas says, "Capistrano had despised the pomps of the world, he had fled from its delights, he had trampled down avarice, he had overcome lust, but he could not contemn glory."[598]{555}

No one could be found worthy to replace Capistrano but his friendly rival, Giacomo della Marca, who was accordingly despatched, in 1457, to the scene of his labors of twenty years previous, armed with the same powers, as inquisitor and crusader. The danger from the Turk was still too pressing for him to waste thought on the former function, and he devoted himself to stimulating and organizing the war against the Moslem until his health gave way, and he returned to Italy, where, as we have seen, he not long afterwards had to defend himself from a charge of heresy brought by his zealous Dominican brethren. He was replaced by his disciples, Giovanni da Tagliacozza and Michele da Tussicino, who were followed in 1461 by Frà Gabriele da Verona; but though Franciscans still continued for a generation to labor for the conversion of the Calixtins, they had little success in the absence of power to employ the customary inquisitorial methods, of which more hereafter.[599]

In fact, the prospects of reducing Bohemia to obedience were steadily diminishing. In the wildest uproar of the Hussite wars{556} there were powerful barons and cities who steadily held out for the pope and kaiser, and under the interregnum there had at first been a dual government, shared equally by Catholic and Calixtin. Under the firm hand of George Podiebrad the orthodox communities submitted one by one, and in spiritual matters Rokyzana was supreme. It is true that there was now little to distinguish the churches in doctrine or practice save the use of the cup; but independence served as a protection against the greed of the Roman curia, and there was small encouragement for a surrender of this independence in the clamor which was now going up from Germany. The Basilian regulations, confirmed by Eugenius, had for a time served as a safeguard to some extent, but now these were coolly treated as obsolete, and complaints were loud that all the old abuses were flourishing as vigorously as ever. Elections were set aside, or heavy sums were extorted for their confirmation, while the country was drained of money by the exaction of tenths and the sale of indulgences. Secure in their isolation, the Bohemians might well submit to some inconvenience to be spared the costly blessing of apostolic paternal care. The only hope of Rome lay in the approaching majority of the Catholic youth Ladislas; but when, on the eve of his marriage with the daughter of Charles VII. of France, he suddenly died, towards the close of 1457, not without suspicions of foul play, and George Podiebrad soon afterwards was elected and crowned, it might well seem that, short of Divine interposition, the peaceful return of Bohemia was not to be looked for.[600]

Yet at first it looked as though an accommodation might be reached. Ladislas, shortly before his death, had proposed to send an embassy to Rome for the purpose of effecting a reconciliation, and Calixtus III. had asked of Podiebrad to gratify his vehement desire of seeing Rokyzana, whose high reputation was well known in

Rome. Podiebrad, moreover, caused himself to be crowned according to the Roman rite; having no bishop of his own, he{557} borrowed from his son-in-law, Matthias Corvinus of Hungary, those of Raab and Bacs, to perform his consecration; in his coronation oath he swore obedience to Calixtus and his successors, to restore the Catholic religion, and to persecute heretics; he wrote to Calixtus as a faithful son of the Church, and obtained from him letters recognizing him as King of Bohemia; he sent envoys to Rome, who held out promises that Rokyzana would follow, and settle on a lasting basis the submission of Bohemia. All this was mere skirmishing for position; but when, a few months later, Calixtus died, and was succeeded by Æneas Sylvius, who took the name of Pius II., men might hope that some reasonable accommodation could be reached. Since he had gone to Basle in the suite of Cardinal Capranica, and had become the mouth-piece of the antipapal party, influenced, as he himself says, by cupidity rather than by truth, and inspired by the hostility to the Church usually felt by the laity, the new pope had been occupied almost exclusively with German and Bohemian affairs, which he knew better than any living man; he had taken part in the negotiations resulting in the Compactata; he was shrewd, clear-headed, and troubled with few scruples, and, sharing fully in the papal anxiety to unite Christendom against the Turks, he might be expected to recognize the vital importance of reconciliation with Bohemia. George made haste to send an embassy to renew his protestations of obedience, and to ask for the confirmation of the Compactata. Pius, who took no shame in issuing a solemn bull condemning and disavowing all his early opinions uttered during his service with the council, was prepared to break with his own traditions rather than with those of his predecessors. He gave a dubious response; George could win his recognition as king by extirpating heresy, and he promised to send legates. They came, but the pope, although he addressed George as king and as his dearest son when soliciting his co-operation in the crusade, shortly afterwards took a step which, with his knowledge of Bohemia, he knew could not but provoke a rupture. Wenceslas, Dean of Prague, was a Catholic, and a bitter enemy of Rokyzana, and this man Pius appointed as administrator of the archbishopric, thus ousting Rokyzana. All at once was in uproar. Wenceslas endeavored to assert himself, but the power remained in Rokyzana's hands. George threw into prison Fantinus, who had been his procurator in the curia, and{558} who had been sent with a commission as papal orator, and detained him there for three months. Frederic III., whom George, by a stroke of happy audacity, had recently liberated from a siege by his rebellious subjects in the castle of Vienna, interposed, and delayed the explosion of the papal wrath; but to his earnest request that George should be acknowledged as king Pius returned an absolute refusal. George was a heretic, incapable of the crown, and his subjects" oaths of allegiance were void; only by returning to the Church could he hope to be fitted for the royal dignity. In June, 1464, Pius, in full consistory, published a bull reciting all the griefs of the Church against Bohemia, pronouncing the Compactata void, as never having been confirmed by the Holy See, and summoning George before him to stand trial for heresy within three terms of sixty days each. In two months Pius was dead, but his successor, Paul II., carried forward the proceedings with the old inquisitorial weapons. Three cardinals were appointed in 1465 to try George as a relapsed heretic, and summoned him in August, as a private person, to appear before them within six months for judgment. Without waiting for the expiration of the term, early in December, Paul issued a bull absolving all George's subjects from their allegiance, alleging as a reason for haste that the sentence would grow more difficult by delay. The papal wrath increased with the obstinacy of the assumed heretic. In 1468 another summons was issued to him to appear before the cardinals for judgment; and in February, 1469, his name was placed as that son of perdition, the Hussite George Podiebrad, together with those of Rokyzana and Gregory of Heimburg, in the curse of the Cœna Domini, to be anathematized thrice a year, in the solemnities of the mass, in all cathedrals, both in Latin and in the vernacular.|601|

All this was not a mere *brutum fulmen*. It was not difficult{559} to excite rebellion among turbulent subjects and attacks from ambitious neighbors. With all his vigor and capacity George found the maintenance of his position by no means easy. When, in 1468, the German princes had agreed upon a five years" truce in order to concentrate their energies against the Moslem, Paul II. threw the empire into confusion by sending the Bishop of Ferrara to preach a crusade with plenary indulgences against Bohemia, adding the special favor that all who joined in the preaching should have the privilege of choosing a confessor, and receiving from him plenary absolution and indulgence. The kingdom was bestowed upon Matthias Corvinus of Hungary, who took the cross, and with an army of crusaders occupied Moravia. A long war ensued, during which George died, in 1471, released from excommunication on his death-bed, and Ladislas II., son of Casimir of Poland, was elected as his successor. In 1475 the rivals came to terms; both were recognized as kings of Bohemia, while Matthias was to have for life Moravia, Silesia, and the greater part of Lusatia, and the survivor was to enjoy the whole kingdom. On the death of Matthias, in 1490, Ladislas recovered the three provinces, and shortly afterwards added Hungary to his dominions.|602|

Ladislas was a good Catholic, and Sixtus IV., who had aided in his election, hoped that the opportunity had at last arrived to break down the stubbornness of the Calixtins. The king made the attempt, but bloody tumults in Prague, which nearly cost him his life, showed that, slight as was the difference between Catholic and Utraquist, the old fanaticism for the cup survived. At length, in 1485, at the Diet of Kuttenberg, mutual toleration was agreed upon, and Ladislas, who was of easy disposition, ran no further risks. Thus the anomalous position of Bohemia, as a member of Latin Christendom, became more remarkable than ever. The great majority of the people were Calixtins and therefore heretics, but the Church had to abandon the attempt to coerce them to salvation. Missionary inquisitors were commissioned from time to time, but practically their efforts were limited to persuasion and controversy. Even Pius II., in 1463, felt obliged to caution Zeger, the Observantine Vicar-general, that his brethren, {560} in dealing with heretics, should restrain their zeal from the customary curses and insults, and should try the effect of gentleness and argument. That these missionaries were mostly Franciscans perhaps explains why the toleration accorded to Catholics could not be enforced against the popular prejudices of which the Order was the object. Even George Podiebrad, in 1460, had permitted the Franciscans to return to Prague, but their zeal was not to be restrained, and they were expelled in 1468. Under Ladislas they came again, in 1482, but in the disturbances of the following year they were glad to escape, their house was levelled to the ground, and was not rebuilt until 1629. From time to time other communities were founded at Hradecz, Glatz, and Neisse, but they were short-lived, and were speedily destroyed by the fanaticism of the people. As the invention of printing facilitated controversy, polemical zeal multiplied treatises to prove the iniquity of the Utraquist heresy, but the Utraquists were not to be converted. They maintained the Compactata as the charter of their religious independence. When, in 1526, King Louis fell in the disastrous day of Mohacz, and the House of Austria, in the person of Ferdinand I., obtained the Bohemian throne, good Catholic though Ferdinand was, he was obliged to pledge himself to preserve the Compactata.[603]

It is not to be imagined that the teachings of Wickliff and Huss were wholly forgotten in Utraquist degeneracy. Their real inheritors were the Taborites, and although these, in their disorderly enthusiasm, vainly contended against the spirit of the age and disappeared from sight under the strong hand of Podiebrad, the seed which they had nurtured was not wholly lost. The profound religious convictions which animated these poor and simple folk are visible through the satire with which Æneas Sylvius requited their hospitality in 1451, on the eve of their suppression. Travelling with some nobles, on a mission from Frederic III., he was benighted{561} near Mount Tabor, and thought it safer to trust himself with the enemies of his faith than to pass the hours of darkness in the open villages. In return for the simple kindliness of his reception the polished scholar and courtier describes them with the liveliest ridicule, and with brutal sneers at their poverty. They were mostly peasants, and as they came forth to greet him in the cold and rain, many were almost naked, having nothing but a shirt or a sheepskin to protect them; one had no saddle, another no reins, another no spurs; this one had lost an eye, that one an arm. Ziska was their patron saint, whose portrait was painted on the city gates. Though they ridiculed the consecration of churches, they were very earnest in listening to the word of God, and if any one was too busy or too lazy to go to the wooden house where they assembled for preaching he was compelled by stripes. Though they paid no tithes, they filled their priests" houses with corn, beer, wood, vegetables, meat, and all the necessaries of life. Firm as they were in defence of their religious independence, they were not intolerant, and wide diversity of opinion was allowed among them.[604]

When such men as these were driven forth and scattered among the people they were much more likely to make converts than to be converted, and though lost to sight they were assuredly not false to their convictions. The reactionary course of Rokyzana and Podiebrad during the succeeding years could hardly fail to provoke discontent among the more earnest even of the Calixtins and to furnish fresh disciples and teachers. Materials existed for a sect representing the doctrines which, a generation earlier, had set Bohemia aflame; and although when that sect timidly appeared it prudently and sedulously disavowed all affiliation with the hated and dreaded Taborites, there can be no doubt that it was, to a great extent, composed of the same elements.

These new sectaries first present themselves in an organized form in 1457. Earnest, humble Christians, who sought to carry out the doctrines of Jesus, they differed from the Taborites in a yet closer approach to Waldensianism, due probably to the influence of Peter Chelcicky, who, without belonging to them, was yet to some extent their teacher. Like the Waldenses, they rejected{562} the oath and the sword—nothing would justify the taking of human life, and consequently they were non-resistants. Since the time of Constantine and Silvester the Roman Church had gone astray in the pursuit of wealth and worldly power. The sacraments were worthless in polluted hands. Priests might hear confessions and impose penances, but they could not absolve; they could only announce the forgiveness of God. Purgatory was a myth invented by cunning priests. As for the mystery of the Eucharist, they prudently adopted the formula of Peter Chelcicky, which eluded the difficulty by affirming that the believer receives the body and blood of Christ, without pretending to explain or daring to discuss the matter. They ridiculed the superstition of the Calixtins, which exaggerated in the absurdest fashion the sanctity of the Eucharist, which carried the sacrament through the streets for adoration, and which held that he whose eye chanced to fall on it was safe from evil happening for that day; and they sometimes incurred martyrdom by publicly reproving the fanatic zeal which regarded the Eucharist as the holiest of idols. On this basis was founded the brotherhood of love and charity, of patient endurance and meekness, which represented more nearly the Christian ideal than anything the world had seen for thirteen centuries. With extreme simplicity of life there was no exaggeration of asceticism. Heaven was not to be stormed by mortification of the flesh, but was to be won by the sedulous discharge of the duties imposed on man by his Creator, in humble obedience to the divine will, and in pious reliance on Christ. Such was the "Unitas Fratrum"—the Bohemian or Moravian Brotherhood—and that a society thus defenceless and unresisting should endure the savage vicissitudes of that transitional period, and maintain itself through four hundred years to the present time, shows that force is not necessarily the last word in human affairs, and that average human nature is capable of a higher moral development than it has been permitted to reach under prevailing influences, secular and spiritual.[605]{563}

At first they seem to have enjoyed the favor of Rokyzana, whose doctrines they claimed to follow, and whose nephew Gregory was one of their earliest leaders, along with Michael, priest of Zamberg. Rokyzana's fluctuating policy, as the archbishopric seemed to approach or recede, soon led him to hold aloof, and when they drew apart from the Calixtins and organized themselves as a separate body he had no objection to see them persecuted. In vain they declared that they were neither Waldenses nor Taborites—the one was a word of bitter reproach, the other a terror. When, about 1461, Gregory, with a few companions, ventured secretly to Prague, they were betrayed as conspiring Taborites and put to the torture. It shows their state of religious exaltation that Gregory swooned on the rack and had a beatific vision. It may be put to the credit of Rokyzana that when he saw his nephew insensible from the torture he burst into tears, exclaiming, "O my Gregory, I would I were where thou art!" and that he soon afterwards obtained from Podiebrad permission for them to settle at Liticz. Here they prospered amid alternate peace and persecution, their numbers rapidly increasing.[606]

In retaining all the sacraments they retained belief in the necessity of apostolical succession for that of ordination; but as the sacraments were vitiated in unworthy hands, they became oppressed with misgivings as to the efficacy of the sacerdotal character of their priests, derived as it was through the Church of Rome. Some of them proposed sending to the legendary Christians of India, but they met with two men who had been in the East, and the accounts they received of the Oriental churches satisfied them that the succession there had been lost. Then they bethought them of the Greeks, but they met some Greeks in{564} Prague, and many Bohemians had been in the Levant and Danubian provinces, from whom they learned that fees were required for ordination, thus rendering it void through simony; moreover, they heard of three Bohemians who had been ordained without inquiry as to their morals, which satisfied them that no true ordination was to be obtained there. Finally they turned to the Waldenses, of whom there was a community on the Austrian border. These claimed to descend from the primitive Church; that their ancestors had separated from Rome when the papacy was secularized under Silvester by the donation of Constantine, and that they had preserved the apostolic succession untainted. It remained for the brethren to see whether it was the will of God that they should organize themselves by means of these Waldenses. At Lhotka, in 1467, an assembly of about sixty chosen deputies was held. After fasting and earnest prayer, recourse was had to the lot, to decide whether they should separate themselves from the Roman priesthood. The result was affirmative. Then they selected nine men, from among whom three or two or one should be drawn, or none, if God so willed it. Twelve cards were taken, on three of which was written "is," and on nine "is not." These were mingled together, and a youth was directed to distribute nine of them among the men selected. All three with "is" proved to have been distributed, and the assembly devoutly thanked God for showing them the path to follow. Michael of Zamberg was sent to the Waldensian Bishop Stephen, who investigated his faith and life, and thanked God, with tears, that it had been vouchsafed him before he died to see such pious men. After episcopal consecration Michael returned; careful inquiry was made as to the antecedents of one of the three elect, named Matthias, and he was duly consecrated as bishop by Michael, who thereupon laid down both his Waldensian episcopate and Catholic priesthood, and was again ordained anew by Matthias.[607]{565}

Thus all connection with Rome was sundered, and intimate relations were established with the Waldenses. Mutual sympathy and the identity of their faith drew the two sects together, although the austere virtue of the Brethren reproached the older heretics with concealing their faith by attending Catholic mass, with accumulating wealth, and with neglecting the poor. The Waldenses took the reproof kindly, promised amendment, and in a short time the two sects united and formed one body. Although the official name remained the "Unity of the Brethren," gradually the despised term of Waldenses came to be recognized, and was freely used by the body to designate themselves, in their confessions of faith and apologetic tracts. I have already alluded to the mission which was sent in 1498 to the Brethren of Italy and France, and to the increased spirit of vigor and independence which the old Alpine communities drew from the resolute steadfastness of their new associates.[608]

Gregory had moulded the Church of the Brethren on the strictest basis. Members on entering were not, it is true, obliged to contribute their property to the common fund, but this was frequently done. The closest watch was kept on the conduct of each, and any dereliction was visited with expulsion, not to be revoked without evidence of change of heart. No one was allowed to take an oath, even in court, to hold an office, to keep an inn, to follow any trade except in the necessaries of life. Any noble desiring to join was required to lay aside his rank and resign whatever offices he might hold. In 1479 two barons and several knights applied for admission, when the rules were strictly enforced, and some submitted while others withdrew. This rigor at last caused violent dissensions, and in 1490 the Synod of Brandeis relaxed the rules. The puritan party recalcitrated and were strong enough to cause a revocation of this action in a subsequent synod.{566} Much ill-feeling was generated, until, in 1495, at the Synod of Reichenau, there was mutual forgiveness and a moderation of the rules. Yet two of the puritan leaders, Jacob of Wodnan and Amos of Stekna, refused to accept the compromise, and founded the sect known as Amosites, or the Little Party, which maintained a separate existence for forty-six years.[609]

During this period the Brethren had been subjected to repeated and severe persecution. Sometimes driven for refuge to the mountain and forest, whence they earned the name of Jamnici, or cave-dwellers, they counted their roll of martyrs who had testified in the dungeon or at the stake to the strength of their convictions. Yet the little band steadily grew. In the year 1500 it was deemed necessary to increase the number of bishops to four. In Bohemia and Moravia they counted between three hundred and four hundred churches with nearly two hundred thousand members. There were few villages and scarce any towns in which they were not to be found, and they had powerful protectors among the nobility, who, by the enslavement of the peasants in 1487, had become practically independent and able to shelter them during periods of persecution. The Brethren were active in education and in the use of the press. Every parish had its school, and there were higher institutions of learning, especially at Jungbunzlau and Litomysl. Of the six Bohemian printing-offices they possessed three, while the Catholics had but one and the Calixtins two. Of the sixty books issued in Bohemia between 1500 and 1510, fifty were printed by the Brethren.[610]

From this period until the death of Ladislas, in 1516, they were subjected to intermittent but severe persecution, especially in Bohemia. Ladislas, in his will, left instructions for their extermination "for the sake of his soul's salvation and of the true faith;" but the minority of his son Louis, only ten years old, the breaking-out of disturbances, and the feuds between Catholic and Calixtin brought them peace. The exiled pastors returned, the churches were reopened, and public service was resumed. With the rise of Lutheranism and the negotiations between the Bohemians and{567} the German Protestants their history passes beyond our present horizon, except to allude to the fidelity with which they endured the shocks of the counter-Reformation, and succeeded in transmitting to our own time the lessons which they had learned from Peter Waldo and John Wickliff. They brought across the Atlantic the union of fearless zeal with the gentler Christian virtues, and in the annals of Pennsylvania the name of Moravian came to represent all that serves as the firmest and surest foundation of social organization. Parkman has well indicated the contrast between the civilizing influence of the kindly Moravian missionaries and the manner in which their Jesuit rivals were content to substitute the cross as a fetich in place of the medicine-bag. The same well-directed enthusiasm endures to the present day. Small as is the Moravian Church, it maintained in 1885 no less than three hundred and nineteen missionaries scattered among the remote places of the earth, with over eighty-one thousand native converts as church members; and the more rugged and inhospitable the fields of labor the more earnest the zeal of the good Brethren. But for them the savage coasts of Greenland would be almost destitute of Christian teaching, and in their truly apostolic work we may recognize that the blood of the martyrs of Constance was not shed in vain.[611]

{568}
{569}

APPENDIX.

I.

EXCOMMUNICATION OF THE MAGISTRATES OF TOULOUSE, JULY 24, 1237. (Doat, XXI. fol. 146.)

Manifestum eit omnibus tam presentibus quam futuris quod nos frater Stephanus de ordine fratrum Minorum et frater Guilhelmus A. de ordine fratrum Predicatorum inquisitores instituti ad faciendam inquisitionem contra hereticos, fautores, receptatores et deffensores hereticorum Tholose et in tota diocesi Tholosana; cum per diligentem inquisitionem a nobis factam constiterit nobis R. Centulli et Sicardum de Tholosa et R. Rogerii et Alamannum de Roaxio et R. Embruni et Ondradam uxorem Arnaldi Petrarii infectos esse heretica pravitate, per sententiam diffinitivam eos esse hereticos condemnaverimus. Petrum de Tholosa vicarium Tholose et capitularios Tholose diligenter et legitime tam per nos quam per alios admonuimus ut dictos hereticos caperent et de dictis hereticis facerent quod est de hereticis faciendum; cumi gitur vicarius et capitularii, neglectis et contemptis omnibus supradictis admonitionibus a nobisfactis, non solum non ceperunt eos nec de terra eos fugaverunt, vel eorum bona occupaverunt ut tenentur, sed etiam in periculum animarum suarum et in prejudicium fidei, pacis et ecclesie R. Rogerii et Alamannum de Roaxio predictos hereticos condemnatos tolerant et sustinent in stratis publicis circa Tholosam et aliis locis eotum jurisdictioni subditis, capere viros religiosos et clericos ac eorum bonis propriis spoliare et ad redemptionem compellere, et vulnerare et injuriis eos afficere, necnon et viros Catholicos cum clericis commorantes occidere mutilare et alia mala ceclesiis et ecclesiasticis viris inferre, maxime cum nos dicti inquisitores publice excommunicaverimus omnem hominem tam virum quam mulierem tanquam fautorem et deffensorem hereticorum qui eis consilium vel auxilium aliquod eis occulte vel manifeste prestaret, et vicarius et capitularii supradicti contra prohibitionem nostram temere supradictos hereticos in supradictis malitiis fovent nequiter et sustentant; et cum insuper ipsi sacramento et constitutionibus ecclesie teneantur hereticos ubique capere et totam terram eorum jurisdictioni subjectam a pravitate heretica extirpare, non attendentes quod scriptura dicit, non est grandis differentia utrum letum admittas vel differas quoniam mortem languentibus probatur infligere qui hanc, cum possit, non excludit et alibi dicatur canone, quod error cui non resistitur probatur, et negligere cum possit arguere perversos{570} nihil aliud est quam fovere, nec caret scrupulo societatis occulte qui manifesto facinori distulit obviare, maxime cum vicarius et capitularii supradicti alia vice tanquam fautores et deffensores hereticorum fuerint excommunicati, predictos vicarium et capitularios, habito diligenti consilio et tractatu, assidentibus nobis venerabili patre R. Dei gratia episcopo Tholosano et B. abbate Mansi sub Verduno, et P. preposito Sancti Stephani, et P. priore ecclesie beate Marie

187

desurate, tanquam fautores et sustentatores hereticorum auctoritate qua fungimur excommunicationis vinculo innodamus.

Lata fuit hec sententia publice in ecclesia sancti Stephani Tholose, coram multis viris religiosis et capellanis parochialium ecclesiarum Tholose et aliis viris ecclesiasticis, IX Kal. Augusti anno Domini MCCXXXVII.

II.
ARGUMENT OF BERNARD DÉLICIEUX BEFORE PHILIPPE LE BEL, TOULOUSE, 1304.
(Bib. Nat. MSS., fonds latin. No. 4270, fol. 138.)

Dixit etiam se dixisse tunc ipse frater Bernardus quod Deus fecerat magnam gratiam patriæ in adventu ipsius domini regis, eo quod dictus frater Guilhelmus Petri, ordinis prædicatorum, tunc prior provincialis, præsentibus inquisitoribus Tolosæ et Carcassonæ et multis aliis fratribus ejusdem ordinis, dixit et confessus est loquens in personam inquisitorum prædictorum, in præsentia ipsius regis et plurium quam quingentarum personarum in aula superiori ipsius domini regis existentium, quod in tota lingua occitana non erant hæretici nisi tantummodo in burgo Carcassonæ, Albiæ vel Corduæ, vel in circuitu per unam leucam vel duas, et quod illi non erant quadraginta, et si erant quadraginta non erant quinquaginta, et quod hoc dictus frater Guilhelmus dixit bis in præsentia prædictorum; et ideo intulit tunc ipse frater Bernardus, ut dixit, quod patria quæ hactenus fuerat diffamata testimonio ipsorum inquisitorum ab infamia prædicta in adventu ipsius domini regis fuerat relevata, et sperabat frater Bernardus, ut dixit tunc se dixisse, quod ex quo tunc secundum verba eorum tota patria erat sana, excepta sex leucis et quinquaginta personis, quod leucæ illæ et personæ ac tres villæ prædictæ adhuc invenientur immunes a labe hæresis prædicta. Dixit etiam tunc se dixisse, quod si hodie viverent beati Petrus et Paulus, et contra eos impingeretur quod hæreticos adorassent, si procederetur contra eos super hujusmodi adoratione, sicut per aliquos inquisitores istarum partium aliquando contra multos fuit processum nec pateret eis via deffensionis. Si enim de fide interrogarentur, responderent sicut magistri et doctores, ubi autem diceretur eis quod hæreticos adorassent, et quærerent quos hæreticos, et dicerentur eis sola nomina dictorum hæreticorum (quæ quidem nomina et cognomina multis conveniunt) et ipsi beati Petrus et Paulus dicerent "Istos nunquam novimus. Dicatis nobis ubi sunt vel unde venerunt et quo iverunt, cujus linguæ, staturæ aut conditionis erant" et nihil eis diceretur per quod notitia dictorum hæreticorum, qui dicuntur adorati haberi posset: si etiam quærerent quo tempore facta fuerit hæc adoratio,{571} et non diceretur dies, mensis nec annus: si etiam quærerent nomina testium et non darentur eis, non est qui possit exprimere, ut dixit tunc se dixisse ipse frater Bernardus quod hi apostoli qui tam sancti sunt, a tali macula coram hominibus se possent deffendere, maxime cum si quis vellet eos deffendere statim impingeretur quod erat fautor hæreticorum, sicut ipse frater Bernardus in se ipso et dicto vicedomino probavit.

III.
SUPPLICATION OF THE CHURCH OF ALBI TO THE COLLEGE OF CARDINALS (1304-5).
(Archives de l'Hôtel-de-ville d'Albi.—Doat, XXXIV. fol. 42.)

Illustrissimæ Dominationis Patribus venerabilibus Dominis Cardinalibus sacrosanctæ Romanæ ecclesiæ sacroque cœtui eorumdem. Capitulum et Canonici ecclesiæ Albiensis et Capitulum et Canonici ecclesiæ Sti. Salvii de Albia, Abbasque et monachi monasterii de Galliaco Albiensis diocesis, et alii religiosi quorum sigilla inferius sunt appensa, suarum sublimitatum imperiis subjectionem debitam et devotam. Juste pater supplicatur a filiis dum cernunt fluctus tumescere et undis insiliantibus ventis et flantibus ex adverso naufragium imminere formidant, præsertim dum necessarium exigente qualitate causaram salus non pateat aut auxilium aliunde. Verum nostra patria quantis sit exposita præcipitiis et ruinis propter quæstiones et dissensiones quibus ad invicem se colliderunt patria et inquisitores hæreticæ pravitatis novit ille qui nihil ignorat, et adeo excrevit turbatio ut idem populus ad iracundian concitatus non videatur aliud anhelare nisi ut discriminibus se committens deducat in ore gladii, nedum quos sibi putat adversarios sed et alios, ac ad talia se convertat quæ non poterunt aliquatenus reparari. Vestræ igitur Paternitatis pedibus provoluti humiliter supplicanus ut circa præmissa sic salutifere et celeriter succurratis quod, præclusa via periculis et ruinis, patria restituatur paci debitæ et quieti. Constet enim vobis quod dictus populus et patria est catholica et fidelis, quantum nos humana fragilitas nosse sinit, et populus civitatis Albiæ et patriæ fidem catholicam corde credens ore profitetur eamdem ut sic perveniat ad salutem et bonis operibus astruit et confirmat.... Paternitatem vestram conservet altissimus ecclesiæ suæ sanctæ per tempora longiora. (Signed with seventeen seals.)

IV.
BULL OF CLEMENT V. IN FAVOR OF THE INQUISITION.
(Doat, XXXIV. fol. 112.)

Clemens episcopus servus servorum Dei ad perpetuam rei memoriam. Dudum venerabili fratri Petro episcopo Prenestino, tunc tituli Sancti Vitalis, et dilecto filio nostro Berengario titulo sanctorum Nerei et Achillei presbyteris cardinalibus, per nostros sub certa forma litteras duximus committendum ut ipsi circa negotium inquisitionis heretice pravitatis in partibus Carcassonensi, Albiensi et{572} Cordue super certis articulis seu dependentibus ab eisdem diligenter inquireretur et nonnulla etiam ordinarent; qui auctoritate litterarum hujusmodi quadam cura dictum officium ordinasse noscuntur. Quia vero nostre intentionis non extitit nec existit ut occasione dicte commissionis seu alicujus mandati nostri super hiis Cardinalibus ipsis facti, Inquisitoribus pravitatia predicte inquirendi vel conjunctim vel divisim cum episcopo seu episcopis ordinariis, aut sine ipsis, prout eis licet secundum canonicas sanctiones facultas aliquatenus restringatur; Nos ordinationem per quam dicti Cardinales facultatem inquirendi per se divisim inquisitoribus ipsis restrinxisse dicuntur utpote intentioni nostre et juri contrariam, juribus carere decernimus et nullatenus observandam, ordinatione ipsorum Cardinalium circa ceteros alios articulos in omnibus et per omnia in suo robore duratura. Nulli ergo omnino hominum liceat hanc paginam nostre constitutionis infringere, vel ei ausu temerario contraire. Si quis autem hec attemptare presumpserit, indignationem omnipot. Dei et beatorum Petri et Pauli apostolorum ejus se noverit incursurum. Datum Pictavis, secundo Idus Augusti, Pontificatus nostri anno tertio. (12 Aug. 1308.)

V.
BRIEF OF CLEMENT V. CONCERNING THE PRISONERS OF ALBI.[612]
(Doat, XXXIV. fol. 89.)

Venerabili fratri Geraldo episcopo Albiensi et dilectis filiis inquisitoribus heretice pravitatis in partibus Albiensibus. Dudum venerabili fratri nostro Bertrando tunc episcopo Albiensi et inquisitoribus dictis nostros direximus litteras in hec verba: {573}

Clemens episcopus, servus servorum Dei venerabili fratri Bertrando episcopo Albiensi et dilectis filiis inquisitoribus heretice pravitatis in partibus Albie, salutem et apostolicam benedictionem. Significarunt nobis Isarnus Colli, P. Fransa, Jo. de Porta, Joannes Pays, Petrus de Raissaco, B. Casas, G. Salavert, G. de Landas, Isarnus de Cardalhaco, G. Borrelli, cives Albienses, quod ipsi olim de mandato venerabilis fratris B. Aniciensis, tunc Albiensis, episcopi et inquisitoris seu inquisitorum qui erant tunc in partibus illis, occasione criminis hereseos, fuerint carceri mancipati, et jam per octo annos et amplius, tam Albie quam Carcassone, diu carceris angustias sustulerunt, sicut adhuc sustinent, quamvis nulla super hoc facta fuerit condempnatio de eisdem; cum autem ex parte dictorum civium pluries fuerimus cum instantia requisiti, ut ad condempnationem vel absolutionem eorumdem, prout jus exigit faceremus procedi: Nos volentes quod circa illos vestri officii debitum exequamini, sicut decet, discretioni vestre per Apostolica scripta mandamus, quatenus apud Albiam tu frater episcope per te vel per alium seu alios idoneos, vos vero inquisitor vel inquisitores prefati, personaliter predictos cives ubicumque detineantur, adduci ad vestram, presentiam sub fida custodia facientes, in eodem negotio quibuscumque processibus factis seu inchoatis per venerabiles fratres Leonardum Albanensem, nunc Prenestinum tunc tituli S. Vitalis et Berengarium Tusculanum episcopum, tunc tituli sanctorum Nerei et Achillei, et dilectos filios nostros Johannem tituli sanctorum Marcellini et Petri presbyteros ac Richardum sancti Eustachii diaconum Cardinales, seu per dilectum filium Arnaldum abbatem Fontisfrigidi Cisterciensis ordinis, Narbonensis diocesis, nunc Sancte Romane Ecclesie Vicecancellarium seu alios quoscumque, commissionum vigore per nos vel per felicis recordationis Benedictum papam undecimum predecessorem nostrum super facto heresis dictos cives tangente factarum, ab subrogatione prefati abbatis et predicti Albiensis episcopi facta, nequaquam obstantibus, in eodem negotio solum Deum habentes pre oculis, ad inquirendum contra illos contra quos inquisitum non est, et contra illos etiam contra quos inquisitum extitit, sed non plene, diligenter ac plenarie secundum formam que consuevit in talibus observari, contra illos vero contra quos plenarie inquisitum est, et contra predictos alios cum plene fuerit inquisitum, ad sententiam ratione previa procedatis, et alias contra illos vestri officii debitum exequamini, prout fuerit rationis, communicato tamen processu prius et inquisitione predictis prefatis Prenestino et Tusculano episcopis, eorum consiliis inherentes; per hoc tamen quoad alios ordinationi facte dudum de mandato nostro, tam Carcassone quam Albie per dictos Prenest. et Tuscul. episcopos tunc, ut predicitur, presbyteros Cardin. ex commissione seu commissionibus tam per nos quam per predecessorem nostrum factis predictis quibuscumque aliis Cardinalibus, et processibus habitis per eosdem super facto hominum illorum de Albia et de diocesi Albiensi, contra quos per dictum Bernardum Aniciensem tunc Albiensem episcopum, et inquisitorem seu inquisitores predictos, condempnationis sententia lata fuit, nullatenus volumus prejudicium generari. Datum Avenione, sexto Idus Februarii pontificatus nostro anno V. (8 Feb. 1310).

Verum sicut accepimus presentatis prefato episcopo et inquisitoribus litteris supradictis, et quibusdam dicentibus quod dicte littere fuerant a nobis subrepticie {574} impetrate, pro eo videlicet quod aliqui ex dictis civibus ante tempus date litterarum ipsarum decesserant, reliqui vero ipso tempore in carcere permanebant, et sic predicta non potuerunt intimasse, et in prefato negotio huc usque procedere neglexerant. Nos itaque nolentes quod propter hoc justitia retardetur, discretioni vestre per apostolica mandamus, quatenus premissis non obstantibus, nec obstante etiam quod aliqui de predictis querelantibus non sint cives Albie, licet sint de diocesi Albie, nec si aliquem de predictis mori contingat, vel ante decessisset quam inquirere inchoaveritis vel inchoavissetis, vel post eorumdem mortem, in aliquo non obstante, tam de mortuis quam de vivis inquirere, et in eodem negotio procedere minime postponatis, juxta predictarum nostrarum tenorem litterarum. Quod si forsan vos filii inquisitores, his nolueritis, aut non potueritis, aut non curaveritis interesse, tu frater episcope, solus per te vel per alium seu alios in negotio eodem procedas, juxta litterarum continentiam earumdem.

VI.
WITHDRAWAL OF SECURITY FROM CITIZENS OF ALBI.
(Archives de l'Inquisition de Carcassonne.—Doat, XXXII. fol. 138.)

Joannes episcopus servus servorum Dei dilectis filiis inquisitoribus hæreticæ pravitatis in partibus Carcassonæ constitutis salutem et apostolicam benedictionem. Ut commissum vobis negotium Catholicæ fidei autore Domino prosperetur in vestris manibus libenter apostolicæ sollicitudinis partes apponimus et quæque obstantia submovemus. Olim quidem felicis recordationis Clementi papæ quinto prædecessori nostro pro parte

189

quorumdam hominum de partibus Carcassonæ suggesto quod inquisitores pravitatis hæreticæ illarum partium qui tunc erant et pro tempore fuerant multa illis gravamina et injurias irrogarunt, iniquos contra eos et alios illarum partium processus contra justitiam facientes, idem prædecessor hujusmodi suggestionibus aurem accommodans, bonæ memoriæ Petro episcopo Prænestinensi tunc tituli Sancti Vitalis et venerabili fratri nostro Berengario episcopo Tusculanensi, tunc tituli SS. Nerei et Achillei presbiteris cardinalibus qui partium illarum notitiam habebant et per partes illas transitum facere tunc habebant, suis dedit litteris in mandatis ut de præmissis suggestionibus et aliis incidentibus se plenius informarent, et nihilominus interim personis prosequentibus negotium memoratum de securitate idonea, pendente dicto negotio, auctoritate apostolica providerent nec permitterent eos per eosdem inquisitores aliquatenus molestari; præfati quoque cardinales hujusmodi commissionis prætextu Aymerico de Castro burgensi Carcassonæ et quibusdam aliis tunc negotium prosequentibus supradictum securitatem hujusmodi, pendente dicto negotio, apostolica auctoritate præstantes, illos sub sua protectione et sedis apostolicæ receperunt; quam receptionem idem prædecessor noster ratam habens et gratam mandavit illam inviolabiliter observari, eisdem inquisitoribus districtius inhibendo ne contra præfatum Aymericum et alios officii eorum prætextu procederent quoquomodo, donec præfatum negotium esset per sedem apostolicam terminatum et a sede ipsa aliud reciperent in mandatis. Quia vero præfati Aymericus{575} et alii circa proposita et objecta per eos ulterius coram prædecessore præfato ac etiam coram nobis negotium ipsum prosequi neglexerunt et quasi negligunt, præfata protectione securi, nos nolentes sicut etiam non debemus propterea vestrum officium impediri, securitatem ipsam penitus revocantes discretioni vestræ per apostolica scripta mandamus quatinus contra eumdem Aymericum et alios in decreta vobis provincia, Deum et justitiam habendo præ oculis, procedentes, non obstantibus securitate prædicta et aliis securitatibus, protectionibus, confirmationibus, ordinationibus, et inhibitionibus quibuscumque dicti prædecessoris aut aliorum quorumlibet, juxta formam vobis traditam ac canonicas sanctiones et de peritorum consilio officii vestri debitum curetis exequi diligenter. Datum Avenione, tertio Kalendas Aprilis, pontificatus nostri anno secundo (30 Mart. 1318).

VII.
Exequatur of on Inquisitor for Champagne.
(Archives de l'Inquisition de Carcassonne.—Doat, XXXII. fol. 127.)

Philippus regis Franciæ primogenitus Dei gratia rex Navarræ, Campaniæ et Briæ comes palatinus dilectis et fidelibus suis universis baillivis, castellanis, vasallis, præpositis, communitatibus villarum et earum rectoribus, cæterisque communia officia gerentibus in nostris comitatibus Campaniæ et Briæ, ad quos præsentes litteræ pervenerint salutem et dilectionem. Tenore præsentium bovis districte præcipitiendo mandamus, quatenus dilecto fratri Guillelmo Altissiodorensi ordinis fratrum prædicatorum præsentium exhibitori domini Papæ inquisitori hæreticorum ac perfidorum Judæorum in regno Franciæ sine mora et qualibet difficultate plenarie obediatis, sicut vobis in citando, capiendo, detinendo, ad eos mittendo seu etiam ducendo et puniendo tam Christianos quam Judæos, quos idem frater inquisitor invenerit culpabiles contra statuta ecclesiæ et fidem Domini nostri Jesu Christi, ipsum nihilominus familiam et res ipsius custodientes et defendientes sicut nos et familiam et res nostras. In cujus rei testimonium præsentibus litteris nostrum fecimus apponi sigillum. Actum et datum Parisius, die Dominica in crastino Sancti Matthiæ apostoli, anno Domini MCC. octuagesimo quarto, mense Februarii (25 Feb. 1285).

VIII.
Sentence of Marguerite la Porete.
(Archives nationales de France.—J. 428, No. 15.)

In Christi nomine amen. Anno ejusdem MCCC decimo, indictione octava, die dominica post Ascensionem Domini (31 Maii), pontificatus beatissimi patris domini C. divina providentia Pape quinti anno quinto, in Gravia Parisius, facta ibidem congregatione sollempni, assistentibus mihi reverendo in Christo patre domino Parisiensi episcopo, magistris Johanne de Frogerio officiali Parisiensi, C. de Chenat, Johanne de Domnomartino, Xaverio de Charmoia, Stephano de{576}Bercondicuria, fratribus Martino de Abbatisvilla bachalario in theologia, Nicolao de Avessiaco ordinis predicatorum, Johanne Marchandi preposito Parisiensi, G. de Choques et pluribus aliis ad hoc specialiter evocatis, presentibus etiam pluribus processionibus ville Parisius et populi multitudine copiosa, et me notario publico infrascripto, religiosus vir et honestus frater G. de Parisius, ordinis predicatorum, inquisitor heretice pravitatis in regno Francie auctoritate apostolica deputatus in scriptis tulit sentientias infrascriptas sub hac forma:

In nomine Patris et Filii et Spiritua Sancti amen. Quia nobis fratri Guillelmo de Parisius ordinis predicatorum inquisitori heretice pravitatis in regno Francie auctoritate apostolica deputato, constat et constitit evidentius argumentis te, Margaritam de Hannonia dictam Perete, super labe heretice pravitatis vehementer esse suspectam, propter quod citari te fecimus ut compareas in judicio coram nobis, in quo existens personaliter a nobis ortata pluries canonice et legitime ut coram nobis juramentum prestares de plena pura et integra veritate dicenda de te et aliis super hiis que ad nobis commissum inquisitionis officium pertinere noscuntur, que facere contempsisti, licet a nobis fueris pluries super hoc et locis pluribus requisita, in hiis fuisti semper contumax et rebellis, pro quibus contumaciis et rebellionibus evidentibus et notoriis hoc exigentibus de multorum peritorum consilio, in te sic rebellem et contumacem sententiam majoris excommunicationis tulimus et in scriptis, quam, licet te notificata fuisset, post notificationem predictam fere per annum et dimidium in tue salutis dispendium

190

sustinuisti animo pertinaci, licet tibi pluries obtulerimus nos tibi absolutionis beneficium impensuros secundum formam ecclesie si hoc humiliter postulares, quod usque nunc petere contempsisti nec jurare nec respondere nobis super premissis hactenus voluisti, propter que secundum sanctiones canonicas pro convicta et confessa, et pro lapsa in heresim seu pro heretica te habemus et habere debemus: Porro dum tu Margarita in istis rebellionibus obstinata maneres, ducti conscientia volentes officii nobis commissi debitum exercere inquisitionem contra te et processum fecimus super predictis, prout exegit ordo vite, ex quibus inquisitione et processu nobis constitit evidenter quondam composuisse te librum pestiferum continentem heresim et errores, ob quam causam fuit dictus liber per bone memorie Guidonem olim Cameracensem episcopum[613] condemnatus et de mandato ipsius in Valencenis in tua combustus presentia publice et patenter; a quo episcopo tibi fuit sub pena excommunicationis expresse inhibitum ne de cetero talem librum componeres vel haberes aut eo vel simili utereris, addens et expresse ponens dominus episcopus in quadem littera suo sigillata sigillo, quod si de cetero libro utereris predicto vel si ca que continebantur in eo verbo vel scripto de cetero attemptares, te condempnabat tanquam hereticam et relinquebat justiciandam justicie seculari. Post vero dicta omnia dictum librum contra dictam prohibitionem pluries habuisti et pluries usa es, sicut et ejus patet recognitionibus factis nedum coram inquisitore Lotharingie et coram reverendo patre et domino, domino Johanne tunc Cameracensi episcopo, nunc archiepiscopo Senonensi,[614] dictum eumdem librum, preter condempnationem{577} et combustionem predictas, sicut bonum et licitum communicasti reverendo patri domino Johanni Cathalonensi episcopo et quibusdam personis aliis, prout ex fidedignorum juratorum et super hiis coram nobis evidentibus testimoniis nobis liquet. Nos igitur super premissis omnibus deliberatione prehabita diligenti communicatoque multorum peritorum in utroque jure consilio, Deum et sancta evangelia pre oculis habentes, de reverendi patris et domini Domini G. Dei gratia Parisiensis episcopi consilio et assensu, te Margaritam non solum sicut lapsum in heresim sed sicut relapsam finaliter condempnamus, et te relinquimus justicie seculari, rogantes eam ut citra mortem et membrorum mutilationem, tecum agat misericorditer quantum permictunt canonice sanctiones; dictum etiam librum tanquam hereticum et erroneum upote errores et heresim continentem, judicio magistrorum in theologia Parisius existentium et de eorumdem consilio finaliter condempnamus ac demum excommunicari volumus et comburi; universis et singulis habentibus dictum librum precipientes districte et sub pena excommunicationis quod infra instans festum Apostolorum Petri et Pauli nobis vel priori fratrum predicatorum Parisius, nostro commissario, sine fraude reddere teneantur. Actum Parisius in Gravia, presente predicto patre reverendo Parisiensi episcopo, clero et populo dicte civitatis ibidem sollempniter congregate, Dominica infra Ascensionem Domini, anno Domini MCCC decimo.

CONSULTATION OF CANON LAWYERS ON THE CASE OF MARGUERITE LA PORETE, HELD MAY 30, 1310.

Universis presentes litteras inspecturis, Guillelmus dictus Frater archidiaconus Laudonie in ecclesia Sancti Andree in Scocia, Hugo de Bisuncio canonicus Parisiensis, Johannes de Tollenz canonicus Sancti Quintini in Veromandua, Henricus de Bitunia canonicus Furnensis et Petrus de Vallibus curatua Sancti Germani Altissiodorensis de Parisius, et etiam regentes Parisius in decretis, salutem in actore salutis. Noveritis virum venerabilem devotum et discretum fratrem Guillelmum de Parisius ordinis predicatorum inquisitorem heretice pravitatis in regno Francie auctoritate sedis apostolice deputatum, inque processum qui sequitur nobis intimasse, consultationemque nobis fecisse inferius annotatam. Processus equidem talis est: Tempore quo Margarita dicta Porete suspecta de heresi fuit in rebellione et in inobedientia, nolens respondere nec jurare coram inquisitore de hiis que ad inquisitionis sibi commisse officium pertinent, ipse inquisitor contra eam nihilominus inquisivit et etiam depositione plurium testium invenit quod dicta Margarita librum quemdam composuerat continentem hereses et errores qui de mandato reverendi patris domini Guidonis condam Cameracensis episcopi publice et sollempniter tanquam talis fuit condempnatus et combustus et per litteram dicti episcopi fuit ordinatum quod si talia sicut ea que continebantur in libro de cetero attemptaret verbo vel scripto earn condempnabat et relinquebat justiciandam justicie seculari. Invenit etiam idem inquisitor quod ipsa recognovit in judicio semel coram inquisitore Lotharingie et semel coram reverendo patre Domino Philippe tunc Cameracensi episcopo, se post condempnationem predictam librum dictum habuisse et alios: invenit etiam idem inquisitor{578} quod dicta Margarita dictum librum in suo consimili eosdem continentem errores post ipsius libri condempnationem reverendo patri Domino Jo. Dei gratia Catbalaunensi episcopo communicavit ac nedum dicto domino sed et pluribus aliis personis simplicibus, begardis et aliis tanquam bonum. Consultatio autem ex predictis resultans per prefatum inquisitorem ut pertactum est nobis facta talis est: Videlicet, utrum in talibus dicta beguina debeat relapsa judicari? Nos autem fidei catholice zelatores, veritatisque canonice professores qualescumque consultationi predicte respondentes, dicimus quod ipsa beguina. supposita veritate facti precedentis, judicanda est relapsa et merito relinquenda est curie seculari. In cujus rei testimonium sigilla nostra presentibus apposuimus. Datum anno Domini MCCC decimo sabbato post festum beati Joannis ante portam latinam.[615]

IX.

EXEQUATUR OF AN INQUISITOR ISSUED BY PHILLIPE LE BON OF BURGUNDY.

(MSS. Bib. Nat., fonds Moreau, 444 fol. 10.)

Philippus universis et singulis seneschallis, baillivis, scultetis, officiariis et justiciariis nostris præsentibus et futuris, et locatenentibus eorumdem per ducatus et diatrictus nostras infra dyoceses Cameracensis et Leodiensis constitutos, ad quos præsentes nostræ litteræ pervenerint salutem et omne bonum. Cum religiosus dilectusque noster frater (Henricus) Kaleyser sacræ theologiæ professor ordinis fratrum prædicatorum inquisitor bæreticæ pravitatis per provincialem provinciæ Theotoniæ in prædictis Cameracensi et Leodiensi dyocesibus auctoritate apostolica specialiter deputatus pro Dei servitio et cultu seu exaltatione sanctæ fidei orthodoxæ utque ipsum hæresis crimen a dictis partibus quibus presidemus si forsan alicubi vigeat seu inoleat valeat extirpare ad loca seu partes nostræ jurisdictioni subjectas et vobis commissas declinare quisquam habeat seu etiam proficisci, nosque velut princeps catholicus qui de manu altissimi multa bona variosque honores recognoscimus recipisse in prædictis et aliis qui divinum continuo obsequium complacere ut convenit plurimum cupiantes intendimus ymo et volumus favorabilem dare locum, ipsumque inquisitorem tanquam Dei specialem ministrum nostris prosequi gratiis et favoribus optamus ideo vobis et cuilibet vestum qui super hoc fueritis requisiti seu fuerit requisitus, districte præcipiendo{579}mandamus sub obtentu gratiæ nostra quatenus dictum fratrem Henricum inquisitorem quotiescumque ad exercendum dictum officium ad dicta loca seu partes vobis commissas contigerit se transferre et supra prædictis sæculare brachium invocando vestrum auxilium postulare, eumdem inquisitorem favorabiliter admittatis, et eidem in et supra prædictis sæculare brachium invocando vestrum auxilium impendatis, capiendo seu capi faciendo quoscumque ipse inquisitor debita informatione seu inquisitione prævia et juris ordine alias desuper observato de memorato facinore suspectos vel diffamatos noverit et hæreticos quosque vobis duxerit nominandos, et captos etiam detinendo, et infra jurisdictionem vestram ad locum de quo dictus inquisitor vobis dixerit deducendo, necnon pœna debita plectendo eosdem sicut ipse decreverit et est fieri consuetum, si videlicet quando et quotiens ac prout ipse inquisitor vos duxerit requirendos. Ut autem inquisitor præfatus suum inquisitionis officium securius et liberius exercere valeat, nostro suffultus presidio et favore, inquisitorem eumdem ipsiusque socium ac ejus notarium et familiam, res et bona eorum, sub nostris protectione, defensione et salvagardia speciali atque securo conductu recepimus et recipimus per præsentes, mandantes vobis omnibus et singulis supradictis ut vestrum cuilibet quatenus nostras protectionem, defensionem et salvagardiam securumque conductum hujusmodi dicto inquisitori ejusque socio ac notario, familiæ, bonis et rebus eorum inviolabiliter observando, nullam injuriam nullumque dispendium, gravamen aut dampnum aliquod ipsis inferre in personis ac bonis a quocumque permittatis, quinnymo provideatis eisdem de securo transitu et salvo conductu si et prout per dictum inquisitorem inde fueritis requisiti. Datum in oppido nostro Bruxellensi mensis novembria die nona, anno Domini MCCCC tricesimo primo.

X.

WALDENSIANISM IN THE SENTENCES OF PIERRE CELLA.

(Doat, XXI.)

I select a few of the sentences of Pierre Cella in 1241-2, illustrating the development of Waldensianism at that period, and the relations between it and Catharism. The sects were perfectly distinct, but frequently the people, in their antagonism to the established Church, looked favorably on both, and considered them equally as "*boni homines.*" It will be borne in mind that, in the language of the Inquisition, "heretic" always means Catharan. The following cases are all from Gourdon and Montauban.

Galterus Archambaut vidit hereticos pluries in diversis locis, audivit predicationes eorum, et comedit cum eis sepe, et adoravit eos sepe, et pacis osculum more hereticorum pluries recepit et interfuit hereticationibus duabus, et adduxit Valdenses ad hereticos in domum suam, ubi disputaverunt, et conduxit hereticos, et fuit depositarius eorum, multociens adoravit eos et comedit cum eis, et dedit{580} eis de bonis suis, et audivit predicationes eorum tociens quod non recordatur, et credebat quod essent boni homines et quod esset salus cum eis, et si moreretur vellet mori in manibus eorum.—Stabit Constantinopoli per quinque annos, de cruce et via sicut alii, et tenebit pauperem quamdiu vixerit (fol. 196-7).

B. Bonaldi vidit P. de Vallibus Valdensem, et audivit predicationem ejus, et credidit aliquando quod non debet homo jurare, et in domo sua propria recepit Joset de Noguer hereticum, et disputavit cum eo, et ipse commendavit sectam Valdensem.—Idem quod proxima, excepta cruce (id est, Ibit ad Podium, Sanctum Egidium, Sanctum Jacobum, Sanctum Salvatorem de Asturia, Sanctum Marcialem, Sanctum Leonardum, Sanctum Dyonisium, Sanctum Thomam Cantuariensem) (fol. 201).

Petrus de Verniolo habuit hereticos et Valdenses in fortia sua, et locutus est alteri eorum, consuluit Valdenses de infirmitate sua.—Ibit ad Podium, Sanctum Egidium et Sanctum Jacobum (fol. 202).

Pana tociens recepit Valdenses quod non recolit, et fuit hospes Valdensium, et misit eis tociens panem, vinum, et alia comestibilia quod non nescit numerum, et fuit in domo sua facta disputatio inter Valdenses et credentes hereticis, et diligebat P. de Vallibus tanquam angelum Dei:—Sicut proxima, excepto paupere et cruce (i.e. Ibit ad Podium, Sanctum Egidium, Sanctum Salvatorem de Asturia, Sanctum Marcialem, Sanctum Leonardum, Sanctum Dyonisium, Sanctum Thomam Cantuariensem) (fol. 203).

Petrona uxor Raimundi Joannis, adduxit P. de Vallibus Valdensem ad domum suam, et tenuit per octo dies, et dedit ad comedendum et bibendum, et audivit eum ibi, et tenuit per tres septimanas Geraldam Valdensem, et credebat quod esset bona mulier, et dedit ei de bonis suis, et vidit hereticos et audivit predicationem eorum, et misit eis panem, vinum, et nuces.—Sicut Huga, excepta cruce (i.e. Ibit ad Podium, ad Sanctum Egidium, Sanctum Jacobum et Sanctum Salvatorem de Asturia, Sanctum Marcialem Lemovicensem, Sanctum Leonardum, Sanctum Dyonisium et Sanctum Thomam Cantuariensem), et tenebit pauperem per annum (fol. 204).

G. de Pradels vidit hereticos, audivit predicationem eorum, dedit eis de bonia suis, et pluries vidit et in diversis locis hereticos, et credebat quod boni homines essent, pluries vidit Valdensem, et credidit quod bonus homo esset, et dedit ei ad comedendum semel, et audivit predicationem ejus.—Portabit crucem per biennium (fol. 208).

G. Ricart pluries vidit hereticos et in diversis locis et sepe audivit predicationem eorum, et interfuit appareilhamento, recepit osculum pacis ab eis, comedit cum eis, recepit pluries eos in domum suam, dedit eis ad comedendum, recepit ab eis forcipes, dedit eis unam capam, unam camisiam, unam tunicam, unam quartam{581} frumenti, duxit Valdenses ad hereticos ad disputandum in die Pasche, associavit hereticos, fuit depositarius eorum, et multociens audivit predicationem hereticorum, credebat quod essent boni homines, et, si moreretur, vellet mori in manibus eorum, tociens adoravit eos quod non recordatur.—Stabit Constantinopoli per tres annos, de cruce et via sicut alii, et tenebit pauperem quamdiu vixerit (fol. 208).

P. de Gaulenas viciit Valdenses et hereticos et locutus est cum eis in quadam navi, et cum audisset hereses quas dicebant, recessit ab eis.—Ibit ad Sanctum Jacobum (fol. 230).

P. Baco vidit Valdenses multociens et dedit eis eleemosynas et audivit predicationem Valdensium, et diligebat eos, et credebat quod essent boni homines, et frequenter dabat eis de suo, et interfuit cene Valdensium, et comedit de pane benedicto, vino et piscibus hereticorum et accepit pacem ab eis; item dedit Valdensibus ad comedendum in domo sua; item interfuit disputationi hereticorum et Valdensium, et dedit eis duodecim denarios.—Idem quod proximus (i.e. Ibit ad Podium, Sanctum Egidium, Sanctum Jacobum et Sanctum Thomam) et amplius ad Sanctum Dyonisium (fol. 231).

P. R. Boca dixit quod vidit multociens Valdenses et in diversis locis, et etiam habuit eos in domo sua, et audivit ibi monitiones eorum; item credebat quod essent boni homines; item pluries venit ad hereticos et audivit predicationem eorum, et alibi vidit hereticos et accepit pacem ab ipsis hereticis; item tercio vidit hereticos et adoravit eos; item quarto vidit hereticos et audivit predicationem eorum et adoravit eos; item recepit in porticu suo hereticum, et duxit eum inde ad quemdam locum, et dedit cuidam heretico unam capam; item credidit a principio quod Valdenses erant boni homines, et idem credidit postea de hereticis.—Stabit Constantinopoli tribus annis, de cruce et via sicut alii (fol. 232).

P. Lanes senior dixit quod vidit Valdenses et dedit eis eleemosinam, et uxor sua dedit se Valdensibus in morte et fuit sepulta in cimiterio eorum, ipse tamen absens erat, ut dixit, et vidit alibi Valdenses.—Ibit ad Podium, Sanctum Egidium et Sanctum Jacobum (fol. 232).

Johannes Toset dixit quod multociens vidit hereticos et in diversis locis, et fuit presens quando quidam fecit se hereticum apud Rabastens, et tunc vidit multos hereticos ibi; item audivit predicationem hereticorum et adoravit eos bis; item dedit sorori sue heretice pluries denarios; item associavit hereticos; item associavit avunculum suum quando fecit se hereticum apud Villamur; item consuluit Valdensibus pro infirmitate sua, et credidit quod essent boni homines.—Stabit tribus annis Constantinopoli, de cruce et via sicut alii (fol. 232-33).

Ramon Carbonel vidit multos Valdeuses et in diversis locis, et induxit fratrem suum ut solveret solidos ducentos Valdensibus legatos eis; item, interfuit{582} disputationi Valdensium et hereticorum; item, interfuit cene Valdensium et comedit de pane et piscibus benedictis ab eis, de vino bibit, et audivit predicationem eorum.—Ibit ad Podium, Sanctum Egidium, Sanctum Jacobum, Sanctum Dyonisium et Sanctum Thomam (fol. 234).

Jacobus Carbonel dixit quod frequenter venit ad scholas Valdensium et legebat cum eis; item interfuit disputationi hereticorum et Valdensium et comedit de pane et pisce benedictis ab eis, de vino bibit, et tunc erat duodecim annorum vel circa, et credidit quod Valdenses erant boni homines usque ad tempus quo ecclesia condemnavit eos.—Ibit ad Podium, Sanctum Egidium, Sanctum Jacobum et Sanctum Dyonisium (fol. 234).

Bartholomeus de Posaca dixit quod adduxit quemdam Valdensem ad uxorem suam infirmam, qui curam illius egit, et audivit predicationem Valdensium, et ex tunc dilexit eos, et venerunt pluries ad domum ejus, et faciebat eis eleemosinas dando eis panem et vinum et multociens et in diversis locis audivit predicationem eorum; item interfuit cene Valdensium et comedit ut supra; item pluries (accepit) pacem ab eis.—Ibit ad Podium, Sanctum Egidium, Sanctum Jacobum et Sanctum Thomam (fol. 236).

Guillelmus de Catus dixit quod cum frater suus et filia ejus infirmarentur adduxit Valdenses ad domum suam ut haberent curam eorum; item, audivit expositionem evangelii a quodam Valdensi; item aliquando iverunt Valdenses ad restringendum dolium suum et tunc dedit eis ad comedendum; item aliquando volebat eis facere eleemosinas sed nolebant accipere; item aliquando accepit pacem ab eis et audivit admonitiones eorum; item credidit quod essent boni homines, et ea quæ dicebant et faciebant placebant ei.—Ibit ad Podium, Sanctum Egidium, Sanctum Jacobum et Sanctum Dyonisium (fol. 236).

P. Austores audivit multociens predicationem Valdensium dum predicarent publice in viis; item quidam apportavit sibi de pane pisceque benedicto a Valdensibus et comedit; item credidit quod essent boni homines et quod homo posset salvari cum ipsis; item dixit quod postquam audivit quod ecclesia condamnaverat eos non dilexit eos.—Ibit ad Podium, Sanctum Egidium et Sanctum Jacobum (fol. 237-8).

Domina de Coutas vidit Valdenses publice predicantes, et dabat eis eleemosinas, et venit ad domum in qua manebant et audivit predicationem eorum, et multociens ivit ad eos pro quodam infirmo; item in die Parasceves venit bis ad Valdenses et audivit predicationem eorum, et confessa fuit Valdensi cuidam peccata sua, et accepit peniteutiam a Valdense; item credebat quod esseut boni homines; item vidit hereticos et comedit cum

193

eis cerasa; et dicebatur quod esset reconciliata; item vidit alibi pluries hereticos; item comedit de pane signato a Valdensibus.—Idem quod proxima excepta cruce (i.e. Ibit ad Podium, Sanctum Egidium, Sanctum Jacobum, Sanctum Thomam) (fol. 241).{583}

B. Remon vidit Valdenses, et audivit predicationem eorum et credebat quod essent boni homines; item, ivit ad hereticos volens tentare qui essent meliores, Valdenses vel heretici, et ibi audivit predicationem eorum; item alibi locutus est cum hereticis, et adoravit eos postquam fuerat confessus quedam de predictis fratri Guillelmo de Belvais; item adduxit sororem suam hereticatam a Tholosa usque ad Montemalbanum, et conduxit eam et alias hereticas usque ad quemdam mansum; item venit ad ipsas et portavit eis piscem et bibit cum eis; item rogavit quemdam quod reciperet illas hereticas in manso suo, quod et fecit, et promisit ei quinquaginta solidos; item, alia vice comedit cum hereticis; item fecit donum dictis hereticis et audivit predicationem eorum et comedit cum eis; item, apportavit hereticis fructus; item, fecit tunicam et capam sorori sue heretice; item, vidit hereticis et credebat quod essent boni homines et haberent bonam fidem, et comedit de pane signato ab eis; item, disputavit cum quodam de fide hereticorum et Valdensium, et approbavit fidem hereticorum.—Stabit Constantinopoli tribus annis, de cruce et via sicut alii (fol. 242).

G. Macips vidit Valdenses qui habuerunt curam ejus in infirmitate sua, et pluries venerunt ad domum ipsius et audivit admonitiones eorum, et dedit eis pluries eleemosinas, et credebat quod essent boni homines; item, posuit fidejussorem quemdam hereticum pro eo pro quindecim solidis; item, vidit hereticos et audivit admonitionem eorum; item, vidit hereticos et audivit predicationem eorum, et promisit cuidam heretico servitium suum.—Ibit ad Podium, Sanctum Egidium, Sanctum Jacobum, Sanctum Salvatorem, Sanctum Dyonisium et Sanctum Thomam (fol. 246).

Guillelmus Laurencii vidit hereticos predicantes, et interfuit disputationi hereticorum et Valdensium, et fecit sibi fieri emplastrum a Valdensibus.—Ibit ad Podium, Egidium et Sanctum Jacobum (fol. 250).

J. Austores vidit hereticos multociens et adoravit eos multociens, et audivit predicationem eorum multociens. et comedit de pane benedicto ab hereticis et de nucibus; item vidit hereticos alibi; item dixit quod multociens vidit et in diversis locis et temporibus, et quotiens videbat hereticos adorabat eos semel; item, vidit Valdenses et audivit predicationem eorum multociens, et dedit eis panem et vinum multociens, et credebat quod essent boni homines.—Stabit Constantinopoli tribus annis, de cruce et via sicut alii (fol. 256).

A. Capra dixit quod multociens duxit quemdam Valdensem ad domuin suam pro infirmitate sue uxoris et dedit Valdensibus multociens panem et vinum et carnes; item, dixit quod portavit panem et piscem Valdensibus ad domum suam; item, dixit quod audivit predicationem Valdensium; item, dixit se audivisse predicationem eorum in platea multociens; item, in die Pasche dedit Valdensibus carnes et comedit de cena Valdensium.—Ibit ad Podium, Sanctum Egidium, Sanctum Jacobum et Sanctum Thomam (fol. 257).{584}

B. Clavelz vidit Valdenses et audivit predicationem eorum in plateis et interfuit cene Valdensium et cenavit cum eis in die Jovis cene, et audivit ibi predicationem eorum, et dedit eis multociens panem et vinum, et credebat quod essent boni homines.—Ibit ad Podium, Sanctum Egidium, Sanctum Jacobum et Sanctum Dyonisium (fol. 258).

XI. LETTERS OF CHARLES I. OF NAPLES.

1.

(Archivio di Napoli, Anno 1269, Reg. 3, Letters A, fol. 64.)

Scriptum est comitibus, marchionibus, baronibus, potestatis et consulibus civitatum et villarum comitatibus, ac omnibus aliis potestatem et jurisdictionem habentibus et aliis amicis et fidelibus suis ad quos presentes littere pervenerint salutem et omne bonum. Cum dilecti nobis in Christo fratres predicatores in terris carissimi domini et nepotis nostri illustris regis Francie inquisitores heretice pravitatis auctoritate apostolica deputati in Lombardia et ad alias partes ytalie sane intelleximus proficisci intendant seu mittere nuncios speciales ad explorandos ibi hereticos et alios pro heresi fugitivos qui de terris predictis aufugerent et se ad partes ytalie transtulerunt et pro ipsis hereticis et fugitivis ad loca unde aufugerint per se vel per eosdem nuncios reducendis, rogamus et requerimus quatenus eisdem fratribus vel predictis eorum nuntiis presentium portatoribus in exigendis predictis vestrum impendatis consilium auxilium et favorem ut per terras et potestates vestras ipsos salvo et secure cum rebus societatis et familia suis conducatis et conduci faciatis eundo redeundo et morando. Ad salvamentum et liberationem eorum efficaciter intendentes quocies sibi necesse fuerit et vos inde credederint requirendos. Datum apud urbem veterem penultimo madii primæ indictionis.

2.

(Anno 1269, Registro 4, Letters B, fol. 47.)

Scriptum est universis justitiariis secretis baiulis judicibus magistris juratis ceterisque officialibus atque fidelibus suis per regnum sicilie constitutis etc. Cum religiosus vir frater benvenutus ordinis Minorum inquisitor heretice pravitatis Regebatium et Jacobucium familiares suos latores presentium pro capiendis quibusdam hereticis per diversas partes regni nostri morantibus quorum nomina inferius continentur mittat ad presens et petiverit nostrum sibi ad hoc favorem et auxilium exhiberi fidelitati tue precipiendo mandamus quatenus ad requisitionem dictorum nunciorum vel alterius eorumdem omnes hujusmodi hereticos cum bonis eorum omnibus tam stabilibus quam mobilibus seseque moventibus capientes faciatis personas illorum in locis tutis cum summa diligentia custodiri. Bona vero ipsorum ad opus nostre curie fideliter et solliciter conservari. Attentius provisuri ne in hoc aliquem adhibeatis negligentiam vel defectum sicut divinam et nostram indignationem cupitis evitare et nihilominus de hiis que ceperitis{585} faciatis fieri quatuor publica consimilia instrumenta, quorum uno penes vos retento alio penes eum qui bona ipsa custodierit dimisso. tercium ad cameram nostram et quartum ad magistros rationales magne nostre curie destinetis. Nomina vero hereticorum ipsorum sunt hec (sequuntur nomina 67). Datum in obsidione lucerie XII. Augusti decime secunde indictionis.

3.
(Anno 1269, Reg. 6, Lettera D, fol. 135.)

Karolus etc. Berardo de Rajona militi etc. Cum te ad justitiariatum aprutii et comitatue molisii pro inveniendis et capiendis patarenis hereticis ac receptatoribus et fautoribus eorum specialiter duximus destinandum fidelitati tue districte precipiendo mandamus quatenus ad partes illas etc. personaliter conferens in inveniendis et capiendis ipsis omnem curam quam poteris et diligentiam et sollicitudinem studeas adhibere, ita quod possis exinde in conspectu nostre celsitudinis commendabili merito apparere. Nos enim scribimus omnibus officialibus nostris ceterisque in eisdem partibus constitutis ut super hiis celeriter exequendis dent tibi consilium et auxilium opportunum. Datum Neapoli XIII. Decembris XIII. indictionia.

4.
(Anno 1270. Reg. 9, Lettera C, fol. 39.)

Xiiij Martii Neapoli scriptum cst Johannutio de Pando magistro portuiano et procuratori curie in principatu et terra laboris etc. Qnia ex insinuatione fratris Mathei de Castro Maris inquisitoris in regno Sicilie heretice pravitatis intelleximus quod idem frater Matheus nuper invenerit in civitate beneventana tres patarenos, unum videlicet lombardum nomine Andream de Vivi Mercato, alium nomine Judicem Johannem de zeccano, et tertium Thomasium Russum nomine de Maula saracena quos judicavit relapsos et tradi fecit ignibus et comburi, quorum bona omnia sunt regie curie tanquam bona Paterenorum juste et rationabiliter applicanta, Devotioni tue etc. quatenus statim receptis presentibus de bonis omnibus tam stabilibus quam mobilibus et semoventibus ipsorum Paterenorum cum omni diligentia inquirere studeas, quibus inventis et captis debeas ea pro parte curie fideliter procurare, faciens redigi in quaterno uno transumptum inquisitionis ipsius in quo quaterno contineantur etiam bona omnia que ceptris, quantitatem et qualitatem ipsorum in quibuscumque consistant et ubi ac valorem annuum eorumdem; quem quaternum cum litteris tuis continentibus processum tuum totum quem in premissis hujusmodi sub sigillo tuo etc. sine dilatione transmittas, in quo quaterno similiter redigi facias formam presentium litterarum. Datum Neapoli ut supra.

5.
(Anno 1271, Reg. 10, Lettera B, fol. 96.)

Pro fratre Trojano inquisitore heretice pravitatis.—Item scriptum est cabellotis seu credentiariis super ferro, pice, et sale Neapolis ut cum scriptum fuerit eis{586} alias ut de pecunia curie etc. fratri Trojano inquisitori heretice pravitatis in justitiariatu provincie terre laboris et aprutii de proventibus ferri picis et salis Neapolis ad requisitionem suam pro expensia suis, alterius socii fratis sui et unius notarii et trium aliarum personarum et equorum suorum pro mensibus martii aprilis madii junii julii et augusti presentis XIIII indictionis ad rationem de augustali uno per diem uncias auri XLVII ponderia generalis in principio videlicet dicti mensis martii deberent ecclesie exhibere etiam mandatum est sub pena dupli ut dictam pecuniam juxta continentiam predictarum litterarum eidem fratri Trojano vel nuncio etc. persolvant. Datum ut supra (apud Montem Flasconem XVIII Martii, XIV indictionis).

XII.
LETTERS OF CHARLES II. OF NAPLES ORDERING THE PROSECUTION OF A REPLAPSED HERETIC.
(MSS. Chioccarelli, T. VIII.)

Scriptum est religioso viro Fratri Roberto de Sancto Valentino Inquisitori in Regno Siciliæ post salutem. Olim religiose viro Fratri Benedicto prædecessori tuo in eodem inquisitionis officio post salutem scripsisse dicimur in hæc verba. Veridica nuper accepimus relatione quod te ex officio tuo contra hæreticæ pravitatis infectos inquirente Petrus de Bucclanico ipsius castri archipresbyter de pluribus articulis contra fidem Catholicam inventus est labefactus, cumque satis expediat in contemptæ religionis vindictam ad reprimendum tam damnabile exemplum hæreticæ pravitatis te satis insurgere viribus ad celerem punitionem tam enormis criminis fidelitati tuæ mandamus quatenus statim receptis presentibus sic omni specie corruptionis procul ejecta in præmissis contra dictum archipresbyterum tam fideliter proscquaris processum quod inde Deo placens honori ordinis tui deservias et apud nos qui dicti negotii plenam habemus fidem et notitiam dignas tibi laudes valeas vindicare. Datum apud Monasterium Regalis Vallis die 10 mensis Martii 4 Indict (1306).—Noviter autem facta nobis assertio continebat quod memoratus archipresbyter ad vomitum rediens in ejusdem hæreticæ pravitatis laqueum est relapsus, quod si veritate fulcitur de tanta profecto obstinatione turbati devotionem tuam attenta exhortatione requirimus ut tam ex processu dicti prædecessoris tui contra dictum archipresbyterum ab olim habito quam habendo per te ut cupimus denuo contra eum meritis (?) sive indagine in prædictis sic tuæ disciplinæ virga in dictum archipresbyterum proinde desæviat aspere ut impunitate non gaudeat hostis fidei orthodoxæ. Tuque propterea digua apud Deum et nos laude attolaris. Datum Neapoli apud Bartholomæum de Capua militem Logothetam et Prothonotarium Regni Siciliæ anno Domini 1307 (1308) die ultimo Augusti, 6 Indict. Regnorum nostrorum anno 24.{587}

XIII.

Archivio di Venezia. Codice ex Brera No. 277.)
Promissio Domini Marini Mauroceno.

In nomine dei eterni amen. Anno ab incarnatione domini nostri Jesu Christi millesimo ducentesimo quadragesimo nono mense Junii die terciodecimo intrante indictione septima Rivoalto. In palatio ducatus Veneciarum feliciter amen.... Ad honorem dei et sacrosancte matris Ecclesie et robur et defensionem fidei catholice studiosi erimus cum consilio nostrorum consiliariorum vel maioris partis quod probi et discreti et catholici viri eligantur et constituantur super inquirendis hereticis in venecia. Et omnes illos qui dati erunt pro hereticis per dominum Patriarchum Gradensem, Episcopum Castellanum vel per alios episcopos provincie duchatus Veneciarum a Grado videlicet usque ad caput aggeris comburi faciemus de consilio nostrorum consiliariorum vel maioris partis ipsorum.... Ego Marinus Maurocenus Dei gratia Dux manu mea subscripsi.

CAPITULARE SUPER PATARENIS ET USURARIIS (1256).

(Dal Registro intitulato, Capitolari di più Magistrati riformato nell" anno 1376. Miscellanea Codici, No. 133, p. 121.)

Item juro quod amodo usque ad unum annum et per totum ipsum annum simul cum meis vel cum altero eorum studiosus ero bona fide sine fraude ad inquirendum et inveniendum patarenos hereticos et suspectos de heresi tam venetos quam forinsecos in civitate Rivoalti et si quem talem vel tales invenero secretum aput me habebo et quam cito potero bona fide sine fraude denunciabo domino Duci et consiliariis ejus vel aliis quibus per dominum ducem et suum consilium fuerint hoc commissum. Hec autem omnia observabo bona fide sine fraude remote odio vel amore prece vel precio, et servitium inde non tollam nec faciam tolli. Item attendam et observabo ea que continentur in capituiari maioris consilii.—Si autem secundo in eodem crimine quis fuerit depreensus penam predictam incurrat et bannizetur et expellatur de veneciis si forinsecus fuerit venetus autem quociens inventus fuerit penam incurrat predictam excepto quod de veneciis non bannizetur nec expellatur. Post anno domini millesimo ducentesimo quinquagesimo quinto (1256) indictione XIIII. mense februarii fuit hoc additum in presente capitulare.

END OF VOL. II.
FOOTNOTES:

[1] Diez, Leben und Werke der Troubadours, pp. 450, 576.--Millot, Hist. Littéraire des Troubadours, III. 244-50.

[2] Teulet, Layettes, II. 185, 226-8. In 1239 we find Raymond asking for six months' delay in the payment of one of the instalments (Ib. p. 406).

[3] Concil. Tarraconens. ann. 1238 c. 11 (Mart. Ampl. Coll. VII. 134).--Ripoll I. 120, 145, 165.--Potthast No. 9452, 11092, 11094, 11515.--Vaissette, III. Pr. 365.--Teulet, Layettes, II. 262.--Arch. des Frères Prêcheurs de Toulouse (Doat, XXXI. 19)--C. 1 Sexto v. 2.--Raynald. ann. 1243, No. 30.--Arch. de l'Inq. de Carc. (Doat, XXXI. 69).--Bern. Guidon, de Trib. Grad. Prædicat. (Bouquet, XXI, 739).--Practica super Inquisit. (MSS. Bib. Nat., fonds latin, No. 14930, fol. 224). When Cardinal Wolsey sought to reform the English Church he found the same difficulty in obtaining bishops to degrade clerical criminals, and he obtained from Clement VII. the same remedy (Rymer, XIV. 239).

[4] Coll. Doat, XXI. 149, 153, 156, 158.--MSS. Bib. Nat., fonds latin, No. 9992.

[5] Practica super Inquisit. (MSS. Bib. Nat., fonds latin, No. 14930, fol. 224).--Guill. Pelisso Chron. (Ed. Molinier. Anicii, 1880, pp. 6, 15).--Epistt. Sæcul. XIII. T. I. No. 688 (Monument. Hist. German.).--Bern. Guidon. Vit. Gregor. PP. IX. (Muratori S. R. I. III. 573). One of the complaints made by Gregory IX. against Raymond, in 1236, was that he had neglected to pay the salaries of the professors, and that the school of Toulouse was dissolved (Teulet, Layettes, II. 315). In 1239, however, a receipt in full for them was exhibited to the papal legate (Ib. p. 397), and in 1242, when Raymond was under peril of death in the Agenois, his chief physician was Loup of Spain, the professor of medicine in the University (Ib. p. 466).

[6] Pelisso Chron. pp. 7-8.

[7] Ibid. pp. 9-10.

[8] Pelisso Chron. pp. 10-11.--Preger, Vorarbeiten zu einer Geschichte der deutschen Mystik, p. 17.

[9] Pelisso Chron. p. 13. Cf. Bern. Guidon. Vit. Gregor. PP. IX. (Muratori S. R. I. III. 573).

[10] Pelisso pp. 10-17.

[11] Ibid. pp. 17-20.

[12] Pelisso Chron. pp. 20-1.

[13] Ibid. p. 22.

[14] Pelisso Chron. pp. 23-5.

[15] Millot, Troubadours, II. 65-77.--Mary-Lafon, Histoire du Midi de la France, III. 396-99.

[16] Vaissette, III. 403.--Martene Thesaur. I. 985.--Pelisso Chron. pp. 13-14, 52-9. Chabanaud (Vaissette, Éd. Privat, X. 330) thinks it probable that this Arnaud Catala is the troubadour of the same name, developing, like Folquet of Marseilles and others, from a poet to a persecutor.

[17] Vaissette, III. 402-3, 406; Pr. 370-1, 379-81.--Coll. Doat, XXXI. 33.--Teulet, Layettes, II. 321, 334.

[18]

"Car del pejors homes que son
Se defen et de tot le mont;
Que Franses ni clergia
Ni las autras gens ne l'affront;
Mas als bos s'humilia
Et l'mal confond."

(Peyrat, Les Albigeois et l'Inquisition, II. 394).

(Peyrat, Les Albigeois et l'Inquisition, II. 394).

[19] Bern. Guidon. Vit. Gregor. PP. IX. (Muratori, S. R I. III. 573)--Archives Nat. de France J. 430, No. 17, 18.--Guill. Pod. Laur. c. 42.--Peyrat, Hist. des Albigeois, I. 287.--Harduin. Concil. VII. 203-8.--D'Achery Spicileg. III. 606.--Potthast No. 9771.--Epistt. Sæculi XIII. T. I. No. 577 (Mon. Germ. Hist.).--Matt. Paris ann. 1334, p. 280.--Vaissette, III. 399-400, 406.--Hist. Diplom. Frid. II. T. IV. pp. 485, 799-802.

[20] Pelisso Chron. pp. 25-8.

[21] Pelisso Chron. pp. 30-40.--Bern. Guidon. Hist. Fundat. Convent. Præidicat. (Martene Thesaur. VI. 460-1).--Epistt. Sæculi XIII. T. I. No. 688 (Mon. Germ. Hist.).--Guill. Pod. Laur. c. 43.

[22] Martene Thesaur. I. 992.--Epistt. Sæculi XIII. T. I. No. 688 (Mon. Germ. Hist.)--Teulet, Layettes, II. 314. The subordination of the bishop to the inquisitors is further shown in the excommunication of the viguier and consuls of Toulouse, July 24, 1237, in which Bishop Raymond and other prelates are mentioned as assessors to the inquisitors (Doat, XXI. 148).

[23] Potthast No. 10152.--Epistt. Sæcul. XIII T. I. No. 700 (Mon. Germ. Hist.).--Hist. Diplom. Frid. II. T. IV. P. II. p. 912.--Vaissette, III. 408.--Pelisso Chron. pp. 40-1.

[24] Pelisso Chron. p. 41-2.

[25] Coll. Doat, XXI. 163.

[26] Pelisso Chron. pp. 43-51.--Coll. Doat, XXI. 149.--It is probable that among these victims perished Vigoros de Bocona, a Catharan bishop. Alberic de Trois Fontaines places his burning in Toulouse in 1233 (Chron. ann. 1233), but there is evidence of his being still alive and active in 1235 or 1236 (Doat, XXII. 222). He was ordained a "filius major" in Montségur about 1229, by the Catharan bishop, Guillabert de Castres (Doat, XXII. 226), and his name as that of a revered teacher continues for many years to occur in the confessions of penitents.

[27] Guill. Pod. Laur. c. 43.--Arch, de l'Évêché de Béziers (Doat, XXXI. 35).--Bern. Guidon. Libell. de Magist. Ord. Prædic. (Martene Ampl. Coll. VI. 422).--Raynald. ann. 1237, No. 32.

[28] Epistt. Sæculi XIII. T. I. No. 706 (Mon. Germ. Hist).--Potthast No. 10357, 10361.--Raynald. ann. 1237, No. 33, 37.--Teulet, Layettes, II. 339, No. 2514.--Vaissette, III. 410.--Coll. Doat, XXI. 146. A deposition of Raymond Jean of Albi, April 30, 1238 (Doat, XXIII. 273), probably marks the term of the activity of the Inquisition before its suspension.

[29] Teulet, Layettes, II. 377, 386.--Epistt. Sæculi XIII. T. I. No. 731 (Mon. Germ. Hist.).--Raynald. ann. 1239, No. 71-3.--Arch. du Vatican T. XIX. (Berger, Actes d'Innocent IV. p. xix.).

[30] Arch. Nat. de France J. 430. No. 19, 20.--Guill. Pod. Laurent, c. 43.--Vaissette, III. 411.

[31] Guill. Pod. Laur. c. 43.--Guill. Nangiac. Gest. S. Ludov. ann. 1239.--Vaissette, III. 420.--Bern. Guidon. Vit. Gregor. PP. IX. (Muratori S. R. I. III. 574).--Teulet, Layettes, II. 457. It was not until 1247 that Trencavel released the consuls of Béziers from their allegiance to him.--Mascaro, Libre de Memorias, ann. 1247.

[32] A. Molinier (Vaissette, Éd. Privat, VII. 448-61).--Douais, Les Albigeois, Paris, 1879; Pieces justif. No. 4.

[33] D'Achery Spicileg. III. 621.--Vaissette, III. 424; Pr. 400.

[34] Guillem de Tudela V. 8980, 9183.--Trésor des Chartes du Roi à Carcassonne (Doat, XXII. 34-49).--Vaissette, Éd. Privat, VIII. 975.--Teulet, Layettes, II. 252, No. 2241.--Vaissette, III. 383, 422-3; Pr. 385, 397-99.--Ripoll VII. 9.--Potthast No. 9024.--Pelisso Chron. pp. 28-9.--Coll. Doat, XXI. 163-164, 166; XXIV. 81.

[35] The document is in the Collection Doat, XXI. 185 sqq.--Although it does not specify that the cases are of voluntary penitents within the time of grace, there is no risk in assuming this. The penances are all of the kind provided for such penitents; and in one case (fol. 220) it is mentioned that the party had not come in within the time, which would infer that the rest had done so. Besides, the extraordinary speed with which the business was transacted is wholly incompatible with prosecutions of accused persons striving to maintain their innocence.

[36] Coll. Doat, XXI. 210, 215, 216, 227, 229, 230, 238, 265, 283, 285, 293, 299, 300, 301, 305, 307, 308, 310.

[37] Concil. Narbonn. ann. 1244 c. 19.

[38] Pelisso Chron. pp. 49-50.--Coll. Doat, XXII. 216-17, 224, 228.--Schmidt, Cathares I. 315, 324.

[39] Coll. Doat, XXI. 153, 155, 158.

[40] Vaissette, III. 431; Pr. 438-42.--Doat, XXIV. 160.--Guill. Pod. Laur. c. 45.--Peyrat, Les Albigeois et l'Inquisition, II. 304.--Diez, Leben und Werke der Troubadours, p. 491.--Ripoll I. 117.--Analecta Franciscana, Quaracchi, 1887, II. 65. The Catholic tradition at Avignonet was that some of the inquisitors' followers escaped to the church, where they were massacred with a number of Catholic inhabitants who had sought refuge there.

In consequence of this pollution the church remained unused for forty years, and the anniversary of its reconciliation, on the first Tuesday in June, was still, in the last century, celebrated with illuminations and rejoicing as a local feast (Bremond *ap*. Ripoll l.c.)

[41] Vaissette, III. 456.--Guill. Pod. Laur. c. 45.--Molinier *ap*. Pelisso Chron. p. 19.--Molinier, L'Ensevelissement de Raimond VI. p. 21.--Vaissette, Éd. Privat, VIII. 1258.

[42] Teulet, Layettes, II. 466.--Maj. Chron. Lemovicens. ann. 1242 (Bouquet, XXI. 765).--Vaissette, III. Pr. 410.--Guill. Pod. Laur. c. 45.--Schmidt. Cathares, I. 320.--Bern. Guidon. Vit. Cœlestin. PP. IV. (Muratori S.R.I. III. 589).

[43] Vaissette, III. 434-7, 439.--Teulet, Layettes, II. 470, 481-2, 484, 487, 488, 489, 493, 495, etc.

[44] Vaissette, III. Pr. 425.--Ripoll I. 118. Innocent's bull is dated July 10, 1243, within a fortnight after his election. The deputation had evidently been sent to Celestin IV., and the bull had been prepared in advance, awaiting the election of a successor.

[45] Archives de l'Évêché d'Albi (Doat, XXXI. 47).--Archives de l'Inq. de Carcassonne (Doat, XXXI. 63, 65, 97).--Berger, Registres d'Innocent IV. No. 31, 102.

[46] Vaissette, III. 443; Pr. 411, 433-4.--Potthast No. 10943, 11187, 11218, 11390, 11638.--Teulet, Layettes, II. 523, 524, 528, 534.--D'Achery, III. 621.--Berger, Registres d'Innocent IV. No. 21, 267, 360, 364, 594, 697, 1283.--Douais. Les sources de l'histoire de l'Inquisition (loc. cit. p. 415).

[47] Guill. Pod. Laur. c. 46.--Coll. Doat, XXII. 204, 210; XXIV. 76, 80, 168-72, 181.--Schmidt, Cathares, I. 325.--Peyrat, Les Albigeois et l'Inquisition, II. 363 sqq.

[48] Collection Doat, XXII. 202, 214, 237; XXIV. 68, 160, 182, 198.

[49] Millot, Troubadours, II. 77.--Berger, Registres d'Innocent IV. No. 37.

[50] Concil. Biterrens. ann. 1246, Consil. ad Inquis. c. 1.--Ripoll, I. 179.

[51] Doat, XXII. 217.--Molinier, L'Inquisition dans le midi de la France, pp. 186-90.--See also Peyrat, Les Albigeois et l'Inq. III. 467-73.--Vaissette, III. Pr. 446-8.--Teulet, Layettes, II. 566. M. l'Abbé Douais (loc. cit. p. 419) tells us that the examinations in the inquest of Bernard de Caux number five thousand eight hundred and four.

[52] Vaissette, III. 457, 459; Pr. 467.--Guill. Pod. Laur. c. 48.--Baluz. et Mansi I. 210.--Arch. de l'Inq. de Carcassonne (Doat, XXXI. 105, 149).--Ripoll, I. 184.

[53] Vaissette, III. 455-6; Pr. 468, 469.--Arcli. de l'Inq. de Carc. (Doat, XXXI. 77, 79, 80).--Martene Thesaur. I. 1040.

[54] Martene Thesaur. I. 1044.--Vaissette, III. 465.--Vaissette, Éd. Privat, VIII. 1255, 1292, 1333, 1583.--Guill. Pod. Laur. c. 48--Mary-Lafon, Hist. du midi de la France, III. 33, 49--Arch. de l'Inq. de Carcass. (Doat, XXXI. 250).

[55] Rainer. Summa (Mart. Thesnur. V. 1768).--Molinier, L'Inquis. dans le midi de la France, pp. 254-55.--MSS. Bib. Nat., fonds latin, No. 11847.--Lib. Sententt. Inq. Tolos. pp. 13, 14.--See also the curious account of Ivo of Narbonne in Matt. Paris, ann. 1243, p. 412-13 (Ed. 1644). The Abbé Douais, in his analysis of the fragments of the "Registre de l'Inquisition de Toulouse" of 1254 and 1256, tells us that it contains the names of six hundred and thirteen accused belonging to the departments of Aude, Ariège, Gers, Aveyron, and Tarne-et-Garonne, the greater part of whom were Perfects. That this is evidently an error is shown by the statistics of Rainerio Saccone, quoted in the text. At this time, in fact, the whole Catharan Church, from Constantinople to Aragon, contained only four thousand Perfects. Still the number of accused shows the continued existence of heresy as a formidable social factor and the successful activity of the Inquisition in tracking it. In this register eight witnesses contribute one hundred and seven names to the list of accused (Sources de l'hist. de l'Inquisition, loc. cit. pp. 432-33).

[56] MSS. Bib. Nat., fonds latin, Nouv. Acquis. 139.--Molinier, op. cit. p. 404.--Ripoll I. 273-4.--Arch. Nat. de France, J. 431, No. 34.--Arch. de l'Inq. de Carc. (Doat, XXXI. 239, 250, 252).--Vaissette, III. Pr. 528, 536.--Arch. di Napoli, Regestro 6, Lettere D, fol. 180.

[57] Concil. Biterrens. ann. 1255.--Vaissette, III. 482-3; IV. 17.--A. Molinier (Vaissette, Éd. Privat, VI. 843).--Peyrat, op. cit. III. 54.

[58] Miguel del Verms, Chronique Bearnaise.--P. Sarnaii Hist. Albigens. c. 6.--Guill. Pod. Laur., c. 8.--Schmidt, Cathares, I. 299.--Vaissette, III. 426, 503; Pr. 383-5, 392-3.--Teulet, Layettes, II. 490.--Bern. Guidon. Vit. Cœlestin. PP. IV. (Muratori, S. R. I. III. 589).--Berger, Registres d'Innocent IV. No. 3530.

[59] Vaissette, III. Pr. 551-3.

[60] Vaissette, III. Pr. 575-77; IV. Pr. 109.

[61] Coll Doat, XXV. XXVI.--Martene Thesaur. V. 1809.

[62] Vaissette, IV. 3-5, 9-11, 16, 24-5.--Baudouin, Lettres inédites de Philippe le Bel, Paris, 1886, p. 125.

[63] Raynald ann. 1303, No. 41.--Vaissette, IV. Note xi.--Guill. Nangiac. Contin. ann. 1303, 1309, 1310.--Nich. Trivetti Chron. ann. 1306.--La Faille, Annales de Toulouse I. 284. The irresistible encroachment of the royal jurisdiction, in spite of perpetual opposition, is most effectively illustrated in the series of royal letters recently printed by M. Ad. Baudouin (Lettres inédites de Philippe le Bel, Paris, 1886).

[64] Bern. Guidon. Gravam. (Doat, XXX. 93, 97).--Molinier op. cit. p. 35.--Doat, XXVI. 197, 245, 265, 266.--Lib. Sententt. Inq. Tolos. p. 282. Sanche Morlana, the archdeacon of Carcassonne, who is represented as

198

bearing a leading part in the conspiracy, belonged to one of the noblest families of the city. His brother Arnaud, who at one time was Seneschal of Foix, was likewise implicated, and died a few years later in the bosom of the Church. In 1328 Jean Duprat, then inquisitor, obtained evidence that Arnaud had been hereticated during a sickness, and again subsequently on his death-bed (Doat. XXVIII. 128). This would seem to lend color to the charge of heresy against the conspirators, but the evidence was considered too flimsy to warrant condemnation.

[65] Doat, XXVI. 254.--Bern. Guidon. Gravam. (Doat, XXX. 93).--Arch. de l'Inq. de Carc. (Doat, XXXII. 132).

[66] MSS. Bib. Nat., fonds latin. No. 11847.--Doat, XXVI. 197.--Lib. Sentent. Inq. Tolos. pp. 54, 109, 111, 130, 137, 138, 139, 143, 144, 146, 147.

[67] There has been great confusion as to the date of Philippe's action. The Ordonnance as printed by Laurière and Isambert is of 1287. As given by Vaissette (IV. Pr. 97-8) it is of 1291. A copy in Doat, XXXI. 266 (from the Regist. Curiæ Franciæ de Carcass.), is dated 1297. Schmidt (Cathares I. 342) accepts 1287; A. Molinier (Vaissette, Éd. Privat, IX. 157)confirms the date of 1291. The latter accords best with the series of events. 1287 would seem manifestly impossible, as Philippe was crowned January 6, 1286, at the age of seventeen, and would scarcely, in fifteen months, venture on such a step so defiant of all that was held sacred; nor would Nicholas IV. in 1290 have praised his zeal in furthering the Inquisition (Ripoll II. 29), while 1297 seems incompatible with his subsequent action on the subject. In 1292 Philippe prohibited the capitouls of Toulouse from employing torture on clerks subject to the jurisdiction of the bishop, a prohibition which had to be repeated in 1307.--Baudouin, Lettres inédites de Philippe le Bel, pp. 16, 73.

[68] Arch. de l'Inq. de Carc. (Doat, XXXII. 251).--Chron. Bardin ann. 1293 (Vaissette IV. Pr. 9).

[69] In 1278 the inquisitors of France applied to Nicholas III. for instructions, stating that some time previous, during a popular persecution of the Jews, many of them through fear, though not absolutely coerced, had received baptism and allowed their children to be baptized. With the passing of the storm they had returned to their Jewish blindness, whereupon the inquisitors had cast them in prison. They were duly excommunicated, but neither this nor the "*squalor carceris*" had been of avail, and they had thus remained for more than a year. The nonplussed inquisitors thereupon submitted to the Holy See the question as to further proceedings, and Nicholas ordered them to treat such Jews as heretics--that is to say, to burn them for continued obstinacy.-- Archives de l'Inq. de Carcassonne (Doat, XXXVII. 191).

[70] Mag. Bull. Roman. I. 151, 155, 159.--Archivio di Napoli, Registro 20, Lett. B, fol. 91.--MSS. Bib. Nat., fonds latin, No. 14930, fol. 227-8.--Wadding, ann. 1290, No. 5, 6.--C. 13, Sexto V. 2--Coll. Doat, XXXII. 127; XXXVII. 193, 206, 209, 242, 255, 258.--Wadding, ann. 1359, No. 1-3.--Lib. Sentent. Inq. Tolos. p. 230. In 1288 Philippe had already ordered the Seneschal of Carcassonne to protect the Jews from the citations and other vexations inflicted on them by the ecclesiastical courts (Vaissette, Éd. Privat, IX. Pr. 232). Yet in 1306 he had all the Jews of the kingdom seized and exiled, and forbidden to return under pain of death (Guill. Nangiac. Contin. ann. 1306).

[71] Regist. Curiæ Franciæ de Carc. (Doat, XXXII. 254, 267, 268, 269).--Vaisette, IV. Pr. 99.

[72] Du Puy, Histoire du Differend, etc. Pr. 14, 15, 23, 24.--D'Argentré, Collect. Judic. de novis Error. I. I. 125.--Vaissette, IV. Pr. 99.--Arch. de l'Inq. de Carc. (Doat, XXXII. 264).--Faucon, Registres de Boniface VIII. No. 2140.

[73] Du Puy, op. cit. Pr. 39, 41, 42, 44.--Faucon, Registres de Boniface VIII. No. 1822-3, No. 1829, No. 1830-1, No. 1930.--C. 18 Sexto v. 2.--Isambert, Anc. Loix Franç. II. 718.--Vaissette, Éd. Privat, X. Pr. 347.-- Archives de l'Évêché d'Albi (Doat, XXXII. 275).

[74] C. Molinier, L'Inq. dans le midi de la France, p. 92.--A. Molinier(Vaissette, Éd. Privat, IX. 307). The character and power of the bishops of Albi are illustrated in a successor of Bernard de Castanet, Bishop Géraud, who in 1312, to settle a quarrel with the Seigneur de Puygozon, raised an army of five thousand men with which he attacked the royal Château Vieux d'Albi, and committed much devastation.--Vaissette, IV. 160.

[75] Bern. Guidon. Hist. Conv. Prædic. (Martene Coll. Ampl. VI. 477-8).--Ejusd. Gravam. (Doat, XXX. 94).

[76] MSS. Bib. Nat., fonds latin, No. 4270, fol. 18, 119-23, 129, 135-6, 292.--Arch. de l'Inq. de Carc. (Doat, XXXII. 283).--Vaissette, IV. 91; Pr. 100-2.--Lib. Sentent. Inq. Tolos. pp. 282-5.--Coll. Doat, XXXIV. 21.

[77] Concil. Biterrens. ann. 1299, c. 3 (Vaissette, IV. 96).--MSS. Bib. Nat., fonds latin, No. 4270, fol. 264, 270.--Archives de l'Evêché d'Albi (Doat, XXXV. 69).--MSS. Bib. Nat., fonds latin, No. 11847.--Lib. Sentent. Inquis. Tolos. p. 266.

[78] Du Puy, Hist. du Differend, Pr. 633 sqq. 653-4.--Martene Thesaur. I. 1320-36.

[79] MSS. Bib. Nat., fonds latin, No. 4270, fol. 125-8, 139.

[80] In a series of confessions extracted from Master Arnaud Matha, a clerk of Carcassonne, in 1285, there are two, of October 4 and 10, in which he describes all the details of the heretication of Castel Fabri on his death-bed, in 1278 (Doat, XXVI. 258-60). While these cannot be positively said to be interpolations, they have the appearance of being so, and it may safely be assumed as impossible that such a matter would have been allowed to lie dormant for fifteen years with so rich a prize within reach. The case is doubtless one of the forged records which, as we have seen, were popularly believed to be customary in the Inquisition.

[81] MSS. Bib. Nat., fonds latin, No. 4270, fol. 14-16, 29-30, 35, 120, 148.--Coll. Doat, XXVII. 178; XXXIV. 123, 189. As late as 1338 the confiscated house of Castel Fabri at Carcassonne was the subject of a reclamation by Pierre de Manse who claimed that Philippe le Bel had given it to his queen, through whom it had come to him. The royal officials asserted that the gift had only been for life, and had seized it again, but Philippe de Valois abandoned it to the claimant.--Vaissette, Éd. Privat. X. Pr. 831-3.

[82] Historia Tribulationum (Archiv für Litteratur. u. Kirchengeschichte, 1886, p. 148).--MSS. Bib. Nat., fonds latin, No. 4270, fol. 231.--Vaissette, Éd. Privat, X. 268.

[83] MSS. Bib. Nat., fonds latin, No. 4270, fol. 9, 19, 22, 24, 26, 32, 40, 63, 70, 73, 81, 82, 84, 119, 128, 149, 155, 163.--Bern. Guidon. Hist. Conv. Albiens. (D. Bouquet, XXI. 748).--Coll. Doat, XXXIV. 26.

[84] MSS. Bib. Nat., fonds latin, No. 4270, fol. 163.--Guillel. Nangiac. Contin. ann. 1303.--Grandes Chroniques, T. V. pp. 156-7.--Girard de Fracheto Chron. contin. ann. 1203 (D. Bouq. XXI. 23).--Vaissette, IV. 112.--Bern. Guidon. Hist. Fund. Conv. (Martene Ampl. Coll. V. 514). When, long years afterwards, in 1319, Bernard Délicieux was carried from Avignon to Toulouse for the trial which led to his death, one of the convoy, a notary named Arnaud de Nogaret, chanced to allude to a report that Pequigny had been bribed with one thousand livres to oppose the Inquisition. Then the old man's temper flashed forth in defence of his departed friend--"Thou liest in the throat: the Vidame was an honest man!"--MSS. Bib. Nat., fonds latin, No. 4270, fol. 263.

[85] Bern. Guidon. Hist. Fund. Conv. (Martene Ampl. Coll. VI. 510-11).--Arch. de l'Inq. de Carc. (Doat, XXVII. 7).--MSS. Bib. Nat., fonds latin, No. 4270. fol. 6, 7, 11, 42, 45, 48, 71, 161, 270.--Arch. de l'hôtel-de-ville d'Albi (Doat. XXXIV. 169).--Vaissette, IV. 143.

[86] MSS. Bib. Nat., fonds latin, No. 4270, fol. 16, 149.

[87] MSS. Bib. Nat., fonds latin, No. 4270, fol. 121, 125, 132, 150, 159, 165.--Vaissette, IV. Pr. 118-20.--Bern. Guidon. Hist. Conv. Prædic. (Martene Ampl. Coll. VI. 510).--Arch. de l'hôtel-de-ville d'Albi (Doat, XXXIV. 169).

[88] Vaissette, IV. Pr. 118-21.--MSS. Bib. Nat., fonds latin, No, 4270, fol. 69.--Isambert, Anc. Loix Franç. II. 747, 789.

[89] Arch, de l'hôtel-de-ville d'Albi (Doat, XXXIV. 169).--MSS. Bib. Nat., fonds latin, No. 4270, fol. 16, 70, 134, 151.--Coll. Doat, XXXIII. 207-72; XXXIV. 189.

[90] Vaissette, Éd. Privat, X. Pr. 409.--MSS. Bib. Nat., fonds latin, No. 4270, fol. 165.--Bern. Guidon. Hist. Conr. Prædic. (Martene Ampl. Coll. VI. 511).

[91] MSS. Bib. Nat., fonds latin, 4270, fol. 8, 17, 19, 20, 32, 44, 49, 58, 156, 162, 229.--Pequigny is also said to have arrested some of the friars connected with the Inquisition (La Faille, Annales de Toulouse I. 34), but I think this impossible.

[92] MSS. Bib. Nat., fonds latin, 4270, fol. 27, 272.--Arch. de l'Inq. de Carc. (Doat, XXXII. 114).--Bern. Guidon. Hist. Conv. Prædic. (Martene Ampl. Coll. VI. 511).--Vaissette, IV. Pr. 128.--Coll. Doat, XXXIV. 26. The Dominican party declared that the statements purporting to come from the prisoners were fraudulent, and Bernard Gui relates with savage satisfaction that a monk named Raymond Baudier, who was concerned in getting them up, hanged himself like Judas (l. c. p. 514).

[93] MSS. Bib. Nat., fonds latin, 4270, fol. 63, 153-55, 272-3.--Hauréau, Bern. Délicieux pp. 187, 190.

[94] Arch. de l'Inq. de Carc. (Doat, XXXI. 10; XXXII. 114).--Bern. Guidon. Hist. Conv. Prædic. (Martene Ampl. Coll. VI. 510-11).--MSS. Bib. Nat., fonds latin, 4270, fol. 88, 109, 122.

[95] Arch. de l'hôtel-de-ville d'Albi (Doat, XXXIV. 45).--Arch. de l'Inq. de Carc. (Doat, XXXIV. 14).--MSS. Bib. Nat., fonds latin, 4270, fol. 23, 25, 31, 86, 132, 137, 140-1, 152, 153.

[96] Grandjean, Registres de Benoit XI. No. 1253-60, 1276.--MSS, Bib. Nat., fonds latin, 4270, fol. 21, 73, 74, 158, 162, 278.--Molinier, L'Inq. dans le midi de la France pp. 126-7.--Geoffroi d'Ablis had sufficient influence with the king to persuade him to found the Dominican convent of Poissy.

[97] Vaissette, IV. Pr. 130-1.--MSS. Bib. Nat., fonds latin, 4270, fol. 139.

[98] MSS. Bib. Nat., fonds latin, 4270, fol. 26, 74-8, 88-9, 98, 103-8, 198, 200-3, 226, 233, 265, 279.--Mascaro, Memorias de Bezes, ann. 1336, 1389. For the tenure of Montpellier by the Kings of Majorca, see Vaissette, IV. 38, 42, 77-8, 151, 235-6. It was not until 1349 that Philippe de Valois bought out the rights of Jayme II., and in 1352 his son Jean was obliged to extinguish the claims still asserted by Pedro IV. of Aragon (Ib. 247, 268, Pr. 219). Bernard's attention was probably drawn to the House of Majorca by its strong adhesion to the Franciscan Order. Ferrand's older brother died in 1304, in the Franciscan habit, under the name of Fray Jayme. Another brother, Felipe, became a "Spiritual Franciscan," as we shall see hereafter.

[99] MSS. Bib. Nat., fonds latin, 4270, fol. 78-80, 90-1, 196, 247, 252-3, 257-9.--Bern. Guidon. Hist. Conv. Prædic. (Martene Ampl. Coll. VI. 479-80).--Vaissette, IV. 129-30.--Vaissette, Éd. Privat, X. Pr. 461.--Bernard Gui's allusion refers to the insults offered to the Dominicans during the troubles of Carcassonne, when those who ventured into the streets were followed with cries of "Coac, Coac!" "ad modum corvi"--MS. No. 4270, fol. 281.

[100] Arch. de l'hôtel-de-ville d'Albi (Doat, XXXIV. 42).--Arch, de l'Évêché d'Albi (Doat, XXXII. 81).

[101] MSS. Bib. Nat., fonds latin, 4270, fol. 10-11, 84, 128, 160-7.--Arch. de l'Inq. de Carc. (Doat, XXXII. 83). Geoffroi's stay at Lyons was prolonged. November 29, we find him issuing commissions to those appointed

by his deputies (Doat, XXXII. 85). Jean de Faugoux had been connected with the Inquisition for at least twenty years (Doat, XXXII. 125).

[102] MSS. Bib. Nat., fonds latin, No. 4270, fol. 254.--Arch, de l'hôtel-de-ville d'Albi (Doat, XXXIV. 45).--Arch. de l'Inq. de Carc. (Doat, XXXIII. 48).

[103] Arch. de l'hôtel-de-ville d'Albi (Doat, XXXIV. 45).--Arch. de l'Inq. de Carc. (Doat, XXXIV. 89, 112).--Bern. Guidon Gravam. (Doat, XXX. 95-6.)--Ripoll II. 112. I designed printing in the Appendix the Gravamina of Bernard Gui and the report of the Cardinals. M. Charles Molinier, however, I understand, is engaged on an edition of these documents, to be accompanied with a complete apparatus, which will render any other publication superfluous.

[104] Arch. de l'Inq. de Carc. (Doat, XXXI. 74; XXXIV. 89).--MSS. Bib. Nat., fonds latin, No. 11847.-- Lib. Sententt. Inq. Tolos. pp. 228, 266-7, 282-5.--Coll. Doat, XXXII. 309, 316.--Vaissette, Éd. Privat, X. Pr. 526.

[105] Archives de l'Inq. de Carcassonne (Doat, XXXVII. 255). The Inquisition seems to have by some means acquired jurisdiction over the Jews of Languedoc. In 1279 there is a charter granted by Bernard, Abbot of S. Antonin of Pamiers, to the Jews of Pamiers, approving of certain statutes agreed upon among themselves concerning their internal affairs, thus showing them subjected to the abbatial jurisdiction. Yet in 1297 we have a letter from the inquisitor, Frère Arnaud Jean, ordering the Jews of Pamiers to live according to the customs of the Jews of Narbonne, and promising not to introduce *"aliquas graves et insolitas novitates."* During the interval they had thus passed into the hands of the Inquisition.--Coll. Doat, XXXVII. 156, 160.

[106] Martin Fuldens. Chron. ann. 1312.--C. 1, 2, 3, Clement, V. iii.--Bern. Guidon. Gravam. (Doat, XXX.).--Bern. Guidon. Practica, P. IV. c. 1. It is due to Clement to say that doubtless he devised a much more thorough reform, and the meagreness of the outcome is probably attributable to the final revision under John XXII. Angelo da Clarino, writing from Avignon in 1313, about the new canons, which were then supposed to be ready for issue, says: *"Inquisitores etiam heretice pravitatis restringuntur et supponuntur episcopis"*--which would argue something much more decisive than the regulations as they finally appeared.--Franz Ehrle, Archiv. für Litteratur-u. Kirchengeschichte, 1885, p. 545.

[107] Du Puy, Histoire du Differend, Preuves, pp. 522-602.

[108] Joann. Canon. S. Victor. Chron. ann. 1314-16.--Rymer, Fœdera, III. 494-5.--Grandes Chroniques, ann. 1314-16--Bern. Guidon. Vit. Joann. PP. XXII.--Ptolmaei Lucens. Append. John XXII. has always passed as the son of a cobbler of Cahors. Recent researches, however, render it probable that he belonged to a well-to-do burgher family.--A. Molinier (Vaissette, Éd. Privat. X. 363.)

[109] Joann. Can. S. Victor. Chron. ann. 1311, 1316-19.--Historia Tribulationum (Archiv. für Litteratur-u. Kirchengeschichte, 1886, pp. 145-8).--Wadding. ann. 1318, No. 26-7.--MSS. Bib. Nat., fonds latin, No. 4270, fol. 1, 39.

[110] MSS. Bib. Nat, fonds latin, No. 4270, fol. 5, 81, 103-4, 146-7, 169. Arnaud Garsia and Pierre Probi were kept in prison until 1325, when they were released on payment of two thousand gold florins, and such penance as Jean Duprat, the inquisitor, might impose on them. Their sequestrated property was ordered to be restored.--Vaissette, Éd. Privat, X. Pr. 645.

[111] Lib. Sententt. Inq. Tolosan. pp. 268-73.--MSS. Bib. Nat., fonds latin, No. 4270, fol. 186-92.--Jo. a S. Victore Memor. Historiale ann. 1319 (Bouquet, XXI. 664).

[112] Isambert, Anc. Loix Franç. III. 123.--Arch. de l'Inq. de Carc. (Doat, XXXII. 138).--MSS. Bib. Nat., fonds latin, No. 11847.--Lib. Sententt. Inq. Tolos. pp. 228, 244-8, 266-7, 277-81.--Arch, de l'hôtel-de-ville d'Albi (Doat, XXXIV. 169, 185).

[113] Bern. Guidon. Gravam. (Doat, XXX. 97).

[114] Ibid. (Doat, XXX. 96, 98).--MSS. Bib. Nat., fonds latin, No. 4270, fol. 138-9, 213.

[115] Molinier, L'Inq. dans le midi de la France, p. 111--MSS. Bib. Nat., fonds latin, No. 4270, fol. 285.

[116] Bern. Guidon. Hist. Conv. Præedic. (Martene Ampl. Coll. VI. 469).--Touron, Hommes illustres de l'Ordre de S. Dominique, II. 94.

[117] Lib. Sententt. Inq. Tolos. pp. 2, 3, 12, 13, 32, 68, 76, 81, 159.--Molinier, L'Inq. dans le midi de la France, pp. 145-56.

[118] Molinier, op. cit. p. 157--Lib. Sententt. Inq. Tolos, p. 102.

[119] Lib. Sententt. Inq. Tolos. p. 37.

[120] Lib. Sententt. Inq. Tolos. pp. 59, 60, 64, 73, 74, 75, 92-3, 132.

[121] Lib. Sententt. Inq. Tolos. pp. 341-2.--Coll. Doat, XXVII. 198-200, 248; XXVIII. 128, 158. The entire disappearance of a sect once so numerous and powerful as the Cathari has appeared so unlikely that there has been a widespread belief that their descendants were to be found in the Cagots--the accursed race of the Pyrenees who in French Navarre were only admitted to common legal rights in 1709, and in the Spanish province in 1818, some of them still existing in the latter. The Cagots themselves even assumed this to be their origin in an appeal to Leo X., in 1517, to be restored to human society, and claimed that their ancestral errors had been long atoned for. Yet among all the conjectures as to the origin of this mysterious class, the descent from Catharans would seem to be the least admissible, and M. de Lagrèze's opinion that they are descendants of lepers is sustained by arguments which appear to be convincing.--Lagrèze, La Navarre Française I. 53-60. Cf. Vaissette, Liv. XXXIV. c. 79.

[122] Coll. Doat, XXVII. 216-25, 234.

[123] Vaissette, III, 362, 496; IV. 104-5, 211.--Archives de l'Évêché de Béziers (Doat, XXXI. 35).--Beugnot, Les Olim I. 1029-30.--Les Olim I. 580.--Coll. Doat, XXXIII. 1. The extent of the change of the proprietorship is well illustrated by a list of the lands and rents confiscated for heresy to the profit of Philippe de Montfort from his vassals. It embraces fiefs and other properties in Lautrec, Montredon, Senegats, Rabastain, and Lavaur. The knights and gentlemen and peasants thus stripped are all named, with their offences--one died a heretic, another was hereticated on his death-bed, a third was condemned for heresy, and a fourth was burned at Lavaur, while in other cases the mother, or the father, or both were heretics (Doat, XXXII. 258-63). Many examples of donations and sales are preserved in the Doat collection. I may instance T. XXXI. fol. 171, 237, 255; T. XXXII. fol. 46, 53, 55, 57, 64, 67, 69, 244, etc. In the possessions of the English crown in Aquitaine the same process was going on, though in a minor degree (Rymer, Fœdera, III. 408).

[124] Coll. Doat, XXXII. 309, 316.

[125] Joinville, P. I. (Ed. 1785. p. 23).

[126] Alberic. Triun. Font. Chron. ann. 1236.--Gregor. PP. IX. Bull. *Gaudemus.* 19 Ap. 1233 (Ripoll I. 45-6).--Raynald. ann. 1233, No. 59.

[127] Greg. PP. IX. Bull. *Olim,* 4 Feb. 1234; Ejusd. Bull. *Dudum,* 21 Aug. 1235; Ejusd. Bull. *Quo inter cæteras,* 22 Aug. 1235; Ejusd. Bull. *Dudum,* 23 Aug. 1235 (Ripoll I. 80-1).--Potthast No. 9386.--Chron. breve Lobiens. ann. 1235 (Martene Thes. III. 1427).--D. Bouquet, XXII. 570.--Chron. Rimée de Philippe Mousket, v. 28871-29025.--Alberic. Trium Font. ann. 1235.

[128] Chron. S. Medardi Suessionens. (D'Achery, II. 491).--Conc. Trevirens. ann. 1238, c. 31 (Martene Ampl. Coll. VII. 130).--Wadding. Annal. ann. 1236, No. 3.--Meyeri Annal. Flandrens. Lib. VIII. ann. 1236.--Raynald. ann. 1238, No. 52.--Matt. Paris ann. 1236, 1238, pp. 293, 326 (Ed. 1644).--Chron. Gaufridi de Collone ann. 1239 (Bouquet, XXII. 3).--Alberic. Trium Font. Chron. ann. 1239.--Chron. Riméc de Phil. de Mousket, v. 30525-34. Frère Bremond endeavors to clear Robert's fame from the accusations brought against him by Matthew Paris, and states that he died in the convent of St. Jacques in Paris in 1235.

[129] Concil. Turonens. ann. 1239, c. 1.--D. Bouquet, XXI. 262, 264, 268, 273, 274, 276, 280, 281.--Ripoll I. 273-4.

[130] Coll. Doat, XXXI. 68.--Martene Coll. Ampl. I. 1284.--Wadding. Annal. ann. 1288, No. 14, 15; ann. 1290, No. 3, 5, 6; ann. 1292, No. 3.

[131] Arch. de l'Inq. de Carc. (Doat. XXXI. 90; XXXII. 41).--Wadding. Annal. ann. 1255, No. 14.--Raynald. ann. 1255, No. 33.--Arch. Nat. de France, J. 431, No. 30, 31, 34, 35, 36.--Ripoll I. 273-4, 291, 362, 472, 512; II. 29.--MSS. Bib. Nat., fonds latin. No. 14930. fol. 226.--Martene Thesaur. V. 1814, 1817.

[132] Ripoll I. 179, 183; II. 29.--Potthast No. 15995.--Lib. Sentt. Inq. Tolos. pp. 252-4.

[133] Martene Thesaur. V. 1809, 1811-13.--Arch. de l'Inq. de Carcass. (Doat, XXXII. 127).

[134] Ripoll II. 1.--Guill. Nangiac. Contin. ann. 1307, 1310.

[135] Martene Ampl. Collect. VII. 1325-7. Cf. Concil. Trident. Sess. xxv. Decret. Reform, c. 3.

[136] Arch. Nat. de France, J. 428, No. 15, 19 *bis.*--Guillel. Nangiac. Contin, ann. 1308, 1310.--Grandes Chroniques, V. 188.

[137] Guillel. Nangiac. Contin. ann. 1323.--Grandes Chroniques, V. 273-4.--Chron. Johann. S. Victor. Contin. ann. 1323 (Bouquet, XXI. 681).

[138] Coll. Doat, XXVII. 119, 132, 140, 146, 156, 178, 192, 198, 232.--Vaissette, IV. Pr. 23.

[139] Vaiseette, Éd. Privat, X. Pr. 782-3, 792, 802, 813-14.--Arch, de l'Évêché d'Albi (Doat. XXXV. 120).--Vaissette, IV. 184.--Martene Ampl. Coll. VI. 433.

[140] Ripoll II. 236.

[141] Raynald. ann. 1365, No. 17; ann. 1373, No. 19, 21.--Gaguini Hist. Francor. Lib. IX. c. 2. (Ed. 1576, p. 158).--Meyeri Annal. Flandr. Lib. XIII. ann. 1372.--Du Cange s. v.*Turlupini.*--Gersoni de Consolat. Theolog. Lib. IV. Prosa 3; Ejusd. de Mystica Theol. Specul. P. I. Consid. 8; Ejusd. de Distinctione verarum Visionum Signum, 5.--Altmeyer, Précurseurs de la Réforme aux Pays-Bas, I. 85. Probably there may be some connection between the Turelupins and certain wandering bands known as *"de Pexariacho"* and suspected of heresy. A member of these, named Bidon de Puy-Guillem, of the diocese of Bordeaux, was condemned to perpetual imprisonment, and was liberated by Gregory XI. in 1371 (Coll. Doat, XXXV. 134).

[142] Grandes Chroniques, ann. 1380-1.--Religieux de S. Denis, Hist. de Charles VI. Liv.I. c. 13, liv. II. c. 1.

[143] Religieux de S. Denis, op. cit. Liv. IV. ch. 13.--D'Argentré, Collect. Judic. de novis error. I. II. 151.

[144] Chron. Bardin, ann. 1322 (Vaissette, IV. Pr. 21-22).

[145] Isambert, Anc. Lois Franç. IV. 364-5.--Coll. Doat, XXVII. 118.--Vaissette, IV. Pr. 23.

[146] Chron. Bardin, ann. 1340, 1368 (Vaissette, IV. Pr. 27, 31).

[147] Chron. Bardin, ann. 1364 (Vaissette, IV. Pr. 30. Cf. A. Molinier, Éd. Privat. X. 763).

[148] Martene Thesaur. I. 1399.

[149] Arch. Administratives de Reims, III. 637-45.--Meyeri Annal. Flandr. Lib. XVI. ann. 1419.--Lafaille, Annales de Toulouse I. 183.--Chron. Bardin, ann. 1423 (Vaissette. IV. Pr. 38).

[150] Arch. Administratives de Reims, III. 639-43.

[151] Isambert, Anc. Lois Franç. IX. 3; X. 393, 396-416, 477.--Bochelli Decret. Eccles. Gallican. Lib. IV. Tit. 4, 5.--Bull. de la Soc. de l'Hist. du Protestantisme en France, 1860, p. 121.--D'Argentré Coll. Judic. de novis Error. I. II. 357.--Fascic. Rer. Expetend. et Fugiend. I. 63 (Ed. 1690). The feelings with which the abrogation of the Pragmatic Sanction in 1461 was received are well expressed in the *"Pragmaticæ Sanctionis Passio,"* Baluz. et Mansi, IV. 29. Pius II. is singularly candid in his account of the simoniacal transaction through which he purchased the abrogation by giving the cardinal's hat to Jean, Bishop of Arras. The suggestion at first provoked the liveliest remonstrances from the members of the Sacred College, who, through their spokesman, the Cardinal of Avignon, warned Pius that there would be no peace in the Consistory, for the bishop would set them all by the ears, and that his unquiet spirit showed that he must be the offspring of an Incubus. Pius admitted all this, but argued that it was an unfortunate necessity; both Louis XI. and Philippe le Bon had asked for his promotion; unless the request was granted the Pragmatic Sanction would not be abolished, for the fury of the disappointed man would convert him into its supporter, and, as he was learned, he would readily find ample Scriptural warrant to adduce in its favor, which would be decisive, as he was the only man in France who urged the abrogation, and he could readily lead the king to change his mind. These arguments were convincing, and Pius enjoyed the supreme triumph of destroying the last relic of the reforms of Constance and Basle. He paid dearly for it, however, in the annoyances inflicted on him by the new cardinal, whom he describes as a liar and a perjurer, avaricious and ambitious, a glutton and a drunkard, and excessively given to women. He was so irascible that at meals he would frequently throw the silver plates and vessels at the servants, and occasionally would push the whole table over, to the dismay of his guests.--Æn. Sylvii Opp. inedd. (Atti della Accad. dei Lincei, 1883, pp. 531, 546-8).

[152] Juvenal des Ursins, ann. 1411, 1413.--Religieux de S. Denis, Hist. de Charles VI. Liv. XXXII. ch. 14; XXXIII. ch. 1, 15, 16; XXXV. ch. 18.

[153] D'Argentré, op. cit. I. II. 370.

[154] Ibid. I. II. 340.

[155] Ibid. I. II. 346.

[156] Wadding, ann. 1375, No. 17; 1418, No. 1, 2; 1419, No. 2; 1434, No. 2, 3; 1472, No. 24.--Ripoll II. 522, 566-9, 637, 644; III. 487; IV. 6.

[157] Wadding. ann. 1409, No. 13; 1418, No. 1, 2, 4.

[158] Baluz. et Mansi I. 288-93,--Arch. Gén. de Belgique, Papiers d'État, v. 405.--MSS. Bib. Nat., fonds Moreau, 444, fol. 10.--Ripoll II. 533; III. 6, 8, 21, 193.

[159] Ripoll III. 301.--Wadding, ann. 1458, No. 12.

[160] Wadding, ann. 1458, No. 13; 1461, No. 3.--Ripoll III. 317, 423, 487; IV. 103, 217, 303, 304, 356, 373. A MS. of Bernard Gui's *Practica*, now in the Municipal Library of Toulouse, bears a marginal note that it was lent by the Inquisition of Toulouse, in 1483, to the Dominicans of Bordeaux to be transcribed, thus showing that there was an Inquisition in operation in the latter city of which the members required instruction in their duties (Molinier, l'Inq. dans le midi de la France, p. 201).

[161] Memoires de Jacques du Clercq, Liv. III. ch. 43.--D'Argentré, op. cit. I. II. 308-18, 319-20, 323, 347.

[162] Bremond, *ap.* Ripoll IV. 373.--Ripoll IV. 390.

[163] Ripoll IV. 376.--Wieri de Præstig. Dæmon. Lib. VI. c. 11.

[164] Coll. Doat, XXI. 197, 203, 208, 223, 225, 232, 233, 234, 236, 238, 241, 244, 250, 252, 254, 261-2, 263, 264, 265, 266, 267, 269, 270, 271, 275, 276, 281, 282, 289, 296. It is perhaps worthy of note that Raymond de Péreille, the Castellan of Montségur, and his companions, when on trial, while freely giving evidence about innumerable Cathari, declared that they knew nothing whatever about Waldenses which would seem to indicate that there was little communication between the sects (Doat, XXII. 217; XXIII. 344; XXIV. 8).

[165] Statut. Synod. Odonis Tullensis ann. 1192, c. ix., x. (Martene Thesaur. IV. 1180).--Ripoll I. 183.-- Douais, Les sources de l'histoire de l'Inq. (Revue des Questions Historiques, Oct. 1881, p. 434).--Peyrat, Les Alb. et l'Inquis. III. 74.--Chabrand, Vaudois et Protestants des Alpes, Grenoble, 1886, p. 34.--Havet, L'heresie et le bras seculier (Bib. de l'École des Chartes, 1880, p. 585).--Vaissette, IV. 17.--A. Molinier (Vaissette, Éd. Privat, VI. 819).--Wadding, ann. 1288, No. 14-15; 1292, No. 3.--Raynald. ann. 1288, No. 27-8.

[166] Lib. Sententt. Inq. Tolos. pp. 200-1, 207-8, 216-43, 252-4, 262-5, 289-90, 340-7, 352, 355, 364-66.-- Arch. de l'Inq. de Carcass. (Doat, XXVII. 7 sqq.).

[167] Bernard. Guidon. Practica P. v. (Doat. XXX.).

[168] Wadding. ann. 1321, No. 21-4.

[169] Arch. de l'Inq. de Carcass. (Doat, XXVII. 119 sqq.).--Raynald. ann. 1335, No. 63; 1344, No. 9; 1352, No. 20.--Chabrand. op. cit. pp. 36-7.--Wadding ann. 1352, No. 14, 15; 1363, No. 14, 15; 1364, No. 14, 15; 1365, No. 3.--Lombard, Pierre Valdo et les Vaudois du Briançonnais, Genève, 1880, pp. 17. 20, 23-7.

[170] Raynald. ann. 1372, No. 34; ann. 1373, No. 19.

[171] Wadding. ann. 1375, No. 11-19.--D'Argentré, op. cit. I. I. 394.--Ripoll II. 289.--Raynald. ann. 1375, No. 26.--Gautier, Hist, de la Ville de Gap, p. 39.

[172] Lombard, op. cit. pp. 27-8.--Wadding, ann. 1375, No. 21-3.--Isambert, Anc. Loix Franç. IV. 491.

[173] Wadding. ann. 1376, No. 3.

[174] Wadding. ann. 1375, No. 24; ann. 1376, No. 2.--Arch. de l'Inq. de Carcass. (Doat, XXXV. 163).

[175] Perrin's Waldenses, translated by Lennard, London, 1624, Bk. 2 pp. 18, 19.--Leger, Hist. des Églises Vaudoises II. 26.--Chabrand, op. cit. pp. 39, 40.

[176] Miroir de Souabe, ch. 89 (Ed. Matile, Neuchatel, 1843).

[177] Wadding. ann. 1409, No. 12.

[178] Mary-Lafon, Hist. du midi de la France, III. 384.--C. Bituricens. ann. 1432 (Harduin. VIII. 1459).-- Martene Ampl. Coll. VII. 161-3.

[179] Leger, Hist. des Églises vaudoises, II. 24.--Duverger, La Vauderie dans les États de Philippe le Bon, Arras, 1885, p. 112. Even in the early part of the sixteenth century, Robert Gaguin, in speaking of riding on a broomstick and worshipping Satan, adds *"quod impietatis genus Valdensium esse dicitur"* (Rer. Gallican. Annal. Lib. X. p. 242. Francof. ad M. 1587).

[180] Martene Ampl. Collect. II. 1506-7.

[181] Isambert, Anc. Loix Franç. X. 793-4.

[182] Chabrand, op. cit. pp. 43, 48-52, 70.--Herzog, Die romanischen Waldenser pp. 277-82.--D'Argentré I. I. 105.--Leger, Hist. des Églises Vaudoises II. 23-5.--Filippo de Boni, I Calabro-Valdesi p. 71.--Comba, Histoire des Vaudois d'Italie, Paris, 1887, I. 160-66, 169. The Waldensian legend relates that in the cavern of Aigue-Fraide the number of victims was three thousand, of whom four hundred were children, but I think that M. Chabrand has sufficiently demonstrated its exaggerated improbability (Op. cit. pp. 53-9).

[183] Herzog, op. cit. pp. 283-5.--Perrin, Hist. Waldens. B. II. ch. 3.--Chabrand. op. cit. pp. 73-4.

[184] Matt. Paris ann. 1234 (p. 270, Ed. 1644).--Reinerii Summa (Martene Thesaur. V. 1767-8).

[185] Archives Nat. de France, J. 426, No. 4.--D'Achery Spicileg III. 598.--Paramo de Orig. Offic. S. Inquis. p. 177.--Zurita, Añales de Aragon, Lib. III. c. 94.--Ripoll I. 38. (Cf. Llorente, Ch. III. Art. i. No. 3).-- Marca Hispanica, pp. 1425-6.

[186] Llorente, Ch. III. Art. i. No. 5--Ripoll I. 91-2.

[187] Vaissette, III. Pr. 383-5, 392-3.--Doat, XXII. 218; XXIV. 184.

[188] Wadding, ann. 1238, No. 6.--Doat, XXIV. 182.--Pet. Rodulphii Hist. Seraph. Lib.II. fol. 285*b*.-- Berger, Registres d'Innoc. IV. No. 2257.--Monteiro, Hist. da Inquisição, P. I. Liv. ii. ch. 36.

[189] Llorente, Ch. III Art. 1. No. 7, 8, 19.--Concil. Tarraconens. ann. 1242.--Paramo, pp. 110, 177-8.

[190] Berger, Registres d'Innocent IV. No. 799, 3904.--Baluz. et Mansi I. 208.--Ripoll I. 245, 427, 429; II. 235.--Eymeric. Direct. Inquis. pp. 129-36.--Paramo, p. 132.

[191] Llorente, Ch. III. Art. i. No. 14, 17.--Monteiro, Hist. da Inquisição, P. I. Liv. ii. ch. 10.--Pelayo, Heterodoxos Españoles, I. 492.--Zurita, Añales de Aragon, Lib. II. c. 76.--Paramo, p. 178.

[192] Concil. Tarraconens. ann. 1291, c. 8 (Martene Ampl. Coll. VII. 294).

[193] Llorente, Ch. III. Art. ii. No. 4, 5, 9, 10, 11, 12, 14.--Eymeric. Direct. Inquis. p. 265.--Ripoll II. 245.- -Zurita, Añales, Lib. VI. c. 61.--Raynald. ann. 1344, No. 9.

[194] Eymeric. Direct. Inq. p. 262.--Ripoll. III. 421; VII. 90.--Wadding. ann. 1351, No. 16, 18, 21; ann. 1462, No. 1-18; 1463, No. 1-5; 1464, No. 1-6.--D'Argentré, I. I. 372; II. 250, 254.--Gradonici Pontif. Brixianorum Series, Brixiæ, 1755, pp. 348-51.--Æn. Sylvii Comment. Lib. XI.; Ejusd. Lib. de Contentione Divini Sanguinis.

[195] Eymeric. Direct. Inquis. pp. 44, 266, 314-6, 351, 357-8, 652-3.--Mag. Bull. Rom. I. 263.--Ripoll II. 268, 269, 270.--Martene Thesaur. II. 1181-2, 1182 *bis*, 1189.--Raynald. ann. 1398, No. 23.--Wadding, ann. 1371, No. 14-24.--Paramo, p. 111.--Pelayo, Heterodoxos Españoles, I. 499-500, 528.

[196] Dameto, Mut, y Alemany, Historia General de Mallorca (Ed. 1840, I. 101-3, II. 652).--Libell. de Magist. Ord. Prædic. (Martene Ampl. Coll. VI. 432).--Paramo, pp. 179, 186-7.--Ripoll II. 579, 594; III. 20, 28.-- Monteiro, P. I. Liv. ii. c. 30.--Llorente, Ch. III. Art. iii. No. 4, 8.

[197] Ripoll II. 613.

[198] Ripoll III. 347.--Arch. de l'Inq. de Carcass. (Doat, XXXV. 192).

[199] Llorente, Ch. III. Art. iii. No. 11.--Albertini Repertor. Inquis. s. v. *Deficiens*.--Ripoll III. 397, 415, 572.

[200] Llorente, Ch. VII. Art. ii. No. 2.--Herculano, Da Origem, etc., da Inquisição em Portugal, I. 44.-- Ripoll III. 422.--Paramo, p. 187.

[201] Monteiro, P. I. Liv. i. c. 38, 44, 46, 48-51; Liv. ii. c. 5-12.--Chron. Eccles. Hamelens. (Scriptt. Rer. Brunsv. II. 508).--Herculano, I. 39.--Baluz. et Mansi, I. 208.--Paramo de Orig. Offic. S. Inquis. p. 131.

[202] Lucæ Tudens. de altera Vita, Lib. III. c. 7, 9. Cf. c. 18, 20.--Florez, España Sagrada, XXII. 120-22, 126-30.

[203] Lucæ Tudens. Lib. III. c. 12.--Raynald. ann. 1236, No. 60.--Rodrigo. Hist. Verdadera de la Inquisicion, II. 10.

[204] Las Siete Partidas, P. I. Tit. vi. I. 58; P.VII. Tit. xxiv. I. 7; Tit. XXV. II. 2-7.--El Fuero real, Lib. IV. Tit. i. II. 1, 2.

[205] Coll. Doat, XXX. 132 sqq.--Archbishop Rodrigo's letter is dated 1315. This I presume to be an error of a copyist, probably misled by the use of the Spanish era in which 1355 is equivalent to 1317.

[206] Ripoll II. 421, 433.--Monteiro, P. I. Liv. ii. c. 35, 36.--Ordenanzas Reales, Lib. VIII. Tit. iv. I. 4.

204

[207] Monteiro, P. I. Liv. ii. c. 30.--Rodrigo, II. 11, 14-15.--Paramo, p. 136.--Raynald. ann. 1453, No. 19.--Alphons. de Spina Fortalic. Fidei Prolog, fol. 56*b* (Ed. 1494).

[208] Alphons. de Castro adv. Hæreses Lib. III. s.v. *Confessio.*--Illescas, Historia Pontifical, Lib. VI. c. 18.--Aguirre Concil. Hispan. V. 351-8.--D'Argentré, I. II. 298-302.

[209] Herculano, I. 40.--Monteiro. P. I. Liv. ii. c. 34.--Pelayo, Heterodoxos Españoles, I. 782-3.

[210] Llorente, Ch. III. Art. ii. No. 24.--Monteiro, P. I. Liv. ii. c. 35, 37, 38, 39.--Wadding, ann. 1394, No. 4; 1413, No. 4.--Ripoll II. 389.

[211] Herculano, Da Origem, etc., da Inquisição, I. 163-5.

[212] Cæsar. Heisterbacens. Dial. Mirac. Dist. V. c. 25.--Muratori Antiq. Ital. Diss. LX. (T. XII. p. 447).

[213] D'Argentré, Coll. Judic. de novis Error. I. i. 86.--Reinerii Summa (Martene Thesaur. V. 1767).

[214] Matt. Paris. ann. 1236, p. 293; ann. 1243, pp. 412-13 (Ed. 1644)--Trithem. Chron. Hirsaug. ann. 1230.--Innoc. PP. III. Regest. XV. 189.--Hist. Diplom. Frid. II. T. IV. p. 881.

[215] Montet, Hist. litt. des Vaudois du Piémont, pp. 40-1.--Innoc. PP. III. Regest. IX. 18, 19, 204; XII. 17; XIII. 63.--Kaltner, Konrad v. Marburg, pp. 42, 44.--Annal. Marbacens. ann. 1231 (Urstisii Germ. Hist. Scriptt. II. 90).

[216] Böhmer, Regest, Imp. V. 110.--Comba, La Riforma in Italia, I. 254-57.--Ejusd. Histoire des Vaudois d'Italie, I. 124 sqq., 140.--Charvaz, Origine dei Valdesi, App. No. XXII. Giuseppe Manuel di S. Giovanni (Un' Episodia della Storia del Piemonte, Torino, 1874, pp. 15-21) argues that the letter of Otho IV. is only the draft of one which the bishop desired to procure, but the question is merely of archæological interest, for in either case it was equally ineffective.

[217] Rescript. Heres. Lombard. (Preger, Beiträge, München, 1875, pp. 56-63).--Reinerii Summa (Martene Thesaur. V. 1775).

[218] Campi, Dell' Historia Ecclesiastica di Piacenza, P. II.. pp. 92 sqq.--Innoc. PP. III. Regest. IX. 131, 166-9; X. 54, 64, 222.--Tocco, L'Heresia nel Medio Evo, pp. 364, 366 (Firenze, 1884).--Cf. Pseudo-Joachim de septem temporibus Ecclesiæ P. V.

[219] Epistt. Sæcul. XIII. T. I. No. 451 (Mon. Hist. Germ.).--Potthast No. 7672.

[220] Epistt. Sæc. XIII. T. I. No. 264-66, 275, 295 (Mon. Hist. Germ.).--Havet, Bibl. de l'École des Chartes, 1880, p. 602.

[221] Epistt. Sæc. XIII. T. I. No. 355.

[222] Raynald. Annal. ann. 1231, No. 13-18.--Constit. Sicular. Lilt. I. Tit. i.--Rich. S. Germ. Chron. (Muratori, S. R. I. VII. 1026).--Vit. Gregor. PP. IX. (Ib. III. 578).--Hist. Diplom. Frid. II. T. IV. pp. 299-300, 409-11.--Verri, Storia di Milano, I. 242.--Bern. Corio, Hist. Milanese, ann. 1228.

[223] Ripoll. 41.

[224] Epistt. Sæc. XIII. T. I. No. 559.--Raynald. ann. 1233, No. 40.--Ripoll I. 69, 71. Probably about this period may have occurred the incident related of Moneta, the disciple of St. Dominic, whose efforts against the heretics of Lombardy are said to have aroused their animosity to the point that a noble named Peraldo hired an assassin to despatch him. Word was brought to Moneta, who seized a crucifix and assembled a band of the faithful, with whom he captured Peraldo and the bravo, delivered them to the secular authorities, and they were both burned alive.--Ricchini Vit. Monetæ, p. viii.

[225] Ripoll I. 48, 56-9.--Matt. Paris, ann. 1238, p. 320.--Chron. Veronens. ann. 1233 (Muratori, S.R.I. VIII. 67).--Gerardi Maurisii Hist. (Ib. pp. 37-9).--Barbarano de' Mironi, Hist. Eccles. di Vicenza, II. 79-84.

[226] Barbarano de' Mironi, op. cit. II. 90-1.

[227] Ripoll I. 60-1--Barbarano de' Mironi op. cit. II. 86, 91-2.

[228] Greg. PP. IX. Bull. *Ille humani generis*, 20 Maii, 1230 (Ripoll I. 95. gives this in 1237, probably a reissue).--Epistt. Sæcul. XIII. T. I. No. 693, 700, 702, 704.--Hist. Diplom. Frid. II. T. IV. P. II. pp. 907-8.--Schmidt, Cathares, I. 161.

[229] Ripoll I. 174-5.--Barbarano de' Mironi, op. cit. II. 94-6.

[230] Jac. de Voragine Legenda Aurea s. V.--Mag. Bull. Rom. I. 94.

[231] Campana, Storia di San Piero-Martire, Milano, 1741, pp. 28-39.

[232] Bern. Corio, Hist. Milanese, ann. 1233, 1242.--Verri, Storia di Milano, I. 241-3.--Ripoll I. 65.--Annal. Mediolanens. c. xiv. (Muratori, S.R.I. XVI. 651).--Sarpi, Discorso (Ed. Helmstad. 1763, IV. 21).

[233] Lami, Antichità Toscane, pp. 497, 500.

[234] Ripoll I. 79-80.--Raynald. ann. 1235, No. 15.--Vit. Gregor. PP. IX. (Muratori, S.R.I. III. 581).--Lami op. cit. pp. 554, 557.

[235] Lami, op. cit. pp. 560-85.--Lami's account of these troubles, based upon original sources, is so complete that I have followed it without reference to other authorities. Most of the documents are still in the Archives of Florence (Archiv. Diplom., Prov. S. Maria Novella, ann. 1245). The Compagnia della Fede, known subsequently as del Bigallo, was changed in the middle of the fifteenth century, by Sant' Antonino, Prior of San Marco, into a charitable association for the care of orphans (Villari, Storia di Girol. Savonarola, Firenze, 1887, I. 37).

[236] Ripoll I. 192-3, 199, 205, 208-14, 231.--Berger, Registres d'Innoc. IV. No. 5065, 5345.--Mag. Bull. Rom. I. 91.

[237] Campana, Vita di San Piero-Martire, pp. 100-1.

[238] Bern. Corio, Hist. Milanese, ann. 1252.--Gualvaneo Flamma c. 286 (Muratori, S. R. I. XI. 684).--Ripoll I. 224, 244, 389.--Campana, Vita di San Piero Martire, pp. 118-20, 125, 128-9, 132-33.--Annal. Mediolanens. c. 24 (Muratori, XVI. 656).--Tamburini, Storia dell' Inquisizione, I. 492-502.--Wadding Annal. ann. 1284, No. 3.--Rodulphii Hist. Seraph. Relig. Lib. I. fol. 126.--Raynald. Annal. ann. 1403, No. 24. There is a Daniele da Giussano who appears as inquisitor in Lombardy in 1279 (Ripoll I. 567), and who may very probably be the same as the accomplice in the murder.

[239] Ripoll I. 212.--Campana, op. cit. 126, 149, 151, 257, 259, 262-3.--Jac. de Vorag. Legenda Aurea s. v.--Mag. Bull. Roman. I. 94.--Wadding Annal. ann. 1291, No. 24.--Juan de Mata, Santoral de los dos Santos, Barcelona, 1637, fol. 28.--Gualvaneo Flamma, Opusc. (Muratori, S. R. I. XII. 1035). Frà Tommaso's disgrace was not perpetual. We shall meet him hereafter as inquisitor, alternately protecting and persecuting the Spiritual Franciscans. If the accounts of the latter be true, his death in 1306 was a visitation of God for the frightful cruelties inflicted upon them (Hist. Tribulationum, *ap.* Archiv für Litteratur-und Kirchengeschichte, 1886, p. 326). The question of the Stigmata was always a burning one between the two Orders. The Dominicans at first refused to accept the miracle until forced to submit by energetic papal measures (Chron. Glassberger ann. 1237--Analecta Franciscana II. 58, Quaracchi, 1887), and when at length they claimed the same honor for St. Catharine of Siena the Franciscans were equally incredulous. In 1473, at Trapani, the two Orders preached against each other on this subject with so much violence as to raise great disorders between their respective partisans among the laity, until the Viceroy of Sicily was obliged to interfere (La Mantia, L'Inquisizione in Sicilia, Torino, 1886, p. 17); and, as already mentioned, Sixtus IV., in 1475, prohibited the ascription of the Stigmata to St. Catharine.

[240] Ripoll VIII. 113.--Chron. Parmens. ann. 1286 (Muratori, S.R.I. IX. 810).--Campana, op. cit. p. 63.--Bernardi Comens. Lucerna Inquis. s. VV. *Bona hæreticor.* No. 6,*Crucesignati. Indulgentia.*

[241] Ripoll I. 144, 168.--Campi, Dell' Hist. Eccles. di Piacenza, P. II. pp. 208-9.

[242] Molinier, Thesis de Fratre Guillelmo Pelisso, Anicii, 1880, pp. lix.-lx.

[243] Ripoll I. 238, 242-3; VII. 31.--Bern. Corio, Hist. Milanese, ann. 1269.

[244] Ripoll I. 254.--Campana, op. cit. p. 114.

[245] Bern. Guidon. Vit. Innocent. PP. IV. (Muratori, S.R.I. III. 592).--Wadding, ann. 1254, No. 8.--Ripoll I. 246.--Sclopis, Antica Legislazione del Piemonte, p. 440.

[246] Ripoll I. 285.--Raynald. ann. 1255, No. 31--Campi, Dell' Hist. Eccles. di Piacenza. P. II. pp. 212-13, 402.

[247] Ripoll I. 300, 326, 327, 399.--Potthast No. 16292.

[248] Campi, Deli' Hist. Eccles. di Piacenza, P. II. pp. 214-15.--Barbarano de Mironi, Hist. Eccles. di Vicenza, II. 99, 104.

[249] Epistt. Sæcul. XIII. T. I. No. 451.--Raynald. ann. 1231, No. 20-22.

[250] Chabaneau (Vaissette, Éd. Privat, X. 314).--Monach. Patavin. Chron. (Muratori, S. R. I. VIII. 707-9).--Frederic II. is similarly described by the papal scribes as a monster delighting in objectless cruelty. See Vit. Gregor. PP. IX. (Muratori, S. R. I. III. 583-4).

[251] Epistt. Sæcul. XIII. T. I. No. 453, 741, 757-9.--Ripoll I. 59, 135, 193.--Potthast No. 12899.--Berger, Registres d'Innocent IV. No. 4095.--Raynald. Annal. ann. 1248. No. 25-6.--Harduin. Concil. VII. 362.

[252] Ripoll I. 230, 247, 249-51, 286, 391.--Mag. Bull. Rom. 1.102-4.--Pegnæ Append. Eymeric. p. 77.--Harduin. Concil. VII. 362.

[253] Raynald. ann. 1357, No. 38-9; 1258, No. 1-4; 1259, No. 1-3.--Rolandini Chron. Lib. IX.-XII. (Muratori, S. R. I. VIII. 299-352).--Monach. Patavin. Chron. (Ib. VIII. 691-705).--Nic. Smeregi Chron. (Ib. VIII. 101).--Wadding, ann. 1258, No. 6.--Mag. Bull. Rom, I. 118. The ferocity of the age is seen in the treatment bestowed on Ezzelin's brother Alberico, when captured with his family. He was gagged and tied to a tree, his wife and daughters were burned alive before his eyes, his sons were slain and their limbs thrown in his face, and then he was deliberately hacked in pieces.--Laurentii de Monacis Ezerinus III. (Muratori, S. R. I. VIII. 150). Alberico was a man of culture, a troubadour, and a patron of the *gai science* (Vaissette, Éd. Privat, X. 313).

[254] Raynald. ann. 1259, No. 6-9.

[255] Ripoll I. 398.--Bern. Corio, Hist. Milanese, ann. 1259.

[256] Arch. de l'Inquis de Carcassonne (Doat. XXXI.).--Ripoll I. 400.

[257] Potthast No. 17984-5.--Arch. de l'Inquis. de Carc. (Doat, XXXI. 216).--Ripoll I. 402, 460, 462, 466, 469, 478.--Raynald. ann. 1260, No. 12.--Mag. Bull. Rom. I. 119. The bull threatening the people of Bergamo with interdict for their legislation is by Urban IV. and dated in 1264, as found in the archives of the Inquisition of Carcassonne (Doat, XXX. 288), while Ripoll (I. 499) gives it as by Clement IV. in 1265, showing that the Bergamese were obstinate. Bergamo had been under interdict for adhering to Frederic and Conrad, and had only been reconciled after the death of the latter in 1255 (Ripoll I. 268).

[258] Epistt. Urbani PP. IV. (Martene Thesaur. II. 9-50, 74-9, 116-18, 220-37.)--Epistt. Clement. PP. IV. (Ibid. pp. 176, 186, 196-200, 213, 218, 241-5, 250, 260, 274).

[259] Epistt. Clem. PP. IV. (Martene Thesaur. II. 174, 319, 327).--Raynald. ann. 1266, No. 23.

[260] Ripoll I. 427, 514.--Campi, Dell' Hist. Eccles. di Piacenza, P. II. pp. 218-31.--Philippi Bergomat. Supplem. Chron. ann. 1261.

[261] Wadding, ann. 1254, No. 7, 8, 11, 16; 1261, No. 2.--Grandjean, Registres de Benoît XI. No. 1167.-- Ripoll II. 87.

[262] Wadding, ann. 1259, No. 3.--Barbarano de' Mironi, Hist. Eccles. di Vicenza, II. 95, 105, 108, 113, 121.

[263] Annal. Mediolanens. cap. 31 (Muratori, S. R. I. XVI. 662).--Muratori Antiq. Ital. XII. 513.-- Wadding, ann. 1277, No. 10, 11; 1278, No. 33; 1289, No. 18.

[264] Grandjean, Registres de Benoit XI. No. 508.

[265] Paramo, p. 264.--Verri, Storia di Milano, I. 244.--Ripoll I. 567.--Raynald. ann. 1278, No. 78.--In Doat, XXXII. 160, is the letter to the authorities of Bergamo, which Bremond (Ripoll ubi sup.) says is not to be found.

[266] Memor. Protestat. Regiens. ann. 1279, 1282 (Muratori, S.R.I. VIII. 1146, 1150).--Bern. Corio, Hist. Milanese, ann. 1279.--Paramo Lib. II. Tit. ii. cap. 30, No. 13.--Pegnæ Append. ad Eymeric. p. 55--Salimbene Chron. pp. 274, 276, 342.--Chron. Parmens. ann. 1279, 1282, 1286, 1287 (Muratori, IX. 792, 799, 809-11).-- Sarpi, Discorso (Opere, IV. 21).--Concil. Mediolanens. ann. 1287, c. xi.

[267] Ripoll I. 241-2.--Wadding. ann. 1258, No. 3, 5; ann. 1278, No. 33; ann. 1279, No. 29; Regest. Nich. PP. III. No. 11.--Mag. Bull. Rom. I. 118.--Martene Thesaur. II. 191.--Raynald. ann. 1278, No. 78.

[268] Muratori Antiq. Ital. XII. 513-14, 521-3, 537-8.--Lib. Sententt. Inq. Tolosan. pp. 2, 3, 12, 13, 32, 68, 75, 76, 81, etc.

[269] Muratori Antiq. Ital. XII. 508-55.--Bern. Guidon. Vit. Bonif. VIII. (S.R.I. III. 671-2).--Barbarano de' Mironi, Hist. Eccles. di Vicenza II. 153.--Salimbene Chron. ann. 1279, p. 276.--Paramo, p. 299. The wide attention attracted by the case of Armanno is shown by the allusion to it in the German chronicles.--Trithem Chron. Hirsaug. ann. 1299.--Chron. Cornel. Zanfliet (Martene Ampl. Coll. V. 142-3).

[270] Introductio ad Zanchini Tract. de Hæres, ed. Campegii, Romæ, 1568. (I owe a copy of this document to the kindness of Prof. Felice Tocco, of Florence.)

[271] Cod. Epist. Rodulphi I. Lipsiæ, 1807, pp. 266-9.--Wadding. ann. 1289, No. 20.--Lami, Antichità Toscane, pp. 497, 536-7.

[272] Faucon, Registres de Boniface VIII. No. 1673, p. 632.--Wadding. ann. 1298, No. 3.--Arch. de l'Inq. de Carc. (Doat, XXVI. 147).

[273] Wadding. ann. 1285, No. 9, 10.

[274] Tocco, L'Eresia nel Medio Evo, p. 403.--Renerii Summa (Martene Thesaur. V. 1767).--Ripoll I. 74.

[275] Raynald. ann. 1231, No. 19.--Rich. de S. German. Chron. ann. 1233.--Giannone, Ist. Civ. di Napoli, Lib. XVII. c. 6, Lib. XIX. c. 5.--Vaissette, IV. 17.

[276] Archivio di Napoli, MSS. Chioccarello T. VIII.--Ib. Regist. 3 Lett. A, fol. 64; Reg. 4 Lett. B, fol. 47; Reg. 5 Lett. C, fol. 224; Reg. 6 Lett. D, fol. 35, 39, 174; Reg. 10 Lett. B. fol. 6, 7, 96; Reg. 11 Lett. C, fol. 40; Reg. 13 Lett. A, fol. 212; Reg. 113 Lett. A, fol. 385; Reg. 154 Lett. C, fol. 81; Reg. 167 Lett. A, fol. 324.

[277] Archivio di Napoli, Reg. 6 Lett. D, fol. 135; Reg. 253 Lett. A, fol. 68.--Giannone, Ist. Civ. di Napoli Lib. XIX. c. 5.

[278] Archivio di Napoli, Regist. 3 Lett. A, fol. 64; Regist. 4 Lett. B, fol. 47; Reg. 9 Lett. C, fol. 39.--MSS. Chioccarello, T. VIII.

[279] Lombard, Jean Louis Paschal et les Martyrs de Calabre, Geneve, 1881, pp. 22-32.--Filippo de Boni, L'Inquisizione e i Calabro-Valdesi, Milano, 1864, pp. 73-77.--Perrin, Hist. des Vaudois, Liv. II. ch. 7.--Comba, Hist. des Vaudois d'Italie, I. 128, 181-6, 190.--Rorengo, Memorie Historiche, Torino, 1649, pp. 77 sqq.--Martini Append. ad Mosheim de Beghardis, p. 638. Vegezzi-Ruscalla (Rivista Contemporanea, 1862) has shown the identity of the dialects of the Calabrian Guardia and of the Val d'Angrogna, proving the reality of the emigration.

[280] Salimbene, p. 330.--Grandjean, Registries de Benoît XI. No. 834-5.--Pelayo Heterodoxos Españoles, I. 730.--La Mantia, Origine e Vicende dell' Inquisizione in Sicilia, Torino, 1886, p. 12.

[281] Sarpi, Discorso (Opere, Ed. Helmstadt, IV. 20).

[282] Archivio Generale di Venezia, Codice ex Brera, No. 277, Carte 5.

[283] Ripoll VII. 25.--Arch. di Venez. Miscellanea, Codice No. 133, p. 121; Cod. ex Brera, No. 277, Carte 5.

[284] Albizio, Risposta al P. Paolo Sarpi, pp. 20-3.--Wadding ann. 1288. No. 23.

[285] Albizio, op. cit. pp. 24-7.--Wadding. ann. 1289, No. 15.--Sarpi. op. cit. p. 21.--Arch. di Venez. Codice ex Brera, No. 277, Carte 41; Maggior Consiglio, Carte 67.

[286] Wadding. ann. 1292, No. 5.--Albanese, L'Inquisizione nella Repubblica di Venezia, 1875, pp. 52-3.-- Sarpi, loc. cit.--Cecchetti, La Repubblica di Venezia e la Corte di Roma, Venezia, 1874, I. 18.

[287] Wadding. ann. 1340, No. 10; ann. 1369, No. 4; ann. 1373, No. 7; Regest. Gregor. PP. XI. No. 45-7; Tom. VII. p. 481.--Raynald. ann. 1372, No. 35.

[288] Archivio Storico Italiano, 1865, No. 39, pp. 46-61.

[289] Archivio Storico Italiano, 1865, No. 39, pp. 33-5.

[290] Archivio Storico Italiano, 1865, No. 39, pp. 4-45.--G. Manuel di S. Giovanni, Un Episodio della Storia del Piemonte, Torino, 1874, pp. 75 sqq.

[291] Raynald. ann. 1403, No. 24.--Archiv. Stor. Ital. 1865, No. 38, p. 22.--Comba, Les Vaudois d'Italie, I. 120.

[292] Processus contra Valdenses (Archivio Storico Italiano, 1865, No. 38, pp. 39-40).--Comba, Hist. des Vaudois d'Italie, I. 354-7.

[293] Comba, Hist. des Vaudois d'Italie, I. 141.--Herzog, Die romanischen Waldenser, p. 273.--Wadding. ann. 1332, No. 6.

[294] Rorengo, Memorie Historiche, Torino, 1649, p. 17.--Wadding. ann. 1364, No. 14, 15.--Cantù, Eretici, I. 86.--D'Argentré, Collect. Judic. I. I. 387.--Comba, Rivista Cristiana, 1887, pp. 65 sqq.

[295] Raynald. ann. 1375, No. 26.--Filippo de Boni, L'Inquiz. e i Calabro-Valdesi, p. 70.

[296] Processus contra Valdenses (Archivio Storico Italiano, 1865, No. 38, pp. 18-52). There is some confusion as to the dates of these events which I cannot remove. Gregory XI., in his letter of April 20, 1375, to Amadeo VI., speaks of the recent murder at "Bricherasio" of the inquisitor Antonius Salvianensis (Raynald. ann. 1375, No. 26). According to the records of Antonio Secco, Antonio Pavo da Savigliano received in 1384 the abjuration of Lorenzo Bandoria (loc. cit. p. 23), and his murder must have taken place the same year, from the evidence of the son of one of his murderers, Giov. Gabriele of "Bricherasio" (Ib. p. 31). Rorengo places the martyrdom of Antonio Pavo in 1374, and tells us that he was honored in Savigliano with a local cult as one of the blessed. Another Dominican, Frà Bartolomeo di Cervere was also slain, and his assistant Ricardo desperately wounded, but the date is not certain (Rorengo, Memorie Historiche, p. 17).

[297] Chabrand, Vaudois et Protestants des Alpes, Grenoble, 1886, p. 39.

[298] Raynald. ann. 1403, No. 24.--Melgares Marin, Procedimientos de la Inquisicion, Madrid, 1886, I. 50.

[299] Rorengo, Memorie Historiche, pp. 18-20.--E. Comba, Rivista Cristiana, Giugno, 1882, p. 204.--Ripoll III. 359.

[300] Hahn, Geschichte der Ketzer im Mittalalter, II. 705.--Rorengo, Memorie Historiche, pp. 22-5.--Martene Ampl. Coll. II. 1510-11.--Leger, Hist. des Églises Vaudoises, II. 8-15, 26, 71.--Perrin, Hist. des Vaudois, L. II. c. 4.--Filippo de Boni, op. cit. p. 71.--Comba, Les Vaudois d'Italie, I. 167, 175-8.--Herzog, Die roman. Waldenser, p. 274.--Montet, Hist. Litt. des Vaudois, pp. 152-55.--D'Argentré, Coll. Judic. I. I. 105-7.

[301] Filippo de Boni, op. cit. pp. 79-81.--Lombard, Jean-Louis Paschale, pp. 29-33.--Perrin, Hist. des Vaudois, B. II. ch. 7, 10.--Comba, La Reforma, I. 269.--Vegezzi-Ruscalla, Rivista Contemporanea, 1862.--Camerarii Hist. Frat. Orthodox. p. 120.

[302] Bremond in Ripoll II. 139.--Raynald. ann. 1344, No. 9, 70.--Antiqua Ducum Mediolani Decreta, Mediolani, 1654.--Albanese, L'Inquisizione religiosa nella Repubblica di Venezia, Venezia, 1875, p. 167.--Giuseppe Cosentino, Archivio Storico Siciliano. 1885, p. 92.

[303] Ripoll II. 351; III. 368.--Wadding. ann. 1452, No. 14.--Raynald. ann. 1457, No. 90: ann. 1459, No. 31.

[304] Wadding. ann. 1447, No. 8, 47; ann. 1450, No. 2.--Raynald. ann. 1446. No. 8.

[305] Ripoll IV. 6, 102, 103, 158, 339.--Brev. Hist. Magist. Ord. Prædic. (Martene Coll. Ampl. VI. 393).

[306] Wadding. ann. 1356, No. 12-19.--Arch. di. Venez. Misti, Conc. X. Vol. VI. p. 26.

[307] Wadding. ann. 1373, No. 15-16; ann. 1376, No. 4-5; ann. 1433, No. 15; ann. 1434, No. 4, 6; ann. 1437, No. 24-8; ann. 1456, No. 108.--Archiv. di Venez. Misti, Cons. X. No. 9, pp. 84, 85.--Cecchetti, La Repubblica di Venezia, etc. I. 18.

[308] Archiv. di Venez. Misti, Cons. X. Vol. XIII. p. 192; Vol. XIX. p. 29.--Wadding. ann. 1455, No. 97.--Mag. Bull. Rom. I. 617.--Albizio, Riposto al P. Paolo Sarpi, pp. 64-70.

[309] Wadding. ann. 1494, No. 6.--When Frà Bernardo endeavored to establish a *mont de piété* at Florence the moneyed interests were strong enough to drive him from the city (Burlamacchi, Vita di Savonarola, Baluz. et Mansi I. 557).

[310] Prediche di Frà Giordano da Rivalto, Firenze, 1831, I. 172.--Wadding. ann. 1340, No. 11.--Archivio di Firenze, Riformagioni, Diplomatico, 27; Classe V. No. 129, fol. 46, 54.

[311] Wadding. T. III. App. p. 3--Ughelli, Italia Sacra, Ed. 1659, II. 1075.--Archiv. di Firenze, Riformag. Classe V. No. 129, fol. 55.

[312] Archiv. di Firenze, Riformag. Atti Pubblici, Lib. XVI. de' Capitolari, fol. 15.--Villani Chron. XI. 138; XII. 55, 58.

[313] Archiv. delle Riformag. Atti Pubblici, Lib. XVI. de' Capitolari, fol. 22; Classe V. No. 129, fol. 62 sqq.--Archiv. Diplomatico XXXVII., XXXVIII., XL., XLI., XLII.--Villani, XII. 58. The amount involved was not small. The revenue of Florence at this period was only three hundred thousand florins (Sismondi, Rep. Ital. ch. 36), and Florence was one of the richest states in Europe. Villani (XI. 92) boasts that France alone enjoyed a larger revenue; that of Naples was less, and the three were the wealthiest in Christendom.

[314] Archiv. delle Riformag. Classe IX., Distinzione i. No. 39; Classe V. No. 129, fol. 62 sqq.; Prov. del Convento di S. Croce, 23 Ott. 1354.--Villani, XII. 58.--Ughelli VII. 1015.

[315] Archiv. delle Riformag. Classe II. Distinz. I. No. 14.--Archiv. Diplom. LXXVIII.-IX., LXXX.-I.; Prov. del Convento di S. Croce, 1371 Febb. 18, Ott. 8, 14; 1372, Marz. 15; 1375, Marz. 9; 1380, Genn. 12; 1380, Dic. 1; 1381, Nov. 18; 1383, Lugl. 12; 1384, Dic. 13.--Werunsky Excerptt. ex Registt. Clement. VI. et Innoc. VI. p. 95.--Villani, XII. 58.--Wadding. ann. 1372, No. 35; ann. 1375, No. 32.--Raynald. ann. 1375, No. 13-17; ann.

1376, No. 1-5.--Poggii Hist. Florentin. Lib. II. ann. 1376.--A document of 1374 (Archiv. Fior. Prov. S. Croce, 1374, Nov. 17) allows that Frà Piero di Ser Lippo, at that time Inquisitor of Florence, was defendant in an action brought against him in the papal curia by the Dominican Frà Simone del Pozzo, Inquisitor of Naples, in which Frà Piero seems to have obtained what was equivalent to a nonsuit.

[316] Wadding. ann. 1377, No. 4-23.

[317] Tamburini, Storia Gen. dell' Inquisizione, II. 433-6.--Raynald. ann. 1418, No. 11.--Archiv. di Firenze, Prov. S. Maria Novella, 1424, Ap. 24.--Wadding. ann. 1437, No. 33; ann. 1438, No. 26; ann. 1439, No. 57; ann. 1440, No. 26; ann. 1441, No. 61; ann. 1452, No. 30; ann. 1471, No. 11; ann. 1496, No. 7.--Ripoll VII. 89, 100. Frà Gabriele, the Inquisitor of Bologna, in the same year, 1461, in which he was sent to Rome, expended twenty-three lire ten sol. in having a copy made of Eymerich's *Directorium Inquisitionis*.--Denifle, Archiv für Litteratur-etc. 1885, p. 144.

[318] Paramo de Orig. Office S. Inq. p. 113.

[319] MSS. Chioccarello, T. VIII.--Raynald. ann. 1344, No. 9; ann. 1368, No. 16; ann. 1372, No. 36; ann. 1375, No. 26.--Tocco. Archivio Storico Napolitan. Ann. XII. (1887), Fasc. 1.--Ripoll II. 311, 324, 364.-- Guiseppe Cosentino, Archivio Storico Siciliano, 1885, pp. 74-5, 87.--La Mantia, Dell' Inquisizione in Sicilia, Torino, 1886, pp. 13-15.

[320] Wadding. T. III. Regesta, p. 392.--Ripoll II. 689. When, in 1447, Nicholas V. issued a cruel edict subjecting the Jews to severe disabilities and humiliations, Capistrano was likewise appointed conservator to enforce its provisions (Wadding. ann. 1447, No. 10).

[321] Giannone, Ist. Civ. di Napoli, Lib. XXXII. c. 5.--Wadding. ann. 1449, No. 13.--Ripoll III. 240, 441, 501.

[322] Paramo, pp. 197-99.--Ripoll III. 510.--La Mantia, L'Inquisizione in Sicilia, pp. 16-18. Giuseppe Cosentino says (Archivio Storico Siciliano, 1885, p. 73) that the confirmation in 1451 by King Alonso of the diploma of Frederic II. is not to be found in the archives of Palermo, but that the royal letters of 1415 allude to a privilege granted by Frederic. See also La Mantia, pp. 8-10, 13, 15.

[323] Pirro, Sicilia Sacra, I. 185-6.--G. Cosentino, loc. cit. p. 76.--Caruso, Memorie Istoriche di Sicilia, P. II. T. i. p. 92.--Giannone, op. cit. Lib. XXXII. c. 5.--Paramo, pp. 191-4.--Zurita, Hist. del Rey Hernando, Lib. V. c. 70; Lib. IX. c. 36.--Mariana, Hist. de España, Lib.XXX. c. 1.

[324] Schmidt, Histoire des Cathares, I. 104-9.--Gregor. PP. VII. Regist. VII. 11.--Batthyani Legg. Eccles. Hung. II. 274, 289-90, 415-17.--Raynald. ann. 1203, No. 22.--Innocent. PP. III. Regest. II. 176.

[325] Innoc. PP. III. Regest. II. 176; III. 3; V. 103, 110; VI. 140, 141, 142, 212.

[326] Schmidt, I. 112-13.

[327] Potthast No. 6612, 6725, 6802.--Raynald. ann. 1225, No. 21.--Klaić, Geschichte Bosniens, nach dem Kroatischen von Ivan v. Bojnicić, Leipzig, 1885, pp. 89-91.

[328] Monteiro, Historia da Sacra Inquisição P. I. Liv. 1, c. 59.--Paramo, p. 111.--Raynald. ann. 1257, No. 13.--Hist. Ord. Prædic. c. 8. (Martene Ampl. Coll. VII. 338).--Ripoll I. 70.--Klaić, pp. 92-4.

[329] Epist. Sæc. XIII. T. I. No. 574, 601.--Ripoll I. 70.--Potthast No. 9726, 9733-8, 10019, 10052.--Klaić, p. 96.--Batthyani Legg. Eccles. Hung. I. 355.--Matt. Paris ann. 1243 (Ed. 1644, pp. 412-13).

[330] Bishop John succeeded in resigning his bishopric, and became Grand Master of his Order. A contemporary, who knew him personally, describes him as a man of apostolic virtue, who distributed in alms the revenue of his see, amounting to 8000 marks, and performed his journeys on foot, with an ass to carry his books and vestments. After his death at Strassburg he shone in miracles.--Thomæ Cantimprat. Bonum universale Lib. II. c. 56.

[331] Potthast No. 10223-6, 10507, 10535, 10631-9, 10688-93, 10822-4, 10842.--Ripoll I. 102-4, 106-7.-- Schmidt, I. 122.--Klaić, pp. 97-107.

[332] Ripoll I. 175-6.--Klaić, pp. 107-13.--Kukuljević, Jura Regni Croatiæ, Dalmatiæ et Slavoniæ, Zagrabiæ, 1862, I. 67.

[333] Rainerii Summa (Martene Thesaur. V. 1768).--Klaić, p. 153.--Theiner Monumenta Slavor. Meridional. I. 90.

[334] Raynald. ann. 1280, No. 8, 9; ann. 1291, No. 42-44.--Klaić, pp. 116-9.--Wadding. ann. 1291, No. 12.

[335] Wadding. ann. 1298, No. 2.--Klaić, pp. 123-4.--Raynald. ann. 1319, No. 24.

[336] Klaić, pp. 124-5, 139-40, 154-6.--Theiner Monument. Slavor. Merid. I. 157, 234.--Raynald. ann. 1325, No. 28; ann. 1327, No. 48.--Wadding. ann. 1325, No. 1-4; ann. 1326, No. 3-7; ann. 1329, No. 16; ann. 1330, No. 10.

[337] Archivio di Venezia, Fontanini MSS. III. 560.

[338] Theiner Monument. Slavor. Merid. I. 174, 175--Wadding. ann. 1331, No. 4; ann. 1337, No. 1.-- Raynald. ann. 1335, No. 62.--Klaić, pp. 157-8.

[339] Klaić, pp. 159-61, 181-3.--Wadding. ann. 1340, No. 6-10.--Theiner, op. cit.

[340] Klaić, pp. 184-5, 187-8, 190-5, 200-1, 223, 262, 268-77, 287, 369.--Theiner Monument. Slavor. Merid. I. 233, 240.--Wadding. ann. 1356, No. 7; ann. 1368, No. 1-3; ann. 1369, No. 11; ann. 1372, No. 31-33; ann. 1373, No. 17; ann. 1382, No. 2.--Raynald. ann. 1368, No. 18; ann. 1372, No. 32.--Pet. Ranzani Epit. Rer.

Hung. XIX. (Schwandtner Rer. Hung. Scriptt, p. 377). In 1367 we find the people of Cattaro appealing to Urban V. for aid against the schismatics of Albania, and the heretics of Bosnia who were endeavoring to convert them by force (Theiner, op. cit. I. 259), which probably refers to some enterprise of the restless Sandalj Hranić. Yet when, in 1383, we hear of a Bishop of Bosnia, recently dead, who had lent 12,000 florins to Louis of Hungary, and had then bequeathed the debt to the Holy See (Ib. p. 337), we can only conclude that the orthodox Bosnian Church continued to exist and was not wholly penniless.

[341] Klaić, pp. 275, 287-8, 291, 297-8, 304-5, 312-13, 324.

[342] Klaić, p. 416.

[343] Ibid. pp. 335-8, 344-6, 351-3.

[344] Wadding, ann. 1433, No. 12-13; ann. 1435, No. 1-7, 9; ann. 1476, No. 39-40; ann. 1498. No. 2.-- Ægid. Carlerii Lib. de Legationibus (Monument. Concil. General. Sæc. XV. T. I. p. 676).

[345] Theiner Monument. Slavor. Merid. I. 375, 376.--Klaić, pp. 354-6, 364-5, 369.

[346] Klaić, pp. 366-7, 369-70, 372-3.--Wadding, ann. 1437, No. 2-3; ann. 1444, No. 42-3.--Ripoll III. 91.- -Raynald. ann. 1444, No. 2; ann. 1445, No. 23: ann. 1447, No. 21.--Theiner, op. cit. I. 388, 389, 395.

[347] Klaić, pp. 373-4.--Raynald. ann. 1449, No. 9.

[348] Klaić, pp. 376-77, 379.--Raynald. ann. 1449, No. 9; ann. 1450, No. 13; ann. 1461, No. 136.-- Wadding. ann. 1451, No. 47, 52-3.--Ripoll III. 286.

[349] Theiner, op. cit. I. 408.--Klaic, pp. 380-2.

[350] Klaić, pp. 398, 408-9, 412, 414-15.--Theiner, I. 432.

[351] Klaić, pp. 424-6.

[352] Klaić, pp. 427-8, 432-6.--Wadding. ann. 1462, No. 82.

[353] Klaić, pp. 437-9, 443.--Wadding. ann. 1478, No. 67; ann. 1498, No. 2-3; ann. 1500, No. 44. There was at least one humorous incident connected with the conquest of Bosnia. On the occupation by the Turks of the capital, Jaicza, the Franciscans fled to Venice, carrying with them the body of St. Luke, which had been translated thither from Constantinople. The possession of so important a relic brought them great consideration, but involved them in a troublesome contest. For three hundred years the Benedictine house of St. Justina at Padua had rejoiced in owning the body of St. Luke, which was the source of much profit. The Benedictines objected to the intrusion of the döppelganger; and as no trustworthy tradition assigned two bodies to the saint, there was no chance of compromise. They appealed to Pius II., who referred the case with full powers of decision to his legate at Venice, Cardinal Bessarion. A trial in all legal form was held, lasting for three months and resulting in the victory of the Franciscans. The Paduan Luke, as an impostor, was forbidden to enjoy in future the devotion of the faithful, but no provision was made to compensate those who for three centuries had wasted on him their prayers and offerings, in the belief that they were securing the suffrages of the genuine Evangelist. The Paduans for years vainly endeavored to get Bessarion's decision set aside, and they were finally obliged to submit. Their strongest argument was that, about the year 580, the Emperor Tiberius II. had given to St. Gregory, then apocrisarius of Pelagius II. in Constantinople, the head of St. Luke, which was still exhibited and venerated in the Basilica of the Vatican. Now the Benedictine St. Luke was a headless trunk, while the Franciscan one was perfect, and they argued with reason that it was highly improbable that St. Luke had possessed two heads. This logic was more cogent than successful, though the Vatican clergy did not feel called upon to discredit their own valuable relic, which they continued to exhibit as genuine. The question was still further complicated by a superfluous arm of the Evangelist which was preserved in the Basilica of S. Maria ad Præsepe (Wadding. ann. 1463, No. 13-23).

[354] Kaltner, Konrad von Marburg, Prag, 1882, pp. 41-5.--Frag. Hist. (Urstisii Scriptt. P.II. p. 89).-- Chronik des Jacob v. Königshofen (Chroniken der deutchen Städte, IX. 649).--Trithem. Chron. Hirsaug. ann. 1215.--H. Mutii Chron. Lib. XIX. ann. 1212.--Innoc. PP. III. Regest. XIV. 138.--Cæsar. Heisterb. Dist. III. cap. 16, 17. On the authority of Daniel Specklin, a Strassburg annalist who died in 1589, Bishop Henry is said to have met St. Dominic in Rome, to have promised him and Innocent III. to introduce the Dominican Order in Strassburg, and to have taken some members home with him, who speedily multiplied to about a hundred, and distinguished themselves by the persecution related in the text (Kaltner, loc. cit.; cf. Hoffman. Geschichte der Inquisition II. 365-71). At this period, as we have seen in a former chapter, Dominic was laboring obscurely in Languedoc, and it was not until 1214 that the liberality of Pierre Cella suggested to him the idea of assembling around him in Toulouse half a dozen kindred spirits. It was not until 1224 that the Dominican convent in Strassburg was founded (Kaltner, p. 45).

[355] Kaltner, p. 45.--Hoffmann, II. 371-2.--Trithem. Chron. Hirsaug. ann. 1215.

[356] Innoc. PP. III. Regest. II. 141, 142, 235.--Alberic. Trium Font. ann. 1200.--Cæsar. Heisterb. Dist. V. c. 20.

[357] Kaltner, op. cit. pp. 69-71.--I am rather inclined to believe that honest Daniel Specklin has drawn to some extent upon his own convictions for this list of errors. Among them he enumerates lay communion in both elements. As the cup at this time had not been withdrawn from the laity, its administration would not have been characterized as a heresy.

[358] Tocco, L'Heresia nel Medio Evo, p. 21.--D'Argentré, Collect. Judic. I. I. 127.--Cæsar. Heisterbac. v. 22.--Nich. Trivetti Chron. ann. 1215 (D'Achery Spicileg. III. 185.)--Rigord. de Gest. Phil. Aug. ann. 1210.--Guillel. Nangiac. ann. 1210.--Eymeric. Direct. Inquis. P. II. Q. vii.--Cf. Renan, Averroès et l'Averroïsme, 3d Ed. pp. 220-4.

[359] Cæsar. Heisterb. VI. 5.

[360] Rigordus de Gest. Phil. Aug. ann. 1210.--Chron. Canon Laudunens. ann. 1212.--Chron. de Mailros ann. 1210.--Chron. Turonens. ann. 1210.--Cæsar. Heisterb. V. 22.--Chron. Breve S. Dionys. ann. 1209.--Grandes Chroniques, IV. 139.--Guillel. Brito (Bouquet XVII. 82 sqq.).--D'Argentré, Coll. Judic. I. I. 128-33.--Harduin. Concil. VI. II. 1994.--Chron. Engelbusii (Leibnitz, S. Rer. Brunsv. II. 1113). William the goldsmith, under the title of Gulielmus Aurifex, retains his place in the Index Librorum Prohibitorum to the present day (Migne, Dictionnaire des Hérésies, II. 1056). Cf. Reusch, Der Index der verbotenen Bücher. I. 17.

[361] Steph. de Borbone (D'Argentré I. I. 88).--Potthast No. 7348.--Pelayo, Heterodoxos Españoles, I. 410,--Concil. Lateran. IV. c. 2. For the connection between the speculations of Erigena and those of Amauri see Poole's "Illustrations of the History of Medieval Thought," London, 1884, p. 77.

[362] Anon. Passaviens. c. 6 (Mag. Bib. Pat. XIII. 300-2).--Kaltner, pp. 64-5.--Haupt, Zeitschrift für Kirchengeschichte, 1885, p. 507.

[363] Kaltner, pp. 90-5.--Hartzheim Concil. German. III. 515-16.--Potthast No. 7260.--Chron. Mont. Sereni ann. 1222 (Menken. Scriptt. Rer. Germ. II. 265).--Chron. Sanpetrin. Erfurt, ann. 1222 (Ib. III. 250).

[364] Conrad of Marburg was too shining a light not to be earnestly and persistently claimed by the Dominicans as an ornament of their Order. Their legend relates that he was miraculously drawn into it in 1220 by St. Dominic himself, who earnestly desired him as a colleague, and who promptly sent him to Germany with a commission as inquisitor (Monteiro, Historia da Sacra Inquisição, P. I. Liv. i. c. 48.--Jac. de Voragine Legend. Aur. fol. 90a, Ed. 1480.--Paramo, pp. 248-9), and Ripoll assumes it as a matter of course, though he failed to furnish us with the promised dissertation to prove it (Bull. Domin. I. 20, 52). See also Kaltner, pp. 76-82. The claim is based upon his inquisitorial activity, his voluntary poverty, and the title of *prædicator*, which he bore in virtue of a papal commission--arguments flimsy enough, but better than that of his latest champion, Hausrath, who cites an expression in a letter of Gregory IX. characterizing Conrad as the watch-dog of the Lord--"*Dominicus canis*" (Hoffman, Geschichte d. Inq,. II. 392). Of course a negative, such as the present, can only be proved by negatives, but these are sufficient. In numerous letters to him from Honorius III. and Gregory IX. he is never addressed as "*Frater*," the term invariably used by the Mendicants. The superscription always is "*Magistro Conrado de Marburo prædicatori Verbi Dei*, or the equivalent--Conrad being presumably a master in theology (Epistt. Sæc. XIII. T. I. No. 51, 117, 118, 126, 361, 362, 484, 533, 537). Similarly in the chronicles of the time he is never spoken of as "*Frater*," but always as "*Magister Conradus*." Besides, Theodoric of Thuringia, himself a Dominican, and almost a contemporary, in his life of St. Elizabeth describes Conrad in the most exalted terms, without claiming him for his Order, which he could not have avoided doing had there been ground for it (Canisii Thesaur. IV. 116).

[365] Theod. Thuring, de S. Eliz. Lib. III. c. 10 (Canisii Thesaur. IV. 130).--Potthast No. 7930.--Epistt. Sæc. XIII. T. I. No. 361.

[366] Kaltner, pp. 96, 121.--De Dictis IV. Ancillarum (Menken. Scriptt. Rer. Germ. II. 2017, 2023, 2029)--Theodor. Vit. S. Eliz. (Ib. 2000-1).--Jundt, Les Amis de Dieu, p. 95

[367] Trithem. Chron. Hirsaug. ann. 1214.--Chron. Sanpetrin. Erfurtens. (Menken. III. 242).--Kaltner, pp. 86-7.--Epistt. Sæcul. XIII. T. I. No. 117, 118, 126, 362.

[368] Hartzheim III. 521. Cf. Concil. Frizlar. ann. 1246, ib. p. 574.--Ripoll I. 21.

[369] Vit. S. Eliz. (Canisii Thesaur. I. 116).--Johann Rohte, Chron. Thuring. (Menken. II. 1715).--Kaltner, pp. 108, 130-33.--Gesta Treviror. Episcopp. c. 172.--Trithem. Chron. Hirsaug. ann. 1230.

[370] Hartzheim III. 539, 540.--Potthast No. 8073-4.--Hist. Diplom. Frid. II. T. III. p. 466.--Gest. Treviror. Archiepp. c. 170. 172.

[371] Kaltner, pp. 135-6, 143.--Theod. Vit. S. Eliz. VII. 1.--Vit. rythmic. S. Eliz. (Menken. II. 2090).--Thür. Fortsetzung d. Sächs. Weltchronik (Pertz, Scriptt. Vernac. II. 292).--Trithem. Chron. Hirsaug. ann. 1232.--Erphurdian. Variloq. (Menken. II. 484).

[372] Kaltner. p. 134.--Hist. Diplom. Frid. II. T. IV. pp. 300-2.

[373] Annal. Wormatiens. (Hist. Diplom. Frid. II. T. IV. p. 616).--Kaltner, p. 138.--Sächsiche Weltchronik ann. 1232.--Gest. Treviror. Archiepp. c. 170.

[374] Pauli Carnotens. Vet. Aganon. Lib. VI. c. 3.--Adhemar. Cabannens. ann. 1022 (Bouquet, X. 159).--Gualteri Mapes de Nugis Curialium Dist. I. c. XXX.

[375] Raynald. ann. 1233, No. 41-6.--Epistt. Sæcul. XIII. T. I. No. 533, 537.--Gest. Treviror. Archiepp. c. 171.

[376] Alberic Trium Font. ann. 1234.--Godefrid S. Pantaleon. annal. ann. 1233. It would seem from this that Henry, Archbishop of Cologne, was performing his functions at this period, although he had been suspended by Gregory IX. in December, 1231, pending an investigation into his criminal turpitude, which the pope declared to be a shame to describe and a horror to hear. In April, 1233, Gregory tried to make him resign, to which he responded in June by an appeal to the Holy See. The immediate consequence of this was a papal

levy on the clergy of Cologne of three hundred sterling marks to defray expenses. In March of the next year further provision for the expenses was requisite. In April, 1235, we find him still under excommunication and deprived of his functions. After this he seems to have re-established himself, and in March, 1238, he was condemned to pay thirteen hundred sterling marks to a Roman banker for expenses incurred many years before by his predecessor. In May, 1239, we find his successor, Conrad von Hochstaden, in Rome as archbishop-elect, and Gregory ordering a levy of eight thousand marks on the province to pay the debts due there by the see (Epistt. Select. Sæcul. XIII. T. I. No. 457, 472, 523, 529-30, 555, 579, 637, 723, 748). This serves to illustrate the relations between the Roman curia and the great German bishoprics, the insatiable greed of the former, and the fruitless efforts at emancipation of the latter.

[377] Hist. Diplom. Frid. II. T. IV. pp. 285-7, 300-2.

[378] Annal. Wormatiens. (Hist. Dip. Frid. II. T. IV. pp. 616-17).--Kaltner, pp. 19, 146-8.--Epistt. Select. Sæc. XIII. No. 514.

[379] Gest. Treviror. Archiepp. c. 174.--Sächsische Weltchronik, ann. 1233 (Pertz, II. 292).--Annal. Wormatiens. (loc. cit.).--Godefrid. S. Pantaleon. Annal. ann. 1233.

[380] Sächsische Weltchronik, loc. cit.--Gest. Treviror. loc. cit--Alberic. Trium Font. ann. 1233.--Erphurdian. Variloq. ann. 1233.--Chron. Erfordiens. ann. 1233 (Schannat Vindem. Literar. I. 93).--Trithem. Chron. Hirsaug. ann. 1233.--Kaltner, pp. 160-1.

[381] Alberic. Trium Font. ann. 1233.--Alban Butler, Vies des Saints, 19 Nov^bre.

[382] Gest. Treviror. c. 174.--Hartzheim III. 549.

[383] Epistt. Select. Sæcul. XIII. T. I. No. 533, 537, 558, 560-1.--Chron. Erfordiens. ann. 1234 (Schannat Vindem. Literar. I. 94).

[384] Epistt. Select. Sæcul. XIII. T. I. No. 503, 572.--Chron. Erfordiens. (Schannat Vindem. Literar. I. 94).--Alberic. Trium Font. ann. 1234.--Gest. Treviror. c. 175.

[385] Alberic. Trium Font. ann. 1233.

[386] Alberic. Trium Font. ann. 1233.--Epistt. Select. Sæcul. XIII. T. I. No. 607, 611-12, 636, 647. There would appear not to be ground for the story told by Philippe Mousket (Chronique Rimée, 28831-42.--Bouquet, XXII. 55) that Gregory sent a cardinal Otho to Germany, who proceeded to degrade sundry ecclesiastics concerned in the matter, and raised such a tempest that he was obliged to escape by night to Tournay, and thence return to Rome. Even if baseless, however, the very circulation of such a report shows the antagonism excited between Rome and Germany.

[387] Kaltner, p. 173.--Annal Wormatiens. (Hist. Diplom. Frid. II. T. IV. p. 617).

[388] Tritbem. Chron. Hirsaug. ann. 1232.--Erphurdian. Variloq. ann. 1232 (Menken. II. 484).--Chron. Sanpetrin. Erfurt. (Ib. III. 254).--Anon. Saxon. Hist. Impp. (Ib. III. 125).--Chron. Erfordiens. ann. 1232 (Schannut Vindem. Literar. I. 92).

[389] Kaltner, pp. 171, 173.--Annal. Dominican. Colmar. ann. 1233 (Urstisii Germ. Hist. II. 6).--Potthast No. 13000, 15995.--Albert. Statdens. Chron. ann. 1248.

[390] Anon. Passaviens. contra Waldens. c. 3, 6, 9, 10 (Mag. Bib. Pat. XIII. 299, 301-2, 308-9).--W. Preger, Beiträge, pp. 9, 49.--Ejusd. Per Tractat des David von Augsburg.

[391] Concil. Mogunt. ann. 1261 c. 1 (Hartzheim III. 596).--Cod. Epist. Rodolph. I. pp. 148-9, Lipsiæ, 1806.

[392] Sachsenspiegel, II. iii., III. i.--Raynald. ann. 1374, No. 12. The papal condemnation was probably elicited by a passage in the Sachsenspiegel (II. 3) declaring that the pope could not issue decretals in prejudice of the local laws and constitutions. The Saxon legists were in no wise disconcerted, and proceeded to reassert and prove their position (Richstich Lnndrecht, II. 24).

[393] Schwabenspiegel, Ed. Senck. c. 29, 116 § 12, 351; Ed. Schilt. c. 111, 166, 308.

[394] Hist. Monast. S. Laurent. Leodiens. Lib. V. c. 54.--Mag. Chron. Belgic. p. 193.--Mosheim de Beghardis, Lipsiae, 1790, pp. 98-100, 114. In popular use the words Lollard and Beghard were virtually convertible, and yet there is a difference between them. The associations of Lollards were founded during a pestilence at Antwerp about the year 1300. They were laymen who devoted themselves to the care of the sick and insane, and specially to the burial of the dead, supplying the funds partly by labor and partly by begging. The name was derived from the low and soft singing of the funeral chants, but they called themselves Alexians, from their patron, St. Alexis, and Cellites from dwelling in cells. They were also known as Matemans, and in Germany as Nollbrüder. The word Lollard gradually grew to have the significance of external sanctity covering secret license, and was promiscuously applied to all the mendicants outside of the regular Orders. The Cellite associations spread from the Netherlands through the Rhinelands and all over Germany. Constantly the subject of persecution, along with the Beghards, their value was recognized by the magistrates of the cities who endeavored to protect them. In 1472 Charles the Bold obtained from Sixtus IV. a bull receiving them into the recognized religious orders, thus withdrawing them from episcopal jurisdiction; and in 1506 Julius II. granted them special privileges. The associations of Alexian Brothers still exist, devoted to the care of the sick, and have flourishing hospitals in the United States, as well as in Europe. (Mosheim de Beghardis pp. 461, 469.--Martini Append. ad Mosheim pp. 585-88.--Hartzheim IV. 625-6.--Addis & Arnold's Catholic Dictionary, New York, 1884, p. 886.)

[395] Miræi Opp. Diplom. II. 948 (Ed. Foppens).--D'Argentré, Coll. Judic. I. I.

[396] Miræi Opp. Diplom. I. 429; II. 998, 1013; III. 398, 523.--Mosheim de Beghardis pp. 43, 105, 127, 131-2.--Wadding, ann. 1485, No. 27.--B. de Jonghe Beigium Dominican, ap. Ripoll II. 170.--Chron. Rimée de Ph. Mousket, 28817 (Bouquet. XXII. 54).

[397] Chron. Senonens. Lib. IV. c. 18 (D'Achery II. 634-6). The cry of *"Brod durch Gott*was already of old usage. It was the first German speech acquired by the Franciscans sent to Germany, in 1221, by St. Francis.-- Frat. Jordani Chron. c. 27 (Analecta Franciscana I. 10).

[398] Haupt, Zeitschrift für Kirchengeschichte, 1885, p. 544.--Hartzheim III. 717; IV. 577.--Concil. Trevirens. ann. 1257 c. 66 (Martene Ampl. Coll. VII. 114-5).--Mosheim p. 199.

[399] C. 3 Clement. V. 3.--Johann. de Ochsenstein (or of Zurich) (Mosheim de Beghardis pp. 255-61).-- Concil. Colon. ann. 1306 c. 1, 2 (Hartzheim IV. 100-2).--Vitodurani Chron. ann. 1344 (Eccard. Corp. Hist. I. 1906-7).--Alvar. Pelag. de Planctu Eccles. Lib. II. art. 52.--Conr. de Monte Puellarum contra Begehardos (Mag. Bib. Pat. XIII. 342-3).--Trithem. Chron. Hirsaug. ann. 1356.--D'Argentré, Coll. Judic. I. I. 377.--Nider Formicar. III. v.--W. Preger, Meister Eckart u. d. Inquisition, pp. 45-7.--Haupt, Zeitschrift für Kirchengeschichte, 1885, 557-8.

[400] Nider. Formicar. III. vi.--Concil. Colon, ann. 1306 c. 1 (Hartzheim IV. 101).--Trithem. Chron. Hirsaug. ann. 1356. Poggio states that in his time a number of ecclesiastics in Venice corrupted many women with this theory of impeccability and of nakedness as an evidence of a state of grace.--Poggii Dial. contra Hypocrisim.

[401] Trithem. Chron. Hirsaug. ann. 1315.--Schrödl, Passavia Sacra, Passau, 1879, pp. 242-3, 247, 284.

[402] Altmeyer, Les Précurseurs de la Réforme aux Pays-Bas, I. 94.--Raynald. ann. 1329, No. 71. For the relations of Master Eckart with the Brethren of the Free Spirit, see Preger, Vorarbeiten zu einer Geschichte der deutschen Mystik (Zeitschrift für die hist. Theol. 1869. pp. 68-78). The fact that the bull of John XXII., *"In agro Dominico"* (Ripoll VII. 57; cf. Herman. Corneri Chron. *ap.* Eccard. Corp. Hist. II. 1036-7), condemning Master Eckart's errors, has until within a few years passed as a general bull against the Brethren, sufficiently shows the connection.

[403] Mosheim de Beghardis, pp. 305, 433-57.--Jundt, Les Amis de Dieu, pp. 65-66.--Gersoni Opp. Ed. 1494, xv. Z-xvi.B.--D'Argentré, Coll. Judic. I. II. 152.--Altmeyer, Les Précurseurs de la Réforme aux Pays-Bas, I. 107-117, 166-188.--Acquoy, Gerardi Magni Epistolæ, Amstelod. 1857, pp. 28, 32-5, 37-8, 40-2, 48-9, 52-4, 57-60, 69, 83, 101.--Von der Hardt, III. 107-20.--Bonet-Maury, Gérard Groot, pp. 37-8, 49-54, 62-4, 83-5.

[404] J. Tauleri Institt. c. 12.--Vitæ D. Johannis Tauleri Historia. It is no wonder that Tauler's writings have been the subject of contradictory opinion and action on the part of the Church. Their tendencies to Illuminism and Quietism were recognized, and, in 1603, the Congregation of the Index proposed to prepare an expurgated edition of his works and of those of Savonarola, but the project was never executed.--Reusch, Der Index der verbotenen Bücher, I. 370, 469, 523, 589.

[405] Vitæ Tauleri Historia. M. Jundt, as the result of a series of elaborate and ingenious investigations, feels himself authorized to assume that the mysterious Friend of God in the Oberland, who has given rise to so much discussion, was John of Rutberg; that he was a resident of Coire, and that his final hermitage was in the parish of Ganterschwyl, Canton of St. Gall (Jundt, Amis de Dieu, Paris, 1879, pp. 334-42). Prof. Ch. Schmidt, however, still considers that the mystery has not been solved.--Précis de l'Histoire de l'Église de l'Occident, Paris, 1885, p. 304.

[406] Jundt, pp. 37-9, 60-2, 83, 106-7, 166, 313.

[407] See Rénan, Averroès et l'Averroïsme, 3ᵉ Éd. pp. 95, 144-6.

[408] Jundt, pp. 143, 164, 308-9, 312-13, 316-17.

[409] Mosheim de Beghardis p. 256.--Jundt, pp. 13, 42-3, 147, 155-60, 282-7, 347.--Nider Formicar. III. 2.--Gerson. de Exam. Doctrinarum P. II. Consid. 3. There is nothing improbable in the freedom of speech attributed to the Friends of God in their interview with Gregory. Apocalyptic inspiration was common at the period, and St. Birgitta of Sweden, and St. Catharine of Siena, were not particularly reticent in their language to the successors of St. Peter.

[410] Raynald. ann. 1296, No. 34.--Annal. Domin. Colmar. ann. 1290 (Urstisii Germ. Histor. II. 25).-- Hartzheim IV. 54, 201.

[411] Concil. Colon, ann. 1306, c. 1, 2 (Hartzheim IV. 100-2).--Wadding, ann. 1305, No. 12.--Mosheim de Beghardis pp. 232-4.

[412] Concil. Trevirens. ann. 1310 c. 51 (Martene Thesaur. IV. 250).--Hocsemii Gest. Pontif. Lend. Lib. I. c. 31 (Chapeaville, II. 350).

[413] C. 3, Clement. V. iii.; C. 1, III. xi.

[414] Mosheim de Beghardis, pp. 255-61, 268-9.--Haupt, Zeitschrift für K.G. 1885, pp. 561-4. Many of the decrees of the Council of Vienne were circulated at the time, but Clement, desiring a revision, ordered them to be destroyed or surrendered. After recasting them, they were adopted by a consistory held March 21, 1314, and copies were sent to some of the universities; but Clement's death, on April 20, caused new delay. John XXII. subjected them to another revision, and they were finally published October 25, 1317.--Franz Ehrle, Archiv für Litteratur-u. Kirchengeschichte, 1885, pp. 541-2. The contradictory character of the provisions

concerning the Beguines is doubtless attributable to these repeated revisions. The manner in which John of Zurich obtained the bishopric of Strassburg is highly illustrative of the methods of the papal curia. On the death of Bishop Frederic, the chapter divided and elected four aspirants, among whom was John of Ochsenstein, a favorite of the Emperor Albert, who, to secure his confirmation, sent to Clement V. his chancellor, John of Zurich, Bishop of Eichstedt, and the Abbot of Pairis. The envoys returned bringing papal briefs, one appointing the chancellor to the contested see, and another filling that of Eichstedt with the abbot.--Closener's Chronik (Chron. der deutschen Städte, VIII. 91).

[415] Guill. Nangiac. Contin. ann. 1317.--Ripoll II. 169.--Wadding, ann. 1319, No. 11; Ejusd. Regest. Johann. PP. XXII. No. 81.--Vitodurani Chron. ann. 1317 (Eccard. Corp. Hist. I. 1785-6).--Chron. Sanpetrin. Erfurt, ann. 1315 (Menken. III. 325).--Chron. Magdeburgens. ann. 1317 (Meibom. Rer. German. II. 337).--Chron. Egmondan. ann. 1317 (Matthæi Analect. IV. 161).--Mosheim de Beghardis, pp. 251, 269.

[416] Mosheim, pp. 189-90.--Martini Append. ad Mosheim, pp. 630-2, 638-40.--C. 1 Extrav. Commun. III. 9.--Ripoll II. 169-70.--Haupt, Zeitschrift für K. G. 1885, pp. 517, 524.

[417] Trithem. Chron. Hirsaug. ann. 1322.

[418] Gesta Treviror. ann. 1323 (Martene Ampl. Coll. IV. 410).--Chron. Egmondan. (Matthæi Analect. IV. 233-4)--Vitodurani Chron. (Eccard. Corp. Histor. I. 1814-15).

[419] Hartzheim IV. 436, 438.

[420] Mosheim de Beghardis, pp. 272, 298-300.--Martini Append. ad Mosheim, p. 537.--Haupt, Zeitschrift für K. G. 1885, p. 534.--Chron. de S. Thiebaut de Metz (Calmet, II. Pr. clxxi.).--Erphurdian. Variloq. ann. 1350 (Menken. II. 507).

[421] Vitodurani Chron. (Eccard. Corp. Hist. I. 1833-4, 1839-40).--Dalham Concil. Salisburg. p. 157.

[422] Vitodurani Chron. (Eccard. I. 1906-7, 1767-8).--Ullman, Reformers before the Reformation, Menzies' Translation, I. 383.

[423] Conrad, de Monte Puellar. contra Begehardos (Mag. Bib. Pat. XIII. 342).--Mosheim de Beghardis p. 307.

[424] Carl Müller, Der Kampf Ludwigs des Baiern mit der römischen Curie, Tubingen, 1879, I. 234 sqq. When that bold thinker, Marsiglio of Padua, endeavored, for the benefit of his patron, the Emperor Louis, to introduce into Germany the principles of the Roman jurisprudence which had enabled the French monarchs to triumph over their feudatories and to become independent of the Church, he handled the subject of the persecution of heresy in a manner which has led some writers to regard him as an advocate of toleration. This is an error. It is true that he denies all Scriptural or apostolical authority for the temporal punishment of infractions of the divine law, and asserts that Christ alone is the judge thereof, and his punishments are reserved for the next world, but this is only to serve as a premise to his conclusion that the persecution of heresy is a matter of human law, to be ordained and enforced by the secular ruler. Though the heretic, he argues, sins against the divine law, he is punished for transgressing a human law; the priest has nothing to do with it, except as an expert to determine the commission of the crime, and has no claim upon the consequent confiscations (Defensor. Pacis P. II. c. ix., x.; P. III. c. ii. Conclus. 3, 30). All this is simply part of his general scheme to exclude the Church from control in secular affairs. Louis was never in a position to give these theories practical effect; they had no influence either on the current of opinion or on the course of events, and are only interesting as an episode in the development of political thought.

[425] Werunsky Excerpta ex Registris Clement. VI. et Innoc. VI., Innsbruck, 1885, pp. 8, 40, 63.--Schmidt, Päbstliche Urkunden und Regesten, Halle, 1886, p. 383.

[426] Boccaccio, Decamerone, Giorn. I--Alberti Argentinens. Chron, ann. 1348-9 (Urstisius, II. 147).--Trithem. Chron. Hirsaug. ann. 1248.--Aventinus, Annal. Boiorum Lib.VII. c. 20.--Grandes Chroniques V. 485-6.--Guillel. Nangiac. Contin. ann. 1348-9.--Froissart, Lib. I. P. ii. ch. 5.--Meyeri Annal. Flandr. ann. 1349.--Henrici Rebdorff. Chron. ann. 1347.--Alberti Argent. de Gestis Bertold. (Urstisius, II. 177).--Mascaro, Memorias de Bezes, ann. 1348.--Gesta Treviror. ann. 1349.--Chron. Cornel. Zantfliet (Martene Ampl. Coll. V. 253-4).--Erphurd. Variloq. ann. 1348-9 (Menken. II. 506-7). Accusations such as were brought against the Jews were no new thing. In 1321 all the lepers throughout Languedoc were burned on the charge that they had been bribed by the Jews to poison the wells. Doubtless torture was employed to obtain the confessions which were freely made. The story went that the King of Granada, finding himself hard pressed by the Christians, gave great sums to leading Jews to effect in this way the desolation of Christendom. The Jews, fearing that they would be suspected, employed the lepers. Four great councils of lepers were held in various parts of Europe, where every lazar-house was represented except two in England; there the attempt was resolved upon, and the poison was distributed. King Philippe le Long was in Poitou at the time; when the news was brought him he returned precipitately to Paris, whence he issued orders for the seizure of all the lepers of the kingdom. Numbers of them were burned, as well as Jews. At the royal castle of Chinon, near Tours, an immense trench was dug, and filled with blazing wood, where, in a single day, one hundred and sixty Jews were burned. Many of them, of either sex, sang gayly as though going to a wedding, and leaped into the flames, while mothers cast in their children for fear that they would be taken and baptized by the Christians present. The royal treasury is said to have acquired one hundred and fifty thousand livres from the property of Jews burned and exiled.--Guillel. Nangiac. Contin. ann. 1321.--Grandes Chroniques V. 245-51.--Chron. Cornel. Zantfliet. ann. 1321.

[427] Amalr. Augerii Hist. Pontif. Roman. ann. 1320 Muratori, S. R. I. III. II. 475.--Johann. S. Victor. Chron. ann. 1320 (Ib. p. 485).--Chron. Anon. ann. 1330 (Ib. p. 499).--Pet. de Herentals ann. 1320 (Ib. p. 500).-- Guillel. Nangiac. Contin. ann. 1320.--Grandes Chroniques, V. 245-6.--Cronaca di Firenze ann. 1335 (Baluz. et Mansi IV. 114).--Villani, Lib. XI. c. 23.--Lami, Antichità Toscane, p. 617. Venturino was acquitted of the charge of heresy, but his free speech offended the pope; he was forbidden to preach or hear confessions, and was sentenced to live in retirement at Frisacca, in the mountains of Ricondona (Villani l. c.). He died in 1346, at Smyrna, whither he had gone as a missionary. He had preached with wonderful success in all the countries of Europe, including Spain, England, and Greece. His face, when preaching, shone with celestial light, and his miracles were numerous (Raynald. ann. 1346, No. 70).

[428] Erphurdian. Variloq. ann. 1349.--Chron. Magdeburgens. ann. 1348 (Meibom. Rer. German. II. 342).--Alberti Argentinens. Chron. ann. 1349.--Closener's Chronik (Chron. der deutschen Städte, VIII. 105 sqq.).--Trithem. Chron. Hirsaug. ann. 1348--Hermann. Corneri Chron. ann. 1350.--Guillel. Nangiac. Contin. ann. 1349.--Grandes Chroniques, V. 492-3.--Froissart, Liv. I. P. II. ch. 5.--Gesta Treviror. ann. 1349.--Meyeri Annal. Flandriæ ann. 1349.--Chron. Ægid. Li Muisis (De Smet, Corp. Chron. Flandr. II. 349-51).--Henr. Rebdorff. Annal. ann. 1347.

[429] Alberti Argentinens. Chron. ann. 1349.--Trithem. Chron. Hirsaug. ann. 1348.

[430] Von der Hardt. T. III. pp. 95-105.

[431] Trithem. Chron. Hirsaug. ann. 1348.--Hartzheim IV. 471-2.--Meyeri Ann. Flandr. ann. 1349.

[432] Raynald, ann. 1353, No. 26, 27.--Trithem. Chron. Hirsaug. ann. 1356.--Naucleri Chron. ann. 1356.-- Hartzheim IV. 483.

[433] Mosheim de Beghardis, pp. 333-4.

[434] Mosheim de Beghardis, pp. 335-7.--Chron. Magdeburg. (Leibnitii Scriptt. R. Brunsv. III. 749).-- Herm. Korneri Chron. (Eccard. II. 1113).--Cat. Prædic. Prov. Saxon. (Martene Ampl. Coll. VI. 344).--Böhmer, Regest. Karl IV. No. 4761.

[435] Mosheim de Beghardis pp. 343-55.

[436] Mosheim de Beghardis pp. 356-62.--Mosheim suggests that the distinction between the houses of the Beghards and the Beguines probably arose from the former being larger and situated in the cities, the latter smaller, more numerous, and scattered among the towns and villages.

[437] Chron. Magdeburg. (Leibnitii S. R. Brunsv. III. 749).--Herm. Corneri Chron. (Eccard. Corp. Hist. III. 1113-4).--Raynald. ann. 1372, No. 34.--Ripoll II. 275.--Mosheim de Beghardis pp. 380-3.

[438] Mosheim de Beghardis pp. 368-74, 378-9.--Böhmer, Regest. Karl. IV. No. 4761.

[439] Mosheim de Beghardis pp. 364-66.--Martini Append. ad Mosheim pp. 541-2.

[440] Cat. Prædic. Prov. Saxon. (Martene Ampl. Coll. VI. 344).--Raynald. ann. 1372, No. 33, 34.-- Mosheim de Beghardis pp. 388-92.--Martini Append. ad Mosheim pp. 647-8.

[441] Martene Thesaur. II. 960-1.--Chron. Cornel. Zantfliet (Martene Ampl. Coll. V. 293, 301-2).-- Raynald. ann. 1372, No. 33.--Meyeri Annal. Flandriæ ann. 1373.--Mag. Chron. Belgic. ann. 1374.--Trithem. Chron. Hirsaug. ann. 1374.--P. de Herentals Vit. Gregor. XI. ann. 1375 (Muratori S. R. I. III. ii. 674-5).

[442] Mosheim de Beghardis pp. 394-8.--Haupt, Zeitschrift für K.G. 1885, pp. 525-6, 553-4, 563-4.-- Hæmmerlin Glosa quarumd. Bullar. per Beghardos impetratar. (Basil. 1497, c. 4 sqq.).

[443] Höfler, Prager Concilien, pp. 26-7.--Trithem. Chron. Hirsaug. ann. 1392.--Jundt, Les Amis de Dieu, p. 3.--Haupt, ubi sup. p. 510.

[444] There has recently been discovered at St. Florian, in Austria, an epistle written in 1368 by the Waldenses of Lombardy to some of their German brethren on the occasion of the withdrawal of certain members of the sect, who alleged in justification that the Waldenses were ignorant, that they had no divine authority, and that they were mercenary. Evidently the local church had appealed to the Lombards as to a central head, for an answer to these accusations, and the reply, together with a rejoinder by one of the apostates, throws valuable light upon the current beliefs of the sectaries. It appears that they carried their origin back to the primitive Church, claiming that their predecessors had opposed the reception of the Donation of Constantine, and that when Silvester refused to reject the perilous gift a voice sounded from heaven, "This day hath poison been spread in the Church of God." As they were unyielding, they were driven out and persecuted, since when they had preserved the genuine tradition of the Church in obscurity and affliction. They asserted that Peter Waldo had been ordained to the priesthood, and that they possessed full authority, transmitted from God, but nothing is said as to the apostolical succession, and the apostate, Sigfried, reproaches them with only hearing confessions and sending their disciples to the Catholic churches for the other sacraments. There is no word as to transubstantiation, which must therefore have been an accepted doctrine among them, and their frequent quotations from Augustine and Bernard show that they admitted the authority of the doctors of the Church. They allude to two Franciscans who had recently joined the sect, to a priest who had done so and had been burned, and to a Bishop Bestardi, who, for the same offence, had been summoned to Rome, whence he had never returned.--Comba, Histoire des Vaudois d'Italie, I. 243-55.

[445] Index Error. Waldens. (Mag. Bib. Pat. XIII. 340).--Petri Herp Annal. Francofurt. ann. 1389 (Senckenberg Select. Juris II. 19).--Gudeni Cod. Diplom. III. 598-600.--Serrarii Hist. Mogunt. Lib. v. p. 707.-- Hist. Ordin. Carthus. (Martene Ampl. Coll. VI. 214).--Modus examinandi Hsereticos (Mag. Bib. Pat. XIII. 341-

2). John Wasmod subsequently wrote a tract against the Beghards which has been printed by Haupt (Zeitschrift fur Kirchengeschichte, 1885, pp. 567-76). Its chief interest lies in its attributing to the Beghards the tenets of the Waldenses. There is no allusion to pantheism, to union with God, to refusal of the sacraments, to the denial of hell and purgatory. Either he confounds the sects, or else the Waldenses concealed themselves under the guise of Beghards, or else there were among the Beghards a certain number who constituted a church separate from that of Rome without adopting the distinctive principles of Amaurianism. Wasmod tells us that they do not easily receive applicants, whose obedience they test by making them eat putrid flesh, drink water foul with maggots, etc., at the risk of their lives. One of their strongest arguments is found in the corruption of the Church, which is thus deprived of the power of the keys. Distinctively referable to Beghardism is the assertion that these heretics are greatly favored and defended by the magistrates of the cities; and not very flattering to Rome is the explanation that the bulls in favor of the Beguines were obtained by the use of money.

[446] Gretseri Prolegom. c. 6 (Mag. Bib. Pat. XIII. 292).--Refutat. Waldens. (Ib. p. 335).--P. de Pilichdorf. c. 15 (Ib. p. 315).--Wattenbach, Sitzungsberichte der Preuss. Akad. 1886, pp. 49-9, 51.

[447] Wattenbach, op. cit. pp. 49-50, 54-55.--Flac. Illyr. Cat. Test. Veritatis Lib. XV. pp. 1506, 1524; Lib. XVIII. p. 1803 (Ed. 1608).

[448] W. Preger, Beiträge, pp. 51, 53-4, 68, 72.--P. de Pilichdorf c. 15 (Mag. Bib. Pat. XIII. 315).

[449] Hoffmann, Geschichte der Inquisition, II. 384-90.--C. Schmidt, Real-Encyklop. s.V. Winkeler.

[450] Martini Append, ad Mosheim pp. 652-66, 674-5.--Mosheim pp. 409-10, 430-1.--Hartzheim V. 676--Haupt. Zeitschrift für K. G. 1885, pp. 565-7.

[451] Mosheim de Beghardis pp. 225-8, 383-4.--Martini Append, ad Mosheim pp. 656-7.--Herm. Corneri Chron. ann. 1402-3 (Eccard. Corp. Hist. II. 1185-6).--Raynald. ann. 1403, No. 23.

[452] Chron. Cornel. Zantfliet ann. 1400 (Martene Amplis. Coll. V. 358.)--Haupt. Zeitschrift für K. G. 1885, pp. 513-15.--Chron. Glassberger ann. 1410 (Analecta Franciscana II. 233-5).--Martini Append. ad Mosheim p. 559.--Mosheim p. 455.--Serrarii Lib. V. (Scriptt. Rer. Mogunt. I. 724). In 1399 an outbreak very similar to that of the Flagellants took place in Italy, stimulated by a pestilence which was ravaging the land. The pilgrims were known as *Bianchi*, from the white linen vestments which they wore, and they first brought to popular notice the "Stabat Mater," which was their favorite hymn. The only reference to flagellation, however, is that in Genoa they were joined by the old fraternities of the Verberati or guilds, founded in 1306, which publicly used the scourge. The Archbishop of Genoa and many of the Lombard bishops lent the movement their countenance; universal peace was proclaimed, enemies forgave each other, and even the strife of Guelf and Ghibelline for a moment was forgotten. When we are told that twenty-five thousand Modenese made the pilgrimage to Bologna, we can readily understand why suspicious rulers, such as Galeazzo Visconti and the Signory of Venice, forbade the entry of their states to such armies. Boniface IX. probably felt the same alarm when the movement reached Rome, and the whole population, including some of the cardinals, put on white garments and marched in procession through the neighboring towns. He caused one of the leaders to be seized at Aquapendente; the free use of torture brought a confession that the whole affair was a fraud, and the poor wretch was burned, when the movement collapsed.--Georgii Stella Annal. Genuens. ann. 1399 (Muratori, S. R. I. XVII. 1170).--Mattæi de Griffonibus Memor. Historial. ann. 1399 (Ib. XVIII. 207).--Cronica di Bologna ann. 1399 (Ib. XVIII. 565).--Annal. Estens. ann. 1398 (Ib. XVIII. 956-8).--Conrad Urspurgens. Chron. Contin. ann. 1399.--Theod. a Niem de Schismate, Lib. II. c. 26.

[453] Nider Formicar. Lib. III. c. 2.--Haupt, Zeitschrift für K. G. 1885, pp. 510-11.--Gersoni de Consolat. Theolog. Lib. IV. Prosa iii.; Ejusd. de Mystica Theol. speculat. P. I. consid. viii.; Ejusd. de Distinct, verar. Vision. a falsis, Signum V.

[454] Baluz. et Mansi I. 288-93.--Altmeyer, Les Précurseurs de la Réforme aux Pays-Bas, I. 84.

[455] Theod. Vrie, Hist. Concil. Constant. Lib. IV. Dist. 13.--Marieta, Los Santos de España, Lib. XI. c. xxviii.--Gobelini Person. Cosmodrom. Æt. VI. c. 93.--Chron. S. Ægid. in Brunswig (Leibnitii S. R. Brunsv. III. 595).--Gieseler, Lehrbuch der Kirchengeschichte, II.III. 317-18.--Herm. Corneri Chron. ann. 1416 (Eccard. Corp. Hist. II. 1206).--Andreæ Gubernac. Concil. P. IV. c. 11 (Von der Hardt VI. 194)--Chron. Magdeburgens. ann. 1454 (Meibom. Rer. German. II. 363).--Haupt, Zeitschrift für Kirchengeschichte, 1887, 114-18.--Herzog, Abriss. II. 405. In 1448, when pestilence and famine in Italy brought men to a sense of their sins, the eloquence of Frà Roberto, a Franciscan, excited multitudes to repentance, and the streets of the cities were again filled with Flagellants, disciplining themselves and weeping (Illescas, Historia Pontifical, II. 130).

[456] Conc. Constant. Decret. Reform. Lib. III. Tit. X. c. 13; Tit. V. c. 5 (Von der Hardt, I. 715-17).--Hemmerlin Glosa quarund. Bullar. (Opp. c. d.).--De Rebus Malthæi Grabon (Von der Hardt, III. 107-20).

[457] Von der Hardt, IV. 1518.--Concil. Salisburg. XXXIV. c. 32 (Dalham, Concil Salisb. p. 186).

[458] Hemmerlin Glosa quarund. Bullar; Ejusd. Lollardorum Descriptio.--Nider Formicar. III. 5, 7, 9.

[459] Concil. Herbipolens. ann. 1446 (Hartzheim V. 336).. Mosheim de Beghardis pp. 173-9, 190, 194-5.--Addis and Arnold's Catholic Dictionary, p. 73.

[460] Trithem. Chron. Hirsaug. ann. 1460.--.Hartzheim V. 464, 507, 560, 578.--Wadding, ann. 1492, No. 8.--Martini Append, ad Mosheim p. 579.

|461| Concil. Senens. ann. 1423 (Harduin. VIII. 1016-17).--.Ullumnn's Reformers before the Reformation, Menzies' Transl. I. 383-4.--Flac. Illyr. Catal. Test. Veritatis Lib. XIX. p. 1836 (Ed. 1608).--Comba, Histoire des Vaudois d'Italie, I. 97.--Hoffmann, Geschichte der Inquisition, II. 390-1.

|462| Wattenbach, Sitzungsberichte der Preuss. Akad. 1886, pp. 57-8,

|463| Hist. Persecut. Eccles. Bohem. pp. 71-2 (s. 1. 1648). Camerarii Hist. Frat.] Orthodox, pp. 116-17 (Heidelbergæ, 1605).--Ripoll III. 577.

|464| Ullmann, op. cit. I. 195-207.--Æn. Sylvii Epist. 400 (Opp. 1571, p. 932).--Fasciculus Rerum Expetendarum et Fugiendarum II. 115-28 (Ed. 1690).--Freber et Struv. II. 187-266.--Wadding. ann. 1461, No. 5.--Ripoll III. 466.--Chron. Glassberger ann. 1462.

|465| Trithem. Chron. Hirsaug. ann. 1476.--Ullmann, op. cit. I. 377 sqq.

|466| D'Argentré I. II. 291-8.--Ullmann, op.cit. I. 258-9, 277-94, 356-7.--Trithem. Chron. Hirsaug. ann. 1479.--Conr. Ursperg. Chron. Continuat. ann. 1479,--Melanchthon. Respons. ad Bavar. Inquis., Witebergæ, 1559, Sig. B 3.

|467| Ripoll IV. 5.--Synod Bamberg. ann. 1491, Tit. 44 (Ludewig Scriptt. Rer. Germ. I. 1242-44).--D'Argentré I. II. 342.

|468| Pauli Langii Chron. Citicens. (Pistorii Rer. Germ. Scriptt. I. 1276-6.)--Gieseler, Lehrbuch der Kirchengeschichte II. IV. 532 sq.--Herzog, Abriss, II. 397-401.--Spalatini Annal. ann. 1515 (Menken. II. 591).--Eleuth. Bizeni Joannis Reuchlin Encomion (sine nota. sed c. ann. 1516).--II. Corn. Agrippæ Epist. II. 54

|469| Ripoll IV. 378.--Lutheri Opp., Jenæ, 1564, I. 185 sqq.--Henke, Neuere Kirchengeschichte, I. 42-6.

|470| Dubrav. Hist. Bohem. Lib. 14 (Ed. 1587, pp. 380-1).

|471| Palacky, Beziehungen der Waldenser, Prag, 1869, p. 10.--Potthast No. 11818. Palacky (pp. 7-8) conjectures that these heretics were Cathari, but his reasoning is quite inadequate to overcome the greater probability that they were of Waldensian origin. He is, however, doubtless correct in suggesting that the allusion to princes and magnates may properly connect the movement with the commencement of the conspiracy which finally dethroned King Wenceslas I. in 1253. Wenceslas was a zealous adherent of the papacy and opponent of Frederic II., and the connection between antipapal politics and heresy was too close for us to discriminate between them without more details than we possess.

|472| Wadding. ann. 1257, No. 16.--Potthast No. 16819.--Höfler, Prager Concilien. Einleitung, p. xix.

|473| Palacky. op. cit. pp. 11-13.--Schrödl, Passavia Sacra, Passau, 1879, p. 242.--Dubravius (Hist. Bohem. Lib. 20) relates that in 1315 King John burned fourteen Dolcinists in Prague. Palacky (ubi sup.) argues, and I think successfully, that this relates to the above affair and that there were no executions.

|474| Wadding. ann. 1318, No. 2-6.--Ripoll II. 138-9, 174-6.--Gustav Schmidt, Päbstliche Urkunden und Regesten, Halle, 1886, p. 105.--Raynald. ann. 1319, No. 43.

|475| Palacky, op. cit. pp. 15-18.--Flac. Illyr. Catal. Test. Veritatis Lib. XV. p. 1505 (Ed. 1608).--Raynald. ann. 1335, No. 61-2.--Wadding. ann. 1335, No. 3-4.

|476| Krasinsky, Reformation in Poland, London, 1838, I. 55-6.--Raynald. ann. 1341, No. 27.

|477| Werunsky Excerptt. ex Registt. Clem. VI. pp. 28, 47.--Raynald. ann. 1347, No. 11.

|478| Œn. Sylvii Hist. Bohem. c. 36.--Naucleri Chron. ann. 1360.--Höfler, Prager Concilien, pp. 2, 3, 5, 7.--Loserth, Hus und Wicklif, Prag, 1884, pp. 261 sqq.--Werunsky Excerptt. ex Registt. Clem. VI. pp. 1, 2, 3, 13, 25. Dispensations for children to hold preferment were an abuse of old date, as we have seen in a former chapter. In 1297 Boniface VIII. authorized a boy of Florence, twelve years old, to take a benefice involving the cure of souls.--Faucon, Registres de Boniface VIII. No. 1761, p. 666.

|479| Werunsky op. cit. pp. 89, 94, 98, 99, 102, 111, 120, 135, 136, 140, 141.--Gudeni Cod. Diplom. III. 509.--Hartzheim Concil. Germ. IV. 510.

|480| Höfler, Prager Concilien, pp. 2, 5, 12, 14, 26-7.--Loserth, Hus und Wiclif, pp. 32-33, 37.--W. Preger, Beiträge, p. 51.--Flac. Illyr. Catal. Test. Veritatis Lib. xv. p. 1506 (Ed. 1608).

|481| Mosheim de Beghardis p. 381.

|482| Loserth, Hus und Wiclif, pp. 49, 50-2.--Lechler (Real Encyklopädie, X. 1-3).--Raynald. ann. 1374, No. 10-11.

|483| Höfler, Prager Concilien, pp. 33, 37-9.--De Schweinitz, History of the Unitas Fratrum (Bethlehem, Pa., 1885, pp. 25-6).

|484| Loserth, Hus und Wiclif, pp. 54, 56-7, 63-4, 68-9.--Montet, Hist. Lit. des Vaudois, p. 150.--Pseudo-Pilichdorf Tract. contra Waldens. c. 15 (Mag. Bib. Pat. XIII. 315).

|485| Arnold's English Works of Wyclif, III. 454-96. Cf. Væ Octuplex (Ib. II. 380); Of Mynystris in the Chirch (Ib. II. 394); Vaughan's Tracts and Treatises, p. 226; Trialogi III. 6, 7; Trialogi Supplem. c. 2.--Losertb, Mittheilungen des Vereines für Gesch. der Deutschen in Böhmen, 1886, pp. 384 sqq.

|486| Trialogi II. 14; IV. 22.--Jo. Hus de Ecclesia, c. 1 (Monument. I. fol. 196-7, Ed. 1558).--Wil. Wodford adv. Jo. Wiclefum (Fascic. Rer. Expetend. et Fugiend. I. 250, Ed. 1690).--In the condemnation of the innovations by the Council of Prague, in 1412, predestination is not among the errors enumerated (Höfler, Prager Concilien, p. 72), though it appears in the final proceedings against Huss in the Council of Constance (P. Mladenowic Relatio, Palacky Documenta. p. 317).

[487] Raynald. ann. 1377, No. 4-6.--Lechler's Life of Wickliff, Lorimer's Translation, II. 288-90, 343-7.-- Loserth, Hus und Wiclif, pp. 101-2, 121.--Palacky Documenta Mag. Johannis Hus, p. 189, 203, 313, 374-6, 426-8, 467.--Harduin. Concil. VIII. 203.--Von der Hardt III. XII. 168; IV. 153, 328.--Jo. Hus Replica contra P. Stokes (Monument. I. 108 *a*).--Höfler, Prager Concilien. p. 53.

[488] Loserth, op. cit. pp. 79, 114, 161 sqq.--Mittheilungen des Vereines für Gesch. d. Deutschen in Böhmen, 1886, 395 sqq.--Jo. Hus Monument. I. 25*a*, 108*a*.--Nider Formicar. Lib. III. c. 9. fol. 50*a*.--Von der Hardt IV. 328.--Gobelin. Personæ Cosmodrom. Ætat. VI. c. 86-7 (Meibom. Rer. German. I. 319-21).

[489] Loserth, op. cit. pp. 13, 75-8, 98-100.--Jo. Hus Monument. II. 25-52. Even Æneas Sylvius (Hist. Bohem. c. 35) speaks of Huss as distinguished for the purity of his life; and the Jesuit Balbinus says that his austerity and modesty, his kindness to all, even to the meanest, won for him universal favor. No one believed that so holy a man could deceive or be deceived, so that the memory of the thief was worshipped at Prague as that of a saint (Bohuslai Balbini Epit. Rer. Bohem. Lib. V. C. V. p. 431).

[490] Palacky Documenta, pp. 3, 56.--Berger, Johannes Hus u. König Sigmund, p. 5.--Loserth, op. cit. pp. 82, 98-100, 103-5, 111-12, 270.--Höfler, Prager Concilien, pp. 43-6, 51-3, 57, 60, 61-2.--Hist. Persecut. Eccles. Bohem. p. 29. Wickliff continued to the end to be the chief authority of the Hussites. A half a century later he is appealed to by both factions into which they were divided. See Peter Chelcicky's reply to Rokyzana, in Goll, Quellen und Untersuchungen zur Geschichte der Böhmischen Brüder, II. 83-4.

[491] Loserth, pp. 105-6.--Palacky Documenta, pp. 345-6, 363-4.

[492] Loserth, op. cit. pp. 106-10, 123-4.--Palacky Documenta, pp. 181, 347, 350--62.--Höfler, Prager Concilien, pp. 64-70.--Raynald. ann. 1409, No. 89.

[493] Æneæ; Sylv. Hist. Bohem. c. 35.--Loserth, op. cit. p. 137.--Palacky Documenta, pp. 184-5, 342-3.--Palacky, Beziehungen, pp. 19-20--Jo. Hus Monument. I. 2-3.

[494] Loserth, op. cit. pp. 120, 123-4.--Höfler, Prager Concilien, pp. 5, 15, 18, 31, 32, 46, 57.

[495] Loserth, op. cit. pp. 121-3, 130.--Palacky Documenta, pp. 19-21, 191, 233.--Mladenowic Relatio (Palacky p. 319).--Jo. Hus Disputatio contra Indulgent. (Monument. I. 174-89); Ejusd. contra Bull. PP. Joannis (Ib. I. 189-91); Ejusd. Serm. XXII. de Remissione Peccatorum (Ib. II. 74-5).

[496] Loserth, op. cit. p. 131.--Palacky Documenta, p. 640.--De Schweinitz, Hist. of the Unitas Fratrum, pp. 41-2.--Stephani Cartus. Antihussus c. 5 (Pez Thesaur. Anecd. IV. II. 380, 382).

[497] Höfler, Prager Concilien, pp. 73, 110.--Loserth, op. cit. pp. 132-5.--J. Hus Monument. I. 17; Ejusd. de Ecclesia c. 14 (Monument. I, 223. Cf. Wicklif. de Eccles. c. 18,*ap*. Loserth, p. 188).--Palacky Documenta, pp. 458, 464-66.

[498] Höfler, Prager Concilien, pp. 73-100.--Loserth, op. cit. pp. 142-5.--Palacky Documenta, p. 510.--Mladenowic Relatio (Palacky Documenta, p. 246).

[499] Von der Hardt IV. 313.

[500] Leonardi Aretini Comment. (Muratori S.R.I. XIX. 927-8). --Harduin. VIII. 231.--Theod. a Niem Vit. Joann. XXIII. Lib. II. c. 37 (Von der Hardt II. 384).--Palacky Documenta, pp. 512-18. For the confusion existing in Germany, caused by the Schism, see Haupt, Zeitschrift für Kirchengeschichte, 1883, pp. 356-8.

[501] Jo. Fistenport. Chron. ann. 1415 (Hahn. Coll. Monum. I. 401).--Dacherii Hist. Magnatum (Von der Hardt V. II. 50).--Theod. a Niem Vita Joann. XXIII. Lib. I. c. 40 (Ib. II. 388).--Nider Formicar. Lib. V. c. ix.

[502] Stephani Cartus. Dial. Volatilis c. 11, 14, 21 (Pez Thesaur. Anecd. IV. II. 465, 473, 492).--The three sermons prepared for this purpose are printed in Huss's works (Monument. I. 44-56). The first is on the sufficiency of the law of Christ for the government of the Church: the second is an elaborate exposition of his belief; the third on Peace, in which he attributes the schisms and troubles of the Church to the pride and greed and vices of the clergy.

[503] Mladenowic Relatio (Palacky Documenta, p. 237).--Von der Hardt IV. 754.--Jo. Hus Monument. I. 2-4, 57, 68.--Palacky Documenta, pp. 70, 73.

[504] Richentals Chronik des Constanzer Concils p. 76 (Tübingen, 1882).--Jo. Hus Epistt. iii. vi. (Monument. I. 57-8).--Monument. I. 4*a*

[505] Richentals Chronik p. 58.--Jo. Hus Epistt. iv. vi. vii. (Monument. I. 58-9).

[506] Hus Epistt. v. vi. (Monument. I. 58).--Monument. I. 4 *b*.--Laur. Byzyn. Diar. Bell. Hussit. ann. 1414 (Ludewig Reliq. MSS. VI. 124).--Palacky Document. p. 170.--Richentals Chronik pp. 76-77.--Mladenowic Relatio (Palacky, pp. 247-8).--Naucleri Chron. ann. 1414.

[507] Richentals Chronik p. 77.--Jo. Hus Monument. I. 5 *b*.--Von der Hardt IV. 22, 32, 212.--Mladenowic Relatio (Palacky Document. pp. 246-52). The special rigor of confinement near the latrines was well understood. In 1317, when John XXII. delivered some Spiritual Franciscans to their brethren for safe-keeping, Friar François Sanche "*posuerunt fratres in quodum carcere juxta latrinas.*"--Historia Tribulationum (Archiv. für Litteratur-u. Kirchengeschichte, 1886, p. 146).

[508] Von der Hardt IV. 11-12, 22.--Mladenowic Relatio (Palacky, p. 251).

[509] Palacky Documenta, p. 238.--Von der Hardt IV. 12, 28.--Richentals Chronik p. 76.--Jo. Hus Epist. lvii. (Monument. I. 75).--Mladenowic Relatio (Palacky, p. 253).

[510] Von der Hardt IV. 189, 209. Berger's labored collection of safe-conducts and their comparison with the one given to Huss (Johann Hus u. König Sigmund pp. 180-208) prove nothing but his own industry. Huss

218

went to Constance as an excommunicate to defend himself and his faith. Sigismund. knowing this, gave him a safe-conduct without limitation or condition. The only contemporaneous documents with which this can fairly be compared are those offered by the council and by Sigismund to John XXIII. when they summoned him back to Constance, May 2, 1415, and the one offered by the council to Jerome of Prague, April 17. Of these the first was limited by the clause "*justitia tamen semper salva*," the second by "*in quantum idem dominus rex tenetur sibi dare de jure et servare alios salvos conductus sibi datos*," the third by "*quantum in nobis est et fides exegit orthodoxa*" (V. d. Hardt IV. 119, 143, 145). No ingenious reasoning can explain this away. The allusion in Sigismund's safe-conduct to other letters already given by him to the pope refers to those which John had required of him and of the city of Constance before he would trust himself there (Raynald. ann. 1413, No. 22-3). These the council set aside as coolly as it did that of Huss. Sigismund, as we shall see, had no power to give a safe conduct that would protect a heretic, but Berger's argument that he therefore could not have designedly issued an unlimited one to Huss (Berger, op. cit. 92-3, 109) is worthless in view of his readiness, which Berger freely concedes (p. 85), to enter into engagements which he knew he could not fulfil. From his indignation it is evident that he was unacquainted with the niceties of the canon law; but even if he were, his giving the letters is easily explicable by the fact, which Berger has well pointed out (pp. 100-1), that Huss's certificates of orthodoxy, obtained in August, were laid before him (Palacky Document, p. 70). He could thus easily persuade himself that there was no risk of his pledge causing him trouble. It was of the greatest moment to him that Huss should be reconciled to the Church, and to a man of his temperament it was inconceivable that Huss's delicate conscientiousness would in the end render martyrdom inevitable. Hefele (Conciliengeschichte VII. 234), following Palacky, calls attention to the absence, in the letter of the Bohemian magnates to the council, September 2, 1415, of any reproach for violating the safe-conduct, and he argues thence that they admitted that it could not protect Huss from judgment as a heretic. So little is this the case that they emphatically declare that Huss was not a heretic, and if there is no allusion to the safe-conduct this is evidently attributable to their referring to certain previous letters to Sigismund which the council had ordered burned, and which they defiantly desired to be considered as embodied and repeated in the present one (Monument I. 78). Anything they might have to say on the subject must have been said in those letters, which presumably were the occasion of the projected decree of September 23, 1415, punishing as fautors of heresy all who vilified Sigismund for permitting the violation of his safe-conduct.

[511] Martene Thesaur. II. 1611.--Von der Hardt II. x. 255; IV. 26.--Palacky Documenta, p. 612.--Berger, Johann Hus u. König Sigmund, pp. 133, 136.--Fistenport. Chron. ann. 1419 (Hahn Collect. Monument. I .404).--Ægid. Carlerii Lib. de Legationibus (Monument. Conc. General. Sæc. XV. T. I. pp. 531, 536-7, 595-6, 612-13, 662-73, 680-4, 688-93, 695-7).--Thomæ Ebendorferi Diar. (Ib. p. 767).--Jo. de Turonis Regestr. (Ib. pp. 834-5). Even in France Sigismund was reproached for surrendering Huss after giving him a safe-conduct, and was accused of disregarding other engagements of the same kind.--(Martene Ampl. Coll. II. 1444-5.) Yet had he persisted he would have been liable to excommunication and heavy penalties as an impeder of the Inquisition; and had he carried out his threat of forcibly liberating Huss, under the bull *Ad extirpanda* he would have been punishable by perpetual relegation and the forfeiture of all his dominions (Mag. Bull. Rom. Ed. Luxemb. 1742, I. 92, 149).

[512] Von der Hardt IV. 32, 311-13, 329.--Martene Thesaur. II. 1611.--Berger, Johann Hus u. König Sigmund, p. 138.--Palacky Documenta, 541, 543, 546-53.--Jo. Hus Epistt. xxxiii., liv., lix., lx.(Monument. I. 68-9, 74-77).--Mladenowic Relat. (Palacky, p. 314-15).--Narr. Hist, de Condemnatione (Monument. II. 346 *a*; Von der Hardt IV. 393).--Ægid. Carlerii Lib. de Legat. (Monument. Concil. Gen. Sæc. XV. Tom. I. p. 435).--Martene Ampl. Coll. VII. 174-6, 179-83.--Jo. de Turonis Regestrum (Monument. Con. Gen. Sæc. XV. T. I. p. 860). The incident of Sigismund's blush has been disputed by some recent writers. It is a matter not worth controversy, but as the only evidence to his credit in the whole affair it may be hoped to be true.

[513] Richentals Chronik p. 78.--Von der Hardt IV. 313, 521-22.--Chron. Glassberger ann. 1415.--Martene Ampl. Collect. VIII. 131-33. Cf. Noel Alexander's justification of the decree of September 23 (Hist. Eccles. Ed. Paris, 1699. T. VIII. p. 496). It is customary with modern Catholic writers to stigmatize as a Protestant calumny the assertion that the Church held the doctrine that faith is not to be kept with heretics. See, for instance, Van Ranst, Regent of the College of Antwerp, in his "Historia Hæreticorum" (4th. Ed. Venet. 1759, p. 263), together with his ingenious endeavor to argue away the case of Huss. I have already alluded to this subject (Vol. I. p. 228), and have shown that it was a recognized principle of the Church that faith and oaths pledged to heretics were void. It has also been seen how the efforts of the popes procured the insertion in the public law of Europe of the principle that suspicion of heresy in the lord released the vassal from the most binding engagement known to the Middle Ages--the oath of allegiance (Lib. V. Extra, VII. xiii. § 3). When thus the basis on which society itself was founded was destroyed by heresy all minor pledges were necessarily invalidated. The Church did not allow this to become obsolete. When, in 1327, John XXII. sentenced the Emperor Louis of Bavaria as a heretic, he not only released all his vassals from their oaths of allegiance, but declared void all compacts and agreements made with him (Martene Thesaur. II. 702, 775-6, 791). So, in 1463, when it pleased Pius II. to declare George Podiebrad a heretic, he released the communities of Breslau and Namslau from their allegiance, and excommunicated all who should lend their aid or service to their monarch (Æn. Sylvii Epist. 401); and when Frederic III. asked him to compel Breslau to submit to George, he replied by arguing that heresy dissolved compacts as effectually as death (Martene Ampl. Coll. I. 1598-99). When, in 1469,

Paul II. again declared George a heretic he pronounced that each and every obligation, promise, and oath made to that heretic was null and void, for faith was not to be kept with him who kept not faith with God. Acting under this, when George released from prison Wenceslas of Biberstein, on bail of six thousand florins furnished by John and Ulric of Hazemburg, the papal legate Rudolph incontinently ordered the bailors neither to surrender the accused nor to pay the forfeit (Ludewig Reliq. MSS. VI. 77). The play upon the double meaning of the word faith by which this was epigrammatically justified was seriously accepted by Christendom. In April, 1415, Fernando of Aragon wrote to Sigismund earnestly remonstrating with him for the delay in judging Huss, and expressing the hope that the safe-conduct would not be allowed to protect him "*quoniam non est frangere fidem in eo qui Deo fidem frangit.*"--Andreæ Ratisponens Chron. ann. 1414 (Pez Thesaur. Anecd. IV. III. 626.--Palacky Documenta, p. 540). All statutes and laws impeding the free action of the Inquisition, directly or indirectly, were null and void *ipso jure*, as we have repeatedly seen above (see also Farinaccii de Hæresi Quæst. 182 No. 76); and what Sigismund could not have done at the head of the Imperial Diet, he certainly could not do by a simple safe-conduct, and no ecclesiastical jurisdiction was bound to respect it. If the Church thus disregarded the pledges of laymen, it was equally unmindful of its own when heretics were concerned. Even late in the sixteenth century the bull *Multiplices inter* of Pius V. annulled all letters of absolution and decrees of acquittal for heresy issued by inquisitors, bishops, popes, and even by the Council of Trent, showing how scant was the ceremony customarily used in such cases, and how completely suspicion of heresy deprived a man of all rights (Lib. V. in Septimo III. x.). Even without this general principle, however, there would have been no difficulty in soothing Sigismund's scruples of conscience, if, perchance, he had any. The system of the mediæval Church so completely confused the ideas of right and wrong that the ordinary notions of morality were superseded. The power of the keys was such that a papal dispensation could release any one from an inconvenient vow or promise, no matter how binding might be its form. Sigismund's father, Charles, when Margrave of Moravia, was released, in 1346, by Clement VI. from a troublesome oath which he had taken (Werunsky Excerptt. ex Regist. Clem. VI. p. 44); and the sin of perjury was one for which the popes were accustomed to grant efficacious pardons when it was committed in their interest (Ludewig op. cit. VI. 14). It was deemed only a reasonable precaution in compacts for the parties to pledge themselves that they would not seek a release by a papal dispensation (Hartzheim IV. 329; Preger, Der kirchenpolitische Kampf unter Ludwig dem Baier, p. 59). Sigismund, in the case of Huss, admitted that his pledge was dissolved by heresy and a dispensation was superfluous, but it could have been had for the asking. In view of these facts all attempts to argue away the betrayal of Huss are useless, nor is it possible to accuse the good fathers of Constance of conscious bad faith. They but accepted and enforced the principles in which they were trained.

[514] Mandata Synodalia ann. 1390 (Höfler, Prager Concilien, p. 40).--Æn. Sylvii. Hist. Bohem. cap. 35.-- Laur. Byzyn. Diar. Bell. Hussit. ann. 1414 (Ludewig Reliq. MSS. VI. 125, 128-9).--Von der Hardt III. 335 sqq.; IV. 288-91, 334, 342.--Jo. Hus Monument. I. 42-44, 62, 72. The relentless obstinacy with which the Church of the fifteenth and sixteenth centuries refused the use of the cup to the laity at the cost of Christian unity and unnumbered troubles is perhaps the most impressive example on record of the perversity of sacerdotalism in sacrificing essentials to non-essentials. No one denied that in the early Church communion in both elements was administered to all the faithful, as it continued to be without interruption in the Greek Church. The refusal of the cup to the laity was originally a Manichæan custom, in imitation of the corresponding ancient Izeshne rite of the Mazdeans. Communion in one element thus became a mark of heresy, and was condemned as such by Leo the Great (Leon. PP. I. Serm. XLII. cap. 5), about the middle of the fifth century, and again towards its end by Gelasius I., whose decretal on the subject is embodied, without comment or contradiction, by Gratian in the Decretum (P. II. Dist. ii. c. 12), showing that it was still good law in the twelfth century. When, however, in the tenth and eleventh centuries the belief in transubstantiation became the accepted dogma of the Church, the supreme veneration felt for the consecrated elements naturally gave rise to the necessity of the utmost care in handling them and to excessive dread as to any accidents which might occur to them; and the penitentials grew full of all manner of penalties inflicted on priests who, through carelessness, let fall a crumb of the body or a drop of the blood, for which, by forged decretals of the early popes, a false antiquity was claimed (Decreti III. ii. 27). Of course the liquid was much more subject to these accidents, and to decomposition, than the solid, and the ministering priests were sorely tried to avert such profanation and its consequences to themselves. At first they adopted the ready expedient of dipping the host in the wine-and-water, and thus administering both elements together, which was conducive both to safety and comfort. This innovation was condemned by the Church, but was suppressed with great difficulty. Under Gregory VII. the author of the Micrologus devotes a chapter to its prohibition (Micrologi c. 19). In 1095 the great Council of Clermont forbade it, except in cases where it was demanded by prudence or necessity for the avoidance of accidents (Conc. Claromont. ann. 1095, c. 28); and some twenty years later Paschal II. laid down the rule that it was only admissible in the communion of infants and the sick who could not swallow the bread (Paschal PP. II. Epist. 535). In a Bohemian document dating about the close of the twelfth century the priest carrying the viaticum to the dying is directed to dip the wafer in the wine so as to avoid accidents and yet be able to administer both elements (Höfler, Prager Concilien, Einleitung, p. ix.). When this resource was denied, while the veneration of the sacrament as the flesh and blood of Christ continued to develop, the custom was gradually introduced of restricting the laity to the solid element, in administering which there was less liability to accident, while the priest continued to partake in both. About

1270 Thomas Aquinas tells us that in some churches the bread only is given to the laity, as a matter of prudence, to avoid spilling, and his dialectics are equal to the task of proving that both body and blood are contained in the wafer (Summa III. lxxx. 12). The convenience of the innovation led to its extension, but it was left to the individual churches, and no authoritative decree was issued withdrawing the cup from the laity until the Bohemian controversy led to the action of the Council of Constance. How universal the custom had become without authority of law is shown by the special privilege granted, about 1345, by Clement VI. to John, Duke of Normandy, son of Philip of Valois, to receive both elements (Martene Ampl. Coll. I. 1456-7). When the question was exhaustively debated before the Council of Basle, the orator of the council, John of Ragusa, freely admitted that the Hussite practice was in accordance with the traditions of the Church, but argued that it could be changed if convenience or other reasons demanded it (Harduin. Concil. VIII. 1712, 1740); and the Cardinal of St. Peter told William, Baron of Kostka, the Bohemian chief, that the cup was refused to children and common people simply as a precaution, adding. "If you were to ask of me I would give it, but not to the careless" (Petri Zaticensis Liber Diurnus; Mon. Concil. Gen. Sæc. XV. T. I. p. 315). The final decision of the Council of Basle, in December, 1437, admits that there is no precept on the subject, but lay communion in one element is a laudable custom, the law of the Church, and not to be modified without authority (Conc. Basiliens. Sess. XXX.; Harduin. VIII. 1234). How thoroughly indefensible the Church felt its position to be, yet how arbitrarily and despotically it was resolved to enforce that position, is most clearly shown by the inquisitor Capistrano, in 1452, when he heard that the cardinal legate, Nicholas of Cusa, was thinking of giving Rokyzana a hearing on the subject at Ratisbon. Capistrano expressed his mind freely to the legate: "If we excuse the heretics we condemn ourselves.... I have always avoided a debate with the Bohemians under the ordinary rules, for they study to justify their heresy from the ancient Scriptures and observances, and they have a perfect knowledge of the texts, which certainly are numerous, in favor of communion in both elements." Capistrano then quotes to the legate the bulls of Nicholas V. sent to him, in which the Bohemians are denounced as schismatics, heretics, and disobedient to the Roman Church, pointedly adding that the disciple is not above the teacher, nor the servant superior to the master; he had never read in the law that heretics were to be rewarded, but were to be sharply punished with confiscation and the bitterest penalties (Wadding. Annal. ann. 1452, No. 12). So it had come to this, that those who admittedly followed the practices of the Church current until the thirteenth century were to be condemned and exterminated as heretics. Disobedience was heresy, and Rome, for a century, endeavored to convulse Europe on this simple punctilio. An episode of this question was the communion of infants. This was the practice of the early Church (Cyprian. de Lapsis c. 25), and St. Innocent I. and St. Gelasius I. had both declared that as soon as infants were baptized the sacrament was necessary to secure them eternal life (Innocent PP. I. Epist. XXX. c. 5; Gelasii PP. I. Ep. VII.). The epistle of Paschal II., quoted above, shows that this was still customary in the twelfth century, but the same causes which led to the withdrawal of the cup from the laity induced the withholding of the sacrament from infants, who were liable at any moment unconsciously to commit sacrilege with the body and blood of Christ. In their enthusiasm for the Eucharist the Bohemians naturally recurred to infantile communion, and their obstinacy in this gave the fathers of Basle infinite trouble. After the reconciliation of 1436 the question still remained disputed. The feeling about it is well defined by the Bishop of Coutances, legate of the Council of Basle in Prague, who was horror-stricken when, April 28, 1437, Rokyzana administered communion to a number of infants, and one of them ejected the wafer from its mouth, forcing Rokyzana quietly to replace it. This incident was evidently regarded as the most convincing argument, and the terms in which it is alluded to show how profound was the terror which it was expected to create (Jo. de Turonis Regestrum; Monument. Conc. Gen. Sæc. XV. T. I. p. 863). At the Council of Constance it was gravely argued that if a layman allowed the wine to moisten his beard he ought to be burned with his beard (Von der Hardt III. 369). Gerson was not quite so absurd, but he did not shrink from alleging such reasons as the expensiveness of wine and its liability to turn sour (ib. 771 sqq.). In 1391, when John Malkaw, in preaching against the concubinary priesthood, hotly declared that he would rather place reverently on the ground a consecrated wafer than violate his vow of chastity, Böckeler, the Strassburg inquisitor, in trying him, made this the ground of a charge of heresy with respect to the sacrament of the altar (Haupt, Zeitschrift für Kirchengeschichte, 1883, pp. 366-7). In older times the Church had felt no such exaggerated reverence for the elements. In 646 Pope Theodore, when he excommunicated Pyrrhus, the refugee Patriarch of Constantinople, mingled consecrated wine from the cup with the ink with which he signed the sentence; and in 869 the Council of Constantinople adopted the same device in condemning Photius.--Chr. Lupi Dissert. de Sexta Synodo c. V. (Opp. III. 25). As a matter of course the vilest stories were circulated to inspire the faithful with abhorrence for the Bohemian innovations. It was said that the wine was consecrated in bottles and barrels; that the sectaries held conventicles in cellars, where they would partake of it to intoxication and then commit all manner of sexual abominations (Laur. Byzyn. Diar. Bell. Hussit,; Ludewig VI. 129-30).

[515] Palacky Documenta, pp. 194-204, 506.--Mladenowic Relatio (Palacky, p. 252). The council itself recognized that its proceedings were inquisitorial. In the sentence of Jerome of Prague it uses the phrase "*Hæc sancta synodus Constantiensis in causa inquisitionis hæreticæ pravitatis per eamdem sanctum synodem mota.*"--Von der Hardt IV. 766.

[516] Palacky, pp. 204-24.--Mladenowic Relatio (Palacky, p. 254).--Martene Thesaur. II. 1635.--Jo. Hus Epist. xlviii. (Monument. I. 72).

[517] Epist. xxxii. (Monument. I. 68).--Von der Hardt IV. 20-8.--Jo. Hus Monument. I. 39-41.--
Mladenowic Relatio (Palacky, pp. 276-8, 303, 318). Already in 1411 Huss energetically disclaimed to John XXIII.
belief in remanence and in the vitiation of sacraments (Palacky, p. 19. Cf. pp. 164-5, 170, 174-85).

[518] Mladenowic Relatio (Palacky, pp. 252-3).--Palacky, pp. 73, 174, 318, 560.--Von der Hardt IV. 308,
420-8.

[519] Mladenowic Relatio (Palacky. pp. 253, 323).--Von der Hardt IV. 188, 212, 289.--Epist. xlix.
(Monument. I. 73 a).

[520] Von der Hardt IV. 47.--Mladenowic Relatio (Palacky, p. 255).--Palacby, p. 541.--Jo. Hus
Monument. I. 7, 29-42.--Epistt. xi., xxvii., xxx., xxxi., xxxii., xxxvi., xlvii., li., lii., lvi. (Monument. I. 60, 65-9, 72-
5).--Laur. Byzyn. Diar. Bell. Hussit. (Ludewig Reliq. MSS. VI. 128-9).

[521] Epist. lii. (Monument. I. 75).--Theod. a Niem de Vit. Joann. XXIII. Lib. III. c. 5.--Raynald. ann.
1419, No. 5.

[522] Jo. Hus Monument. I. 118, 128.--Epist. xliii. (Ib. 71 a).--Palacky Documenta, pp. 60, 185, 523-8.--
Mladenowic Relatio (Palacky, p. 301).

[523] Von der Hardt IV. 100, 118, 136, 153, 189, 209, 212-13, 288-90, 296, 306.--Martene Thesaur. II.
1635.--Harduin. VIII. 280.--Mladenowic Relatio (Palacky, pp. 256-72).

[524] Epistt. xliii., xlvii. (Monument. I. 71, 72).--Von der Hardt IV. 291, 306-7.

[525] Jo. Hus Monument. I. 25 b.--Von der Hardt IV. 307, 311-29.--Epistt. xii., xv., xxxvi. (Monument. I.
60-2, 69),--Palacky, pp. 275, 308-15. The attempt to deny to Huss the inalienable privilege of recantation was
based upon a mistranslated passage of his Bohemian address to his disciples, in which he was made to assure
them that if he was forced to abjure, it would only be with the lips and not with the heart (Palacky, pp. 274, 311).
In such matters the council was at the mercy of Huss's Bohemian enemies.

[526] Von der Hardt IV. 432-33.

[527] Huss was by no means the first to suffer from this technical necessity of confession in abjuring. In
the case of the English Templars, William de la More, Preceptor of England, and Humbert Blanc, Preceptor of
Aquitaine, refused to abjure because they would not confess to heresies which they had never entertained.--
Wilkins, Concil. II. 390, 393.

[528] Epistt. xxx., xxxi., xxxii. (Monument. I. 67-8).--Von der Hardt IV. 342-5.

[529] Mladenowic Relatio (Palacky, p. 309).--Epistt. xxvii., xxix., xxx., xxxviii., xxxix., xl., xli. (Monument.
I. 63-66, 67, 70).--Von der Hardt IV. 329-30.--Palacky, pp. 225-34.

[530] Mladenowic Relatio (Palacky, pp. 316-17).--Von der Hardt IV. 345-6, 386.--Palacky, p. 560. To
appreciate properly the extent of the concessions offered to Huss it is necessary to bear in mind the elaborately
careful formulas of abjuration which the inquisitors were accustomed to use, so as to allow no loophole for the
avoidance of the penalties of relapse, and to force the penitent to betray his fellow-heretics. See Modus
Procedendi (Martene Thesaur. V. 1800-1).--Lib. Sententt. Inq. Tolosan. p. 215.--Bern. Guidon. Practica pp. 92-3
(Éd. Douais).

[531] Mladenowic Relatio (Palacky, pp. 318-21).--Von der Hardt IV. 389-96, 432-40.--Harduin. VIII. 408-
10.--Richentals Chronik p. 80.--Richental says that Huss was delivered to the secular arm with the customary
adjuration for mercy, but the text of the sentence as printed by Von der Hardt contains no such clause. It may
well have been omitted at Sigismund's request, as he had already incurred sufficient obloquy, but the same
omission is noticeable in the sentence of Jerome of Prague (Von der Hardt IV. 771).

[532] Richentals Chronik pp. 80-2.--Von der Hardt IV. 445-8.--Mladenowic Relatio (Palacky, pp. 321-4).--
Æn. Sylvii Hist. Bohem. c. 36.--Laur. Byzyn. Diar. Bell. Hussit. (Ludewig VI. 135-6).--Andrew Ratispon. Chron.
(Pez Thes. Anecdot. IV. III. 627).

[533] P. d'Ailly (Theod. a Niem) de Necess. Reform. c. 28, 29 (Von der Hardt I. VI. 306-9).--Theod. Vrie
Hist. Concil. Constant. Lib. VI. Dist. 11; Lib. VII. Dist. 3 (Ibid. I. 170-1, 181-2). It is simply a lack of familiarity
with the ecclesiastical jurisprudence of the Middle Ages that has led historians to regard the cases of Huss and
Jerome as exceptional. Even so well informed an authority as Lechler does not hesitate to say "Hussens
Verbrennung war, mit dem Massstab des damaligen Rechts gemessen, ein warer Justizmord" (Herzog's Real-
Encyklop. VI. 392).

[534] Loserth, Huss u. Wiclif p. 156.--Epistt. lxi., lxii., lxiv. (Monument. I. 77-9, 81).--Von der Hardt IV.
489-90, 494-7.--Palacky Documenta, pp. 580-4, 593-4.--Laur. Byzyn. Diar. Bell. Hussit. (Ludewig VI. 136). The
temper of the Bohemians had been excited, a few days before the burning of Huss, by the news that in Olmütz a
student of Prague named John, described as a zealous follower of God, had been, within the short space of
twelve hours, arrested, tortured, convicted, and burned.--Palacky Documenta, p. 561.

[535] Von der Hardt IV. 634-91, 756.--Palacky Documenta, pp. 63, 336-7, 408-9, 417-20, 506, 572.--
Loserth, Mittheilungen des Vereins für Gesch. der Deutschen in Böhmen, 1885, pp. 108-9.--Schrödl, Passavia
Sacra, pp. 284-5.

[536] Von der Hardt IV. 103-5, 134bis.--Palacky Documenta, p. 541-2.--Richentals Cronik, p. 78.--Laur.
Byzyn. Diar. Bell. Hussit. ann. 1415 (Ludewig VI. 132).

[537] Von der Hardt IV. 119, 134, 139, 142, 148-9, 216-18.

[538] Richentals Cronik p. 70.--Theod. Vrie Hist. Concil. Constant. Lib. VI. Dist. 12.--Theod. a Niem de Vita Joann. PP. XXIII. Lib. III. c. 8.--Palacky Documenta, pp. 596-9.

[539] Von der Hardt IV. 501-7.--Richentals Cronik p. 79.--In the final official articles drawn up against Jerome by the *Promotor Hæreticæ Pravitatis*, his absolute refusal to write to Bohemia, after promising to do so, is made a special point of accusation. Yet his letter to that effect, of September 12, is still on record, and in his last defiant address to the council he speaks of having written it under fear of burning, and now desires to withdraw it (V. d. Hardt IV. 688, 761).

[540] Von der Hardt III. IV. 39; IV. 634-91.--Laur. Byzyn Diar. Bell. Hussit (Ludewig VI. 137-8).

[541] Von der Hardt IV. 600-1, 732-33, 748-56.

[542] Von der Hardt III. 64-9.

[543] Ibid. IV. 754-62.

[544] Von der Hardt III. 55-60; IV. 763-71.--Theod. Vrie Hist. Conc. Constant. Lib. VII. Dist. 4.

[545] Von der Hardt III. 64-71; IV. 771-2.--Richentals Cronik p. 83.--Theod. Vrie Hist. Conc. Constant. Lib. VII. Dist. 3.--Laur. Byzyn. Diar. Bell. Hussit. (Ludewig VI. 141).--Æn. Sylvii Hist. Bohem. c. 36.

[546] Chron. Glassberger ann. 1416.

[547] Palacky Documenta, pp. 566-7, 572-9, 602-3.--Von der Hardt IV. 528, 609-12, 724, 781-2, 823-40.--Æn. Sylvii. Hist. Bohem. c. 35.--Theod. a Niem Vit. Joann. PP. XXIII. Lib.III. c. 12.

[548] Epistt. lxiii., lxv. (Jo. Hus Monument. I. 79-80, 82).--Palacky Documenta, pp. 611-14, 621.--Ludewig Rel. MSS. VI. 69.--Stepbani Cartus. Epist. ad Hussitas P. I. c. 5 (Pez Thesaur. Anecd. IV. II. 521).

[549] Von der Hardt IV. 1077-82, 1410-13.--Palacky Documenta, pp. 652-4. Doubtless there was much ill-treatment of such of the clergy as remained faithful to Rome. In 1417 Stephen of Olmütz complains that they were driven from their benefices, beaten, and slain.--Steph. Cartus. Epist. ad Hussit. P. I. c. 3 (Pez Thesaur. Anecd. IV. II. 517).

[550] Von der Hardt IV. 1514-18.--Palacky Documenta, pp. 676-77.

[551] Von der Hardt IV. 1518-31.--Palacky pp. 684-6.

[552] Palacky Documenta, pp. 631-2, 633-8, 654-6, 679.--Laur. Byzyn. Diar. Bell. Hussit. (Ludewig VI. 138-9).--Jo. Hus Monument. II. 364.--Ægid. Carlerii Lib. de Legation. (Monument Concil. General. Sæc. XV. T. I. pp. 385-6).

[553] Laur. Byzyn. Diar. Bell. Hussit. (Ludewig VI. pp. 142-44).--Æn. Sylvii Hist. Bohem. c. 36, 37.

[554] Laur. Byzyn. Diar. Bell. Hussit. (Ludewig VI. 145-52, 154-56).--Hist. Persecut. Eccles. Bohem. pp. 37-8.--Camerarii Hist. Frat. Orthod. p. 49.

[555] Ægid. Carlerii Lib. de Legation. (Mon. Concil. General. Sæc. XV. T. I. p. 387).--Laur. Byzyn. Diar. Bell. Hussit. (Ludewig VI. 152-4, 157-8, 168, 172).

[556] Laur. Byzyn. Diar. Bell. Hussit. (Ludewig VI. 159).--Raynald. ann. 1420, No. 13.--Hist. Persecut. Eccles. Bohem. pp. 39-40.--Ægid. Carlerii Lib. de Legation. loc. cit. There was warning also to the democratic party among the Bohemians in the vengeance taken by Sigismund on citizens of Breslau who had been concerned in an uprising similar to that of Prague. On March 7 he caused twenty-three of them to be beheaded.--Bezold, König Sigmund und die Reichskriege gegen die Husiten, München, 1872, p. 37.

[557] Laur. Byzyn. Diar. Bell. Hussit. (Ludewig VI. 161-3, 167-70, 181).--Andreæ Ratispon. Chron. (Eccard. Corp. Hist. I. 2147).--Schrödl, Passavia Sacra, p. 289.--Naucleri Chron. p. 933 (Ed. 1544).--Hist. Persecut. Eccles. Bohem. pp. 43-44.

[558] Palacky, Beziehungen, pp. 20-1.--Æn. Sylvii Hist. Bohem. c. 41.--Dubravii Hist. Bohem. Lib. 27.

[559] Laur. Byzyn. Diar. Bell. Hussit. (Ludewig VI. 202-7).--Palacky, Beziehungen, p. 31.--J. Goll, Quellen u. Untersuchungen zur Geschichte der Böhmischen Brüder, Prag, 1882, II. 10-11, 57-60.--Hist. Persecut. Eccles. Bohem. pp. 46-8.--Palacky, Præf. in Mon. Conc. Gen. Sæc. XV. p. xx.

[560] Ægid. Carlerii Lib. de Legation. (Mon. Conc. Gen. Sæc. XV. T. I. p. 389).--Epistt. lxvi. lxvii. (Jo. Hus Monument. I. 82-4).--Laur. Byzyn. Diar. (Ludewig VI. 175-81).

[561] Conciliab. Pragens. ann. 1421 (Hartzheim V. 199-201). Cf. Johann. de Przibram Profess. Cath. Fidei (Cochlæi Hist. Hussit. pp. 501 sqq.).

[562] Jo. de Turonis Regestrum (Mon. Conc. Gen. Sæc. XV. T. I. p. 833, 858). Yet these Puritans were represented to Europe in the papal bulls for the crusades as not only subverting all political and social order, but as condemning marriage and abandoning themselves to all manner of license and bestiality.--Martini PP. V. Bull. *Permisit Deus*, 25 Oct. 1427 (Fascic. Rer. Expetendarum et Fugiend, II. 613).

[563] Jo. de Turonis Regestrum (Mon. Conc. Gen. Sæc. XV. T. I. pp. 843, 858, 865).--Wratislaw, Diary of an Embassy from George of Bohemia, London, 1871.

[564] Æn. Sylvii Hist. Bohem. c. 35; Ejusd. Epist. 130 (Opp. Ed. 1571, p. 678).--Pet. Zatecens. Lib. Diurnus (Monument. Conc. Gen. Sæc. XV. T. I. p. 352).--Concil. Bituricens. ann. 1432 (Harduin. VIII. 1459).--Goll, Quellen u. Untersuchungen zur Geschichte der Böhmischen Brüder, I. 106.

[565] Goll, Quellen u. Untersuchungen, II. 40-1.--Preger, Beiträge zur Geschichte der Waldesier, pp. 68-71.--Laur. Byzyn. Diar. (Ludewig VI. 183-4, 194-202).--Johann. de Przibram Profess. Fidei (Cochlæi Hist. Huss. p. 507).--Huss, Sermo de Exequiis (Monument. II. 50). See also Æneas Sylvius's statement of the identity between the Waldensian and Hussite teachings (Hist. Bohem. c. 35).

[566] Laur. Byzyn. (loc. cit. p. 195).--Martene Ampl. Coll. VIII. 19-27, 249-51, 596-99.--Jo. de Turonis Regest. (Mon. Conc. Gen. Sæc. XV. T. I. p. 842, 846).--Jo. de Ragusio Tractatus (Ibid. T. I. pp. 272-4, 278, 285).--Goll, Quellen, II. 17-18, 61-1.--Æn. Sylvii Epist. 130 (Ed. 1571, p. 661). Even Rokyzana, in 1436, was with great difficulty forced to express his disbelief in the remanence of the substance of the bread.--Jo. de Turonis Regest. (loc. cit. pp. 426-7). Yet nothing can exceed the strength of his affirmation of the existence of the body and blood, in his *Tractatus de Septem Sacramentis* (Cochlæi Hist. Hussit. pp. 473-4). In view of the exaggerated superstitious adoration of the Eucharist by the Calixtins, the assertion of Cardinal Giuliano, in 1431, that the Hussites were wont to manifest their contempt for it by trampling it in the blood of the slain, is a good illustration of the stories invented to stimulate popular abhorrence (Cochlæi op. cit. p. 240).

[567] Herburt. de Fulstin Statut. Regni Poloniæ, Samoscii, 1597, p. 191.

[568] Balbin. Epit. Rer. Hung. pp. 475-6.--Sommersberg Silesiac. Rer. Scriptt. L. 75.--A popular rhyme of the period described:

"Meissen und Sachsen verderbt,	Oesterreich verhergt,
Schliesien und Laussnitz zerscherbt,	Mähren verzerht,
Bayern aussgenehrt,	Böheimb umbgekehrt."

(Balbin. p. 478.)

[569] C. Constant. Decr. *Frequens* (Von der Hardt IV. 1435).

[570] Ludewig Reliq. MSS. XI. 385, 409.

[571] Concil. Senens. ann. 1423 (Harduin. VIII. 1015).

[572] Jo. de Ragusio Init. et Prosec. Conc. Basil. (Mon. Conc. Gen. Sæc. XV. T. I. pp. 28-30, 32-35, 53-61, 64).--Concil. Senens. (Harduin. VIII. 1025-6).--Act. Conc. Basil. (Harduin. VIII. 1108-10).--Raynald. ann. 1425, No. 3, 4. John of Ragusa was the delegate of the University of Paris to Siena, and subsequently played an active part at Basle.

[573] Jo. de Ragusio Init. etc. (Mon. Con. Gen. Sæc. XV. T. I. pp. 66-7).--Cochlæi Hist. Hussit. pp. 237-9. The repulsion of the papacy for general councils was not unnatural. On June 3, 1435, the Council of Basle, with virtual unanimity, abrogated the annates and decreed that in future no charges should be made for sealing collations and confirmations of sees and benefices, except the scrivener's moderate fees. The Bishops of Otranto and Padua protested in the name of the pope, and finding this unheeded arose and left the council, followed by a few others, while the rest gave themselves up to rejoicing and thanking God.--Ægid. Carlerii Lib. de Legation, (op. cit. I. 568).

[574] Martene Ampl. Coll. VIII. 15-18.--Chron. Concil. Zantfliet (Ibid. V. 425-7).--Jo. de Ragusio Tractatus (Mon. Conc. Gen. Sæc. XV. T. I. pp. 135, 138).

[575] Harduin VIII. 1575-8.--Raynald. ann. 1431, No. 26.--Epist. Card. Juliani (Æn. Sylv. Opp. Ed. 1571, pp. 66-9). The letter of Cardinal Giuliano and Æneas Sylvius's Commentaries on the Council of Basle were subsequently put in the Index Expurgatorius (Reusch, Der Index der verbotenen Bücher, I. 40).

[576] Hemmerlin Lollardor. Descriptio.--Duverger, La Vauderie dans les États de Philippe le Bon, Arras, 1885, p. 24--Harduin. VIII. 1141, 1172-82, 1263, 1280, 1582. 1606.--Martene Ampl. Coll. VIII. 80-2.

[577] Martene Ampl. Coll. VIII. 131-33.--Pet. Zatecens. Lib. Diurn. (Mon. Conc. Gen. Sæc. XV. T. I. p. 304-5, 324, 328-31, 348).--Naucleri Chron. ann. 1434.

[578] Ægid. Carlerii Lib. de Legation (Ibid. T. I. pp. 447-71, 495-7).--Martene Ampl. Coll. VIII. 305-40, 356-415, 698-704.--Hartzheim V. 768-9.--Kukuljević, Jura Regni Croatiæ, Zagrabiæ, 1862, I. 192.--Batthyani Legg. Eccles. Hung. III. 419. The question of infantile communion affords an illustration of the skilful casuistry of the orthodox. After the reconciliation, when Sigismund was ruling in Prague, infantile communion was forbidden by the legate of the council, on the ground that the Compactata only guaranteed the privilege to those who had been accustomed to it, and that infants born since then were therefore not entitled to it.--Jo. de Turonis Regest. (Mon. C. Gen. Sæc. XV. T. I. p. 865).

[579] Martene Ampl. Coll. VIII. 710-19.--Harduin. VIII. 1604, 1650-2.--Ægid. Carlerii Liber de Legationibus (Mon. Conc. Gen. Sæc. XV. T. I. pp. 522, 529-39, 544).--Raynald. ann. 1435, No. 22-3.--Naucleri Chron. ann. 1434. The democratic insubordination characteristic of the Taborites is seen in an incident occurring in September, 1433. Procopius sent a detachment to invade Bavaria, and appointed as leader a captain named Pardus. The men mutinied before setting out, and, on Procopius interposing, one of them felled him to the ground with a blow on the head with a stool. The man who struck him was elected leader, and under his guidance the Taborites lost two thousand of their best veterans.--Ægid. Carlerii l.c. pp. 466-7. The reduction to serfdom of the Bohemian peasantry, in 1487, may be regarded as the final result of the overthrow of the Taborites.

[580] Martene Ampl. Coll. VIII. 354-6.--Ægid. Carlerii Lib. de Legationibus (Mon. Conc. Gen. Sæc. XV. T. I. pp. 368-9, 516-17, 519, 595, 597, 600, 632-4, 662-4, 674-6, 678, 684-6, 688).--Th. Ebendorferi Diar. (Ib. pp. 767-9, 776-9, 782-3).--Jo. de Turonis Regest. (Ib. 834-5, 837-8, 848, 868).

[581] Th. Ebendorferi Diar. (loc. cit. 82).--Jo. de Turonis Regest. (Ib. 821-22).--Naucleri Chron. ann. 1436.

[582] Jo. de Turonis Regest. (loc. cit. pp. 862, 865).--Æn. Sylvii Hist. Bohem. c. 59.--Naucleri Chron. ann. 1437.

[583] Æn. Sylvii Epist. lxxi. (Opp. inedd. *ap.* Atti della Accademia dei Lincei, 1883, p. 465).--Jo. de Turonis Regest. (Mon. Conc. Gen. Sæc. XV. T. I. pp. 855, 857).--Camerarii Hist. Frat. Orthod. pp. 57-8.-- Naucleri Chron. ann. 1436, 1438. Concil. Basiliens. Sess. XXX. (Harduin. VIII. 1244).--Petitiones Bohemorum (Fascic. Rer. Expetend. et Fugiend. I. 319, Ed. 1690).--Martene Ampl. Coll. VIII. 942-3--Æn. Sylvii Epist. 101 (Ed. 1571, p. 591).--Chron. Cornel. Zantfliet (Martene Ampl. Coll. V. 445).--De Schweinitz, Hist. of Unitas Fratrum, pp. 91-2, 94.

[584] Æn. Sylvii Hist. Bohem. c. 58.--Ejusd. Epist. xix. (Opp. inedd. p. 397).--Raynald. ann. 1448, No. 3-5.

[585] Ægid. Carlerii. Lib. de Legation. (Monument. Conc. Gen. Sæc. XV. T. I. pp. 691, 694).--Cochlæi Hist. Hussit. Lib. XII. ann. 1462.--Wadding, ann. 1452, No. 1-4.--Raynald. ann. 1446, No. 3, 4; ann. 1447, No. 5-7.--Harduin. VIII. 1307-9. The papal view of the permission to use the cup, as set forth by Pius II. (Æneas Sylvius) in 1464, was that it was only conceded to those accustomed to it until the Council of Basle should decide the question. Had this been observed those who used it would in time have died out, and it was an infraction of the agreement to give it to children and new communicants, through whom the custom was perpetuated.--Æn. Sylvii Epist. lxxi. (Opp. inedd. pp. 465).

[586] Loserth, Mittheilungen des Vereins für Gesch. der Deutschen in Böhmen, 1885, pp. 102-4, 107.-- Wadding. ann. 1436, No. 1-11.--Ægid. Carlerii. Lib. de Legation. (Mon. Conc. Gen. Sæc. XV. T. I. p. 691).

[587] Wadding. ann. 1437, No. 6-12.--Synodd. Strigonens. ann. 1450, 1480 (Batthyani Legg. Eccles. Hung. III. 481, 557).

[588] Wadding. ann. 1437, No. 13-21; ann. 1438, No. 12-16; ann. 1439, No. 41-6; ann. 1440, No. 7; ann. 1444, No. 44; ann. 1446, No. 10.--Herburt de Fulstin Statuta Regni Poloniæ, Samoscii, 1597, p. 192.--Raynald. ann. 1446, No. 10.--Theiner Monument. Slavor. Meridian. I. 394.

[589] Æn. Sylvii. Epistt. 130, 246-7, 259, 404 (Ed. 1571, pp. 667, 782-3, 788, 947).--Wadding. ann. 1455, No. 2; ann. 1456, No. 11-12. In George Podiebrad's letter of 1468 to his son-in-law Matthias Corvinus, complaining of his treatment by the Holy See, he says, "In truth there were formerly in Bohemia many errors concerning the sacrament, and also concerning the ornaments and vestments in administering the rite, and the veneration of saints, but by divine grace these have been so reduced that there is scarcely any difference now existing with the Roman Church. By comparing what was customary thirty or forty years ago with the present, it will be seen that little remains to do in comparison with what has been accomplished."--D'Achery Spieileg. III. 834. A notable part of this retrogression occurred in 1454, when edicts were issued in the name of Ladislas, with the consent of Rokyzana, ordering that the epistles and gospels, in the canon of the mass, should be recited in Latin and not in the vulgar tongue; that confession should be a prerequisite to communion; that children should not receive communion without due preparation; that the blood of the Eucharist should not be carried beyond the churches for fear of accidents; that no one should administer it without letters authenticating his priesthood; that no marriage should be celebrated without banns published in full church.--Chron. Cornel. Zantfliet. ann. 1454 (Martene Ampl. Coll. V. 486-7).

[590] Wadding. ann. 1451, No. 1-16; ann. 1452, No. 34.

[591] Wadding. ann. 1451, No. 17-20; ann. 1452, No. 18, 26; ann. 1453, No. 2-8.

[592] Wadding. ann. 1451, No. 24-36; ann. 1452, No. 1, 12,--Sommersberg Silesiac. Rer. Scriptt. I. 84-5.-- Cochlæi Hist. Hussit. Lib. X. ann. 1451.

[593] Wadding. ann. 1452, No. 2-4, 13-14.--Cochlæi Hist. Hussit. Lib. XI. ann. 1452.

[594] Chron. Glassberger ann. 1452.

[595] Wadding, ann. 1453, No. 9-10; ann. 1254, No. 12-13, 17-19--Chron. Cornel. Zantfliet (Martene Ampl. Coll. V. 486-7).--Æn. Sylvii Epist. 404 (Ed. 1571, p. 947).

[596] Wadding, ann. 1254, No. 7-12; ann. 1255, No. 2-7.--Æn. Sylv. Epist. 405 (p. 947).--Ejusd. Epistt. xxxix.-xliii., xlvi., lviii., lx. (Opp. inedd. pp. 415-24. 426-9, 440-1, 448).

[597] Wadding, ann. 1455, No. 8-13; ann. 1456, No. 9-12.

[598] Wadding. ann. 1456, No. 16-67, 83-4.--Æn. Sylv. Hist. Bohem. cap. lxv. Six several attempts were made, at various times, to canonize Capistrano, but the fates were against it. The earlier efforts were neutralized by the opposition of the legate, Nicholas of Cusa, and the jealousy of the rival orders of Dominicans and Conventual Franciscans. Repeated requests came from Germany, but they remained unheeded. In 1462 urgent letters were written by Frederic III., the Margrave of Brandenburg, and innumerable bishops and magistrates of cities from Cracow to Ratisbon; these were intrusted to a Franciscan friar to take to Rome, but he died on the road, and confided them to a knight of Assisi. The latter brought them to his home, and then departed for Germany, where he died. The trunk containing them was piously preserved by his descendants until, towards the middle of the seventeenth century, Wadding chanced to see it, and took the letters to Rome, in the hopes of their still accomplishing their object. At the inquest held by Leo X. a classified record of the miracles wrought by the thaumaturge shows, of dead brought to life, more than thirty; of deaf made to hear, three hundred and

seventy; of blind restored to sight, one hundred and twenty-three; of cripples and gouty persons cured, nine hundred and twenty, and miscellaneous cases innumerable. This resulted in his admission to the inferior order of the Blessed, to be worshipped by the Franciscans of the diocese of Capistrano. In 1622 Gregory XV. enlarged his cult to the whole Franciscan Order; and in 1690 Alexander VIII. enrolled him in the calendar of saints.--Wadding, ann. 1456, No. 114-22; ann. 1462, No. 29-78.--Weizfäcker, ap. Herzog's Real Encyklop. s. v.

[599] Wadding, ann. 1457, No. 5, 10; ann. 1461, No. 1-2; ann. 1465, No. 6; ann. 1467, No. 5.

[600] Æn. Sylvii Epist. 162, 324, 334-5, 337-40, 356, 369, 387 (Ed. 1571, pp. 714, 815, 821-22, 825, 831, 837, 840).--Ejusd. Hist. Bohem. c. 71-2. Pius II. did not hesitate to publish to Christendom a positive assertion that George poisoned Ladislas, and said that, though the facts were obscure, the Viennese physicians in attendance attributed his death to poison.--Æn. Sylv. Epist. lxxi. (Opp. inedd. p. 467).

[601] Æn. Sylvii Hist. Bohem. c. 69.--Ejusd. Epist. lxxi. (Opp. inedd. pp. 461-70).--Ejusd. Tractatus (Ib. pp. 566, 581).--Raynald. ann. 1457, No. 69; ann. 1458, No. 20-8; ann. 1459, No. 18-23; ann. 1463, No. 96-102.--Cochlæi Hist. Lib. XII.--Dubrav. Hist. Bohem. Lib. 30.--Wadding, ann. 1462, No. 87.--Pii PP. II. Bull. *In minoribus.*--Sommersberg Silesiac. Rer. Scriptt. II. 1025-6, 1031.--Wadding, ann. 1456, No. 12; ann. 1469, No. 4, 6.--Ludewig Reliq. MSS. VI. 61.--Martene Ampl. Coll. I. 1598-9.--D'Achery Spicileg. III. 830-4.--Ripoll III. 466.

[602] Raynald. ann. 1468, No. 1-14.--Chron. Glassberger ann. 1468.--Dubrav. Hist. Bohem. Libb. XXX.-XXXI.--Cochlæi Hist. Hussit. Lib. XII. ann. 1471.

[603] Wadding, ann. 1460, No. 55; ann. 1462, No. 87; ann. 1471, No. 5; ann. 1475, No. 28, 37-9; ann. 1489, No. 21; ann. 1491, No. 8, 78.--Chron. Glassberger ann. 1463, 1466, 1479, 1483.--Dubrav. Hist. Bohem. Lib. XXXI.--De Schweinitz, Hist. of Unitas Fratrum, p. 168.--Camerarii Hist. Frat. Orthod. pp. 72-3.--Georgisch Regest. Chron. Diplom. III. 158.

[604] Æn. Sylvii Epist. 130 (Ed. 1571 pp. 661-2).

[605] Goll, Quellen u. Untersuchungen, I. 10, 32-33, 92, 99; II. 72, 87-88, 94.--De Schweinitz, Hist. of Unitas Fratrum, pp. 111-12, 159, 204-5.--Von Zezschwitz, Real-Encyklop. II. 652-3.--Hist. Persecutionum pp. 58-60, 90.--Palacky, Die Beziehungen der Waldenser, pp. 32-33.--Camerarii Hist. Frat. Orthod. pp. 59-66.--For the Calixtin views on the Eucharist see the treatises of Rokyzana and of John of Przibram in Cochlæi Hist. Hussit. pp. 474, 508; also the latter's articles against Peter Payne (Ib. 230). When the Brethren undertook to explain their views on the Eucharist they become somewhat difficult to understand. The bread and wine became the body and blood, and they would have believed it had the bread been stone, but still the substance remained, and Christ was not present.--Fascic. Rer. Expetend. et Fugiend. I. 165, 170, 174, 183, 185.

[606] Camerarii Hist. Frat. Orthod. pp. 84-9.--Hist. Persecut. p. 65.--Von Zezschwitz, I. c. p. 653-4.

[607] Wie sich die Menschen u.s.w. (Goll, II. 99-100).--Das Buch der Prager Magister (Ib. 104-5). The Calixtins had the same trouble about the apostolic succession. A letter from the Church of Constantinople, in 1451, warmly urging union, and offering to supply spiritual pastors, shows that overtures had been made to the Greek Church to remove the difficulty; but apparently the Bohemians were not prepared to cut loose definitely from Catholicism (Flac. Illyr. Catal. Test. Veritatis, Lib. XIX. p. 1834-5, Ed. 1608). The trouble was renewed after the death of Rokyzana. At length, in 1482, Agostino Luciano, an Italian bishop, came to Prague in search of a purer religion, and was joyfully received. He served them until 1493, when he died. Then Filippo, Bishop of Sidon, came, but after three years he was recalled by the pope. In 1499 a mission was sent to Armenia, where some of them were ordained.--Hist. Persecutionum pp. 95-6.

[608] Goll. op. cit. II. 101.--De Schweinitz, op. cit. p. 156, 200-1.--Édouard Montet, Hist. Litt. des Vaudois, pp. 152, 156.

[609] De Schweinitz, op. cit. pp. 122-7, 172-5, 180-1.

[610] Hist. Persecut. Eccles. Bohem. pp. 63-66, 73-4.--Ripoll III. 577.--Camerarii Hist. Frat. Orthod. pp. 104-22.--De Schweinitz, op. cit. 170, 225-6.--Von Zezschwitz, Real-Encyklop. II. 656-7, 660.

[611] Parkman's Montcalm, II. 144-5.--I owe to the kindness of Bishop De Schweinitz the statistics of the Moravian Missions.

[612] Hauréau (Bernard Délicieux, p. 194) prints the bull of 1210 (Doat, XXXII. fol. 60), contained in the above, but has apparently overlooked the subsequent and far more significant one. The earlier bull also appears in T. V. p. 40, of the Regestum Clementis PP. V. just issued in Rome. In the same publication, received too late for reference to be made in the proper place (see above, p. 78), there arc several letters throwing light on the troubles of Bernard de Castanet, Bishop of Albi. In 1307 two of his cathedral canons, Sicard Aleman and Bernard Astruc, accused him before the pope of numerous crimes. Berenger, Cardinal of SS. Nereo and Achille, to whom the matter was referred, after examining the articles of accusation, suspended him from all his functions during an investigation. "Executors" were ordered to proceed to Albi to take testimony, giving three months to the prosecution, then two to the defence, and finally two more to the prosecution in rebuttal. A vicar-general was appointed, July 31, to take charge of the see, and three procurators to collect its revenues. One of the "executors" was Arnaud Novelli, Abbot of Fontfroide, whom we have seen (p. 87) replacing, by order of Philipe le Bel, the bishop in his inquisitorial capacity. Arnaud was soon afterwards appointed vice-chancellor of the curia; this, with other impediments, delayed the investigation, and on November 20 two additional months were granted to the prosecution. Nothing apparently came of the trial except that it probably quickened Bernard's desire to abandon his thorny seat. There is a papal brief of October 31, 1308, addressed to Bertrand

de Bordes as Bishop of Albi, in which Bernard is alluded to as late of Albi and now of Puy (Ibid. T. II. pp. 52, 165; T. III. pp. 3, 255).

[613] Gui II., Bishop of Cambrai from 1296 to 1305.

[614] Philippe de Marigny, Bishop of Cambrai in 1306, transferred to Sens in April, 1310, in time to burn the Templars who retracted their confessions.

[615] In the Register of Clement V., received since the text of this volume was in type, there is a brief addressed September 3, 1310, to the Inquisitor of Langres ordering him to proceed vigorously against the heretics of that diocese who have been reported by the bishop as multiplying so that, unless prompt measures are taken, grave injury to the faith is to be apprehended. The nature of the heresy is not described, but it was probably that of the Brethren of the Free Spirit which Marguerite la Porete had been disseminating throughout that region. The incident has further interest as showing how completely the French episcopate had transferred to the Inquisition its jurisdiction over heresy, in spite of its renewed activity at the moment in the affair of the Templars.

CPSIA information can be obtained at www.ICGtesting.com
Printed in the USA
BVOW06s0003300915

420275BV00013B/51/P